RANDOM
HOUSE
WEBSTER'S

LEGAL
SPELL CHECKER

James E. Clapp
*Member of the New York and
District of Columbia Bars*

RANDOM HOUSE
NEW YORK

Random House Webster's Legal Spell Checker by James E. Clapp

Copyright © 1998 by Random House, Inc.

Trademarks

This book is available for special purchases in bulk by organizations and institutions, not for resale, at special discounts. Please direct your inquiries to the Random House Special Sales Department, toll-free 888-591-1200 or fax 212-572-4961.

Please address inquiries about electronic licensing of this division's products, for use on a network or on software or on CD-ROM, to the Subsidiary Rights Department, Random House Reference & Information Publishing, fax 212-940-7370.

Library of Congress Cataloging-in-Publication Data
Clapp, James E. (James Edward), 1943–
   Random House Wesbter's legal spell checker / by James E. Clapp—
1st ed.
      p.   cm.
   ISBN 0-375-40155-5
   1. Law—Terminology.   2. English language—Syllabification.
3. Speller. I. Title.
K50.C58   1998
340'.1'4—dc21   98-27428
                                      CIP

Visit the Random House Web site at www.randomhouse.com

Typeset and printed in the United States of America.

First Edition
0 9 8 7 6 5 4 3 2 1
September 1998

ISBN 0-375-40155-5

New York   Toronto   London   Sydney   Auckland

CONTENTS

STAFF

Project Editor: Enid Pearsons
Assistant Editors: Joanne Grumet, Meredith Josey,
                     Rima McKinzey
Editorial Production Services: Jennifer Dowling,
                     Seaside Press
Database Associate: Diane M. Joao
Database Manager: Constance A. Baboukis
Director of Production: Patricia W. Ehresmann
Managing Editor: Andrew Ambraziejus
Editorial Director: Wendalyn Nichols
Associate Publisher: Page Edmunds
Publisher: Charles M. Levine

PREFACE: WHY THIS BOOK?

The *Random House Webster's Legal Spell Checker* makes available in one compact and easy-to-use book a range of information and features otherwise scattered in many different reference sources—and some features not readily available anywhere else. The principal purpose is to enable anyone concerned with legal matters or issues to identify with ease the best way to spell, divide, and abbreviate most of the terms likely to be encountered or needed.

The book includes:

➤ Over 40,000 words, phrases, and abbreviations in a compact alphabetical list and specialized appendices.

➤ Technical legal terms (like *remittitur* and *cestui*) not found in general purpose dictionaries.

➤ Nontechnical terms (like *egregious* and *oxymoron*) likely to arise in legal discourse but not included in legal dictionaries.

➤ Brief definitions or other distinguishing information, not available in computerized spell checkers, to enable the user to make the right choice between easily confused terms (like *forceable* and *forcible* or *bailer* and *bailor*).

➤ Standard legal citation forms (like *Ex'x* for "Executrix" or §§ for "sections")—ordinarily found only in legal style books—for terms that are normally shortened when they appear in case names, journal references, and other citations of legal authority.

➤ Irregular or potentially confusing plurals and verb forms.

➤ All terms divided into syllables, clearly marked to show which divisions would be appropriate at the end of a line.

➤ Language labels identifying foreign-language legal terms.

➤ Labels identifying trademarks and service marks, as well as technical names of controlled substances.

➤ Appendices giving the official names, customary abbreviations, and structure of the principal organizational units of the United States government, the United Nations, and the European Union, and listing other important international bodies.

➤ A table giving legal citation forms and official postal abbreviations for the states, provinces, and other geographic jurisdictions of the United States and Canada.

PRINCIPLES
OF WORD DIVISION

The entries in this book are divided into syllables by means of bullets. In a sequence of phrases, repeated words are syllabified the first time they appear:

> **ob•ses•sive**
>
> **obsessive-com•pul•sive**
>
> **obsessive-compulsive dis•or•der**

Syllable division is a general guide to pronunciation, and therefore helpful in identifying the exact word you have in mind when looking up the spelling. And when a word must be divided between two lines of text, the division must occur between syllables.

But not all syllable divisions are acceptable as end-of-line word breaks. There are guidelines for dividing words between lines so as to minimize confusion for the reader.

In this book, syllable divisions that are acceptable when a word must be hyphenated at the end of a line are indicated by a solid bullet, •, as in **ab•duct**. Syllable divisions that are less acceptable or not acceptable as end-of-line word breaks are indicated by a hollow bullet, ○, as in **a○buse**.

The principal guidelines used in indicating word-division points in this book—and that should be followed in applying them—are these:

➤ One-syllable words cannot be divided: **breathe, pledge.** This includes one-syllable words in the past tense **(breathed, pledged)**, which should never be split before the *-ed* ending.

➤ Word segments like **-ceous, -scious, -tion,** and **-tious** cannot be divided: **de•vo•lu•tion•ist** (not **-tio∘nist**).

➤ It is best not to divide a word of five letters or less: **hu∘man** should not be divided, but **hu•mane** may be.

➤ Words should never be divided in such a way that a single letter is left at the beginning or end of a line: **a∘but•tal** should not be divided after the initial **a,** leaving **a-** at the end of a line; **mi•nu•ti∘a** should not be divided before the final **a,** isolating the letter **a** on the next line.

➤ It is preferable not to split off just the last two letters of a word:

> **cham•per∘ty** (divide as **cham-perty,** not **champer-ty**)
>
> **spe•cif∘ic** (divide as **spe-cific,** not **specif-ic**)
>
> **me•di∘um** (divide as **me-dium,** not **medi-um**)

➤ It is usually preferable to divide after rather than before a syllable consisting of a single vowel:

> **em∘i•gra•tion** (divide as **emi-gration,** not **em-igration**)
>
> **sep∘a•rate** (divide as **sepa-rate,** not **sep-arate**)

But it is better to avoid this division when it would suggest a misleading pronunciation or would cause an awkward division of a compound or a word with a prefix or suffix.

gen∘e∘sis (gene-sis might be confusing)
hold•o∘ver
dis•a∘buse
rea•son•a∘ble

➤ In words with prefixes, the best division point is usually right after the prefix. Prefixes of more than one syllable should be kept intact:

> non•es•sen•tial (best division is
>   non-essential)

> an∘ti•smok•ing (best division is
>   anti-smoking; an-tismoking is
>   unacceptable)

➤ Hyphenated terms are best divided at the hyphen. If the portion of the compound lying on either side of the hyphen is a single letter, however, the rule against splitting off a single letter at the beginning or end of a line should be followed. Thus **e-mail** or **e-mailed** should not be divided; and because of the rule against dividing words of only five letters (like "ratio" and "rated"), **Q-ra∘tio** and **X-rat∘ed** should not be divided either.

Although permissible breaks are shown within the individual words that form hyphenated compounds **(con•tent-neu•tral),** those division points should be used only if it is difficult or impermissible to break at the hyphen. For example, although it would be best not to divide *e-mailing* at all, an end-of-line division after *e-mail-* is less confusing than one after just the initial *e-*.

➤ If an unhyphenated compound must be divided the preferred break point is between the words that make up the compound:

mud•sling•ing (the better division is
mud-slinging, not mudsling-ing)

These rules mean that sometimes a fairly long word
cannot or should not be divided (straight, qual∘i∘fy).
But these standards have evolved to facilitate communication: they avoid forcing readers to retrace their
steps or hesitate even fleetingly in order to grasp what
is written. Attention to these principles is a mark of
consideration for the reader and professionalism in the
writer.

GUIDE

Word Order

Entries are alphabetized word by word, so that all phrases beginning with the same word are listed together. For example, Latin phrases beginning with the word *per* (such as **per annum, per curiam,** and **per stirpes**) are grouped together before words such as **percipient, peremptory,** and **perjurious.**

Hyphenated entries are alphabetized according to whether the underlying form is one word or two. If the hyphen merely sets off a prefix, the entry is treated as a single word:

> **antigestational**
> **anti-intellectual**
> **antisocial**

But hyphenated phrases are alphabetized word by word:

> **all fours**
> **all-points bulletin**
> **all right**

Periods and slashes are disregarded: **J.D.** is alphabetized as "JD"; **d/b/a** as "dba." Ampersands (&) are treated as if spelled out: **P&L** is alphabetized as "P and L."

Inflected Forms

When we add an ending to a word or otherwise change its form in order to satisfy rules of grammar, we are *inflecting* it. In this book, the principal inflected forms of nouns, verbs, and adjectives are spelled out and syllabified whenever they are formed irregularly or otherwise might be confusing.

Nouns

Nouns that have plurals normally form them by adding *-s* (or *-es* for nouns ending in *s*, *x*, *z*, *sh*, or *ch*): *law, laws; heiress, heiresses.* Unless otherwise indicated, any noun in this book that has a plural follows this regular pattern.

Plurals that in standard American legal usage are formed in any other way are shown in full:

> **ad•den•dum** *n., pl.* **ad•den•da**
>
> **a∘nal•y•sis** *n., pl.* **a∘nal•y•ses**

In addition, the plurals of many words and phrases that might be confusing are spelled out even if formed regularly:

> **em•bry∘o** *n., pl.* **em•bry∘os** [not *embryoes*]
>
> **prac•ti•cum** *n., pl.* **prac•ti•cums** [not *practica*]
>
> **deed poll** *n., pl.* **deeds poll** [not *deed polls*]

When two plural forms are commonly used in different contexts or with different shades of meaning, both are shown and a brief explanation is given. For example, the entry

> **in∘dex** *n., pl.* **in•dex∘es** or (esp. in scientific contexts) **in•di•ces**

indicates that a lawyer would most appropriately say "The treatise has two indexes: a subject index and an index of cases cited," but "The expert witness explained the different indices used to measure cognitive development."

The plural forms indicated for nouns labeled *Latin* represent the nominative plural (e.g., **jus** *n., pl.* **ju∘ra; res** *n., pl.* **res**). Users familiar with Latin will understand that many other singular and plural forms exist (e.g., the forms used in the phrases *de jure* and *in rem*).

Verbs

Verbs normally form the past tense and past participle by adding *-ed,* and the present participle by adding *-ing:* I *call,* I *called,* I have *called,* I am *calling.*

When a verb listed in this book forms its principal parts in any other way, they are spelled out in full:

> **ad•judge** *v.,* **ad•judged, ad•judg•ing**
>
> **a∘ver** *v.,* **a∘verred, a∘ver•ring**
>
> **qual∘i∘fy** *v.,* **qual∘i•fied, qual∘i•fy•ing**
>
> **buy** *v.,* **bought, buy•ing**

When the past tense and past participle are different, both are shown:

> **drive** *v.,* **drove, driv∘en, driv•ing** [I *drive,* I *drove,* I have *driven,* I am *driving*]

Occasionally the principal parts of a verb are shown to make it clear that they are formed in the regular way:

> **im•plead** *v.,* **im•plead∘ed, im•plead•ing** [not "impled"]

> **li•bel** *v.,* **li•beled, li•bel•ing** [rather than
> the British spellings "libelled" and
> "libelling"]

Adjectives

The comparative and superlative forms of adjectives are normally formed by adding *-er* and *-est* or using *more* and *most: clever, cleverer, cleverest; eloquent, more eloquent, most eloquent.* Adjectives inflected otherwise are shown:

> **bad** *adj.,* **worse, worst**
>
> **can∘ny** *adj.,* **can•ni∘er, can•ni•est**

Variant Spellings and Forms

Omitted Variants

The spellings and inflected forms given in this book are those commonly found or widely accepted in contemporary American legal usage.

The law is a linguistically conservative profession —in part because the quest for certainty and clarity in law counsels adherence to long established language, and in part because much of the most important legal writing is addressed to or handed down by judges, who generally prefer a scholarly and traditional style over linguistic innovation. Accordingly, forms that may be accepted in other fields or may be emerging in popular culture, but that have not yet become widely used or accepted in careful legal writing—such as *memorandums* as a plural or *criteria* as a singular—are not included here; instead, this book gives:

> **mem∘o•ran•dum** *n., pl.* **mem∘o•ran∘da**
>
> **cri•te•ri∘on** *n., pl.* **cri•te•ri∘a**

British spellings, such as *honour* and *counselled,* are generally omitted unless they are also common in the United States. Certain British forms, however, are important in special contexts; for example, the words **organisation** and **programme** appear in the names of international organizations. Such terms are included in this book (and marked as British spellings).

Terms used only in historical contexts, which typically have had many variant spellings over the centuries, are listed only with the spelling regarded as most likely to be used today; e.g., **feud** (in the sense of a feudal estate), not *feod,* and **aiel** (a word meaning "grandfather" used in the names of certain ancient writs), not *aile, ayle, ayel, ael,* etc.

Listed Variants

When two forms are widely used or accepted, both are given, with the one generally preferred in legal contexts—usually the more traditional form—listed first:

> a○bet•tor or a○bet•ter
>
> ad•vis○er or ad•vi•sor
>
> court-mar•tial *n., pl.* **courts-mar•tial** or **court-mar•tials**
>
> plead *v.,* **plead○ed** or **pled, plead•ing**

As a general rule, a careful writer or speaker should choose the first alternative.

Finding Exactly the Right Word

Often words that are very similar in sound or spelling have different meanings or uses. A computerized spell checker can tell you that *imminent* is a word, but cannot tell whether the word you want is *imminent* or *eminent* or *immanent* or *emanent.* In this book, entries for easily confused terms like these contain short definitions or other distinguishing information, and include cross-references to each other so that if the term you find first is not what you had in mind you can find the correct term. For example, the entries

>**force•a◦ble** (capable of being forced: cf. FORCIBLE)
>**for•ci•ble** (accomplished through force: cf. FORCEABLE)

make it clear that one would write "The burglar found that the lock was forceable, and so was able to make a forcible entry."

In cross-references, "cf."—from Latin *confer*—means "compare." Other entries in the book are referred to in SMALL CAPITAL LETTERS. The cross-references may be omitted if the two entries fall directly adjacent to each other in the alphabetical listing.

Clarifying definitions are also included for a few pairs of terms that are often confused even though they do not sound similar, such as **lay** and **lie,** or **oral** and **verbal.**

Occasionally a distinguishing definition is given even though the term with which an entry might be confused is too far removed from normal legal contexts to be included as an independent entry in this book. In such cases, the contrasting term is shown in italics rather than small capitals and is signaled by "vs." (versus) to call attention to the potential for confusion. For example, in the entry

>**jibe** *v.,* **jibed, jib•ing** (to fit; to be in harmony or accord: vs. *jive;* cf. GIBE)

the addition of "vs. *jive*" serves as a caution against the common mistake of substituting *jive* (which means "to dance to or play jazz or swing music") for *jibe*—often to amusing effect.

When there is a need to distinguish two different meanings or uses for the same word—or different words with the same spelling—the form is usually given two separate listings, with numbered superscripts. Typical situations include:

1. Terms that are inflected differently depending upon the sense in which they are used:

    hang[1] *v.,* **hanged, hang•ing** (to suspend by the neck until dead)

    hang[2] *v.,* **hung, hang•ing** (to suspend generally)

    Thus: "He hung a rope from the light fixture and hanged himself with it."

2. Words that are divided differently depending upon the sense:

    in•val∘id[1] (not valid)

    in•va•lid[2] (sick person)

3. Terms, originally from Latin, treated differently depending upon whether they are used as English or as Latin:

    bo∘na fide[1] *adj. English* (genuine)

    bo∘na fi∘de[2] *adv. Latin* (in good faith)

4. Terms having some meanings that overlap with other terms and others that do not:

    bet•ter[1] (superior: cf. BETTOR)

    better[2] See BETTOR.

    bet•tor or **bet•ter** (wagerer: cf. BETTER[1])

In such cases it is clearly the best practice to confine each spelling to its unique senses—in this example, to write "bettor" whenever referring to one who places bets, and "better" only in other senses: "The one who wins more money is the better bettor."

Legal Citation Forms and Other Abbreviations

Common Abbreviations

In entries for terms that are often abbreviated in text, the abbreviation is supplied parenthetically; and except in some cases where the abbreviation would fall alphabetically right next to the full term, the abbreviation is also given its own entry with a parenthetical explanation of what it stands for. The modern tendency to omit periods from initialisms—abbreviations made up of the first letter of each word in a phrase—is followed here except for initialisms that have clearly resisted the trend:

> **an•nu◦al per•cent•age rate (APR)**
> **APR** (annual percentage rate)
> **J.D.** (Juris Doctor)
> **Ju◦ris Doc•tor (J.D.)** *Latin.*

Labels or other explanatory matter pertaining to an abbreviated term are given at the entry for the spelled-out form and sometimes repeated at the entry for the abbreviation; explanatory matter relating specifically to the abbreviation is given at the entry for the abbreviation:

> **LSD** *Controlled Subst.* (lysergic acid diethylamide: abbr. from German

> *lysergsäure-diäthylamid*)
> **ly•ser•gic ac○id di•eth•yl•am•ide (LSD)**
> *Controlled Subst.*

A few abbreviations are so much a part of the language that the words they stand for are never spelled out. These are entered only as abbreviations:

> **a.m.** (before noon: from Latin *ante meridiem*)

For customary abbreviations of the names of governmental bodies and international agencies, and the official two-letter postal abbreviations for names of states, provinces, and other geographic jurisdictions of the United States and Canada, see the appendices at the end of the book.

Citation Forms

In legal writing, the many necessary citations to legal authority (judicial opinions, statutes, treatises, law review articles, and the like) are greatly shortened through the use of generally recognized abbreviations—many of them for words that would never be abbreviated in ordinary text. For example, when lawyers see "U.S." in a case reference, they instantly recognize it as short for *United States Reports*—the official source for opinions of the Supreme Court of the United States.

In this book, entries for terms that are customarily shortened in legal citations include the standard legal abbreviation, labeled *"citation form."*[1] Separate entries

---

[1]With rare exceptions, the citation forms given here conform to the rather complex dictates and recommendations of the most widely used legal style manual, called *The Bluebook: A Uniform System of Citation*, compiled jointly by the *Columbia Law Review*, the *Harvard Law Review*, the *University of Pennsylvania Law Review*, and *The Yale Law Journal*.

for the citation forms themselves, with parenthetical explanations of what they stand for, are included except in some cases where they would fall alphabetically right next to the full form. Most citation forms are capitalized because in actual citations they stand for words used in names or titles:

> **Ins.** (Insurance)
> **in•sur•ance** (*citation form:* **Ins.**)
> **in∘ter•na•tion∘al** (*citation form:* **Int'l**)
> **Int'l** (International)
> **J.**[1] (Journal)
> **jour•nal** (*citation form:* **J.**)

These entries show that a periodical named "Journal of International Insurance" would be cited as "J. Int'l Ins."

Terms that are not normally capitalized in citations—including terms giving editorial information or referring to parts of a book or statute—have uncapitalized citation forms:

> **cl.** (clause)
> **clause** (*citation form:* **cl.**)
> **n.d.** (no date)
> **no date** (*citation form:* **n.d.**)

When different terms have the same citation form or more than one citation form is used for a particular term, the variations are all shown:

> **Pet.** (Petition; Petitioner)
> **pe•ti•tion** (*citation form:* **Pet.**)
> **pe•ti•tion∘er** (citation form: **Pet'r** or **Pet.**)
> **Pet'r** (Petitioner)

Standard citation forms for the names of states, provinces, and other geographic jurisdictions of the United States and Canada—important in citing judicial opinions from the various jurisdictions—are listed in the table at the back of the book.

Citation Forms for Plurals

Some terms for which there are citation forms have no plural (**probate,** citation form **Prob.**); some are so rarely used in the plural in citations that no particular citation form has become established for the plural (**executrix,** citation form **Ex'x; journal,** citation form **J.**); some are so rarely used in the singular in citations that no citation form has become established for the singular (**problems,** citation form **Probs.**).

Most terms that appear in citations, however, may appear as either singular or plural. The citation form for the plural of such a term is normally made by simply adding *s* to the citation form for the singular (before the period, if any): Thus **Adm'r, Adm'rs** for **Administrator(s); pt., pts.** for **part(s)**.

When a citation form is pluralized in any other way, this is indicated both at the entry for the citation form and at the entry for the underlying term. Often the citation form for the plural is the same as for the singular:

> **Est.** (Estate; Estates)
>
> **es•tate** (*citation form for sing. and pl.:* **Est.**)

Otherwise, the plural of the citation form is shown:

> **l.** *pl.* **ll.** (line)
>
> **line** (*citation form:* **l.,** *pl.* **ll.**)

Labels

Part of Speech Labels

Labels identifying a word or phrase as a noun, adjective, or the like are included when helpful to distinguish one entry from another or one use of a term from another. Labels are shown in italics.

When inflected forms are shown for a word in one or more parts of speech, for completeness the other parts of speech in which the word is commonly used are also listed:

> base *n., adj.,* bas∘er, bas∘est, *v.,* based, bas•ing

> pred∘i•cate *v.,* pred∘i•cat∘ed, pred∘i•cat•ing, *adj., n.*

Part of speech labels are also employed when helpful in drawing a distinction between similar words or phrases with different spellings or other features, or in breaking up an entry that would otherwise be unnecessarily complex. For example,

> prec∘e∘dent[1] *n.*

> pre•ce•dent[2] *adj.*

indicates that the word *precedent* is divided one way as a noun (as in the phrase "judicial precedent"—pronounced PRESSedent) and another way as an adjective (as in the phrase "condition precedent"—pronounced preSEEdent). And for convenience,

> in•sti•tute[1] *n.* (*citation form:* Inst.)

> institute[2] *v.,* in•sti•tut∘ed, in•sti•tut•ing

separates into two entries material that would be cumbersome if included in a single entry.

Often the way in which a two-word phrase or compound is used determines whether it should be written as one word, two words, or hyphenated. For example,

> **eve°ry day** *adv.* (cf. EVERYDAY)
>
> **eve°ry•day** *adj.* (cf. EVERY DAY)

shows that one would write "She has come to the trial every day," but "In the United States murder is an everyday occurrence." When two such entries fall directly adjacent to each other in the alphabetical list, the cross references are omitted:

> **break in** *v.*
>
> **break-in** *n.*

Singular and Plural Nouns

Plural nouns for which there is no singular (**environs, estovers**), or that have a special meaning different from the singular (**premises, presents**), are given their own listings with a special label:

> **en•vi•rons** *n.pl.*
>
> **prem•is°es** *n.pl.*

Nouns that looks as if they might be plural, but actually are singular, are similarly flagged to prevent misuse:

> **ku°dos** *n.sing.*
>
> **fi°des** *n.sing. Latin.*

Some nouns take either a singular or a plural verb, depending upon the sense in which they are used. For example, *economics* may be used as a singular noun meaning "the study of economic systems," or as a plural noun meaning "financial considerations." Words having this dual character are labeled accordingly:

da∘ta *n.sing. or pl.*

ec∘o•nom•ics *n.sing. or pl.*

Language Labels

Foreign-language terms are given a label, in italics, naming the language. This helps to identify the words and distinguish them from similarly spelled English words with which they might otherwise be confused.

The most important legal languages are Latin, law French (a language used in early English law and quite different from modern French), and French (still an important language in international law and diplomacy). Words that are fully integrated into English (like the Latin **appendix,** the French **fiancé,** or the law French **tort**) are not labeled. A few words with distinct meanings in English and Latin (e.g., **post**—an English noun and verb and a Latin adverb and preposition) are labeled *English and Latin.*

Category Labels

Terms that are known to be claimed as proprietary names (e.g., **Lexis, Westlaw, Seeing Eye, Mace, Breathalyzer, Quaalude**) are labeled *Trademark* or *Service Mark* as appropriate.

Scientific and statutory names for drugs that because of their addicting, intoxicating, or mood-altering properties are classified as controlled substances under federal law are labeled *Controlled Subst.* This helps to distinguish that large class of terms from scientific terms for other substances of legal significance (such as the DNA building blocks **adenine** and **cytosine,** the abortifacients **methotrexate** and **mifepristone,** or the substances **alcohol** and **nicotine**).

ABBREVIATIONS

abbr.	abbreviation
adj.	adjective
adv.	adverb
Brit.	British
cf.	compare (Latin *confer*)
Controlled Subst.	Controlled Substance
e.g.	for example (Latin *exempli gratia*)
esp.	especially
etc.	et cetera
i.e.	that is (Latin *id est*)
interj.	interjection
n.	noun
n.pl.	plural noun
n.sing.	singular noun
pl.	plural
pron.	pronoun
sing.	singular
v.	verb
vs.	versus
• solid bullet	good syllable break
◦ hollow bullet	poor syllable break

All syllable divisions recommended for use as end-of-line hyphenation points are marked with a bold, centered dot, or bullet (•). This symbol is the one used most frequently in dictionaries to mark word divisions.

The mark used in this book to divide syllables where end-of-line hyphenation is NOT recommended is a hollow bullet (◦).

RANDOM
HOUSE
WEBSTER'S

LEGAL
SPELL CHECKER

A (adenine)

A. (Atlantic Reporter)

a&b (assault and battery)

a&r (assault and robbery)

à a∘ver et te∘ner *Law French.*

a coe∘lo us∘que ad cen•trum *Latin.*

a coelo usque ad in•fe∘ros *Latin.*

a con•si•li∘is *Latin.*

a for•ti•o∘ri *Latin.*

a gra•ti∘a *Latin.*

a men∘sa et tho∘ro *Latin.*

a pos•te•ri•o∘ri *Latin.*

à pren•dre *Law French.*

a pri•o∘ri *Latin.*

a quo *Latin.*

à ren•dre *Law French.*

à tort *Law French.*

a vin•cu∘lo ma•tri•mo•ni∘i *Latin.*

a while *n.* (a short time: cf.AWHILE)

A.B. (Bachelor of Arts: from Latin *Artium Baccalaureus*)

ab ae•ter∘no *Latin.*

ab an∘te *Latin.*

ab an•ti•quo *Latin.*

ab ex∘tra *Latin.*

ab in•con•ve•ni•en∘ti *Latin.*

ab i∘ni•ti•o *Latin.*

ab in•vi∘to *Latin.*

ab o∘ri•gi•ne *Latin.*

a∘ban•don

a∘ban•don•a∘ble

a∘ban•doned prop•er∘ty

a∘ban•don•ee

a∘ban•don•er

a∘ban•don•ment

a∘base *v.*, a∘based, a∘bas∘ing

a∘base•ment

a∘bas∘er

a∘bat•a∘ble

abatable nui•sance

a∘bate *v.*, a∘bat∘ed, a∘bat•ing

a∘bate•ment

abatement clause

a∘bat∘er (an abating; a plea in abatement: cf. ABATOR)

a∘ba•tor (one who abates: cf. ABATER)

abbr. (abbreviated; abbreviation)

ab•bre•vi•ate *v.*, ab•bre•vi•at∘ed, ab•bre•vi•at∘ing

ab•bre•vi•at∘ed (abbr.)

ab•bre•vi•a•tion (abbr.)

ab•bre•vi•a•tor

ABC trans•ac•tion

ab•di•cant

ab•di•cate *v.*, ab•di•cat∘ed, ab•di•cat∘ing

ab•di•ca•tion

ab•di•ca•tor

ab•do•men

ab•dom∘i•nal

ab•dom∘i•nal∘ly

ab•duct

ab•duct∘ee

ab•duc•tion

ab•duc•tor

ab•er•rance

ab•er•ran•cy

ab•er•rant

ab•er•rant∘ly

ab•er•ra•tion

ab•er•ra•tion∘al

a∘bet *v.*, a∘bet•ted, a∘bet•ting

a∘bet•ment

a∘bet•tor or a∘bet•ter

a∘bey•ance

a∘bey•ant

ab∘hor *v.*, ab•horred, ab•hor•ring

ab•hor•rence

ab•hor•rent

ab•hor•rent∘ly

a∘bid•ance

a∘bide *v.*, a∘bode or a∘bid∘ed, a∘bid•ing

abide the event

a∘bid•ing *adj.*

abiding con•vic•tion

a∘bid•ing∘ly

a∘bil∘i∘ty

ab•ject

ab•jec•tion

ab•ject∘ly

ab•ject•ness

ab•ju•ra•tion (renunciation: cf. ADJURATION)

ab•jur∘a•to∘ry

ab•jure *v.*, ab•jured, ab•jur∘ing (renounce; forswear: cf. ADJURE)

ab•jur∘er

a∘ble

able-bod∘ied

able-bodied sea•man

able sea•man

a•ble•ism
a•ble•ist
a•bler
a•blest
a•bly
ab•ne•gate v., ab•
 ne•gat•ed, ab•ne•
 gat•ing
ab•ne•ga•tion
ab•ne•ga•tor
ab•nor•mal
abnormal psy•
 chol○o•gy
abnormal spoil•age
ab•nor•mal○i○ty
ab•nor•mal○ly
abnormally dan•ger•
 ous ac•tiv○i○t○y
a•board
a•board•age
a•bode
a•bol•ish
a•bol•ish•a•ble
ab○o○li•tion
ab○o○li•tion•ism
ab○o○li•tion•ist
a•bom○i•na•ble
a•bom○i•na•bly
a•bom○i•nate
a•bom○i•na•tion
ab○o○rig○i•nal
aboriginal cost
aboriginal peo•ples
ab○o○rig○i•nal○i○ty
ab○o○rig○i•nal○ly
a•bort
a•bor•ti•fa•cient
a•bor•tion
abortion pill
a•bor•tion•ist
a•bor•tive
a•bor•tive•ly
a•bor•tus n., pl.
 a•bor•tus○es
a•bout

a•bove
above the line
a•bove•men•tioned
abr. (abridged; abridg-
 ment
a•brade v.,
 a•brad○ed, a•brad•
 ing (to scrape: cf. UP-
 BRAID)
a•bra•sion
a•bra•sive
a•bra•sive•ly
a•bra•sive•ness
a•bridg•a•ble
a•bridge v.,
 a•bridged, a•bridg•
 ing
a•bridged (citation
 form: abr.)
a•bridg○er
a•bridg•ment (citation
 form: abr.)
a•broad
ab•ro•ga•ble
ab•ro•gate v., ab•ro•
 gat○ed, ab•ro•gat•
 ing
ab•ro•ga•tion
ab•ro•ga•tive
ab•ro•ga•tor
abs. re. (absente reo)
ab•scess
ab•scessed
ab•scond•ence
ab•scond○er
ab•scond•ing
ab•sence
absence with•out
 leave (AWOL)
ab•sent
absent with•out
 leave (AWOL)
ab•sen○te Latin.
absente re○o (abs.
 re.) Latin.

ab•sen•tee
absentee bal•lot
absentee land•lord
absentee man•age•
 ment
absentee vote
absentee vot○er
ab•sen•tee•ism
ab•so•lute
absolute con•vey•
 ance
absolute deed
absolute dis•cre•tion
absolute di•vorce
absolute es•tate
absolute gift
absolute im•ped○i•
 ment
absolute law
absolute li•a•bil○i○ty
absolute ma•jor○i○ty
absolute mon•arch
absolute mon•ar•chy
absolute nui•sance
absolute priv○i•lege
absolute right
absolute sale
absolute ti•tle
ab•so•lute•ly
ab•so•lute•ness
ab•so•lu•tion
ab•so•lut•ism
ab•so•lut•ist
ab•so•lu•to○ry
ab•solv•a•ble
ab•solve v., ab•
 solved, ab•solv•ing
ab•sorb
ab•sorb•a•ble risk
ab•sorp•tion
absorption cost•ing
abs•que Latin.
ab•stain
ab•stain○er
ab•sten•tion

ab•sten•tion•ism
ab•sten•tion•ist
ab•sti•nence
abstinence syn•drome
ab•sti•nent
ab•stract
abstract of ti•tle
ab•stract•er
ab•strac•tion
ab•stract•ly
ab•stract•ness
ab•struse
ab•struse•ly
ab•struse•ness
ab•surd
ab•surd•i•ty
ab•surd•ly
a•bus•a•ble
a•buse n., v.,
  a•bused, a•bus•ing
abuse ex•cuse
abuse of dis•cre•tion
abuse of proc•ess
a•bus•er
a•bu•sive
a•bu•sive•ly
a•bu•sive•ness
a•but v., a•but•ted,
  a•but•ting
a•but•tal
a•but•ter
A/C or a/c (account; ac-
  count current; ac-
  counts current)
Acad. (Academic; Acad-
  emy)
ac•a•deme
ac•a•de•mese
ac•a•de•mi•a
ac•a•dem•ic (citation
  form: Acad.)
academic free•dom
academic ques•tion
ac•a•dem•i•cal•ly
ac•a•de•mi•cian
ac•a•dem•i•cism

a•cad•e•o•my (citation
  form: Acad.)
ac•cede v., ac•
  ced•ed, ac•ced•ing
  (to assent; to attain a
  high position: cf. EX-
  CEED)
ac•ced•er
ac•cel•er•a•ble
ac•cel•er•ant
ac•cel•er•ate v., ac•
  cel•er•at•ed, ac•
  cel•er•at•ing
ac•cel•er•at•ed cost
re•cov•er•y sys•
tem
accelerated de•pre•
ci•a•tion
ac•cel•er•a•tion
acceleration clause
ac•cen•tu•ate v., ac•
  cen•tu•at•ed, ac•
  cen•tu•at•ing
ac•cen•tu•a•tion
ac•cept (to receive or
  agree to: cf. EXCEPT)
ac•cept•a•bil•i•ty
ac•cept•a•ble
ac•cept•a•bly
ac•cept•ance
ac•cept•er
ac•cept•ee
ac•cep•tor
ac•cess (ability to
  reach: cf. EXCESS)
access charge
ac•ces•sa•ry See AC-
  CESSORY.
ac•ces•si•bil•i•ty
ac•ces•si•ble
ac•ces•si•bly
ac•ces•sion
ac•ces•sion•al
ac•ces•sions tax
ac•ces•so•ri•al
ac•ces•so•ri•ly or
  ac•ces•sa•ri•ly

ac•ces•so•ri•ness
ac•ces•so•ry or ac•
  ces•sa•ry n., pl. ac•
  ces•so•ries or ac•
  ces•sa•ries
accessory af•ter the
fact
accessory be•fore the
fact
ac•ci•dent
accident in•sur•ance
accident-prone
ac•ci•dent•al
accidental death
accidental death
ben•e•fit
ac•ci•dent•al•ly
ac•claim
ac•claim•er
ac•cla•ma•tion
ac•clam•a•to•ry
ac•com•mo•da•ble
ac•com•mo•date v.,
  ac•com•mo•dat•ed,
  ac•com•mo•dat•ing
ac•com•mo•dat•ed
par•ty
ac•com•mo•da•tion
accommodation bill
accommodation in•
dorse•ment
accommodation
pa•per
accommodation
par•ty
ac•com•mo•da•
tion•al
ac•com•mo•da•tion•
ist
ac•com•mo•da•tive
ac•com•mo•da•tive•
ness
ac•com•plice
ac•com•plish
ac•com•plish•a•ble
ac•com•plish•ment

ac•cord

accord and sat•is•fac•tion

ac•cord•ance

ac•cord•ant

ac•cord•ing•ly

ac•cost

ac•count (A/C or a/c) (citation form: Acct.)

account book

account cur•rent (A/C or a/c) n., pl. ac•counts cur•rent

account debt•or

account of (A/O or a/o)

account par•ty

account pay•a•ble (A/P) n., pl. ac•counts pay•a•ble

account re•ceiv•a•ble (A/R) n., pl. ac•counts re•ceiv•a•ble

account ren•dered

account stat•ed

ac•count•a•bil•i•ty

ac•count•a•ble

ac•count•an•cy (citation form: Acct.)

ac•count•ant (citation form for sing. and pl.: Acct.)

ac•count•ant's re•port

ac•count•ing (citation form: Acct.)

accounting meth•od

accounting pe•ri•od

ac•cred•it

ac•cred•it•a•ble

ac•cred•i•ta•tion

ac•cred•it•ed

ac•crete v., ac•cret•ed, ac•cret•ing

ac•cre•tion

ac•cre•tion•ar•y

ac•cre•tive

ac•croach (to usurp: cf. ENCROACH)

ac•croach•ment

ac•cru•a•ble

ac•cru•al

accrual ac•count•ing

accrual ba•sis

ac•crue v., ac•crued, ac•cru•ing

accrued de•pre•ci•a•tion

accrued div•i•dend

accrued ex•pense

accrued in•come

accrued in•ter•est

accrued li•a•bil•i•ty

ac•cru•er

Acct. (Account; Accountant; Accountants; Accounting; Accountancy)

ac•cul•tur•ate v., ac•cul•tur•at•ed, ac•cul•tur•at•ing

ac•cul•tur•a•tion

ac•cul•tur•a•tion•al

ac•cul•tur•a•tive

ac•cul•tu•rize v., ac•cul•tu•rized, ac•cul•tu•riz•ing

ac•cu•mu•la•ble

ac•cu•mu•late v., ac•cu•mu•lat•ed, ac•cu•mu•lat•ing

ac•cu•mu•lat•ed de•pre•ci•a•tion

accumulated earn•ings cred•it

accumulated earnings tax

accumulated sur•plus

ac•cu•mu•la•tion

accumulation trust

ac•cu•mu•la•tive

ac•cu•mu•la•tive•ly

ac•cu•ra•cy

ac•cu•rate

ac•cu•rate•ly

ac•cu•sa•tion

ac•cu•sa•to•ri•al

accusatorial sys•tem

ac•cu•sa•to•ri•al•ly

ac•cu•sa•to•ry

accusatory in•stru•ment

ac•cuse v., ac•cused, ac•cus•ing

ac•cused n., pl. ac•cused, adj.

ac•cus•er

ac•cu•sing•ly

ACE (adjusted current earnings)

a•ce•nes•the•sia

a•ceph•a•lous

a•cer•bic

a•cer•bi•cal•ly

a•cer•bi•ty

a•ce•tone

a•cet•or•phine Controlled Subst.

a•cet•yl-al•pha-meth•yl-fen•tan•yl Controlled Subst.

a•cet•yl•di•hy•dro•co•deine Controlled Subst.

a•cet•yl•meth•a•dol Controlled Subst.

ache v., ached, ach•ing, n.

a•chiev•a•ble

a•chieve v., a•chieved, a•chiev•ing

a•chieve•ment

achievement age

achievement quo•tient

achievement test

a∘chiev∘er
ac∘id
acid rain
acid-test ra∘tio
a∘cid∘ic
a∘cid∘i∘ty
ac∘knowl∘edge
ac∘knowl∘edge∘
a∘ble
ac∘knowl∘edg∘er
ac∘knowl∘edg∘ment
ac∘me (pinnacle: vs. acne)
acq. (acquiescence)
ac∘quaint
ac∘quaint∘ance
acquaintance rape
ac∘quaint∘ance∘ship
ac∘quaint∘ed
ac∘quaint∘ed∘ness
ac∘quest
ac∘quet
ac∘qui∘esce v., ac∘qui∘esced, ac∘qui∘esc∘ing
ac∘qui∘es∘cence (citation form: acq.)
ac∘qui∘es∘cent
ac∘qui∘es∘cent∘ly
ac∘qui∘es∘cing∘ly
ac∘quire v., ac∘quired, ac∘quir∘ing
ac∘quired im∘mu∘no∘de∘fi∘cien∘cy (or im∘mune de∘fi∘cien∘cy) syn∘drome (AIDS)
ac∘quir∘er
ac∘quis com∘mu∘nau∘taire French.
ac∘qui∘si∘tion
acquisition cost
ac∘quis∘i∘tive
acquisitive re∘or∘gan∘i∘za∘tion
ac∘quis∘i∘tive∘ly

ac∘quis∘i∘tive∘ness
ac∘quit v., ac∘quit∘ted, ac∘quit∘ting
ac∘quit∘tal
ac∘quit∘tance
ac∘quit∘ter
a∘cre
a∘cre∘age
ac∘ri∘mo∘ni∘ous
ac∘ri∘mo∘ni∘ous∘ly
ac∘ri∘mo∘ni∘ous∘ness
ac∘ri∘mo∘ny
a∘crit∘i∘cal
ac∘ro∘nym
ac∘ro∘nym∘ic
ac∘ro∘nym∘i∘cal∘ly
ac∘ron∘y∘mous
a∘cross the board adv.
across-the-board adj.
ACRS (accelerated cost recovery system)
act
act of bank∘rupt∘cy
act of com∘mis∘sion
act of God
act of in∘sol∘ven∘cy
act of o∘mis∘sion
act of state
act of state doc∘trine
act of war
ac∘ta n.pl. Latin.
acta pub∘li∘ca Latin.
act∘ing
acting out
ac∘ti∘o n., pl. ac∘ti∘o∘nes Latin.
actio in per∘so∘nam Latin.
actio in rem Latin.
actio mix∘ta Latin.
ac∘tion
action grant
action in per∘so∘nam
action in rem

action on the case
ac∘tion∘a∘bil∘i∘ty
ac∘tion∘a∘ble
ac∘tion∘a∘bly
ac∘tive
active con∘trol du∘ty
active duty
active in∘come
active ingredient
active in∘volve∘ment du∘ty
active serv∘ice
active trust
ac∘tive∘ly
ac∘tive∘ness
ac∘tiv∘ism
ac∘tiv∘ist
ac∘tiv∘i∘ty
ac∘tor
ac∘tu∘al
actual au∘thor∘i∘ty
actual cash val∘ue (ACV)
actual cost
actual dam∘ag∘es
actual de∘liv∘er∘y
actual e∘vic∘tion
actual know∘ledge
actual mal∘ice
actual no∘tice
actual pos∘ses∘sion
ac∘tu∘ar∘i∘al
ac∘tu∘ar∘i∘al∘ly
ac∘tu∘ar∘y
ac∘tum n., pl. ac∘ta Latin.
ac∘tus n., pl. ac∘tus Latin.
actus re∘us Latin.
a∘cu∘men
a∘cute
acute stress dis∘or∘der
acute stress re∘ac∘tion
a∘cute∘ly

a•cute•ness

ACV (actual cash value)

A.D.¹ (in the year of the Lord: from Latin *anno Domini*)

A.D.² (assembly district)

ad au•di•en•dum et ter•mi•nan•dum *Latin.*

ad dam•num *Latin.*

ad damnum clause

ad de•li•be•ran•dum *Latin.*

ad fa•ci•en•dum et re•ci•pi•en•dum *Latin.*

ad hoc *Latin.*

ad ho•mi•nem *Latin.*

ad i•dem *Latin.*

ad inf. (ad infinitum)

ad in•fi•ni•tum (ad inf.) *Latin.*

ad init. (ad initium)

ad in•i•ti•um (ad init.) *Latin.*

ad in•qui•ren•dum *Latin.*

ad int. (ad interim)

ad in•te•rim (ad int.) *Latin.*

ad li•tem *Latin.*

ad nau•se•am *Latin.*

ad pro•se•quen•dum *Latin.*

ad quem *Latin*

ad quod dam•num *Latin.*

ad res•pon•den•dum *Latin.*

ad sa•tis•fa•ci•en•dum *Latin.*

ad sec•tam (ads.) *Latin.*

ad sub•ji•ci•en•dum *Latin.*

ad tes•ti•fi•can•dum *Latin.*

ad val. (ad valorem)

ad va•lo•rem (ad val. or A/V or a.v.) *Latin.*

ad valorem tax

ad•age

ad•o•a•mance

ad•o•a•man•cy

ad•o•a•mant

a•dapt (to modify; to adjust: cf. ADEPT; ADOPT)

a•dapt•a•bil•i•ty

a•dapt•a•ble

ad•ap•ta•tion

a•dapt•ed

a•dapt•er

a•dap•tive

a•dap•tive•ly

ad•ap•tiv•i•ty

ADD (attention deficit disorder)

add-on

add-on in•ju•ry

ad•den•dum *n., pl.* ad•den•da

ad•dict

ad•dict•ed

ad•dict•ing

ad•dic•tion

ad•dic•tive

ad•dic•tive•ness

ad•di•tion

ad•di•tion•al

additional in•sur•ance

additional in•sured

additional paid-in cap•i•tal

ad•di•tur *Latin.*

ad•dress

ad•dress•a•ble

ad•dress•ee

ad•dres•sor or ad•dress•er

ad•duce *v.*, ad•duced, ad•duc•ing (to put forth: cf. EDUCE)

ad•duc•i•ble or ad•duce•a•ble

a•deem

a•demp•tion

ad•e•o•nine **(A)**

a•dept (skilled: cf. ADAPT, ADOPT)

a•dept•ly

a•dept•ness

ad•e•qua•cy

ad•e•quate

adequate and full con•sid•er•a•tion

adequate de•scrip•tion

adequate pro•tec•tion

adequate rem•e•dy at law

adequate state grounds

ad•e•quate•ly

ad•e•quate•ness

ad•her•a•ble

ad•here *v.*, ad•hered, ad•her•ing

ad•her•ence

ad•her•er

ad•he•sion con•tract

ad•ja•cence

ad•ja•cen•cy *n., pl.* ad•ja•cen•cies

ad•ja•cent

ad•ja•cent•ly

ad•jec•tive

adjective law

ad•join

ad•join•ing

ad•journ

ad•journed meet•ing

ad•journ•ment

ad•judge *v.*, ad•judged, ad•judg•ing
ad•ju•di•cate *v.*, ad•ju•di•cat•ed, ad•ju•di•cat•ing
ad•ju•di•cat•ed
ad•ju•di•ca•tion
ad•ju•di•ca•tive
ad•ju•di•ca•tor
ad•ju•di•ca•to•ry
ad•junct
ad•junc•tion
ad•ju•ra•tion (earnest comment or request: cf. ABJURATION)
ad•ju•ra•to•ry
ad•jure *v.*, ad•jured, ad•jur•ing (to command or entreat: cf. ABJURE)
ad•jur•er or ad•ju•ror
ad•just
ad•just•a•bil•i•ty
ad•just•a•ble
adjustable-rate mort•gage (ARM)
ad•just•a•bly
ad•just•ed
adjusted ba•sis
adjusted book val•ue
adjusted cur•rent earn•ings (ACE)
adjusted gross es•tate
adjusted gross in•come (AGI)
adjusted grossed-up ba•sis (AGUB)
adjusted or•di•nar•y gross in•come (AOGI)
ad•just•er or ad•jus•tor
ad•just•ing en•try
ad•jus•tive

ad•just•ment
adjustment dis•or•der
adjustment of loss
ad•just•ment•al
ad•ju•vant
Adm. (Admiralty; Admiralty Court; Admiralty Division)
ad•mea•sure *v.*, ad•mea•sured, ad•mea•sur•ing
ad•mea•sure•ment
ad•mea•sur•er
Admin. (Administration; Administrative)
ad•min•is•ter
ad•min•is•tered price
ad•min•is•tra•tion (*citation form:* Admin.)
ad•min•is•tra•tion•al
ad•min•is•tra•tive (*citation form:* Admin.)
administrative a•gen•cy
administrative dis•cre•tion
administrative ex•pense
administrative hear•ing
administrative law
Administrative Law Judge (A.L.J.)
administrative leave
administrative pro•ce•dure
administrative re•lief
administrative rem•e•dy
administrative re•view
administrative tri•bu•nal

ad•min•is•tra•tive•ly
ad•min•is•tra•tor (*citation form:* Adm'r)
administrator ad li•tem
administrator c.t.a. (cum testamento annexo)
administrator d.b.n. (de bonis non)
administrator pen•den•te li•te
administrator with will an•nexed
ad•min•is•tra•tor•ship
ad•min•is•tra•trix *n.*, *pl.* ad•min•is•tra•tri•ces
ad•mi•ral•ty (*citation form:* Adm.)
Admiralty Court (*citation form:* Adm.)
Admiralty Di•vi•sion (*citation form:* Adm.)
admiralty ju•ris•dic•tion
admiralty law
admiralty side
ad•mis•si•bil•i•ty
ad•mis•si•ble
admissible for a lim•it•ed pur•pose
ad•mis•si•bly
ad•mis•sion
admission to the bar
ad•mit *v.*, ad•mit•ted, ad•mit•ting
ad•mit•tance
ad•mit•ted com•pa•ny
ad•mit•ted•ly
ad•mit•tee
ad•mon•ish
ad•mon•ish•ment

ad•mo•ni•tion
ad•mon•i•to•ri•ly
ad•mon•i•to•ry
Adm'r (Administrator)
Adm'x (Administratrix)
ad•o•les•cence
ad•o•les•cent
a•dopt (to take as one's own: cf. ADAPT, ADEPT)
a•dopt•a•bil•i•ty
a•dopt•a•ble
a•dopt•ed child
a•dopt•ee
a•dopt•er
a•dop•tion
a•dop•tive
adoptive par•ent
a•dop•tive•ly
ADP (automatic data processing)
ADR (alternative dispute resolution; asset depreciation range; American depository receipt)
ads. (at the suit of: from Latin *ad sectam*)
ADSP (aggregate deemed sales price)
a•dult
a•dul•ter•ant
a•dul•ter•ate *v.*, a•dul•ter•at•ed, a•dul•ter•at•ing
a•dul•ter•a•tion
a•dul•ter•a•tor
a•dul•ter•er
a•dul•ter•ess
a•dul•ter•ine
a•dul•ter•ous
a•dul•ter•ous•ly
a•dul•ter•y
a•dult•hood
a•dult•like
a•dult•ly

a•dult•ness
adv. (adversus)
ad•vance *n.*, *v.*, ad•vanced, ad•vanc•ing
advance di•rec•tive
ad•vance•ment
ad•van•tage
ad•van•ta•geous
ad•van•ta•geous•ly
ad•van•ta•geous•ness
ad•ven•ti•tious
ad•ven•ti•tious•ly
ad•ven•ti•tious•ness
ad•ven•ture
Adver. (Advertising)
ad•ver•sar•i•al
ad•ver•sar•i•ness
ad•ver•sar•y *n.*, *pl.* ad•ver•sar•ies, *adj.*
adversary pro•ceed•ing
adversary sys•tem
ad•verse (contrary to one's interests; opposing: cf. AVERSE)
adverse in•ter•est
adverse o•pin•ion
adverse pos•ses•sion
adverse se•lec•tion
adverse use
adverse us•er
adverse wit•ness
ad•verse•ly
ad•verse•ness
ad•ver•si•ty
ad•ver•sus (adv.) *Latin.*
ad•ver•tis•a•ble
ad•ver•tise *v.*, ad•ver•tised, ad•ver•tis•ing
ad•ver•tise•ment
ad•ver•tis•er
ad•ver•tis•ing

ad•vice (a suggestion: cf. ADVISE)
advice and con•sent
ad•vis•a•bil•i•ty
ad•vis•a•ble
ad•vise *v.*, ad•vised, ad•vis•ing (to offer a suggestion: cf. ADVICE)
advise and con•sent
ad•vis•ed•ly
ad•vise•ment
ad•vis•er or ad•vi•sor
ad•vi•so•ry
advisory o•pin•ion
Advoc. (Advocacy; Advocate)
ad•vo•ca•cy (*citation form:* Advoc.)
ad•vo•cate[1] *n.* (*citation form:* Advoc.)
advocate[2] *v.*, ad•vo•cat•ed, ad•vo•cat•ing
ad•vow•ee
ad•vow•son
ae•gis
ae•qui•tas se•qui•tur le•gem *Latin.*
ae•quo a•ni•mo *Latin.*
aer•o•sol
aes•thet•ic
AET *Controlled Subst.* (alpha-ethyltryptamine)
Aff. (Affidavit; Affirmation; Affairs)
af•fa•ble
af•fa•bly
af•fair
af•fairs (*citation form:* Aff.)
affairs of state
aff'd (affirmed)

af•fect (to act on; emotional state: cf. EFFECT)

af•fect•a•bil•i•ty

af•fect•a•ble

af•fect•ing com•merce

af•fec•tion

af•fec•tive (pertaining to one's emotional state: cf. EFFECTIVE)

affective dis•or•der

af•fect•less

af•feer

af•fee•ror

aff'g (affirming)

af•fi•ance v., af•fi•anced, af•fi•anc•ing

af•fi•ant

af•fi•bil•i•ty

af•fi•da•vit (citation form: Aff.)

affidavit of serv•ice

af•fil•i•a•ble

af•fil•i•ate n., v., af•fil•i•at•ed, af•fil•i•at•ing

affiliate trans•ac•tion

af•fil•i•at•ed

affiliated en•ter•prise

af•fil•i•a•tion

affiliation or•der

af•fil•i•a•tive

af•fi•nal

af•fine

af•fined

af•fine•ly

af•fin•i•tive

af•fin•i•ty n., pl. af•fin•i•ties

affinity card

af•firm

af•firm•a•ble

af•firm•a•bly

af•firm•ance

af•fir•ma•tion (citation form: Aff.)

af•firm•a•tive

affirmative act

affirmative ac•tion

affirmative action pro•gram

affirmative de•fense

affirmative dis•clo•sure

affirmative ease•ment

affirmative plea

affirmative preg•nant

affirmative proof

affirmative re•lief

affirmative war•ran•ty

af•firmed (citation form: aff'd)

af•firm•er

af•firm•ing (citation form: aff'g)

af•firm•ing•ly

af•fix

af•fix•a•tion

af•flict

af•flic•tion

af•flu•ence (wealth: a flowing toward: cf. EFFLUENCE)

af•flu•ent (rich; abundant; a tributary: cf. EFFLUENT)

af•flu•ent•ly

af•force v., af•forced, af•forc•ing

af•force•ment

af•ford

af•ford•a•bil•i•ty

af•ford•a•ble

af•ford•a•bly

af•fran•chise v., af•fran•chised, af•fran•chis•ing (to free: cf. ENFRANCHISE)

af•fran•chise•ment

af•fray

af•fray•er

af•freight

af•freight•er

af•freight•ment

af•front

AFLP (amplified fragment length polymorphism)

a•fore•men•tioned

a•fore•said

a•fore•thought

a•foul

Afr. (Africa; African)

a•fraid

Af•ri•ca (citation form: Afr.)

Af•ri•can (citation form: Afr.)

af•ter

after-ac•quired

after-acquired prop•er•ty

after-acquired ti•tle

after-born

after-born child

after cost

after hours adv.

after-hours adj.

after-tax or af•ter•tax

after-tax in•come

after the fact

af•ter•care

af•ter•ef•fect

af•ter•mar•ket

af•ter•math

af•ter•tax See AFTER-TAX.

af•ter•thought

AG (Attorney General)

a•gain

a•gainst

against the weight of the ev•i•dence

age n., v., aged, ag•ing or age•ing

age-ap•pro•pri•ate

age dis•crim•i•na•tion

age group

age of con•sent

age of dis•cre•tion

age of ma•jor•i•ty

age of rea•son

ag•ed *adj., n.*

ag•ed•ness

age•ism

age•ist (age-discriminatory; one who discriminates on the basis of age: cf. AGIST)

a•gen•cy *n., pl.* a•gen•cies

agency ac•tion

agency con•tract

agency dis•cre•tion

agency shop

a•gen•da *n., pl.* a•gen•das

a•gen•dum *n., pl.* a•gen•da or a•gen•dums

a•gent

agent pro•vo•ca•teur *n., pl.* a•gents pro•vo•ca•teurs *French.*

a•gent•ory

Ag•ga•dah

ag•gran•dize *v.,* ag•gran•dized, ag•gran•diz•ing

ag•gran•dize•ment

ag•gra•vate *v.,* ag•gra•vat•ed, ag•gra•vat•ing

ag•gra•vat•ed

aggravated as•sault

ag•gra•va•ting cir•cum•stance

aggravating fac•tor

ag•gra•va•tion

ag•gre•ga•ble

ag•gre•gate *n., v.,* ag•gre•gat•ed, ag•gre•gat•ing

aggregate con•cen•tra•tion

aggregate deemed sales price (ADSP)

ag•gre•gate•ly

ag•gre•ga•tion

ag•gre•ga•tive

ag•gre•ga•tive•ly

ag•gress

ag•gres•sion

ag•gres•sive

aggressive war

ag•gres•sive•ly

ag•gres•sive•ness

ag•gres•sor

ag•grieve *v.,* ag•grieved, ag•griev•ing

ag•grieved

ag•griev•ed•ly

ag•griev•ed•ness

ag•grieve•ment

a•ghast

AGI (adjusted gross income)

ag•o•ing sched•ule

ag•o•i•o *n., pl.* ag•o•i•os

ag•o•i•o•tage

a•gist (to pasture livestock for a fee: cf. AGE-IST)

a•gist•er

a•gist•ment

ag•i•tate *v.,* ag•i•tat•ed, ag•i•tat•ing

ag•i•tat•ed

agitated de•pres•sion

ag•i•tat•ed•ly

ag•i•ta•tion

ag•i•ta•tor

ag•it•prop

ag•it•prop•ist

ag•o•nist

ag•o•nis•tic

ag•o•nis•ti•cal•ly

ag•o•nize *v.,* ag•o•nized, ag•o•niz•ing

ag•o•nized

ag•o•niz•ed•ly

ag•o•niz•ing

ag•o•niz•ing•ly

ag•o•ny *n., pl.* ag•o•nies

a•grar•i•an

agrarian laws

a•grar•i•an•ism

a•gré•a•tion *French.*

a•gree *v.,* a•greed, a•gree•ing

a•gree•a•bil•i•ty

a•gree•a•ble

a•gree•a•ble•ness

a•gree•a•bly

a•greed

agreed case

a•gree•ment

agreement to a•gree

a•gré•ment *French.*

ag•ri•busi•ness

Agric. (Agricultural; Agriculture)

ag•ri•chem•i•cal

ag•ri•cul•tur•al (*citation form:* **Agric.**)

agricultural a•gent

ag•ri•cul•tur•al•ly

ag•ri•cul•ture (*citation form:* **Agric.**)

ag•ro-ec•o•nom•ic

ag•ro-in•dus•tri•al or ag•ro•in•dus•tri•al

ag•ro-in•dus•try

a•ground

AGUB (adjusted grossed-up basis)

aid (assistance; to assist: cf. AIDE)

aid and a•bet

aid prayer or **aid-prayer**

aide (helper: cf. AID)

aide-mé•moire *n., pl.* **aide-mé•moire** *French.*

aid∘er

aider and a∘bet•tor (or a∘bet•ter)

aider by ver•dict

aid•ing and a∘bet•ting

AIDS (acquired immunodeficiency (or immune deficiency) syndrome)

AIDS-re•lat∘ed com•plex (ARC)

ai∘el *Law French.*

aim

aim•less

aim•less∘ly

aim•less•ness

air car∘go

air carr•i∘er

air ex•press

air freight

air pi•ra∘cy

air pi•rate

air pol•lu•tion

air right

air way•bill

air•bill

air∘craft

air∘fare

air∘ing

air•plane

air•wor•thy

a.k.a. (also known as)

a∘kin

a∘larm

a∘larm•ing

a∘larm•ing∘ly

a∘larm•ism

a∘larm•ist

a∘lar∘um

al∘be∘it

al•cai∘ode or **al•cay∘ode** *n., pl.* **al•cai∘odes** or **al•cay∘odes** *Spanish.*

al•cal∘ode *n., pl.* **al•cal•des** *Spanish.*

al•co∘hol

alcohol a∘buse

alcohol de•pend•ence

alcohol-in•duced dis•or∘der

alcohol-induced per•sist•ing am•nes•tic disorder

alcohol-induced psy•chot∘ic disorder

alcohol in•tox∘i•ca•tion

alcohol intoxication de•li•ri∘um

alcohol with•draw∘al delirium

al•co∘hol∘ic

alcoholic hal•lu•ci•no∘sis

alcoholic jeal•ous∘y

alcoholic par∘a•noi∘a

alcoholic psy•cho∘sis

al•co∘hol∘i•cal∘ly

al•co∘hol•ism

al•der•man *n., pl.* **al•der•men**

al•der•man∘cy

al•der•man∘ic

al•der•man∘ry

al•der•man•ship

al•der•per•son

al•der•wom∘an *n., pl.* **al•der•wom∘en**

a∘le∘a•to∘ry

aleatory con•tract

a∘lert

a∘lert∘ly

a∘lert•ness

ALF (assisted living facility)

al•fen•ta•nil *Controlled Subst.*

Al∘ford plea

al•go•rithm

al•go•rith•mic

a∘li∘as *n., pl.* **a∘li•as∘es**, *adv.*

alias sum•mons

alias writ

al∘i∘bi *n., pl.* **al∘i•bis**, *adj.*

alibi wit•ness

a∘li∘en

alien cor•po•ra•tion

alien en∘e•my

al•ien•a•bil∘i•ty

al•ien•a•ble

al•ien∘age

al•ien•ate *v.,* **al•ien•at∘ed**, **al•ien•at•ing**

al•ien•a•tion

alienation of af•fec•tions

al•ien•a•tive

al•ien•a•tor

al•ien•ee

a∘li∘e∘ni ju∘ris *Latin.*

al•ien•ism

al•ien•ist

al•ien∘or

a∘lign•ment

a∘li•ment

a∘li•men•ta•tion

a∘li•mo∘ny

a∘li•quot

a∘li•ter *Latin.*

a∘li•un∘de *Latin.*

aliunde rule

a∘live

A.L.J. (Administrative Law Judge)

al•ka∘li

al•ka•line

al•ka•lin∘i∘ty

al•ka•loid
al•ka•loid•al
all dis•putes clause
all-in•clu•sive
all-lines in•sur•ance
all-points bul•le•tin (APB)
all-pur•pose pub•lic fig•ure
all read•y (fully prepared: cf. ALREADY)
all right
all-risk in•sur•ance
all risks pol•i•cy
all the world
all to•geth•er (collectively: cf. ALTOGETHER)
al•le•ga•ta et pro•ban•da *Latin.*
al•le•ga•tion
al•lege
al•lege•a•ble
al•leg•ed•ly
al•leg•er
al•le•giance
al•lele
allele fre•quen•cy
allele-spe•cif•ic ol•i•go•nu•cle•o•tide (ASO) probe
Al•len charge
al•le•vi•ate *v.,* al•le•vi•at•ed, al•le•vi•at•ing
al•le•vi•a•tion
al•li•a•ble
al•li•ance
al•lied
al•li•sion
al•lo•ca•bil•i•ty
al•lo•ca•ble
al•lo•cate
al•lo•ca•tion
al•lo•ca•tive
al•lo•ca•tur *Latin.*

al•lo•cute *v.,* al•lo•cut•ed, al•lo•cut•ing
al•lo•cu•tion
al•lo•di•al or a•lo•di•al
al•lo•di•al•i•ty or a•lo•di•al•i•ty
al•lo•di•al•ly or a•lo•di•al•ly
al•lo•di•um or a•lo•di•um *n., pl.* al•lo•di•a or a•lo•di•a
al•lo•graph
al•lo•graph•ic
al•longe
al•lo•path
al•lo•path•ic
al•lo•path•i•cal•ly
al•lop•a•thist
al•lop•a•thy
al•lot *v.,* al•lot•ted, al•lot•ting
al•lot•ment
al•lot•ta•ble
al•lot•tee
al•lot•ter
al•low
al•low•a•bil•i•ty
al•low•a•ble
al•low•a•bly
al•low•ance
allowance for bad debts
allowance for doubt•ful ac•counts
al•lowed (permitted: cf. ALOUD)
al•lude *v.,* al•lud•ed, al•lud•ing (to refer: cf. ELUDE)
al•lu•sion (reference: cf. ILLUSION)
al•lu•sive (containing allusions: cf. ELUSIVE; ILLUSIVE)

al•lu•sive•ly
al•lu•sive•ness
al•lu•vi•on (gradual depositing of land by water: cf. ALLUVIUM)
al•lu•vi•um (land deposited by water: cf. ALLUVION)
al•ly *n., pl.* al•lies, *v.,* al•lied, al•ly•ing
al•lyl•pro•dine *Controlled Subst.*
al•moign *Law French.*
alms
alms•house
a•lo•di•al See ALLODIAL.
a•lo•di•al•i•ty See ALLODIALITY.
a•lo•di•al•ly See ALLODIALLY.
a•lo•gi•a
a•loud (vocally; out loud: cf. ALLOWED)
al•pha•ce•tyl•meth•a•dol *Controlled Subst.*
al•pha-eth•yl•tryp•ta•mine (AET) *Controlled Subst.*
al•pha-mep•ro•dine *Controlled Subst.*
al•pha-meth•a•dol *Controlled Subst.*
alpha-meth•yl•fen•tan•yl *Controlled Subst.*
alpha-meth•yl•thi•o•fen•tan•yl *Controlled Subst.*
al•pha-pro•dine *Controlled Subst.*
al•praz•o•lam *Controlled Subst.*
A.L.R. (American Law Reports)

al•read•y (previously:
cf. ALL READY)

al○so known as
(a.k.a)

al○ter

alter e○go

al•ter•a•bil○i•ty

al•ter•a•ble

al•ter•a•bly

al•ter○a•tion

al•ter•ca•tion

alt•er○er

al•ter•nate n., adj., v.,
al•ter•nat○ed, al•
ter•nat○ing

alternate ju○ror

alternate val○u•a•
tion

alternate valuation
date

al•ter•nate○ly

al•ter•na•tion

al•ter•na•tive

alternative dis•pute
res○o•lu•tion (ADR)

alternative hy•
poth○e○sis

alternative min○i•
mum tax (AMT)

alternative minimum
tax•a•ble income
(AMTI)

alternative plead•ing

alternative re•lief

alternative rem○e•dy

alternative writ

al•ter•na•tive○ly

al•to•geth○er (com-
pletely: cf. ALL TO-
GETHER)

al•tru•ism

al•tru•ist

al•tru•is•tic

a○lum○na n., pl.
a○lum•nae

a○lum•nus n., pl.
a○lum○ni

Alz•hei○mer's dis•
ease

A.M. (Master of Arts:
from Latin *Artium
Magister*)

Am. (America; Ameri-
can; Americas)

a.m. (before noon: from
Latin *ante meridiem*)

a○mal•ga•ma•ble

a○mal•ga•mate v.,
a○mal•ga•mat○ed,
a○mal•ga•mat○ing

a○mal•ga•ma○tion

a○mal•ga•ma•tive

a○mal•ga•ma•tor

am○a•teur

am○a•teur•ism

am○a•tol

am•bas•sa•dor

am•bas•sa•
dor-at-large n., pl.
am•bas•sa•
dors-at-large

ambassador ext○ra•
or•di•nar○y and
plen○i•po•ten•ti•
ar○y

am•bas•sa•do•ri•al

am•bas•sa•do•ri•
al○ly

am•bas•sa•dor•ship

am•bi•ent

am•big•u•ous (having
two meanings: cf. AM-
BIVALENT)

am•big•u•ous○ly

am•big•u•ous•ness

am○bit

am•bi•tion

am•bi•tion•less

am•bi•tious

am•bi•tious○ly

am•bi•tious•nesʂ

am•biv•a•lence

am•biv•a•lent (of two
minds: cf. AMBIGUOUS)

am•biv•a•lent○ly

am•bu○lance

ambulance chas○er

ambulance chas•ing

am•bu•la•to•ri○ly

am•bu•la•to○ry

ambulatory sur•gi•cal
cen○ter (ASC)

am•bush

am•bush○er

a○mel•io•ra•ble

a○mel•io•rate v.,
a○mel•io•rat○ed,
a○mel•io•rat○ing
waste

a○mel•io•ra•tion

a○mel•io•ra•tive

a○mel•io•ra•tor

a○me•na•bil○i•ty

a○me•na•ble

a○me•na•bly

a○mend (to alter text
in any way: cf. EMEND)

amend. (amendment)

a○mend•a○ble

a○mend○a•to○ry

a○mend○ed re•turn

a○mend○er

a○mend•ment (*cita-
tion form: amend.*)

a○mends n.sing. or pl.

a○men○i•ty n., pl.
a○men○i•ties

a○merce v., a○merced,
a○merc○ing

a○merce•a○ble

a○merce•ment

a○merc○er

A○mer○i•ca (*citation
form: Am.*)

A○mer○i•can (*citation
form: Am.*)

American de•pos•i•to•ry re•ceipt (ADR)

American Law Re•ports (*citation form:* A.L.R.)

American Sign Lan•guage (ASL)

American Stand•ard Code for In•for•ma•tion In•ter•change (ASCII)

A•mer•i•can•ism

A•mer•i•can•ist

A•mer•i•can•i•za•tion

A•mer•i•can•ize v., A•mer•i•can•ized, A•mer•i•can•iz•ing

A•mer•i•cas

Am•e•slan

a•mi *Law French.*

a•mi•a•ble (good-natured: cf. AMICABLE)

am•i•ca•bil•i•ty

am•i•ca•ble (peaceable: cf. AMIABLE)

amicable ac•tion

am•i•ca•bly

a•mi•cus n., pl. a•mi•ci *Latin.*

amicus cu•ri•ae n., pl. amici cu•ri•ae *Latin.*

a•mi•no•rex Con•trolled Subst.

am•i•ty (friendship: cf. ENMITY)

am•mu•ni•tion

am•ne•sia

am•ne•si•ac

am•ne•sic

am•nes•tic

amnestic dis•or•der

am•nes•ty n., pl. am•nes•ties, v., am•nes•tied, am•nes•ty•ing

a•mni•o•cen•te•sis

n., pl. am•ni•o•cen•te•ses

am•o•bar•bi•tal Con•trolled Subst.

a•mok or a•muck

a•mor•al (lacking moral standards: cf. IMMORAL)

amoral per•son•al•i•ty

a•mor•al•ism

a•mo•ral•i•ty

a•mor•al•ly

a•mor•phous

a•mor•phous•ly

a•mor•phous•ness

am•or•tiz•a•ble

am•or•ti•za•tion

am•or•tize v., am•or•tized, am•or•tiz•ing

a•mo•tion

a•mount (amt.)

amount at risk

amount in con•tro•ver•sy

a•move v., a•moved, a•mov•ing

AMP-FLP (amplified fragment length polymorphism)

am•phet•a•mine Con•trolled Subst.

amphetamine-in•duced dis•or•der

am•ple

am•ple•ness

am•pli•fi•a•ble

am•pli•fi•ca•tion

am•plif•i•ca•to•ry

am•pli•fied frag•ment length pol•y•mor•phism (AFLP or AMP-FLP)

am•pli•fi•er

am•pli•fy v., am•pli•fied, am•pli•fy•ing

am•ply

am•pule

AMT (alternative minimum tax)

amt. (amount)

a•muck See AMOK.

a•muse•ment tax

am•yl ni•trite

Am•y•tal *Trademark.*

an•a•bol•ic ster•oid Controlled Subst.

a•nach•ro•nism

a•nach•ro•nis•tic

a•nach•ro•nis•ti•cal•ly

an•a•cri•sis n., pl. an•a•cri•ses

a•nal

an•a•lep•tic

an•al•ge•si•a

an•al•ge•sic

a•nal•ly

an•a•log adj. (cf. ANALOGUE)

a•nal•o•gism

a•nal•o•gist

a•nal•o•gize v., a•nal•o•gized, a•nal•o•giz•ing

a•nal•o•gous

analogous art

a•nal•o•gous•ly

a•nal•o•gous•ness

an•a•logue (preferred spelling for noun: cf. ANALOG)

a•nal•o•gy n., pl. a•nal•o•gies

analogy test

a•nal•y•sis n., pl. a•nal•y•ses

an•a•lyst (one who analyzes: cf. ANNALIST)

an•a•lyt•i•cal

analytical ju•ris•pru•dence

an•a•lyt•i•cal•ly

an•a•lyt•ics

an•a•lyz•a•bil•i•ty

an•a•lyz•a•ble

an•a•lyze

an•ar•chic

an•ar•chi•cal

an•ar•chi•cal•ly

an•ar•chism

an•ar•chist

an•ar•chis•tic

an•ar•chy

a•nath•e•ma n., pl. a•nath•e•mas

a•nath•e•ma•tize v., a•nath•e•ma•tized, a•nath•e•ma•tiz•ing

an•a•tom•i•cal

anatomical do•na•tion

anatomical gift

an•a•tom•i•cal•ly

anatomically cor•rect

a•nat•o•mist

a•nat•o•my n., pl. a•nat•o•mies

an•ces•tor

an•ces•tral

an•ces•tral•ly

an•ces•try

an•chor

an•chor•a•ble

an•chor•age

an•cient

ancient de•mesne

ancient doc•u•ment

an•cient•ly

an•cient•ness

an•cil•lar•y adj., n., pl. an•cil•lar•ies

ancillary ad•min•i•stra•tion

ancillary ju•ris•dic•tion

ancillary pro•ceed•ing

and (citation form: &)

and a•noth•er (et al.)

and oth•ers (et al.)

and the fol•low•ing (et seq.; ff.)

an•dro•cen•tric

an•dro•cen•trism

an•dro•cen•trist

an•droc•ra•cy n., pl. an•droc•ra•cies

an•dro•crat•ic

an•dro•gen

an•ec•do•tal (incidental; unsystematic: cf. ANTIDOTAL)

an•ec•do•tal•ly

an•ec•dote (account of an incident: cf. ANTIDOTE)

an•en•ce•phal•ic

an•en•ceph•a•lous

an•en•ceph•a•oly

an•es•the•sia

an•es•the•si•ol•o•gist

an•es•the•si•ol•o•gy

an•es•thet•ic

an•es•thet•i•cal•ly

an•es•the•tist

an•es•the•ti•za•tion

an•es•the•tize v., an•es•the•tized, an•es•the•tiz•ing

an•ga•ry

an•ger

An•glo-A•mer•i•can

an•gri•ly

an•gry adj., an•gri•er, an•gri•est

an•guish

an•guished

an•oi•ler•oi•dine Controlled Subst.

an•oi•mos•oi•ty n., pl. an•oi•mos•oi•ties

an•oi•mus[1] English. (animosity)

a•ni•mus[2] Latin. (intention)

animus do•nan•di Latin.

animus et fac•tum Latin.

animus fu•ran•di Latin.

animus ma•lus Latin.

ann. (annotated; annual)

an•nal•ist (a chronicler: cf. ANALYST)

an•nals n.pl.

an•nex

an•nex•a•ble

an•nex•a•tion

an•nex•a•tion•al

an•nex•a•tion•ism

an•nexed

an•oni nu•bi•les Latin.

an•ni•hi•late v., an•ni•hi•lat•ed, an•ni•hi•lat•ing

an•ni•hi•la•tion

an•ni•ver•sa•ry n., pl. an•ni•ver•sa•ries

an•no Do•mi•ni (A.D.) Latin.

annot. (annotation)

an•no•tate v., an•no•tat•ed, an•no•tat•ing

an•no•tat•ed (citation forms: Ann. in title of a work; ann. in descriptive material)

an•no•ta•tion (citation form: annot.)

an•no•ta•tive

an•no•ta•to•ry
an•nounce *v.*, an•
nounced, an•nounc•
ing
an•nounce•a•ble
an•nounce•ment
an•nounc•er
an•noy
an•noy•ance
an•noy•er
an•noy•ing
an•noy•ing•ly
an•noy•ing•ness
an•nu•al *(citation form:* **Ann.***)*
annual per•cent•age rate (APR)
annual percentage yield (APY)
annual report
an•nu•al•ize *v.*, an•
nu•al•ized, an•nu•
al•iz•ing
an•nu•al•ly
an•nu•i•tant
an•nu•i•ty *n., pl.* an•
nu•i•ties
annuity cer•tain *n., pl.* an•nu•i•ties cer•
tain
annuity de•pre•ci•a•
tion
an•nul *v.*, an•nulled, an•nul•ling
an•nul•la•ble
an•nul•ment
an•nun•ci•ate *v.*, an•
nun•ci•at•ed, an•
nun•ci•at•ing (to proclaim: cf. ENUNCI-
ATE
an•nun•ci•a•tion
an•nun•ci•a•tive
an•nun•ci•a•to•ry
an•o•o•log•i•cal
an•o•o•log•i•cal•ly

a•nom•a•lous
a•nom•a•lous•ly
a•nom•a•lous•ness
a•nom•a•ly *n., pl.* a•nom•a•lies
a•nom•ic
an•o•mie or an•o•my
anon. (anonymous)
a•non•y•mous *(citation forms:* **Anon.** as name of person; **anon.** as description)
a•non•y•mous•ly
a•non•y•mous•ness
an•o•rec•tic
an•o•rex•i•a
anorexia ner•vo•sa
an•o•rex•i•ant
an•o•rex•ic
an•swer
an•swer•a•bil•i•ty
an•swer•a•ble
an•swer•a•bly
an•swer•er
ans•wer•ing brief
an•swer•less
An•ta•buse *Trademark.*
an•tag•o•nism
an•tag•o•nist
an•tag•o•nis•tic
an•tag•o•nis•ti•
cal•ly
an•tag•o•nize *v.*, an•
tag•o•nized, an•
tag•o•niz•ing
an•te *Latin.* (before: cf. ANTI-)
ante li•tem mo•tam *Latin.*
ante mor•tem *Latin.*
an•te•cede *v.*, an•te•
ced•ed, an•te•ced•
ing
an•te•ced•ence

an•te•ced•en•cy
an•te•ced•ent
antecedent debt
an•te•ced•ent•ly
an•te•ces•sor
an•te•date *v.*, an•te•
dat•ed, an•te•dat•
ing
an•te•na•tal
an•te•na•tal•ly
an•te•na•tus *n., pl.* an•te•na•ti *Latin.*
an•te•nup•tial
antenuptial a•gree•
ment
an•te•par•tum
an•ter•o•grade am•
ne•sia
an•thra•co•sil•i•co•s
is or an•thra•sil•i•
co •sis
an•thra•co•sis
an•thra•cot•ic
an•ti- (against: cf.
ANTE)
an•ti•a•bor•tion
an•ti•an•xi•e•ty
an•ti•a•part•heid
an•ti•au•thor•i•
tar•i•an
an•ti•au•thor•i•
tar•i•an•ism
an•ti•bi•ot•ic
an•ti•bi•ot•i•cal•ly
an•ti•black
an•ti•bod•y *n., pl.*
an•ti•bod•ies
an•ti•bus•ing or
an•ti•bus•sing
an•ti•cen•sor•ship
an•ti•chre•sis *n., pl.*
an•ti•chre•ses
an•tic•i•pat•a•ble
an•tic•i•pate *v.*, an•
tic•i•pat•ed, an•
tic•i•pat•ing

an•tic•i•pa•tion
an•tic•i•pa•tive
an•tic•i•pa•tive•ly
an•tic•i•pa•tor
an•tic•i•pa•to•ri•ly
an•tic•i•pa•to•ry
anticipatory breach
anticipatory of•fense
anticipatory re•pu•
di•a•tion
an•ti•com•mu•nist
an•ti•com•pet•i•tive
anticompetitive ef•
fect
an•ti•com•pet•i•
tive•ly
an•ti•com•pet•i•
tive•ness
an•ti•con•vul•sant
an•ti•de•fi•cien•cy
stat•ute
an•ti•de•pres•sant
an•ti•de•pres•sive
an•ti•dis•crim•i•na•
tion
an•ti•do•tal (tending
to counteract: cf. ANEC-
DOTAL)
an•ti•do•tal•ly
an•ti•dote (something
that counteracts: cf.
ANECDOTE)
an•ti•dump•ing
an•ti•es•tab•lish•
ment
an•ti•es•tab•lish•
men•tar•i•an
an•ti•es•tab•lish•
men•tar•i•an•ism
an•ti•fem•i•nist
an•ti•fer•til•i•ty
an•ti•gay
an•ti•gen
an•ti•gen•ic
an•ti•gen•i•cal•ly
an•ti•ge•nic•i•ty

an•ti•ges•ta•tion•al
antigestational drug
an•ti•gov•ern•ment
an•ti•gov•ern•men•
tal
an•ti•his•ta•mine
an•ti-im•pe•ri•al•
ism
an•ti-im•pe•ri•al•ist
an•ti-im•pe•ri•al•is•
tic
an•ti-in•fla•tion
an•ti-in•fla•tion•
ar•y
an•ti-in•tel•lec•tu•al
an•ti-in•tel•lec•tu•
al•ism
an•ti•lapse stat•ute
an•ti•nep•o•tism
rule
an•ti•noise
an•ti•no•mic
an•tin•o•my n., pl.
an•tin•o•mies
an•ti•ob•scen•i•ty
an•ti•pa•thet•ic
an•ti•pa•thet•i•
cal•ly
an•tip•a•thy n., pl.
an•tip•a•thies
an•ti•por•nog•ra•
phy
an•ti•pro•lif•er•a•
tion
an•ti•psy•chot•ic
an•ti•rack•e•teer•
ing
an•ti•re•al•ism
an•ti-Se•mit•ic
an•ti-Sem•i•tism
an•ti•sex
an•ti•slav•e•o•ry
an•ti•smok•ing
an•ti•so•cial
antisocial be•hav•ior

antisocial per•son•
al•i•ty
antisocial personality
dis•or•der
an•ti•so•cial•ly
an•ti•stuf•fing rule
an•ti•take•o•ver
leg•is•la•tion
an•ti•ter•ror•ism
an•ti•ter•ror•ist
an•tith•e•sis n., pl.
an•tith•e•ses
an•ti•thet•ic
an•ti•thet•i•cal
an•ti•thet•i•cal•ly
an•ti•to•bac•co
an•ti•tox•ic
an•ti•tox•in
an•ti•trust
antitrust in•ju•ry
antitrust laws
an•ti•un•ion
an•ti•un•ion•ism
an•ti•un•ion•ist
an•ti•white
an•ti•wom•an
a•nus n., pl. a•nus•es
an•xi•e•ty n., pl. an•
xi•e•ties
anxiety dis•or•der
anxiety neu•ro•sis
anx•i•o•lyt•ic
anxiolytic-in•duced
dis•or•der
anx•ious
anx•ious•ly
anx•ious•ness
AOGI (adjusted ordi-
nary gross income)
A/P (account payable;
accounts payable)
ap•a•nage See APPA-
NAGE.
a•part•heid
ap•a•thet•ic
ap•a•thet•i•cal•ly

ap•a•thy
APB (all-points bulletin)
a•pha•sia
a•pha•sic
aph•o•rism
aph•ro•dis•i•ac
a•pol•o•get•ic
a•pol•o•get•i•cal•ly
ap•o•lo•gi•a *n., pl.*
  a•po•lo•gi•as
a•pol•o•gist
a•pol•o•gize *v.,*
  a•pol•o•gized,
  a•pol•o•giz•ing
a•pol•o•giz•er
a•pol•o•gy *n., pl.*
  a•pol•o•gies
ap•o•si•o•pe•sis *n.,*
  pl. ap•o•si•o•pe•
  ses
ap•o•si•o•pet•ic
a•pos•tille *French*
ap•o•thegm
ap•o•theg•mat•i•
  cal•ly
App. (Appeal; Appeals;
  Appellate)
app. (appendix)
App. Ct. (Appeals
  Court; Appellate
  Court)
App. Dep't (Appellate
  Department)
App. Div. (Appellate
  Division)
ap•pall
ap•palled
ap•pal•ling
ap•pal•ling•ly
ap•pa•nage or ap•a•
  nage
ap•pa•rat
ap•pa•rat•chik
ap•pa•rat•ous *n., pl.*
  ap•pa•rat•us•es
ap•par•ent

apparent au•
  thor•i•ty
apparent de•fect
apparent ease•ment
apparent heir
ap•par•ent•ly
ap•par•ent•ness
ap•peal (*citation form
  for sing. and pl.:*
  App.)
appeal as of right
appeal bond
appeal by per•mis•
  sion
ap•peal•a•bil•i•ty
ap•peal•a•ble
appealable or•der
Ap•peals Court (*cita-
  tion form:* App. Ct.)
ap•pear
ap•pear•ance
ap•peas•a•ble
ap•peas•a•ble•ness
ap•peas•a•bly
ap•pease *v.,* ap•
  peased, ap•peas•ing
ap•pease•ment
ap•peas•er
ap•peas•ing•ly
ap•pel•lant
ap•pel•late (*citation
  form:* App.)
Appellate Court (*cita-
  tion form:* App. Ct.)
Appellate De•part•
  ment (*citation form:*
  App. Dep't)
Appellate Di•vi•sion
  (*citation form:* App.
  Div.)
appellate ju•ris•dic•
  tion
ap•pel•la•tion
appellation con•tro•
  lée *French.*
ap•pel•lee

ap•pend
ap•pend•age
ap•pend•aged
ap•pend•ance or ap•
  pend•ence
ap•pend•an•cy or
  ap•pend•en•cy
ap•pend•ant or ap•
  pend•ent
ap•pen•dix[1] *n., pl.*
  ap•pen•di•ces (ad-
  dendum to a writing;
  citation form: app.
)(See also JOINT APPEN-
  DIX.)
appendix[2] *n., pl.* ap•
  pen•dix•es (an inter-
  nal organ)
ap•per•ceive *v.,* ap•
  per•ceived, ap•per•
  ceiv•ing
ap•per•cep•tion
ap•per•cep•tive
ap•per•cep•tive•ly
ap•per•tain
ap•pe•tite sup•pres•
  sant
ap•pli•ca•bil•i•ty
ap•pli•ca•ble
ap•pli•ca•bly
ap•pli•cant
ap•pli•ca•tion
ap•plied
ap•ply *v.,* ap•plied,
  ap•ply•ing
ap•point
ap•point•a•ble
ap•point•ed
ap•point•ee
ap•poin•tive
ap•point•ment
ap•poin•tor
ap•por•tion
ap•por•tion•
  a•bil•i•ty
ap•por•tion•a•ble

ap•por•tion∘er

ap•por•tion•ment

ap•po•site (pertinent: cf. OPPOSITE)

ap•po•site•ly

ap•po•site•ness

ap•prais•a•ble

ap•prais∘al

appraisal rights

ap•praise *v.*, ap•praised, ap•prais•ing (to evaluate: cf. APPRISE)

ap•prais∘er

ap•pre•ci•a•ble

ap•pre•ci•a•bly

ap•pre•ci•ate *v.*, ap•pre•ci•at∘ed, ap•pre•ci•at•ing

ap•pre•ci•at∘ed

ap•pre•ci•a•tion

ap•pre•hend

ap•pre•hend∘er

ap•pre•hen•sion

ap•pre•hen•sive

ap•pre•hen•sive•ly

ap•pre•hen•sive•ness

ap•pren•tice *n., v.*, ap•pren•ticed, ap•pren•tic∘ing

ap•pren•tice•ship

ap•prise *v.*, ap•prised, ap•pris•ing (to inform: cf. APPRAISE)

ap•proach

ap•proach•a•bil∘i•ty

ap•proach•a•ble

ap•pro•bate *v.*, ap•pro•bat∘ed, ap•pro•bat•ing

ap•pro•ba•tion

ap•pro•ba•tive

ap•pro•ba•tive•ness

ap•pro•ba•tor

ap•pro•ba•to∘ry

ap•pro•pri•a•ble

ap•pro•pri•ate *v.*, ap•pro•pri•at∘ed, ap•pro•pri•at∘ing, *adj.*

ap•pro•pri•at∘ed re•tained earn•ings

ap•pro•pri•ate•ly

ap•pro•pri•ate•ness

ap•pro•pri•a•tion

ap•pro•pri•a•tive

ap•pro•pri•a•tor

ap•prov∘al

ap•prove *v.*, ap•proved, ap•prov•ing

ap•prove•ment

ap•prov∘er

ap•prox∘i•mate *adj., v.*, ap•prox∘i•mat∘ed, ap•prox∘i•mat•ing

ap•prox∘i•ma•tion

approximation of laws

ap•prox∘i•ma•tive

ap•pur•te•nance

ap•pur•te•nant

APR (annual percentage rate)

Apr. (April)

A∘pril (*citation form:* Apr.)

ap•ro•pos

apt

ap•ti•tude

aptitude test

ap•ti•tu•di•nal

ap•ti•tu•di•nal•ly

apt∘ly

apt•ness

APY (annual percentage yield)

A/R (account receivable; accounts receivable)

A.R. (Army Regulation; Army Regulations)

Arb. (Arbitration; Arbitrator)

ar•bi•ter

ar•bi•tra•bil∘i•ty

ar•bi•tra•ble

ar•bi•trage

ar•bi•tra•geur or ar•bi•trag∘er

ar•bi•tral

ar•bit•ra•ment

ar•bi•trar∘i•ly

primed PCR

ar•bi•trar∘i•ness

ar•bi•trar∘y

arbitrary and ca•pri•cious

ar•bi•trate *v.*, ar•bi•trat∘ed, ar•bi•trat•ing

ar•bi•tra•tion (*citation form:* **Arb.**)

arbitration clause

ar•bi•tra•tion∘al

ar•bi•tra•tor (**Arb.**)

ARC (AIDS-related complex)

ar•cha∘ic

ar•cha•i•cal∘ly

ar•cha•i•cism

ar•cha•ism

arch•en∘e∘o•my *n., pl.* arch•en∘e∘o•mies

ar•chi•tect

ar•chi•tect's lien

ar•chi•tec•tur∘al

ar•chi•tec•tur•al•ly

ar•chi•tec•ture

ar•chi•val

ar•chive *n., v.*, ar•chived, ar•chiv•ing

ar•chiv•ist

ar∘e∘a stand•ards

area standards pick•et•ing

area-wide bar•gain•
ing
A•ree•da-Tur•ner
test
ar•got
ar•gu•a•ble
ar•gu•a•bly
ar•gue v., ar•gued,
ar•gu•ing
ar•gu•en•do Latin.
ar•gu•ment
ar•gu•men•ta•tion
ar•gu•men•ta•tive
argumentative ques•
tion
ar•gu•men•ta•
tive•ly
ar•gu•men•ta•tive•
ness
ar•gu•men•tum n.,
pl. ar•gu•men•ta
Latin.
ar•gu•men•tum a si•
mi•li Latin.
argumentum ab auc•
to•ri•ta•te Latin.
argumentum ab im•
pos•si•bi•li Latin.
argumentum ab in•
con•ve•ni•en•ti
Latin.
argumentum ad cru•
me•nam Latin.
argumentum ad ho•
mi•nem Latin.
argumentum ad ig•
no•ran•ti•am Latin.
argumentum ad ve•
re•cun•di•am Latin.
a•rise v., a•rose,
a•ris•en, a•ris•ing
a•ris•ing out of
arising un•der
ar•is•toc•ra•cy
a•ris•to•crat
a•ris•to•crat•ic

a•ris•to•crat•i•cal•ly
a•ris•to•crat•ic•ness
a•rith•me•tic[1] n.
ar•ith•met•ic[2] adj.
ARM (adjustable-rate
mortgage)
aro•ma n.pl. Latin.
armed con•flict
armed forc•es
armed rob•ber•y
armed serv•ic•es
ar•mi•stice
arms n.pl.
arms con•trol
arm's length n.
arm's-length adj.
aro•my n., pl. ar•mies
Army Reg•u•la•tion
(A.R.)
ar•o•mat•ic hy•dro•
car•bon
ar•raign
ar•raign•ment
ar•range v., ar•
ranged, ar•rang•ing
ar•range•a•ble
ar•range•ment
arrangement with
cred•i•tors
ar•ray
ar•rear
ar•rear•age
ar•rear•ag•es n.pl.
ar•rears n.pl.
ar•rest
arrest of judg•ment
arrest rec•ord
arrest war•rant
ar•rest•a•ble
ar•rest•ee
ar•rest•er or ar•res•
tor
ar•rest•ing
ar•ro•gance of
pow•er
ar•ro•gate v., ar•ro•

gat•ed, ar•ro•gat•
ing
ar•ro•ga•tion
ar•ro•ga•tor
ar•se•nal
ar•se•nic[1] n.
ar•se•nic[2] adj.
ar•son
ar•son•ist
ar•son•ous
ART (assisted reproduc-
tive technology)
art. (article)
art•ful
artful plead•ing
ar•ti•cle (citation form:
art.)
article of man•u•fac•
ture
ar•ti•cled
articled clerk
ar•ti•cles of a•gree•
ment
articles of as•so•ci•
a•tion
Articles of Con•fed•
er•a•tion
articles of im•peach•
ment
articles of in•cor•po•
ra•tion
articles of war
ar•tic•u•la•ble
ar•tic•u•late v., ar•
tic•u•lat•ed, ar•
tic•u•lat•ing, adj.
ar•tic•u•late•ly
ar•tic•u•late•ness
ar•tic•u•la•tion
ar•ti•fact
ar•ti•fice
ar•ti•fic•er
ar•ti•fi•cial
artificial in•sem•i•
na•tion

artificial in•tel•li•gence

artificial per•son

artificial res•pi•ra•tion

ar•ti•fi•ci•al•i•ty

ar•ti•fi•cial•ly

ar•ti•san

ar•ti•san's lien

as a mat•ter of law

as ap•plied

as is

as•bes•tos

as•bes•to•sis

ASC (ambulatory surgical center)

as•cend

as•cend•a•ble

as•cend•ance

as•cend•an•cy

as•cend•ant

as•cent (upward movement: cf. ASSENT)

as•cer•tain

as•cer•tain•a•ble

as•cer•tain•a•bly

as•cer•tain•ment

ASCII (American Standard Code for Information Interchange)

as•crib•a•ble

as•cribe v., as•cribed, as•crib•ing

as•crip•tion

as•crip•tive

as•crip•tive•ly

a•sex•u•al

asexual re•pro•duc•tion

a•sex•u•al•i•ty

a•sex•u•al•ly

a•shamed

a•sham•ed•ly

A•sia•dol•lar

as•i•nine

as•i•nine•ly

as•i•nin•i•ty

a•skance

asked price

ask•ing price

ASL (American Sign Language)

ASO probe (allele-specific oligonucleotide probe)

a•so•cial

asocial per•son•al•i•ty

as•pect

as•per•i•ty n., pl. as•per•i•ties

as•perse v., as•persed, as•pers•ing

as•pers•er

as•per•sion

as•per•sive

as•per•sive•ly

as•phyx•i•a

as•phyx•i•al

as•phyx•i•ate v., as•phyx•i•at•ed, as•phyx•i•at•ing

as•phyx•i•a•tion

as•port

as•por•ta•tion

as•sail

as•sail•a•ble

as•sail•a•ble•ness

as•sail•ant

as•sas•sin

as•sas•si•nate v., as•sas•si•nat•ed, as•sas•si•nat•ing

as•sas•si•na•tion

as•sault

assault and bat•ter•y (a&b)

assault and rob•ber•y (a&r)

assault weap•on

assault with a dead•ly weapon

as•sault•er

as•saul•tive

as•saul•tive•ly

as•saul•tive•ness

as•say (to analyze; an analysis: cf. ESSAY)

assay of•fice

as•say•a•ble

as•say•er

as•sem•ble

as•sem•bly

assembly dis•trict (A.D.)

assembly line

as•sem•bly•man n., pl. as•sem•bly•men

as•sem•bly•per•son n., pl. as•sem•bly•per•sons

as•sem•bly•wom•an n., pl. as•sem•bly•wom•en

as•sent (concurrence; to concur: cf. ASCENT)

as•sen•tive

as•sen•tor or as•sent•er

as•sert

as•sert•ed

as•sert•ed•ly

as•sert•er

as•sert•i•ble

as•ser•tion

as•ser•tive

as•ser•tive•ly

as•ser•tive•ness

assertiveness train•ing

as•sess

as•sess•a•ble

assessable stock

assessed val•ue

as•sess•ment

as•ses•sor

as•ses•so•ri•al

as•ses•sor•ship

as•set
asset al•lo•ca•tion
asset de•pre•ci•a•tion range (ADR)
asset for•fei•ture laws
as•sets
as•sev•er•ate v., as•sev•er•at•ed, as•sev•er•at•ing
as•sev•er•a•tion
as•sev•er•a•tive
as•sev•er•a•tive•ly
as•sev•er•a•to•ry
as•sign
as•sign•a•bil•i•ty
as•sign•a•ble
as•sign•a•bly
as•sig•na•tion
as•signed coun•sel
assigned risk
assigned-risk plan
as•sign•ee
as•sign•ment
assignment for the ben•e•fit of cred•i•tors
assignment of er•ror
as•sign•or
as•signs n.pl.
as•sim•i•late v., as•sim•i•lat•ed, as•sim•i•lat•ing
as•sim•i•la•tion
as•sim•i•la•tive
as•sim•i•la•tive•ness
as•sim•i•la•tor
as•sim•i•la•to•ry
as•si•o•sa n., pl. as•si•sae Latin.
assisa de no•cu•men•to Latin.
assisa fris•cae for•ti•ae Latin.
assisa mor•tis an•te•ces•so•ris Latin.

assisa no•vae dis•sei•si•nae Latin.
assisa ul•ti•mae prae•sen•ta•ti•o•nis Latin.
assisa u•trum Latin.
as•si•sor
as•sist
as•sis•tance
as•sis•tant
Assistant U•nit•ed States At•tor•ney (AUSA)
as•sist•ed con•cep•tion
assisted dy•ing
assisted liv•ing
assisted liv•ing fa•cil•i•ty (ALF)
assisted re•pro•duc•tive tech•nol•o•gy (ART)
assisted su•i•cide
as•size
assize of dar•rein pre•sent•ment
assize of fresh force
assize of mort d'an•ces•tor
assize of no•vel dis•sei•sin
assize of nui•sance
assize u•trum
Ass'n (Association)
Assoc. (Associate)
as•so•ci•a•bil•i•ty
as•so•ci•a•ble
as•so•ci•a•ble•ness
as•so•ci•ate[1] n., adj. (citation form: **Assoc.**)
associate[2] v., as•so•ci•at•ed, as•so•ci•at•ing
as•so•ci•ate•ship
as•so•ci•a•tion (citation form: **Ass'n**)

association a•gree•ment
as•so•ci•a•tion•al
associational stand•ing
as•soil•er Law French.
as•suage v., as•suaged, as•suag•ing
as•suage•ment
as•sum•a•bil•i•ty
as•sum•a•ble
as•sume v., as•sumed, as•sum•ing
as•sum•er
as•sump•sit Latin.
as•sump•tion
assumption of risk
as•sur•ance
as•sure v., as•sured, as•sur•ing
as•sur•ed•ly
as•sur•ed•ness
as•sur•er or as•su•ror
as•trict
as•tric•tion
Astroturf lob•by•ing
a•sy•lum n., pl. a•sy•lums
at bar
at large
at-risk lim•i•ta•tions
at-risk rules
at will
Atl. (Atlantic)
At•lan•tic (citation form: **Atl.**)
Atlantic Re•port•er (citation form: **A.**)
ATM (automated-teller machine)
a•tom•ic en•er•gy
atomic pow•er
atomic re•ac•tor
atomic weap•on

a•tone v., a•toned, a•ton•ing
a•tone•ment
a•tro•cious
atrocious as•sault and bat•te•ry
a•tro•cious•ly
a•tro•cious•ness
a•troc•i•ty
at•tach
at•tach•a•ble
at•ta•ché
at•tached
at•tach•er
at•tach•ment
attachment bond
at•tack
at•tack•a•ble
at•tack•er
at•tain
at•tain•a•bil•i•ty
at•tain•a•ble
at•tain•a•ble•ness
at•tain•der
at•tain•er
at•tain•ment
at•taint
at•tempt
at•tempt•a•bil•i•ty
at•tempt•a•ble
at•tempt•ed
at•tempt•er
at•tend
at•tend•ance
at•tend•ant
attendant cir•cum•stanc•es
at•tend•ee
at•ten•tion
attention def•i•cit dis•or•der (ADD)
attention-deficit/hy•per•ac•tiv•i•ty dis•or•der
at•ten•tive
at•ten•tive•ly

at•ten•tive•ness
at•ten•u•ate v., at•ten•u•at•ed, at•ten•u•at•ing
at•ten•u•a•tion
at•test
at•test•a•ble
at•test•ant
at•tes•ta•tion
at•tes•ta•tive
at•tes•ta•tor
at•test•ed cop•y
at•test•er or at•tes•tor
at•test•ing wit•ness
at•torn
at•tor•ney n., pl. at•tor•neys (citation form: Att'y)
attorney at law n., pl. attorneys at law
attorney-cli•ent priv•i•lege
attorney gen•er•al (AG) n., pl. attorneys general or attorney ge•ner•als (citation form: Att'y Gen.)
attorney in fact n., pl. attorneys in fact
attorney of rec•ord
attorney work prod•uct
at•tor•ney's lien
at•torn•ment
at•trac•tive nui•sance
at•trib•u•ta•ble
at•trib•ute v., at•trib•ut•ed, at•trib•ut•ing, n.
at•trib•ut•er
at•tri•bu•tion
at•tri•tion
at•tri•tion•al
at•tri•tive

Att'y (Attorney)
Att'y Gen. (Attorney General)
a•typ•ic
a•typ•i•cal
a•typ•i•cal•i•ty
a•typ•i•cal•ly
auc•tion
auc•tion•a•ble
auc•tion•eer
au•da•cious
au•da•cious•ly
au•dac•i•ty n., pl. au•dac•i•ties
au•di•ence
au•dit
audit com•mit•tee
audit o•pin•ion
audit pro•gram
audit re•port
audit trail
au•di•ta que•re•la Latin.
au•dit•a•ble
au•di•tor
au•di•tor's o•pin•ion
auditor's re•port
au•di•tor•ship
au•di•to•ry hal•lu•ci•na•tion
Aug. (August)
Au•gust (citation form: Aug.)
au•ral (by ear: cf. ORAL)
AUSA (Assistant United States Attorney)
Austl. (Australia)
Aus•tral•ia (citation form: Austl.)
au•tarch
au•tar•chic
au•tar•chi•cal
au•tar•chi•cal•ly
au•tar•chist

au•tar•chy *n., pl.* au•tar•chies
Auth. (Authority)
au•then•tic
authentic act
au•then•ti•cal•ly
au•then•ti•ca•ta•ble
au•then•ti•cate *v.,* au•then•ti•cat•ed, au•then•ti•cat•ing
au•then•ti•ca•tion
au•then•ti•ca•tor
au•then•tic•i•ty
au•thor
au•tho•ri•al
au•thor•i•tar•i•an
au•thor•i•tar•i•an•ism
au•thor•i•ta•tive
au•thor•i•ta•tive•ly
au•thor•i•ta•tive•ness
au•thor•i•ty *n., pl.* au•thor•i•ties *(citation form:* AUTH.*)*
au•thor•iz•a•ble
au•thor•i•za•tion
au•thor•ize *v.,* au•thor•ized, au•thor•iz•ing
au•thor•ized
authorized cap•i•tal
authorized deal•er•ship
authorized stock
au•thor•ship
au•tism
au•tis•tic
autistic dis•or•der
Auto. (Automobile)
au•to-da-fé *n., pl.* au•tos-da-fé *Portuguese.*
au•to•cide
au•toc•ra•cy *n., pl.* au•toc•ra•cies

au•to•crat
au•to•crat•ic
au•to•crat•i•cal•ly
au•to•graph
au•to•graph•ic
au•to•graph•i•cal
au•to•graph•i•cal•ly
au•to•mat•a•ble
au•to•mate *v.,* au•to•mat•ed, au•to•mat•ing
au•to•mat•ed-tel•ler ma•chine (ATM)
au•to•mat•ic
automatic da•ta proc•ess•ing (ADP)
automatic stay
automatic weap•on
au•to•ma•tion
au•tom•a•tism
au•tom•a•tist
au•to•mo•bile *(citation form:* Auto.*)*
automobile guest stat•ute
automobile in•sur•ance
au•ton•o•mous
au•ton•o•mous•ly
au•ton•o•my
au•top•sy *n., pl.* au•top•sies, *v.,* au•top•sied, au•top•sy•ing
au•top•tic
autoptic ev•i•dence
au•to•rad
au•to•ra•di•o•gram
au•to•ra•di•o•graph
au•to•ra•di•o•graph•ic
au•to•ra•di•o•graph•i•cal•ly
au•to•ra•di•og•ra•phy
au•to•some
au•tre *Law French.*

autre vie *Law French.*
au•tre•fois ac•quit *Law French.*
autrefois at•taint *Law French.*
autrefois con•vict *Law French.*
aux•il•ia•ry *adj., n., pl.* aux•il•ia•ries
auxiliary eq•ui•ty
A/V or a.v. (ad valorem)
a•vail
a•vail•a•bil•i•ty
a•vail•a•ble
a•vails *n.pl.*
av•a•rice
av•a•ri•cious
av•a•ri•cious•ly
Ave. (Avenue)
a•venge *v.,* a•venged, a•veng•ing
a•veng•er
a•veng•ing•ly
av•e•nue (Ave.)
a•ver *v.,* a•verred, a•ver•ring
av•er•age *n., adj., v.,* av•er•aged, av•er•ag•ing
av•er•age•a•ble
av•er•age•ly
av•er•age•ness
a•ver•ment
a•verse (reluctant; antipathetic; cf. ADVERSE)
a•verse•ly
a•verse•ness
a•ver•sion
aversion ther•a•py
a•ver•sive
aversive con•di•tion•ing
aversive ther•a•py

a◦vert
a◦vert•i◦ble
a◦vi•at◦ic
a◦vi•a•tion
aviation tort
av◦o•ca•tion
av◦o•ca•tion◦al
av◦o•ca•tion•al◦ly
a◦void
a◦void•a◦ble
a◦void•a◦bly
a◦void•ance
a◦void◦er
a◦vo•li•tion
a◦vo•li•tion◦al
a◦vow

a◦vow◦al
a◦vow•ant
a◦vowed
a◦vow•ed◦ly
a◦vow◦er
a◦vow◦ry n., pl.
  a◦vow•ries
a◦vulse v., a◦vulsed,
  a◦vuls•ing
a◦vul•sion
a◦wait
a◦ward
a◦ward•a◦bil◦i◦ty
a◦ward•a◦ble
a◦ward◦er
a◦ware

a◦ware•ness
a◦way-go◦ing crop
a◦while adv. (for a
  short time: cf. A WHILE)
AWOL (absent without
  leave; absence without
  leave)
a◦wry
ax◦io•log◦i•cal eth•
  ics
ax◦i◦om
ax◦io•mat◦ic
ax◦io•mat◦i•cal◦ly
ax◦is n., pl. ax◦es
ay◦ant cause French.
aye

B

B. (Bar; Baron)
B.A. (Bachelor of Arts:
  from Latin *Baccal-
  aureus Artium*)
ba◦by n., pl. ba•bies,
  adj., v., ba•bied, ba•
  by•ing
baby act
baby-sit or ba◦by•sit
  v., baby-sat or ba•
  by•sat, baby-sit•ting
  or ba•by•sit•ting
baby-sit•ter or ba•
  by•sit•ter or baby
  sit•ter
ba◦by•hood
ba◦by•ish
ba◦by•ish◦ly
ba◦by•ish•ness
ba◦by•like
ba◦by•proof
BAC (blood alcohol con-
  tent)
bac◦ca•lau•re•ate
bach◦e•lor
Bachelor of Arts (B.A.
  or A.B.)

Bachelor of Laws
  (LL.B.)
Bachelor of Sci•ence
  (B.S.)
bach◦e•lor•hood
bach◦e•lor's de•gree
bac◦il•lar◦y
ba◦cil•lus n., pl. ba•
  cil◦li
back-al◦ley adj.
back burn◦er
back-door fi•nanc•ing
back down v. (cf. BACK-
  DOWN)
back-haul al•low•
  ance
back-load
back of•fice n.
back-office adj.
back or◦der n.
back-order v.
back pay
back street n.
back-street adj.
back tax◦es
back-to-ba•sics adj.

back up v. (cf. BACKUP)
back•bite v., back•bit,
  back•bit•ten, back•
  bit•ing
back•bit◦er
back•date v., back•
  dat◦ed, back•dat•
  ing
back•down n. (cf. BACK
  DOWN)
back◦er
back•ground
back•ground◦er
back•hand◦ed
back•hand•ed◦ly
back•hand•ed•ness
back•haul
back•ing
back•lash
back•load•ing
back•log n., v., back•
  logged, back•log•
  ging
back•stab v., back•
  stabbed, back•stab•
  bing
back•stab•ber

back○up n. (cf. BACK
  UP)
back•ward¹ adj.
backward² or back•
  wards adv.
backward ver•ti•cal
  merg○er
back•ward○ly
back•ward•ness
bac•te•ri○a See BACTE-
  RIUM.
bac•te•ri○al
bac•te•ri•al○ly
bac•te•ri•o•log○ic
bac•te•ri•o•log○i•cal
bacteriological war•
  fare
bac•te•ri•o•log○i•
  cal○ly
bac•te•ri•ol○o○gist
bac•te•ri•ol○o○gy
bac•te•ri○um n., pl.
  bac•te•ri○a
ba•cu•lus n., pl. ba•
  cu○li Latin.
baculus nun•ti•a•to•
  ri○us Latin.
bad adj., worse, worst
bad act
bad ac○tor
bad check
bad con•duct dis•
  charge
bad debt
bad faith n.
bad-faith adj.
bad law
bad-mouth v., bad-
  mouthed,
  bad-mouth•ing
bad ti○tle
badge
badge of fraud
badge of ser•vi•tude
badg○er
bad○i•nage

bad○ly
bad•ness
baf•fle v., baf•fled,
  baf•fling
baf•fle•gab
baf•fle•gab•ber
baf•fle•ment
baf•fling
baf•fling○ly
bail (security money:
  cf. BALE)
bail bond (b.b.)
bail bonds•man n., pl.
  bail bonds•men
bail for•fei•ture
bail jump•ing
bail revo○ca•tion
bail•a○ble
bailable of•fense
bail○ee (holder of
  goods: cf. BAILIE; BAI-
  LEY)
bail○er (one who posts
  bail for another: cf.
  BAILOR)
Bai•ley (London crimi-
  nal court (Old Bailey):
  cf. BAILEE; BAILIE)
bail○ie (bailiff; Scottish
  magistrate: cf. BAILEE;
  BAILEY)
bail•iff
bail•iff•ship
bail○i•wick
bail•ment
bailment for hire
bailment for mu•
  tu○al ben○e•fit
bailment lease
bail○or (one who en-
  trusts goods to an-
  other: cf. BAILER)
bails•man n., pl.
  bails•men
bait (a lure: cf. BATE)
bait ad•ver•tis•ing

bait and switch n.
bait-and-switch adj.
bal•ance n., v., bal•
  anced, bal•anc•ing
balance due
balance of con•ven•
  ience
balance of pay•ments
balance of pow○er
balance of trade
balance sheet
bal•ance•a○ble
bal•anced
balanced
  e○con○o○my
balanced fund
bal•anc•ing of in•
  ter•ests
balancing of the eq•
  ui•ties
balancing test
bale n., v., baled, bal•
  ing (a bundle; to bun-
  dle: cf. BAIL)
bale•ful
bale•ful○ly
bale•ful•ness
bal○er
balk
Balk•an•ism
Bal•kan○i•za•tion
Bal•kan•ize v., Bal•
  kan•ized, Bal•kan•
  iz•ing
balk○er
balk○i•ness
balk○y adj. balk○i•er,
  balk○i•est
bal•last
bal•lis•ti•cian
bal•lis•tics n.sing.
bal•loon
balloon loan
balloon mort•gage
balloon note
balloon pay•ment

bal•lot n., v., bal•lot•ed, bal•lot•ing

ballot box

bal•lot•er

bal•ly•hoo n., pl. bal•ly•hoos, v., bal•ly•hooed, bal•ly•hoo•ing

ba•lo•ney

bam•boo•zle v., bam•boo•zled, bam•boo•zling

ban v., banned, ban•ning, n. (to prohibit; a prohibition; a proclamation: cf. BANNS)

ba•nal

ba•nal•i•ty

ba•nal•ly

banc Law French.

ban•cus n., pl. ban•ci Latin.

Bancus Re•gi•nae (B.R.) Latin.

Bancus Re•gis (B.R.) Latin.

ban•dit n., pl. ban•dits or ban•dit•ti

ban•di•to•ry

B&P costs (bid and proposal costs)

ban•ish

ban•ish•ment

bank

bank ac•cept•ance

bank ac•count

bank bal•ance

bank bold•ing com•pa•ny

bank card

bank check

bank cred•it

bank credit card

bank de•pos•it

bank deposit in•sur•ance

bank de•pos•i•tor

bank dis•count

bank draft

bank ex•am•in•er

bank loan

bank note or bank•note

bank of is•sue

bank pa•per

bank rate

bank state•ment

bank•a•bil•i•ty

bank•a•ble

bank•er

bank•er's ac•cep•tance

banker's bill

banker's lien

bank•ing

banking day

bank•note See BANK NOTE.

Bankr. (Bankruptcy; Bankruptcy Court)

bank•rupt

bank•rupt•cy n., pl. bank•rupt•cies (citation form: **Bankr.**)

Bankruptcy Ap•pel•late Pan•el (citation form: **B.A.P.**)

Bankruptcy Court (citation form: **Bankr.**)

bankruptcy es•tate

bankruptcy pe•ti•tion

bankruptcy pro•ceed•ing

bankruptcy trust•ee

ban•na•ble

banns n.pl. (marriage notice: cf. BAN)

B.A.P. (Bankruptcy Appellate Panel)

bar[1] (the legal profession; citation form: **B.**)

bar[2] n., v., barred, bar•ring (an impediment; to preclude)

bar as•so•ci•a•tion

bar ex•am•i•na•tion

bar-press guide•lines

bar•bar•ism

bar•bar•i•ty

bar•bar•i•za•tion

bar•bar•ize v., bar•bar•ized, bar•bar•iz•ing

bar•bar•ous

bar•bar•ous•ly

bar•bar•ous•ness

bar•bi•tal Controlled Subst.

bar•bi•tu•rate

bar•bi•tu•ric ac•id de•riv•a•tive Controlled Subst.

bar•bi•tur•ism

bare adj., bar•er, bar•est, v., bared, bar•ing (mere; naked; to expose: cf. BEAR)

bare li•cen•see

bare•boat

bareboat char•ter

bare•boat•ing

bare•ly

bare•ness

bar•gain

bargain and sale

bargain and sale deed

bargain col•lec•tive•ly

bargain sale

bar•gain•a•ble

bar•gained for

bargained-for ex•change

bar•gain•ee

bar•gain•er (one who bargains: cf. BARGAI•NOR)

bar•gain•ing

bargaining a∘gent
bargaining pow∘er
bargaining u∘nit
bar•gain∘or (the seller in a real estate contract: cf. BARGAINER)
bar∘on (B.)
ba∘ron et feme *Law French.*
bar•on•age
bar∘o•net (Bart.)
bar∘o∘ny
barr. (barrister)
bar•ra•ble
bar∘rage *n., v.,* bar∘raged, bar∘rag•ing
bar•ra•tor or bar•rat∘er
bar•ra•trous
bar•ra•trous•ly
bar•ra•try
barred
bar•ren
bar•ren•ness
bar•ri∘er
bar•ring the en•tail
bar•ris•ter (barr.)
bar•ris•te•ri•al
bar•ris•ter•ship
Bart. (Baronet)
bar•ter
bar•ter∘er
base *n., adj.,* bas∘er, bas•est, *v.,* based, bas•ing
base es•tate
base fee
base line or base•line
base pair
base pay
base price
base rate
base sal∘a∘ry
base serv•ic∘es
base ten•ant

base ten•ure
base•less
base•line See BASE LINE.
base∘ly
base•ness
ba∘sic
basic pat•ent
ba∘sis *n., pl.* ba∘ses
basis point
bas•tard
bastard eigne
bas•tard∘i•za•tion
bas•tard•ize *v.,* bas•tard•ized, bas•tard•iz•ing
bas•tar∘dy
bastardy ac•tion
bastardy pro•ceed•ing
bas•tion
bas•tioned
batch
bate *v.,* bat∘ed, bat•ing (to restrain or diminish: cf. BAIT)
ba•thet•ic (mawkish: cf. PATHETIC)
ba•thet•i•cal•ly
ba•thos (anticlimax; insincerity: cf. PATHOS)
bat•tal•ion
bat•ter
bat•tered child syn•drome
battered per•son syndrome
battered wom∘an syndrome
bat•ter∘er
bat•ter∘y *n., pl.* bat•ter•ies
bat•tle *n., v.,* bat•tled, bat•tling
battle of the ex•perts
battle of the forms
bat•tler

bawd
bawd∘i•ly
bawd•i•ness
bawd∘y *adj.,* bawd∘i∘er, bawd∘i•est
bawdy house or bawd∘y•house
ba•zaar (marketplace: cf. BIZARRE)
b.b. (bail bond)
Bd. (Board)
bear *v.,* bore, borne or born, bearing, *n.* (to carry; a pessimist: cf. BARE) See also BORN; BORNE.
bear mar•ket
bear∘er
bearer bond
bearer in•stru•ment
bearer pa∘per
bear•ish
bear•ish∘ly
bear•ish•ness
beat *v.,* beat, beat∘en, beat•ing, *n.*
beat•a∘ble
beat∘er
bed and board
beer
be∘fit *v.,* be•fit•ted, be•fit•ting
be•fit•ting∘ly
be•fit•ting•ness
be∘fog *v.,* be•fogged, be•fog•ging
be•fore
before the fact
be•fore•hand
be∘foul
be•foul∘er
be•friend
be•fud•dle *v.,* be•

fud•dled, be•fud•dling

be•fud•dle•ment

beg v., begged, beg•ging

beg the ques•tion

be•get v., be•got, be•got•ten or be○got, be•get•ting

be•get•ter

beg•gar

be•gin v., be•gan, be○gun, be•gin•ning

be•gin•ner

be•gin•ning

beginning in•ven•to○ry

be•got•ten

be•half

Behav. (Behavior; Behavioral

be•have v., be•haved, be•hav•ing

be•hav•ior (citation form: Behav.)

behavior mod○i•fi•ca○tion

be•hav•ior○al (citation form: Behav.)

behavioral dis•turb•ance

behavioral sci•ence

be•hav•ior•al○ly

be•hav•ior•ism

be•hav•ior•ist

be•hav•ior•is•tic

be•hav•ior•is•ti•cal○ly

be•hest

be•hind the scenes adv.

behind-the-scenes adj.

be•hold○en

be•hoof

be•hoove v., be•

hooved, be•hoov•ing

be•la•bor

be•lat○ed

be•lat•ed○ly

be•lat•ed•ness

be•lea•guer

be•lie v., be•lied, be•ly○ing

be•lief

be•liev•a○bil○i○ty

be•liev•a○ble

be•liev•a○bly

be•lieve v., be•lieved, be•liev•ing

be•liev○er

bel•lig•er•en○cy

bel•lig○er•ent

belligerent rights

belligerent status

bel•lig•er•ent○ly

bel•lum n., pl. bel○la Latin.

bell•weth○er

be•long

be•long•ing

be•loved[1] or be•lov○ed adj.

be•lov○ed[2] n.

be•low

below-mar•ket in•ter•est

below par

below the line

be•muse v., be•mused, be•mus•ing

be•mused

be•mus•ed○ly

be•muse•ment

Ben○a•dryl Trademark.

bench

bench con•fer•ence

bench tri○al

bench war•rant

bench•mark

bend v., bent, bend•ing, n.

be○ne es○se Latin.

be•neath

ben○e○fac•tion

ben○e○fac•tor

ben○e○fac•tress

ben○e○fice

be•nef○i•cence

be•nef○i•cent

ben○e○fi•cial

beneficial as•so•ci•a○tion

beneficial en•joy•ment

beneficial hold○er

beneficial in•ter•est

beneficial own○er

beneficial pow○er

beneficial use

ben○e○fi•cial○ly

ben○e○fi•cial•ness

ben○e○fi•ci•ar○y n., pl. ben○e○fi•ci•ar•ies

be•ne•fi•ci○um n., pl. be•ne•fi•ci○a Latin.

ben○e○fit n., v., ben○e○fit○ed, ben○e○fit•ing

benefit as•so•ci•a○tion

benefit of ces•sion

benefit of cler•gy

benefit of coun•sel

benefit of the bar•gain

benefit of the doubt

benefit so•ci•e○ty

be•nev○o○lence

be•nev○o○lent

benevolent as•so•ci•a○tion

be•nev○o○lent○ly

be•night○ed

be•nign

be•nig•nan•cy
be•nig•nant
be•nig•nant•ly
be•nig•ni•ty
be•nign•ly
Ben•ze•drine *Trademark.*
ben•zeth•o•i•dine *Controlled Subst.*
ben•zo•di•az•e•pine
benz•phet•a•mine *Controlled Subst.*
ben•zyl•fen•ta•nyl *Controlled Subst.*
ben•zyl•mor•phine *Controlled Subst.*
be•queath
be•queath•a•ble
be•queath•er
be•quest
be•reave *v.,* be•reaved or be•reft, be•reav•ing
be•reaved
be•reave•ment
ber•serk
ber•serk•ness
berth (space for a vessel: cf. BIRTH
bes•ai•el *Law French.*
be•set *v.,* be•set, be•set•ting
be•set•ment
be•set•ter
be•side (next to; apart from: cf. BESIDES)
be•sides (moreover; in addition to: cf. BESIDE)
be•siege *v.,* be•sieged, be•sieg•ing
be•siege•ment
be•sieg•er
be•smirch
be•smirch•er
be•speak *v.,* be•

spoke, be•spok•en, be•speak•ing
best and fi•nal of•fer
best and high•est use
best-case sce•nar•i•o
best ef•forts
best efforts con•tract
best-efforts un•der•writ•ing
best ev•i•dence rule
best in•ter•ests of the child
best mode
best use
bes•tial
bes•ti•al•i•ty
be•stow
be•stow•al
bet *v.,* bet, bet•ting, *n.*
be•ta•ce•o•tyl•meth•a•dol *Controlled Subst.*
be•ta-hy•drox•y•fen•ta•nyl *Controlled Subst.*
be•ta•mep•ro•dine *Controlled Subst.*
be•ta•meth•o•a•dol *Controlled Subst.*
be•ta•pro•dine *Controlled Subst.*
be•tide *v.,* be•tid•ed, be•tid•ing
be•times
be•to•ken
be•tray
be•tray•al
be•tray•er
be•troth
be•troth•al
be•trothed
bet•ter¹ (superior: cf. BETTOR
better² See BETTOR.

better law (or better rule) ap•proach
bet•ter•ment
betterment tax
bet•ting
bet•tor or bet•ter (wagerer: cf. BETTER¹)
be•tween
be•tween•ness
bev•er•age
be•ware
be•wil•der
be•wil•dered
be•wil•der•ing
be•wil•der•ing•ly
be•wil•der•ment
be•yond a rea•son•a•ble doubt
beyond the scope
be•zit•ra•mide *Controlled Subst.*
BFOQ (bona fide occupational qualification)
Bhd. (Brotherhood)
bi•as
bias crime
bi•ased
bi•ble (authoritative work in any field: cf. BIBLE)
Bi•ble (sacred book: cf. BIBLE)
Bib•li•cal
bib•li•o•graph•ic
bib•li•o•graph•i•cal
bib•li•o•graph•i•cal•ly
bib•li•og•ra•phy *n., pl.* bib•li•og•ra•phies
bi•cam•er•al
bi•cam•er•al•ism
bi•cam•er•al•ist
bid¹ *v.,* bid, bid•ding, *n.* (to propose a sum

of money; the proposal of a sum of money)

bid² v., bade, bid•den or bid, bid•ding (to invite or command)

bid and asked

bid and pro•pos•al (B&P) costs

bid price

bid rig•ging or bid-rig•ging n.

bid-rigging adj.

bid shop•ping

bid up v.

bid-up n.

bid•der

bid•ding

bi•en•ni•al

bi•en•ni•al•ly

bi•en•ni•um n., pl. bi•en•ni•a or bi•en•ni•ums

bi•fur•cate v., bi•fur•cat•ed, bi•fur•cat•ing

bi•fur•cat•ed

bifurcated trial

bi•fur•ca•tion

big•a•mist

big•a•mous

big•a•mous•ly

big•a•my

big•ot

big•ot•ed

big•ot•ry

bi•lat•er•al

bilateral con•tract

bilateral mis•take

bilateral trea•ty

bi•lat•er•al•ism

bi•lat•er•al•ly

bi•lat•er•al•ness

bi•lin•gual

bilingual ed•u•ca•tion

bi•lin•gual•ism

bi•lin•gual•ly

bill

bill in chan•cer•y

bill in eq•ui•ty

bill in the na•ture of a bill of re•view

bill o•blig•a•to•ry

bill of at•tain•der

bill of cer•ti•o•ra•ri

bill of costs

bill of dis•cov•er•y

bill of en•try

bill of ex•cep•tions

bill of ex•change

bill of goods

bill of health

bill of in•dict•ment

bill of in•ter•plead•er

bill of lad•ing (B/L or b/l)

bill of pains and pen•al•ties

bill of par•tic•u•lars

bill of peace

bill of re•view

bill of re•vi•vor

bill of rights (the generic concept of a list of rights: cf. BILL OF RIGHTS)

Bill of Rights (a specific list, esp. in U.S. Constitution: cf. BILL OF RIGHTS)

bill of sale (B/S or b/s)

bill of sight

bill pay•a•ble n., pl. bills pay•a•ble

bill qui•a ti•met

bill re•ceiv•a•ble

bil•la ve•ra Latin.

bill•a•ble

bill•er

bil•let n., v., bil•let•ed, bil•let•ing

bill•ing

billing cy•cle

bil•ly n., pl. bil•lies

billy club

bi•mod•al

bi•na•tion•al

bind v., bound, bind•ing, n.

bind o•ver v. (cf. BIND-OVER)

bind•a•ble

bind•er

bind•ing

binding au•thor•i•ty

binding force

binding re•ceipt

bind•ing•ly

bind•ing•ness

bind•o•ver or bind-o•ver adj. (cf. BIND OVER)

bindover

bindover (or bind-over) hear•ing

bi•o•as•say

bi•o•a•vail•a•bil•i•ty

bi•o•a•vail•a•ble

bi•o•di•ver•si•ty

bi•o•e•quiv•a•lence

bi•o•e•quiv•a•len•cy

bi•o•e•quiv•a•lent

bi•o•haz•ard

bi•o•log•i•cal

biological war•fare

biological weap•on

bi•o•log•ics n.pl.

bi•ol•o•gy

bi•o•tech•ni•cal

bi•o•tech•no•log•i•cal

bi•o•tech•no•log•i•cal•ly

bi•o•tech•nol•o•gist

bi•o•tech•nol•o•gy

bi•par•ti•san

bi•par•ti•san•ism
bi•par•ti•san•ship
bi•par•tite
bi•par•tite◦ly
bi•par•ti•tion
bi•po•lar
bipolar af•fec•tive dis•or•der
bipolar disorder
birth cer•tif◦i•cate
birth con•trol
birth par•ent
birth•right
bi•sex•u◦al
bi•sex•u•al◦i◦ty
Biv•ens ac•tion
bi•zarre (strange: cf. BAZAAR)
bi•zarre◦ly
bi•zarre•ness
bk. (book)
B/L or b/l (bill of lading)
Black Book of the Ad•mi•ral•ty
black cap
black let•ter law
black lung
black lung dis•ease
Black Ma◦ri◦a
black mar•ket n.
black-market adj., v.
black-mar•ke•teer
black-mar•ke•teer•ing
black-mar•ket◦er
black mon◦ey
Black•a◦cre
black•ball
black•bal•ler
black•list
black•mail
black•mail◦er
blam•a◦ble or blame• a◦ble

blam•a◦bly or blame• a◦bly
blame v., blamed, blam•ing
blame•less
blame•less◦ly
blame•less•ness
blame•wor•thi•ness
blame•wor•thy
blank
blank check
blank in•dorse•ment (or en•dorse•ment)
blan•ket a◦gree• ment
blanket bond
blanket im•mu•ni◦ty
blanket lien
blanket pol◦i◦cy
blas•pheme v., blas• phemed, blas• phem◦ing
blas•phem◦er
blas•phe•mous
blas•phe•mous◦ly
blas•phe•mous•ness
blas•phe•my n., pl. blas•phe•mies
bla•tant
bla•tant◦cy
bla•tant◦ly
Bldg. (Building)
bleed v., bled, bleed• ing
blend◦ed trust
blight
blight◦ed
blight•ing◦ly
blind
blind al◦ley
blind cor•ner
blind in◦ter•sec•tion
blind spot
blind trust
blind•ing
blind•ing◦ly

blind◦ly
blind•ness
bloc (a group united in interest: cf. BLOCK)
bloc-vote v., bloc-vot◦ed, bloc-vot•ing
bloc vot•ing
block (a solid mass; to obstruct: cf. BLOC)
block grant
block trade
block trad◦er
block•a◦ble
block•ade n., v., block•ad◦ed, block• ad•ing
blockade-run•ner
blockade-run•ning
block•ad◦er
block•age
blockage rule
block•bust◦er
block•bust•ing
blood
blood al•co•hol con• tent (BAC)
blood dop•ing
blood feud
blood group
blood mon◦ey
blood re•la•tion
blood re•la•tion•ship
blood rel◦a•tive
blood test
blood test•ing
blood type
blood•bath
blood•hound
blood•less
blood•less◦ly
blood•less•ness
blood•let•ting
blood•shed
blood◦y adj., blood◦i◦er, blood◦i•

est, *v.*, blood•ied,
blood•y•ing
blot•ter
blow•out
bludg•eon
blue chip *n.*
blue-chip *adj.*
blue-col•lar
blue-collar work•er
blue law
blue-pen•cil *v.*,
blue-pen•ciled,
blue-pen•cil•ing
blue pencil rule
blue rib•bon ju•ry or
blue-rib•bon ju•ry
blue sky law or blue-
sky law
Blue•book, The: A
U•ni•form Sys•tem
of Ci•ta•tion
blue•print
blue•print•er
blue•wa•ter sea•man
bluff
bluff•er
blund•er
blund•er•buss
blund•er•er
blund•er•ing•ly
blunt
blunt•ly
blunt•ness
blurb
blus•ter
blus•ter•er
board (*citation form:*
Bd.)
board of com•mis•
sion•ers
board of di•rec•tors
board of ed•u•ca•
tion
board of e•lec•tions
board of e•qual•i•
za•tion

board of es•ti•mate
board of gov•er•nors
board of health
board of o•ver•se•
ers
board of par•dons
board of pa•role
board of re•gents
board of su•per•vi•
sors
board of trade
board of trust•ees
board•er (lodger: cf.
BORDER)
board•ing house
board•room or board
room
bode *v.*, bod•ed,
bod•ing
bod•ied
bod•i•ly
bodily harm
bodily heirs
bodily in•ju•ry
bodily injury li•a•
bil•i•ty in•sur•ance
bod•y *n.*, *pl.* bod•ies
body bag
body-cav•i•ty search
body cor•po•rate
body ex•e•cu•tion
body lan•guage
body of the crime
body pol•i•tic
bod•y•guard
bog•gle *v.*, bog•gled,
bog•gling
bog•gling•ly
bo•gus
bo•gus•ly
boil•er room
boiler-room sales
boil•er•plate
boi•ster•ous
boi•ster•ous•ness

bol•de•none *Con-
trolled Subst.*
bol•ster
bomb
bom•bard
bom•bard•ment
bom•bast
bom•bas•tic
bom•bas•ti•cal•ly
bon vi•vant *n.*, *pl.*
bons vi•vants *French.*
bo•na *n.pl.*, *adj. Latin.*
bona et ca•tal•la *n.pl.
Latin.*
bona fide[1] *adj. English.*
(genuine)
bona fi•de[2] *adv. Latin.*
(in good faith)
bona fide occupa-
tional qualifica-
tion (BFOQ)
bona fide pur•
chas•er
bona fide purchaser
for val•ue
bona fides[1] *n.pl. Eng-
lish.* (credentials)
bona fi•des[2] *n.sing.
Latin.* (good faith)
bona gra•ti•a *Latin.*
bona im•mo•bi•li•a
n.pl. Latin.
bona mo•bi•li•a *n.pl.
Latin.*
bona va•can•ti•a
n.pl. Latin.
bo•nae fi•de•i *Latin.*
bonae fidei emp•tor
Latin.
bo•nan•za
bond
bond fund
bond im•mu•ni•za•
tion
bond in•den•ture
bond rat•ing

bond re•fund•ing
bond serv•ice
bond slav•er•y
bond•a•bil•i•ty
bond•a•ble
bond•age
bond∘ed
bonded debt
bonded ware•house
bond∘er
bond•hold•er
bond•hold•ing
bond•ing com•pa•ny
bond•maid or bond•
  maid∘en
bond•man or bonds•
  man *n., pl.* bond•
  men or bonds•men
  (male slave or serf: cf.
  BONDSMAN[1])
bond•serv•ant
bond•slave
bonds•man[1] *n., pl.*
  bonds•men (surety:
  cf. BONDMAN)
bondsman[2] See BOND-
  MAN.
bonds•wom∘an[1] *n.,
  pl.* bonds•wom∘en
  (a woman who is a
  surety: cf. BONDWOMAN)
bondswoman[2] See
  BONDWOMAN.
bond•wom∘an or
  bonds•wom∘an *n.,
  pl.* bond•wom∘en or
  bonds•wom∘en (fe-
  male slave or serf: cf.
  BONDSWOMAN[1])
bon∘i•fi•ca•tion
bo∘no et ma∘lo *Latin.*
bo∘num fac∘tum
  Latin.
bo∘nus *n., pl.* bo•
  nus∘es
bonus stock
boo∘by trap *n.*

booby-trap *v.,* booby-
  trapped,
  booby-trap•ping
book[1] *n. (citation form:*
  bk.)
book[2] *v.*
book in•ven•to•ry
book of ac•count
book of o∘rig∘i•nal
  en∘try
book share
book val∘ue
book-val∘ue shares
book∘ie
book•ing
book•keep∘er
book•keep•ing
book•mak∘er
book•mak•ing
books and pa•pers
boom
boom-and-bust *adj.*
boom-or-bust *adj.*
boom•let
boon
boon•dog•gle *n., v.,*
  boon•dog•gled,
  boon•dog•gling
boon•dog•gler
boost
boost∘er
boost•er•ism
boot
boot•leg *n., v.,* boot•
  legged, boot•leg•
  ging
boot•leg•ger
boot•leg•ging
boot•less
boot•strap *v.,* boot•
  strapped, boot•
  strap•ping, *n., adj.*
boo∘ty
Bor. Ct. (Borough
  Court)

bor•del∘lo *n., pl.* bor•
  del•los
bor•der (boundary; to
  bound: cf. BOARDER)
border line *n.* (cf. BOR
  DERLINE)
border search
border tax
bor•der•land
bor•der•less
bor•der•line *adj.* (cf.
  BORDER LINE)
borderline in•tel•lec•
  tu∘al func•tion•ing
borderline per•son•
  al∘i•ty
borderline personality
  dis•or•der
bore *v.,* bored, bor•
  ing, *n.*
bore•dom
bor•ing
born (brought forth by
  birth: cf. BORNE)
borne (carried; given
  birth to: cf. BORN)
bor•ough
Borough Court (*cita-
  tion form:* Bor. Ct.)
borough-Eng•lish
bor•row
bor•row•a∘ble
bor•rowed serv•ant
bor•row∘er
bor•row•ing stat•ute
boss•ism
bo•tan•i•cal
bot∘a•nist
bot∘a•ny
botch
botched
botch∘er
botch∘y
bote
both-to-blame clause
bot•tle law

bot•tle•neck
bot•tom line *n.*
bottom-line *adj.*
bottom-lin•er
bottom man•age•ment
bottom-of-the-line *adj.*
bot•tom•less
bot•tom•less•ness
bot•tom•most
bot•tom•ry
bottomry bond
bought
Boul•war•ism or Boul•ware•ism
bounce *v.,* bounced, bounc•ing
bounc•er
bound
bound•a•ble
bound•a•ry *n., pl.* bound•a•ries
boundary line
boundary wa•ters
bound•ed
bound•ed•ness
bound•less
bound•less•ly
bound•ness
boun•ti•ful
boun•ti•ful•ly
boun•ty *n., pl.* boun•ties
bounty hunt•er
bounty hunt•ing
bour•geois *n., pl.* bour•geois, *adj.*
bour•geoise *n., pl.* bour•geoises
bour•geoi•sie
bourse
bowd•ler•ism
bowd•ler•i•za•tion
bowd•ler•ize *v.,* bowd•ler•ized, bowd•ler•iz•ing

boy•cott
boy•cott•er
B.R. (Bancus Regis; Bancus Reginae)
Br. (Brief)
Bra•dy ma•te•ri•al
braille
brain
brain dam•age
brain-dam•aged
brain-dead
brain death
brain•pow•er
brain•storm
brain•storm•er
brain•storm•ing
brain•wash
brain•wash•er
brain•wash•ing
brake *n., v.,* braked, brak•ing (device for slowing down; to slow down: cf. BREAK)
brake•less
branch
branch ac•count•ing
branch bank
branch prof•its tax
brand
brand a•ware•ness
brand im•age
brand lead•er
brand loy•al•ty
brand name *n.*
brand-name *adj.*
brand switch•ing
brand•ed
Bran•deis brief
brand•ing
brass knuck•les
bra•va•do
brave *adj.,* brav•er, brav•est
brav•er•y
brawl

brawl•er
brawl•ing
bra•zen
bra•zen•ly
breach
breach of close
breach of con•tract
breach of cov•e•nant
breach of du•ty
breach of faith
breach of fi•du•ci•ar•y du•ty
breach of priv•i•lege
breach of prom•ise
breach of promise of mar•riage
breach of promise to mar•ry
breach of the peace
breach of trust
breach of war•ran•ty
breach•er
bread-and-but•ter *adj.*
breadth
break *v.,* broke, bro•ken, break•ing, *n.* (to interrupt, shatter, or violate; an instance of breaking: cf. BRAKE)
break a case
break a quo•rum
break down *v.* (cf. BREAKDOWN)
break e•ven *v.*
break-even *adj.*
break-even point
break in *v.*
break-in *n.*
break out *v.* (cf. BREAK-OUT)
break the close
break through *v.* (cf. BREAKTHROUGH)
break up *v.* (cf. BREAKUP)
break•a•ble

break•a•ble•ness
break•a•bly
break•age
break•down n. (cf. BREAK DOWN)
breakdown clause
break•ing and en•ter•ing
breaking bulk
break•out n. (cf. BREAK OUT)
break•through n. (cf. BREAK THROUGH)
break•up n. (cf. BREAK UP)
breast im•plant
breath
breath an•a•lyz•er
breath•a•bil•i•ty
breath•a•ble
Breath•a•lyz•er
breathe v., breathed, breath•ing
breath•er
breed v., bred, breed•ing, n.
breed•er
breth•ren See BROTHER[1].
Bret•ton Woods in•sti•tu•tions
bre•ove n., pl. bre•vi•a Latin.
breve de cur•su Latin.
breve de in•gres•su Latin.
breve de rec•to Latin.
breve de recto pa•tens Latin.
breve de recto te•nen•do Latin.
breve o•ri•gi•na•le Latin.
brev•i•ty
brew
brew•er

brib•a•bil•i•ty
brib•a•ble
bribe n., v., bribed, brib•ing
brib•ee
brib•er
brib•er•y n., pl. brib•er•ies
bride
bride price
bride•groom
bridge n., v., bridged, bridg•ing
bridge fi•nanc•ing
bridge loan
bridge•a•ble
brief (citation form: Br.)
brief in op•po•si•tion
brief in sup•port
brief of ti•tle
brief psy•chot•ic dis•or•der
brief•er
brief•less
brief•less•ly
brief•less•ness
brief•ly
brig
brig•and
brig•and•age
brig•and•ry
bril•liance
bril•liant
bril•liant•ly
bring v., brought, bring•ing
bring on
bring•er
brink•man or brinks•man
brink•man•ship or brinks•man•ship
Brit. (British)

Brit•ish (citation form: Brit.)
broach
Broad. (Broadcast; Broadcasting)
broad-based
broad con•struc•tion
broad-form in•sur•ance
broad seal
broad•band com•mu•ni•ca•tions
broad•cast[1] n., adj. (citation form: Broad.)
broadcast[2] v., broad•cast or broad•cast•ed, broad•cast•ing
broad•cast•er
broad•cast•ing (citation form: Broad.)
broad•side n., adv., v., broad•sid•ed, broad•sid•ing
broke
bro•ken
broken-down adj.
broken lot
bro•ker
broker-deal•er
bro•ker•age
bro•ker's lien
bro•ker•ship
bro•ma•ze•o•pam Controlled Subst.
bro•mide
Bros. (Brothers)
broth•el
broth•er[1] n., pl. breth•ren (fellow judge)
brother[2] n., pl. broth•ers (male sibling)
broth•er-in-law n., pl. broth•ers-in-law

brother-sis•ter cor•
po•ra•tions
broth•er•hood (cita-
tion form: **Bhd.**)
broth•er•li•ness
broth•er•ly
broth•ers (citation
form: **Bros.**)
brou•ha•ha
brow•beat v., brow•
beat, brow•beat∘en,
brow•beat•ing
brow•beat∘er
brown•wa•ter sea•
man
brows•a∘ble
browse v., browsed,
brows•ing
brows∘er
bruise n., v., bruised,
bruis•ing
bruit (to spread as a ru-
mor: cf. BRUTE)
brusque
bru•tal
bru•tal•ism
bru•tal∘i∘ty n., pl.
bru•tal∘i•ties
bru•tal∘ly
brute (an animal or an
animal-like person: cf.
BRUIT)
brut•ish
brut•ish∘ly
brut•ish•ness
bru•tum ful•men
Latin.
B.S. (Bachelor of Science)
B/S or **b/s** (bill of sale)
bub•ble
buck∘et shop
budg∘et
budget res∘o•lu•tion
budget var∘i•ance
budg•et•ar∘y

budg•et•eer
budg•et∘er
buff∘er
buffer stock
buffer zone
bu•fo•ten•ine Con-
trolled Subst.
bug n., v., bugged,
bug•ging
bug•ger∘y
build v., built, build•
ing
build•ing (citation
form: **Bldg.**)
building code
building line
building per•mit
built-in de•duc•tion
built-in gain
built-in loss
built-in ob∘so•les•
cence
bu•lim∘i∘a
bulimia ner∘vo∘sa
bulk
bulk break•ing
bulk dis•count
bulk freight
bulk sale
bulk trans•fer
bull
Bull. (Bulletin)
bull mar•ket
bul•let
bul•le•tin (citation
form: **Bull.**)
bul•let•proof
bul•lion (gold or silver;
vs. bouillon)
bull•ish
bull•ish∘ly
bull•ish•ness
bul∘ly pul•pit
bum•ble v., bum•
bled, bum•bling
bum•bler

bum•bling
bun∘co or bun∘ko n.,
pl. bun•cos or bun•
kos, v., bun•coed or
bun•koed, bun•co∘
ing or bun•ko•ing
bunco (or bunko)
scheme
bunco (or bunko)
squad
bun•combe See BUN-
KUM.
bun•dle v., bun•dled,
bun•dling, n.
bun•dled
bun•gle v., bun•gled,
bun•gling
bun•gler
bun•gling∘ly
bunk
bun•kum or bun•
combe
bu∘oy
bu∘oy•age
bu•pren∘or•phine
Controlled Subst.
bur•den
burden of per•sua•
sion
burden of plead•ing
burden of pro•duc•
ing ev∘i•dence
burden of proof
burden shift•ing
bur•dened
burdened ves•sel
bur•den•some
bur•den•some∘ly
bur•den•some•ness
bu•reau n., pl. bu•
reaus
bu•reauc•ra∘cy n., pl.
bu•reauc•ra•cies
bu•reau•crat
bu•reau•crat•ese
bu•reau•crat∘ic

bu•reau•crat•i•cal•ly
bu•reauc•ra•tism
bu•reauc•ra•ti•za•tion
bu•reauc•ra•tize
Bur•ford ab•sten•tion
bur•gage
burgage ten•ure
bur•ga•tor
bur•geon
bur•gess
burgh
burgh•al
burgh•er
bur•glar
burglar a•larm
bur•glar•i•ous
bur•glar•i•ous•ly
bur•glar•ize v., bur•glar•ized, bur•glar•iz•ing
bur•glar•proof
bur•gla•ry n., pl. bur•gla•ries
burglary tools
bur•gle v., bur•gled, bur•gling
bur•i•al
burial in•sur•ance
Burn•side rem•e•dy
bur•sar
bur•sar•i•al
bur•y v., bur•ied, bur•y•ing
bus n., pl. bus•es or bus•ses, v., bused or bussed, bus•ing or bus•sing
Bus. (Business)
busi•ness (*citation form:* **Bus.**; occupation: cf. BUSYNESS)
business a•gent
business cor•po•ra•tion

business cy•cle
business de•vel•op•ment cen•ter
business en•try
business en•vi•ron•ment
business eth•ics
business ex•pense
business guest
business in•cen•tive
business in•sur•ance
business in•ter•rup•tion insurance
business in•vi•tee
business judg•ment rule
business league
business name
business plan
business pur•pose
business rec•ord
business risk
business-risk in•dem•ni•ty
business si•tus
business tort
business trust
busi•ness•man n., pl. busi•ness•men
busi•ness•per•son n., pl. busi•ness•peo•ple
busi•ness•wom•an n., pl. busi•ness•wom•en
bust
bust•er
bus•y adj., bus•i•er, bus•i•est, v., bus•ied, bus•y•ing
bus•y•bod•y n., pl. bus•y•bod•ies
bus•y•ness (state of being busy: cf. BUSI-NESS)
bus•y•work

but-for rule
but-for test
but•ler•age
but•tals n.pl.
but•tress
butts and bounds
bu•tyl ni•trite
buy v., bought, buy•ing, n.
buy back v. (cf. BUY-BACK)
buy down v.
buy-down n.
buy-down mort•gage
buy in v.
buy-in n.
buy off v. (cf. BUYOFF)
buy on mar•gin
buy out v. (cf. BUYOUT)
buy-sell a•gree•ment
buy•a•ble
buy•back or buy-back n. (cf. BUY BACK)
buy•er
buyer in the or•di•nar•y course of busi•ness
buy•er's (or buy•ers') market
buy•ers' strike
buy•ing pow•er
buy•off or buy-off n. (cf. BUY OFF)
buy•out or buy-out n. (cf. BUY OUT)
by-bid•der
by-bid•ding
by op•er•a•tion of law
by-prod•uct
by the en•tire•ty
by•law
by•stand•er
Byz•an•tine or byz•an•tine

C

C. (Chancellor; College)
C.&F. (cost and freight)
C cor•po•ra•tion
C short year
C (cytosine)
C.A. See COURT OF AP-
PEAL.
C/A (current account)
ca. (circa)
C.A.A.F. (United States
Court of Appeals for
the Armed Forces)
ca•bal n., v., ca•
balled, ca•bal•ling
cab•a•lism
cab•a•list
cab•a•lis•tic
cab•a•lis•ti•cal•ly
ca•bal•ler
cab•a•ret
cabaret li•cense
cabaret tax
cab•i•net
cabinet gov•ern•
ment
cabinet min•is•ter
cab•i•net•eer
ca•ble n., v., ca•bled,
ca•bling
cable tel•e•vi•sion
ca•ble•cast n., adj., v.,
ca•ble•cast or ca•
ble•cast•ed, ca•ble•
cast•ing
ca•ble•cast•er
ca•ble•cast•ing
ca•ble•gram
ca•ble•vi•sion
cab•o•tage
cache n., v., cached,
cach•ing (hiding
place; something hid-
den; to hide: cf. CASH)

ca•chet
ca•coph•o•nous
ca•coph•o•nous•ly
ca•coph•o•ny n., pl.
ca•coph•o•nies
ca•das•tral
ca•das•tral•ly
ca•das•tre or ca•das•
ter
ca•dav•er
ca•dav•er•ic
ca•dav•er•ous
ca•dav•er•ous•ly
ca•dav•er•ous•ness
ca•det
Cad•me•an vic•to•ry
ca•dre
ca•dre•man n., pl.
ca•dre•men
ca•du•ca•ry
CAF (computer-assisted
fraud)
caf•e•te•ri•a plan
caf•fein•at•ed
caf•feine
caf•feine-in•duced
an•xi•e•ty dis•or•
der
caffeine in•tox•i•ca•
tion
caf•fein•ic
caf•fein•ism
cage n., v., caged,
cag•ing
cag•ey or cag•y adj.,
cag•i•er, cag•i•est
cag•i•ly
cag•i•ness or cag•
ey•ness
ca•hoots n.pl.
ca•jole v., ca•joled,
ca•jol•ing
ca•jole•ment

ca•jol•er
ca•jol•er•y n., pl. ca•
jol•er•ies
ca•jol•ing•ly
ca•lam•i•tous•ly
ca•lam•i•tous•ness
ca•lam•i•ty n., pl.
ca•lam•i•ties
cal•cu•la•bil•i•ty
cal•cu•la•ble
cal•cu•la•bly
cal•cu•late v., cal•cu•
lat•ed, cal•cu•lat•
ing
cal•cu•lat•ed
calculated risk
cal•cu•lat•ed•ly
cal•cu•lat•ed•ness
cal•cu•lat•ing
cal•cu•lat•ing•ly
cal•cu•la•tion
cal•cu•la•tion•al
cal•cu•la•tive
cal•cu•la•tor
cal•cu•lus n., pl. cal•
cu•li or cal•cu•
lus•es
cal•en•dar
calendar call
calendar day
calendar month
calendar year
ca•len•dri•cal or ca•
len•dric
cal•i•ber
cal•i•bered
cal•i•brate v., cal•i•
brat•ed, cal•i•brat•
ing
cal•i•bra•tion
cal•i•bra•tor
call

call back v. (cf. CALL-BACK)
call girl
call-in pay
call loan
call mar•ket
call mon•ey
call op•tion
call out v.
call-out n.
call pre•mi•um
call price
call rate
call the cal•en•dar
call the roll
call to arms
call to or•der
call to the bar
call up v.
call-up n.
call•a•ble
callable bond
callable se•cur•i•ty
call•back n. (cf. CALL BACK)
callback pay
call•er
call•ing
cal•lous (hard-hearted: vs. *callus*)
cal•lous•ly
cal•lous•ness
ca•lum•ni•ate v., ca•lum•ni•at•ed, ca•lum•ni•at•ing
ca•lum•ni•a•tion
ca•lum•ni•a•tor
ca•lum•ni•a•to•ry
ca•lum•ni•ous
ca•lum•ni•ous•ly
ca•lum•ni•ous•ness
cal•um•ny n., pl. cal•um•nies
Cal•vo doctrine
CAM (computer-aided manufacturing)

ca•ma•ra•de•rie
ca•ma•ri•lla n., pl. ca•ma•ri•llas *Spanish*.
cam•azo•e•pam *Controlled Subst.*
cam•bist
cam•bist•ry
ca•me•ra n., pl. ca•me•rae *Latin*. See also IN CAMERA.
cam•er•al
cam•er•a•lis•tic
cam•er•a•lis•tics n. sing.
cam•ou•flage n., adj., v., cam•ou•flaged, cam•ou•flag•ing
cam•ou•flage•a•ble
cam•ou•flag•er
cam•ou•flag•ic
cam•paign
campaign chest
campaign fund
cam•paign•er
cam•pus n., pl. cam•pus•es
ca•nard
can•cel v., can•celed, can•cel•ing
can•cel•a•ble
can•celed check
can•cel•er
can•cel•la•tion or can•cel•a•tion
can•cer
can•cer•ous
can•cer•ous•ly
can•cer•ous•ness
can•croid
can•did
can•di•da•cy
can•di•date
can•did•ly
can•did•ness
can•dor

cane n., v., caned, can•ing
can•ing
can•na•bic
can•nab•i•noid
can•nab•i•nol
can•na•bis *Controlled Subst.* (Cannabis sativa L.)
cannabis a•buse
cannabis de•pend•ence
can•na•bis-in•duced dis•or•der
cannabis in•tox•i•ca•tion
can•ni•bal•ism
can•ni•bal•is•tic
can•ni•bal•is•ti•cal•ly
can•ni•bal•i•za•tion
can•ni•bal•ize v., can•ni•bal•ized, can•ni•bal•iz•ing
can•ni•ness
can•non n., pl. can•nons or can•non (mounted gun: cf. CA-NON)
can•ny adj., can•ni•er, can•ni•est
can•on (fundamental rule: cf. CANNON)
canon law
canon law•yer
canon of con•struc•tion
ca•non•ic
ca•non•i•cal
canonical dis•a•bil•i•ty
ca•non•i•cal•ly
can•on•oi•ci•ty
can•on•ist
can•on•is•tic
can•on•is•ti•cal

can•on•ize *v.*, can•
on•ized, can•on•iz•
ing
cant (hypocritical plati-
tudes; underworld jar-
gon: vs. *can't*)
can•tan•ker•ous
can•tan•ker•ous•ly
can•tan•ker•ous•
ness
cant•ing
can•vass (to solicit or
survey: vs. *canvas*)
can•vass•er
cap *n.*, *v.*, capped,
cap•ping
ca•pa•bil•i•ty *n.*, ca•
pa•bil•i•ties
ca•pa•ble
ca•pa•ble•ness
ca•pa•bly
ca•pac•i•tate *v.*, ca•
pac•i•tat•ed, ca•
pac•i•tat•ing
ca•pac•i•ta•tion
ca•pac•i•ty *n.*, *pl.* ca•
pac•i•ties
capacity costs
ca•pax do•li *Latin.*
capax ne•go•ti•i
Latin.
ca•per
ca•per•er
ca•per•ing•ly
ca•pi•as *Latin.*
capias ad re•spon•
den•dum *Latin.*
capias ad sa•tis•fa•
ci•en•dum *Latin.*
capias in with•er•
nam
capias pro fi•ne *Latin.*
capias ut•la•ga•tum
Latin.
ca•pi•ta *n.pl. Latin.*
See also PER CAPITA.

cap•i•tal (wealth; gov-
ernment city: cf. CAPI-
TOL)
capital ac•count
capital ap•pre•ci•a•
tion
capital as•set
capital bud•get
capital case
capital con•tri•bu•
tion
capital ex•pen•di•
ture
capital gain
capital gains tax
capital goods
capital im•prove•
ment
capital-in•ten•sive
capital in•vest•ment
capital lease
capital lev•y
capital loss
capital mar•ket
capital of•fense
capital out•lay
capital pun•ish•ment
capital ra•tion•ing
capital shares
capital stock
capital struc•ture
capital sum
capital sur•plus
capital turn•o•ver
cap•i•tal•ism
cap•i•tal•ist
cap•i•tal•is•tic
cap•i•tal•is•ti•cal•ly
cap•i•tal•iz•a•ble
cap•i•tal•i•za•tion
capitalization rate
cap•i•tal•ize *v.*,
cap•i•tal•ized,
cap•i•tal•iz•ing
cap•i•tal•iz•er
cap•i•tal•ly

cap•i•ta•tion
capitation tax
cap•i•ta•tive
Cap•i•tol (legislative
building: cf. CAPITAL)
Capitol Hill
ca•pit•u•lar•y *n.*, *pl.*
ca•pit•u•lar•ies
ca•pit•u•late *v.*, ca•
pit•u•lat•ed, ca•
pit•u•lat•ing
ca•pit•u•la•tion
ca•pit•u•la•tion•ism
ca•pit•u•la•tion•ist
ca•pit•u•la•tor
ca•pit•u•la•to•ry
ca•po *n.*, *pl.* ca•pos
ca•price
ca•pri•cious
ca•pri•cious•ly
ca•pri•cious•ness
cap•tain
captain of in•dus•try
cap•tain•cy
cap•tain's mast
cap•tain•ship
cap•tion
cap•tion•less
cap•tious
cap•tious•ly
cap•tious•ness
cap•tive
captive in•sur•ance
com•pa•ny
cap•tiv•i•ty
cap•tor
cap•tur•a•ble
cap•ture *v.*, cap•
tured, cap•tur•
ing, *n.*
cap•tur•er
ca•put *n.*, *pl.* ca•pi•ta
Latin.
car bomb
car seat
car•bine

car•bon cop∘y

carbon di•ox•ide

carbon mo∘nox•ide

carbon tet∘ra•chlor•ide

car•cin∘o•gen

car•ci•no•gen∘e•sis

car•ci•no•gen∘ic

car•ci•no•ge•nic∘i•ty

card-car•ry•ing

card count∘er

card count•ing

card•hold∘er

car•di•nal

cardinal change

car•di•o•vas•cu•lar

care *n., v.,* cared, car•ing

care of (c/o)

ca•reen

ca•reer

career crim∘i•nal

ca•reer•ism

ca•reer•ist

care•ful

care•ful∘ly

care•giv∘er

care•giv•ing

care•less

care•less∘ly

care•less•ness

care•tak∘er

car•fen•ta•nil *Controlled Subst.*

car∘go *n.,* car•gos or car•goes

car∘i•ca•tur•a∘ble

car∘i•ca•tur∘al

car∘i•ca•ture *n. v.,* car∘i•ca•tured, car∘i•ca•tur•ing

car∘i•ca•tur•ist

car•jack∘er

car•jack•ing

car•load

carload lot

carload rate

car•nage

car•nal

carnal a∘buse

carnal knowl•edge

car•nal∘i∘ty

car•nal∘ly

car•net *French.*

ca•rous∘al

ca•rouse *v.,* ca•roused, ca•rous•ing, *n.*

ca•rous∘er

ca•rous•ing∘ly

carp

car•pal tun•nel syn•drome

carp∘er

car•pet•bag•ger

car•pet•bag•ger∘y

carp•ing

car•pool

car•pool∘er

car•pool•ing

car•ri•a∘ble or car•ry•a∘ble

car•riage

carriage of goods

car•ried interest

car•ri∘er

car•ri•er's lien

car∘ry *v.,* car•ried, car•ry•ing

carry back *v.* (cf. CARRY-BACK)

carry forward *v.* (cf. CARRYFORWARD)

carry over *v.* (cf. CARRY-OVER)

car•ry•a∘ble See CAR-RIABLE.

car•ry•back *n.* (cf. CARRY BACK

car•ry•for•ward *n.* (cf. CARRY FORWARD)

car•ry•ing ca•pac∘i∘ty

carrying charge

carrying costs

car•ryo∘ver or car∘ry-o∘ver *n., adj.* (cf. CARRY OVER)

car•ry∘o•ver ba∘sis

cart

car∘ta *n., pl.* car•tae *Latin.*

cart•a∘ble

cart•age

carte *n., pl.* cartes *French.*

carte blanche *n., pl.* cartes blanches *French.*

car•tel

car•tel•ism

car•tel•ist

car•tel•is•tic

car•tel∘i•za•tion

car•tel•ize *v.,* car•tel•ized, car•tel•iz•ing

car•ter

Car•tha•gin∘i•an peace

cart•ridge

cartridge belt

cartridge clip

car•tu•lar∘y See CHAR-TULARY.

carve *v.,* carved, carv•ing

carve out *v.*

carve-out *n.*

carved out o∘ver•rid•ing roy•al∘ty

Cas. (Cases; Casualty

case *n., v.,* cased, cas•ing

case in chief

case in point

case law

case load See CASELOAD.
case man•age•ment
case meth•od
case note
case of first im•pres•sion
case or con•tro•ver•sy
case stat•ed
case stud•y
case sys•tem
case•book
case•load or case load
cas•es (*citation form:* Cas.)
case•work
case•work•er
cash (money: cf. **cache**)
cash ac•count
cash ac•count•ing
cash-and-car•ry
cash-and-carry whole•sal•er
cash au•dit
cash bail
cash ba•sis
cash before de•liv•er•y (C.B.D.)
cash book
cash bud•get
cash cow
cash crop
cash cus•tom•er
cash dis•count
cash e•quiv•a•lent
cash flow
cash-flow cy•cle
cash in *v.*
cash-in *n.*
cash jour•nal
cash let•ter
cash ma•chine
cash on de•liv•er•y See C.O.D.
cash on hand
cash out *v.*

cash-out *n.*
cash reg•is•ter
cash sale
cash sur•ren•der val•ue
cash trad•ing
cash val•ue
cash•a•bil•i•ty
cash•a•ble
cash•book
cash•box
cash•ier
cash•iered
cash•ier's check
cash•less
cashless so•ci•e•ty
ca•si•no *n.,* pl. ca•si•nos
cas•sa•tion *French.*
cast *v.,* cast, cast•ing, *n.* (to throw; a mold: cf. CASTE)
cast•a•bil•i•ty
cast•a•ble
caste (social class: cf. CAST)
caste mark
caste•ism
caste•less
cas•tel•lan
cas•tel•lan•ship
cas•tel•la•ny *n.,* pl. cas•tel•la•nies
cast•er
cas•ti•gate *v.,* cas•ti•gat•ed, cas•ti•gat•ing
cas•ti•ga•tion
cas•ti•ga•tive
cas•ti•ga•tor
cas•ti•ga•to•ry *adj., n.,* pl. cas•ti•ga•to•ries
cast•ing voice
casting vote

cas•trate *v.,* cas•trat•ed, cas•trat•ing
cas•tra•tion
cas•tra•tor
ca•su con•si•mi•li *Latin.*
cas•u•al (irregular; fortuitous: cf. CAUSAL)
casual e•jec•tor
casual em•ploy•ee
casual em•ploy•ment
casual sale
cas•u•al•ly
cas•u•al•ness
cas•u•al•ty *n.,* pl. cas•u•al•ties (*citation form:* Cas.)
casualty in•sur•ance
casualty loss
cas•u•ist
cas•u•is•tic
cas•u•is•ti•cal
cas•u•is•ti•cal•ly
cas•u•ist•ry *n.,* pl. cas•u•ist•ries
ca•sus *n.,* pl. ca•sus *Latin.*
casus bel•li *Latin.*
casus for•tu•i•tus *Latin.*
casus o•mis•sus *Latin.*
cat•a•chre•sis *n.,* pl. cat•a•chre•ses
cat•a•chres•tic
cat•a•chres•ti•cal
cat•a•chres•ti•cal•ly
cat•a•clysm
cat•a•clys•mal
cat•a•clys•mic
cat•a•clys•mi•cal•ly
cat•a•lep•sy
cat•a•lep•tic
cat•a•lep•ti•cal•ly
ca•tal•la *n.pl. Latin.*
cat•a•log or cat•a•logue *n., v.,* cat•a•

loged or cat•a•
logued, cat•a•log•
ing or cat•a•logu•
ing
cat•a•log•er or
cat•a•logu•er
cat•a•log•ic
ca•tal•y•sis n., ca•
tal•y•ses
cat•a•lyst
cat•a•lyt•ic
catalytic con•vert•er
cat•a•lyt•i•cal
cat•a•lyt•i•cal•ly
cat•a•lyze v., cat•a•
lyzed, cat•a•lyz•ing
cat•a•lyz•er
cat•a•plec•tic
cat•a•plex•y
ca•tas•tro•phe
cat•a•stroph•ic
cat•a•stroph•i•cal•ly
cat•a•to•ni•a
cat•a•to•ni•ac
cat•a•ton•ic
catatonic dis•or•der
catatonic schiz•o•
phre•ni•a
catch v., caught,
catch•ing
catch phrase
catch time char•ter
Catch-22 n., pl. Catch-
22's
catch•all
catch•i•ness
catch•ing bar•gain
catch•ment
catchment ar•e•a
catch•pole or catch•
poll
catch•word
catch•y adj.,
catch•i•er, catch•i•
est
cat•e•chism

cat•e•chis•mal
cat•e•chist
cat•e•chis•tic
cat•e•chis•ti•cal•ly
cat•e•chiz•a•ble
cat•e•chi•za•tion
cat•e•chize v.,
cat•e•chized,
cat•e•chiz•ing
cat•e•chiz•er
cat•e•gor•ic
cat•e•gor•i•cal
categorical im•per•a•
tive
cat•e•gor•i•cal•ly
cat•e•gor•ist
cat•e•gor•i•za•tion
cat•e•go•rize v.,
cat•e•go•rized,
cat•e•go•riz•ing
cat•e•go•ry n., pl.
cat•e•go•ries
cat•e•nate v.,
cat•e•nat•ed,
cat•e•nat•ing
cat•e•na•tion
Cath. (Catholic)
ca•thar•sis n., pl. ca•
thar•ses
ca•thar•tic
ca•thar•ti•cal•ly
ca•thec•tic
ca•thex•is n., pl. ca•
thex•es
cath•ine Controlled
Subst.
cath•i•none Controlled
Subst.
cath•o•lic (wide-
ranging; broad-
minded: cf. CATHOLIC)
Cath•o•lic (citation
form: Cath.; pertaining
to a Catholic church:
cf. CATHOLIC)
cath•o•lic•i•ty

cat•ti•ly
cat•ti•ness
cat•ty
CATV (community an-
tenna television)
cau•cus n., pl. cau•
cus•es, v., cau•
cused, cau•cus•ing
cau•di•llo n., pl. cau•
di•llos Spanish
caught See CATCH.
cau•sa n., pl. cau•sae
Latin.
causa cau•sans Latin.
causa mor•tis Latin.
causa prox•i•ma
Latin.
causa re•mo•ta Latin.
causa si•ne qua non
Latin.
caus•a•bil•i•ty
caus•a•ble
cau•sal (of a cause: cf.
CASUAL)
cau•sal•i•ty
cau•sal•ly
cau•sa•tion
cau•sa•tion•al
cau•sa•tive
cau•sa•tive•ly
cause n., v., caused,
caus•ing
cause and ef•fect n.
cause-and-effect adj.
cause cé•lè•bre n., pl.
cause cé•lè•bres
French.
cause of ac•tion
caus•er
cau•tion
cau•tion•ar•y
cautionary in•struc•
tion
cau•tion•er
cau•tious
cau•tious•ly

cau•tious•ness

cave n., v., **caved,
cav•ing**

cave in v.

cave-in n.

ca•ve•at

caveat emp•tor Latin.

caveat ven•di•tor Latin.

ca•ve•a•tor

cav•il v., **cav•iled,
cav•il•ing**

cav•il•er

cav•il•ing•ly

CB (citizens band)

C.B. (Chief Baron)

C.B.D. (cash before delivery)

CCRC (continuing care retirement community)

CD (certificate of deposit)

C.D. (Central District; Congressional district)

cease v., **ceased, ceas•ing,** n.

cease-and-de•sist or•der

cease-fire

cease•less

cease•less•ly

cease•less•ness

cede v., **ced•ed, ced•ing**

ced•er

ceil•ing

cel•e•brate v., **cel•e•brat•ed, cel•e•brat•ing**

cel•e•brat•ed

cel•e•bra•tion

cel•e•bra•tor

ce•leb•ra•to•ry

ce•leb•ri•ty n., pl. **ce•leb•ri•ties**

cell (prison room; bio-

logical structure: cf. SELL)

cell phone

cell•u•lar

cellular tel•e•phone

cem•e•te•ri•al

cem•e•ter•y n., **cem•e•ter•ies**

cen•sor (supervisor of morals; to suppress: cf. CENSURE)

cen•sor•a•ble

cen•so•ri•al

cen•so•ri•ous

cen•so•ri•ous•ly

cen•so•ri•ous•ness

cen•sor•ship

cen•su•al (relating to a census: cf. SENSUAL)

cen•sur•a•bil•i•ty

cen•sur•a•ble

cen•sur•a•ble•ness

cen•sur•a•bly

cen•sure n., v., **cen•sured, cen•sur•ing** (a reprimand; to reprimand: cf. CENSOR)

cen•sur•er

cen•sus n., **cen•sus•es,** v.

census tak•er

census tract

Cent. (Central)

cen•ter (citation form: **Ctr.**)

center of grav•i•ty doc•trine

cen•ter•a•ble

cen•ter•less

cen•ter•piece

cen•tral (citation form: **Cent.**)

central bank

central cor•po•rate ex•pen•ses

Cen•tral Dis•trict (citation form: **C.D.**)

central ner•vous sys•tem

cen•tral•i•ty

cen•tral•oi•za•tion

cen•tral•ize v., **cen•tral•ized, cen•tral•iz•ing**

cen•tral•ly

cen•tre (British spelling for CENTER; citation form: **Ctr.**)

cent•ric

cen•tri•cal

cen•tri•cal•ly

cen•tric•i•ty

cen•trif•ou•gal

cen•trif•ou•gal•ly

cen•trip•oe•tal

cen•trip•oe•tal•ly

cen•trism

cen•trist

cen•tu•ory n., pl. **cen•tu•ries**

CEO (Chief Executive Officer)

ce•pit Latin.

cer•e•brate v., **cer•e•brat•ed, cer•e•brat•ing**

cer•e•bra•tion

cer•e•mo•ni•a•lism

cer•e•mo•ni•al•ly

cer•e•mo•ni•ous

cer•e•mo•ni•ous•ly

cer•e•mo•ni•ous•ness

cer•e•mo•ny n., pl. **cer•e•mo•nies**

cert. (certiorari)

cer•tain

cer•tain•ly

cer•tain•ty n.,pl. **cer•tain•ties**

cer•ti•fi•a•ble

cer•ti•fi•a•bly
cer•tif•oi•cate
certificate of ad•meas•ure•ment
certificate of de•pos•it (CD)
certificate of en•roll•ment
certificate of in•cor•po•ra•tion
certificate of in•debt•ed•ness
certificate of in•sur•ance
certificate of need
certificate of oc•cu•pan•cy
certificate of oro•i•gin
certificate of par•ti•ci•pa•tion
certificate of pub•lic con•ven•ience
certificate of reg•is•try
certificate of stock
certificate of ti•tle
cer•ti•fi•ca•tion
certification mark
cer•tif•oi•ca•to•ry
cer•ti•fied
certified check
certified copy
certified fi•nan•cial state•ment
certified in•ter•nal au•di•tor (CIA)
certified mail
certified pro•fes•sion•al sec•re•tar•y (CPS)
certified pub•lic account•ant (CPA)
certified ques•tion
cer•ti•fi•er
cer•ti•fy v., cer•ti•fied, cer•ti•fy•ing

certify the rec•ord
cer•ti•o•o•ra•ri Latin. (citation form: cert.)
ces•sa•tion
ces•sa•vit Latin.
ces•ser (cessation; neglect: cf. CESSOR)
cesser clause
cesser of hire clause
ces•sion (a yielding; territory yielded: cf. SESSION)
ces•sion•ar•y n.,pl. ces•sion•ar•ies
ces•sor (one who ceases or neglects: cf. CESSER)
ces•tui n., pl. ces•tuis Law French
cestui que trust n., pl. cestuis que trust or cestuis que trustent Law French.
cestui que use n., pl. cestuis que use Law French.
cestui que vie n., pl. cestuis que vie Law French.
cf. (compare: from Latin confer)
CFA (chartered financial analyst)
CFO (Chief Financial Officer)
C.F.R. (Code of Federal Regulations)
Ch. (Chancery; Court of Chancery; Chancery Court; Chancery Division)
ch. (chapter)
Ch. Div. (Chancery Division)
chaf•fer
cha•grin n., v., cha•grined, cha•grin•ing

chain letter
chain of com•mand
chain of cus•to•dy
chain of evoi•dence
chain of ti•tle
chair
chair•man n., pl. chair•men
chairman of the board
chair•man•ship
chair•per•son n., pl. chair•per•sons
chair•per•son•ship
chair•wom•an n., pl. chair•wom•en
chal•lenge n., v., chal•lenged, chal•leng•ing
challenge for cause
challenge to the ar•ray
chal•lenge•a•ble
chal•lenged
chal•leng•er
chal•leng•ing
chal•leng•ing•ly
cham•ber
cham•ber•lain
cham•bers n.pl.
cham•per•tor
cham•per•tous
cham•per•ty
cham•pi•on
chance n., v., chanced, chanc•ing
chance-med•ley
chance ver•dict
chan•cel•ler•oy n., pl. chan•cel•ler•ies
chan•cel•lor (C.)
Chan•cel•lor of the Ex•cheq•uer
chan•cel•lor•ship
chan•cer•oy (citation form: Ch.)

Chan•cer•y Court (*ci
tation form:* **Ch.**)

Chancery Di•vi•sion
(*citation form:* **Ch.** or
Ch. Div.)

chan○i•ness

chan○y *adj.*,
chan○i•er, chan○i•
est

change *v.*, changed,
chang•ing, *n.*

change a○gent

change of ven○ue

change or○der

change•a○bil•i○ty

change•a○ble

change•a○bly

changed cir•cum•
stanc○es

change•less

change•less○ly

change•less•ness

change•ling

change•o○ver

chang○er

chan•nels of dis•tri•
bu•tion

cha○os

cha•ot○ic

cha•ot○i•cal○ly

chap•ter (*citation form:*
ch.)

Chapter 7 bank•
rupt○cy

Chapter 11 bank-
ruptcy

Chapter 12 bank-
ruptcy

Chapter 13 bank-
ruptcy

char•ac○ter

character as•sas•sl•
na○tion

character dis•or•der

character ev○i•dence

character trait

character wit•ness

char•ac•ter•ful

char•ac•ter•is•tic

char•ac•ter•is•ti
cal○ly

char•ac•ter•iz•a○ble

char•ac•ter○i•za•tion

char•ac•ter•ize *v.*,
char•ac•ter○ized,
char•ac•ter•iz•ing

char•ac•ter•iz○er

cha•rade

charge *n.*, *v.*, charged,
charg•ing

charge ac•count

charge and dis•
charge state•ment

charge back *v.* (cf.
CHARGEBACK)

charge card

charge con•fer•ence

char○gé d'af•faires *n.*,
pl. char•gés d'af•
faires *French.*

chargé d'affaires ad
in•ter○im *n.,pl.*
char•gés d'affaires
ad in•ter○im *French
and Latin.*

charge off *v.*

charge-off *or* charge•
off *n.*

charge plate

charge•a○ble

charge•a○bly

charge•back *n.* (cf.
CHARGE BACK)

charged

charge•off See CHARGE-
OFF.

charg•ing docu•
ment

charging lien

charging or○der

charging par○ty

char○i○ly

char○i•ness

cha•ris○ma

char•is•mat○ic

char•is•mat○i•cal○ly

char○i•ta•ble

charitable be•quest

charitable con•tri•
bu•tion

charitable de•duc•
tion

charitable gift

charitable in•come
trust

charitable or•gan○i•
za•tion

charitable pur•pose

charitable re•main•
der trust

charitable trust

charitable use

char○i•ta•ble•ness

char○i•ta•bly

char○i○ty *n.*, *pl.*
char○i•ties

char•la•tan

char•la•tan○ic

char•la•tan○i•cal

char•la•tan○i•cal○ly

char•la•tan•ish

char•la•tan•ism

char•la•tan•is•tic

char•la•tan○ry *n.*, *pl.*
char•la•tan•ries

charm

charmed

charm○er

charm•ing

charm•less

charm•less○ly

char•nel

charnel house

char○ta *n.*, *pl.* char•
tae *Latin.*

char•ter[1] (authorizing
document; to lease)

chart•er² (one who charts)

char•ter mem•ber

char•ter mem•bers•hip

charter par•ty

char•ter•a•ble

char•ter•age

char•tered fi•nan•cial an•a•lyst (CFA)

chartered life un•der•writ•er (CLU)

char•ter•er

char•ter•less

char•tist

char•tu•lar•y or car•tu•lar•y n., pl. char•tu•lar•ies or car•tu•lar•ies

chase v., chased, chas•ing, n.

chase•a•ble

chas•er

chasm

chas•mal

chas•mic

chaste

chaste•ly

chas•ten

chas•tened

chas•ten•er

chaste•ness

chas•ten•ing•ly

chas•ten•ment

chas•tis•a•ble

chas•tise v., chas•tised, chas•tis•ing

chas•tise•ment

chas•tis•er

chas•ti•ty

chat•room or chat room

chat•tel

chattel mort•gage

chattel pa•per

chattel re•al

chau•vin•ism

chau•vin•ist

chau•vin•is•tic

chau•vin•is•ti•cal•ly

cheap•en

cheat

cheat•a•ble

cheat•er

cheat•ing•ly

check

check fraud

check kit•ing

check off v. (cf. CHECK-OFF)

check pro•tec•tor

check reg•is•ter

check up v. (cf. CHECKUP)

check•a•bil•i•ty

check•a•ble

check•book

check•er

check•ered

check•ing ac•count

check•less

checkless so•ci•e•ty

check•list

check•off n. (cf. CHECK OFF)

check•point

checks and bal•anc•es

check•up n. (cf. CHECK UP)

check•writ•er

Chem. (Chemical)

chem•i•cal (citation form: Chem.)

chemical cas•tra•tion

chemical com•pound

chemical de•pend•en•cy

Chemical Mace Trademark.

chemical proc•ess

chemical syn•the•sis

chemical weap•on

chemo•i•cal•ly

che•mo•ther•a•peu•tic

che•mo•ther•a•peu•ti•cal•ly

che•mo•ther•a•peu•tics n.sing.

che•mo•ther•a•pist

che•mo•ther•a•py

cher•ry-pick

cher•ry pick•ing

chew•ing to•bac•co

chi•ca•ner•y n., pl. chi•ca•ner•ies

chief

Chief Bar•on (C.B.)

chief ex•ec•u•tive (head of a state or other government)

Chief Executive (president of the United States)

chief executive of•fi•cer (CEO)

chief fi•nan•cial offi•cer (CFO)

Chief Judge (C.J. or Ch.J.)

Chief Jus•tice (C.J. or Ch.J.)

Chief Justice of the U•nit•ed States

chief jus•tice•ship

chief of state

chief op•er•at•ing of•fi•cer (COO)

child n., pl. chil•dren

child a•buse

child-bat•ter•er

child-bat•ter•ing

child care

Child. Ct. (Children's Court)

child cus•to•dy

child in need of

su•per•vi•sion (CHINS)
child la•bor
child mo•les•ta•tion
child mo•lest•er
child ne•glect
child por•nog•ra•phy
child psy•chi•a•try
child psy•chol•o•gy
child-re•sist•ant
child sup•port
child wel•fare
child•bear•ing
child•birth
child•hood
child•ish
child•ish•ly
child•less
child•less•ness
child•like
child•proof or child-proof
Chil•dren's Court
chill•ing ef•fect
chi•me•ra n., pl. chi•me•ras
chi•mer•ic
chi•mer•i•cal
chi•mer•i•cal•ly
Chi•nese wall
CHINS (child in need of supervision)
chiv•al•rous
chiv•al•rous•ly
chiv•al•rous•ness
chiv•al•ry
Ch.J. (Chief Judge; Chief Justice)
chlor•al be•ta•ine Controlled Subst.
chlor•al hy•drate Controlled Subst.
chlor•di•az•e•pox•ide Controlled Subst.
chlor•hex•a•dol Controlled Subst.

chlor•o•fluor•o•car•bon Controlled Subst.
chlor•o•fluor•o•meth•ane
chlor•o•tes•tos•ter•one Controlled Subst.
chlor•phen•ter•mine Controlled Subst.
choice of e•vils
choice of fo•rum clause
choice of law
choice of law clause
choke v., choked, chok•ing
choke•hold
chok•er
chol•er (anger: cf. COL-LAR)
cho•les•ter•ol
cho•re•o•graph
cho•re•o•graph•ic
choreographic work
cho•re•og•ra•phy
chose n., pl. chos•es Law French.
chose in ac•tion n., pl. chos•es in ac•tion
chose in pos•ses•sion n., pl. chos•es in pos•ses•sion
chro•mo•so•mal
chromosomal ab•er•ra•tion
chro•mo•so•mal DNA
chro•mo•so•mal•ly
chro•mo•some
Chron. (Chronicle)
chron•ic
chron•i•cal•ly
chro•nic•i•ty
chron•i•cle[1] n. (citation form: Chron.)
chron•i•cle[2] v.,

chron•i•cled, chron•i•cling
chron•i•cler
chron•o•log•i•cal
chronological age
chronological sta•bi•li•za•tion
chron•o•log•i•cal•ly
chro•nol•o•gize v., chro•nol•o•gized, chro•nol•o•giz•ing
chro•nol•o•gy n., pl. chro•nol•o•gies
churl
churl•ish
churl•ish•ly
churl•ish•ness
churn
churn•er
churn•ing
CIA (certified internal auditor)
Cia. Portuguese. (Companhia)
Cía. Spanish. (Compañía)
CID civil investigative demand
Cie French. (Compagnie)
C.I.F. (cost, insurance, and freight)
ci•gar
cig•a•rette
ci•pher
Cir. (Circuit)
Cir. Ct. (Circuit Court)
cir•ca (ca.) Latin.
cir•cuit (citation form: CIR.)
circuit break•er
Circuit Court (citation form: CIR. CT.)
circuit judge
cir•cu•i•tous
cir•cu•i•tous•ly

cir•cu•i•tous•ness
cir•cu•lar•oi•za•tion
cir•cu•lar•ize v., cir•cu•lar•ized, cir•cu•lar•iz•ing
cir•cu•lat•ing cap•i•tal
circulating capital goods
cir•cum•lo•cu•tion
cir•cum•scrib•a•ble
cir•cum•scribe v., cir•cum•scribed, cir•cum•scrib•ing
cir•cum•scrip•tion
cir•cum•scrip•tive
cir•cum•scrip•tive•ly
cir•cum•spect
cir•cum•spec•tion
cir•cum•spect•ly
cir•cum•spect•ness
cir•cum•stance
cir•cum•stan•tial
circumstantial evoi•dence
cir•cum•stan•ti•al•i•ty
cir•cum•stan•tial•ly
cir•cum•vent
cir•cum•vent•er or cir•cum•ven•tor
cir•cum•vent•ing
cir•cum•ven•tion
cir•cum•ven•tive
cir•rhosed
cir•rho•sis
cir•rhot•ic
cit•a•ble or cite•a•ble
ci•ta•tion
ci•ta•tion•al
ci•ta•tor
cite v., cit•ed, cit•ing, n. (to refer to; citation: cf. SIGHT; SITE)
cit•i•zen

cit•i•zen•ly
cit•i•zen•ry
cit•i•zen's ar•rest
citizens band (CB)
cit•i•zen•ship
citizenship pa•pers
cit•y n., pl. cit•ies
city clerk
city coun•cil
Cit•y Court (citation form: CITY CT.)
City Ct. (City Court)
city hall
city man•ag•er
city plan
city plan•ner
city planning
cit•y-state
cit•y•wide
Civ. (Civil)
Civ. App. (Civil Appeals; Court of Civil Appeals)
Civ. Ct. (Civil Court)
Civ. Ct. Rec. (Civil Court of Record)
civ•ic
civ•ics n.sing.
civ•il (citation form: Civ.)
civil ac•tion
Civil Ap•peals (citation form: Civ. App.)
civil ar•rest
civil case
civil code
civil com•mit•ment
civil com•mo•tion
civil con•fine•ment
civil con•tempt
Civil Court (citation form: Civ. Ct.)
Civil Court of Rec•ord (citation form: Civ. Ct. Rec.)
civil death

civil de•fense
civil dis•a•bil•i•ty
civil dis•o•be•di•ence
civil dis•or•der
civil dis•tur•bance
civil fine
civil for•fei•ture
civil fraud
civil in•ves•ti•ga•tive de•mand (CID)
civil law
civil lib•er•tar•i•an
civil lib•er•ties
civil lib•er•ty
civil mar•riage
civil pen•al•ty
civil pro•ce•dure
civil pros•e•cu•tion
civil rights
civil serv•ant
civil serv•ice
civil side
civil war
Civil War a•mend•ments
ci•vil•ian
civilian re•view board
ci•vil•ian•i•za•tion
ci•vil•ian•ize v., ci•vil•ian•ized, ci•vil•ian•iz•ing
ci•vil•i•ty
civ•il•ly
ci•vi•tas n., pl. ci•vi•ta•tes Latin.
C.J. or > Ch.J. (Chief Judge; Chief Justice)
Cl. (Claims)
cl. (clause)
Cl. Ct. (Claims Court)
Claf•lin trust
claim
claim join•der
claim of right
claim pre•clu•sion

claim•a•ble
claim•ant
claims ad•just•er
Claims Court (*citation form:* **Cl. Ct.**)
clam•or
clam•or•ous
clam•or•ous•ly
clam•or•ous•ness
clan•des•tine
clan•des•tine•ly
clan•des•tine•ness
clap•trap
clar•i•fi•ca•tion
clar•i•fi•er
clar•i•fy v., clar•i•fied, clar•i•fy•ing
clar•i•ty
clash
clash•ing
clash•ing•ly
class
class ac•tion n.
class-action adj.
class con•flict
class-con•scious
class con•scious•ness
clas•si•cal ec•o•nom•ics
classical e•con•o•mist
clas•si•fi•a•ble
clas•si•fi•ca•tion
clas•si•fied
clas•si•fy v., clas•si•fied, clas•si•fy•ing
clause (*citation form:* **cl.**)
clause par•a•mount
clau•sum n., pl. clau•sa Latin.
clausum fre•git Latin.
clean
clean bill
clean bill of health
clean bill of lad•ing

clean-hand•ed
clean hands
clean hands doc•trine
clean slate doctrine
clean up v. (cf. CLEANUP)
clean•a•bil•i•ty
clean•a•ble
clean•hand•ed•ness
clean•li•ness
clean•ly
clean•ness
clean•up n. (cf. CLEAN UP)
cleanup costs
clear
clear and con•vinc•ing ev•i•dence
clear and pres•ent dan•ger
clear-cut adj., n., v., clear-cut, clear-cut•ting
clear-cut•ting
clear-eyed
clear-sight•ed
clear-sight•ed•ly
clear-sight•ed•ness
clear ti•tle
clear•a•ble
clear•ance
clear•er
clear•head•ed
clear•head•ed•ly
clear•head•ed•ness
clear•ing
clearing ac•count
clearing loan
clear•ing•house or clear•ing house
clear•ly
clearly er•ro•ne•ous
clem•en•cy
clem•ent
clem•ent•ly
cler•gy n.,pl. cler•gies

clergy-com•mu•ni•cant priv•i•lege
cler•ic
cler•i•cal
clerical er•ror
clerical mis•take
cle•ri•ca•le pri•vi•le•gi•um Latin.
clerk
clerk of the court
clerk•ship
clev•er adj., clev•er•er, clev•er•est
clev•er•ly
clev•er•ness
cli•ent
client state
cli•en•tele
cli•ent•less
cliff vest•ing
Clif•ford trust
cli•mac•tic (culminating: cf. CLIMATIC)
cli•mac•ti•cal•ly
cli•mate
cli•mat•ic (pertaining to climate: cf. CLIMACTIC)
cli•mat•i•cal•ly
cli•max
clinch
clinch•er
clin•ic
clin•i•cal
clinical de•pres•sion
clinical psy•chol•o•gist
clinical psy•chol•o•gy
clinical symp•tom
clin•i•cal•ly
cli•ni•cian
clique
cloak•room
clo•ba•zam Controlled Subst.

clog v., clogged, clog•ging, n.

clog•ging the eq•ui•ty of re•demp•tion

clo•naz•e•pam Controlled Subst.

clone n., v., cloned, clon•ing

clon•ing

clo•nit•a•zene Controlled Subst.

clo•raz•e•pate Controlled Subst.

clor•ter•mine Controlled Subst.

clos•a•ble or close•a•ble

close v., closed, clos•ing, adj., clos•er, clos•est, n.

close-con•nect•ed•ness doc•trine

close (or closed) cor•po•ra•tion

close down v. (cf. CLOSEDOWN)

close out v. (cf. CLOSE-OUT)

closed-cap•tioned

closed-cap•tion•ing

closed cor•po•ra•tion See CLOSE CORPORATION.

closed-end

closed-end cred•it

closed-end in•vest•ment com•pa•ny

closed-end mort•gage bond

closed-mind•ed

closed pri•ma•ry

closed rule

closed sea•son

closed shop

closed un•ion

close•down n. (cf. CLOSE DOWN)

close•ly

closely held

closely held cor•po•ra•tion

close•mouthed

close•ness

close•out n. (cf. CLOSE OUT)

clos•et

clos•et•ed

clos•ing

closing costs

closing date

closing in•ven•to•ry

closing price

closing state•ment

clos•te•bol Controlled Subst.

clo•sure[1] n. (act of closing: cf. CLOTURE)

closure[2] n., v., clo•sured, clo•sur•ing Chiefly Brit. (See CLO-TURE)

clo•ti•az•e•pam Controlled Subst.

clo•ture n., v., clo•tured, clo•tur•ing (cutting off of debate; to cut off debate: cf. CLOSURE[1]; see also CLO-SURE[2])

cloud on ti•tle

clox•az•o•lam Controlled Subst.

CLU (chartered life underwriter)

club n., v., clubbed, club•bing

clue n., v., clued, clu•ing

clus•ter con•cept

cluster zon•ing

C.M.R. (Court of Military Review)

cmt. (comment)

Co. (Company)

c/o (care of)

coach

coach•a•bil•i•ty

coach•a•ble

co•a•li•tion

coalition bar•gain•ing

co•a•li•tion•ism

co•a•li•tion•ist

coarse adj., coars•er, coars•est (harsh; crude: cf. COURSE)

coarse•ly

coars•en

coarse•ness

co•as•sign•ee

coast•al wa•ters

cob•ble v., cob•bled, cob•bling

COBRA (Consolidated Omnibus Budget Reconciliation Act of 1985)

co•ca Controlled Subst. (Erythroxylon coca)

co•caine Controlled Subst.

cocaine a•buse

cocaine al•ka•loid

cocaine de•pend•ence

cocaine-in•duced dis•o•rder

cocaine in•tox•i•ca•tion

cocaine with•draw•al

co•chair

co•chair•man

co•chair•per•son

co•cli•ent

co•con•spir•a•tor or co•con•spir•a•tor

co•coun•sel

C.O.D. or c.o.d. (collect

on delivery; colloqui-
ally, cash on delivery)
cod•dle v., cod•dled,
cod•dling
code
Code Ci•vil French.
Code Na•po•lé•on
French.
Code of Fed•er•al
Reg•u•la•tions (cita-
tion form: **C.F.R.**)
Code of Ham•mu•
ra•bi
code plead•ing
co•de•fen•dant
co•deine Controlled
Subst.
codeine meth•yl•
bro•mide Controlled
Subst.
codeine-N-ox•ide Con-
trolled Subst.
co•de•ter•mi•na•
tion
co•dex n., co•di•ces
English and Latin
Codex Ju•ris Ca•no•
ni•ci Latin.
cod•i•cil
cod•i•cil•la•ry
cod•i•fi•a•bil•i•ty
cod•i•fi•ca•tion
cod•i•fi•er
cod•i•fy v., cod•i•
fied, cod•i•fy•ing
CODIS (Combined DNA
Identification System)
co•ed•u•ca•tion
co•ed•u•ca•tion•al
co•ed•u•ca•tion•
al•ly
co•emp•tion
co•emp•tion•al
co•emp•tive
co•e•qual

co•erce v., co•erced,
co•erc•ing
co•erc•er
co•er•ci•ble
co•er•cion
co•er•cive
co•er•cive•ly
co•er•cive•ness
co•ex•ec•u•tor
co•ex•ist
co•ex•ist•ence
co•ex•ist•ent
co•ex•tend
co•ex•ten•sive
co•ex•ten•sive•ly
co•ex•ten•sive•ness
cof•fer
co•gen•cy
co•gen•er•a•tion
co•gent
cog•i•tate v., cog•i•
tat•ed, cog•i•tat•
ing
cog•i•ta•tion
cog•ni•tion
cog•ni•tive
cognitive def•i•cit
cognitive de•vel•op•
ment
cognitive dis•or•der
cognitive dis•so•
nance
cog•ni•tive•ly
cog•ni•tiv•ism
cog•ni•tor
cog•ni•za•ble
cog•ni•za•bly
cog•ni•zance
cog•ni•zant
cog•nize v., cog•
nized, cog•niz•ing
cog•ni•zee
cog•niz•er (one who
takes cognizance gen-
erally: cf. COGNIZOR)
cog•ni•zor (party ac-

knowledging another's
right to land: cf. COG-
NIZER)
cog•no•men
co•gno•scen•ti n.pl.
cog•no•vit Latin.
cognovit note
co•hab•it
co•hab•i•tant
co•hab•i•ta•tion
co•hab•it•er
co•heir or co-heir
co•heir•ess or
co-heir•ess
co•heir•ship or
co-heir•ship
co•here v., co•hered,
co•her•ing
co•her•ence
co•her•en•cy
co•her•ent
co•her•ent•ly
co•he•sion
co•he•sive
co•he•sive•ly
co•he•sive•ness
co•hort
coif
coin of the realm
coin•age
co•in•cide v., co•in•
cid•ed, co•in•cid•
ing
co•in•ci•dence
co•in•ci•dent
co•in•ci•dent•al
co•in•ci•dent•al•ly
co•in•her•it•ance
co•in•sur•ance
co•in•sure v., co•in•
sured, co•in•sur•ing
co•in•sur•er
co•i•tal
co•i•tal•ly
co•i•tion
co•i•tus

col. (column)

COLA (cost-of-living adjustment)

cold-blood∘ed

cold war

cold war∙ri∘or

col∙lab∘o∘rate *v.*, col∙lab∘o∙rat∘ed, col∙lab∘o∙rat∙ing

col∙lab∘o∙ra∙tion

col∙lab∘o∙ra∙tion∙ism

col∙lab∘o∙ra∙tion∙ist

col∙lab∘o∙ra∙tive

col∙lab∘o∙ra∙tive∙ly

col∙lapse *v.*, col∙lapsed, col∙laps∙ing, *n.*

col∙laps∘i∙bil∘i∘ty

col∙laps∘i∙ble

collapsible cor∘po∙ra∙tion

col∙lar

col∙lat∙er∙al

collateral an∙ces∙tor

collateral as∙sur∙ance

collateral at∙tack

collateral dam∙age

collateral de∙scent

collateral es∙top∙pel

collateral heir

collateral im∙peach∙ment

collateral is∘sue

collateral lim∘i∙ta∙tion

collateral prom∙ise

collateral se∙cur∘i∘ty

collateral source rule

collateral un∙der∙tak∙ing

col∙lat∙er∙al∘i∘ty

col∙lat∙er∙al∘i∙za∙tion

col∙lat∙er∙al∙ize *v.*,

col∙lat∙er∙al∙ized,

col∙lat∙er∙al∙iz∙ing

collateralized mort∙gage ob∙li∙ga∙tion

col∙lat∙er∙al∘ly

col∙la∙tion

col∙lect

collect on de∙liv∙er∘y (C.O.D. or c.o.d.)

col∙lect∘i∙ble

col∙lec∙tion

collection a∘gen∘cy

collection i∘tem

col∙lec∙tive

collective a∘gree∙ment

collective bar∙gain∙ing

collective bargaining a∘gree∙ment

collective bargaining u∘nit

collective mark

collective work

col∙lec∙tive∙ly

col∙lec∙tiv∙ism

col∙lec∙tiv∙ist

col∙lec∙tiv∙is∙tic

col∙lec∙tiv∙is∙ti∙cal∘ly

col∙lec∙tiv∘i∘ty

col∙lec∙tor

col∙lege (*citation form:* **C.**, used in periodical names only)

col∙le∙gial

col∙le∙gi∙al∘i∘ty

col∙le∙gial∘ly

col∙le∙gi∘um *n., pl.* col∙le∙gi∘a *Latin.*

col∙lide *v.*, col∙lid∘ed, col∙lid∙ing

col∙li∙sion

collision course

collision in∙sur∙ance

col∙lo∙qui∘um *n., pl.*

col∙lo∙qui∘a or col∙lo∙qui∘ums

col∙lo∙quy *n., pl.* col∙lo∙quies

col∙lude *v.*, col∙lud∘ed, col∙lud∙ing

col∙lud∘er

col∙lu∙sion

col∙lu∙sive

collusive suit

col∙lu∙sive∙ly

col∙lu∙sive∙ness

co∙lo∙ni∙al

co∙lo∙ni∙al∙ism

co∙lo∙ni∙al∙ist

co∙lo∙ni∙al∙is∙tic

co∙lo∙ni∙al∘i∙za∙tion

co∙lo∙ni∙al∙ize *v.*, co∙lo∙ni∙al∙ized, co∙lo∙ni∙al∙iz∙ing

co∙lo∙ni∙al∘ly

col∘o∙nist

col∘o∙ni∙za∙tion

col∘o∙nize *v.*, col∘o∙nized, col∘o∙niz∙ing

col∘o∙niz∘er

col∘o∘ny *n., pl.* col∘o∙nies

col∘or

color-blind

color of au∙thor∘i∘ty

color of law

color of of∙fice

color of ti∘tle

col∙or∙a∘ble

colorable im∘i∙ta∙tion

col∙or∙a∘ble∙ness

col∙or∙a∘bly

Col∘o∙rad∘o Riv∘er doc∙trine

col∙umn (*citation form:* col.)

Com. (Commerce; Commercial)

co∘ma *n., pl.* co∘mas

co•mak∘er
com∘a•tose
com∘a•tose∘ly
com∘a•tose•ness
com•bat *v.*, com•
bat∘ed, com•bat•
ing
combat zone
com•bat•a∘ble
com•bat•ant
com•bat•ive
com•bat•ive∘ly
com•bat•ive•ness
com•bi•na•tion
combination pat•ent
com•bi•na•tive
com•bine *v.*, com•
bined, com•bin•
ing, *n.*
com•bined
Combined DNA
I∘den•ti•fi•ca•tion
Sys•tem (CODIS)
com•bust
com•bus•ti•ble
com•bus•tion
co•mes•ti•ble
com•fort let•ter
co•mi•tas *Latin.*
co•mi•ta•tus *n., pl.*
co•mi•ta•tus *Latin.*
com∘i∘ty
comity of na•tions
Comm. (Committee;
Communication;
Communications)
com•mand (order: cf.
COMMEND)
com•mand•a∘ble
com•man•deer
com•mand∘er
Com•mand∘er in
Chief
com•mand•ment
com•mence *v.* com•

menced, com•menc•
ing
com•mence•ment
com•mend (to praise:
cf. COMMAND)
com•mend•a∘ble
com•mend•a∘bly
com•men•da•tion
com•mend•a•to∘ry
com•mend•ing∘ly
com•men•su•ra•
bil∘i∘ty
com•men•su•ra•bly
com•men•su•rate
com•men•su•rate∘ly
com•men•su•rate•
ness
com•ment (*citation
form:* cmt.)
com•ment•a∘ble
com•men•tar∘y *n., pl.*
com•men•tar•ies
com•men•ta•tor
com•ment∘er
com•merce (*citation
form:*
Com.
Com•merce Clause
commerce pow∘er
com•mer•cial (*citation
form:* Com.)
commercial at•ta•ché
commercial bank
commercial bri•ber∘y
commercial bur•
glar∘y
commercial cred∘it
commercial crime
commercial ex•ploi•
ta•tion
commercial frus•tra•
tion
commercial goods
commercial im•prac•
ti•ca•bil∘i∘ty
commercial law

commercial on•line
serv•ice pro•vid∘er
(COSP)
commercial pa∘per
commercial rob•ber∘y
commercial speech
commercial suc•cess
com•mer•cial•ism
com•mer•cial•ist
com•mer•cial•is•tic
com•mer•ci•al∘i∘ty
com•mer•cial•i•za•
tion
com•mer•cial•ize *v.*,
com•mer•cial•ized,
com•mer•cial•iz•ing
commercialized vice
com•mer•cial•iz∘er
com•mer•cial•iz∘er
com•mer•cial∘ly
com•min•gle *v.*, com•
min•gled, com•min•
gling
com•min•gler
com•mis•sar∘y
com•mis•sion (*citation
form:* Comm'n
commission mer•
chant
commission plan
com•mis•sion•a∘ble
com•mis•sion•al
com•mis•sion∘er (*ci-
tation form:* Comm'r)
com•mis•sion•er•
ship
com•mis•sive
commissive waste
com•mis•sive∘ly
com•mit *v.*, com•mit•
ted, com•mit•ting
com•mit•ment
commitment fee
com•mit•ta•ble
com•mit•tal
com•mit•ted cost

com•mit•tee (*citation form:* Comm.

committee of the whole

com•mit•tee•man *n.,* *pl.* com•mit•tee• men

com•mit•tee•ship

com•mit•tee• wom•an *n. pl.* com• mit•tee•wom•en

com•mit•ter

Comm'n (Commission)

com•mod•i•ty *n. pl.* com•mod•i•ties

commodity exchange

com•mon

common ap•pend• ant

common ap•pur•te• nant

common ar•e•a

common as•sump•sit

common as•sur•ance

common at large

common av•er•age

common be•cause of vic•i•nage

Common Bench

common car•riage

common car•ri•er *n.*

common-carrier *adj.*

common carrier stan• dard

common chase

common cost

common coun•cil

common counts

common de•sign

common di•sas•ter

common fish•er•y

common hang•man

common in gross

common in the soil

common in•tend• ment

common ju•ry

common law *n.*

common-law or com• mon law *adj.* (Note: Although phrases like those that follow are often written without the hyphen, the hy- phen aids in clarity, especially in works likely to be read by nonlawyers.)

common-law ac•tion

common-law crime

common-law form of ac•tion

common-law mar• riage

common-law prop• er•ty states

common-law side

common-law state

common-law trade• mark

common law•yer

common mar•ket

common nui•sance

common of dig•ging

common of es•to• vers

common of fish•er•y

common of pas•ture

common of pis•ca•ry

common of shack

common of tur•ba•ry

common pas•tur•age

common pleas (*cita- tion form:* C.P.)

common prop•er•ty

common re•cov•er•y

common scold

common sense *n.*

common-sense or com•mon•sense *adj.*

common share

common si•tus pick• et•ing

common stock

common stock fund

common weal See OMMONWEAL.

com•mon•a•ble

com•mon•age

com•mon•al•oi•ty *n.,* *pl.* com•mon•al•oi• ties

com•mon•al•ty

com•mon•er

com•mon•ness

com•mon•place

com•mons

com•mon•sense See COMMON-SENSE.

com•mon•weal or com•mon weal

com•mon•wealth

Com•mon•wealth Court (*citation form:* Commw. Ct.)

com•mo•ran•cy *n.,* *pl.* com•mo•ran•cies

com•mo•rant

com•mo•tion

Comm'r (Commis- sioner)

com•mu•nal

communal court

com•mu•nal•ism

com•mu•nal•ist

com•mu•nal•is•tic

com•mu•nal•ly

com•mu•nard

com•mune *n., v.,* com•muned, com• mun•ing

com•mu•ni•a pla• ci•ta *Latin.*

com•mu•ni•ca• bil•i•ty

com•mu•ni•ca•ble

communicable dis•ease

com•mu•ni•ca•ble•ness

com•mu•ni•cate *v.*, com•mu•ni•cat•ed, com•mu•ni•cat•ing

com•mu•ni•ca•tion (*citation form for sing. and pl.:* Comm.)

communication dis•or•der

com•mu•ni•ca•tion•al

com•mu•ni•ca•tions *n.sing.* (*citation form:* Comm.)

communications law

com•mu•ni•ca•tive

com•mu•ni•ca•tive•ly

com•mu•ni•ca•tive•ness

com•mu•ni•ca•tor

com•mu•nism

com•mu•nist

com•mu•nis•tic

com•mu•nis•ti•cal•ly

com•mu•ni•tar•i•an

com•mu•ni•ty *n.*, *pl.* com•mu•ni•ties

community an•ten•na tel•e•vi•sion (CATV)

community med•i•cine

community men•tal health cen•ter

community no•ti•fi•ca•tion laws

community of in•ter•est

community-plan•ning leg•is•la•tion

community prop•er•ty

community property state

community serv•ice

com•mu•ta•bil•i•ty

com•mu•ta•ble

com•mu•ta•tion

com•mu•ta•tive jus•tice

com•mute *v.*, com•mut•ed, com•mut•ing, *n.*

com•mut•er

commuter tax

Commw. Ct. (Commonwealth Court)

comp. (comparative; compilation; compiled)

com•pact

compact of free as•so•ci•a•tion

com•pan•ion case

com•pa•ny *n.*, *pl.* com•pa•nies (*citation form:* Co.)

company loan

company-spon•sored tax shel•ter

company store

company town

company un•ion

com•pa•ra•bil•i•ty

com•pa•ra•ble

comparable worth

com•pa•ra•ble•ness

com•pa•ra•bly

com•par•a•tive (*citation form:* Comp.)

comparative ad•ver•tis•ing

com•par•a•tive fault

comparative fi•nan•cial state•ment

comparative im•pair•ment

comparative impairment doc•trine

comparative law

comparative neg•li•gence

comparative state•ment

com•par•a•tive•ly

com•pare *v.*, com•pared, com•par•ing

com•par•i•son

comparison-shop *v.*, comparison-shopped, comparison-shop•ping

comparison shop•per

com•pas•sion•ate

com•pas•sion•ate•ly

com•pas•sion•ate•ness

com•pat•a•bil•i•ty

com•pat•i•ble

com•pat•i•bly

com•pa•tri•ot

com•pel *v.*, com•pelled, com•pel•ling

com•pel•la•ble

com•pel•la•bly

com•pel•ling

compelling gov•ern•men•tal in•ter•est

compelling interest

compelling state interest

com•pel•ling•ly

com•pen•di•ous

com•pen•di•ous•ly

com•pen•di•ous•ness

com•pen•di•um *n.*, *pl.* com•pen•di•ums or com•pen•di•a

com•pen•sa•ble

compensable in•ju•ry

com•pen•sate *v.*, com•pen•sat•ed, com•pen•sat•ing

compensating bal•ance

compensating use tax

com•pen•sa•tion

compensation lien

com•pen•sa•to•ry

compensatory dam•ag•es

com•pete v., com•pet•ed, com•pet•ing

com•pe•tence

com•pe•ten•cy

com•pe•tent

competent ev•i•dence

com•pe•tent•ly

com•pet•ing

com•pe•ti•tion

com•pet•i•tive

competitive bid•ding

competitive im•pact state•ment

competitive in•ju•ry

competitive mar•ket

com•pet•i•tive•ly

com•pet•i•tive•ness

com•pet•i•tor

com•pi•la•tion (citation forms:: Comp. in title of a work; comp. in descriptive material)

com•pile v., com•piled, com•pil•ing

com•piled (citation forms:: Comp. in title of a work; comp. in descriptive material)

com•pil•er

com•plain

com•plain•ant

com•plain•ing wit•ness

com•plaint

com•plete adj., v.,

com•plet•ed, com•plet•ing

complete liq•ui•da•tion

com•plet•ed-con•tract meth•od

com•ple•tion

completion bond

com•plex

complex trust

com•plex•i•ty n., pl. com•plex•i•ties

com•pli•ance

com•pli•ant

com•plic•it

com•plic•i•tous

com•plic•i•ty

com•ply v., com•plied, com•ply•ing

com•po•nent

com•pos men•tis Latin.

com•pos•ite

composite work

com•pos•ite•ness

com•po•si•tion

composition of mat•ter

composition with cred•i•tors

com•pound

compound in•terest

com•pound lar•ce•ny

compound ques•tion

com•pound•er

com•pound•ing a crime

compounding a fel•on•y

com•pre•hen•sive

comprehensive in•sur•ance

comprehensive ma•jor med•i•cal in•sur•ance

com•pre•hen•sive•ly

com•pre•hen•sive•ness

com•pro•mis n., pl. com•pro•mis French.

compromis d'ar•bi•trage French.

com•pro•mise n., v., com•pro•mised, com•pro•mis•ing

compromise ver•dict

com•pro•mis•er

com•pro•mis•ing•ly

comp•trol•ler

Comp•trol•ler of the Cur•ren•cy

comp•trol•ler•ship

com•pul•sion

com•pul•sive

com•pul•sive•ly

com•pul•sive•ness

com•pul•so•ri•ly

com•pul•so•ri•ness

com•pul•so•ry

compulsory ar•bi•tra•tion

compulsory coun•ter•claim

compulsory join•der

compulsory li•cense

compulsory pi•lot

compulsory proc•ess

compulsory self-in•crim•i•na•tion

com•punc•tion

com•pur•ga•tion

com•pur•ga•tor

com•put•a•bil•i•ty

com•put•a•ble

com•put•a•bly

com•pu•ta•tion

com•pu•ta•tion•al

com•pute v., com•put•ed, com•put•ing

com•put•er

computer-aid•ed

man•u•fac•tur•ing (CAM)
computer-as•sist•ed fraud (CAF)
computer crime
computer crim•i•nal
computer law
computer pro•gram
com•put•er te•leph•o•ny
computer vi•rus
com•put•er•ese
com•put•er•iz•a•ble
com•put•er•i•za•tion
com•put•er•ize v., com•put•er•ized, com•put•er•iz•ing
com•put•ing
Com•stock laws
Com•stock•er•y
Com•stock•i•an
con adv., v., conned, con•ning, n.
con art•ist
con man n., pl. con men
Con. Res. (Concurrent Resolution)
con•ceal
con•ceal•a•bil•i•ty
con•ceal•a•ble
con•cealed weap•on
con•ceal•er
con•ceal•ment
con•cede v., con•ced•ed, con•ced•ing
con•ced•ed•ly
con•ceiv•a•bil•i•ty
con•ceiv•a•ble
con•ceiv•a•ble•ness
con•ceiv•a•bly
con•ceive v., con•ceived, con•ceiv•ing
con•ceiv•er
con•cen•trate v.,

con•cen•trat•ed, con•cen•trat•ing, n.
con•cen•trat•ed
con•cen•tra•tion
concentration camp
concentration ra•tio
con•cept
con•cep•tion
con•cep•tive
con•cep•tu•al
con•cep•tu•al•i•za•tion
con•cep•tu•al•ize v., con•cep•tu•al•ized, con•cep•tu•al•iz•ing
con•cep•tu•al•ized
con•cep•tu•al•iz•er
con•cep•tu•al•ly
con•cern
con•cerned
con•cern•ing
con•cert
concert of ac•tion
con•cert•ed
concerted ac•tiv•i•ty
concerted prac•tice
con•cert•ed•ly
con•cert•ed•ness
con•ces•si•ble
con•ces•sion
concession a•gree•ment
con•ces•sion•aire
con•ces•sion•al
con•ces•sion•ar•y
con•ces•sion•er
con•ces•sive
con•ces•sive•ly
con•ces•sor
con•ces•sus
con•cil•i•a•ble
con•cil•i•ate v., con•cil•i•at•ed, con•cil•i•at•ing
con•cil•i•at•ing•ly

con•cil•i•a•tion
con•cil•i•a•tive
con•cil•i•a•tor
con•cil•i•a•to•ri•ly
con•cil•i•a•to•ri•ness
con•cil•i•a•to•ry
con•clave
con•clude v., con•clud•ed, con•clud•ing
con•clu•sion
conclusion of law
con•clu•sion•al
con•clu•sion•al•ly
con•clu•sive
conclusive pre•sump•tion
con•clu•sive•ly
con•clu•sive•ness
con•clu•so•ry
conclusory al•le•ga•tion
con•com•i•tance
con•com•i•tant
con•com•i•tant•ly
con•cord
con•cor•dat
con•cu•bi•nage
con•cu•bine
con•cur v., con•curred, con•cur•ring
con•cur•rence
con•cur•ren•cy
con•cur•rent
concurrent cause
concurrent con•di•tions
concurrent ju•ris•dic•tion
concurrent neg•li•gence
concurrent pow•er
concurrent res•o•lu•tion (*citation form:* **Con. Res.**)

concurrent sen•
tenc•es
concurrent tort•fea•
sor
con•cur•rent•ly
con•cur•ring in the
re•sult
concurring o•pin•ion
con•cur•ring•ly
con•cur•sus
concursus of claims
concursus pro•ceed•
ing
con•demn (to censure:
cf. CONTEMN)
con•dem•na•ble
con•dem•na•bly
con•dem•na•tion
con•dem•na•to•ry
con•dem•nee
con•demn•er
con•demn•ing•ly
con•di•tion
condition of bail
condition pre•ce•
dent
condition sub•se•
quent
con•di•tion•a•ble
con•di•tion•al
conditional be•quest
conditional bind•ing
re•ceipt
conditional dis•
charge
conditional es•tate
conditional fee
conditional leg•a•cy
conditional par•don
conditional priv•i•
lege
conditional re•lease
conditional sale
con•di•tion•al•i•ty
con•di•tion•al•ly

conditionally sus•
pend•ed sen•tence
con•di•tioned re•
sponse
con•di•tion•ing
con•do•min•i•um n.,
pl. con•do•min•i•
ums
con•don•a•ble
con•do•na•tion
con•done v., con•
doned, con•don•ing
con•don•er
con•duct
conduct dis•or•der
conduct un•be•com•
ing an of•fic•er and
a gen•tle•man
con•du•it
Conf. (Conference)
con•fab•u•late v.,
con•fab•u•lat•ed,
con•fab•u•lat•ing
con•fab•u•la•tion
con•fab•u•la•tor
con•fab•u•la•to•ry
confederacy n., pl.
con•fed•er•a•cies
(an alliance or conspir-
acy)
Con•fed•er•a•cy, the
(11 secessionist states
in the Civil War: cf.
CONFEDERATION)
con•fed•er•al
con•fed•er•ate adj.,
n., v., con•fed•er•
at•ed, con•fed•er•
at•ing
**Confederate States of
A•mer•i•ca**
con•fed•er•a•tion
(an alliance)
Confederation, the
(first 13 U.S. states un-
der the Articles of

Confederation: cf. CON•
FEDERACY)
con•fed•er•a•tive
con•fer v., con•
ferred, con•fer•ring
con•fer•ee
con•fer•ence (citation
form: **Conf.**)
conference com•mit•
tee
con•fer•ment
con•fer•ra•ble
con•fer•ral
con•fer•rer
con•fess
con•fess•a•ble
con•fess•ed•ly
con•fes•sion
confession and
a•void•ance
confession of judg•
ment
con•fes•sion•al
con•fes•sor
con•fide v., con•
fid•ed, con•fid•ing
con•fi•dence
confidence game
confidence man n., pl.
confidence men
con•fi•den•tial
confidential com•mu•
ni•ca•tion
confidential dis•clo•
sure
confidential re•la•
tion•ship
con•fi•den•ti•al•i•ty
confidentiality or•der
confidentiality
stip•u•la•tion
con•fi•den•tial•ly
con•fid•er
con•fig•u•ra•tion
con•fig•ure v., con•

fig•ured, con•fig•ur•ing

con•fin•a•ble

con•fine *v.*, con•fined, con•fin•ing

con•fined

con•fin∘ee

con•fine•ment

con•fin∘er

con•firm

con•firm•a∘bil∘i∘ty

con•firm•a∘ble

con•fir•ma•tion

con•fir•ma•tion∘al

con•firm∘a•tive

con•firm∘a•to∘ry

con•firmed

con•firm•ed∘ly

con•firm•ed•ness

con•firm∘ee

con•firm∘er (one who confirms generally: cf. CONFIRMOR)

con•firm•ing∘ly

con•fir•mor (maker of a deed or contract of confirmation: cf. CON-FIRMER)

con•fis•cat•a∘ble

con•fis•cate *v.*, con•fis•cat∘ed, con•fis•cat•ing

con•fis•ca•tion

con•fis•ca•tor

con•fis•ca•to∘ry

con•fla•gra•tion

con•flate *v.*, con•flat∘ed, con•flat•ing

con•fla•tion

con•flict

conflict of in•ter•est

conflict of laws

conflict res∘o∘lu•tion

con•flict•ing

con•flict•ing∘ly

con•flic•tion

con•flic•tive

con•flic•to∘ry

con•flu•ence

con•flu•ent

con•form

con•form•a∘ble

con•form•ance

con•for•ma•tion

con•for•ma•tion∘al

con•formed copy

con•form∘er

con•form•ing

conforming a∘mend•ment

conforming goods

conforming use

con•form•ing∘ly

con•form∘i∘ty

con•front

con•front∘al

confrontation

Con•fron•ta•tion Clause

con•fron•ta•tion∘al

con•fron•ta•tion∘ist

con•fron•ta•tive

con•fron∘ter

con•front•ment

con•fu•sa•bil∘i∘ty

con•fu•sa•ble

con•fu•sa•bly

con•fuse *v.*, con•fused, con•fus•ing

con•fus•ed∘ly

con•fus•ed•ness

con•fus•ing

con•fus•ing∘ly

confusingly sim∘i•lar

con•fus•ing•ness

con•fu•sion

con•fu•sion∘al

con•fut•a∘ble

con•fu•ta•tion

con•fu•ta•tive

con•fute *v.*, con•fut∘ed, con•fut•ing

Cong. (Congress; Congressional)

Cong. Rec. (Congressional Record)

con•gé *n.*, *pl.* con•gés *French.*

con•gen∘i•tal

congenital a∘nom∘a∘ly

con•gen∘i•tal∘ly

con•gen∘i•tal•ness

con•glom•er•ate *n.*, *adj.*, *v.*, con•glom•er•at∘ed, con•glom•er•at•ing

conglomerate merg∘er

con•glom•er∘a•teur

con•glom•er∘a•tion

con•glom•er∘a•tive

con•glom•er∘a•ti∘za•tion

con•glom•er∘a•tize *v.*, con•glom•er∘a•tized, con•glom•er∘a•tiz•ing

con•glom•er∘a•tor

con•gress (assembly)

Congress (*citation form:* **Cong.**; national legislature of U.S.)

con•gres•sion∘al (*citation form:* **Cong.**)

Congressional dis•trict (**C.D.**)

congressional in•tent

Congressional Rec•ord (*citation form:* **Cong. Rec.**)

con•gres•sion•al∘ly

con•gress•man *n.*, *pl.* con•gress•men

con•gress•mem•ber

con•gress•per•son *n.*,

pl. con•gress•per•sons
con•gress•wom•an *n., pl.* con•gress•wom•en
con•gru•ence
con•gru•en•cy
con•gru•ent
con•gru•ent•ly
con•gru•i•ty
con•gru•ous
con•gru•ous•ly
con•gru•ous•ness
con•jec•tur•al
con•jec•tur•al•ly
con•jec•ture *n, v.,* con•jec•tured, con•jec•tur•ing
con•joint
con•joint•ly
con•joint•ness
con•joints *n.pl.*
con•ju•gal
conjugal rights
conjugal vis•it
conjugal vis•it•a•tion
con•ju•gal•i•ty
con•ju•gal•ly
con•ju•ra•tion
con•jur•a•tor
con•nect
connect up
con•nec•tion
con•niv•ance
con•nive
con•niv•er
con•niv•er•y
con•niv•ing•ly
con•no•ta•tion
con•no•ta•tive
con•no•ta•tive•ly
con•note *v.,* con•noted, con•not•ing
con•no•tive
con•no•tive•ly
con•nu•bi•al

con•nu•bi•al•i•ty
con•nu•bi•al•ly
con•quis•i•tor
con•san•guin•e•ous
con•san•guin•i•ty
con•science
con•science clause
conscience mon•ey
conscience of the court
conscience-strick•en
con•sci•en•tious
conscientious ob•jec•tion
conscientious ob•jec•tor
con•sci•en•tious•ly
con•sci•en•tious•ness
con•scion•a•ble
con•scious
conscious par•al•lel•ism
con•scious•ly
con•scious•ness
con•script
conscript fa•thers
con•script•a•ble
con•script•ee
con•scrip•tion
con•sec•u•tive
consecutive sen•tenc•es
con•sec•u•tive•ly
con•sec•u•tive•ness
con•sen•su•al
con•sen•su•al•ly
con•sen•sus *n., pl.* con•sen•sus•es
consensus gen•ti•um *Latin.*
con•sent
consent a•gree•ment
consent de•cree
consent judg•ment
consent or•der

consent search
con•sen•ta•ne•i•ty
con•sen•ta•ne•ous
con•sen•ta•ne•ous•ly
con•sen•ta•ne•ous•ness
con•sent•ed use
con•sent•er
con•sen•tience
con•sen•tient
con•sen•tient•ly
con•sent•ing
consenting a•dult
con•se•quence
con•se•quent
con•se•quen•tial
consequential dam•ag•es
con•se•quen•tial•ism
con•se•quen•tial•ist
con•se•quen•ti•al•i•ty
con•se•quen•tial•ly
con•se•quen•tial•ness
con•se•quent•ly
con•ser•va•tion
conservation ease•ment
conservation law
con•ser•va•tion•al
con•ser•va•tion•ist
con•ser•va•tism
con•serv•a•tive
con•serv•a•tive•ly
con•serv•a•tive•ness
con•serv•a•tor
con•serv•a•to•ri•al
con•serv•a•tor•ship
con•serve *v.,* con•served, con•serv•ing
con•sid•er
con•sid•er•a•ble
con•sid•er•ate
con•sid•er•ate•ly

con•sid•er•ate•ness
con•sid•er•a•tion
con•sid•ered
con•sign
con•sign•a•ble
con•sign•ee
con•sign•ment
con•sign•or
con•si•mi•li ca•su
Latin.
con•sist•en•cy *n., pl.*
  con•sist•en•cies
con•sist•ent
con•sist•ent•ly
con•sis•to•ri•al
consistorial law
con•sis•to•ry
Consol. (consolidated)
con•sol•i•date *v.,*
  con•sol•i•dat•ed,
  con•sol•i•dat•ing
con•sol•i•dat•ed (*citation form:* Consol.)
consolidated ap•peal
consolidated case
consolidated fi•nan•
  cial state•ment
Consolidated Om•ni•
  bus Budg•et Rec•
  on•cil•i•a•tion Act
  of 1985 (COBRA)
consolidated re•turn
consolidated tri•al
con•sol•i•da•tion
consolidation loan
con•sol•i•da•tive
con•sol•i•da•tor
con•sor•ti•al
con•sor•ti•um *n., pl.*
  con•sor•ti•a
con•spic•u•ous
con•spic•u•ous•ly
con•spic•u•ous•ness
con•spir•a•cy *n., pl.*
  con•spir•a•cies
conspiracy of si•lence

con•spir•a•tive
con•spir•a•tor
con•spir•a•to•ri•al
con•spir•a•to•ri•
  al•ly
con•spir•a•to•ry
con•spir•er
con•spir•ing•ly
Const. (Constitution;
  Constitutional)
con•sta•ble
con•sta•ble•ship
con•stab•u•lar
con•stab•u•lar•y *n.,*
  pl. con•stab•u•lar•
  ies, *adj.*
con•stan•cy
con•stant
constant dol•lar
con•stit•u•en•cy *n.,*
  pl. con•stit•u•en•
  cies
con•stit•u•ent
con•stit•u•ent•ly
con•sti•tute *v.,* con•
  sti•tut•ed, con•sti•
  tut•ing
con•sti•tu•tion (*citation form:* Const.)
con•sti•tu•tion•al (*citation form:* Const.)
constitutional con•
  ven•tion
constitutional is•sue
constitutional law
constitutional mon•
  arch
constitutional mon•
  ar•chy
constitutional right
constitutional tort
con•sti•tu•tion•al•
  ism

con•sti•tu•tion•al•
  ist
con•sti•tu•tion•
  al•i•ot y
con•sti•tu•tion•al•i•
  za•tion
con•sti•tu•tion•al•
  ize *v.,* con•sti•tu•
  tion•al•ized, con•
  sti•tu•tion•al•iz•
  ing
con•sti•tu•tion•al•ly
con•sti•tu•tive
con•sti•tu•tive•ly
Constr. (Construction)
con•strain
con•strain•a•ble
con•strained
con•strain•ed•ly
con•strain•er
con•strain•ing•ly
con•straint
con•struct
con•struct•i•ble
con•struc•tion (*citation form:* Constr.)
construction loan
construction war•
  ran•ty
con•struc•tion•ism
con•struc•tion•ist
con•struc•tive
constructive de•liv•
  er•y
constructive de•ser•
  tion
constructive dis•
  charge
constructive e•vic•
  tion
constructive fraud
constructive know•
  ledge
constructive no•tice
constructive pos•ses•
  sion

constructive re•ceipt
constructive serv•ice of proc•ess
constructive tak•ing
constructive trust
constructive trust◦ee
con•struc•tive•ly
con•struc•tive•ness
con•struc•tor
con•strue v., con•strued, con•stru•ing
con•stru◦er
con◦sue•tude
con•sul (diplomatic officer: cf. COUNCIL; COUNSEL)
consul gen•er◦al n., pl. con•suls gen•er◦al
con•su•lar (of a consul: cf. COUNCILOR; COUNSELOR)
consular a◦gent
con•su•lar◦i•za•tion
con•su•lar•ize v., con•su•lar•ized, con•su•lar•iz•ing
con•su•late
consulate gen•er◦al n., pl. con•su•lates gen•er◦al
con•sul•ship
con•sult
con•sult•an◦cy n., pl. con•sult•an•cies
con•sult•ant
con•sult•ant•ship
con•sul•ta•tion
con•sul•ta•tive
con•sul•ta•tive•ly
con•sul•ta•to◦ry
con•sul•tive
con•sum◦er
consumer ad•vo•cate
consumer cred◦it
consumer fraud

consumer goods
consumer price in◦dex (CPI)
con•sum◦er product
consumer pro•tec•tion
consumer rights
consumer strike
con•sum•er•ism
con•sum•er•ist
con•sum•er•ship
con•sum•mate v., con•sum•mat◦ed, con•sum•mat•ing, adj.
con•sum•mate•ly
con•sum•ma•tion
con•sum•ma•tive
con•sum•ma•tor
con•sum•ma•to◦ry
con•sump•tion
consumption tax
Cont. (Contract; Contracts)
con•ta•gion
con•ta•gious
con•ta•gious•ness
con•tain
con•tain•a◦ble
con•tained
con•tain◦er
container ship or con•tain•er•ship
con•tain•er◦i•za•tion
con•tain•er•ize v., con•tain•er•ized, con•tain•er•iz•ing
con•tain•er•port
con•tain•er•ship See CONTAINER SHIP.
con•tain•ment
con•tam◦i•nate v., con•tam◦i•nat◦ed, con•tam◦i•nat•ing, n.

con•tam◦i•na•tion
con•temn (to scorn: cf. CONDEMN)
con•temn◦er (one who behaves scornfully in general: cf. CONTEMNOR)
con•tem•ni•ble
con•tem•ni•bly
con•tem•nor (one legally guilty of contempt: cf. CONTEMNER)
Contemp. (Contemporary)
con•tem•plate v., con•tem•plat◦ed, con•tem•plat•ing
con•tem•pla•tion
contemplation of bank•rupt◦cy
contemplation of death
con•tem•pla•tive
con•tem•po•ra•ne•i◦ty
con•tem•po•ra•ne•ous
con•tem•po•ra•ne•ous◦ly
con•tem•po•ra•ne•ous•ness
con•tem•po•rar◦y (citation form: Contemp.)
con•tempt
contempt of Con•gress
contempt of court
con•tempt•i◦ble
con•tempt•i◦ble•ness
con•tempt•i◦bly
con•temp•tu•ous
con•temp•tu•ous◦ly
con•temp•tu•ous•ness
con•tend

con•tent
content-based
content-based reg•ou•la•tion
content-neu•tral
content-neutral reg•ou•la•tion
con•ten•tion
con•ten•tion°al
con•ten•tious
con•ten•tious•oly
con•ten•tious•ness
con•test
con•test•a•ble
con•test•a•ble•ness
con•test•a•bly
con•test•ant
con•tes•ta•tion
con•test°ed
con•test°er
con•text
con•tex•tu•al
con•tex•tu•al•oi•za•tion
con•tex•tu•al•ize *v.*, con•tex•tu•al•ized, con•tex•tu•al•iz•ing
con•tex•tu•al•oly
con•ti•gu•i•ty
con•tig•u•ous
con•tig•u•ous•oly
con•tig•u•ous•ness
con•ti•nen•tal shelf
continental shelf in•come
con•tin•gen°cy *n.*, *pl.* con•tin•gen•cies
contingency fee
contingency fund
contingency re•serve
contingency tax
con•tin•gent
contingent ben°e°fi•ci•ar°y
contingent busi•ness-in•ter•rup•tion in•sur•ance
contingent claim
contingent es•tate
contingent fee
contingent fund
contingent in•ter•est
contingent leg•o•acy
contingent li•a•bil•i•ty
contingent re•main•der
con•tin•gent•oly
con•tin•u•a•ble
con•tin•u•al (re•peated; intermittent; cf. CONTINUOUS)
continual claim
con•tin•u•al•oly
con•tin•u•ance
con•tin•u•a•tion
continuation ap•pli•ca•tion
continuation of ben•e•fits
con•tin•ue *v.*, con•tin•ued, con•tin•ou•ing
con•tin•ued
con•tin•u•ing
continuing care re•tire•ment com•mu•ni•ty (CCRC)
continuing in•ju•ry
continuing ju•ris•dic•tion
continuing le•gal ed•ou•ca•tion
continuing nui•sance
continuing ob•jec•tion
continuing of•fense
continuing res•o•lu•tion
con•ti•nu•i•ty

continuity of in•ter•est
con•tin•u•ous (unin•terrupted: cf. CONTINU•AL)
continuous com•pound•ing
continuous in•no•va•tion
con•tin•u•ous•oly
con•tin•u•ous•ness
con•tra
contra ac•count
contra as•oset
contra bo•ona mo•ores *Latin.*
contra le•ogem *Latin.*
contra pa•ocem *Latin.*
contra pro•fe•ren•tem *Latin.*
con•tra•band
contraband of war
con•tra•band•ism
con•tra•band•ist
con•tra•cep•tion
con•tra•cep•tive
con•tract (*citation form for sing. and pl.:* Cont.)
contract bond
contract car•ri•oer
contract for deed
contract im•plied in fact
contract implied in law
contract la•obor
contract of af•freight•ment
contract sal•vage
contract to sell
contract un•oder seal
con•trac•tor
con•trac•tu•al
contractual li•a•bil•i•ty

con•trac•tu•al•ly
con•trac•tus *n., pl.*
  con•trac•tus *Latin.*
con•tra•dict
con•tra•dict•a•ble
con•tra•dic•tion
con•tra•dic•tive
con•tra•dic•tive•ly
con•tra•dic•tive•ness
con•tra•dic•to•ri•ly
con•tra•dic•to•ri•
  ness
con•tra•dic•to•ry
  adj., n., con•tra•dic•
  to•ries
con•tra•dis•tinc•tion
con•tra•dis•tinc•tive
con•tra•dis•tinc•
  tive•ly
con•tra•dis•tin•guish
con•tra•in•di•cate *v.,*
  con•tra•in•di•
  cat•ed, con•tra•in•
  di•cat•ing
con•tra•in•di•ca•
  tion
con•trar•i•ly
con•trar•i•ness
con•trar•y *adj., n.,*
  con•trar•ies
con•tra•vene *v.,* con•
  tra•vened, con•tra•
  ven•ing
con•tra•ven•er
con•tra•ven•tion
con•tre•temps *n., pl.*
  con•tre•temps
con•trib•ute *v.,* con•
  trib•ut•ed, con•
  trib•ut•ing
contributed cap•i•tal
con•trib•ut•ing cause
contributing to the
  de•lin•quen•cy of a
  mi•nor
con•tri•bu•tion

con•tri•bu•tion•al
con•trib•u•tor
con•trib•u•to•ry *adj.,*
  n., con•trib•u•to•
  ries
contributory in•
  fringe•ment
contributory neg•li•
  gence
contributory pen•sion
  plan
con•trite
con•trite•ly
con•trite•ness
con•tri•tion
con•triv•a•ble
con•triv•ance
con•trive *v.,* con•
  trived, con•triv•ing
con•trived
con•triv•er
con•trol *v.,* con•
  trolled, con•trol•
  ling, *n.*
control ac•count
control per•son
control pre•mi•um
con•trol•la•bil•i•ty
con•trol•la•ble
controllable cost
con•trol•la•ble•ness
con•trol•la•bly
con•trolled
controlled en•vi•ron•
  ment
controlled for•eign
  cor•po•ra•tion
controlled sub•stance
con•trol•ler
con•trol•ler•ship
con•trol•ling ac•
  count
controlling in•ter•est
controlling le•gal au•
  thor•i•ty
con•trol•ling•ly

con•tro•ver•sial
con•tro•ver•sial•ly
con•tro•ver•sy *n., pl.*
  con•tro•ver•sies
con•tro•vert
con•tro•vert•i•ble
con•tro•vert•i•bly
con•tu•ma•cious
con•tu•ma•cious•ly
con•tu•ma•cious•
  ness
con•tu•ma•cy *n., pl.*
  con•tu•ma•cies
con•tu•me•ly *n., pl.*
  con•tu•me•lies
con•tu•sion
co•nun•drum *n., pl.*
  co•nun•drums
con•ven•a•ble
con•ven•a•bly
con•vene *v.,* con•
  vened, con•ven•ing
con•ven•er or con•v
  e•nor
con•ven•tion
con•ven•tion•al
conventional loan
con•ven•tion•al•ism
con•ven•tion•al•ist
con•ven•tion•al•ly
con•ven•tion•eer
con•verge *v.,* con•
  verged, con•verg•
  ing
con•ver•gence
convergence of mar•
  kets
con•ver•gent
con•ver•gent•ly
con•ver•sion
conversion dis•or•der
con•vert
con•vert•er
con•vert•i•bil•i•ty
con•vert•i•ble
convertible bond

convertible de•ben•ture

convertible in•sur•ance

convertible pre•ferred stock

convertible se•cur∘i∘ty

con•vert•i•bly

con•vey

con•vey•a•ble

con•vey•ance

con•vey•anc•er

con•vey•anc•ing

con•vey∘ee

con•vey∘or or con•vey∘er

con•vict

con•vict•a•ble or con•vict•i•ble

con•vic•tion

con•vince v., con•vinced, con•vinc•ing

con•vin•ci•ble

con•vinc∘ing

con•vinc∘ing∘ly

con•vo•lut∘ed

COO (Chief Operating Officer)

co-ob•li•gor

cool•ing-off law

cooling-off pe•ri∘od

co-op n., v., co-oped, co-op•ing

Coop. (Cooperative)

co-op∘er

co•op•er•ate v., co•op•er•at∘ed, co•op•er•at•ing

co•op•er•a•tion

co•op•er•a•tion•ist

co•op•er•a•tive (citation form: **Coop.**)

cooperative as•so•ci•a•tion

cooperative bank

cooperative buy•ing

cooperative cor•po•ra•tion

cooperative cred∘it un∘ion

cooperative store

co•op•er•a•tive•ly

co•op•er•a•tive•ness

co•op•er•a•tor

co-opt

co-op•ta•tion

co-op•tive

co•or•di•nate adj., n., v., co•or•di•nat∘ed, co•or•di•nat•ing

coordinate ju•ris•dic•tion

co-own

co-own∘er

co-own•er•ship

co•par•ce•nar∘y n., pl. co•par•ce•nar•ies

co•par•ce•ner

co•par•ce•ny n., pl. co•par•ce•nies

co•part•ner

co•part•ner•ship

co-par∘ty or co-par∘ty

co∘pay

co•pay•ment

co•pend•en∘cy

co•plain•tiff

Copr. (Copyright)

co•prin•ci•pal

cop•ro•la•li•a

co•pros∘e•cu•tor

cop∘u•late v., cop∘u•lat∘ed, cop∘u•lat•ing

cop∘u•la•tion

cop∘u•la•to∘ry

cop∘y n., pl. cop•ies,

v., cop•ied, cop∘y•ing

cop∘y•hold

cop∘y•hold∘er

cop∘y•right

cop∘y•right•a∘bil∘i∘ty

cop∘y•right•a•ble

cop∘y•right∘ed

co∘ram Latin.

coram ju•di∘ce Latin.

coram no∘bis Latin.

coram non ju•di∘ce Latin.

coram vo∘bis Latin.

cor•don sa•ni•taire n., pl. cor•dons sa•ni•taires French.

core (center; central: cf. CORPS)

core pro•ceed•ing

co•re•spond•ent or co-re•spond•ent (joint respondent: cf. CORRESPONDENT)

cor•ner n., v., cor•nered, cor•ner•ing

corner the mar•ket

cor∘o∘dy or cor•ro∘dy n., pl. cor∘o∘dies or cor•ro∘dies

cor•ol•lar∘y n., pl. cor•ol•lar•ies

cor∘o∘ner

cor∘o∘ner's in•quest

coroner's ju∘ry

cor∘o∘ner•ship

Corp. (Corporation; Corporate)

cor•po∘ra See CORPUS.

cor•po∘ral (of the body; a military officer: cf. CORPOREAL)

corporal pun•ish•ment

cor•po•rate (*citation form:* **Corp.**

corporate ac•qui•si•tion

corporate a•gent

corporate bond

corporate char•ter

corporate cul•ture

corporate im•age

corporate in•come tax

corporate lad•der

corporate law

corporate op•por•tu•ni•ty doc•trine

corporate pur•pose

corporate raid•er

corporate re•or•gan•i•za•tion

corporate seal

corporate se•cur•i•ty

corporate stock

corporate tax•a•tion

corporate veil

corporate wel•fare

cor•po•rate•ly

cor•po•rate•ness

cor•po•ra•tion (*citation form:* **Corp.**

cor•pó•ra•tion•al

cor•po•rat•ism

cor•po•rat•ist

cor•po•ra•tive

cor•po•ra•ti•za•tion

cor•po•ra•tize *v.*, cor•po•ra•tized, cor•po•ra•tiz•ing

cor•po•ra•tor

cor•po•re et a•ni•mo *Latin.*

cor•po•re•al (tangible; of the body: cf. CORPORAL)

corporeal her•e•dit•a•ment

corporeal prop•er•ty

corps *n., pl.* corps (group: cf. CORE

corps di•plo•ma•tique *n., pl.* corps di•plo•ma•tiques *French.*

corpse

cor•pus *n., pl.* cor•po•ra *English and Latin.*

corpus de•lic•ti

corpus ju•ris *Latin.*

Corpus Juris Ca•no•ni•ci *Latin.*

Corpus Juris Ci•vi•lis *Latin.*

cor•rect

cor•rect•a•bil•i•ty

cor•rect•a•ble

cor•rec•tion

cor•rec•tion•al

correctional (or cor•rec•tion or cor•rec•tions) fa•cil•i•ty

cor•rec•tions *n.sing. or pl.*

corrections (or cor•rec•tion or cor•rec•tion•al) of•fi•cer

cor•rec•tive

corrective ad•ver•tis•ing

cor•rec•tive•ly

cor•rect•ly

cor•rect•ness

cor•rec•tor

cor•rel•o•a•tive

correlative rights

cor•re•spond

cor•re•spond•ence

correspondence au•dit

cor•re•spond•ent (letter writer; distant business partner or agent: cf. ORESPOND•ENT)

correspondent bank

correspondent bank•ing

cor•re•spond•ing

cor•re•spond•ing•ly

cor•rob•o•o•rate *v.*, cor•rob•o•o•rat•ed, cor•rob•o•o•rat•ing

cor•rob•o•o•rat•ing

cor•rob•o•o•ra•tion

cor•rob•o•o•ra•tive

cor•ro•o•dy See CORODY.

cor•rupt

corrupt prac•tic•es

cor•rupt•er or cor•rup•tor

cor•rupt•i•bil•i•ty

cor•rupt•i•ble

cor•rupt•i•ble•ness

cor•rupt•i•bly

cor•rup•tion

corruption of blood

cor•rup•tive

cor•rup•tive•ly

cor•rupt•ly

cor•rupt•ness

cor•rup•tor See COR•RUPTER.

cor•vée

Co•sa Nos•tra

co•sign

co•sig•na•to•ry *adj., n. pl.* co•sig•na•to•ries

co•sign•er

cos•in•age *Law French.*

COSP (commercial online service provider)

co•spon•sor

co•spon•sor•ship

cost[1] *n. v.*, cost, cost•ing (the price; to require payment of a price)

cost[2] *v.*, cost•ed,

cost•ing to calculate cost)

cost ac•count•ing

cost and freight (C. & F.)

cost ba∘sis

cost-ben•e•fit

cost-benefit a∘nal∘y•sis

cost de•ple•tion

cost-ef•fec•tive

cost-ef•fec•tive∘ly

cost-ef•fec•tive•ness

cost-ef•fi•cien∘cy

cost-ef•fi•cient

cost-ef•fi•cient∘ly

cost, in•sur•ance, and freight (C.I.F.)

cost ledg∘er

cost of com•ple•tion

cost of goods man∘u•fac•tured

cost of goods sold

cost of liv•ing n.

cost-of-living adj.

cost-of-living ad•just•ment (COLA)

cost-of-living es•ca•la•tor

cost-of-living in∘dex

cost out

cost o∘ver•run

cost-plus

cost-plus-a∘ward-fee (CPAF) con•tract

cost-plus contract

cost-plus-fixed-fee (CPFF) contract

cost-plus-in•cen•tive-fee (CPIF) con•tract

cost-plus-per•cent•age-of-cost (CPPC) contract

cost-plus price reg∘u•la•tion

cost-plus pric•ing

cost-re•im•burse•ment contract

cost-sharing contract

cost u∘nit

cost•ing

cost•less

cost•less•ness

costs n.pl.

costs to a∘bide the e∘vent

co•ten•an∘cy

co•ten•ant

co•ten•ure

co-trust∘ee

cot•tage in∘dust∘ry

coun•cil assembly: cf. CONSUL; COUNSEL)

coun•cil-man•ag∘er plan

coun•cil•man n., pl. coun•cil•men

coun•cil•man∘ic

coun•cil•mem•ber

coun•ci∘lor or esp. Brit.) coun•cil•lor (member of a council: cf. CONSULAR; COUNSE-LOR)

coun•cil•per•son n. pl. coun•cil•per•sons

coun•cil•wom∘an n., pl. coun•cil•wom∘en

Couns. Counsel; Counselor; Counselors· Counselor's; Counselors')

coun•sel[1] n., pl. coun•sel (citation form for sing. and pl.: **Couns.**; legal adviser: cf. CON-SUL; COUNCIL)

coun•sel[2] n., v., coun•seled, coun•sel•ing

(advice; to advise: cf. ⌒ONSUL; COUNCIL)

coun•sel•a•ble

coun•sel∘ee

coun•sel•ing

coun•sel•lor British spelling for COUNSELOR

coun•se•lor (citation form for sing. and pl.: **Couns.**; one who counsels: cf. CONSULAR; COUNCILOR)

counselor at law or counselor-at-law n., pl. coun•se•lors at law or coun•se•lors-at-law

coun•se•lor's (citation form: **Couns.**)

coun•se•lors' (citation form: **Couns.**)

coun•se•lor•ship

count

coun•te•nance v., coun•te•nanced, coun•te•nanc∘ing, n.

coun∘ter v., coun∘tered, coun∘ter•ing, n., adv., adj.

counter check

coun∘ter•ac•cu•sa•tion

coun∘ter•act

coun∘ter•ac•tion

coun∘ter•ad•ver•tis•ing

coun∘ter•ar•gu•ment

coun∘ter•at•tack

coun∘ter•bal•ance n., v., coun∘ter•bal•anced, coun∘ter•bal•anc∘ing

coun∘ter•bid n., v.,

coun○ter•bid,
coun○ter•bid•ding

coun○ter•block•ade
n., v., coun○ter•
block•ad○ed,
coun○ter•block•ad•
ing

coun○ter•cam•paign

coun○ter•charge n.,
v., coun○ter•
charged, coun○ter•
charg•ing

coun○ter•check

coun○ter•claim

coun○ter•claim•ant

coun○ter•con•ven•
tion

coun○ter•coup

coun○ter•cy•cli•cal

coun○ter•de•mand

coun○ter•dem•on•
stra•tion

coun○ter•dem•on•
stra•tor

coun○ter•es•pi○o•
nage

coun○ter•ev○i•dence

coun○ter•ex•am•ple

coun○ter•feit

counterfeit drug

coun○ter•feit○er

coun○ter•feit•ing

coun○ter•foil

coun○ter•in•sur•
gen○cy n., pl.
coun○ter•in•sur•
gen•cies

coun○ter•in•sur•gent

coun○ter•in•tel•li•
gence

coun○ter•in•tu○i•tive

coun○ter•mand

coun○ter•mand•
a○ble

coun○ter•marque

coun○ter•mea•sure

coun○ter•of•fen•sive

coun○ter•of•fer

coun○ter•part

coun○ter•pe•ti•tion

coun○ter•pick○et

coun○ter•plea

coun○ter•pose v.,
counter•posed,
counter•pos•ing

coun○ter•pro•ceed•
ings n., pl.

coun○ter•pro•duc•
tive

coun○ter•pro•duc•
tive○ly

coun○ter•pro•pos○al

coun○ter•pur•chase

coun○ter•rev○o•lu•
tion

coun○ter•rev○o•lu•
tion•ar○y n., pl.
counter•rev○o•lu•
tion•ar•ies

coun○ter•sign

coun○ter•sig•na•ture

coun○ter•spy

coun○ter•state•ment

coun○ter•strat○e•gy
n., pl. coun○ter•
strat○e•gies

coun○ter•sue v.,
coun○ter•sued,
coun○ter•su•ing

coun○ter•sug•ges•
tion

coun○ter•suit

coun○ter•sur•veil•
lance

coun○ter•tac•tics

coun○ter•ter•ror•ism

coun○ter•ter•ror•ist

coun○ter•vail

coun○ter•vail•ing

coun•try n., pl. coun•
tries, adj.

count•ship

coun○ty n., pl. coun•
ties

county board

county clerk

county com•mis•
sion○er

County Court (citation
form: County Ct.)

County Ct. (County
Court)

County J. Ct. County
Judge's Court)

County Judge's Court
(citation form: County
J. Ct.)

county seat

coup n., pl. coups

coup de grâce n., pl.
coups de grâce
French.

coup d'é○tat n., pl.
coups d'é○tat French.

cou•pled with an in•
te•rest

cou•pon

coupon bond

coupon rate

cour○i○er

course n., v., coursed,
cours•ing (manner of
proceeding; duration;
schooling; sporting
site; to flow; cf.
COARSE)

course of busi•ness

course of con•duct

course of dea•ling

course of em•ploy•
ment

course of per•form•
ance

court (citation form:
Ct.)

court a○bove

court be○low

court cal•en•dar

court Chris•tian *n., pl.* courts Chris•tian
court clerk
court costs
court hand
court-mar•tial *n., pl.* courts-mar•tial, *v.,* court-mar•tialed, court-mar•tial•ing
Court of Ap•peal *(citation forms:* **Ct. App.** for American courts; **C.A.** for the British court)
Court of Ap•peals *(citation form:* **Ct. App.***)*
Court of Ap•peals for the Armed Forc•es *(citation form:* **C.A. A.F.***)*
Court of Chan•cer•y *(citation form:* **Ch.***)*
Court of Civil Ap•peals *(citation form:* Civ. App.*)*
Court of Claims *(citation form:* **Ct. Cl.***)*
Court of Com•mon Pleas *(citation form:* **C.P.***)*
Court of Crim•i•nal Ap•peals *(citation form:* Crim. App.*)*
court of eq•ui•ty
Court of Er•rors *(citation form:* **Ct. Err.***)*
Court of Errors and Ap•peals *(citation form:* Ct. Err. & App.*)*
Court of Ex•cheq•uer *(citation form:* **Ex.***)*
Court of Fed•er•al Claims *(citation form:* Fed. Cl.*)*
court of first in•stance

court of gen•er•al ju•ris•dic•tion
Court of Gen•er•al Ses•sions *(citation form:* **Ct. Gen. Sess.***)*
court of hon•or
court of in•quir•y
Court of In•ter•na•tion•al Trade *(citation form:* **Ct. Int'l Trade***)*
court of last re•sort
court of law
court of lim•it•ed ju•ris•dic•tion
Court of Mil•i•tar•y Re•view *(citation form:* **C.M.R.***)*
court of o•rig•i•nal ju•ris•dic•tion
Court of Oy•er and Ter•min•er
court of rec•ord
Court of Ses•sions *(citation form:* **Ct. Sess.***)*
Court of Spe•cial Ap•peals *(citation form:* Ct. Spec. App.*)*
Court of Special Ses•sions *(citation form:* Ct. Spec. Sess.*)*
Court of Star Cham•ber
Court of Vet•er•ans Ap•peals *(citation form:* Vet. App.*)*
court or•der
court pack•ing
court re•port•er
court rules
cour•te•ous
cour•te•ous•ly
cour•te•san
cour•te•sy *(politeness:* cf. CURTESY*)*
courtesy cop•y
court•house

court•room
cov•e•nant
covenant a•gainst en•cum•branc•es
covenant ap•pur•te•nant
covenant for fur•ther as•sur•ance
covenant in gross
covenant mar•riage
covenant not to com•pete
covenant not to sue
covenant of quiet en•joy•ment
covenant of sei•sin
covenant of war•rant•y
covenant re•al
covenant run•ning with the land
covenant to stand seised
cov•e•nan•tal
cov•e•nan•tee
cov•e•nan•tor
cov•e•nants of ti•tle
co-ven•ture
cov•er
cover up *v.*
cover-up *n.*
cov•er•a•ble
cov•er•age
cov•er•er
co•vert
covert ac•tion
covert bar•on
covert op•er•a•tion
co•vert•ly
co•vert•ness
cov•er•ture
C.P. (Common Pleas; Court of Common Pleas)
CPA (certified public ac•countant)

CPAF (cost plus award fee)

CPFF (cost plus fixed fee)

CPI (consumer price index)

CPIF (cost plus incentive fee)

CPPC (cost plus percentage of cost)

CPS (certified professional secretary)

crack

crack co•caine

crack house or crack•house

craft un○ion

cram v., crammed, cram•ming

cram•down n.

cram•ming

crash

crash•proof

crash•wor•thi•ness

crash•wor•thy

crass

crass○ly

crass•ness

crave v., craved, crav•ing

cra•ven

cra•ven○ly

cra•ven•ness

crav•ing

crav•ing○ly

craze v., crazed, craz•ing, n.

crazed

craz•ed○ly

cra•zi○ly

cra•zi•ness

cra•zy adj., cra•zi○er, cra•zy○est, n., pl. cra•zies

cream skim•ming

cre•at•a○ble

cre•ate v., cre•at○ed, cre•at•ing

cre•a•tion

cre•a•tion•ism

cre•a•tion•ist

cre•a•tion•is•tic

cre•a•tive

cre•a•tiv○i○ty

cre•a•tor

cre•den•tial n., v., cre•den•tialed, cre•den•tial•ing

cre•den•tialed

cre•den•tials n.pl.

cred•i○bil○i○ty

cred•i○ble

cred•i○bly

cred○it

credit a○gency

credit bal•ance

credit bu•reau

credit card

credit card fraud

credit in•sur•ance

credit life in•sur•ance

credit line

credit mem○o•ran•dum

credit rat•ing

credit re•port

credit risk

credit sale

credit stand•ing

credit un○ion

cred•it•a○bil○i○ty

cred•it•a○ble

cred•it•a○ble•ness

cred•it•a○bly

cred•it•less

cred○i○tor

creditor ben○e○fi○ci•ar○y

cred○i○tors' com•mit•tee

cred○i○tor•ship

cred•it•wor•thi•ness

cred•it•wor•thy

cre•du•li○ty

cred○u○lous

cred○u○lous○ly

cred○u○lous•ness

creep•ing ac•qui•si•tion

cri○er

Crim. (Criminal)

Crim. App. (Criminal Appeals; Court of Criminal Appeals)

Crim. Ct. (Criminal Court)

crime

crime a○gainst hu•man○i○ty

crime against na•ture

crime-fight○er

crime in○dex

crime in•sur•ance

crime of pas•sion

crime of vi○o○lence

crime rate

crime score

cri○men n., pl. cri•mi○na Latin.

crimen fal○si Latin.

crim○i○nal (citation form: **Crim.**)

criminal ac•tion

criminal an•ar•chy

Crim○i○nal Ap•peals (citation form: **Crim. App.**)

criminal as•sault

criminal case

criminal charge

criminal code

criminal con•spir○a○cy

criminal con•tempt

criminal con•ver•sa•tion

Criminal Court (citation form: **Crim. Ct.**)

criminal for•feit•ure
criminal fraud
criminal hom•i•cide
criminal in•for•ma•tion
criminal in•tent
criminal jus•tice
criminal law
criminal law•yer
criminal li•bel
criminal mis•chief
criminal neg•li•gence
criminal of•fense
criminal pos•ses•sion
criminal pro•ce•dure
criminal pro•ceed•ing
criminal side
criminal syn•di•cal•ism
criminal tres•pass
crim•i•nal•ist
crim•i•nal•is•tics n. sing.
crim•i•nal•i•ty
crim•i•nal•i•za•tion
crim•i•nal•ize v., crim•i•nal•ized, crim•i•nal•iz•ing
crim•i•nal•ly
criminally neg•li•gent hom•i•cide
crim•i•nate v., crim•i•nat•ed, crim•i•nat•ing
crim•i•na•tion
crim•i•na•tive
crim•i•na•tor
crim•i•na•to•ry
crim•i•no•gen•ic
crim•i•no•log•ic
crim•i•no•log•i•cal
crim•i•no•log•i•cal•ly
crim•i•nol•o•gist
crim•i•nol•o•gy
crim•o•gen•ic

cri•sis n., pl. cri•ses
crisis man•age•ment
cri•te•ri•a See CRITERION.
cri•te•ri•al
cri•te•ri•on n., pl. cri•te•ri•a
crit•ic (one who evaluates: cf. CRITIQUE)
crit•i•cal
critical le•gal stud•ies
critical race the•o•rist
critical race the•o•ry
critical stage
crit•i•cal•i•ty
crit•i•cal•ly
crit•i•cism
crit•i•ciz•a•ble
crit•i•cize v., crit•i•cized, crit•i•ciz•ing
crit•i•ciz•er
cri•tique n., v., cri•tiqued, cri•ti•quing (evaluation; to evaluate: cf. CRITIC)
crook•ed
crook•ed•ly
crook•ed•ness
cross
cross-ac•tion
cross-ad•dict•ed
cross-ap•peal
cross-bill
cross-bor•der
cross-check
cross-claim
cross-claim•ant
cross-col•lat•er•al
cross-collateral clause
cross-col•lat•er•al•ize v., cross-col•lat•er•al•ized, cross-col•lat•er•al•iz•ing
cross-col•lat•er•i•za•tion

cross-com•plaint
cross-con•tam•o•i•na•tion
cross-cul•tur•al
cross-cul•tur•al•ly
cross-de•mand
cross-e•las•tic•i•ty
cross-elasticity of de•mand
cross-er•rors
cross-ex•am•i•na•tion
cross-ex•am•ine v., cross-ex•am•ined, cross-ex•am•in•ing
cross-ex•am•in•er
cross-file v., cross-filed, cross-fil•ing
cross-li•bel
cross-li•cens•ing
cross-me•di•a
cross-media own•er•ship
cross-own•er•ship
cross-ques•tion
cross-re•fer v., cross-re•ferred, cross-re•fer•ring
cross-ref•er•ence n., v., cross-ref•er•enced, cross-ref•er•enc•ing
cross-ref•er•enc•ing
cross-sub•si•di•za•tion
cross-sub•si•dize v., cross-sub•si•dized, cross-sub•si•diz•ing
cross-sub•si•dy
cross-trade
cross-trad•ing
cross•a•bil•i•ty
cross•a•ble
crown
crown case
cru•el

cruel and un•u•su•al pun•ish•ment
cru•el•ly
cru•el•ty
Crum•mey trust
cryp•tog•ra•pher
cryp•to•graph•ic
cryp•tog•ra•phy
cryp•tol•o•gist
cryp•tol•o•gy
CSOP (commercial on-line service provider)
Ct. (Court)
Ct. App. (Court of Appeal; Court of Appeals)
Ct. Cl. (Court of Claims)
Ct. Err. (Court of Errors)
Ct. Err. & App. (Court of Errors and Appeals)
Ct. Gen. Sess. (Court of General Sessions)
Ct. Int'l Trade (United States Court of International Trade)
Ct. Spec. App. (Court of Special Appeals)
Ct. Spec. Sess. (Court of Special Sessions)
c.t.a. (cum testamento annexo)
Ctr. (Center; Centre)
cuck•ing stool
cuck•old
cuck•old•ry
cul•mi•nate v., cul•mi•nat•ed, cul•mi•nat•ing
cul•mi•na•tion
cul•pa Latin.
cul•pa•bil•i•ty
cul•pa•ble (blameworthy: cf. INCULPABLE)
cul•pa•bly
cul•prit

cult
cult•ish
cult•ism
cult•ist
cul•tur•al
cultural plu•ral•ism
cultural rel•a•tiv•i•ty
Cul•tural Rev•o•lu•tion
cul•tur•al•ly
cul•ture n., v., cul•tured, cul•tur•ing
culture-bound syn•drome
culture-spe•cif•ic dis•or•der
culture-specific syn•drome
cum Latin.
cum. (cumulative)
cum cau•sa Latin.
cum div•i•dend
cum lau•de Latin.
cum rights
cum tes•ta•men•to an•nex•o (c.t.a.) Latin.
cu•mu•la•tive (cum.)
cumulative ev•i•dence
cumulative pre•ferred stock
cumulative sen•tenc•es
cumulative vot•ing
cumulative zon•ing
cu•mu•la•tive•ly
cu•mu•la•tive•ness
cun•ni•lin•gus
cur•a•bil•i•ty
cur•a•ble
cur•a•ble•ness
cur•a•bly
cur•a•tive
curative in•struc•tion
cur•a•tive•ly

cu•ra•tor
cu•ra•to•ri•al
cu•ra•tor•ship
curb
curb mar•ket
curb•a•ble
cure n., v., cured, cur•ing
cur•few
cu•ri•a n., pl. cu•ri•ae Latin.
cur•ren•cy n., pl. cur•ren•cies
currency ex•change
currency spec•u•la•tion
currency trans•ac•tion
currency trans•la•tion
cur•rent
current ac•count (C/A)
current as•sets
current bal•ance
current cost
current ex•pens•es
current li•a•bil•i•ties
current ra•tio
current val•ue
current yield
cur•ric•u•lar
cur•ric•u•lum n., pl. cur•ric•u•la or cur•ric•u•lums
curriculum vi•tae (CV) n., pl. cur•ric•u•la vi•tae
cur•si•tor
cur•te•sy (a common-law property right: cf. COURTESY)
curtesy con•sum•mate
curtesy in•i•ti•ate
cur•ti•lage
Cust. (Customs)

cus•to•di•a le•gis *Latin.*
cus•to•di•al
custodial ac•count
custodial ar•rest
custodial in•ter•fer•ence
custodial in•ter•ro•ga•tion
custodial search
cus•to•di•an
cus•to•di•an•ship
cus•to•dy
custody bill of lad•ing
cus•tom
custom and u•sage
cus•tom•a•ble

cus•tom•a•ble•ness
cus•tom•ar•oi•ly
cus•tom•ar•y
customary in•ter•na•tion•al law
customary law
cus•tom•er
customer list
cus•toms (*citation form:* Cust.)
customs bro•ker
customs du•ty
customs un•ion
cut•throat
CV (curriculum vitae)
cy pres *Law French.*
cy•ber•crime
cy•ber•fraud

cy•ber•na•tion
cy•ber•net•ic
cy•ber•net•ics *n.sing.*
cy•ber•porn
cy•ber•squat•ter
cy•ber•squat•ting
cy•clo•thy•mic dis•or•der
cyn•ic
cyn•i•cal
cyn•i•cal•ly
cyn•i•cism
cy•pren•or•phine *Controlled Subst.*
cy•to•sine (C)
czar
czar•dom

D

D. (District)
D&C (dilation and curettage)
D&E (dilation and evacuation)
D&O in•sur•ance (directors' and officers' liability insurance)
D&X (dilation and extraction)
D.A. (District Attorney)
dac•ty•log•ra•pher
dac•ty•log•ra•phy
DAF (DNA amplification fingerprinting)
dag•ger
da•is
dal•li•ance
dam•age *n., v.* dam•aged, dam•ag•ing
damage ac•tion
damage con•trol *n.*
damage-control *adj.*
dam•age•a•bil•i•ty
dam•age•a•ble

dam•ag•er
dam•ag•es *n.pl.*
dam•ag•ing
dam•ag•ing•ly
dam•ni•fy *v.,* dam•ni•fied, dam•ni•fy•ing
damn•ing
damn•ing•ly
dam•num *n.,* pl. dam•na *Latin.*
damnum abs•que in•ju•ri•a *Latin.*
Dane•law
dan•ger
dan•ge•rous
dangerous in•stru•men•tal•i•ty
dangerous per•son
dangerous weap•on
dan•ger•ous•ly
dan•ger•ous•ness
dare *v.,* dared, dar•ing
dare•dev•il

dare•dev•il•try
dar•er
dar•ing
dar•ing•ly
dark horse
dar•rein *Law French.*
darrein pre•sent•ment *Law French.*
Dar•von *Trademark.*
da•ta *n.sing. or pl.* See also DATUM.
data bank
da•ta•base
dat•a•ble
date *n., v.,* dat•ed, dat•ing
date cer•tain
date of is•sue
date of rec•ord
date rape
date stamp *n.*
date-stamp *v.*
dat•ed
date•less

da◦tum *n., pl.* da◦ta

daugh•ter

daughter-in-law *n., pl.* daugh•ters-in-law

daunt

daunt◦ed

daunt•ing•ly

daunt•ing•ness

daunt•less

daunt•less•ly

daunt•less•ness

Da◦vid and Go•li•ath

day care

day-in-the-life film

day loan

day-trade *v.*, day-trad◦ed, day-trad•ing

day-trad◦er

day•book

day•care[1] or day care *n.*

daycare[2] or day-care *adj.*

day•time

daytime cur•few

d/b/a (doing business as)

d.b.n. (de bonis non)

D.C. Cir. (District of Columbia Circuit; United States Court of Appeals for the District of Columbia Circuit)

de be◦ne es◦se *Latin.*

de bien et de mal *Law French.*

de bo◦nis as•por•ta•tis *Latin.*

de bonis non (d.b.n.) *Latin.*

de bonis non ad•min•is•tra•tis *Latin.*

de bo◦no et ma◦lo *Latin.*

de con•su•e•tu•di•

ni•bus et ser•vi•ti◦is *Latin.*

de cu•ro◦su *Latin.*

de do◦lo ma◦lo *Latin.*

de e◦jec•ti•o◦ne fir◦mae *Latin.*

de fac◦to *Latin.*

de facto cor•po•ra•tion

de facto gov•ern•ment

de facto seg•re•ga•tion

de gra◦ti◦a *Latin.*

de ho•mi◦ne re•ple•gi•an◦do *Latin.*

de ju◦re *Latin.*

de min◦i•mis *Latin.*

de no◦vo *Latin.*

de novo re•view

de novo tri◦al

de o◦di◦o et a◦ti◦a *Latin.*

de pla◦no *Latin.*

de ra•ti•o◦na•bi◦li par◦te *Latin.*

de ra•ti•o◦na•bi•li•bus di•vi◦sis *Latin.*

de ri◦gueur *French.*

de sa vie *Law French.*

de son tort *Law French.*

de u◦na par◦te *Latin.*

de ven•tre in•spi•ci•en◦do *Latin.*

de•ac•cel•er•ate *v.*, de•ac•cel•er•at◦ed, de•ac•cel•er•at•ing

de•ac•cel•er◦a•tion

dead

dead end *n.*

dead-end *adj.*

dead freight

dead hand

dead-hand con•trol

dead let•ter

dead man's stat•ute

dead set

dead ship

dead time

dead to rights

dead•beat

dead•line

dead•lock

dead•locked

dead◦ly *adj.*, dead•li◦er, dead•li•est

dead◦ly force

deadly weap◦on

deaf

deaf◦en

deaf•en•ing

deaf•en•ing•ly

deaf◦ly

deaf•ness

deal *v.*, dealt, deal•ing, *n.*

deal◦er

deal•er•ship

deal•ing

deal•ings

death

death ben◦e•fit

death cer•tif◦i•cate

death cham•ber

death pen•al◦ty

death-qual◦i•fied ju◦ry

death row

death sen•tence

death squad

death tax

death war•rant

death•bed

deathbed con•fes•sion

deathbed dec•la•ra•tion

death•blow

death•less

death•less◦ly

decimation

death•less•ness
de•ba•cle
de○bar v. de•barred, de•bar•ring (to preclude: cf. DISBAR)
de•bar•ment
de•base v. de•based, de•bas•ing
de•bas○ed•ness
de•base•ment
de•bas○er
de•bas•ing○ly
de•bat•a○ble
de•bate n., v., de•bated, de•bat•ing
de•bat○er
de•bat•ing○ly
de•bauch
de•bauch○ee
de•bauch○er
de•bauch•er○y n., pl. de•bauch•er•ies
de•bauch•ment
de•ben•ture
debenture bond
de•ben•tured
de○bet Latin.
de•bil○i•tate v., de•bil○i•tat○ed, de•bil○i•tat•ing
de•bil○i•ta•tion
de•bil○i•ta•tive
de•bil○i○ty n., pl. de•bil○i•ties
deb○it
debit bal•ance
debit card
de•bi•tum n., pl. de•bi○ta Latin.
de•brief
de•brief○er
de•brief•ing
debt
debt cap○i•tal
debt col•lec○tor
debt-eq•ui○ty ra○tio

debt in•stru•ment
debt is○sue
debt lim○it
debt se•cu•ri○ty
debt serv•ice
debt-service cost
debt serv○i•cing
debt•less
debt○or
debtor in pos•ses•sion
debtor to la○bor
de○bug v., de•bugged, de•bug•ging
de•bug•ger
de•bunk
de•bunk○er
de•bunk•ing
Dec.[1] pl., Dec. or Decs (Decision)
Dec.[2] (December)
dec○a•dence
dec○a•dent
dec○a•dent○ly
de•caf•fein•ate v., de•caf•fein•at○ed, de•caf•fein•at•ing
de•caf•fein○a•tion
de•cap○i•tal○i•za•tion
de•cap○i•tal•ize v., de•cap○i•tal•ized, de•cap○i•tal•izing
de•cap○i•tate v., de•cap○i•tat○ed, de•cap○i•tat•ing
de•cap○i•ta•tion
de•cap○i•ta•tor
de○cay
de•cease n., v., de•ceased, de•ceas•ing
de•ceased
de•ce○dent
decedent's es•tate
de•ceit

de•ceit•ful
de•ceit•ful○ly
de•ceit•ful•ness
de•ceiv•a○bil○i○ty
de•ceiv•a○ble
de•ceiv•a○ble•ness
de•ceiv•a○bly
de•ceive v., de•ceived, de•ceiv•ing
de•ceiv○er
de•ceiv•ing○ly
De•cem•ber (citation form: Dec.)
de•cen○cy n., pl. de•cen•cies
de•cent (proper: cf. DESCENT; DISSENT)
de•cent○ly
de•cent•ness
de•cen•tral○i•za•tion
de•cen•tral•ize v., de•cen•tral•ized, de•cen•tral•iz•ing
de•cep•tion
de•cep•tive
deceptive la•bel•ing
deceptive pack•ag•ing
de•cep•tive○ly
de•cep•tive•ness
de•cer•ti•fi•ca•tion
de•cer•ti○fy v., de•cer•ti•fied, de•cer•ti•fy•ing
de•cid•a○bil○i○ty
de•cid•a○ble
de•cide v., de•cid○ed, de•cid•ing
de•cid○ed
de•cid○ed○ly
de•cid•ing
dec○i•mate v., dec○i•mat○ed, dec○i•mat•ing
dec○i•ma•tion

dec○i•ma•tor
de•ci•sion (*citation form:* Dec., *pl.* Dec. or Decs.)
decision-mak○er
decision-mak•ing
de•ci•sion-mak•ing proc•ess
decision on the mer•its
decision tree
de•ci•sion○al
decisional law
de•ci•sive
de•ci•sive•ly
de•ci•sive•ness
deck car○go
deck load
Decl. (Declaration)
declaim
de•claim○er
dec•la•ma•tion
de•clam•a•to○ry
de•clar•a○ble
de•clar•ant
dec•la•ra•tion (*citation form:* Decl.)
declaration a○gainst in•ter•est
Declaration of In•de•pend•ence
declaration of trust
declaration of war
de•clar•a•tive
de•clar○a•tive•ly
de•clar○a•to○ry
declaratory judg•ment
declaratory re•lief
de•clare v., de•clared, de•clar•ing
de•clared war
de•clar○er
de•clas•si•fi•a○ble
de•clas•si•fi•ca○tion
de•clas•si•fy v., de•

clas•si•fied, de•clas•si•fy•ing
de•cline v., de•clined, de•clin•ing, n.
de•clin•ing-bal•ance
de•pre•ci•a•tion
de•co•cain•ize v., de•co•cain•ized, de•co•cain•iz•ing
de•code v., de•cod○ed, de•cod•ing
de•cod○er
de•col○o•ni•za•tion
de•col○o•nize v., de•col○o•nized, de•col○o•niz•ing
de•com•mis•sion
de•con•cen•trate v., de•con•cen•trat○ed, de•con•cen•trat•ing
de•con•cen•tra•tion
de•con•struct
de•con•struc•tion
de•con•struc•tion•ist
de•con•trol v., de•con•trolled, de•con•trol•ling
dec○o•rous
dec○o•rous•ly
dec○o•rous•ness
de•co•rum
de•coy
de•crease v., de•creased, de•creas•ing
de•cree n., v., de•creed, de•cree•ing
decree-law
decree ni○si
de•crep○it
de•crep•it•ly
de•crep•it•ude
de•cre•tal
De•cre•tals
de•cre•tist

de•cre•tive
dec•re•to○ry
de•cri○er
de•crim○i•nal○i•za•tion
de•crim○i•nal•ize v., de•crim○i•nal•ized, de•crim○i•nal•iz•ing
de○cry v., de•cried, de•cry•ing
de•crypt
de•cryp•tion
de•cul•tur○ate v., de•cul•tur•at○ed, de•cul•tur•at•ing
de•cul•tur•a•tion
de○di et con•ces•si *Latin.*
ded○i•cate v., ded○i•cat○ed, ded○i•cat•ing
ded○i•ca○ted
ded○i•cat•ed•ly
ded○i•ca•tee
ded○i•ca•tion
ded○i•ca•tor
ded○i•ca•to○ri•ly
ded○i•ca•to○ry
de•duce v., de•duced, de•duc•ing
de•duc○i•bil○i○ty
de•duc○i•ble
de•duc○i•bly
de•duct
de•duct•i○bil○i○ty
de•duct•i○ble
deductible clause
de•duc•tion
de•duc•tive
de•duc•tive•ly
deed
deed of cov○e•nant
deed of trust
deed poll n., pl. deeds poll

deed•less

deem

deep pock○et

deep sea•bed

Def. (Defense; Defend-ant)

de•face *v.*, de•faced, de•fac•ing

de•face•ment

de•fac○er

de•fal•cate *v.*, de•fal•cat○ed, de•fal•cat•ing

de•fal•ca•tion

de•fal•ca•tor

def○a•ma○tion

de•fam○a•to○ry

de•fame *v.*, de•famed, de•fam•ing

de•fam○er

de•fam•ing○ly

de•fault

default judg•ment

de•fault○er

de•fea•sance

de•fease *v.*, de•feased, de•feas•ing

de•fea•si•bil•i•ty

de•fea•si•ble

defeasible fee

de•fea•si•bly

de•feat

de•feat○er

de•feat•ism

de•feat•ist

de•fect

de•fec•tive

defective prod○uct

defective ti○tle

de•fec•tive○ly

de•fec•tive•ness

de•fect•less

de•fec○tor

de•fed•er•al•i•za-tion

de•fed•er•al•ize *v.*,

de•fed•er•al•ized, de•fed•er•al•iz•ing

de•fend

de•fend•a○ble

de•fend•ant (*citation form:* **Def.**)

defendant in er○ror

de•fend○er

de•fen•es•tra•tion

de•fense (*citation form:* **Def.**)

defense at•tor•ney

defense mech•an•ism

de•fense•less

de•fense•less○ly

de•fense•less•ness

de•fen•si•bil•i•ty

de•fen•si•ble

de•fen•si•bly

de•fen•sive

defensive lock•out

defensive med○i•cine

de•fen•sive○ly

de•fen•sive•ness

de○fer *v.*, de•ferred, de•fer•ring (to post-pone; to yield: cf. DIF-FER)

def○er•ence (respect: cf. DIFFERENCE)

def•er•en•tial

def•er•en•tial○ly

de•fer•ment

de•fer•ra•ble

de•fer•ral

de•ferred

deferred an•nu•i○ty

deferred charge

deferred com•pen•sa•tion

deferred in•come

deferred in•te•rcom•pa○ny trans•ac•tion

de•fer•rer

de•fi•a○ble

de•fi•ance

de•fi•ant

de•fi•ant○ly

de•fi•ant•ness

de•fi•cien○cy *n., pl.* de•fi•cien•cies

deficiency ac•count

deficiency judg•ment

de•fi•cient

de•fi•cient○ly

def○i•cit

deficit fi•nan•cing

deficit spend•ing

de•fi○er

de•fil•a○ble

de•file *v.*, de•filed, de•fil•ing

de•file•ment

de•fil○er

de•fil•ing○ly

de•fin•a•bil•i•ty

de•fin•a○ble

de•fin•a○bly

de•fine *v.*, de•fined, de•fin•ing

de•fined

defined ben•e•fit plan

defined con•tri•bu•tion plan

def○i•nite

definite fail•ure of is○sue

definite sen•tence

def○i•nite○ly

def○i•nite•ness

def○i•ni○tion

def○i•ni•tion○al

def○i•ni•tion•al○ly

de•fin○i•tive

de•fin○i•tive○ly

de•fin○i•tive•ness

de•flate *v.*, de•flat○ed, de•flat•ing

de•fla•tion

de•fla•tion•ar○y

deflationary spi•ral

de•flect
de•flect•a•ble
de•flec•tion
de•flec•tor
de•force v., de•
forced, de•forc•ing
de•force•ment
de•forc•er
de•for•ciant
de•for•est
de•for•est•a•tion
de•for•est•er
de•form•i•ty n., pl.
de•form•i•ties
de•fraud
de•fraud•a•tion
de•fraud•er
de•fraud•ing
de•fraud•ment
de•funct
de•funct•ness
de•fund
de•fus•a•ble
de•fuse v., de•fused,
de•fus•ing (to make
less explosive: cf. DIF-
FUSE)
de•fus•er
de•fy v., de•fied, de•
fy•ing
de•fy•ing•ly
de•gen•er•a•cy
de•gen•er•ate v.,
de•gen•er•at•ed,
de•gen•er•at•ing,
adj., n.
de•gen•er•ate•ly
de•gen•er•ate•ness
de•gen•er•a•tion
de•gen•er•a•tive
de•grad•a•bil•i•ty
de•grad•a•ble
deg•ra•da•tion
deg•ra•da•tion•al
deg•ra•da•tive
de•grade v., de•

grad•ed, de•grad•
ing
de•grad•ed•ly
de•grad•er
de•grad•ing
de•grad•ing•ly
de•gree
degree of care
degree of con•san•
guin•i•ty
degree of crime
degree of neg•li•
gence
degree of proof
de•gres•sion
de•gres•sive
de•gres•sive•ly
de hors Law French.
de•hu•man•i•za•
tion
de•hu•man•ize v.,
de•hu•man•ized,
de•hu•man•iz•ing
de•hy•dro•chlor•
meth•yl•t es•tos•
ter•one Controlled
Subst.
deign
de•in•sti•tu•tion•
al•i•za•tion
de•in•sti•tu•tion•al•
ize v., de•in•sti•tu•
tion•al•ized, de•in•
sti•tu•tion•al•iz•
ing
de•i•so•late v., de•
i•so•lat•ed, de•
i•so•lat•ing
de•i•so•la•tion
de•ject•ed
de•ject•ed•ly
de•ject•ed•ness
del cre•de•re Italian.
del credere a•gent
del credere com•mis•
sion

de•lay v., de•layed,
de•lay•ing, n.
delay rent•al
de•lay•a•ble
de•layed
delayed stress re•ac•
tion
delayed stress syn•
drome
de•lay•er
de•lay•ing•ly
de•lec•tus per•so•
nae Latin.
del•e•ga•ble
del•e•ga•cy n., pl.
del•e•ga•cies
de•le•gal•ize v., de•
le•gal•ized, de•le•
gal•iz•ing
del•e•gate n., v.,
del•e•gat•ed,
del•e•gat•ing
del•e•gat•ed pow•er
del•e•ga•tee
del•e•ga•tion
delegation doc•trine
delegation of pow•er
del•e•ga•tor
del•e•ga•to•ry
de•le•git•i•mate v.,
de•le•git•i•mat•ed,
de•le•git•i•mat•ing
de•le•git•i•ma•tion
de•le•git•i•ma•tize
v., de•le•git•i•ma•
tized, de•le•git•i•
ma•tiz•ing
de•le•git•i•mi•za•
tion
de•le•git•i•mize v.,
de•le•git•i•mized,
de•le•git•i•miz•ing
de•let•a•ble
de•lete v., de•let•ed,
de•let•ing
del•e•te•ri•ous

del•e•te•ri•ous•ly
del•e•te•ri•ous•ness
de•le•tion
de•lib•er•ate v., de•
  lib•er•at•ed, de•
  lib•er•at•ing, adj.
deliberate speed
de•lib•er•ate•ly
de•lib•er•ate•ness
de•lib•er•a•tion
de•lib•er•a•tive
de•lib•er•a•tive•ly
de•lib•er•a•tive•
  ness
del•i•ca•cy n., pl.
  del•i•ca•cies
del•i•cate
del•i•cate•ly
del•i•cate•ness
de•lict
de•lic•tu•al
de•lic•tum n., pl. de•
  lic•ta Latin.
de•lim•it
de•lim•i•ta•tion
de•lim•it•er
de•lin•e•a•ble
de•lin•e•ate v., de•
  lin•e•at•ed, de•
  lin•e•at•ing
de•lin•e•a•tion
de•lin•e•a•tive
de•lin•e•a•tor
de•link
Delinq. (Delinquency)
de•linq•uen•cy (cita-
  tion form: **Delinq.**)
de•lin•quent
de•lin•quent•ly
de•lir•i•ant
de•lir•i•ous
de•lir•i•ous•ly
de•lir•i•ous•ness
de•lir•i•um n., pl.
  de•lir•i•ums or de•
  lir•i•a

delirium tre•mens
  (d.t.'s) Latin.
de•list
de•liv•er
de•liv•er•a•bil•i•ty
de•liv•er•a•ble
de•liv•er•ance
de•liv•ered cost
delivered price
de•liv•er•er
de•liv•er•y n., pl.
  de•liv•er•ies
de•lo•cal•ize v., de•
  lo•cal•ized, de•lo•
  cal•iz•ing
de•lor•az•e•pam
  Controlled Subst.
de•lu•sion
delusion of ref•er•
  ence
de•lu•sion•al
delusional dis•or•der
delusional jeal•ous•y
de•lu•sive
de•lu•sive•ly
de•lu•sive•ness
dem•a•gog•ic
dem•a•gog•i•cal
dem•a•gog•i•cal•ly
dem•a•gog•ism
dem•a•gogue
dem•a•gogu•er•y
dem•a•go•gy
de•mand
demand bill
demand de•pos•it
demand for re•lief
demand in•stru•ment
demand let•ter
demand loan
demand note
demand pa•per
de•mand•a•ble
de•mand•ant
de•mand•er
de•mand•ing

de•mand•ing•ly
de•mar•cate v., de•
  mar•cat•ed, de•
  mar•cat•ing
de•mar•ca•tion
de•mar•ca•tive
de•mar•ca•tor
dé•marche French.
de•mean
de•mean•ing
de•mea•nor
de•ment•ed
de•ment•ed•ly
de•ment•ed•ness
dé•men•ti French.
de•men•tia
dementia in•fan•ti•
  lis Latin.
dementia of the Alz•
  hei•mer's type
dementia prae•cox
  Latin.
de•men•tial
de•mer•it
Dem•e•rol Trademark.
de•mesne Law French.
de•mesn•i•al
de•mil•i•tar•i•za•
  tion
de•mil•i•ta•rize v.,
  de•mil•i•ta•rized,
  de•mil•i•ta•riz•ing
dem•i•monde
de•mis•a•bil•i•ty
de•mis•a•ble
de•mise n., v., de•
  mised, de•mis•ing
demise char•ter
demised ship
de•mis•sion
de•mit v., de•mit•
  ted, de•mit•ting
de•mo•bi•li•za•tion
de•mo•bi•lize v., de•
  mo•bi•lized, de•
  mo•bi•liz•ing

de•moc•ra•cy *n., pl.*
 de•moc•ra•cies
dem•o•crat
dem•o•crat•ic
Democratic par•ty
dem•o•crat•i•cal•ly
de•moc•ra•ti•za•
 tion
de•moc•ra•tize *v.,*
 de•moc•ra•tized,
 de•moc•ra•tiz•ing
de•moc•ra•tiz•er
de•mog•ra•pher
dem•o•graph•ic *adj.*
 (cf. DEMOGRAPHICS)
dem•o•graph•i•
 cal•ly
dem•o•graph•ics *n.*
 sing. (cf. DEMOGRAPHIC)
de•mog•ra•phy
de•mol•ish
de•mol•ish•er
dem•o•li•tion
dem•o•li•tion•ist
de•mon•e•ti•za•tion
de•mon•e•tize *v.,*
 de•mon•e•tized,
 de•mon•e•tiz•ing
de•mon•ic
de•mon•i•za•tion
de•mon•ize *v.,* de•
 mon•ized, de•mon•
 iz•ing
de•mon•stra•bil•i•ty
de•mon•stra•ble
de•mon•stra•bly
dem•on•strate *v.,*
 dem•on•strat•ed,
 dem•on•strat•ing
dem•on•stra•tion
demonstration per•
 mit
de•mon•stra•tive
demonstrative ev•i•
 dence

demonstrative
 leg•a•cy
de•mon•stra•tive•ly
de•mon•stra•tive•
 ness
dem•on•stra•tor
de•mor•al•i•za•tion
de•mor•al•ize *v.,* de•
 mor•al•ized, de•
 mor•al•iz•ing
de•mor•al•iz•ing•ly
de•mote *v.,* de•
 mot•ed, de•mot•
 ing
de•mo•tion
de•mur *v.,* de•
 murred, de•mur•
 ring
de•mur•ra•ble
demurrable for want
 of eq•ui•ty
de•mur•rage
de•mur•al
de•mur•rant (one
 who demurs: cf. DE-
 MURRER)
de•mur•rer (a chal-
 lenge to the sufficiency
 of allegations or evi-
 dence: cf. DEMURRANT)
de•mu•tu•al•ize *v.,*
 de•mu•tu•al•ized,
 de•mu•tu•al•iz•ing
de•mys•ti•fi•ca•tion
de•mys•ti•fi•er
de•mys•ti•fy *v.,* de•
 mys•ti•fied, de•
 mys•ti•fy•ing
de•na•tion•al•i•za•
 tion
de•na•tion•al•ize *v.,*
 de•na•tion•al•ized,
 de•na•tion•al•iz•
 ing
de•nat•u•ral•i•za•
 tion
de•nat•u•ral•ize *v.,*

de•nat•u•ral•ized,
 de•nat•u•ral•iz•ing
de•na•tur•o•a•tion
de•na•ture *v.,* de•
 na•tured, de•na•
 tur•ing
de•na•tur•i•za•tion
de•na•tur•ize *v.,* de•
 na•tur•ized, de•na•
 tur•iz•ing
de•na•tur•iz•er
de•ni•a•bil•i•ty
de•ni•a•ble
de•ni•al
de•nic•o•tin•ize *v.,*
 de•nic•o•tin•ized,
 de•nic•o•tin•iz•ing
de•ni•er
den•i•grate *v.,*
 den•i•grat•ed,
 den•i•grat•ing
den•i•gra•tion
den•i•gra•tive
den•i•gra•tor
den•i•gra•to•ry
den•i•zen
de•nom•i•nate *v.,*
 de•nom•i•nat•ed,
 de•nom•i•nat•ing
de•nom•i•na•tion
de•nom•i•na•tion•al
de•nom•i•na•tion•
 al•ly
de•nom•i•na•tive
de•nom•i•na•tive•ly
de•nom•i•na•tor
de•no•ta•ble
de•no•ta•tion
de•no•ta•tive
de•no•ta•tive•ly
de•no•ta•tive•ness
de•note *v.,* de•
 not•ed, de•not•ing
de•noue•ment or dé•
 noue•ment *French.*
de•nounce

de•nounc•er
dense adj., dens•er, dens•est
dense•ly
dense•ness
den•si•ty n., pl. den•si•ties
de•nu•cle•ar•oi•za•tion
de•nu•cle•ar•ize v., de•nu•cle•ar•ized, de•nu•cle•ar•iz•ing
de•nun•ci•a•ble
de•nun•ci•a•tion
de•nun•ci•a•tive
de•nun•ci•a•tive•ly
de•nun•ci•a•tor
de•nun•ci•a•to•ry
de•ny v., de•nied, de•ny•ing
de•ny•ing•ly
de•o•dand
de•on•to•log•oi•cal
deontological eth•ics
de•on•tol•o•gist
de•on•tol•o•gy
de•ox•y•ri•bo•nu•cle•ase (DNAase or DNase)
de•ox•y•ri•bo•nu•cleoic ac•id (DNA)
de•ox•y•ri•bo•nu•cle•o•tide
de•part•ment (citation form: Dep't.
de•part•men•tal
de•part•men•tal•ism
de•part•men•tal•i•za•tion
de•part•men•tal•ize v., de•part•men•tal•ized, de•part•men•tal•iz•ing
de•part•men•tal•ly
de•pe•cage or dé•pe•çage French.

de•pend
de•pend•a•bil•i•ty
de•pend•a•ble
de•pend•a•ble•ness
de•pend•ence
dependence syn•drome
de•pend•en•cy n., pl. de•pend•en•cies
de•pend•ent
dependent per•son•al•i•ty dis•or•der
de•pend•ent•ly
de•per•son•al•i•za•tion
depersonalization dis•or•der
de•per•son•al•ize v., de•per•son•al•ized, de•per•son•al•iz•ing
de•plet•a•ble
de•plete v., de•plet•ed, de•plet•ing
de•ple•tion
depletion al•low•ance
de•ple•tive
de•plor•a•bil•i•ty
de•plor•a•ble
de•plor•a•ble•ness
de•plor•a•bly
de•plore v., de•plored, de•plor•ing
de•plor•er
de•ploy
de•ploy•a•bil•i•ty
de•ploy•a•ble
de•ploy•ment
de•pone v., de•poned, de•pon•ing
de•po•nent
de•port
de•port•a•ble
deportable a•li•en
de•por•ta•tion (ex-

pulsion: cf. DEPORT-MENT)
de•por•tee
de•port•ment (behav-ior: cf. DEPORTATION)
de•pos•a•ble
de•pose v., de•posed, de•pos•ing
de•pos•er
de•pos•it
deposit mon•ey
deposit slip
de•pos•i•tar•y n., pl. de•pos•i•tar•ies, adj.
dep•o•si•tion
deposition de be•ne es•se
deposition in aid of ex•e•cu•tion
dep•o•si•tion•al
de•pos•i•tor
de•pos•i•to•ry n., pl. de•pos•i•to•ries, adj.
dep•ra•va•tion (act of corrupting; state of being corrupt: cf. DEP-RIVATION)
de•prave v., de•praved, de•prav•ing
de•praved (corrupt: cf. DEPRIVED)
depraved in•dif•fer•ence
de•praved•ly
de•praved•ness
de•prav•er
de•prav•ing•ly
de•prav•i•ty n., pl. de•prav•i•ties
dep•re•cate v., dep•re•cat•ed, dep•re•cat•ing (to belittle: cf. DEPRECIATE)
dep•re•cat•ing•ly
dep•re•ca•tion

dep•re•ca•tive
dep•re•ca•tive•ly
dep•re•ca•tor
dep•re•ca•to•ri•ly
dep•re•ca•to•ri•ness
dep•re•ca•to•ry
de•pre•ci•a•ble
depreciable as•set
depreciable prop•
erty
de•pre•ci•ate v., de•
pre•ci•at•ed, de•
pre•ci•at•ing (to
lessen in value: cf.
DEPRECATE)
de•pre•ci•a•tion
dep•re•date v., dep•
re•dat•ed, dep•re•
dat•ing
dep•re•da•tion
de•press
de•pres•sant
de•pressed
de•press•ing
de•press•ing•ly
de•pres•sion
de•pres•sive
depressive dis•or•der
depressive ep•i•sode
depressive per•son•
al•i•ty
de•pres•sive•ly
de•pres•sive•ness
dep•ri•va•tion (act of
depriving; state of be-
ing deprived: cf. DEPRA-
VATION
de•prive v., de•
prived, de•priv•ing
de•prived (lacking ne-
cessities: cf. DEPRAVED)
de•pro•gram v., de•
pro•grammed or
de•pro•gramed, de•
pro•gram•ming or
de•pro•gram•ing

de•pro•gram•mer or
de•pro•gram•er
Dep't (Department)
dep•u•ta•ble
dep•u•ta•tion
de•pute v., de•
put•ed, de•put•ing
dep•u•ti•za•tion
dep•u•tize v.,
dep•u•tized,
dep•u•tiz•ing
dep•u•ty n., pl.
dep•u•ties
deputy sher•iff
dep•u•ty•ship
de•raign
de•raign•ment
de•rail
de•rail•ment
de•range v., de•
ranged, de•rang•ing
de•ranged
de•range•ment
de•re•al•i•za•tion
de•rec•og•ni•tion
de•rec•og•nize v.,
de•rec•og•nized,
de•rec•og•niz•ing
de•reg•u•late v., de•
reg•u•lat•ed, de•
reg•u•lat•ing
de•reg•u•la•tion
de•reg•u•la•tor
de•reg•u•la•to•ry
der•e•lict
der•e•lic•tion
dereliction of du•ty
der•e•lict•ly
der•e•lict•ness
de•ride v., de•rid•ed,
de•rid•ing
de•rid•er
de•rid•ing•ly
de•ris•i•ble
de•ri•sion
de•ri•sive

de•ri•sive•ly
de•ri•sive•ness
de•riv•a•ble
der•i•va•tion
der•i•va•tion•al
der•i•va•tion•al•ly
de•riv•a•tive
derivative ac•tion
derivative li•a•
bil•i•ty
derivative suit
derivative tort
derivative work
de•riv•a•tive•ly
de•riv•a•tive•ness
de•rive v., de•rived,
de•riv•ing
de•riv•er
der•o•ga•ble
der•o•gate v., der•o•
gat•ed, der•o•gat•
ing
der•o•ga•tion
de•rog•a•tive
de•rog•a•tive•ly
de•rog•a•to•ri•ly
de•rog•a•to•ri•ness
de•rog•a•to•ry
DES (diethylstilbestrol)
de•sa•pa•re•ci•do
Spanish and Portu-
guese.
de•scend
de•scend•ant n. (off-
spring: cf. DESCENDENT)
de•scend•ent adj. (de-
scending: cf. DESCEND-
ANT)
de•scend•i•bil•i•ty
de•scend•i•ble
de•scent (passing
down: cf. DECENT; DIS-
SENT)
descent and dis•tri•
bu•tion
de•scrib•a•bil•i•ty

de•scrib•a•ble
de•scrib•a•bly
de•scribe *v.*, de•scribed, de•scrib•ing
de•scrib•er
de•scrip•tion
de•scrip•tive
descriptive bill•ing
descriptive mark
de•scrip•tive•ly
de•scrip•tive•ness
des•e•crate *v.*, des•e•crat•ed, des•e•crat•ing
des•e•crat•er *or* des•e•cra•tor
des•e•cra•tion
de•seg•re•gate *v.*, de•seg•re•gat•ed, de•seg•re•gat•ing
de•seg•re•ga•tion
de•seg•re•ga•tion•ist
de•se•lect
de•sen•si•ti•za•tion
de•sen•si•tize *v.*, de•sen•si•tized, de•sen•si•tiz•ing
de•sert¹ *v.* (to leave: vs. *dessert*)
des•ert² *n.* (arid place)
de•sert•ed
de•sert•er
de•ser•ti•fi•ca•tion
de•ser•tion
des•ert•like
de•serts *n.pl.* (deserved reward or punishment: vs. *desserts*)
de•sid•er•a•tum *n.*, *pl.* de•sid•er•a•ta
de•sign
design de•fect
design pat•ent
design reg•i•stra•tion

des•ig•nate *v.*, des•ig•nat•ed, des•ig•nat•ing, *adj.*
des•ig•nat•ed dri•ver
des•ig•na•tion
des•ig•na•tive
des•ig•na•tor
des•ig•na•to•ry
de•signed
de•sign•ed•ly
de•sign•ed•ness
de•sig•nee
de•sign•er
designer drug
designer gene
de•sign•ing
de•sign•ing•ly
de•sir•a•bil•i•ty
de•sir•a•ble
de•sir•a•ble•ness
de•sir•a•bly
de•sire *v.*, de•sired, de•sir•ing, *n.*
de•sired
de•sir•er
de•sir•ous
de•sir•ous•ness
de•sist
de•sist•ance
de•so•cial•i•za•tion
de•so•cial•ize *v.*, de•so•cial•ized, de•so•cial•iz•ing
des•o•late *adj., v.*, des•o•lat•ed, des•o•lat•ing
des•o•late•ly
des•o•late•ness
des•o•lat•er *or* des•o•la•tor
des•o•la•tion
des•o•mor•phine *Controlled Subst.*
de•spair
de•spair•ing

de•spair•ing•ly
des•per•a•do *n.*, *pl.* des•per•a•does *or* des•per•a•dos
des•per•ate (in urgent circumstances: cf. DIS-PARATE)
des•per•ate•ly
des•per•ate•ness
des•per•a•tion
des•pi•ca•ble
des•pi•ca•ble•ness
des•pi•ca•bly
de•spis•a•ble
de•spis•a•ble•ness
de•spise *v.*, de•spised, de•spis•ing
de•spis•er
de•spis•ing•ly
de•spite
de•spite•ful
de•spite•ful•ly
de•spite•ful•ness
de•spoil
de•spoil•er
de•spoil•ment
de•spo•li•a•tion
de•spond
de•spond•en•cy
de•spond•ent
de•spond•ent•ly
de•spond•ing•ly
des•pot
des•pot•ic
des•pot•i•cal•ly
des•pot•ism
de•ster•oi•li•za•tion
de•ster•oi•lize *v.*, de•ster•oi•lized, de•ster•oi•liz•ing
des•ti•na•tion
destination con•tract
des•ti•na•to•ry *n.*, *pl.* des•ti•na•to•ries
des•tine *v.*, des•tined, des•tin•ing

des•tined
des•ti•ny n., pl des•
ti•nies
des•ti•tute adj., v.,
des•ti•tut•ed, des•
ti•tut•ing
des•ti•tute•ly
des•ti•tute•ness
des•ti•tu•tion
de•stroy
de•stroy•a•ble
de•stroy•er
de•struct
de•struct•i•bil•i•ty
de•struct•i•ble
destructible trust
de•struct•i•ble•ness
de•struc•tion
de•struc•tion•ist
de•struc•tive
de•struc•tive•ly
de•struc•tive•ness
de•struc•tiv•i•ty
des•ue•tude
des•ul•to•ri•ly
des•ul•to•ri•ness
des•ul•to•ry
DET Controlled Subst.
(diethyltryptamine)
de•tach
de•tach•a•bil•i•ty
de•tach•a•ble
de•tach•a•bly
de•tached
de•tach•ed•ly
de•tach•ed•ness
de•tach•er
de•tach•ment
de•tail
de•tailed
de•tailed•ness
de•tail•er
de•tain
de•tain•a•ble
de•tain•ee

de•tain•er
de•tain•ment
de•tect
de•tect•a•bil•i•ty
de•tect•a•ble
de•tect•a•bly
de•tec•tion
de•tec•tive
de•tec•tor
dé•tente French.
de•ten•tion
detention camp
detention cen•ter
detention home
de•ter v., de•terred,
de•ter•ring
de•te•ri•o•rate v.,
de•te•ri•o•rat•ed,
de•te•ri•o•rat•ing
de•te•ri•o•ra•tion
de•te•ri•o•ra•tive
de•ter•mi•na•
bil•i•ty
de•ter•mi•na•ble
determinable fee
de•ter•mi•na•bly
de•ter•mi•na•cy
de•ter•mi•nant
de•ter•mi•nate
determinate sen•
tence
de•ter•mi•nate•ly
de•ter•mi•nate•ness
de•ter•mi•na•tion
determination let•ter
de•ter•mi•na•tive
de•ter•mi•na•tive•ly
de•ter•mine v., de•
ter•mined, de•ter•
min•ing
de•ter•mined
de•ter•mined•ly
de•ter•mined•ness
de•ter•min•er
de•ter•min•ism
de•ter•min•ist

de•ter•min•is•tic
de•ter•min•is•ti•
cal•ly
de•ter•rence
de•ter•rent
de•ter•rent•ly
de•test
de•test•a•bil•i•ty
de•test•a•ble
de•test•a•ble•ness
de•test•a•bly
de•tes•ta•tion
de•test•er
de•ti•net Latin.
det•i•nue
de•to•o•na•bil•i•ty
de•to•o•na•ble
de•to•o•nate v., det•o•o•
nat•ed, det•o•o•nat•
ing
de•to•o•na•tion
de•to•o•na•tor
de•tour
de•tox•i•fi•ca•tion
detoxification treat•
ment
de•tox•i•fy v., de•
tox•i•fied, de•
tox•i•fy•ing
de•tract
de•tract•ing•ly
de•trac•tion
de•trac•tive
de•trac•tive•ly
de•trac•tive•ness
de•trac•tor
det•ri•ment
det•ri•men•tal
detrimental re•li•
ance
det•ri•men•tal•i•ty
det•ri•men•tal•ly
det•ri•men•tal•ness
de•un•ion•i•za•tion
de•un•ion•ize v., de•

un•ion•ized, de•
un•ion•iz•ing
Deu•ter•on•o•my
Dev. (Development)
de•val•u•ate v., de•
val•u•at•ed, de•
val•u•at•ing
de•val•u•a•tion
de•val•ue v., de•val•
ued, de•val•u•ing
dev•as•tate v., dev•
as•tat•ed, dev•as•
tat•ing
dev•as•tat•ing
dev•as•tat•ing•ly
dev•as•ta•tion
dev•as•ta•tive
dev•as•ta•tor
de•va•sta•vit Latin.
de•vel•op
de•vel•op•a•bil•i•ty
de•vel•op•a•ble
de•vel•op•er
de•vel•op•ing
developing coun•try
(or state or nation)
de•vel•op•ment (cita-
tion form: **Dev.**)
development costs
development rights
development train•
ing
de•vel•op•men•tal
developmental dis•
a•bil•i•ty
developmental psy•
chol•o•gy
de•vel•op•men•tal•
ist
de•vel•op•men•
tal•ly
de•vel•op•men•
ta•ry
de•vest or di•vest (to
annul or take away a

vested right: cf. DI-
VEST)
de•vi•a•bil•i•ty
de•vi•a•ble
de•vi•ance
de•vi•an•cy n., pl.
de•vi•an•cies
de•vi•ant
deviant be•hav•ior
de•vi•ate v., de•vi•
at•ed, de•vi•at•ing,
adj., n.
de•vi•a•tion
deviation de•lay
de•vi•a•tive
de•vi•a•tor
de•vi•a•to•ry
de•vice (a contrivance:
cf. DEVISE)
de•vice•ful
de•vice•ful•ly
de•vice•ful•ness
dev•il•try
de•vi•ous
de•vi•ous•ly
de•vi•ous•ness
de•vis•a•bil•i•ty (ca-
pability of being de-
vised: cf. DIVISIBILITY)
de•vis•a•ble (capable
of being devised: cf.
DIVISIBLE)
de•vise v., de•vised,
de•vis•ing, n. (to
contrive; to give by
will; a testamentary
gift: cf. DEVICE)
de•vi•see
de•vis•er (one who
contrives: cf. DEVISOR;
DIVISOR)
de•vi•sor (one who
gives by will: cf. DE-
VISER; DIVISOR)
dev•o•lu•tion
dev•o•lu•tion•ar•y

dev•o•lu•tion•ist
de•volve v., de•
volved, de•volv•ing
de•vote v., de•
vot•ed, de•vot•ing
de•vot•ed
de•vot•ed•ly
de•vot•ed•ness
dev•o•tee
de•vo•tion
de•vo•tion•al
de•vo•tion•al•ly
de•vout
de•vout•ly
de•vout•ness
Dex•e•drine Trade-
mark.
dex•fen•flur•a•mine
dex•tro•mor•am•ide
Controlled Subst.
dex•tro•pro•pox•y•
phene Controlled
Subst.
dhar•ma
dhar•mic
di•ag•nos•a•ble
di•ag•nose v., di•ag•
nosed, di•ag•nos•
ing
di•ag•no•sis n., pl
di•ag•no•ses
di•ag•nos•tic
diagnostic fea•ture
di•ag•nos•ti•cal•ly
di•ag•nos•tics n.sing.
di•al n., v., di•aled,
di•al•ing
dial-a-porn
di•a•lec•tic
di•a•lec•ti•cal
di•a•lec•tics n.sing.
di•al•y•sis n., pl. di•
al•y•ses
di•am•pro•mide Con-
trolled Subst.
di•a•tribe

di•az•e•pam

di•chot•o•mist

di•chot•o•mi•za•tion

di•chot•o•mize v., di•chot•o•mized, di•chot•o•miz•ing

di•chot•o•mous

di•chot•o•mous•ly

di•chot•o•mous•ness

di•chot•o•my n., pl. di•chot•o•mies

dic•ta See DICTUM.

dic•tate v., dic•tat•ed, dic•tat•ing

dic•ta•tion

dic•ta•tor

dic•ta•to•ri•al

dic•ta•to•ri•al•ly

dic•ta•to•ri•al•ness

dic•ta•tor•ship

dic•tion

dic•tion•al

dic•tion•al•ly

dic•tum n., pl. dic•ta

di•dact

di•dac•tic

di•dac•ti•cal•ly

di•dac•ti•cism

die v., died, dy•ing

die•hard

di•em clau•sit ex•tre•mum Latin.

di•es n., pl. di•es Latin.

di•es non ju•ri•di•cus or di•es non Latin.

di•et pill

di•eth•yl•pro•pi•on Controlled Subst.

di•eth•yl•stil•bes•trol (DES)

di•eth•yl•thi•am•bu•tene Controlled Subst.

di•eth•yl•tryp•ta•mine (DET) Controlled Subst.

di•fen•ox•in Controlled Subst.

dif•fer (to disagree; to be dissimilar: cf. DE•FER)

dif•fer•ence (disagreement; dissimilarity: cf. DEFERENCE)

dif•fer•ent

dif•fer•en•ti•a•bil•i•ty

dif•fer•en•ti•a•ble

dif•fer•en•tial

differential cost

differential di•ag•no•sis

differential rate

dif•fer•en•tial•ly

dif•fer•en•ti•ate v., dif•fer•en•ti•at•ed, dif•fer•en•ti•at•ing

dif•fer•en•ti•a•tor

dif•fer•ent•ly

dif•fer•ent•ness

dif•fi•cult

dif•fi•cul•ty n., pl. dif•fi•cul•ties

dif•fi•dence

dif•fi•dent

dif•fi•dent•ly

dif•fuse adj., v., dif•fused, dif•fus•ing (unfocused; to spread out or disseminate: cf. DEFUSE)

dif•fuse•ly

dif•fuse•ness

Dig. (Digest)

di•gest (citation form: Dig.)

di•gest•er

dig•it•al

digital wrap•per

dig•it•al•ly

dig•ni•fied

dig•ni•fy v., dig•ni•fied, dig•ni•fy•ing

dig•ni•ty n., pl. dig•ni•ties

di•gress

di•gres•sion

di•gres•sive

di•gres•sive•ly

di•gres•sive•ness

di•hy•dro•co•deine Controlled Subst.

di•hy•dro•co•de•i•none Controlled Subst.

di•hy•dro•mor•phine Controlled Subst.

di•hy•dro•tes•tos•ter•one Controlled Subst.

dik•tat

di•lap•oi•dat•ed

di•lap•oi•da•tion

di•lap•oi•da•tor

di•lo•a•ta•tion

di•la•tion and cur•et•tage (D&C)

dilation and e•vac•u•a•tion (D&E)

dilation and ex•trac•tion (D&X)

di•lo•a•to•ri•ly

di•lo•a•to•ri•ness

di•lo•a•to•ry

dilatory ac•tion

dilatory de•fense

dilatory plea

Di•lau•did Trademark.

di•lem•o•ma

di•lem•mat•ic

dil•et•tante n., pl. dil•et•tantes or dil•et•tan•ti

dil•et•tant•ish

dil•et•tant•ism

dil○i•gence

dil○i•gent

dil○i•gent○ly

di•lute *v.*, di•lut○ed, di•lut•ing, *adj.*

di•lut○er or di•lu•tor

di•lu•tion

di•lu•tive

di•men•ox○a•dol *Controlled Subst.*

di•meph•ep•ta•nol *Controlled Subst.*

di•meth•yl•thi•am•bu•tene *Controlled Subst.*

di•meth•yl•tryp•ta•mine (DMT) *Controlled Subst.*

di•min•ish

di•min•ish•a○ble

di•min•ished

di•min•ished ca•pac○i○ty

diminished re•spon•si•bil○i•ty

di•min•ish•ing re•turns

di•min•ish•ment

dim○i•nu•tion

di•ox○a•phe•tyl bu•ty•rate *Controlled Subst.*

di•phen•ox○y•late *Controlled Subst.*

di•pip○a•none *Controlled Subst.*

Dipl. (Diplomacy)

dip•loid

dip•loi○dy

di•plo•ma

di•plo•ma○cy *(citation form:* Dipl.)

dip•lo•mat (government representative: cf. DIPLOMATE)

dip•lo•mate (holder of a specialized diploma: cf. DIPLOMAT)

dip•lo•mat○ic

diplomatic a○sy•lum

diplomatic corps

diplomatic im•mu•ni○ty

diplomatic pouch

diplomatic re•la•tions

diplomatic sec•re•tar○y

dip•lo•mat○i•cal○ly

di•plo•ma•ti•za•tion

di•plo•ma•tize *v.*, di•plo•ma•tized, di•plo•ma•tiz•ing

dip•so•ma•ni○a

dip•so•ma•ni○ac

dip•so•ma•ni○a•cal

Dir. (Director)

dire *adj.*, dir○er, dir•est

di•rect

direct ac•tion

direct con•tempt

direct cost

direct cost•ing

direct de•pos○it

direct e○lec•tion

direct ev○i•dence

direct ex•am•i•na•tion

direct ex•pense

direct ex•port•ing

direct la○bor

direct loss

direct mail

direct mar•ket•ing

direct pri•ma○ry

direct tax

direct trust

di•rect•a○ble

di•rect○ed

directed ver•dict

di•rect•ed•ness

di•rec•tion

di•rec•tion○al

di•rec•tive

di•rect○ly

di•rect•ness

di•rec•tor *(citation form:* Dir.)

director gen•er○al *n.*, *pl.* di•rec•tors gen•eral

di•rec•tor•ate

di•rec•to•ri○al

di•rec•tors' and of•fi•cers' li•a•bil○i•ty in•sur•ance (D&O insurance)

di•rec•tor•ship

di•rec•to○ry *n.*, *pl.* di•rec•to•ries, *adj.*

directory trust

dire○ly

dire•ness

dirt○i•ness

dirt○y *adj.*, dirt•i○er, dirt•i•est, *v.*, dirt•ied, dirt○y•ing, *adv.*

dirty tricks

dirty war

dis•a○bil○i•ty *n.*, *pl.* dis•a○bil○i•ties

disability ben•e•fit

disability clause

disability dis•crim•i•na•tion

disability in•sur•ance

dis•a○ble *v.*, dis•a○bled, dis•a○bling

dis•a○bled

dis•a○ble•ment

dis•a○bler

dis•a○bus○al

dis•a○buse *v.*, dis•a○bused, dis•a○bus•ing

dis•ac•cred○it

dis•ac•cred•i•ta•tion

dis•ad•van•tage v.,
dis•ad•van•taged,
dis•ad•van•tag•ing
dis•ad•van•taged
dis•ad•van•ta•geous
dis•ad•van•ta•
geous•ly
dis•ad•van•ta•
geous•ness
dis•af•fect
dis•af•fect•ed
dis•af•fil•i•ate v.,
dis•af•fil•i•at•ed,
dis•af•fil•i•at•ing
dis•af•fil•i•a•tion
dis•af•firm
dis•af•fir•mance
dis•a•gree v., dis•
a•greed, dis•
a•gree•ing
dis•a•gree•a•bil•i•ty
dis•a•gree•a•ble
dis•a•gree•a•ble•
ness
dis•a•gree•a•bly
dis•a•gree•ment
dis•al•low
dis•al•low•a•ble
dis•al•low•a•ble•
ness
dis•al•low•ance
dis•ap•pear
dis•ap•pear•ance
dis•ap•point
dis•ap•point•ed
dis•ap•point•ing
dis•ap•point•ing•ly
dis•ap•point•ment
dis•ap•pro•ba•tion
dis•ap•prov•al
dis•ap•prove v., dis•
ap•proved, dis•ap•
prov•ing
dis•ap•prov•er
dis•ap•prov•ing•ly
dis•arm

dis•ar•ma•ment
dis•arm•ing
dis•arm•ing•ly
dis•ar•ray
dis•as•ter
disaster ar•e•a
dis•as•trous
dis•as•trous•ly
dis•as•trous•ness
dis•band
dis•band•ment
dis•bar v., dis•barred,
dis•bar•ring (to ex-
pel from legal practice:
cf. DEBAR)
dis•bar•ment
dis•be•lief
dis•burs•a•ble
dis•burse v., dis•
bursed, dis•burs•ing
(to hand out: cf. DIS-
PERSE)
dis•burse•ment
dis•burs•er
DISC (domestic interna-
tional sales corpora-
tion)
dis•cern
dis•cern•er
dis•cern•i•ble
dis•cern•i•ble•ness
dis•cern•i•bly
dis•cern•ing
dis•cern•ing•ly
dis•cern•ment
dis•charge n., v., dis•
charged, dis•charg•
ing
discharge in bank•
rupt•cy
dis•charge•a•ble
dis•char•gee
dis•charg•er
dis•ci•ple
dis•ci•plin•a•ble
dis•ci•plin•al

dis•ci•pli•nar•i•an
dis•ci•pli•nar•y
disciplinary ac•tion
disciplinary prac•ti•
ces
disciplinary pro•ceed•
ing
dis•ci•pline n., v.,
dis•ci•plined, dis•
ci•plin•ing
dis•ci•plined
dis•ci•plin•er
dis•claim
dis•claim•er
dis•clam•a•to•ry
dis•close v., dis•
closed, dis•clos•ing
dis•clos•er
dis•clo•sure
disclosure a•gree•
ment
disclosure state•ment
dis•com•fit v., dis•
com•fit•ed, dis•
com•fit•ing (to dis-
concert: cf. DISCOM-
FORT)
dis•com•fi•ture
dis•com•fort n., v.
(uncomfortableness: to
make uncomfortable:
cf. DISCOMFIT)
dis•com•mon
dis•con•cert
dis•con•cert•ed
dis•con•cert•ing•ly
dis•con•cert•ing•
ness
dis•con•cer•tion
dis•con•cert•ment
dis•con•nect
dis•con•nec•tion
dis•con•so•late
dis•con•so•late•ly
dis•con•so•late•ness
dis•con•so•la•tion

dis•con•tent
dis•con•tent•ed
dis•con•tent•ed•ly
dis•con•tent•ed•ness
dis•con•tin•u•ance
dis•con•tin•ue *v.*,
  dis•con•tin•ued,
  dis•con•tin•u•ing
dis•con•tin•u•er
dis•con•ti•nu•i•ty
  n., pl. dis•con•ti•
  nu•i•ties
dis•con•tin•u•ous
dis•con•tin•u•ous•ly
dis•con•tin•u•ous•
  ness
dis•cord
dis•cord•ance
dis•cord•ant
dis•cord•ant•ly
dis•count
discount bro•ker
discount bro•ker•age
discount mar•ket
discount points
discount rate
dis•count•a•ble
dis•count•er
dis•cour•age *v.*, dis•
  cour•aged, dis•
  cour•ag•ing
dis•cour•age•a•ble
dis•cour•age•ment
dis•cour•ag•er
dis•cour•ag•ing•ly
dis•course *n., v.*, dis•
  coursed, dis•cours•
  ing
dis•cours•er
dis•cour•te•sy
dis•cov•er
dis•cov•er•a•bil•i•ty
dis•cov•er•a•ble
dis•cov•er•a•bly
dis•cov•ered per•il
  doc•trine

dis•cov•er•er
dis•cov•ert
dis•cov•er•ture
dis•cov•er•y *n., pl.*
  dis•cov•er•ies
dis•cred•it
dis•cred•it•a•bil•i•ty
dis•cred•it•a•ble
dis•cred•it•a•bly
dis•creet (circumspect:
  cf. DISCRETE)
dis•creet•ly
dis•creet•ness
dis•crep•an•cy
dis•crep•ant
dis•crep•ant•ly
dis•crete (separate: cf.
  DISCREET)
discrete com•pound•
  ing
dis•crete•ly
dis•crete•ness
dis•cre•tion
dis•cre•tion•ar•i•ly
dis•cre•tion•ar•y
discretionary ac•
  count
discretionary ap•peal
discretionary in•come
discretionary or•der
discretionary pow•er
discretionary re•view
discretionary trust
dis•crim•i•nate *v.*,
  dis•crim•i•nat•ed,
  dis•crim•i•nat•ing,
  adj.
dis•crim•i•nate•ly
dis•crim•i•nat•ing
dis•crim•i•nat•ing•ly
dis•crim•i•na•tion
dis•crim•i•na•tor
dis•crim•i•na•to•
  ri•ly
dis•crim•i•na•to•ry
dis•cum•fit•er

dis•cur•sion
dis•cur•sive
dis•cur•sive•ly
dis•cur•sive•ness
dis•cuss
dis•cus•sant
dis•cuss•er
dis•cuss•i•ble
dis•cus•sion
dis•cus•sion•al
dis•dain
dis•dain•ful
dis•dain•ful•ly
dis•dain•ful•ness
dis•ease
dis•eased
dis•e•con•o•my *n.,
  pl.* dis•e•con•o•
  mies
dis•em•bow•el *v.*,
  dis•em•bow•eled,
  dis•em•bow•el•ing
dis•em•pow•er
dis•em•pow•er•
  ment
dis•en•chant
dis•en•chant•ing
dis•en•chant•ing•ly
dis•en•chant•ment
dis•en•cum•ber
dis•en•fran•chise See
  DISFRANCHISE.
dis•en•fran•chise•
  ment See DISFRANCHISE-
  MENT.
dis•en•gage *v.*, dis•
  en•gaged, dis•en•
  gag•ing
dis•en•gag•ed•ness
dis•en•gage•ment
dis•en•tail
dis•en•tail•ment
dis•e•quil•i•brate *v.*,
  dis•e•quil•i•
  brat•ed, dis•
  e•quil•i•brat•ing

dis•e•qui•li•bra•tion
dis•e•qui•lib•ri•um
dis•fa•vor
dis•fa•vored
dis•fa•vor•er
dis•fig•ure *v.*, dis•fig•ured, dis•fig•ur•ing
dis•fig•ure•ment
dis•fran•chise or dis•en•fran•chise *v.*, dis•fran•chised or dis•en•fran•chised, dis•fran•chis•ing or dis•en•fran•chis•ing
dis•fran•chise•ment or dis•en•fran•chise•ment
dis•gav•el *v.*, dis•gav•eled, dis•gav•el•ing
dis•gorge *v.*, dis•gorged, dis•gorg•ing
dis•gorge•ment
dis•gorg•er
dis•grace *v.*, dis•graced, dis•grac•ing
dis•grace•ful
dis•grace•ful•ly
dis•grace•ful•ness
dis•grac•er
dis•grun•tle *v.*, dis•grun•tled, dis•grun•tling
dis•grun•tled
dis•grun•tle•ment
dis•guis•a•ble
dis•guise *v.*, dis•guised, dis•guis•ing, *n.*
dis•guised
disguised div•i•dend
dis•guis•ed•ly
dis•guis•ed•ness
dis•guise•ment

dis•guis•er
dis•gust
dis•gust•ed
dis•gust•ed•ly
dis•gust•ed•ness
dis•gust•ing
dis•gust•ing•ly
dis•ha•bit•u•ate *v.*, dis•ha•bit•u•at•ed, dis•ha•bit•u•at•ing
dis•har•mo•ny
dis•heart•en
dis•heart•ened
dis•heart•en•ing•ly
dis•heart•en•ment
dis•hon•est
dis•hon•est•ly
dis•hon•es•ty *n., pl.* dis•hon•es•ties
dis•hon•or
dis•hon•or•a•ble
dishonorable dis•charge
dis•hon•or•a•bly
dis•hon•or•er
dis•il•lu•sion
dis•il•lu•sion•ment
dis•in•cen•tive
dis•in•cli•na•tion
dis•in•cline *v.*, dis•in•clined, dis•in•clin•ing
dis•in•clined
dis•in•cor•po•rate *v.*, dis•in•cor•po•rat•ed, dis•in•cor•po•rat•ing
dis•in•cor•po•ra•tion
dis•in•flate *v.*, dis•in•flat•ed, dis•in•flat•ing
dis•in•fla•tion
dis•in•fla•tion•ar•y
dis•in•form
dis•in•form•ant

dis•in•for•ma•tion
dis•in•form•er
dis•in•gen•u•ous
dis•in•gen•u•ous•ly
dis•in•gen•u•ous•ness
dis•in•her•it
dis•in•her•i•tance
dis•in•hib•it•ed
dis•in•hi•bi•tion
dis•in•te•grate *v.*, dis•in•te•grat•ed, dis•in•te•grat•ing
dis•in•te•gra•tion
dis•in•te•gra•tive
disintegrative psy•cho•sis
dis•in•ter *v.*, dis•in•terred, dis•in•ter•ring
dis•in•ter•est
dis•in•ter•est•ed (unbiased: cf. UNINTERESTED)
dis•in•ter•est•ed•ly
dis•in•ter•est•ed•ness
dis•in•ter•me•di•a•tion
dis•in•ter•ment
dis•in•vest
dis•in•vest•ment
dis•junc•tion
dis•junc•tive
disjunctive al•le•ga•tion
dis•lik•a•ble or dis•like•a•ble
dis•like *v.*, dis•liked, dis•lik•ing
dis•lo•cate *v.*, dis•lo•cat•ed, dis•lo•cat•ing
dis•lo•ca•tion
dis•loy•al
dis•loy•al•ly

disproportionality

dis•loy•al•ty *n., pl.*
  dis•loy•al•ties
dis•mal
dis•mal○ly
dis•mal•ness
dis•man•tle *v.,* dis•
  man•tled, dis•man•
  tling
dis•man•tle•ment
dis•man•tler
dis•may
dis•mem•ber
dis•mem•ber•ment
dis•miss
dis•miss○al
dismissal for want of
  eq•ui○ty
dismissal for want of
  pros○e•cu○tion
dismissal in the in•
  ter•est of jus•tice
dismissal with leave
  to re•plead
dismissal with
  prej○u•dice
dismissal without
  prej○u•dice
dis•miss•i○ble
dis•mis•sive
dis•mis•sive○ly
dis•o○be•di•ence
dis•o○be•di•ent
dis•o○be•di•ent○ly
dis•o○bey
dis•o○bey○er
dis•or•der
dis•or•dered
dis•or•der•li•ness
dis•or•der○ly
disorderly con•duct
disorderly house
disorderly per•son
dis•or•gan○i•za•tion
dis•or•gan•ized
disorganized schiz○o•
  phre•ni○a

dis•o○ri•ent
dis•o○ri•en•ta•tion
dis•o○ri•ent○ed
dis•own
dis•own•ment
Disp. (Dispute)
dis•par•age *v.,* dis•
  par•aged, dis•par•
  ag○ing
dis•pa•rage•ment
disparagement of
  goods
disparagement of
  ti○tle
dis•par•ag○er
dis•par•ag•ing
dis•par•ag•ing○ly
dis•par•ate (varied: cf.
  DESPERATE)
disparate im•pact
dis•par•ate○ly
dis•par•ate•ness
dis•par○i○ty *n., pl.*
  dis•par○i•ties
dis•pas•sion
dis•pas•sion•ate
dis•pas•sion•ate○ly
dis•pas•sion•ate•
  ness
dis•patch
dis•patch○er
dis•pau•per
dis•pel *v.,* dis•pelled,
  dis•pel•ling
dis•pel•la•ble
dis•pel•ler
dis•pen•sa•bil•i○ty
dis•pen•sa•ble
dis•pen•sa•ble•ness
dis•pen•sa•tion
dis•pen•sa•tion○al
dis•pense *v.,* dis•
  pensed, dis•pens•
  ing
dis•pen•si•ble
dis•perse *v.,* dis•

persed, dis•pers•ing
  (to scatter: cf. DIS-
  BURSE)
dis•per•si•bil○i○ty
dis•per•si•ble
dis•per•sion
dis•per•sive
dis•per•sive○ly
dis•per•sive•ness
dis•pir•it○ed
dis•pir•it○ed○ly
dis•pir•it○ed•ness
dis•place *v.,* dis•
  placed, dis•plac•ing
dis•place•a○ble
dis•placed
displaced home•ma•
  ker
displaced per•son
dis•place•ment
dis•play
dis•please *v.,* dis•
  pleased, dis•pleas•
  ing
dis•pleas•ure
dis•pos•a○bil○i○ty
dis•pos•a○ble
disposable in•come
dis•pos•a○bly
dis•pos○al
dis•pose *v.,* dis•
  posed, dis•pos•ing
dis•pos•ing mind
dis•pos•ing○ly
dis•po•si•tion
dis•po•si•tion○al
dis•pos•i•tive
dis•pos•sess
dis•pos•sessed
dis•pos•ses•sion
dis•pos•ses•sor
dis•pos•ses•so○ry
dis•pro•por•tion
dis•pro•por•tion○al
dis•pro•por•tion•al•
  i○ty

dis•pro•por•tion•ate
dis•pro•por•tion•
ate•ly
dis•pro•por•tion•
ate•ness
dis•prov•a•ble
dis•prove v., dis•
proved, dis•prov•
ing
dis•prov•er
dis•pu•ta•bil•i•ty
dis•pu•ta•ble
dis•pu•ta•bly
dis•pu•tant
dis•pu•ta•tion
dis•pu•ta•tious
dis•pu•ta•tious•ly
dis•pu•ta•tious•ness
dis•pute¹ n. (citation
form: Disp.)
dispute² v., dis•
put•ed, dis•put•ing
dis•put•er
dis•qual•i•fi•a•ble
dis•qual•i•fi•ca•tion
dis•qual•i•fied prop•
er•ty
dis•qual•i•fy v., dis•
qual•i•fied, dis•
qual•i•fy•ing
dis•qui•et
dis•qui•et•ing
dis•qui•et•ing•ly
dis•qui•si•tion
dis•qui•si•tion•al
dis•re•gard
dis•re•gard•a•ble
dis•re•gard•er
dis•re•gard•ing the
cor•po•rate en•
ti•ty
dis•rep•u•ta•ble
dis•rep•u•ta•ble•
ness
dis•rep•u•ta•bly
dis•re•pute

dis•re•spect
dis•re•spect•ful
dis•re•spect•ful•ly
dis•re•spect•ful•ness
dis•rupt
dis•rupt•able
dis•rupt•er
dis•rup•tive
disruptive be•hav•ior
dis•or•der
dis•rup•tive•ly
dis•rup•tive•ness
dis•sat•is•fac•tion
dis•sat•is•fied
dis•save v., dis•
saved, dis•saving,
dis•sav•er
dis•seise v., dis•
seised, dis•seis•ing
dis•sei•see
dis•sei•sin
dis•sei•sor
dis•sem•ble v., dis•
sem•bled, dis•sem•
bling
dis•sem•bler
dis•sem•i•nate v.,
dis•sem•i•nat•ed,
dis•sem•i•nat•ing,
dis•sem•i•na•tion
dis•sem•i•na•tive
dis•sem•i•na•tor
dis•sen•sion
dis•sent (to disagree;
expression of disagree-
ment: cf. DECENT; DE-
SCENT)
dis•sent•er
dis•sent•ing o•pin•
ion
dissenting share•
hold•er
dis•sent•ing•ly
dis•sen•tious
dis•ser•ta•tion

dis•serve v., dis•
served, dis•serv•ing
dis•serv•ice
dis•si•dence
dis•si•dent
dis•sim•i•lar
dis•sim•i•lar•i•ty n.,
pl. dis•sim•i•lar•i•
ties
dis•sim•i•lar•ly
dis•sim•u•late v.,
dis•sim•u•lat•ed,
dis•sim•u•lat•ing
dis•sim•u•la•tion
dis•sim•u•la•tive
dis•sim•u•la•tor
dis•si•pate v., dis•si•
pat•ed, dis•si•pat•
ing
dis•si•pat•ed
dis•si•pat•ed•ly
dis•si•pa•ted•ness
dis•si•pa•tion
dis•so•cial
dissocial per•son•al•
i•ty dis•or•der
dis•so•ci•al•i•ty
dis•so•ci•ate v., dis•
so•ci•at•ed, dis•so•
ci•at•ing
dis•so•ci•a•tion
dis•so•ci•a•tive
dissociative am•ne•
si•a
dissociative dis•or•
der
dissociative fugue
dissociative i•den•
ti•ty dis•or•der
dissociative re•ac•
tion
dis•so•lute
dis•so•lute•ly
dis•so•lute•ness
(looseness; licentious-
ness: cf. DISSOLUTION)

dis•so•lu•tion (termi-
nation; a breaking up:
cf. DISSOLUTENESS)
dis•so•lu•tive
dis•solv•a•bil•i•ty
dis•solv•a•ble
dis•solve v., dis•
solved, dis•solv•ing
dis•solv•er
dis•suad•a•ble
dis•suade v., dis•
suad•ed, dis•suad•
ing
dis•suad•er
dis•sua•sion
dis•sua•sive
dis•sua•sive•ly
dis•sua•sive•ness
Dist. (District)
Dist. Ct. (District Court)
Dist. Ct. App. (District
Court of Appeal; Dis-
trict Court of Appeals)
dis•tance n., v., dis•
tanced, dis•tanc•ing
dis•tant
dis•tant•ly
dis•tant•ness
dis•taste
dis•taste•ful
dis•taste•ful•ly
dis•taste•ful•ness
dis•till
dis•till•a•ble
dis•til•la•tion
dis•tilled spir•its
dis•till•er•y n., pl.
dis•till•er•ies
dis•tinct
dis•tinc•tion
dis•tinc•tive
dis•tinc•tive•ly
dis•tinc•tive•ness
dis•tinct•ly
dis•tin•guish

dis•tin•guish•
a•bil•i•ty
dis•tin•guish•a•ble
dis•tin•guish•a•bly
dis•tin•guished
dis•tin•guish•ing
dis•tort
dis•tort•ed
dis•tort•er
dis•tor•tion
dis•tor•tive
dis•tract
dis•tract•ed
dis•tract•ed•ly
dis•tract•ed•ness
dis•tract•i•bil•i•ty
dis•tract•i•ble
dis•trac•tion
dis•train
dis•train•a•ble
dis•train•ee
dis•trai•nor or dis•
train•er
dis•traint
dis•tress
distress mer•chan•
dise
distress sale
dis•tressed
distressed ar•e•a
distressed goods
distressed mer•chan•
dise
dis•tress•ed•ly
dis•tress•ing
dis•tress•ing•ly
Distrib. (Distributing;
Distributor)
dis•trib•ut•a•ble
dis•trib•ute v., dis•
trib•ut•ed, dis•trib•
ut•ing
dis•trib•u•tee
dis•trib•ut•ing (cita-
tion form: Distrib.)
dis•tri•bu•tion

distribution ex•pense
dis•tri•bu•tion•al
dis•trib•u•tive
distributive jus•tice
distributive share
dis•trib•u•tor (cita-
tion form: Distrib.)
dis•trib•u•tor•ship
dis•trict (citation form:
Dist. or D.)
district at•tor•ney
(D.A.)
district court (citation
form: Dist. Ct.)
District Court of Ap•
peal (citation form:
Dist. Ct. App.)
District Court of Ap•
peals (citation form:
Dist. Ct. App.)
district judge
District of Co•lum•
bi•a Cir•cuit (citation
form: D.C. Cir.)
dis•trin•gas Latin.
distringas in det•i•
nue
distringas ju•ra•to•
res Latin.
dis•turb
dis•turb•ance
dis•turbed
dis•turb•er
dis•turb•ing
disturbing the peace
dis•turb•ing•ly
dis•u•nite v., dis•
u•nit•ed, dis•u•nit•
ing
dis•u•ni•ty n., dis•
u•ni•ties
dis•use n., v., dis•
used, dis•us•ing
dis•u•til•i•ty
Div. (Division)

di•verge v., di•
verged, di•verg•ing
di•ver•gence
di•ver•gent
di•ver•gent•ly
di•vers (several; sun-
dry: cf. DIVERSE)
di•verse (differing: cf.
DIVERS)
di•ver•si•fi•
a•bil•i•ty
di•ver•si•fi•a•ble
di•ver•si•fi•ca•tion
di•ver•si•fied in•
vest•ment com•
pa•ny
di•ver•si•fi•er
di•ver•si•fy v., di•
ver•si•fied, di•ver•
si•fy•ing
di•ve•rsion
di•ver•sion•ar•y
di•ver•sion•ism
di•ver•sion•ist
di•ver•si•ty n., pl.
di•ver•si•ties
diversity case
diversity ju•ris•dic•
tion
diversity of cit•i•
zen•ship
di•vert
di•vert∘ter
di•vert∘i•ble
di•vest[1] (to free from
or deprive; to sell off:
cf. DEVEST)
divest[2] See DEVEST.
di•ves•ti•ble
di•vest∘i•ture
di•vest•ment
di•ves•ture
di•vid•a∘ble
di•vid•a∘ble•ness
di•vide
di•vid∘ed

divided dam•ag∘es
di•vid•ed•ness
div•i•dend
dividend on
di•vin•a∘ble
di•vine v., di•vined,
di•vin•ing, adj., n.
di•vis•i•bil∘i•ty (ca-
pability of being di-
vided: cf. DEVISABILITY)
di•vis∘i•ble (capable
of being divided: cf.
DEVISABLE)
divisible con•tract
divisible di•vorce
di•vis∘i•bly
di•vi•sion (citation
form: Div.)
division of la∘bor
division of the house
di•vi•sion∘al
divisional ap•pli•ca•
tion
di•vi•sion•al∘ly
di•vi•sive
divisive re•or•gan•i•
za•tions
di•vi•sive•ly
di•vi•sive•ness
di•vi•sor (a number by
which another is di-
vided: cf. DEVISER; DEVI-
SOR)
di•vorce n., v., di•
vorced, di•vorc•ing
di•vor•cé (divorced
man: cf. DIVORCÉE)
divorce a men∘sa et
tho∘ro
divorce a vin•cu•lo
ma•tri•mo•ni∘i
divorce court
divorce mill
di•vorce•a∘ble
di•vor•cée (divorced
woman: cf. DIVORCÉ)

di•vorce•ment
di•vor•cer
di•vor•cive
di•vul•ga•tion
di•vulge v., di•
vulged, di•vulg•ing
di•vul•gence
di•vul•ger
DMT Controlled Subst.
(dimethyltryptamine)
DNA (deoxyribonucleic
acid)
DNA am•pli•fi•ca•
tion
DNA amplification
fin•ger•print•ing
(DAF)
DNA band
DNA ex•trac•tion
DNA fin•ger•print•
ing
DNA i∘den•ti•fi•ca•
tion
DNA pol∘y•mer•ase
DNA probe
DNA pro•fil•ing
DNA rep•li•ca•tion
DNA test
DNA typ•ing
DNAase or Dnase (de-
oxyribonuclease)
DNR (do not resusci-
tate)
do v., did, done,
do∘ing
do-good∘er
do-good•ism
do-it-your∘self adj.
do-it-yourself di•
vorce
do-it-yourself kit
do not re•sus•ci•tate
(DNR)
Doc. (Document)
dock
dock re•ceipt

dock•age

dock∘et

doc•tor

Doctor of Ju•rid∘i•cal Sci∘ence

Doctor of Laws (LL.D.)

Doctor of Med∘i•cine (M.D.)

Doctor of Phi•los•o•phy (Ph.D.)

Doctor of Sci∘ence (D.Sc. or Sc.D.)

Doctor of the Sci∘ence of Law (J.S.D.)

doctor-pa•tient priv∘i•lege

doc•tor∘al

doc•tor∘ate

doc•tri•naire

doc•tri•nal

doc•tri•nal•i∘ty

doc•tri•nal∘ly

doc•trine

doctrine of e∘quiv•a•lents

doctrine of finds

doctrine of slight chang∘es

doctrine of wor•thi∘er ti∘tle

doc∘u•ment (*citation form:* Doc.)

document of ti∘tle

doc∘u•ment•a•ble

doc∘u•men•tar•i∘ly

doc∘u•men•ta∘ry *adj., n., pl.* doc∘u•men•ta•ries

documentary cred∘it

documentary draft

documentary ev∘i•dence

doc∘u•men•ta∘tion

doc∘u•ment∘er

dodge *v.,* dodged, dodg•ing, *n.*

dodg∘er

dodg∘y *adj.,* dodg•i∘er, dodg•i•est

D'Oench Duhme doc•trine

dog•ma *n., pl.* dog•mas or dog•ma∘ta

dog•mat∘ic

dog•mat∘i•cal∘ly

dog•ma∘tism

dog•ma•tist

dog•ma•ti•za•tion

dog•ma•tize *v.,* dog•ma∘tized, dog•ma•tiz•ing

dog•ma•tiz∘er

do∘ing busi•ness

doing business as (d/b/a)

dole *n., v.,* doled, dol•ing

do∘li ca∘pax *Latin.*

doli in•ca•pax *Latin.*

dol•lar

dollar ar∘e∘a

dol•lar-av•er•age *v.,* dol•lar-av•er•aged, dol•lar-av•er•ag•ing

dollar av•er•ag•ing

dollar cost averaging

dol•lar-de•nom•i•nat∘ed ac•count

dollar di•plo•ma∘cy

do∘lus *Latin.*

Dom. Rel. (Domestic Relations)

Dom. Rel. Ct. (Domestic Relations Court)

do•main

domain name

do•ma•ni∘al

do•mes•tic

domestic an∘i•mal

domestic com•merce

domestic cor•po•ra•tion

domestic in•ter•na•tion∘al sales cor•po•ra•tion (DISC)

domestic part•ner

domestic part•ner•ship

domestic re•la•tions (*citation form:* Dom. Rel.)

Domestic Relations Court (*citation form:* Dom. Rel. Ct.)

domestic tran•quil∘i•ty (spelling used in U.S. Constitution: cf. TRANQUILLITY)

domestic vi•o•lence

do•mes•ti•cal∘ly

dom∘i•cile *n., v.,* dom∘i•ciled, dom∘i•cil•ing

dom∘i•ciled

dom∘i•cil•i•ar∘y *n., pl.* dom∘i•cil•i•ar•ies, *adj.*

dom∘i•nance

dom∘i•nant

dominant es•tate

dominant ten∘e∘ment

dominant trait

dom∘i•nant∘ly

dom∘i•nate *v.,* dom∘i•nat∘ed, dom∘i•nat•ing

dom∘i•nat•ing∘ly

dom∘i•na•tion

dom∘i•na∘tor

dom∘i•neer

dom∘i•neer•ing

dom∘i•neer•ing∘ly

do•min∘i•on

do•min∘i•um *Latin.*

do•mi•tae na•tu•rae *Latin.*

do•na•ble

do•nate v., do•
nat•ed, do•nat•ing

do•na•ti•o n., pl. do•
na•ti•o•nes Latin.

donatio cau•sa mor•
tis Latin.

donatio in•ter vi•vos
Latin.

do•na•tion

donation land

don•a•tive

donative in•tent

don•a•to•ry n., pl.
don•a•to•ries

done (completed: cf.
DUN)

do•nee

donee ben•e•fi•ci•
ar•y

do•nor

do•nor•ship

Don't Ask, Don't Tell

Don't Ask, Don't Tell,
Don't Pur•sue

doom

dope n., v., doped,
dop•ing

dor•man•cy

dor•mant

dormant part•ner

do•sage

dose n., v. dosed,
dos•ing

dos•si•er

do•tal

dotal prop•er•ty

dou•ble adj., n., v.,
dou•bled, dou•bling

double a•gent

dou•ble-bar•reled

dou•ble-bill v.

double bind

dou•ble-breast•ing

double-check

double-cross

double-cross•er

double-dam•age ac•
tion

double dam•ag•es

double-deal v., dou•
ble-dealt, dou•
ble-deal•ing

double-deal•er

double-deal•ing

double-de•clin•
ing-bal•ance de•
pre•ci•a•tion

double-dip v., dou•
ble-dipped, dou•
ble-dip•ping

double-dip•per

double-dip•ping

double-edged

double-edged sword

double-en•try book•
keep•ing

double he•lix

double in•dem•ni•ty

double jeop•ar•dy

double li•a•bil•i•ty

double pat•ent•ing

double patenting
doc•trine

double re•cov•er•y

double stand•ard

double strin•gen•cy
pol•y•mer•ase
chain re•ac•tion
(DS-PCR)

double-talk

double-talk•er

double tax•a•tion

double time

dou•ble•speak

dou•ble•speak•er

dou•bly

doubt

doubt•a•ble

doubt•a•bly

doubt•er

doubt•ful

doubt•ful•ly

doubt•ful•ness

doubt•ing•ly

dow•a•ble

dow•a•ger

dow•a•ger•ism

dow•er

dow•er•ess

dow•er•less

down pay•ment

down•er

down•heart•ed

down•heart•ed•ly

down•heart•ed•ness

down•right

Down's syn•drome or
Down syn•drome

down•side

down•size v., down•
sized, down•siz•ing

down•stream

downstream merg•er

down•time

down•turn

down•zone v., down•
zoned, down•zon•
ing

dow•ry n., pl. dow•
ries

dra•co•ni•an (harsh;
severe)

Draconian (of Draco or
his laws)

dra•co•ni•an•ism

dra•con•ic

dra•con•i•cal•ly

draft

draft•a•ble

draft•ee

draft•er

drag•net

dragnet clause

dram shop acts

dra•ma

dra•mat•ic

dramatic work

dra•mat•i•cal•ly
dram•a•tist
dram•a•tiz•a•ble
dram•a•ti•za•tion
dram•a•tize *v.*,
  dram•a•tized,
  dram•a•tiz•ing
dram•a•tiz•er
dram•shop
draught (British spell
  ing for draft: cf.
  DROUGHT)
draw *v.*, drew, drawn,
  draw•ing
draw and quar•ter
draw down *v.* (cf.
  DRAWDOWN)
draw•a•bil•i•ty
draw•a•ble
draw•back
draw•down *n.* (cf.
  DRAW DOWN)
draw•ee
draw•er
draw•ing
drawing ac•count
drear•i•ly
drear•i•ness
drear•y *adj.*, drear•
  i•er, drear•i•est
Dred Scott Case
drink *v.*, drank, drunk,
  drink•ing
drive *v.*, drove,
  driv•en, driv•ing, *n.*
drive-through *adj.*
drive-through de•liv•
  er•y
driv•el *n.*, *v.*, driv•
  eled, driv•el•ing
driv•en
driv•en•ness
driv•er
driver ed•u•ca•tion
driv•er's li•cense

driv•ing un•der the
  in•flu•ence (DUI)
driving under the in-
  fluence of al•co•hol
driving under the in-
  fluence of drugs
driving while
  a•bil•i•ty im•paired
  (DWAI)
driving while im-
  paired (DWI)
driving while in•
  tox•i•cat•ed (DWI)
droit *French*
droit à la pa•ter•
  ni•té *French.*
droit au re•spect de
  l'oeu•vre *French*
droit au respect du
  nom *French.*
droit d'au•teur *French.*
droit de di•vul•ga•
  tion *French.*
droit de re•pen•tir
  French.
droit de re•trait
  French.
droit de suite *French.*
droit des gens *French.*
droit mo•ral *n.*, *pl.*
  droits mo•raux
  French.
droits *n.pl.*
droits of ad•mir•
  al•ty
droits voi•sins *n.pl.*
  French.
droi•tu•ral
dro•nab•i•nol *Con-
  trolled Subst.*
drop-dead of•fer
drop-down trans•ac•
  tion
drop out *v.* (cf. DROP-
  OUT; DROPOUT)
drop-out *adj.* (cf. DROP
  OUT; DROPOUT)

drop-out rate
drop-ship *v.*, drop-
  shipped, drop-ship•
  ping
drop ship•ment
drop ship•per
drop•out *n.* (cf. DROP
  OUT; DROP-OUT)
dro•stan•o•o•lone *Con-
  trolled Subst.*
dro•te•ba•nol *Con-
  trolled Subst.*
drought (dry period: cf.
  DRAUGHT)
drown
drow•sy *adj.*, drow•
  si•er, drow•si•est
drug *n.*, *v.*, drugged,
  drug•ging
drug a•buse
drug a•bus•er
drug ad•dict
drug ad•dic•tion
drug con•trols
drug de•pen•dence
drug ed•u•ca•tion
drug-free
drug in•ter•dic•tion
drug par•a•pher•na•
  lia
drug screen•ing
drug test
drug test•ing
drug treat•ment
drug treatment fa•
  cil•i•ty
drug•less
drug•push•er
drunk
drunk driv•ing *n.*
drunk-driving *adj.*
drunk tank
drunk•ard
drunk•en
drunk•en•ly
drunk•en•ness

drunk•om•e•ter
dry bulk n.
dry-bulk adj.
dry law
dry rent
dry trust
D.Sc. (Doctor of Science)
DS-PCR (double stringency polymerase chain reaction)
d.t.'s (delirium tremens)
du•al (double: cf. DUEL)
dual a•gen•cy
dual ca•pac•i•ty
dual cit•i•zen
dual cit•i•zen•ship
dual-cli•ent doc•trine
dual na•tion•al•i•ty
dual pur•pose
du•al•ism
du•al•ist
du•al•is•tic
du•al•is•ti•cal•ly
du•al•i•ty
du•bi•ous
du•bi•ous•ly
du•bi•ous•ness
du•bi•ta•ble
du•bi•tan•te Latin.
du•bi•ta•tive
du•bi•ta•tive•ly
du•ces te•cum Latin.
dudg•eon (indignation: cf. DUNGEON)
due
due bill
due course of law
due date
due de•mand
due dil•i•gence
due-on-sale clause
due proc•ess
due process of law
du•el n., v., du•eled,

du•el•ing (a fight; to fight: cf. DUAL)
du•el•ist
dues n pl.
dues check•off
dues-pay•ing
DUI (driving under the influence)
du•ly
dum•my n., pl. dum•mies, adj., v., dum•mied, dum•my•ing
dummy cor•po•ra•tion
dump
dump•er
dump•ing
dun v., dunned, dun•ning, n. (to demand payment: cf. DONE)
dun•geon (prison: cf. DUDGEON)
du•op•o•ly n., pl. du•op•o•lies
du•op•so•ny n., pl. du•op•so•nies
dupe
du•plex
du•pli•ca•bil•i•ty
du•pli•ca•ble
du•pli•cate n., v., du•pli•cat•ed, du•pli•cat•ing, adj.
duplicate o•rig•i•nal
du•pli•ca•tion
du•pli•ca•tive
du•plic•i•tous
du•plic•i•tous•ly
du•plic•i•ty n., pl. du•plic•i•ties
du•ra•bil•i•ty
du•ra•ble
durable goods
durable pow•er of at•tor•ney
durable power of at-

torney for health care
du•ra•bly
dur•ance
durance vile
du•ra•tion
du•ra•tion•al
du•ress
du•res•sor
du•ti•a•bil•i•ty
du•ti•a•ble
du•ti•ful
du•ti•ful•ly
du•ty n., pl. du•ties
duty-free
duty of can•dor
duty to in•ter•vene
duty to mit•i•gate dam•age
duty to su•per•vise and in•spect
duty to warn
DWAI (driving while ability impaired)
dwell v., dwelt or dwelled, dwell•ing
dwell•ing
dwelling house
dwelling place
DWI (driving while impaired; driving while intoxicated)
dying dec•la•ra•tion
dy•nam•ic
dy•nam•i•cal•ly
dy•nam•ics
dy•nast
dy•nas•tic
dy•nas•ti•cal•ly
dy•nas•ty n., pl. dy•nas•ties
dys•func•tion
dys•func•tion•al
dys•so•cial

E. (East; Eastern)
E&O in•sur•ance (errors and omissions insurance)
e-com•merce
e con•ver•so *Latin.*
e-mail
ear•ful *n., pl.* ear•fuls
ear•ly *adv., adj.,* ear•li•er, ear•li•est
early re•tire•ment
early retirement ben•e•fits
ear•mark
earn
earned in•come
earned income cred•it
earned sur•plus
earn•er
ear•nest
earnest mon•ey
ear•nest•ly
ear•nest•ness
earn•ing ca•pac•i•ty
earn•ings *n.pl.*
earnings per share
ear•wit•ness
ease•ment
easement ap•pur•te•nant
easement by pre•scrip•tion
easement in gross
easement of ac•cess
easement of light and air
easement of ne•ces•si•ty
east (E.)
east•ern (E.)
East•ern Dis•trict (*citation form:* E.D.)

eas•y *adj.,* eas•i•er, eas•i•est, *adv.*
eas•y•go•ing
eaves•drop *v.,* eaves•dropped, eaves•drop•ping
eaves•drop•per
EBT (examination before trial)
e•bul•lience
e•bul•lient
ec•cen•tric
ec•cen•tri•cal•ly
ec•cen•tric•i•ty *n., pl.* ec•cen•tric•i•ties
ec•cle•si•as•tic
ec•cle•si•as•ti•cal
ecclesiastical court
ecclesiastical law
ec•cle•si•as•ti•cal•ly
ec•go•nine *Controlled Subst.*
ech•e•lon
ec•o•ca•tas•tro•phe
ec•o•cid•al
ec•o•cide
ec•o•haz•ard
ec•o•log•i•cal
ecological niche
ec•o•log•i•cal•ly
e•col•o•gist
e•col•o•gy
Econ. (Economy; Economic; Economics; Economical)
e•con•o•met•ric
e•con•o•met•ri•cal
e•con•o•me•tri•cian
e•con•o•met•rics *n. sing.*
e•con•o•met•rist
ec•o•nom•ic (*citation form:* Econ.)

economic block•ade
economic du•ress
economic growth
economic in•di•ca•tor
economic loss
economic mod•el
economic strike
ec•o•nom•i•cal (*citation form:* Econ.)
ec•o•nom•i•cal•ly
ec•o•nom•ics *n.sing. or pl.* (*citation form:* Econ.)
e•con•o•mies of scale
e•con•o•mist
e•con•o•mize *v.,* e•con•o•mized, e•con•o•miz•ing
e•con•o•miz•er
e•con•o•my *n., pl.* e•con•o•mies, *adj.* (*citation form:* Econ.)
ec•o•sys•tem
ECU (European currency unit)
E.D. (Eastern District)
ed. (edition; editor)
e•dict
ed•i•fi•ca•tion
ed•i•fi•er
ed•i•fy *v.,* ed•i•fied, ed•i•fy•ing
ed•i•fy•ing•ly
ed•it
e•di•tion (*citation form:* ed.)
ed•i•tor (*citation form:* ed.)
ed•i•to•ri•al
editorial ad•ver•tis•ing

ed•i•to•ri•al•i•za•
tion
ed•i•to•ri•al•ize v.,
ed•i•to•ri•al•ized,
ed•i•to•ri•al•iz•ing
ed•i•to•ri•al•ly
EDP (Electronic Data
Processing)
EDTA (ethylenediamine-
tetraacetic acid)
Educ. (Education; Educational)
ed•u•ca•bil•i•ty
ed•u•ca•ble
ed•u•cate v., ed•u•
cat•ed, ed•u•cat•
ing
ed•u•cat•ed
ed•u•ca•tion (citation
form: **Educ.**)
ed•u•ca•tion•al (cita-
tion form: **Educ.**)
educational psy•
chol•o•gist
educational psy•
chol•o•gy
ed•u•ca•tion•al•ly
ed•u•ca•tion•ese
ed•u•ca•tion•ist
ed•u•ca•tor
ed•u•ca•to•ry
e•duce v., e•duced,
e•duc•ing (to draw
out: cf. ADDUCE)
EEG (electroencephalo-
gram)
ef•fect (to bring about;
consequence: cf. AF-
FECT)
ef•fect•i•ble
ef•fec•tive (operative;
actual; ready for serv-
ice: cf. AFFECTIVE)
effective as•sist•ance
of coun•sel
effective date
effective tax rate

effective yield
ef•fec•tive•ly
ef•fec•tive•ness
ef•fects n.pl.
ef•fec•tu•al
ef•fec•tu•al•i•ty
ef•fec•tu•al•ness
ef•fec•tu•ate v., ef•
fec•tu•at•ed, ef•
fec•tu•at•ing
ef•fec•tu•a•tion
ef•fi•ca•cious
ef•fi•ca•cious•ly
ef•fi•ca•cious•ness
ef•fi•ca•cy n., pl. ef•
fi•ca•cies
ef•fi•cien•cy n., pl.
ef•fi•cien•cies
ef•fi•cient
efficient cause
ef•fi•cient•ly
ef•fi•gy n., pl. ef•fi•
gies
ef•flu•ence (action of
flowing out; something
that flows out: cf. AF-
FLUENCE)
ef•flu•ent (flowing
out; something that
flows out: cf. AFFLUENT)
ef•fort
ef•fort•ful
ef•fort•ful•ly
ef•fort•less
ef•fort•less•ly
ef•fort•less•ness
ef•frac•tion
ef•frac•tor
ef•fuse v., ef•fused,
ef•fus•ing
ef•fu•sion
ef•fu•sive
ef•fu•sive•ly
ef•fu•sive•ness
EFT (electronic funds
transfer)

e.g. (for example: from
Latin exempli gratia;
cf. I.E.)
e•gal•oi•tar•i•an or
e•qual•oi•tar•i•an
e•gal•oi•tar•i•an•ism
or e•qual•oi•tar•i•
an•ism
egg•shell skull
e•go n., pl. e•gos
e•go•cen•tric
e•go•cen•tric•i•ty
e•go•cen•trism
e•go•ism
e•go•ist
e•go•is•tic
e•go•is•ti•cal
e•go•is•ti•cal•ly
e•go•ma•ni•a
e•go•ma•ni•ac
e•go•ma•ni•a•cal
e•go•tism
e•go•tist
e•go•tis•tic
e•go•tis•ti•cal
e•go•tis•ti•cal•ly
e•gre•gious
e•gre•gious•ly
e•gre•gious•ness
e•gress
EIA (enzyme immuno-
assay)
ei•det•ic
ei•dos
eigne Law French.
ei•ther
e•jac•u•late v.,
e•jac•u•lat•ed,
e•jac•u•lat•ing
e•jac•u•la•tion
e•jac•u•la•to•ry
e•ject
e•jec•tion
e•jec•ti•o•ne fir•
mae Latin.
e•jec•tive

e·jec·tive·ly
e·ject·ment
e·jec·tor
e·jus·dem ge·ne·ris *Latin.*
e·lab·o·o·rate *adj., v.,* e·lab·o·o·rat·ed, e·lab·o·o·rat·ing
e·lab·o·o·rate·ly
e·lab·o·o·rate·ness
e·lab·o·o·ra·tion
e·lab·o·o·ra·tive
e·lab·o·o·ra·tor
e·lapse *v.,* e·lapsed, e·laps·ing
e·las·tic
elastic clause
e·las·ti·cal·ly
e·las·tic·i·ty
e·late *v.,* e·lat·ed, e·lat·ing
e·lat·ed
e·lat·ed·ly
e·lat·ed·ness
e·la·tion
el·der
elder a·buse
elder law
el·der·li·ness
el·de·orly
eld·est
Elec. (Electric; Electrical; Electricity; Electronic)
e·lect
e·lect·a·bil·i·ty
e·lect·a·ble
e·lect·ed
e·lec·tion
election board
election day
election dis·trict
election of de·fens·es
election of rem·e·dies

election re·turns
election un·der the will
e·lec·tion·eer *v.*
e·lec·tion·eer·er *n.*
e·lec·tive
elective fran·chise
elective of·fice
elective share
e·lec·tive·ly
e·lec·tive·ness
e·lec·tor
e·lec·tor·al
electoral col·lege
electoral vote
e·lec·tor·al·ly
elec·tor·ate
e·lec·tric *(citation form:* **Elec.**)
electric chair
e·lec·tri·cal *(citation form:* **Elec.**)
e·lec·tric·i·ty *(citation form:* **Elec.**)
e·lec·tri·fi·ca·tion
e·lec·tri·fy *v.,* e·lec·tri·fied, e·lec·tri·fy·ing
e·lec·tro·cute *v.,* e·lec·tro·cut·ed, e·lec·tro·cut·ing
e·lec·tro·cu·tion
e·lec·tro·en·ceph·a·lo ·gram (EEG)
e·lec·tron·ic *(citation form:* **Elec.**)
electronic bank·ing
electronic crime
electronic da·ta ex·change
electronic data proc·ess·ing (EDP)
electronic eaves·drop·ping

electronic funds trans·fer (EFT)
electronic mail
electronic pub·lish·ing
electronic sur·veil·lance
e·lec·tron·i·cal·ly
e·lec·tron·ics *n.sing.*
e·lec·tro·pho·re·sis
el·ee·mos·y·nar·y
e·le·git *Latin.*
el·e·ment
el·e·men·tal
el·e·men·tal·ly
el·e·men·ta·ry
el·e·vate *v.,* el·e·vat·ed, el·e·vat·ing
elevated mood
el·e·va·tion
e·lic·it (to bring out: cf. ILLICIT)
e·lic·i·ta·tion
e·lide *v.,* e·lid·ed, e·lid·ing
el·i·gi·bil·i·ty
el·i·gi·ble (qualified; available: cf. ILLEGIBLE)
eligible pa·per
el·i·gi·bly
e·lim·i·na·bil·i·ty
e·lim·i·nate *v.,* e·lim·i·nat·ed, e·lim·i·nat·ing
e·lim·i·na·tion
e·lim·i·na·tive
e·lim·i·na·tor
e·lim·i·na·to·ry
e·lis·or
e·lite
e·lit·ism
e·lit·ist
el·lip·sis *n., pl.* el·lip·ses
el·lip·ti·cal

el•lip•ti•cal•ly
el•lip•ti•cal•ness
e•loign or e•loin (to remove: cf. ELOIGNE)
e•loigne *Law French.* (removed: cf. ELOIGN)
e•loign•ment
e•lope *v.,* e•loped, e•lop•ing
e•lope•ment
e•lop•er
el•o•quence
el•o•quent
el•o•quent•ly
else
else•where
e•lu•ci•date *v.,* e•lu•ci•dat•ed, e•lu•ci•dat•ing
e•lu•ci•da•tion
e•lu•ci•da•tive
e•lu•ci•da•tor
e•lude *v.,* e•lud•ed, e•lud•ing
e•lu•sion (evasion: cf. ILLUSION)
e•lu•sive (evasive: cf. ALLUSIVE; ILLUSIVE)
e•ma•ci•ate *v.,* e•ma•ci•at•ed, e•ma•ci•at•ing
e•ma•ci•at•ed
e•ma•ci•a•tion
em•a•nant (issuing forth: cf. EMINENT; IM-MANENT; IMMINENT)
em•a•nate *v.,* em•a•nat•ed, em•a•nat•ing
em•a•na•tion
em•a•na•tive
e•man•ci•pate *v.,* e•man•ci•pat•ed, e•man•ci•pat•ing
e•man•ci•pat•ed
emancipated mi•nor

e•man•ci•pa•tion
E•man•ci•pa•tion Proc•la•ma•tion
e•man•ci•pa•tion•ist
e•man•ci•pa•tive
e•man•ci•pa•tor
e•mas•cu•late *v.,* e•mas•cu•lat•ed, e•mas•cu•lat•ing
e•mas•cu•la•tion
e•mas•cu•la•tive
e•mas•cu•la•tor
e•mas•cu•la•to•ry
em•bar•go *n., pl.* em•bar•goes, *v.,* em•bar•goed, em•bar•go•ing
em•bark
em•bar•ka•tion
em•bar•rass
em•bar•rassed•ly
em•bar•rass•ing•ly
em•bar•rass•ment
em•bas•sy *n., pl.* em•bas•sies
em•bat•tle *v.,* em•bat•tled, em•bat•tling
em•bat•tled
em•bel•lish
em•bel•lish•er
em•bel•lish•ment
em•bez•zle *v.,* em•bez•zled, em•bez•zling
em•bez•zle•ment
em•bez•zler
em•bit•ter
em•bit•ter•ment
em•blem
em•blem•at•ic
em•blem•at•i•cal
em•blem•at•i•cal•ly
em•blem•at•i•cal•ness
em•ble•ments *n.pl.*

em•bod•i•er
em•bod•i•ment
em•bod•y *v.,* em•bod•ied, em•bod•y•ing
em•brace *v.,* em•braced, em•brac•ing, *n.*
em•brace•ment (a physical or mental embracing: cf. EMBRACERY)
em•brace•or or em•brac•er (one guilty of embracery)
em•brac•er (one who embraces)
em•brac•er•y *n., pl.* em•brac•er•ies (corrupt influencing of judge or jury: cf. EM-BRACEMENT)
em•bry•o *n., pl.* em•bry•os
em•bry•o•log•ic
em•bry•o•log•i•cal
em•bry•o•log•i•cal•ly
em•bry•ol•o•gy
em•bry•on•ic
embryonic de•vel•op•ment
em•bry•on•i•cal•ly
e•mend (to correct a text: cf. AMEND)
e•mend•a•ble
e•men•date *v.,* e•men•dat•ed, e•men•dat•ing
e•men•da•tion
e•men•da•tor
e•men•da•to•ry
Emer. (Emergency)
e•merge *v.,* e•merged, e•merg•ing
e•mer•gence
e•mer•gen•cy *n., pl.*

e∘mer•gen•cies (*citation form:* Emer.)

emergency con•tra•cep•tion

emergency con•tra•cep•tive

emergency pow∘er

e∘mer•gent

e∘mer•gent•ly

e∘mer•gent•ness

e∘merg•ing

emerging mar•ket

e∘mer∘i•tus *adj., n., pl.* e∘mer∘i∘ti

em∘i•grant (departing person: cf. IMMIGRANT)

em∘i•grate *v.,* em∘i•grat∘ed, em∘i•grat•ing (to leave one's country: cf. IMMIGRATE)

em∘i•gra•tion

em∘i•gra•tion•al

é∘mi•gré

em∘i•nence

é∘mi•nence grise *n., pl.* é∘mi•nences grises *French.*

em∘i•nen∘cy *n., pl.* em∘i•nen•cies

em∘i•nent (outstanding: cf. EMANANT; IMMANENT; IMMINENT)

eminent do•main

em∘i•nent•ly

em•is•sar∘y *n., pl.* em•is•sar•ies

e∘mis•sion

emission stan•dards

e∘mis•sive

e∘mit *v.,* e∘mit•ted, e∘mit•ting

e∘mit•ter

e∘mol∘u•ment

e∘mote *v.,* e∘mot∘ed, e∘mot•ing

e∘mot∘er

e∘mo•tion

e∘mo•tion•al

emotional dep∘ri•va•tion

e∘mo•tion•al•ism

e∘mo•tion•al∘i•ty

e∘mo•tion•al•ize *v.,* e∘mo•tion•al•ized, e∘mo•tion•al•iz•ing

e∘mo•tion•al•ly

e∘mo•tion•less

e∘mo•tive

e∘mo•tive•ly

e∘mo•tive•ness

e∘mo•tiv∘i•ty

em•pan∘el *v.,* em•pan•eled, em•pan•el•ing

em•pa•thet∘ic

em•pa•thet∘i•cal•ly

em•path∘ic (sharing another's feelings: cf. EMPHATIC)

em•path∘i•cal•ly

em•pa•thize *v.,* em•pa•thized, em•pa•thiz•ing (to share another's feelings: cf. EMPHASIZE)

em•pa•thy

em•per∘or

em•pha•sis *n., pl.* em•pha•ses

em•pha•size *v.,* em•pha•sized, em•pha•siz•ing (to stress: cf. EMPATHIZE)

em•phat∘ic (stated strongly: cf. EMPATHIC)

em•phat∘i•cal•ly

em•phat∘i•cal•ness

em•phy•steu•sis

em•pire

em•pir∘ic

em•pir•i•cal

em•pir•i•cal•ly

em•pir•i•cism

em•pir•i•cist

em•ploy

em•ploy•a∘bil∘i•ty

em•ploy•a∘ble

em•ploy∘ee

employee ben∘e•fit plan

employee in•sur•ance

employee life insur-ance

Em•ploy∘ee Re•tire•ment In•come Se•cu∘ri∘ty Act of 1974 (ERISA)

employee stock op∘tion

employee stock own•er•ship plan (ESOP)

em•ploy∘er

em•ploy•ers' as•so•ci∘a•tion

employers' li∘a•bil∘i∘ty act

employers' liability in•sur•ance

em•ploy•ment

employment a∘gency

employment at will

employment tax

em•pow∘er

em•pow•er•ment

em•press (female ruler: cf. IMPRESS)

emp•ti•ly

emp•ti•ness

emp•tor *n., pl.* emp•to∘res *Latin.*

emp•ty *adj.,* emp•ti∘er, emp•ti•est, *n., pl.* emp•ties, *v.,* emp•tied, emp•ty•ing

empty-hand∘ed

EMS (European Monetary System)
em•u•late *v.*, em•u•lat•ed, em•u•lat•ing
em•u•la•tion
em•u•la•tive
em•u•la•tive•ly
em•u•la•tor
en banc or (in a few jurisdictions) in bank or in banc *Law French.*
en clair *French.*
en fait *Law French.*
en gros *Law French.*
en masse *French.*
en ven•tre sa mère *Law French.*
en vie *Law French.*
en•a•ble *v.*, en•a•bled, en•a•bling
en•a•ble•ment
en•a•bler
en•a•bling
enabling clause
enabling leg•is•la•tion
en•act
en•act•a•ble
en•act•ing clause
en•ac•tive
en•act•ment
en•ac•tor
en•ac•to•ry
en•am•or
en•am•ored
en•am•ored•ness
en•cap•su•late *v.*, en•cap•su•lat•ed, en•cap•su•lat•ing
en•cap•su•la•tion
en•chain
en•chant
en•chant•er
en•chant•ing

en•chant•ing•ly
en•chant•ment
en•chant•ress
en•clave *n.*, *v.*, en•claved, en•clav•ing
en•close•a•ble
en•close *v.*, en•closed, en•clos•ing
en•clos•er
en•clos•ure
en•code *v.*, en•cod•ed, en•cod•ing
en•cod•er
en•com•pass
en•com•pass•ment
en•count•er
en•count•er•er
en•cour•age *v.*, en•cour•aged, en•cour•ag•ing
en•cour•age•ment
en•cour•ag•er
en•cour•ag•ing•ly
en•croach (to trespass: cf. ACCROACH)
en•croach•er
en•croach•ment
en•crypt
en•cryp•tion
en•cum•ber
en•cum•ber•ing•ly
en•cum•brance
en•cum•branc•er
en•cy•clo•pe•dic
en•cy•clo•pe•di•cal•ly
en•dan•ger
en•dan•gered
endangered spe•cies
en•dan•ger•ment
en•dear
en•dear•ing
en•dear•ing•ly
en•dear•ment
en•deav•or
en•deav•or•er

en•dem•ic
en•dem•i•cal•ly
en•de•mic•i•ty
en•de•mism
end•ing in•ven•to•ry
end•less
end•less•ly
end•less•ness
end•note For citation forms, see NOTE[1].
en•dog•e•nous
endogenous de•pres•sion
endogenous drug
en•dor•phin
en•dors•a•ble
en•dorse[1] *v.*, en•dorsed, en•dors•ing (to express support; to write a notation on a document)
en•dorse[2] See INDORSE.
en•dor•see See INDORSEE.
en•dorse•ment
en•dors•er
en•dor•sive
en•dow
en•dow•er
en•dow•ment
endowment in•sur•ance
endowment life insurance
en•dur•ance
en•dur•ant
en•dure *v.*, en•dured, en•dur•ing
en•dur•er
en•dur•ing
en•dur•ing•ly
en•dur•ing•ness
en•e•my *n.*, *pl.* en•e•mies, *adj.*
enemy al•ien
enemy bel•lig•er•ent

en•er•get•ic
en•er•get•i•cal•ly
en•er•gize v., en•er•gized, en•er•giz•ing
en•er•giz•er
en•er•gy n., pl. en•er•gies
energy au•dit
energy serv•ic•es com•pa•ny (ESCO)
en•er•vate v., en•er•vat•ed, en•er•vat•ing (to weaken: vs. *in•nervate*)
en•er•vat•ed
en•er•va•tion
en•er•va•tive
en•feoff
en•feoff•ment
en•force v., en•forced, en•forc•ing
en•force•a•bil•i•ty
en•force•a•ble
en•force•ment
en•forc•er
en•for•cive
en•fran•chise v., en•fran•chised, en•fran•chis•ing (to grant the right to vote: cf. AFFRANCHISE)
en•fran•chise•ment
en•fran•chis•er
Eng. (England; English)
en•gage v., en•gaged, en•gag•ing
en•ga•gé French.
en•gaged
engaged in com•merce
en•gag•ed•ly
en•gag•ed•ness
en•gage•ment
en•gag•er
en•gag•ing
en•gag•ing•ly

en•gen•der
en•gen•der•er
en•gen•der•ment
Eng'g (Engineering)
en•gine
en•gi•neer[1] n. (citation form: Eng'r)
engineer[2] v.
en•gi•neer•ing (citation form: Eng'g)
Eng•land (Eng.)
Eng•lish (citation form: Eng.)
English-on•ly law
English side
Eng'r (Engineer)
en•grave v., en•graved, en•grav•ing
en•gross
en•grossed bill
en•gross•ed•ly
en•gross•er
en•gross•ment
en•gulf
en•gulf•ment
en•hance
en•hance•ment
en•hanc•er
en•ig•ma n., pl. en•ig•mas or en•ig•ma•ta
en•ig•ma•tic
en•ig•ma•ti•cal
en•ig•mat•i•cal•ly
en•join
en•join•der
en•join•er
en•join•ment
en•joy
en•joy•a•ble
en•joy•a•ble•ness
en•joy•a•bly
en•joy•er
en•joy•ment
en•large v., en•larged, en•larg•ing

en•large•a•ble
en•large•ment
enlargement of time
en•light•en
en•light•ened
en•light•en•ing
en•light•en•ment
en•list
en•list•ed per•son•nel
en•list•ee
en•list•er
en•list•ment
en•liv•en
en•liv•en•er
en•liv•en•ing•ly
en•liv•en•ment
en•mesh
en•mesh•ment
en•mi•ty n., pl. en•mi•ties (hatred: cf. AMITY)
en•no•ble v., en•no•bled, en•no•bling
en•no•ble•ment
en•no•bler
en•no•bling•ly
E•noch Ar•den stat•utes
e•nor•mi•ty n., pl. e•nor•mi•ties (atrociousness: cf. ENORMOUSNESS)
e•nor•mous
e•nor•mous•ly
e•nor•mous•ness (hugeness: cf. ENORMITY)
e•nough
en•quire See INQUIRE.
en•quir•er See INQUIRER.
en•quir•y See INQUIRY.
en•rage v., en•raged, en•rag•ing
en•rich

en•rich•ing
en•rich•ing•ly
en•rich•ment
en•roll
en•rolled
enrolled bill
en•roll◦ee
en•roll◦er
en•roll•ment
en•sconce v., en•
  sconced, en•sconc•
  ing
en•serf
en•slave v., en•
  slaved, en•slav•ing
en•slave•ment
en•slav◦er
en•snare v., en•
  snared, en•snar•ing
en•snare•ment
en•snar◦er
en•snar•ing•ly
en◦sue v., en•sued,
  en•su•ing
en•sure v., en•sured,
  en•sur•ing (to make
  certain: cf. INSURE)
Ent. (Entertainment)
en•tail
en•tail◦er
en•tail•ment
en•tan•gle v., en•
  tan•gled, en•tan•
  gling
en•tan•gled•ness
en•tan•gle•ment
en•tan•gling•ly
en•tente n., pl. en•
  tentes French.
entente cor•diale n.,
  pl. ententes cor•
  diales French.
en◦ter
Enter. (Enterprise)
en•ter•a◦ble
en•ter◦er

en•ter•prise
enterprise fund
enterprise li•a•
  bil◦i◦ty
enterprise zone
en•ter•pris•ing
en•ter•pris•ing•ly
en•ter•tain
en•ter•tain◦er
en•ter•tain•ing
en•ter•tain•ing•ly
en•ter•tain•ment (ci-
  tation form: **Ent.**)
entertainment ex•
  pense
en•throne v., en•
  throned, en•thron•
  ing
en•throne•ment
en•thu•si•asm
en•thu•si•ast
en•thu•si•as•tic
en•thu•si•as•ti•
  cal◦ly
en•tice v., en•ticed,
  en•tic◦ing
en•tice•ment
en•tic◦ing•ly
en•tic◦ing•ness
en•tire
entire con•tract
en•tire•ly
en•tire•ness
en•tire◦ty n., pl. en•
  tire•ties
en•ti•tle
en•ti•tled
en•ti•tle•ment
en•ti•ty n., pl. en•ti•
  ties
en•tou•rage
en•trance n., v., en•
  tranced, en•tranc•
  ing
entrance ex•am◦i•
  na•tion

en•trance•ment
en•tranc◦ing
en•tranc◦ing•ly
en•trant
en•trap v., en•
  trapped, en•trap•
  ping
en•trap•ment
en•trap•per
en•trap•ping•ly
en•treat
en•treat•ing•ly
en•treat◦y n., pl. en•
  treat•ies
en•trée
en•trench
en•trenched
en•trench•ment
en•tre•pôt French.
en•tre•pre•neur (ad-
  venturous business
  owner: cf. INTRAPRE-
  NEUR)
en•tre•pre•neur◦i◦al
en•tre•pre•neur◦i•
  al◦ly
en•tre•pre•neur•ism
en•tre•pre•neur•ship
en•trust
en•trust•ment
en◦try n., pl. en•tries
entry bar•ri◦er
entry lev◦el n.
entry-level adj.
entry wound
e◦nu•mer•a◦ble
  (countable; listable: cf.
  INNUMERABLE)
e◦nu•mer•a◦bly
e◦nu•mer•ate v.,
  e◦nu•mer•at◦ed,
  e◦nu•mer•at•ing
e◦nu•mer•at◦ed
  pow◦er
e◦nu•mer◦a•tion
e◦nu•mer◦a•tive

e•nu•mer•a•tor

e•nun•ci•a•bil•i•ty

e•nun•ci•a•ble

e•nun•ci•ate *v.*, e•nun•ci•at•ed, e•nun•ci•at•ing (to articulate: cf. ANNUNCI-ATE)

e•nun•ci•a•tion

e•nun•ci•a•tive

e•nun•ci•a•tive•ly

e•nun•ci•a•tor

e•nun•ci•a•to•ry

e•nure See INURE.

en•vel•op *v.*, en•vel•oped, en•vel•op•ing

en•ve•lope *n.*

en•vel•op•ment

en•vi•a•ble

en•vi•a•ble•ness

en•vi•a•bly

en•vi•ous

en•vi•ous•ly

en•vi•ous•ness

en•vi•ron•ment (*citation form:* Env't)

en•vi•ron•men•tal (*citation form:* Envtl.)

environmental au•dit

environmental im•pact state•ment

environmental pro•tec•tion

environmental protection leg•is•la•tion

en•vi•ron•men•tal•ism

en•vi•ron•men•tal•ist

en•vi•ron•men•tal•ly

en•vi•rons *n.pl.*

en•vis•age *v.*, en•vis•aged, en•vis•ag•ing

en•vis•age•ment

en•vi•sion

en•voy

envoy ex•traor•di•nar•y

Env't (Environment)

Envtl. (Environmental)

en•vy *v.*, en•vied, en•vy•ing

en•zyme

enzyme im•mu•no•as•say (EIA)

e•o di•o Latin.

e•o in•stan•te Latin.

e•o no•mi•ne Latin.

e•phem•er•al

e•phem•er•al•i•ty

e•phem•er•al•ly

e•phem•er•al•ness

ep•ic (heroic and sweeping in scope; a sweeping narrative: cf. EPOCH

ep•i•cal•ly

ep•i•dem•ic

ep•i•dem•i•cal•ly

ep•i•de•mic•i•ty

ep•i•de•mi•o•log•i•cal

ep•i•de•mi•o•log•i•&spb rk;cal•ly

ep•i•de•mi•olo•gist

ep•i•de•mi•ol•o•gy

e•piph•a•ony *n., pl.* e•piph•a•nies

ep•i•phe•nom•e•non *n., pl.* ep•i•phe•nom•e•na

ep•i•sode

ep•i•sod•ic

episodic ex•ces•sive drink•er

ep•i•sod•i•cal•ly

ep•i•ste•mic

ep•i•ste•mi•cal•ly

e•pis•te•mo•log•i•cal

e•pis•te•mo•log•i•cal•ly

e•pis•te•mol•o•gist

e•pis•te•mol•o•gy

ep•i•taph

ep•i•thet

ep•i•thet•ic

ep•i•thet•i•cal

e•pit•o•ome

e•pit•o•mi•za•tion

e•pit•o•mize *v.*, e•pit•o•mized, e•pit•o•miz•ing

ep•och (era: cf. EPIC)

epoch-mak•ing

ep•och•al

ep•och•al•ly

Eq. (Equity; Equity Court; Equity Division)

e•qual *adj., n., v.*, e•qualed, e•qual•ing

Equal. (Equality)

equal ac•cess

equal em•ploy•ment op•por•tu•ni•ty (EEO) laws

equal opportunity

equal pro•tec•tion

equal time

e•qual•i•tar•i•an See EGALITARIAN.

e•qual•i•tar•i•an•ism See EGALITARIANISM.

e•qual•i•ty *n., pl.* e•qual•i•ties (*citation form:* Equal.)

e•qual•i•za•tion

e•qual•ize *v.*, e•qual•ized, e•qual•iz•ing

e•qual•iz•er

e•qual•ly

equally di•vid•ed
court

e•quat•a•bil•i•ty

e•quat•a•ble

e•quate v.,
e•quat•ed, e•quat•
ing

e•quil•i•bra•to•ry

e•qui•lib•ri•um n.,
pl. e•qui•lib•ri•ums
or e•qui•lib•ri•a

equilibrium price

e•quip v., e•quipped,
e•quip•ping

Equip. (Equipment)

e•quip•ment (citation
form: Equip.)

equipment trust

e•quip•per

eq•ui•ta•ble

equitable ab•sten•
tion

equitable ac•tion

equitable as•sets

equitable as•sign•
ment

equitable charge

equitable de•fense

equitable dis•tri•bu•
tion

equitable es•tate

equitable es•top•pel

equitable in•ter•est

equitable lien

equitable mort•gage

equitable own•er

equitable re•coup•
ment

equitable re•demp•
tion

equitable re•lief

equitable rem•e•dy

equitable re•plev•in

equitable right

equitable ser•vi•tude

equitable sub•ro•ga•
tion

equitable ti•tle

equitable waste

eq•ui•ta•ble•ness

eq•ui•ta•bly

eq•ui•ty n., pl. eq•
ui•ties (citation form:
Eq.)

equity cap•i•tal

equity con•ver•sion

Equity Court (citation
form: Eq.)

Equity Di•vi•sion (ci-
tation form: Eq.)

equity kick•er

equity of re•demp•
tion

equity par•tic•i•pa•
tion

equity real es•tate
in•vest•ment trust

equity se•cu•ri•ty

equity side

equity stock

e•quiv•o•a•lence

e•quiv•o•a•len•cy n.,
pl. e•quiv•o•a•len•
cies

e•quiv•o•a•lent

e•quiv•o•a•lent•ly

e•quiv•o•a•lents, doc•
trine of

e•quiv•o•o•cal

e•quiv•o•o•cate v.,
e•quiv•o•o•cat•ed,
e•quiv•o•o•cat•ing

e•quiv•o•o•cat•ing•ly

e•quiv•o•o•ca•tion

e•quiv•o•o•ca•tor

e•rad•i•ca•ble

e•rad•i•cate v.,
e•rad•i•cat•ed,
e•rad•i•cat•ing

e•rad•i•ca•tion

e•rad•i•ca•tive

e•ras•a•bil•i•ty

e•ras•a•ble

e•rase v., e•rased,
e•ras•ing

e•ra•sure

e•rect

e•rect•a•ble

e•rec•tion

er•go Latin.

er•go•no•met•ric

er•go•nom•ic

er•go•nom•i•cal•ly

er•go•nom•ics n.sing.
or pl.

er•gon•o•mist

er•got

E•rie doc•trine

ERISA (Employee Re-
tirement Income Secu-
rity Act of 1974)

e•rod•a•bil•i•ty

e•rod•a•ble

e•rode v., e•rod•ed,
e•rod•ing

e•rod•i•bil•i•ty

e•rod•i•ble

e•ros•i•ble

e•ro•sion

e•rot•ic

e•rot•i•ca n.sing. or
pl.

e•rot•i•cal•ly

e•rot•i•cism

e•rot•i•ci•za•tion

e•rot•i•cize v.,
e•rot•i•cized,
e•rot•i•ciz•ing

e•rot•o•ma•ni•a

e•rot•o•ma•ni•ac

e•rot•o•man•ic

erotomanic de•lu•
sion

err

Err. (Error; Errors)

er•rant

er•rant•ly

er•ra•re hu•ma•num est *Latin.*
er•rat∘ic
er•rat•i•cal∘ly
er•rat∘i•cism
er•ra•tum *n., pl.* er•ra∘ta
er•ro•ne•ous
er•ro•ne•ous∘ly
er•ro•ne•ous•ness
er∘ror (*citation form for sing. and pl.:* **Err.**)
er•ror•less
er•ror•less∘ly
er•rors and o∘mis•sions (E&O) in•sur•ance
er•rors in ex•tre•mis doc•trine
er∘ou•dite
er∘ou•dite∘ly
er∘ou•dite•ness
er∘ou•di∘tion
e∘rupt
e∘rup•tion
Er∘y•throx∘y•lon co∘ca *Controlled Subst.* (the coca plant)
es•ca•late *v.,* es•ca•lat∘ed, es•ca•lat•ing
es•ca•la•tion
es•ca•la•tor
escalator clause
es•ca•la•to∘ry
es•cap•a∘ble
es•cape *v.,* es•caped, es•cap∘ing, *adj.*
escape clause
es•cap∘ee
es•cap∘er
es•cheat
es•cheat•a∘ble
es•cheat•age
es•cheat∘or

ESCO (energy services company
es•cort
es•crow
escrow ac•count
escrow a∘gree•ment
es•crow∘ee
es∘ne∘cy
ESOP (employee stock ownership plan)
es∘o•ter∘ic
es∘o•ter∘i∘ca *n.pl.*
es∘o•ter•i•cal∘ly
es∘o•ter•i•cism
es•pe•cial
es•pe•cial∘ly
es•pi∘o•nage
es•plees *n.pl.*
es•pous∘al
es•pouse *v.,* es•poused, es•pous•ing
es•pous∘er
es•prit
esprit de corps *French.*
Esq. (Esquire)
Es•quire (Esq.)
es∘say (a written work; to attempt: cf. ASSAY)
es∘se *Latin.*
es•sence
es•sen•tial
essential fa•cil•i•ty
essential pur•pose
es•sen•ti•al∘i∘ty
es•sen•tial∘ly
es•sen•tial•ness
es•soin
Est. (Estate; Estates)
es•tab•lish
es•tab•lish•a∘ble
es•tab•lish∘er
es•tab•lish•ment
establishment of re•li•gion
es•tab•lish•men•tar∘i•an

es•tab•lish•men•tar∘i•an•ism
es•tate (*citation form for sing. and pl.:* **Est.**)
estate at suf•fer•ance
estate at will
estate by pur•chase
estate by the en•tire∘ty
estate for life
estate for years
estate from year to year
estate in bank•rupt∘cy
estate in com•mon
estate in co•par•ce•nar∘y
estate in ex•pect•an∘cy
estate in fee
estate in pos•ses•sion
estate in sev•er•al∘ty
estate of in•her•it•ance
estate plan•ning
estate pur au∘tre vie
estate tail
estate tax
estate up∘on con•di•tion
es•taz∘o∘lam *Controlled Subst.*
es•teem
es∘ter
es•ti•mate *v.,* es•ti•mat∘ed, es•ti•mat•ing, *n.*
es•ti•mat∘ed tax
es•ti•ma•tion
es•ti•ma•tive
es•ti•ma•tor
es∘top *v.,* es•topped, es•top•ping

es•top•page
es•top•pel
estoppel by deed
estoppel by e•lec•tion
estoppel by judg•ment
estoppel by rec•ord
estoppel in pais
es•to•vers *n.pl.*
es•trange *v.*, es•tranged, es•trang•ing
es•tranged
es•trange•ment
es•tray
es•treat
es•trepe•ment *Law French.*
es•tro•gen
et al. (and another: from Latin *et alius*; and others: from Latin *et alii*)
et cet•er•a (etc.) *Latin.*
et seq. (and those following: from Latin *et sequentia*)
et ux. (et uxor)
et ux•or (et ux.) *Latin.*
et vir *Latin.*
etc. (et cetera)
eth•a•nol
eth•chlor•vy•nol *Controlled Subst.*
e•ther
eth•ic
eth•i•cal
ethical drug
eth•i•cal•i•ty
eth•i•cal•ly
eth•i•cal•ness
eth•i•cist

eth•i•cize *v.*, eth•i•cized, eth•i•ciz•ing
eth•ics *n.sing. or pl.*
e•thin•o•a•mate *Controlled Subst.*
eth•nic
ethnic cleans•ing
eth•ni•cal•ly
eth•nic•i•ty *n., pl.* eth•nic•i•ties
eth•no•cen•tric
eth•no•cen•tri•cal•ly
eth•no•cen•tric•i•ty
eth•no•cen•trism
ethyl al•co•hol
ethyl lo•flaz•o•e•pate *Controlled Subst.*
eth•yl•ene•di•am•ine•tet•ra•a•ce•tic ac•id (EDTA)
eth•yl•es•tre•nol *Controlled Subst.*
eth•yl•meth•yl•thi•am•bu• tene *Controlled Subst.*
eth•yl•mor•phine *Controlled Subst.*
e•oti•o•log•ic
e•oti•o•log•i•cal
e•oti•o•log•i•cal•ly
e•oti•ol•o•gy *n., pl.* e•oti•ol•o•gies
et•i•quette
e•oton•oi•taz•ene *Controlled Subst.*
e•otor•phine *Controlled Subst.*
etorphine hy•dro•chlor•ide *Controlled Subst.*
e•otox•er•oi•dine *Controlled Subst.*
eu•gen•ic
eu•gen•oi•cal•ly
eu•gen•ics *n.sing.*

eu•lo•gize *v.*, eu•lo•gized, eu•lo•giz•ing
eu•lo•giz•er
eu•lo•o•gy *n., pl* eu•lo•gies
eu•phe•mism
eu•phe•mis•tic
eu•phe•mis•ti•cal•ly
eu•phe•mize *v.*, eu•phe•mized, eu•phe•miz•ing
eu•pho•ri•a
eu•phor•ic
Eur. (Europe; European)
Eur. Ct. H.R. (European Court of Human Rights)
eu•ro *n., pl.* eu•ros
Eu•ro•bank
Eu•ro•bank•er
Eu•ro•bank•ing
Eu•ro•bond
Eu•ro•cur•ren•cy *n., pl.* Eu•ro•cur•ren•cies
Eu•ro•dol•lar
Eu•ro•mon•ey
Eu•ro•pat•ent
Eu•rope *(citation form:* Eur.*)*
Eu•ro•pe•an *(citation form:* Eur.*)*
European Court of Hu•man Rights *(citation form:* Eur. Ct. H.R.*)*
European cur•ren•cy u•nit (ECU)
European Mon•e•ta•ry Sys•tem (EMS)
Eu•ro•pe•an•ism
Eu•ro•pe•an•ist
eu•tha•na•sia
eu•tha•nize *v.*, eu•

tha•nized, eu•tha•
niz•ing
e•vac•u•ate *v.*,
e•vac•u•at•ed,
e•vac•u•at•ing
e•vac•u•a•tion
e•vac•u•a•tive
e•vac•u•ee
e•vad•a•ble *or*
e•vad•i•ble
e•vade *v.*, e•vad•ed,
e•vad•ing
e•vad•er
e•val•u•a•ble
e•val•u•ate *v.*,
e•val•u•at•ed,
e•val•u•at•ing
e•val•u•a•tion
e•val•u•a•tive
e•val•u•a•tor
ev•a•nesce *v.*, ev•a•
nesced, ev•a•nesc•
ing
ev•a•nes•cence
ev•a•nes•cent
ev•a•nes•cent•ly
e•va•sion
e•va•sive
e•va•sive•ly
e•va•sive•ness
e•ven
even-tem•pered
e•ven•er
e•ven•hand•ed
e•ven•hand•ed•ly
e•ven•hand•ed•ness
e•ven•ly
e•ven•ness
e•vent
e•vent•ful
e•vent•ful•ly
e•vent•ful•ness
e•ven•tu•al
e•ven•tu•al•i•ty
e•ven•tu•al•ly
e•ven•tu•ate *v.*,

e•ven•tu•at•ed,
e•ven•tu•at•ing
e•ven•tu•a•tion
ever•green con•tract
eve•ry
every day *adv.* (cf. EVE
RYDAY)
eve•ry•bod•y
eve•ry•day *adj.* (cf..
EVERY DAY)
Eve•ry•man
eve•ry•one
eve•ry•thing
eve•ry•where
Eve•ry•wom•an
e•vict
e•vict•ee
e•vic•tion
e•vic•tor
ev•i•dence *n., v.*,
ev•i•denced, ev•i•
denc•ing
evidence of in•sur•a•
bil•i•ty
evidence tech•ni•cian
ev•i•dent
ev•i•den•tial
ev•i•den•tial•ly
ev•i•den•tia•ry
evidentiary fact
evidentiary priv•i•
lege
ev•i•dent•ly
ev•i•dent•ness
e•vil
evil-mind•ed
e•vil•do•er
e•vil•do•ing
e•vil•ly
e•vince *v.*, e•vinced,
e•vinc•ing
e•vin•ci•ble
e•vin•cive
ev•o•ca•ble
ev•o•ca•tion
e•voc•a•tive

e•voc•a•tive•ly
e•voc•a•tive•ness
e•voke *v.*, e•voked,
e•vok•ing
e•vok•er
ev•o•lu•tion
ev•o•lu•tion•al
ev•o•lu•tion•al•ly
ev•o•lu•tion•ar•i•ly
ev•o•lu•tion•ar•y
ev•o•lu•tive
e•volv•a•ble
e•volve *v.*, e•volved,
e•volv•ing
ex *English and Latin*
Ex. (Exhibit; Exchequer;
Court of Exchequer)
ex ae•quo et bo•no
Latin.
ex ca•the•dra *Latin.*
ex con•trac•tu *Latin*
ex cu•ri•a *Latin.*
ex de•lic•to *Latin.*
ex div•i•dend
ex gra•ti•a *Latin.*
ex hy•poth•e•si
Latin.
ex in•ter•est
ex le•ge *Latin.*
ex ma•le•fi•ci•o
Latin.
ex me•ro mo•tu
Latin.
ex mo•re *Latin.*
ex ne•ces•si•ta•te
Latin.
ex of•fi•ci•o *Latin.*
ex par•te *Latin.*
ex post fac•to *Latin.*
ex post facto law
ex pro•pri•o mo•tu
Latin.
ex proprio vi•go•re
Latin.
ex qua•si con•trac•tu
Latin.

ex rel. (ex relatione; for the use of; on behalf of; on the relation of)

ex re•la•ti•o•ne *Latin. (citation form:* **ex rel.**)

ex rights

ex vo•lun•ta•te *Latin*

ex vo•to *Latin.*

ex•ac•er•bate *v.,* ex•ac•er•bat•ed, ex•ac•er•bat•ing

ex•ac•er•bat•ing•ly

ex•ac•er•ba•tion

ex•act

ex•act•a•ble

ex•act•ing

ex•act•ing•ly

ex•act•ing•ness

ex•ac•tion

ex•act•i•tude

ex•act•ly

ex•act•ness

ex•ac•tor *or* ex•act•er

ex-ad•dict

ex•ag•ger•ate *v.,* ex•ag•ger•at•ed, ex•ag•ger•at•ing

ex•ag•ger•at•ed

ex•ag•ger•at•ed•ly

ex•ag•ger•at•ing•ly

ex•ag•ger•a•tion

ex•ag•ger•a•tive

ex•ag•ger•a•tive•ly

ex•ag•ger•a•tor

ex•am•in•a•ble

ex•am•i•na•tion

examination be•fore trial (EBT)

examination in aid of ex•e•cu•tion

examination in chief

ex•am•ine *v.,* ex•am•ined, ex•am•in•ing

examined cop•y

ex•am•oi•nee

ex•am•in•er *(citation form:* **Exam'r**)

ex•am•ple

Exam'r (Examiner)

ex•as•per•ate *v.,* ex•as•per•at•ed, ex•as•per•at•ing

ex•as•per•at•ed•ly

ex•as•per•at•ing•ly

ex•as•per•a•tion

ex•ca•vate *v.,* ex•ca•vat•ed, ex•ca•vat•ing

ex•ca•va•tion

ex•ceed (to surpass: cf. ACCEDE)

ex•ceed•ing•ly

ex•cel

ex•cel•lence

ex•cel•len•cy *n., pl.* ex•cel•len•cies

ex•cel•lent

ex•cel•lent•ly

ex•cept (to exclude; to object: cf. ACCEPT)

ex•cept•a•ble

ex•cept•ing

ex•cep•ti•o *n., pl.* ex•cep•ti•o•nes *Latin.*

ex•cep•tion

ex•cep•tion•a•ble

ex•cep•tion•a•ble•ness

ex•cep•tion•a•bly

ex•cep•tion•al

ex•cep•tion•al•i•ty

ex•cep•tion•al•ly

ex•cep•tion•al•ness

ex•cep•tion•less

ex•cerpt

ex•cess (surplus: cf. ACCESS)

excess con•tri•bu•tion

excess dis•tri•bu•tion

excess in•sur•ance

excess of ju•ris•dic•tion

excess prof•its tax

ex•ces•sive

excessive bail

excessive fine

excessive force

excessive ver•dict

ex•ces•sive•ly

ex•ces•sive•ness

Exch. (Exchange)

ex•change *(citation form:* **Exch.**)

exchange con•trols

exchange gain

exchange loss

exchange rate

ex•change•a•bil•i•ty

ex•change•a•ble

ex•change•a•bly

ex•chang•ee

ex•chang•er

ex•cheq•uer *(citation form:* **Ex.**)

ex•cis•a•ble

ex•cise *n., v.,* ex•cised, ex•cis•ing

excise tax

ex•ci•sion

ex•cit•a•bil•i•ty

ex•cit•a•ble

ex•cit•a•bly

ex•ci•ta•tion

ex•cit•a•tive

ex•cite *v.,* ex•cit•ed, ex•cit•ing

ex•cit•ed

excited ut•ter•ance

ex•cit•ed•ly

ex•cite•ment
ex•claim
ex•cla•ma•tion
ex•clam•a•to•ri•ly
ex•clam•a•to•ry
ex•clud•a•bil•i•ty
ex•clud•a•ble
excludable al•ien
ex•clude *v.*, ex•
clud•ed, ex•clud•
ing
ex•clu•sion
exclusion clause
ex•clu•sion•ar•y
exclusionary rule
exclusionary zon•ing
ex•clu•sion•ism
ex•clu•sive
exclusive a•gen•cy
exclusive bar•gain•
ing a•gent
exclusive con•tract
exclusive deal•ing
exclusive ju•ris•dic•
tion
exclusive li•cense
exclusive list•ing
exclusive pos•ses•
sion
exclusive rep•re•sen•
ta•tion
exclusive right
exclusive zon•ing
ex•clu•sive•ly
ex•clu•sive•ness
ex•clu•siv•ism
ex•clu•so•ry
ex•com•mu•ni•cate
v., ex•com•mu•ni•
cat•ed, ex•com•
mu•ni•cat•ing, *n.*,
adj.
ex•com•mu•ni•ca•
tion
ex•cru•ci•ate *v.*, ex•

cru•ci•at•ed, ex•
cru•ci•at•ing
ex•cru•ci•at•ing
ex•cru•ci•at•ing•ly
ex•cru•ci•a•tion
ex•cul•pa•ble
ex•cul•pate *v.*, ex•
cul•pat•ed, ex•cul•
pat•ing
ex•cul•pa•tion
exculpation clause
ex•cul•pa•to•ry
exculpatory no
exculpatory state•
ment
ex•cur•sive
ex•cur•sive•ly
ex•cur•sive•ness
ex•cur•sus
ex•cus•a•ble
excusable hom•i•cide
excusable ne•glect
ex•cus•a•ble•ness
ex•cus•a•bly
ex•cus•a•to•ry
ex•cuse *v.*, ex•cused,
ex•cus•ing, *n.*
ex•cuse•less
ex•cus•er
ex•cuss
ex•cus•sion
Exec. (Executive)
ex•e•cra•ble
ex•e•cra•ble•ness
ex•e•cra•bly
ex•e•crate *v.*, ex•e•
crat•ed, ex•e•crat•
ing
ex•e•cra•tion
ex•e•cra•tive
ex•e•cra•tor
ex•e•cra•to•ry
ex•e•cut•a•ble
ex•e•cute *v.*, ex•e•
cut•ed, ex•e•cut•
ing

ex•e•cut•ed
executed con•sid•
er•a•tion
executed con•tract
executed trust
ex•e•cu•tion
execution sale
ex•e•cu•tion•er
ex•ec•u•tive (*citation
form:* **Exec.**)
executive a•gen•cy
executive a•gree•
ment
executive clem•en•cy
executive com•mit•
tee
executive con•trol
executive of•fi•cer
executive or•der
executive priv•i•lege
executive proc•la•
ma•tion
executive sec•re•
tar•y
executive ses•sion
ex•ec•u•tor[1] (one
who administers an
estate under a will; *ci-
tation form:* **Ex'r**)
ex•e•cu•tor[2] or
ex•e•cut•er (one
who carries out, per-
forms, or puts into ef-
fect generally)
ex•ec•u•to•ri•al
ex•ec•u•tor•ship
ex•ec•u•to•ry
executory ac•cord
executory con•tract
executory in•ter•est
executory trust
ex•ec•u•trix *n.*, *pl.*
ex•ec•u•tri•ces
or ex•ec•u•trix•es (*ci-
tation form:* **Ex'x**)

ex•e•ge•sis *n.*, *pl.*
  ex•e•ge•ses
ex•em•plar
ex•em•pla•ri•ly
ex•em•pla•ri•ness
ex•em•pla•ry
exemplary dam•
  ag•es
ex•em•pli gra•ti•a
  (e.g.) *Latin.*
ex•em•pli•fi•a•ble
ex•em•pli•fi•ca•tion
ex•em•pli•fied cop•y
ex•em•pli•fi•er
ex•em•pli•fy *v.*, ex•
  em•pli•fied, ex•
  em•pli•fy•ing
ex•empt
exempt car•ri•er
exempt in•come
exempt or•gan•i•za•
  tion
exempt per•son•nel
exempt prop•er•ty
exempt se•cu•ri•ty
exempt trans•ac•tion
ex•emp•ti•ble
ex•emp•tion
ex•o•e•qua•tur *Latin.*
ex•er•cis•a•ble
ex•er•cise *n.*, *v.*, ex•
  er•cised, ex•er•cis•
  ing
exercise price
ex•ert
ex•e•rtion
Exh. (Exhibit)
ex•haust
ex•haust•i•bil•i•ty
ex•haust•i•ble
ex•haust•ing
ex•haust•ing•ly
ex•haus•tion
exhaustion of ad•
  min•i•stra•tive
  rem•e•dies

exhaustion of in•ter•
  nal un•ion remedies
exhaustion of reme-
  dies
exhaustion of state
  remedies
exhaustion of tri•bal
  remedies
ex•hib•it (*citation
  form:* Exh. *or* Ex.)
ex•hib•it•a•ble
ex•hi•bi•tion
ex•hi•bi•tion•ism
ex•hi•bi•tion•ist
ex•hib•i•to•ry
ex•hil•o•a•rate *v.*, ex•
  hil•o•a•rat•ed, ex•
  hil•o•a•rat•ing
ex•hil•o•a•rat•ing•ly
ex•hil•o•a•ra•tion
ex•hort
ex•hor•ta•tion
ex•hort•a•tive
ex•hort•a•tive•ly
ex•hort•er
ex•hu•ma•tion
ex•hume
ex-hus•band
ex•i•gence
ex•i•gen•cy *n.*, *pl.*
  ex•i•gen•cies
ex•i•gent
exigent cir•cum•
  stanc•es
ex•i•gent•ly
ex•i•gi fa•ci•as *Latin.*
ex•i•gi•ble
ex•il•a•ble
ex•ile *n.*, *v.*, ex•iled,
  ex•il•ing
ex•il•er
ex•ist•ence
ex•ist•ent
ex•ist•ing
ex•it

exit in•ter•view
exit strat•e•gy
exit wound
ex•og•e•nous
exogenous drug
ex•og•e•nous•ly
ex•on•er•ate *v.*, ex•
  on•er•at•ed, ex•
  on•er•at•ing
ex•on•er•a•tion
exoneration clause
ex•on•er•a•tive
ex•on•er•a•tor
ex•or•bi•tance
ex•or•bi•tan•cy
ex•or•bi•tant
exorbitant ju•ris•dic•
  tion
ex•or•bi•tant•ly
ex•ot•ic
ex•pand
ex•pand•a•bil•i•ty
ex•pand•a•ble
ex•pan•si•bil•i•ty
ex•pan•si•ble
ex•pan•sion
ex•pan•sion•ar•y
ex•pan•sion•ism
ex•pan•sion•ist
ex•pan•sion•is•tic
ex•pan•sive
ex•pa•tri•ate *v.*, ex•
  pa•tri•at•ed, ex•
  pa•tri•at•ing, *adj.*,
  n.
ex•pa•tri•a•tion
ex•pect
ex•pect•a•ble
expectable loss
ex•pect•a•bly
ex•pect•an•cy
ex•pect•ant
expectant es•tate
expectant heir
expectant right
ex•pect•ant•ly

ex•pec•ta•tion
expectation dam•
 ag•es
expectation of pri•
 va•cy
ex•pect•ed
expected re•turn
expected yield
ex•pect•ed•ly
ex•pect•ed•ness
ex•pe•di•ent
ex•pe•di•ent•ly
ex•pe•dite v., ex•pe•
 dit•ed, ex•pe•dit•
 ing
ex•pe•dit•ed
ex•pe•dit•er
ex•pe•di•tion
ex•pe•di•tious
ex•pe•di•tious•ly
ex•pe•di•tious•ness
ex•pel v., ex•pelled,
 ex•pel•ling
ex•pel•la•ble
ex•pelled
ex•pel•lee
ex•pend
ex•pend•a•bil•i•ty
ex•pend•a•ble
ex•pend•i•ture
ex•pen•sa•ble or ex•
 pen•si•ble
ex•pense n., v., ex•
 pensed, ex•pens•ing
expense ac•count
ex•pen•sive
ex•pen•sive•ly
ex•pen•sive•ness
ex•pe•ri•ence n., v.,
 ex•pe•ri•enced, ex•
 pe•ri•enc•ing
experience rat•ing
experience ta•ble
ex•pe•ri•enced
ex•pe•ri•en•tial
ex•pe•ri•en•tial•ly

ex•per•i•ment
ex•per•i•men•tal
ex•per•i•men•tal•ist
ex•per•i•men•tal•ly
ex•per•i•men•ta•
 tion
ex•per•i•ment•er
ex•pert
expert o•pin•ion
expert tes•ti•mo•ny
expert wit•ness
ex•per•tise
ex•pert•ly
ex•pert•ness
ex•pi•a•ble
ex•pi•ate v., ex•pi•
 at•ed, ex•pi•at•ing
ex•pi•a•tion
ex•pi•a•to•ry
ex•pi•ra•tion
expiration date
ex•pire v., ex•pired,
 ex•pir•ing
ex•plain
ex•plain•a•ble
ex•plain•er
ex•pla•na•tion
ex•pla•na•tor
ex•plan•a•to•ri•ly
ex•plan•a•to•ry
ex•ple•tive
ex•pli•ca•ble
ex•pli•cate v., ex•
 pli•cat•ed, ex•pli•
 cat•ing
ex•pli•ca•tion
ex•pli•ca•tive
ex•pli•ca•tive•ly
ex•pli•ca•tor
ex•pli•ca•to•ry
ex•plic•it
ex•plic•it•ly
ex•plic•it•ness
ex•plode v., ex•
 plod•ed, ex•plod•
 ing

ex•ploit
ex•ploit•a•bil•i•ty
ex•ploit•a•ble
ex•ploi•ta•tion
ex•ploi•ta•tive
ex•ploit•er
ex•ploi•tive
ex•ploi•tive•ly
ex•plor•a•bil•i•ty
ex•plor•a•ble
ex•plo•ra•tion
exploration costs
ex•plor•a•tive
ex•plor•a•tive•ly
ex•plor•a•to•ry
ex•plore v., ex•
 plored, ex•plor•ing
ex•plor•er
ex•plor•ing•ly
ex•plo•sion
ex•plo•sive
ex•plo•sive•ly
ex•plo•sive•ness
ex•po•nent
ex•po•nen•tial
ex•po•nen•tial•ly
ex•port
ex•port•a•bil•i•ty
ex•port•a•ble
ex•por•ta•tion
ex•port•er
ex•pos•a•bil•i•ty
ex•pos•a•ble
ex•posed
ex•pos•ed•ness
ex•pos•er
ex•po•si•tion
ex•po•si•tion•al
ex•pos•i•tor
ex•pos•i•to•ry
ex•pos•tu•late v.,
 ex•pos•tu•lat•ed,
 ex•pos•tu•lat•ing
ex•pos•tu•lat•ing•ly
ex•pos•tu•la•tion

ex•pos•tu•la•tor
ex•pos•tu•la•to°ry
ex•po°sure
ex•pound
ex•pound°er
ex-pres°i•dent
ex•press
express ad•vo•ca°cy
express as•sump•sit
express au•thor°i•ty
express con•di•tion
express con•tract
express mal•ice
express per•mis•sion
express re•peal
express trust
express waiv°er
express war•ran°ty
ex•press°i•ble
ex•pres•sion
ex•pres•sion•less
ex•pres•sion•less•
ness
ex•pres•sive lan•
guage dis•or•der
ex•pres•siv°i°ty
ex•press°ly
ex•pro•pri•a•ble
ex•pro•pri•ate v.,
ex•pro•pri•at°ed,
ex•pro•pri•at•ing
ex•pro•pri•a•tion
ex•pro•pri•a•tion•ist
ex•pro•pri•a•tor
ex•pul•sion
ex•pul•sive
ex•punge v., ex•
punged, ex•pung•
ing
ex•punge•ment
ex•pur•gate v., ex•
pur•gat°ed, ex•
pur•gat•ing
ex•pur•gat°ed
ex•pur•ga•tion
ex•pur•ga•tor

ex•pur•ga•to•ri•al
ex•pur•ga•to°ry
ex•quis•ite
Ex'r (Executor)
ex•tant (existing: cf.
EXTENT)
ex•tem•po•ra•ne•
i°ty
ex•tem•po•ra•ne•
ous
ex•tem•po•ra•ne•
ous°ly
ex•tem•po•ra•ne•
ous•ness
ex•tem•po°re
ex•tem•po•ri•za•
tion
ex•tem•po•rize v.,
ex•tem•po•rized,
ex•tem•po•riz•ing
ex•tend
ex•tend°ed
extended care fa•
cil°i•ty
extended cov•er•age
extended term in•
sur•ance
ex•tend•ed°ly
ex•tend•ed•ness
ex•tend•i•bil°i•ty
ex•tend•i•ble
ex•ten•si•bil°i•ty
ex•ten•si•ble
ex•ten•sion
extension of time
ex•ten•sive
ex•ten•sive°ly
ex•ten•sive•ness
ex•tent (scope; a writ
of execution upon a
debt: cf. EXTANT)
extent in aid
extent in chief
ex•ten•u•ate v., ex•
ten•u•at°ed, ex•
ten•u•at•ing

ex•ten•u•at•ing
extenuating cir•cum•
stanc°es
ex•ten•u•a•tion
ex•ten•u•a•to°ry
ex•ter•mi•nate v.,
ex•ter•mi•nat°ed,
ex•ter•mi•nat•ing
ex•ter•mi•na•tion
ex•ter•mi•na•to°ry
ex•ter•nal
external au•di•tor
external re•port•ing
ex•ter•nal•ism
ex•ter•nal°ly
ex•ter•ri•to•ri•
al°i•ty
ex•tinct
ex•tinc•tion
ex•tin•guish
ex•tin•guish•a•ble
ex•tin•guish°er
ex•tin•guish•ment
ex•tir•pate v., ex•tir•
pat°ed, ex•tir•pat•
ing
ex•tir•pa•tion
ex•tir•pa•tive
ex•tir•pa•tor
ex•tol v., ex•tolled,
ex•tol•ling
ex•tor•sive
ex•tor•sive°ly
ex•tort
ex•tort°er
ex•tor•tion
ex•tor•tion•ar°y
ex•tor•tion•ate
ex•tor•tion•ate°ly
ex•tor•tion•ist
ex•tor•tive
ex°tra
extra-ex•pense in•
sur•ance
extra work
ex•tra-budg•et•ar°y

ex•tract
ex•tract•a•bil•i•ty
ex•tract•a•ble
ex•trac•tion
ex•trac•tive
extractive ac•tiv•i•
ties
ex•tra•dit•a•ble
ex•tra•dite v., ex•
tra•dit•ed, ex•tra•
dit•ing
ex•tra•di•tion
ex•tra•do•tal
extradotal prop•er•ty
ex•tra•ju•di•cial
extrajudicial state•
ment
ex•tra•ju•di•cial•ly
ex•tra•lat•er•al
extralateral rights
ex•tra•le•gal
ex•tra•le•gal•ly
ex•tra•mar•i•tal
ex•tra•ne•ous
ex•tra•ne•ous•ly
ex•tra•ne•ous•ness
ex•traor•di•nar•i•ly
ex•traor•di•nar•i•
ness
ex•traor•di•nar•y
extraordinary care

extraordinary div•i•
dend
extraordinary ex•
pense
extraordinary i•tem
extraordinary re•lief
extraordinary
rem•e•dy
extraordinary ses•
sion
extraordinary writ
ex•trap•o•late v.,
ex•trap•o•lat•ed,
ex•trap•o•lat•ing
ex•trap•o•la•tion
ex•trap•o•la•tive
ex•tra•ter•ri•to•ri•al
extraterritorial ju•ris•
dic•tion
ex•tra•ter•ri•to•ri•
al•i•ty
ex•tra•ter•ri•to•ri•
al•ly
ex•trav•a•gance
ex•trav•a•gan•cy
ex•trav•a•gant
ex•trav•a•gant•ly
ex•treme
ex•treme•ly
ex•tre•mis Latin.
ex•trem•ism

ex•trem•ist
ex•trem•i•ty n., pl.
ex•trem•i•ties
ex•tri•ca•ble
ex•tri•cate v., ex•tri•
cat•ed, ex•tri•cat•
ing
ex•tri•ca•tion
ex•trin•sic
extrinsic am•bi•gu•
i•ty
extrinsic ev•i•dence
extrinsic fraud
ex•trin•si•cal•ly
ex•u•ber•ant
ex•ude v., ex•ud•ed,
ex•ud•ing
ex•ult
ex•ult•ant
ex•ul•ta•tion
ex•urb
ex•ur•ban
ex•ur•ban•ite
ex•ur•bi•a
ex-wife
Ex'x (Executrix)
eye•ful n., pl. eye•
fuls
eyes-on•ly
eye•wit•ness
eyre

F

F. (Federal; Federal Re•
porter; Forum)
F. Supp. (Federal Sup•
plement)
fab•ri•cate v., fab•ri•
cat•ed, fab•ri•cat•
ing
fab•ri•cat•ed ev•i•
dence
fab•ri•ca•tion
fab•ri•ca•tor

Fac. (Faculty)
face n., v., faced, fac•
ing
face a•mount
face-sav•er
face-sav•ing
face to face adv.
face-to-face adj.
face val•ue
face•less
face•less•ness

fac•et
fac•et•ed
fa•ce•tious
fa•ce•tious•ly
fa•ce•tious•ness
fa•cial
fa•cial•ly
fac•ile
fac•ile•ly
fac•ile•ness
fa•cil•i•tate v., fa•

cil•i•tat•ed, fa•
cil•i•tat•ing
fa•cil•i•ta•tion
fa•cil•i•ta•tive
fa•cil•i•ta•tor
fa•cil•i•ty n., pl. fa•
cil•i•ties
fac•sim•i•le
facsimile sig•na•ture
fact
fact wit•ness
fac•ta See FACTUM.
fact•find•er
fact•find•ing
fac•tion
fac•tion◦al
fac•tious (contentious:
cf. FACTITIOUS)
fac•tious•ly
fac•tious•ness
fac•ti•tious (artificial;
contrived: cf. FACTIOUS;
FICTITIOUS)
factitious dis•or•der
factitious disorder by
prox•y
fac•ti•tious•ly
fac•ti•tious•ness
fac•tor
fac•tor•age
fac•tor•ing
fac•tor•i•za•tion
fac•tor•ize v., fac•
tor•ized, fac•tor•iz•
ing
fac•tor's lien
fac•to•ry n., pl. fac•
to•ries
fac•to•tum n., pl.
fac•to•tums
fac•tu◦al
factual is◦sue
fac•tu•al•i◦ty
fac•tu•al◦ly
fac•tu•al•ness

fac•tum n., pl. fac◦ta
Latin.
factum pro•ban•dum
Latin.
factum pro•bans
Latin.
fac•ul◦ty n., pl. fac•
ul•ties (citation form:
Fac.)
fail
fail•ing
failing cir•cum•
stanc◦es
failing com•pa◦ny
de•fense
fail•ure
failure of con•sid•
er◦a•tion
failure of is◦sue
failure of proof
failure to bar•gain
col•lec•tive•ly
failure to make de•
liv•er◦y
failure to pros◦e•cute
failure to state a
claim for re•lief
failure to state cause
of ac•tion
faint (collusive or de-
ceitful; weak; to
swoon; a swoon: cf.
FEINT)
faint ac•tion
faint plead•ing or
faint plead◦er
fair (unbiased; moder-
ately good; an exhibi-
tion: cf. FARE)
fair and im•pa•rtial
ju◦ry
fair com•ment
fair em•ploy•ment
fair employment
prac•tice laws
fair hear•ing
fair hous•ing

fair mar•ket price
fair market va◦lue
fair pre•pon•der•
ance of the ev◦i•
dence
fair re•port priv◦i•
lege
fair re•turn
fair sale
fair trade n.
fair-trade adj.
fair trial
fair use
fair◦ly
fair•ness
fairness doc•trine
fait ac•com•pli n., pl.
faits ac•com•plis
French.
faith
faith•ful
faith•ful◦ly
faith•ful•ness
faith•less
faith•less◦ly
fake v., faked, fak•
ing, n., adj.
fak◦er
fak•er◦y n., pl. fak•
er•ies
fall v., fell, fall◦en,
fall•ing, n.
fal•la•cious
fal•la•cious◦ly
fal•la•cious•ness
fal•la◦cy n., pl. fal•
la•cies
fal•li•ble
fal•ling-out n., pl. fal•
lings-out
fall•out
false
false ad•ver•tis•ing
false and fraud◦u•
lent

false and mis•lead•ing

false an•swer

false ar•rest

false col•ors

false con•flict

false ex•cul•pa•to•ry state•ment

false im•per•son•a•tion

false im•pli•ca•tion

false im•pris•on•ment

false in•stru•ment

false light

false mem•o•ry

false memory syn•drome (FMS)

false neg•a•tive

false pos•i•tive

false pre•tens•es

false rep•re•sen•ta•tion

false state•ment

false swear•ing

false ver•dict

false•hood

false•ly

false•ness

fal•si cri•men *Latin.*

fal•si•fi•a•bil•i•ty

fal•si•fi•a•ble

fal•si•fi•ca•tion

fal•si•fi•er

fal•si•fy *v.,* fal•si•fied, fal•si•fy•ing

fal•si•ty *n., pl.* fal•si•ties

fal•sum *n., pl.* fal•sa *Latin.*

fal•sus *Latin.*

fal•ter

fal•ter•er

fal•ter•ing•ly

Fam. (Family)

Fam. Ct. (Family Court)

fame

famed

fa•mil•ial

familial pat•tern

fa•mil•iar

fa•mil•iar•i•za•tion

fa•mil•iar•ize *v.,* fa•mil•iar•ized, fa•mil•iar•iz•ing

fa•mil•iar•ly

fa•mil•iar•ness

fam•i•ly *n., pl.* fam•i•lies (*citation form:* Fam.)

family busi•ness

family car doc•trine

Family Court (*citation form:* Fam. Ct.)

family es•tate trust

family law

family leave

family plan•ning

family pur•pose doc•trine

family ther•a•py

fa•mous

fa•mous•ly

fa•mous•ness

fa•nat•ic

fa•nat•i•cal

fa•nat•i•cal•ly

fa•nat•i•cism

fan•ci•ful

fan•ci•ful•ly

fan•ci•ful•ness

fan•fare

fan•ta•size *v.,* fan•ta•sized, fan•ta•siz•ing

fan•ta•siz•er

fan•tas•tic

fan•tas•ti•cal

fan•tas•ti•cal•i•ty

fan•tas•ti•cal•ly

fan•tas•ti•cal•ness

fan•ta•sy *n., pl.* fan•ta•sies, *v.,* fan•ta•sied, fan•ta•sy•ing.

fa•qih *n., pl.* fa•qihs or fu•qa•ha'

far *adj.,* far•ther or fur•ther, far•thest or fur•thest

far-fetched

far-fetched•ness

far-flung

farce

far•ci•cal

far•ci•cal•i•ty

far•ci•cal•ly

far•ci•cal•ness

fare *n., v.,* fared, far•ing (fee for transportation; to get on or turn out: cf. FAIR)

farm•work•er

F.A.S. (free alongside; free alongside ship)

fas•ci•nate *v.,* fas•ci•nat•ed, fas•ci•nat•ing

fas•ci•nat•ed•ly

fas•ci•nat•ing

fas•ci•nat•ing•ly

fas•ci•na•tion

fas•cism

fas•cist

fas•cis•tic

fas•cis•ti•cal•ly

fast

fast-mov•ing

fast track *n.*

fast-track or fast track *adj.*

fast-track ap•prov•al

fast-track leg•is•la•tion

fast-track ne•go•ti•a•ting au•thor•i•ty

fas•tid•i•ous

fas•tid•i•ous•ly

fas•tid•i•ous•ness

fa•tal

fatal er•ror

fatal var•i•ance

fa•tal•ist

fa•tal•is•tic

fa•tal•is•ti•cal•ly

fa•tal•i•ty *n., pl.* fa•
tal•i•ties

fa•tal•ly

fa•tal•ness

fate *n., v.,* fat•ed,
fat•ing

fate•ful

fate•ful•ly

fate•ful•ness

fa•ther

father-in-law *n., pl.*
fa•thers-in-law

fa•ther•hood

fa•ther•less

fa•ther•ly

fath•om

fath•om•a•ble

fa•tigue *n., adj., v.,*
fa•tigued, fa•ti•
guing

fa•tigued

fa•ti•guing•ly

fat•u•ous

fat•u•ous•ly

fat•u•ous•ness

fat•wa

fault

fault•find•er

fault•find•ing

fault•i•ly

fault•i•ness

fault•less

fault•less•ly

fault•less•ness

fault•y *adj.,*
fault•i•er, fault•i•
est

faux *French and Law
French.*

faux pas *n., pl.* faux
pas *French.*

fa•vor

fa•vor•a•ble

fa•vor•a•ble•ness

fa•vor•a•bly

fa•vored

fa•vor•er

fa•vor•ite

fa•vor•it•ism

faze *v.,* fazed, faz•ing
(to disconcert: cf.
PHASE)

f/b/o (for the benefit
of)

FCN trea•ties (friendship, commerce, and
navigation treaties)

fe•al•ty *n., pl.* fe•al•
ties

fear

fear•ful

fear•ful•ly

fear•ful•ness

fear•less

fear•less•ly

fear•less•ness

fear•some

fear•some•ly

fear•some•ness

fea•sance

fea•sant

fea•si•bil•i•ty

feasibility stud•y

fea•si•ble

fea•si•bly

fea•sor

feat

feath•er•bed *v.,*
feath•er•bed•ded,
feath•er•bed•ding

fea•ture *n., v.,* fea•
tured, fea•tur•ing

fea•tured

Feb. (February)

Feb•ru•ar•y (*citation
form:* **Feb.**)

feck•less

feck•less•ly

feck•less•ness

Fed. (Federal)

Fed. Cir. (Federal Circuit; United States
Court of Appeals for
the Federal Circuit)

Fed. Cl. (United States
Court of Federal
Claims)

Fed. R. App. P. (Fed-
eral Rules of Appellate
Procedure)

Fed. R. Civ. P. (Federal
Rules of Civil Proce-
dure)

Fed. R. Crim. P. (Federal Rules of Criminal
Procedure)

Fed. R. Evid. (Federal
Rules of Evidence)

Fed. Reg. (Federal Register)

fed•er•al (*citation
form:* **Fed.** or **F.**)

federal case

Federal Cir•cuit (*citation form:* **Fed. Cir.**)

federal com•mon law

federal court

federal crime

federal gov•ern•
ment

federal in•stru•men•
tal•i•ty

**Federal In•sur•ance
Con•tri•bu•tions
Act (FICA)**

federal ju•ris•dic•
tion

federal of•fense

federal ques•tion

federal question ju•
ris•dic•tion

Federal Reg•is•ter (*citation form:* **Fed. Reg.**)
federal reg•u•la•tion
Federal Re•port•er (*citation form:* **F.**)
Federal Re•serve bank
Federal Reserve note
Federal Rules of Ap•pel•late Pro•ce•dure (*citation form:* **Fed. R. App. P.**)
Federal Rules of Civ•il Pro•ce•dure (*citation form:* **Fed. R. Civ. P.**)
Federal Rules of Crim•i•nal Pro•ce•dure (*citation form:* **Fed. R. Crim. P.**)
Federal Rules of Ev•i•dence (*citation form:* **Fed. R. Evid.**)
Federal Sup•ple•ment (*citation form:* **F. Supp.**)
fed•er•al•ism
fed•er•al•ist
fed•er•al•i•za•tion
fed•er•al•ize *v.,* fed•er•al•ized, fed•er•al•iz•ing
fed•er•al•ly
fed•er•ate *v.,* fed•er•at•ed, fed•er•at•ing
fed•er•a•tion (*citation form:* **Fed'n**)
fed•er•a•tive
fed•er•a•tive•ly
fed•er•a•tor
Fed'n (Federation)
fee
fee ar•bi•tra•tion
fee ex•pect•ant
fee farm
fee-for-serv•ice *adj.*

fee sim•ple
fee simple ab•so•lute
fee simple con•di•tion•al
fee simple de•fea•si•ble
fee simple de•ter•min•a•ble
fee split•ting *n.*
fee-splitting *adj.*
fee tail
fee tail fe•male
fee tail male
feed•back
feel *v.,* felt, feel•ing
feel•er
feel•ing
feel•ing•ly
feign
feigned
feign•er
feign•ing•ly
feint (a deception; to make a deceptive move: cf. FAINT)
feist•i•ly
feist•i•ness
feist•y *adj.,* feist•i•er, feist•i•est
fe•lic•i•ta•tion
fe•lic•i•tous
fe•lic•i•tous•ly
fe•lic•i•tous•ness
fel•la•ti•o
fel•la•tion
fel•low
fellow serv•ant
fellow-servant rule
fel•on
fe•lo•ni•ous
felonious as•sault
felonious en•try
felonious hom•i•cide
felonious in•tent
felonious tak•ing
fe•lo•ni•ous•ly

fe•lo•ni•ous•ness
fel•on•ry
fel○○ony *n., pl.* fel○○•nies
felony mur•der
fe•male gen•i•tal mu•ti•la•tion
feme *Law French.*
feme co•vert *Law French.*
feme sole *Law French.*
feme sole trad•er
fem•i•cide
fem•i•nism
fem•i•nist
fen•cam•fam•in *Controlled Subst.*
fence *n., v.,* fenced, fenc•ing
fend•er bend•er or fen•der•bend•er
fen•er•a•tion (usury: cf. VENERATION)
fen•eth•yl•line *Controlled Subst.*
fen•flur•a•mine *Controlled Subst.*
fenfluramine-phen•ter•mine (fen-phen)
fen-phen (fenfluramine-phentermine)
fen•pro•po•rex *Controlled Subst.*
fen•tan•yl *Controlled Subst.*
feo•da•ry *n., pl.* feo•da•ries
feoff
feoff•ee
feoffee to us•es
feoff•ment
feoffment to us•es
feof•for
fe•rae na•tu•rae *Latin.*
fe•ral

Feres doc•trine
fer•ment (unrest; to
change to alcohol: cf.
FOMENT)
fer•men•ta•tion
fe•ro•cious
fe•ro•cious•ly
fe•ro•cious•ness
fe•roc•i•ty
fer•ret
fer•tile
fer•til•i•ty
fer•ti•liz•a•bil•i•ty
fer•ti•liz•a•ble
fer•ti•li•za•tion
fer•ti•lize v., fer•ti•
lized, fer•ti•liz•ing
fer•ti•liz•er
fer•ven•cy
fer•vent
fer•vent•ly
fer•vent•ness
fer•vor
fes•ter
fe•tal
fetal al•co•hol ef•
fect
fetal alcohol syn•
drome
fetal drug tox•ic•i•ty
fe•ti•cid•al
fe•ti•cide
fet•ish
fet•ish•ism
fet•ish•ist
fet•ish•is•tic
fet•ish•is•ti•cal•ly
fet•ish•ize v., fet•
ish•ized, fet•ish•iz•
ing
fe•tus n., pl. fe•
tus•es
feud
feu•dal
feudal court
feudal law

feudal sys•tem
feu•dal•ism
feu•dal•ist
feu•dal•is•tic
feu•dal•i•ty n., pl.
feu•dal•i•ties
feu•dal•i•za•tion
feu•dal•ize v., feu•
dal•ized, feu•dal•
iz•ing
feu•dal•ly
feu•da•to•ry n., pl.
feu•da•to•ries, adj.
feu•dum n., pl.
feu•da Latin.
fe•ver
fe•vered
fe•ver•ish
fe•ver•ish•ly
fe•ver•ish•ness
ff. (and those follow-
ing
fi. fa. (fieri facias)
fi•an•cé (engaged
man
fi•an•cée (engaged
woman)
fi•at
FICA (Federal Insurance
Contributions Act)
fic•tion
fic•tion•al
fic•tion•al•i•za•tion
fic•tion•al•ize v., fic•
tion•al•ized, fic•
tion•al•iz•ing
fic•tion•al•iz•er
fic•tion•al•ly
fic•ti•tious (imaginary;
cf. FACTITIOUS)
fictitious fare
fictitious name
fictitious pay•ee
fictitious per•son
fic•ti•tious•ly
fic•ti•tious•ness

fic•tive
fic•tive•ly
fi•de•i•com•mis•
sar•i•ly
fi•de•i•com•mis•
sar•y adj., n. pl. fi•
de•i•com•mis•sar•
ies
fi•de•i•com•mis•
sion
fi•de•i•com•mis•
sion•er
fi•de•i•com•mis•sor
fi•de•i•com•mis•
sum n., pl. fi•de•i•
com•mis•sa Latin.
fi•del•i•ty
fidelity bond
fidelity in•sur•ance
fi•des n.sing. Latin.
fi•du•ci•ar•i•ly
fi•du•ci•ar•y n., pl.
fi•du•ci•ar•ies, adj.
fiduciary bond
fiduciary du•ty
fiduciary re•la•tion•
ship
fief
field au•dit
field ware•hous•ing
fierce adj., fierc•er,
fierc•est
fierce•ly
fierce•ness
fi•e•ri fa•ci•as (fi.
fa.) Latin.
FIFO (first in, first out)
fig. (figure)
fight
fight•a•bil•i•ty
fight•a•ble
fight•er
fight•ing words
fig•ment
fig•ur•a•tive
fig•ur•a•tive•ly (in a

metaphorical or rhetor-ical sense: cf. LITER-ALLY)

fig•ur•a•tive•ness

fig•ure (citation form: fig.)

figure of speech

fikh See FIQH.

filch

filch•er

file n., v., filed, fil•ing

file un•der seal

file wrap•per

file wrapper es•top•pel

file•a•ble

fil•er

fil•i•al

fil•i•ate v., fil•i•at•ed, fil•i•at•ing

fil•i•a•tion

fil•i•bus•ter

fil•i•bus•ter•er

fil•i•cid•al

fil•i•cide

fil•ing fee

filing sta•tus

fil•i•ous nul•li•us Latin.

Fin. (Finance; Financial; Financing)

fin•a•ble

fi•nal

final ap•peal•a•ble or•der

final de•ci•sion

final de•cree

final de•ter•mi•na•tion

final dis•po•si•tion

final hear•ing

final judg•ment

final or•der

final read•ing

final set•tle•ment

fi•nal•i•ty n., pl. fi•nal•i•ties

fi•nal•i•za•tion

fi•nal•ize v., fi•nal•ized, fi•nal•iz•ing

fi•nal•iz•er

fi•nal•ly

fi•nance n., v., fi•nanced, fi•nanc•ing (citation form: Fin.)

finance charge

finance com•pa•ny

fi•nance•a•ble

fi•nanc•es n.pl.

fi•nan•cial (citation form: Fin.)

financial ac•count•ing

financial lease

financial plan•ning

financial re•spon•si•bil•i•ty

financial responsibility law

financial state•ment

fi•nan•cial•ly

fin•an•cier

fi•nanc•ing (citation form: Fin.)

financing lease

financing state•ment

find v., found, find•ing, n.

find•a•ble

find•er

finder of fact

finder of the facts

find•er's fee

find•ing

finding of fact n., pl. find•ings of fact

find•ings and con•clu•sions

findings of fact and conclusions of law

finds n.pl.

fine n., v., fined, fin•ing, adj., fin•er, fin•est, adv.

fine print

fin•esse n., v., fin•essed, fin•ess•ing

fin•ger•print

fin•ger•printing

fin•ick•y adj., fin•ick•i•er, fin•ick•i•est

fin•ish

fi•nite

fi•nite•ly

fi•nite•ness

F.I.O. (free in and out)

fiqh or fikh

fire n., v., fired, fir•ing

fire in•sur•ance

fire-re•sist•ant

fire-re•tard•ant

fire•arm

fire•proof

fire•trap

firm

firm-fixed-price con•tract

firm of•fer

firm or•der

firm•ly

firm•ness

first

first-de•gree mur•der

first-dol•lar cov•er•age

first im•pres•sion

first in, first out (FIFO)

first lien

first meet•ing of cred•i•tors

first mort•gage

first of•fend•er

first read•ing

first re•fu•sal

first-sale doc•trine
first•hand
firsthand knowl•edge
fisc
fis•cal (financial: cf. PHYSICAL)
fiscal a•gent
fiscal year (FY)
fis•cal•ly
fish•er•y n., pl. fish•er•ies
fish•i•ly
fish•i•ness
fish•ing ex•pe•di•tion
fish•y adj., fish•i•er, fish•i•est
fis•sile ma•te•ri•al
fis•sion
fis•sion•a•ble
fit adj., fit•ter, fit•test, v., fit•ted or fit, fit•ting, n.
fit•ness
fitness for par•tic•u•lar pur•pose
fit•ting
fit•ting•ly
fit•ting•ness
fix
fix•a•bil•i•ty
fix•a•tion
fixed
fixed as•set
fixed cap•i•tal
fixed charge
fixed cost
fixed ex•pense
fixed in•come n.
fixed-income adj.
fixed li•a•bil•i•ty
fixed o•ver•head
fixed-price con•tract
fixed-rate mort•gage
fix•ed•ly
fix•ed•ness

fix•er
fix•ture
flag n., v., flagged, flag•ging
flag of con•ven•ience
flag of truce
flag state
fla•grance
fla•gran•cy
fla•grant
fla•gran•te de•lic•to Latin.
fla•grant•ly
flail
flair (talent; style: cf. FLARE)
flam•boy•ance
flam•boy•an•cy
flam•boy•ant
flam•boy•ant•ly
flare (to flame; a torch: cf. FLAIR)
flash
flash•back
flash•er
flat rate
flat tax
flat•ter
flat•ter•y
flaunt (to display: cf. FLOUT)
flaunt•er
flaunt•ing•ly
flee v., fled, flee•ing
flee to the wall
fleece n., v., fleeced, fleec•ing
fleece•a•ble
fleec•er
flesh out (to add detail to: cf. FLUSH OUT)
flex•dol•lars
flex•i•bil•i•ty
flex•i•ble
flex•i•ble•ness
flex•i•bly

flex•time or flex•i•time
flight
flight of i•de•as
flight•y adj., flight•i•er, flight•i•est
flim•si•ly
flim•si•ness
flim•sy adj., flim•si•er, flim•si•est
flip v., flipped, flip•ping, n.
float
float•a•bil•i•ty
float•a•ble
float•ing ease•ment
floating in•ter•est rate
floating lien
floating pol•i•cy
floating rate note
floating stock
floating zone
flog v., flogged, flog•ging
flog•ger
flood
flood con•trol
flood in•sur•ance
flood•gate
flood•plain
floor
floor bro•ker
floor de•bate
floor plan•ning
floor trad•er
flo•tage
flo•ta•tion
flo•til•la
flotilla doc•trine
flotilla rule
flot•sam
floun•der (to struggle clumsily: cf. FOUNDER[2])
floun•der•ing•ly

flout (to ignore: cf. FLAUNT)

flow of com•merce

flow•chart

flow∘er bond

fluc•tu•ate v., **fluc•tu∘at•ed, fluc•tu•at•ing**

fluc•tu•a•tion

flu•di•az∘e∘pam Controlled Subst.

flu•ni•traz∘e∘pam Controlled Subst.

flun∘ky n., pl. **flun•kies**

fluor∘o∘car•bon

flu∘ox∘y∘mes•ter•one Controlled Subst.

flu•raz∘e∘pam Controlled Subst.

flur∘ry n., pl. **flur•ries**

flush

flush out (to force into the open: cf. FLESH OUT)

flush∘ly

flush•ness

flus•ter

fly v., **flew, flown, fly•ing**

FMS (false memory syndrome)

F.O.B. (free on board)

fo∘cus[1] n., pl. **fo•cus∘es** or (esp. in scientific contexts) **fo•ci**

focus[2] v., **fo•cused, fo•cus•ing**

fog rule

FOIA (Freedom of Information Act)

fol. (folio)

fo∘lie à deux n., pl. **fo∘lies à deux** French.

fo∘li∘o[1] n., pl.

fo∘li∘os, adj. (citation form: fol.)

folio[2] v., **fo•li∘oed, fo•li∘o•ing**

folk•right

fol•low

follow-on adj.

follow through v.

follow-through n

follow up v.

follow-up n., adj.

fol•low∘a•ble

fol•low∘er

fol•low•ing See also ET SEQ.; FF.

fo•ment (to instigate: cf. FERMENT)

fo•men•ta•tion

fon•dle v., **fon•dled, fon•dling**

fon•dler

fon•dling (caressing: cf. FOUNDLING)

fon•dling∘ly

fond∘ly

fond•ness

food stamps

fool

fool•er∘y n., pl **fool•er•ies**

fool•har∘dy

fool•ish

fool•ish∘ly

fool•ish•ness

fool•proof

fools•cap

foot•ing

foot•note For citation forms, see NOTE[1].

foot•print

for cause

for col•lec•tion

for de•pos∘it

for good cause shown

for hire

for-prof∘it adj.

for-profit cor•po•ra•tion

for the ben∘e∘fit of (f/b/o)

for the rec∘ord

for the use of (citation form: ex rel.)

for val∘ue re•ceived

for•as•much as

for∘ay

for•bear v., **for•bore, for•borne, for•bear•ing**

for•bear•ance

for•bear∘er

for•bear•ing

for•bear•ing∘ly

for•bid v., **for•bade, for•bid•den, for•bid•ding**

for•bid•dance

for•bid•den

for•bid•den•ness

for•bid•der

for•bid•ding (grim∙ intimidating; sinister: cf. FOREBODING)

for•bid•ding∘ly

for•bid•ding•ness

force n., v., **forced, forc•ing**

force and arms

force ma•jeure French.

force of law

force•a∘ble (capable of being forced; cf. FORCIBLE)

forced

forced heir

forced sale

forc•ed∘ly

forc•ed•ness

force•ful

force•ful∘ly

force•ful•ness

forc∘er

for•ci•ble (accom
plished through force:
cf. FORCEABLE)
forcible de•tain∘er
forcible en∘try
forcible entry and de•
tain∘er
forcible rape
forcible tres•pass
for•ci•ble•ness
for•ci•bly
fore•bear (ancestor: cf.
FORBEAR)
fore•bode v., fore•
bod∘ed, fore•bod•
ing
fore•bod•ing n., adj.
(a portent; a sense of
impending evil; tend
ing or seeming to pre-
dict or portend: cf.
FORBIDDING)
fore•bod•ing•ly
fore•bod•ing•ness
fore•cast v., fore•cast
or fore•cast∘ed,
fore•cast•ing
fore•cast•a∘ble
fore•cast∘er
fore•cast•ing
fore•clos•a∘ble
fore•close v., fore•
closed, fore•clos•ing
fore•clo•sure
foreclosure by ju•di•
cial sale
foreclosure by
pow∘er of sale
foreclosure sale
fore•fa•ther
fore∘go v., fore•
went, fore•gone,
fore•go∘ing (to pre-
cede: cf. FORGO)
fore•go∘er
fore•go•ing

for•eign
foreign at•tach•ment
foreign bill of ex•
change
foreign com•merce
foreign cor•po•ra•
tion
foreign di•vorce
foreign ex•change
foreign-exchange
con•tract
foreign-exchange rate
foreign ex•ec∘u•tor
foreign-flag ves•sel
foreign judg•ment
foreign law
foreign serv•ice
foreign si•tus trust
foreign sov•er•eign
im•mu•ni•ty
foreign tax cred∘it
foreign trade
foreign will
for•eign∘er
for•eign•ness
fore•judge[1] v., fore•
judged, fore•judg•
ing (to prejudice: cf.
FORJUDGE)
forejudge[2] See FOR-
JUDGE.
fore•judg∘er
fore•judg•ment
fore•know•ledge
fore•la∘dy n., pl.
fore•la•dies
fore•man n., pl. fore•
men
fore•man•ship
fore•most
fore•mo•ther
fo•ren•sic
forensic med∘i•cine
forensic psy•chi•
a∘try
forensic sci•ence

fo•ren•si•cal∘ly
fore•or•dain
fore•or•dain•ment
fore•per•son n., pl.
fore•per•sons
fore•run v., fore•ran,
fore•run, fore•run•
ning
fore•run•ner
fore•see v., fore•saw
fore•seen, fore•
see•ing
fore•see•a∘bil•i•ty
fore•see•a∘ble
foreseeable con•se•
quence
foreseeable in•ju•ry
fore•shad∘ow
fore•short∘en
fore•sight
fore•sight∘ed
fore•sight•ed∘ly
fore•sight•ed•ness
for•est
fore•stall
forestall the mar•ket
fore•stall∘er
fore•stall•ment
fore•sta•tion
for•est∘ed
for•est∘er
for•est•ory
fore•taste n., v., fore•
tast∘ed, fore•tast•
ing
fore•tell v., fore•told,
fore•tell•ing
fore•thought
fore•thought•ful
fore•thought•ful∘ly
fore•thought•ful•
ness
fore•to•ken
for•ev∘er
fore•warn
fore•warn∘er

fore•warn•ing∘ly
fore•wom∘an *n., pl.*
  fore•wom∘en
fore•word (introduc-
  tory statement: cf. FOR
  WARD)
for•feit
for•feit•a•bil∘i∘ty
for•feit•a∘ble
for•feit∘er
for•fei•ture
for•fend
forge *v.,* forged, forg•
  ing, *n.*
forge•a∘ble
forg∘er
for•ger∘y *n., pl.* for•
  ger•ies
for•get *v.,* for•got,
  for•got•ten or for•
  got, for•get•ting
for•get•ful
for•get•ful∘ly
for•get•ful•ness
for•get•ta•ble
for•get•ter
for•giv•a∘ble
for•give *v.,* for•gave,
  for•giv∘en, for•giv•
  ing
for•give•ness
for•giv∘er
for•giv•ing
for•giv•ing∘ly
for•giv•ing•ness
for∘go *v.,* for•went,
  for•gone, for•go•
  ing (to abstain from:
  cf. FOREGO)
for•judge or fore•
  judge *v.,* for•judged
  or fore•judged, for•
  judg•ing or fore•
  judg•ing (to expel or
  deprive by judgment:
  cf. FOREJUDGE[1])

for•judg•ment
fo•rlorn
for•lorn∘ly
for•lorn•ness
form
form of ac•tion
for∘ma pau•pe•ris
  Latin.
formal
for•malism
for•mal•ist
for•mal•is•tic
for•mal∘i•ti•cal∘ly
for•mal∘i∘ty *n., pl.*
  for•mal∘i•ties
for•mal∘i•za•tion
for•mal•ize *v.,* for•
  mal•ized, for•mal•
  iz•ing
for•mal∘ly (with for-
  mality: cf. FORMERLY)
for•mal•ness
for•ma•tion
for•ma•tion∘al
form∘a•tive
form∘a•tive∘ly
form∘a•tive•ness
for•meb∘u•lone *Con-
  trolled Subst.*
for•me•don
formedon in the des•
  cend∘er
formedon in the re•
  main•der
formedon in the re•
  vert∘er
for•mer[1] *adj.* (earlier)
form∘er[2] *n.* (a person
  or thing that forms)
for•mer jeop•ard∘y
for•mer∘ly (in the
  past: cf. FORMALLY)
for•mi•da•ble
for•mi•da•ble•ness
for•mi•da•bly
for•mu∘la *n., pl.* for•

mu•las or (esp. in sci
entific contexts) for•
mu•lae
for•mu•la•ble
for•mu•la∘ic
for•mu•la•i•cal∘ly
for•mu•lar∘y *n., pl.*
  for•mu•lar•ies, *adj.*
formulary sys•tem
for•mu•late *v.,* for•
  mu•lat∘ed, for•mu•
  lat•ing
for•mu•la•tion
for•mu•la•tor
for•ni•cate *v.,* for•
  ni•cat∘ed, for•ni•
  cat•ing
for•ni•ca•tion
for•ni•ca•tor
for•ni•ca•to∘ry
for•ni•ca•trix *n., pl.*
  for•ni•ca•tri•ces
for•sake *v.,* for•sook,
  for•sak∘en, for•
  sak•ing
for•sak∘en
for•sak•en∘ly
for•sak•en•ness
for•sak∘er
for•swear *v.,* for•
  swore, for•sworn,
  for•swear•ing
for•swear∘er
for•sworn
for•sworn•ness
Fort. (Fortnightly)
forte[1] *n.* (strong point;
  specialty: vs. *fort*)
for∘te[2] *adj., adv.* (loud)
forth (onward: vs.
  fourth)
forth•com•ing
forth•com•ing•ness
forth•right
forth•right∘ly
forth•right•ness

forth•with

for•ti•tude

for•ti•tu•di•nous

fort•night•ly (*citation form:* **Fort.**)

for•tu•i•tous (happening by chance: cf. FORTUNATE)

fortuitous col•li•sion

for•tu•i•tous•ly

for•tu•i•tous•ness

for•tu•i•ty n., pl for•tu•i•ties

for•tu•nate (lucky: cf. FORTUITOUS)

for•tune

fo•rum n., pl. fo•ra or fo•rums (*citation form:* **F.**)

forum con•trac•tus Latin.

forum do•mi•cil•i•i Latin.

forum non con•ve•ni•ens Latin.

forum pro•ro•ga•tum Latin.

forum re•i Latin.

forum rei ges•tae Latin.

forum rei si•tae Latin.

forum se•lec•tion clause

forum shop•ping

for•ward (ahead; in advance: cf. FOREWORD)

forward buy•ing

forward con•tract

forward de•liv•er•y

forward ex•change

forward quo•ta•tion

for•ward•a•ble

for•ward•er

for•warding a•gent

for•ward•ly

for•ward•ness

fos•ter

foster bro•ther

foster care

foster child

foster home

foster par•ent

foster sis•ter

fos•ter•er

fos•ter•ing•ly

foul

foul bill of lad•ing

foul•ly

foul-mouthed or foul-mouthed

foul•ness

found

Found. (Foundation)

foun•da•tion (*citation form:* **Found.**)

foun•da•tion•al

foun•da•tion•al•ly

found•er' n. (one who founds)

foun•der² v. (to sink or fail: cf. FLOUNDER)

found•ers' shares

found•ling (abandoned child: cf. FONDLING)

four cor•ners

four corners rule

four free•doms

four•square

frac•tion

frac•tion•al

fractional as•sign•ment

fractional share

frac•tion•al•i•za•tion

frac•tion•al•ize v., frac•tion•al•ized, frac•tion•al•iz•ing

frac•tion•al•ly

frac•tious

frac•tious•ly

frac•tious•ness

frac•tur•a•ble

frac•ture n., v., frac•tured, frac•tur•ing

frag•ile

fra•gil•i•ty

frag•ment

frag•men•tar•i•ly

frag•men•tar•i•ness

frag•men•tar•y

frag•men•tation

frag•ment•ed

fram•a•ble or frame•a•ble

frame v., framed, fram•ing, n.

frame of ref•er•ence n., pl. frames of ref•er•ence

frame-up

Fram•ers, the

frame•work

fran•chis•a•bil•i•ty

fran•chis•a•ble

fran•chise n., v., fran•chised, fran•chis•ing

franchise clause

franchise tax

fran•chi•see

fran•chise•ment

fran•chi•sor

frank adj., n., v.

frank al•moign Law French.

frank and free

frank chase

frank fee

frank ferme

frank law

frank mar•riage

frank pledge

frank ten•ant

frank ten•e•ment

frank ten•ure

frank•a•ble

franked mail

frank•fold

frank•ing priv•i•lege

frank•ly

frank•ness

fran•tic

fran•ti•cal•ly or fran•tic•ly

fran•tic•ness

fra•ter•nal

fraternal in•sur•ance

fraternal or•gan•i•za•tion

fraternal so•ci•e•ty

fra•ter•nal•ism

fra•ter•nal•ly

fra•ter•ni•ty n., pl. fra•ter•ni•ties

frat•er•ni•za•tion

frat•er•nize v., frat•er•nized, frat•er•niz•ing

frat•er•niz•er

frat•ri•cid•al

frat•ri•cide

fraud

fraud in fact

fraud in law

fraud in the ex•e•cu•tion

fraud in the fac•tum

fraud in the in•duce•ment

fraud on the court

fraud•u•lence

fraud•u•lent

fraudulent con•ceal•ment

fraudulent con•vey•ance

fraudulent in•duce•ment

fraudulent mis•rep•re•sen•ta•tion

fraudulent pro•cure•ment

fraudulent rep•re•sen•ta•tion

fraudulent sale

fraudulent trans•fer

fraud•u•lent•ly

free *adj.*, fre•er, fre•est, *v.*, freed, free•ing.

free a•gen•cy

free a•gent

free alms

free a•long•side (F.A.S.)

free alongside ship (F.A.S.)

free and clear

free and com•mon soc•age

free ex•er•cise of re•li•gion

free in and out (F.I.O.)

free on board (F.O.B.)

free press

free ride

free-rid•er

free-rid•ing

free soc•age

free speech

free ten•ure

free trade *n.*

free-trade *adj.*

free will

free•board

free•born

free•dom

freedom of as•sem•bly

freedom of as•so•ci•a•tion

freedom of con•tract

freedom of ex•pres•sion

Freedom of In•for•ma•tion Act (FOIA)

freedom of re•li•gion

freedom of speech

freedom of the press

freedom of the seas

freed•wom•an *n.*, pl. freed•wom•en

free•hold

freehold es•tate

free•hold•er

free•lance *n.*, *v.*, free•lanced, free•lanc•ing, *adj.*, *adv.*

free•lanc•er

free•man *n.*, pl. free•men

free•ness

fre•er

freez•a•bil•i•ty

freez•a•ble

freeze *v.*, froze, froz•en, freez•ing, *n.*

freeze out *v.*

freeze-out *adj.*, *n.*

freight

freight a•gent

freight for•ward•er

freight•age

freight•er

fre•net•ic

fre•net•i•cal•ly

fren•zied

fren•zi•ly

fren•zy *n.*, pl. fren•zies, *v.*, fren•zied, fren•zy•ing.

fre•quen•cy *n.*, pl. fre•quen•cies

fre•quent

fre•quen•ta•tion

fre•quent•er

fre•quent•ly

fresh dis•sei•sin

fresh force

fresh pur•suit

fresh suit

fret *v.*, fret•ted, fret•ting

Freud○i○an slip
fric•tion
fric•tion○al
fric•tion○al○ly
fric•tion•less
fric•tion•less○ly
friend
friend of the court
friend•less
friend•less•ness
friend•li○ly
friend•li•ness
friend○ly
friendly fire
friendly suit
friendly take•o○ver
friendly ten•der
    of○fer
friend•ship
friendship, com•
    merce, and nav○i•
    ga○tion trea○ties
    (FCN treaties)
fright
fright○en
fright•en•a○ble
fright•ened
fright•en•ing
fright•en•ing○ly
fright•ful
fright•ful○ly
fright•ful•ness
fringe ben○e•fit
frisk
frisk○er
fri•vol○i○ty n., pl. fri•
    vol○i•ties
friv○o○lous
frivolous ac•tion
frivolous ap•peal
frivolous com•plaint
frivolous mo•tion
frivolous ob•jec•tion
frivolous plead•ing
frivolous re•turn

frivolous suit
friv○o○lous○ly
friv○o•lous•ness
frol○ic of one's own
front
front end n.
front-end adj.
front-end fee
front-end load
front-end load fund
front load n.
front-load adj., v.
front-load○ed
front-load•ing
front mon○ey
front of•fice n.
front-office adj.
front•age
fron•tal
fron•tal○ly
fron•tier
frot•tage
frot•teur
fro•tteur•ism
frown
frown•ing○ly
fro•zen
fro•zen•ness
fruc•tus n., pl. fruc•
    tus Latin.
fructus ci•vi•les Latin.
fructus in•dus•tri•a•
    les Latin.
fructus na•tu•ra•les
    Latin.
fructus pen•den•tes
    Latin.
fructus re○i a○li•e○ni
    Latin.
fructus se•pa•ra○ti
    Latin.
fruit
fruit of the poi•son•
    ous tree
fruit•ful
fruit•ful○ly

fruit•ful•ness
fru•i•tion
fruit•less○ly
fruit•less•ness
fruits of a search
fruits of crime
frus•trate v., frus•
    trat○ed, frus•trat•
    ing
frus•trat○ed
frus•trat○er
frus•trat•ing○ly
frus•tra•tion
frus•tra•tive
Frye test
FTE (full-time equiva-
    lent employee)
fudge v., fudged,
    fudg•ing
fu•gi•tive
fugitive from jus•tice
fu•gi•tive○ly
fu•gi•tive•ness
fugue
fugue state
fugue•like
ful•fill
ful•fill○er
ful•fill•ment
full (complete: cf. FUL-
    SOME)
full age
full and fair hear•ing
full court
full cov•er•age
full dis•clo•sure
full faith and cred○it
full-fledged
full par•don
full par•tner
full-scale
full speed
full time n.
full-time adj., adv.
full-time e○quiv○a•

lent em•ploy•ee (FTE)
full-tim•er
full war•ran•ty
full•ness
fullness of time
ful•ly
fully di•lut•ed earn•ings per share
fully paid stock
ful•mi•nate v., ful•mi•nat•ed, ful•mi•nat•ing
ful•mi•na•tor
ful•mi•na•to•ry
ful•some (disgusting: cf. FULL)
ful•some•ly
ful•some•ness
func•tion
func•tion•a•bil•i•ty
func•tion•al
functional dis•or•der
functional il•lit•er•o•a•cy
functional il•lit•er•ate
functional im•pair•ment
functional pat•ent
functional rep•re•sen•ta•tion
func•tion•al•ism
func•tion•al•ist
func•tion•al•i•ty
func•tion•al•ly

functionally il•lit•er•ate
func•tion•ar•o•y n., pl. func•tion•ar•ies
fund
fund-rais•er or fund•rais•er
fund-rais•ing or fund•rais•ing
fun•da•men•tal
fundamental breach
fundamental er•ror
fundamental fair•ness
fundamental law
fundamental right
fun•da•men•tal•ly
fund•ed debt
fund•ing
funds n.pl.
fun•gi•bil•i•ty
fun•gi•ble
fur•eth•oi•dine Controlled Subst.
fu•ri•ous
fu•ri•ous•ly
fu•ri•ous•ness
fur•lough
fur•nish
fur•nish•er
fu•ror
fur•ther
further as•sur•ance
further pro•ceed•ings
fur•ther•ance
fur•ther•er

fur•ther•more
fu•rtive
fu•ry n., pl. fu•ries
fu•sil•lade n., v., fu•sil•lad•ed, fu•sil•lad•ing
fu•sion
fu•sion•al
fus•tian
fus•ti•gate v., fus•ti•gat•ed, fus•ti•gat•ing
fus•ti•ga•tion
fus•ti•ga•tor
fus•ti•ga•to•ry
fu•tile
fu•tile•ly
fu•til•i•oi•ty n., pl. fu•til•i•o•ties
fu•ture
future dam•ag•es
future earn•ings
future es•tate
future goods
future in•ter•est
fu•tures n.pl.
futures con•tract
futures ma•rket
fu•tu•o•ri n.pl. Latin.
fu•tur•is•tic
fu•tur•is•ti•cal•ly
fu•tu•ri•o•ty n., pl. fu•tu•ri•ties
fu•tu•rum Latin.
FY (fiscal year)

G

G (guanine)
GAAP (generally accepted accounting principles)
GAAS (generally accepted auditing standards)
gad•a•bout
gad•get
gad•get•eer
gad•get•ry
gaffe
gag v., gagged, gag•ging, n.

gag law
gag order
gag rule
gage n., v., gaged, gag•ing (something pledged as security; a pledge of security; to

make such a pledge:
cf. GAUGE)
gage cred○i•tor
gage debt○or
ga○gee
ga○ger¹ (the pledging
of security: cf. GAGOR;
GAUGER)
gag○er² See GAUGER.
gag•ger
ga○gor (one who
pledges something as
security: cf. GAGER;
GAUGER)
gain
gain•a○ble
gain○er
gain•ful
gainful em•ploy•
ment
gain•ful○ly
gain•ful•ness
gain•less
gain•less•ness
gain•say v., **gain•**
said, gain•say•ing
gain•say○er
gall
gal•lant
gal•lant○ly
gal•lant•ness
gal•lant○ry n., pl.
gal•lant•ries
gall•ing
gall•ing○ly
gall•ing•ness
gal•li•vant
gal•li•vant○er
gal•lon
gal•lon•age
gal•lows n., pl. **gal•**
lows○es or gal•lows
gam•bit
gam•ble v., gam•
bled, gam•bling, n.
gam•bler

gam•bling
game
game law
game of chance
game park
game plan
game pre•serve
game the•o○ry
game war•den
game•keep○er
game•keep•ing
game•less
game○ly
game•ness
gam○er
games•man n., pl.
games•men.
games•man•ship
gam•ete
ga•met○ic
ga•met○i•cal○ly
gam•ing
gaming ta○ble
gam○ut
Gan•dhi○an
Gan•dhi•ism
gang
gang rape n.
gang-rape v., gang-
raped, gang-rap•ing
gang up v.
gang-up n.
gang war
gang war•fare
gang•bust○er
gang•bust•ers
gang•land
gang•ling
gang○ly adj., gang•
li○er, gang•li•est
gang•ster
gang•ster•ism
gang•way
gan○ja

gaol (a British spelling
for JAIL)
gaol○er (a British spelling for JAILER)
gap n., v., gapped,
gap•ping.
gape v., gaped, gap•
ing
gap○er
gar•bage
gar•bage in, gar•
bage out (GIGO)
gar•ble v., gar•bled,
gar•bling
gar•ble•a○ble
gar•bler
gar•nish
gar•nish•a○ble
gar•nish○ee
gar•nish○er or gar•
nish○or
gar•nish•ment
gar•ri•son
gar•rote n., v., gar•
rot○ed, gar•rot•ing
gar•rot○er
gar•ru•li○ty
gar•ru•lous
gar•ru•lous○ly
gar•ru•lous•ness
gas n., pl. gas○es, v.,
gassed, gas•sing
gas-guz•zler
gas-guz•zling
gas○e○ous
gas○i•fi•a○ble
gas○i•fi•ca•tion
gas○i•fi○er
gas○i•fy v., gas○i•
fied, gas○i•fy•ing
gas○o•hol
gas○o•line
gas○o•line•less
gas○o•lin○ic
gasp

gate *n., v.,* gat○ed, gat•ing.

gate-crash○er

gate-crash•ing

gate•keep○er

gate•keep○ing

gate•way

gateway drug

gath○er

gath•er•ing

gauche

gauche○ly

gauche•ness

gauge *v.,* gauged, gaug•ing, *n.* (to measure or estimate; a measure or device for measuring: cf. GAGE)

gauge•a○ble

gauge•a○bly

gaug○er or gag○er (a measurer; a customs officer who determines duty owed: cf. GAGER[1]; GAGOR)

gaunt

gaunt•let

gaunt○ly

gaunt•ness

ga•vage

gav○el

gavel to gavel *adv.*

gavel-to-gavel *adj.*

gav•el•kind

gawk○i○ly

gawk○i•ness

gawk○y *adj.,* gawk○i○er, gawk○i•est

gay

gay•ness

ga•zette

gDNA (genomic DNA)

GDP (gross domestic product)

gel *n., v.,* gelled, gel•ling. (substance used in DNA analysis; to form such a gel: cf. JELL)

gel e○lec○tro•pho•re○sis

Ge•ma○ra

Gen. (General)

Gen. Sess. (General Sessions)

gen•darme *n., pl.* gen•darmes. *French.*

gen•dar•me•rie *French.*

gen•der

gender gap

gender i○den○ti○ty

gender role

gender-spe•cif○ic

gen•der•less

gene

gene am•pli•fi•ca•tion

gene fre•quen○cy

gene map•ping

gene pool

gene splic○ing

gene ther○a○py

gene trans•fer

ge•ne•a•log○ic

ge•ne•a•log○i•cal

ge•ne•a•log○i•cal○ly

ge•ne•al○o○gist

ge•ne•al○o○gy *n., pl.* ge•ne•al○o•gies

gen•er○a See GENUS.

gen•er•a○bil○i○ty

gen•er•a○ble

gen•er○al *(citation form:* Gen.)

general ap•pear•ance

General As•sem•bly

general as•sump•sit

general av•er•age

general average loss

general be•quest

general con•trac•tor

general coun•sel

General Court

general court-mar•tial

general de•liv•er○y

general dis•charge

general e○lec•tion

general in•tel•lec•tu○al func•tion•ing

general ju•ris•dic•tion

general mar○i•time law

general med○i•cal con•di•tion

general-ob•li•ga•tion bond

general or•ders

general part•ner

general part•ner•ship

general pow○er of at•tor•ney

general rule

general ses•sions *(citation form:* Gen. Sess.)

general strike

general ver•dict

gen•er•al○cy

gen•er•al•ist

gen•er•al○i○ty *n., pl.* gen•er•al○i•ties

gen•er•al•iz•a○ble

gen•er•al○i○za•tion

gen•er•al•ize *v.,* gen•er•al•ized, gen•er•al•iz•ing

gen•er•al•ized an•xi○e○ty dis•or•der

generalized sys•tem of pref•er•enc○es

generalized tar•iff pref•er•ence

gen•er•al•iz○er

gen•er•al○ly

generally ac•cept○ed

ac•count•ing prin•
ci•ples (GAAP)
generally accepted
au•dit•ing stand•
ards (GAAS)
gen•er•al•ness
gen•er•al•ship
gen•er•ate v., gen•
er•at•ed, gen•er•
at•ing.
gen•er•a•tion
generation gap
generation-skip•ping
tax
generation-skipping
trans•fer
generation-skipping
transfer tax
generation-skipping
trust
gen•er•a•tion•al
gen•er•a•tion•al•ly
gen•er•a•tive
gen•er•a•tive•ly
gen•er•a•tive•ness
gen•er•a•tor
ge•ner•ic
generic claim
generic mark
generic name
generic prod•uct
ge•ner•i•cal•ly
ge•ner•ic•ness
gen•er•os•i•ty n., pl.
gen•er•os•i•ties
gen•er•ous
gen•er•ous•ly
gen•er•ous•ness
gen•e•sis n., pl.
gen•e•ses
ge•net•ic
genetic code
genetic coun•sel•ing
genetic dis•crim•i•
na•tion
genetic di•ver•si•ty

genetic en•gi•neer
genetic en•gi•neer•
ing
genetic fin•ger•print
genetic fin•ger•
print•ing
genetic map
genetic mark•er
genetic pri•va•cy
genetic red•lin•ing
genetic screen•ing
genetic test
genetic test•ing
ge•net•i•cal•ly
ge•net•i•cist
ge•net•ics n.sing.
Ge•ne•va Con•ven•
tion
gen•ial
ge•ni•al•i•ty
gen•ial•ly
gen•ial•ness
gen•ic
gen•i•tal
gen•i•ta•li•a n.pl.
gen•i•tals n.pl.
gen•ius n., pl. gen•
ius•es
gen•o••cid•al
gen•o••cide
ge•nome
ge•no•mic
genomic DNA (gDNA)
ge•no•mics n.sing.
ge•no•type
ge•no•typ•ic
ge•no•typ•i•cal
ge•no•typ•i•cal•ly
ge•no•typ•ing
gens n., pl. gen•tes
Latin.
gen•teel
gen•teel•ism
gen•teel•ly
gen•teel•ness

gen•til•i•ty
gen•tle adj., gen•tler,
gen•tlest, v., gen•
tled, gen•tling
gen•tle•folk n.pl.
gen•tle•man n., pl.
gen•tle•men
gen•tle•man•ly
gen•tlemen's a•gree•
ment
gen•tle•ness
gen•tle•per•son n.,
pl. gen•tle•peo•ple
gen•tle•wom•an n.,
pl. gen•tle•wom•en
gen•tle•wom•an•ly
gen•tly
gen•tri•fi•ca•tion
gen•tri•fied
gen•tri•fi•er
gen•tri•fy v., gen•
tri•fied, gen•tri•fy•
ing
gen•try
gen•u•ine
gen•u•ine•ly
gen•u•ine•ness
ge•nus n., pl. gen•
er•a
ge•o-ec•o•nom•ics n.
sing.
ge•og•ra•pher
ge•o•graph•ic
geographic ju•ris•
dic•tion
geographic mar•ket
geographic market
ex•ten•sion
merg•er
ge•o•graph•i•cal
ge•o•graph•i•cal•ly
ge•og•ra•phy
ge•o•log•i•cal•ly
ge•o•po•lit•i•cal
ge•o•po•lit•i•cal•ly

ge•o•pol•i•tics *n.*
sing.
ger•i•a•tric *adj.*
ger•i•a•tri•cian
ger•i•at•rics *n.sing.*
ger•i•at•rist
germ
germ-free
ger•mane
ger•mane•ly
ger•mane•ness
ger•mi•nal
ger•mi•nal•ly
ger•mi•nance
ger•mi•nan•cy
ger•mi•nant
ger•mi•nate *v.,* ger•
mi•nat•ed, ger•mi•
nat•ing.
ger•mi•na•tion
ger•mi•na•tive
ger•mi•na•tive•ly
germ•less
germ•like
ge•ron•to•log•i•cal
ger•on•tol•o•gist
ger•on•tol•o•gy
ger•ry•man•der
ger•ry•man•der•er
Ge•sell•schaft or ge•
sell•schaft, *n., pl.*
Ge•sell•schaf•ten or
ge•sell•schaf•ten
German.
Gesellschaft mit Be•
schränk•ter Haf•
tung (GmbH) *Ger-
man.*
ge•stalt *n., pl.* ge•
stalts or ge•stal•ten
ges•tate *v.,* ges•
tat•ed, ges•tat•ing
ges•ta•tion
ges•ta•tion•al
gestational car•ri•er
gestational moth•er

gestational sac
gestational sur•ro•
ga•cy
gestational sur•ro•
gate
ges•ta•tive
ges•tic•u•late *v.,*
ges•tic•u•lat•ed,
ges•tic•u•lat•ing
ges•tic•u•la•tion
ges•tic•u•la•tive
ges•tic•u•la•tor
ges•tic•u•la•to•ry
ges•tum *n., pl.* ges•ta
Latin.
ges•tur•al
ges•ture *n., v.,* ges•
tured, ges•tur•ing
ges•tur•er
get[1] *v.,* got, got or
got•ten, get•ting
get[2] *n., pl.* git•tin or
gi•tim *Hebrew.*
get to•geth•er *v.*
get-together *n.*
get-tough *adj.*
get•ter
ghast•i•ly
ghast•li•ness
ghast•ly
ghet•to *n., pl.* ghet•
tos.
ghoul
ghoul•ish
ghoul•ish•ly
ghoul•ish•ness
GI *n., pl.* GI's, *adj., v.,*
GI'd, GI'ing
gib•ber•ish
gib•bet *n., v.,* gib•
bet•ed, gib•bet•ing
gibe *v.,* gibed, gib•
ing, *n.* (to taunt; a
taunt: cf. JIBE)
gib•er
gib•ing•ly

gift
gift and lease•back
gift cau•sa mor•tis
gift cer•tif•oi•cate
gift in con•tem•pla•
tion of death
gift in•ter vi•vos
gift o•ver
gift tax
gift•ed
gift•ed•ly
gift•ed•ness
GIGO (garbage in, gar-
bage out)
gig•o•lo *n., pl.*
gig•o•los
gild *v.,* gild•ed or gilt,
gild•ing (to coat with
gold; to give a decep-
tively good appearance
to: cf. GUILD)
gild•ed
gilt (a veneer of gold:
cf. GUILT)
gilt-edged
gilt-edged se•
cur•i•ty
gird *v.,* gird•ed or
girt, gird•ing
gird•ed
gist
give *v.,* gave, giv•en,
giv•ing, *n.*
give-and-take *n.*
give a•way *v.* (cf. GIVE-
AWAY)
give back *v.* (cf. GIVE-
BACK)
give o•ver
give up *v.*
give-up *n.*
give way *v.* (cf.
GIVEWAY VESSEL)
give•a•ble or giv•
a•ble

give•a•way n. (cf. GIVE AWAY)

give•back n. (cf. GIVE BACK)

giv•en

given name

giv•er

give•way ves•sel

glam•our stock

glare n., v., glared, glar•ing.

glar•ing

glar•ing•ly

glar•ing•ness

glass ceil•ing

glass•ine

glassine en•ve•lope

glib adj., glib•ber, glib•best

glib•ly

glib•ness

glimpse v., glimpsed, glimps•ing.

gloat

gloat•er

gloat•ing•ly

glob•al

global sett•le•ment

global vil•lage

global warm•ing

glob•al•ism

glob•al•ist

glob•al•i•za•tion

glob•al•ize v., glob•al•ized, glob•al•iz•ing

globe

gloom

gloom•y adj., gloom•i•er, gloom•i•est

glo•ri•fi•a•ble

glo•ri•fi•ca•tion

glo•ri•fi•er

glo•ri•fy v., glo•ri•fied, glo•ri•fy•ing

gloss

glos•sa•tor

glos•sa•to•ri•al

gloss•ing•ly

glos•sog•ra•pher

glos•so•graph•i•cal

glos•sog•ra•phy

glu•teth•oi•mide Controlled Subst.

GMAT Trademark. (Graduate Management Admission Test)

GmBH (Gesellschaft mit Beschränkter Haftung)

gnome

gno•mic

gno•mi•cal•ly

gnom•ish

gnos•tic

gnos•ti•cal•ly

GNP (gross national product)

go v., went, gone, go•ing, n.

go for•ward

go forward with ev•oi•dence

go pri•vate

go pub•lic

go to

goad

goal

goal•less

gob•ble•dy•gook or gob•ble•de•gook

god•child n., pl. god•chil•dren

god•daugh•ter

god•fa•ther

god•moth•er

god•par•ent

god•send

god•sent

god•son

go•ing

going con•cern

gold re•serve

gold•en

golden hand•cuffs

golden hand•shake

golden par•a•chute

golf

golf course

golf•er

go•li•ath

good adj., bet•ter, best, n., interj., adv.

good and val•u•a•ble con•sid•er•a•tion

good be•hav•ior

good cause

good cause hav•ing been shown

good con•sid•er•a•tion

good de•liv•er•y

good faith

good faith ex•cep•tion

good faith pur•chas•er

good faith purchaser for val•ue

good-for-noth•ing

good-heart•ed or good•heart•ed

good-hu•mored

good law

good-na•tured

good of•fic•es n.pl.

Good Sa•mar•oi•tan law

good-till-can•celed or•der

good time

glum adj., glum•mer, glum•mest

glum•ly

glum•ness

glut v., glut•ted, glut•ting, n.

good ti•tle
good•li•ness
good•ly *adj.*, good•
li•er, good•li•est
good•ness
goods *n.pl.*
good•will or good
will
goon
Gov. (Governor)
gov•ern
gov•ern•a•bil•i•ty
gov•ern•a•ble
gov•ern•a•ble•ness
gov•ern•ance
gov•ern•ess
gov•ern•ment (*citation form:* Gov't)
government bond
government con•
trac•tor
government in the
sun•shine
government is•sue or
government-issue
government se•
cur•i•ty
government-spon•
sored en•ter•prise
(GSE)
gov•ern•men•tal
governmental in•ter•
est a•nal•y•sis
gov•ern•men•tal•ese
gov•ern•men•tal•ly
gov•ern•ment•ese
gov•er•nor (Gov.)
governor gen•er•al
or governor-gen•
er•al *n., pl.* gover-
nors gen•er•al or
governor gen•er•als
or governors-gen•
er•al or
governor-gen•er•als

governor-gen•er•al•
ship
gov•er•nor•ate
gov•er•nor•ship
Gov't (Government)
grace *n., v.,* graced,
grac•ing.
grace pe•ri•od
grad•a•bil•i•ty
grad•a•ble
gra•da•tion
gra•da•tion•al
gra•da•tion•al•ly
grade *n., v.,* grad•ed,
grad•ing
grad•er
grad•u•al
grad•u•al•ism
grad•u•al•ist
grad•u•al•is•tic
grad•u•al•ly
grad•u•al•ness
grad•u•ate *n., adj., v.,*
grad•u•at•ed,
grad•u•at•ing
Graduate Man•age•
ment Ad•mis•sion
Test (GMAT) *Trade-
mark.*
grad•u•at•ed
graduated in•come
tax
graduated pay•ment
mort•gage
graduated payment
note
graduated re•lease
graduated tax
grad•u•a•tion
grad•u•a•tor
graf•fi•to *n., pl.* graf•
fi•ti
grain al•co•hol
grand
grand as•size
grand ju•ror

grand ju•ry
grand lar•ce•ny
grand ser•jeant•y
grand theft
grand•child *n., pl.*
grand•chil•dren
grand•daugh•ter
grand•fa•ther
grandfather clause
gran•dil•o•quence
gran•dil•o•quent
gran•dil•o•quent•ly
gran•di•ose
grandiose de•lu•sion
gran•di•ose•ly
gran•di•os•i•ty
grand•ly
grand•moth•er
grand•ness
grand•par•ent
grand•son
grand•stand
grand•stand•er
grand•stand•ing
grant
grant-back clause
grant-in-aid *n., pl.*
grants-in-aid.
grant•a•ble
grant•ed•ly
gran•tee
grant•er (one who
makes a grant of any
kind: cf. GRANTOR)
gran•tor (one who
makes a formal legal
grant: cf. GRANTER)
grantor trust
grants•man•ship
grape•vine
graph
graph•ic
graph•i•cal
graph•i•cal•ly
graph•ic•ness
grasp

grasp•a•ble
grasp•er
grasp•ing
grasp•ing•ly
grasp•ing•ness
grass•land
grass•roots
grassroots lob•by•ing
grate v., grat•ed, grat•ing, n.
grate•ful
grate•ful•ly
grate•ful•ness
grat•i•fi•a•ble
grat•i•fi•ca•tion
grat•i•fi•ed•ly
grat•i•fi•er
grat•i•fy v., grat•i•fied, grat•i•fy•ing
grat•i•fy•ing
grat•i•fy•ing•ly
grat•ing
grat•is
grat•i•tude
gra•tu•i•tous
gratuitous in•ter•med•dler
gratuitous prom•ise
gra•tu•i•tous•ly
gra•tu•i•tous•ness
gra•tu•i•ty n., pl. gra•tu•i•ties
gra•va•men n., pl. gra•vam•i•na
grave adj. grav•er, grav•est, n.
grave rob•ber
grave•less
grave•like
grave•ly
grave•ness
grave•rob•ber or grave rob•ber
grave•rob•bing
grave•yard shift
grav•i•tate v.,

grav•i•tat•ed, grav•i•tat•ing.
grav•i•tat•er
grav•i•ty n., pl. grav•i•ties
gray mar•ket
gray•mail
Gray's Inn
graze v., grazed, graz•ing
graze•a•ble
graz•ing•ly
great
Great Char•ter
great seal
Great Writ
great writ of lib•er•ty
great•ly
great•ness
greed
greed•i•ly
greed•i•ness
greed•y adj., greed•i•er, greed•i•est
green
green card
green pow•er
green•belt
green•house ef•fect
greenhouse gas
green•mail
green•mail•er
gre•gar•i•ous
gre•gar•i•ous•ly
gre•gar•i•ous•ness
grid•lock
grid•locked
grief
grief-strick•en
griev•ance
grievance com•mit•tee
grievance pro•ce•dure

griev•ant
grieve v., grieved, griev•ing.
griev•ed•ly
griev•er
griev•ing•ly
griev•ous
griev•ous•ly
griev•ous•ness
grift
grift•er
grim adj., grim•mer, grim•mest
grim•ace n., grim•aced, grim•ac•ing
grim•ac•er
grim•ac•ing•ly
grim•ly
grim•ness
gripe v., griped, grip•ing
grip•er
grip•ing
gris•li•ness
gris•ly adj., gris•li•er, gris•li•est
groan
groan•er
groan•ing•ly
groom
grope v., groped, grop•ing
grop•er
grop•ing
grop•ing•ly
gross
gross an•nu•al wag•es
gross do•mes•tic prod•uct (GDP)
gross in•come
gross lease
gross na•tion•al prod•uct (GNP)
gross neg•li•gence
gross prof•it
gross profit ra•tio

gross re•ceipts
gross receipts tax
gross rev○e○nue
gross sales
gross stress re•act•ion
gross up
gross weight
gross work•ing cap○i○tal
gross○ly
gross•ness
gro•tesque
gro•tesque○ly
gro•tesque•ness
grouch
grouch○i○ly
grouch○i•ness
grouch○y adj., grouch○i○er, grouch○i○est
ground
ground lease
ground rent
ground rule
ground•a○ble
ground•a○bly
ground•break○er
ground•break•ing
ground○ed
ground•ed•ness
ground•less
ground•less○ly
ground•less•ness
grounds n.pl.
ground•swell
group
group an•nu○i○ty
group boy•cott
group de•pre•ci•a•tion
group home
group in•sur•ance
group life
group life insurance

group prac•tice
group rep•re•sen•ta•tion
group•ing
group•think
grouse v., groused, grous•ing
grous○er
grov○el v., grov•eled, grov•el•ing
grov•el○er
grov•el•ing○ly
grow v., grew, grown, grow•ing
grow•a○ble
grow○er
grow•ing
growing-eq•ui○ty mort•gage
growing-equity note
grown
grown-up adj.
grown○up n.
growth
growth fund
growth stock
grub•stake n., v., grub•staked, grub•stak•ing
grub•stak○er
grudge n., adj., v., grudged, grudg•ing
grudge•less
grudg○er
grudg•ing
grudg•ing○ly
gru○el
gru•el•ing
gru•el•ing○ly
grue•some
grue•some○ly
grue•some•ness
gruff
gruff○ly
gruff•ness

grum•ble v., grum•bled, grum•bling
grum•bler
grum•bling○ly
grum•bly
grump
grump○i○ly
grump○i•ness
grump○y adj., grump○i○er, grump○i•est
grunginess
grun○gy adj., grun•gi○er, grun•gi•est
grunt
GSE (government sponsored enterprise)
gua•nine (G)
Guar. (Guaranty)
guar•an•tee n., v., guar•an•teed, guar•an•tee•ing
guar•an•teed
guaranteed an•nu○al in•come
guaranteed annual wage
guaranteed au○to•mo•bile pro•tec•tion
guaranteed bond
guaranteed in•come
guaranteed se•cur○i○ty
guaranteed stock
guaranteed stu•dent loan
guar•an•tor
guar•an○ty[1] n., pl. guar•an•ties (citation form: **Guar.**)
guaranty[2] v., guar•an•tied, guar•an•ty•ing
guaranty in•sur•ance
guard

guard•a•ble
guard•ed
guard•ed•ly
guard•ed•ness
guard•house law•yer
guard•i•an
guardian ad li•tem
guardian an•gel
guardian of the per•
son
guardian of the prop•
er•ty
guard•i•an•less
guard•i•an•ship
guard•room
gu•ber•na•to•ri•al
guer•ril•la (soldier: vs.
gorilla)
guerrilla war•fare
guess
guess•a•ble
guess•er
guest
guest stat•ute
guest work•er
guid•a•ble
guid•ance
guide *v.*, guid•ed,
guid•ing.
guide dog
guide•line
guide•post

guid•er
guild (an association:
cf. GILD)
guild•ship
guilds•man *n., pl.*
guilds•men.
guile
guile•ful
guile•ful•ly
guile•ful•ness
guile•less
guile•less•ly
guile•less•ness
guil•lo•tine *n., v.,*
guil•lo•tined, guil•
lo•tin•ing
guilt (criminal responsi-
bility: cf. GILT)
guilt phase
guilt•i•ly
guilt•i•ness
guilt•less
guilt•less•ly
guilt•less•ness
guilt•y *adj.,*
guilt•i•er, guilt•i•
est
guise *n., v.,* guised,
guis•ing.
gu•lag
gump•tion
gump•tion•less

gump•tious
gun *n., v.,* gunned,
gun•ning.
gun belt or gun•belt
gun con•trol
gun-shy
gun-tot•ing
gun•boat di•plo•
ma•cy
gun•fight
gun•fight•er
gun•fire
gung-ho
gun•mak•er
gun•mak•ing
gun•man *n., pl.* gun•
men.
gun•ning
gun•play
gun•point
gun•run•ning
gun•shot
gun•sling•er
gun•smith
gun•smith•ing
gut•si•ness
guts•y *adj.,* guts•i•er,
guts•i•est
guz•zle *v.,* guz•zled,
guz•zling
guz•zler

H

ha•be•as *Latin.*
habeas cor•po•ra ju•
ra•to•rum *Latin.*
habeas cor•pus *Latin.*
habeas corpus ad de•
li•be•ran•dum *Latin.*
habeas corpus ad fa•
ci•en•dum et re•ci•
pi•en•dum *Latin.*
habeas corpus ad

pro•se•quen•dum
Latin.
habeas corpus ad sa•
tis•fa•ci•en•dum
Latin.
habeas corpus ad
sub•ji•ci•en•dum
Latin.
habeas corpus ad tes•
ti•fi•can•dum *Latin.*

habeas corpus cum
cau•sa *Latin.*
ha•ben•dum *Latin.*
habendum clause
habendum et te•nen•
dum *Latin.*
ha•bil•i•tate *v.,* ha•
bil•i•tat•ed, ha•
bil•i•tat•ing
ha•bil•i•ta•tion

habilitation serv•ic•es

ha•bil•i•ta•tive

ha•bil•i•ta•tor

ha•bit

habit-form•ing

hab•it•a•bil•i•ty

hab•it•a•ble

hab•it•a•ble•ness

hab•it•a•bly

hab•i•tan•cy n., pl. hab•i•tan•cies

hab•i•tant

hab•i•tat

hab•i•ta•tion

hab•i•ta•tion•al

ha•bit•u•al

habitual crim•i•nal

habitual of•fend•er

ha•bit•u•al•ly

ha•bit•u•al•ness

ha•bit•u•ate v., ha•bit•u•at•ed, ha•bit•u•at•ing

ha•bit•u•a•tion

hab•i•tude

hab•i•tu•di•nal

ha•bit•u•é n., pl. ha•bit•u•és

hab•i•tus n., pl. hab•i•tus

hack

hack li•cense

hack•er

hack•neyed

haec ver•ba n.pl. Latin.

hae•res or he•res n., pl. hae•ri•des or he•ri•des Latin.

hag•gard

hag•gard•ly

hag•gard•ness

hag•gle v., hag•gled, hag•gling

hag•gler

Hague rules

hail (to greet, salute, or call out; icy precipita•tion: cf. HALE[1])

Ha•la•khah

ha•lal

ha•laz•e•pam Con•trolled Subst.

Hal•ci•on Trademark.

hale[1] v., haled, hal•ing (to haul; to com•pel to come: cf. HAIL)

hale[2] adj., hal•er, hal•est (healthy)

half n., pl. halves

half-baked

half broth•er

half-con•vinced

half-crazed

half-cra•zy

half-dead

half-heart•ed

half-heart•ed•ly

half-heart•ed•ness

half-lie

half-life n., pl. half-lives

half-pi•lot•age

half-share

half sis•ter

half-truth

half•way

halfway house

hall•mark

hal•lu•ci•nate v., hal•lu•ci•nat•ed, hal•lu•ci•nat•ing

hal•lu•ci•na•tion

hal•lu•ci•na•tive

hal•lu•ci•na•tor

hal•lu•ci•na•to•ry

hal•lu•ci•no•gen

hallucinogen a•buse

hallucinogen de•pend•ence

hallucinogen-in•duced dis•or•der

hallucinogen in•tox•i•ca•tion

hallucinogen per•sist•ing per•cep•tion disorder

hal•lu•ci•no•gen•ic

hallucinogenic sub•stance

hal•lu•ci•no•sis

ha•lox•az•o•lam Controlled Subst.

Ham•burg rules

ham•let

Ham•mu•ra•bi, Code of

ham•per

ham•pered•ly

ham•pered•ness

ham•per•er

Han•a•fi

Han•ba•li

hand

hand and seal

hand-car•ry v., hand-car•ried, hand-car•ry•ing

hand-de•liv•er

hand de•liv•er•y

hand down

hand-held

hand out v. (cf. HAND•OUT)

hand o•ver v. (cf. HANDOVER)

hand to hand adv.

hand-to-hand adj.

hand to mouth adv.

hand-to-mouth adj.

hand up

hand•bill

hand•bill•ing

hand•book

hand•cuff

hand•ful *n.*, *pl.* hand•
fuls
hand•hold•ing
hand◦i•cap *n.*, *v.*,
hand◦i•capped,
hand◦i•cap•ping
hand◦i•capped
hand◦i•cap•per
hand◦i•ly
hand◦i•ness
hand◦i•work
han•dle *n.*, *v.*, han•
dled, han•dling
han•dle•a◦bil◦i◦ty
han•dle•a◦ble
hand•ler
hand•ling
hand•out *n.* (cf. HAND
OUT)
hand•o◦ver *n.* (cf.
HAND OVER)
hand•pick
hand•picked
hands-off
hands-on
hand•write *v.*, hand•
wrote, hand•writ•
ten, hand•writ•ing
hand•writ•ing
hand•writ•ten
hand◦y *adj.*,
hand◦i•er, hand◦i•
est
hang[1] *v.*, hanged,
hang•ing (to suspend
by the neck until
dead)
hang[2] *v.*, hung, hang•
ing (to suspend gener-
ally)
hang out *v.*, hung
out, hang•ing out
hang•a◦bil◦i◦ty
hang•a◦ble
hang◦er-on *n.*, *pl.*
hang◦ers-on

hang•man *n.*, *pl.*
hang•men
hang•out *n.* (cf. HANG
OUT)
hang•o◦ver
han◦ky-pan◦ky
Han•sard
hap•haz•ard
hap•haz•ard◦ly
hap•haz•ard•ness
hap•haz•ard◦ry
hap•less
hap•less◦ly
hap•less•ness
hap•loid
hap•loi◦dy
hap•pen
hap•pen•ing
hap•pen•stance
hap•pi◦ly
hap•pi•ness
hap•py *adj.*, hap•
pi◦er, hap•pi•est
hap•py-go-luck◦y
ha◦ra-ki◦ri
ha•rangue *v.*, ha•
rangued, ha•rangu•
ing
ha•rass
ha•rass•a◦ble
ha•rass◦er
ha•rass•ing◦ly
ha•rass•ment
har•ber mas•ter or
har•bor•mas•ter
har•bin•ger
har•bor
harbor work◦er or
har•bor•work◦er
har•bor•age
har•bor◦er
har•bor•less
har•bor•ous
har•bor•side
hard
hard-and-fast

hard-and-fast•ness
hard as◦set *n.*
hard-as◦set *adj.*
hard-bit•ten
hard-boiled
hard-boiled•ness
hard case
hard cash
hard-core
hard-core por•nog•
ra•phy
hard cur•ren◦cy
hard drug
hard goods
hard-hit•ting
hard la◦bor
hard law
hard line *n.*
hard-line *adj.*
hard-lin◦er
hard mon◦ey
hard-nosed
hard sell *n.*
hard-sell *adj.*
hard time
hard•ball
hard◦en
hard•en•a◦bil◦i◦ty
hard•en•a◦ble
hard•ened
hard•en◦er
hard•en•ing
hard-head◦ed
hard-head•ed◦ly
hard-head•ed•ness
hard-heart◦ed
hard-heart•ed◦ly
hard-heart•ed•ness
hard◦ly
hard•ness
hard•ship
hard•ware
hard-work•ing
har◦dy *adj.*, har•
di◦er, har•di•est

hare•brained
hare•brained•ly
hare•brained•ness
har•lot
har•lot∘ry
harm
harm∘er
harm•ful
harm•ful•ness
harm•less
harmless er∘ror
harm•less∘ly
harm•less•ness
har•mo•ni•ous
har•mo•ni•ous∘ly
har•mo•ni•ous•ness
har•mo•niz•a•ble
har•mo•ni•za•tion
har•mo•nize v., har•
  mo•nized, har•mo•
  niz•ing
har•mo•niz∘er
har•mo∘ny n., pl.
  har•mo•nies
har•row
har•rowed
har•row•ing
har∘ry v., har•ried,
  har•ry•ing
harsh
harsh∘ly
harsh•ness
har∘um-scar∘um
has-been
hash•ish
has•sle n., v., has•
  sled, has•sling
has•ten
hast∘i∘ly
hast∘i•ness
hast∘y adj., hast∘i∘er,
  hast∘i•est
hatch∘et job
hatchet man
hatch•et∘work

hate v., hat∘ed, hat•
  ing,
hate crime
hate mail
hate sheet
hate speech
hate•a∘ble
hate•ful
hate•ful∘ly
hate•ful•ness
hate•mon•ger
hate•mon•ger•ing
hat∘er
ha•tred
haugh•ti∘ly
haugh•ti•ness
haugh∘ty adj.,
  haugh•ti∘er,
  haugh•ti•est
haul
haul•age
haul∘er
haunts n., pl.
hau•teur
have v., had, hav•ing,
have-not n., pl. have-
  nots
have the floor
ha•ven
ha•ven•less
hav∘oc n., v., hav•
  ocked, hav•ock•ing
hawk
hawk∘er
haz•ard
haz•ard•a∘ble
haz•ard∘er
haz•ard•less
haz•ard•ous
hazardous em•ploy•
  ment
hazardous oc•cu•pa•
  tion
hazardous sub•stance
hazardous waste
haz•ard•ous∘ly

haz•ard•ous•ness
haze v., hazed, haz•
  ing
haz∘er
haz•ing
H.C. (House of
  Commons)
HDTV (high definition
  television)
He Said, She Said
head char•ter
head mon∘ey
head of house•hold
head of state
head-on
head tax
head∘ed
head•hunt∘er
head•hunt•ing
head•ing
head•long
head•man n., pl.
  head•men
head•note
head•quar•ters
head•right
heads up interj.
heads-up n., adj.
head•ship
heads•man n., pl.
  heads•men
head•way
head∘y adj.,
  head∘i∘er, head∘i•
  est
heal
heal•a∘ble
heal∘er
health
health care
health care prox∘y
health code
health in•sur•ance
health main•te•nance
  or•gan∘i•za•tion
  (HMO)

health of•fi•cer
health•ful (producing
  health: cf. HEALTHY)
health•ful•ly
health•ful•ness
health∘i∘ly
health∘i•ness
health•y adj.,
  health∘i∘er,
  health∘i•est (pos-
  sessing health: cf.
  HEALTHFUL)
hear v., heard, hear•
  ing
hear and de•ter•mine
hear and re•port
hear ye
hear•a∘ble
hear∘er
hear•ing
hearing aid
hearing dog or hear-
  ing-ear dog
hearing ex•am•in∘er
hearing-im•paired
hearing of•fi•cer
hear•say
hearsay ev∘i•dence
hearsay ex•cep•tion
hearsay rule
heart
heart balm stat•ute
heart to heart adv.
heart-to-heart adj., n.
heart•break
heart•break∘er
heart•break•ing
heart•break•ing∘ly
heart•bro•ken
heart•bro•ken∘ly
heart•bro•ken•ness
heart∘en
heart•en•ing∘ly
heart∘i∘ly
heart∘i•ness
heart•land

heart•less
heart•less∘ly
heart•less•ness
heart•rend•ing
heart•rend•ing∘ly
heart•sick
heart•sick•en∘ing
heart•sick•ness
heart•sore
heart•warm•ing
heart∘y adj.,
  heart∘i∘er, heart∘i•
  est
heat
heat of pas•sion
heat∘ed
heat•ed∘ly
heat•ed•ness
heav∘i∘ly
heav∘i•ness
heav•y adj.,
  heav∘i∘er, heav∘i•
  est
heavy-hand∘ed
heavy-heart∘ed
heav∘y•set
heck∘le v., heck•led,
  heck•ling
heck•ler
hec•tic
hec•ti•cal∘ly or hec•
  tic∘ly
hec•tic•ness
hedge n., v., hedged,
  hedg∘ing
hedge fund
hedg∘er
hedg•ing
he•don∘ic
hedonic dam•ag∘es
he•don•i•cal∘ly
he•don•ist
he•don•is•tic
he•don•is•ti•cal∘ly
heed
heed∘er

heed•ful
heed•ful∘ly
heed•ful•ness
heed•less
heed•less∘ly
heed•less•ness
heg∘e∘mon
heg∘e∘mon∘ic
heg∘e∘mon∘i•cal
he•gem∘o∘nism
he•gem∘o∘nist
he•gem∘o∘nis•tic
he•gem∘o∘ny n., pl.
  he•gem∘o∘nies
height
height∘en
height•ened
heightened scru•ti∘ny
height•en∘er
hei•nous
hei•nous∘ly
hei•nous•ness
heir
heir ap•par•en∘cy
heir ap•par•ent n., pl.
  heirs ap•par•ent
heir at law n., pl.
  heirs at law
heir pre•sump•tive
  n., pl. heirs pre•
  sump•tive
heir•dom
heir•ess
heir•less
heir•loom
heirs and as•signs
heir•ship
heist
heist∘er
held
he∘lix n., pl. hel∘i•ces
  or he•lix∘es
hell-rais∘er
hell•hole
hel•lion
hell•ish

hell•ish•ly
hell•ish•ness
helm
helms•man n., pl.
 helms•men
help
help•a•ble
help•er
help•ful
help•ful•ly
help•ful•ness
help•ing
helping hand
help•ing•ly
help•less
help•less•ly
help•less•ness
help•mate
help•meet
hel•ter-skel•ter
hem•or•rhage n., v.,
 hem•or•rhaged,
 hem•or•rhag•ing
hem•or•rhag•ic
hemp
hence
hence•forth
hench•man n., pl.
 hench•men
Her Hon•or
her•ald
herb•age
here•af•ter
here•at
here•by
he•red•i•ta•bil•i•ty
he•red•i•ta•ble
he•red•i•ta•bly
her•e•dit•a•ment
he•red•i•tar•i•ly
he•red•i•tar•i•ness
he•red•i•tar•y
hereditary suc•ces•
 sion
he•red•i•ty

here•in
here•in•a•bove
here•in•af•ter
here•in•be•fore
here•in•be•low
here•of
here•on
he•res See HAERES.
here•to
here•to•fore
here•un•der
here•un•to
here•up•on
here•with
Her•fin•dahl-Hirsch•
 man in•dex (HHI)
her•i•ot
her•it•a•bil•i•ty
her•it•a•ble
her•it•age
her•it•ance
her•i•tor
he•ro n., pl. he•roes
he•ro•ic
he•ro•i•cal•ly
her•o•in Controlled
 Subst. (opium deriva-
 tive: cf. HEROINE)
her•o•ine (admired
 woman: cf. HEROIN)
her•o•ism
hes•i•tan•cy n., pl.
 hes•i•tan•cies
hes•i•tant
hes•i•tant•ly
hes•i•tate v., hes•i•
 tat•ed, hes•i•tat•
 ing
hes•i•tat•er or
 hes•i•ta•tor
hes•i•tat•ing•ly
hes•i•ta•tion
hes•i•ta•tive
hes•i•ta•tive•ly
het•er•o•dox

het•er•o•dox•y n.,
 pl. het•er•o•dox•ies
het•er•o•ge•ne•i•ty
het•er•o•ge•ne•ous
het•er•o•ge•ne•
 ous•ly
het•er•o•ge•ne•
 ous•ness
het•er•on•o•mous
het•er•on•o•
 mous•ly
het•er•on•o•my
het•er•o•sex•ism
het•er•o•sex•ist
het•er•o•sex•u•al
het•er•o•sex•u•
 al•i•ty
het•er•o•zy•
 gos•i•ty
het•er•o•zy•gote
het•er•o•zy•gous
heu•ris•tic
heu•ris•ti•cal•ly
hew v., hewed,
 hewed or hewn,
 hew•ing (to adhere,
 uphold, conform; to
 chop: cf. HUE)
HHI (Herfindahl-
 Hirschman index)
hi•a•tal
hi•a•tus n., pl. hi•a•
 tus•es
hid•a•bil•i•ty
hid•a•ble
hid•den
hidden a•gen•da
hidden as•set
hidden de•fect
hidden re•serves
hidden tax
hid•den•ly
hid•den•ness
hide[1] v., hid, hid•den
 or hid, hid•ing (to
 conceal)

hide² *n., v.,* hid∘ed, hid•ing (a pelt; to thrash)

hide out *v.,* hid out, hid•den out or hid out, hid•ing out (cf. HIDEOUT)

hide•bound

hide•bound•ness

hid∘e∘ous

hid∘e∘ous•ly

hid∘e∘ous•nesss

hide•out *n.* (cf. HIDE OUT)

hid∘er

hid•ing

hi•er•arch

hi•er•ar•chal

hi•er•ar•chic

hi•er•ar•chi•cal

hi•er•ar•chi•cal∘ly

hi•er•ar•chism

hi•er•ar•chist

hi•er•ar•chize *v.,* hi•er•ar•chized, hi•er•ar•chiz•ing

hi•er•ar•chy *n., pl.* hi•er•ar•chies

high-and-might∘i•ness

high and might∘y *n., adv.*

high-and-mighty *adj.*

high com•mis•sion∘er

High Court (*citation form:* High Ct.)

High Court of Jus•tice

high crimes and mis•de•mean•ors

High Ct. (High Court)

high def∘i•ni•tion tel∘e∘vi•sion (HDTV)

high fi•nance

high-flown

high-hand∘ed

high-hand•ed∘ly

high-hand•ed•ness

high-lev∘el

high-mind∘ed

high-mind•ed∘ly

high-mind•ed•ness

high-pow∘er ri∘fle

high-pow•ered

high-pres•sure *adj., v.,* high-pres•sured, high-pres•sur•ing

high-rise

high roll∘er

high-sea *adj.*

high seas *n.*

high-tech *n., adj.*

high tech•nol∘o∘gy *n.*

high-technology *adj.*

high trea•son

high∘er court

higher law

high•est and best use

highest de•gree of care

high-fa•lu•tin

high-fli∘er or high-fli∘er

high-fly•ing or high-fly•ing

high∘jack See HIJACK.

high•jack∘er See HI-JACKER.

high•jack•ing See HI-JACKING.

high∘ly

high•ness (loftiness)

High•ness (royal title)

high•way

highway pa•trol

high•way rob•ber

highway rob•ber∘y

high•way•man *n., pl.* high•way•men

hi•jack or high•jack

hi•jack∘er or high•jack∘er

hi•jack•ing or high•jack•ing

hin•der

hin•der∘er

hin•der•ing pros∘e∘cu•tion

hin•der•ing∘ly

hin•drance

hind∘sight

hir•a∘bil∘i∘ty

hir•a∘ble or hire•a∘ble

hire *v.,* hired, hir•ing,

hire clause

hire out

hire-pur•chase

hire-purchase a∘gree•ment

hire-purchase sys•tem

hire•a∘ble See HIRABLE.

hired gun

hired hand

hir∘ee

hire•ling

hir∘er

hir•ing hall

His Hon∘or

Hist. (Historical; History)

his•to•ri∘an

his•tor∘ic

historic dis•trict

historic site

his•tor∘i•cal (*citation form:* Hist.)

historical cost

historical school

his•tor∘i•cal∘ly

his•tor∘i•cal•ness

his•tor∘i•cism

his•tor∘i•cist

his•to•ric∘i∘ty

his•tor∘i•cize *v.,* his•

tor•oi•cized, his•
tor•oi•ciz•ing
his•to•ried
his•to•ri•og•ra•pher
his•to•ri•og•ra•
pher•ship
his•to•ri•o•
graph•i•al
his•to•ri•o•graph•ic
his•to•ri•o•graph•i•
cal•ly
his•to•ri•og•ra•phy
his•to•ry *n., pl.* his•
to•ries (*citation form:*
Hist.)
his•tri•on•ic
histrionic per•son•
al•i•ty dis•or•der
his•tri•on•i•cal•ly
his•tri•on•ics *n.sing
or pl.*
hit *v.,* hit, hit•ting
hit-and-miss
hit-and-run
hit-and-run•ner
hit list
hit man
hit-run
hit-skip
hit squad
hith•er•to
hit•ta•ble
hit•ter
HIV (human immunode-
ficiency virus)
H.L. (House of Lords)
HLA (human leukocyte
antigen)
HMO (health mainte-
nance organization)
hoard (to amass; an accumulation: cf. HORDE)
hoard•er
hoard•ing
hob•by *n., pl.* hob•
bies

hobby ex•pense
hob•by•ist
hob•nob *v.,* hob•
nobbed, hob•nob•
bing
hock
Hoh•feld•i•an
hoi pol•loi *Greek.*
hoist by one's own
pe•tard
ho•kum
hold *v.,* held, hold•
ing
hold back *v.* (cf. HOLD-
BACK)
hold harm•less
hold-harmless
a•gree•ment
hold out *v.* (cf. HOLD-
OUT)
hold o•ver *v.* (cf. HOLD-
OVER)
hold up (to rob; to de-
lay: cf. HOLDUP; HOLED
UP)
hold•a•ble
hold•back *n.* (cf. HOLD
BACK)
hold•er
holder in due course
holder-of-rec•ord
date
hold•er•ship
hold•ing
holding cell
holding com•pany
holding per•i•od
hold•out *n.* (cf. HOLD
OUT)
hold•o•ver *n., adj.* (cf.
HOLD OVER)
holdover ten•an•cy
holdover ten•ant
hold•up *n.* (a robbery;
a delay: cf. HOLD UP;
HOLED UP)

holdup man
hole up *v.,* holed up,
hol•ing up
holed up (hidden; bar-
ricaded: cf. HOLD UP;
HOLDUP)
hol•i•day
ho•li•er-than-thou
ho•lism
ho•list
ho•lis•tic
ho•lis•ti•cal•ly
hol•o•caust
hol•o•graph
hol•o•graph•ic
holographic will
hol•o•graph•i•cal
hol•ster
hom•age
home *n., adj., adv., v.,*
homed, hom•ing
home care *n.*
home-care *adj.*
home eq•ui•ty con•
ver•sion mort•gage
home equity loan
home health care
home of•fice
home office de•duc•
tion
home own•er's war•
ran•ty
home port doc•trine
home rule
home•bound
home•build•er
home•build•ing
home•buy•er
home•grown
home•land
home•less
home•less•ly
home•less•ness
home•like
home•made
home•mak•er

home•mak•ing
home•own•er
home•own•ers' in•sur•ance or home•own•er's in•sur•ance
homeowner's pol•i•cy
home•site
home•stead
homestead ex•emp•tion
home•stead•er
home•stead•ing
homesteading pro•gram
home•ward
home•wards
home•work
home•work•er
home•wreck•er
hom•i•cid•al
hom•i•cid•al•ly
hom•i•cide
hom•i•ness See HOM•EYNESS.
ho•mo•ge•ne•i•ty
ho•mo•ge•ne•ous
ho•mo•ge•ne•ous•ly
ho•mo•ge•ne•ous•ness
ho•mol•o•gate v., ho•mol•o•gat•ed, ho•mol•o•gat•ing
ho•mol•o•ga•tion
ho•mo•phobe
ho•mo•pho•bi•a
ho•mo•pho•bic
ho•mo•pho•bi•cal•ly
ho•mo•sex•u•al
ho•mo•sex•u•al•i•ty
ho•mo•zy•gos•i•ty
ho•mo•zy•gote
ho•mo•zy•gous
Hon. (Honorable)
hon•est

hon•est•ly
hon•es•ty n., pl. hon•es•ties
hon•or
honor pol•i•cy
honor sys•tem
hon•or•a•ble (honest; respectable: cf. HONOR•ABLE)
Honorable (Hon.) (title for judges and certain other officials: cf. HON•ORABLE)
honorable dis•charge
hon•or•a•ble•ness
hon•or•a•bly
hon•o•rar•i•ly
hon•o•rar•i•um n., pl. hon•o•rar•i•a or hon•o•rar•i•ums
hon•or•ar•y
honorary trust
hon•or•ee
hon•or•er
hon•or•if•ic
ho•no•ris cau•sa *Latin.*
hon•or•less
hon•ors of war
hoo•ey (nonsense: cf. HUI)
hook•er
hoo•li•gan
hoo•li•gan•ism
hope n., v., hoped, hop•ing
hope•ful
hope•ful•ly
hope•ful•ness
hope•less
hope•less•ly
hope•less•ness
horde (a large group: cf. HOARD)
hor•i•zon•tal

horizontal com•bi•na•tion
horizontal di•vest•oi•ture
horizontal in•te•gra•tion
horizontal mar•ket al•lo•ca•tion
horizontal market di•vi•sion
horizontal merg•er
horizontal price fix•ing
horizontal priv•i•ty
horizontal re•straint
horizontal un•ion
hor•i•zon•tal•i•ty
hor•i•zon•tal•ly
hor•i•zon•tal•ness
hor•mone
horn•book
hornbook law
hor•ren•dous
hor•ren•dous•ly
hor•ri•ble
hor•ri•ble•ness
hor•ri•bly
hor•rid
hor•rid•ly
hor•rid•ness
hor•rif•ic
hor•rif•i•cal•ly
hor•ri•fy v., hor•ri•fied, hor•ri•fy•ing
hor•ri•fy•ing•ly
hor•ror
hors de com•bat *French.*
hor•ta•tive
hor•ta•tive•ly
hor•ta•to•ri•ly
hor•ta•to•ry
Hosp. (Hospital)
hos•pice
hos•pi•ta•ble
hos•pi•ta•bly

hos•pi•tal (*citation form:* **Hosp.**)

hos•pi•tal•ism

hos•pi•tal•i•ty

hos•pi•tal•i•za•tion

hospitalization in•sur•ance

hos•pi•tal•ize *v.*, hos•pi•tal•ized, hos•pi•tal•iz•ing

hos•tage *n., v.,* hos•taged, hos•tag•ing

hos•tile

hostile au•di•ence

hostile en•vi•ron•ment

hostile environment ha•rass•ment

hostile fire

hostile pos•ses•sion

hostile take•o•ver

hostile ten•der of•fer

hostile wit•ness

hostile wor•king en•vi•ron•ment

hos•tile•ly

hos•til•i•ty *n., pl.* hos•til•i•ties

hot *adj.*, hot•ter, hot•test

hot blood

hot-blood•ed

hot ca•rgo a•gree•ment

hot mon•ey

hot pur•suit

hot spot

hot-tem•pered

hot war

hotch•pot

hour•ly

hours *n.pl.*

Hous. (Housing; Houston)

house *n. v.*, housed, hous•ing

House Bill (*citation form:* **H.R.;** a bill in the House of Representatives)

house coun•sel

house de•tec•tive

house mark

House of Com•mons (*citation form:* **H.C.**)

house of cor•rec•tion

House of Del•e•gates

house of de•ten•tion

house of ill fame

house of ill re•pute

House of Lords (*citation form:* **H.L.**)

house of pros•ti•tu•tion

House of Rep•re•sen•ta•tives (*citation form:* **H.R.**)

house rule

house•break•ing

house•ful

house•hold

household bur•gla•ry

household crimes

household ef•fects

household goods

household lar•ce•ny

house•hold•er

house•hold•er•ship

house•hus•band

house•keep•er

house•keep•ing

house•mate

house•wife *n., pl.* house•wives

house•work•er

hous•ing (*citation form:* **Hous.**)

housing de•vel•op•ment

housing proj•ect

hov•er

hov•er•er

hov•er•ing

hovering act

hovering ves•sel

hov•er•ing•ly

how•ev•er

H.R. (House of Representatives; House Bill)

huck•ster

huck•ster•ism

hue (clamor; color: cf. HEW)

hue and cry

hui (Hawaiian form of association: cf. HOOEY)

hull in•sur•ance

hull pol•i•cy

Hum. (Human)

hu•man (*citation form:* **Hum.**)

Human. (Humanity; Humanities)

human im•mu•no•de•fi•cien•cy vi•rus (HIV)

human leu•ko•cyte an•ti•gen (HLA)

human na•ture

human re•la•tions

human re•sourc•es

human rights

human serv•ic•es

hu•mane

hu•mane•ly

hu•mane•ness

hu•man•ism

hu•man•ist

hu•man•is•tic

hu•man•is•ti•cal•ly

hu•man•i•tar•i•an

hu•man•i•tar•i•an•ism

hu•man•i•tar•i•an•ist

hu•man•i•ties *n., pl.* (*citation form:* **Human.**)

hu•man•i•ty (*citation form:* **Human.**
hu•man•i•za•tion
hu•man•ize *v.*, hu•man•ized, hu•man•iz•ing
hu•man•iz•er
hu•man•kind
hu•man•ly
hu•man•ness
hum•ble *adj.*, hum•bler, hum•blest, hum•bling•ly
hum•bly
hu•mil•i•ate *v.*, hu•mil•i•at•ed, hu•mil•i•at•ing
hu•mil•i•at•ing
hu•mil•i•at•ing•ly
hu•mil•i•a•tion
hu•mil•i•a•tor
hu•mil•i•ty
hu•mor
hu•mor•less
hu•mor•less•ly
hu•mor•less•ness
hu•mor•ous
hu•mor•ous•ly
hu•mor•ous•ness
hunch
hun•dred
Hundred Court
hung ju•ry
hun•ger
hunger strike *n.*
hunger-strike *v.* hunger-struck, hunger-strik•ing
hunger strik•er
hun•gri•ly
hun•gry *adj.*, hun•gri•er, hun•gri•est
hun•ker
hunt
hunt•a•ble
hunt•ed

hunt•er
hunt•ing
hurl•y-burl•y
hur•ried
hur•ried•ly
hur•ried•ness
hur•ry *v.*, hur•ried, hur•ry•ing
hurt *v.*, hurt, hurt•ing
hurt•a•ble
hurt•er
hurt•ful
hurt•ful•ly
hurt•ful•ness
hus•band
hus•band•ry
hush mon•ey
hus•tings
hustings court
hus•tle *v.*, hus•tled, hus•tling,
hus•tler
hus•tling
hy•brid
hybrid rule•mak•ing
hybrid stock
hy•brid•ism
hy•brid•ist
hy•brid•i•ty
hy•brid•iz•a•ble
hy•brid•i•za•tion
hy•brid•ize *v.*, hy•brid•ized, hy•brid•iz•ing
hy•brid•iz•er
hy•brid•o•o•ma
hy•drate *v.*, hy•drat•ed, hy•drat•ing
hy•dra•tion
hy•dro•car•bon
hy•dro•co•done *Controlled Subst.*
hy•dro•mor•phin•ol *Controlled Subst.*

hy•dro•mor•phone *Controlled Subst.*
hy•drox•y•peth•oi•dine *Controlled Subst.*
hype *v.*, hyped, hyp•ing
hy•per•ac•tive
hyperactive-im•pul•sive
hy•per•ac•tive•ly
hy•per•ac•tiv•i•ty
hy•per•bo•le
hy•per•bol•ic
hy•per•bol•i•cal•ly
hy•per•crit•i•cal
hy•per•crit•i•cal•ly
hy•per•in•fla•tion
hy•per•in•fla•tion•ar•y
hy•per•ki•net•ic
hyperkinetic con•duct dis•or•der
hyperkinetic disorder
hy•per•sen•si•tive
hy•per•sen•si•tive•ness
hy•per•sen•si•tiv•i•ty
hyp•no•sis *n.*, *pl.* hyp•no•ses
hyp•no•ther•o•a•pist
hyp•no•ther•o•a•py
hyp•not•ic
hypnotic a•buse
hypnotic de•pend•ence
hypnotic-in•duced dis•or•der
hypnotic in•tox•i•ca•tion
hypnotic with•draw•al
hyp•not•i•cal•ly
hypnotically re•freshed rec•ol•lec•tion

hyp•no•tism
hyp•no•tist
hyp•no•tiz•a•bil•i•ty
hyp•no•tiz•a•ble
hyp•no•tize v., hyp•no•tized, hyp•no•tiz•ing
hy•po•ac•tive
hy•po•chon•dri•a
hy•po•chon•dri•ac
hy•po•chon•dri•a•cal
hypochondriacal dis•or•der
hy•po•chon•dri•a•cal•ly
hy•po•chon•dri•a•sis

hy•poc•ri•sy n., pl. hy•poc•ri•sies
hypo•o•crite
hyp•o•crit•i•cal
hyp•o•crit•i•cal•ly
hy•po•der•mic
hypodermic nee•dle
hypodermic sy•ringe
hy•po•der•mi•cal•ly
hy•po•ma•ni•a
hy•po•man•ic
hypomanic ep•i•sode
hy•poth•ec
hy•poth•e•o•car•y
hy•poth•e•o•cate v., hy•poth•e•o•cat•ed, hy•poth•e•o•cat•ing
hy•poth•e•o•ca•tion
hy•poth•e•o•ca•tor

hy•poth•o•e•sis n., pl. hy•poth•o•e•ses
hy•poth•o•e•sist
hy•poth•o•e•size v., hy•poth•o•e•sized, hy•poth•o•e•siz•ing
hy•poth•o•e•siz•er
hy•po•thet•oi•cal
hypothetical ques•tion
hy•po•thet•oi•cal•ly
hys•te•ri•a
hys•ter•oic
hys•ter•oi•cal
hysterical per•son•al•i•ty dis•or•der
hys•ter•oi•cal•ly
hys•ter•ot•o•o•my n., pl. hys•ter•ot•o•o•mies

I

i•at•ro•gen•oic
i•at•ro•ge•nic•oi•ty
ibid. (ibidem)
i•bi•dem (ibid.) Latin.
i•bo•gaine Controlled Subst.
I.C.J. (International Court of Justice)
ID[1] n., pl. ID's or IDs (identification)
ID[2] v., ID'd or ID'ed or IDed, ID'ing or IDing (to identify)
id. (idem)
id est (i.e.) Latin.
IDB (industrial development bond)
i•de•a
i•de•al
i•de•al•ism
i•de•al•ist
i•de•al•is•tic
i•de•al•oi•za•tion

i•de•al•ize v., i•de•al•ized, i•de•al•iz•ing
i•de•al•ized
i•de•al•iz•er
i•de•as of ref•er•ence
i•de•a•tion
i•de•a•tion•al
i•de•a•tion•al•ly
i•dée fixe n., pl. i•dées fixes French.
i•dem Latin. (citation form: id.)
idem so•nans Latin.
i•den•tic
i•den•ti•cal
i•den•ti•cal•ly
i•den•ti•cal•ness
i•den•ti•fi•a•bil•i•ty
i•den•ti•fi•a•ble
i•den•ti•fi•ca•tion

i•den•ti•fied goods
i•den•ti•fi•er
i•den•ti•fy v., i•den•ti•fied, i•den•ti•fy•ing
I•den•ti-Kit Trademark.
i•den•ti•ty n., pl. i•den•ti•ties
identity card
i•de•o•o•log•ic
i•de•o•o•log•oi•cal
i•de•o•o•log•oi•cal•ly
i•de•o•oloo•gist
i•de•o•oloo•gize v., i•de•o•oloo•gized, i•de•o•oloo•giz•ing
i•de•o•o•logue
i•de•o•oloo•gy n., pl. i•de•o•oloo•gies
id•i•o•o•cy n., pl. id•i•o•o•cies
id•i•o•o•syn•cra•o•sy

id•i•o•o•syn•crat•ic
id•i•o•o•syn•crat•i•
  cal•ly
id•i•o•ot
id•i•ot•ic
id•i•ot•i•cal•ly
i•dle *adj., v.,* i•dled,
  i•dling (not working;
  to put out of work: cf.
  IDOL)
i•dle•ness
i•dler
i•dly
i•dol (revered person
  or object: cf. IDLE)
i•dol•i•za•tion
i•dol•ize *v.,* i•do•
  lized, i•do•liz•ing
i.e. (that is: from Latin
  td est; cf. E.G.)
IFB (invitation for bids)
if•fi•ness
if•fy
ig•no•bil•i•ty
ig•no•ble
ig•no•ble•ness
ig•no•bly
ig•no•min•i•ous
ig•no•min•i•ous•ly
ig•no•min•i•ous•
  ness
ig•no•min•y *n., pl.*
  ig•no•min•ies
ig•nor•a•ble
ig•no•ra•mus[1] *n., pl.*
  ig•no•ra•mus•es
  English. (ignorant person)
ig•no•ra•mus[2] *Latin.*
  (we take no notice of
  it)
ig•no•rance
ig•no•rant
ig•no•rant•ly
ig•nore *v.,* ig•nored,
  ig•nor•ing

ig•nor•er
ij•ma'
ij•ti•had
ilk
ill
ill-ad•vised
ill-ad•vis•ed•ly
ill-con•ceived
ill-con•sid•ered
ill-de•fined
ill-dis•posed
ill-e•quipped
ill fame
ill-famed
ill-fat•ed
ill-fa•vored
ill-fit•ted
ill-found•ed
ill-got•ten
ill-hu•mored
ill-in•ten•tioned
ill-judged
ill-kempt
ill-man•nered
ill-na•tured
ill-o•omened
ill-pre•pared
ill-spent
ill-starred
ill-suit•ed
ill-tem•pered
ill-timed
ill-treat
ill-treat•ment
ill-us•age
ill-use *v.,* ill-used, ill-
  us•ing, *n.*
ill-used
ill will
ill-willed
ill-wish•er
il•le•gal
illegal al•ien
illegal en•try
illegal immigrant

il•le•gal•i•ty *n., pl.*
  il•le•gal•oi•ties
il•le•gal•ly
il•leg•i•bil•i•ty
il•leg•i•ble (unreada-
  ble: cf. ELIGIBLE)
il•leg•i•bly
il•le•git•i•ma•cy *n.,*
  pl. il•le•git•i•ma•
  cies
il•le•git•i•mate *adj.,*
  n., v., il•le•git•oi•
  mat•ed, il•le•git•oi•
  mat•ing
il•le•git•i•mate•ly
il•le•git•i•ma•tion
il•le•git•i•ma•tize *v.,*
  il•le•git•i•ma•
  tized, il•le•git•oi•
  ma•tiz•ing
il•le•git•oi•mize *v.,* il•
  le•git•oi•mized, il•
  le•git•oi•miz•ing
il•lic•it (illegal or im-
  proper: cf. ELICIT)
illicit co•hab•i•ta•
  tion
il•lic•it•ly
il•lic•it•ness
il•lit•er•a•o•cy *n., pl.*
  il•lit•er•o•a•cies
il•lit•er•ate
il•lit•er•ate•ly
il•lit•er•ate•ness
ill•ness
il•log•ic
il•log•i•cal
il•log•i•cal•i•ty *n.,*
  pl. il•log•i•cal•oi•
  ties
il•log•i•cal•ly
il•log•i•cal•ness
il•lu•mi•na•ble
il•lu•mi•nate *v.,* il•
  lu•mi•nat•ed, il•lu•
  mi•nat•ing
il•lu•mi•nat•ing

il•lu•mi•nat•ing•ly
il•lu•mi•na•tion
il•lu•mi•na•tive
il•lu•mi•na•tor
il•lu•mine *v.*, il•lu•mined, il•lu•min•ing
illus. (illustration; illustrations)
il•lu•sion (false idea: cf. ALLUSION; ELUSION)
il•lu•sion•ar•y
il•lu•sive (deceptive: cf. ALLUSIVE; ELUSIVE)
il•lu•sive•ly
il•lu•sive•ness
il•lu•so•ri•ly
il•lu•so•ri•ness
il•lu•so•ry
illusory con•sid•er•a•tion
illusory con•tract
illusory prom•ise
illusory trust
il•lus•trat•a•ble
il•lus•trate *v.*, il•lus•trat•ed, il•lus•trat•ing
il•lus•trat•ed
il•lus•tra•tion (*citation form for sing. and pl.:* illus.)
il•lus•tra•tive
il•lus•tra•tive•ly
il•lus•tra•tor
il•lus•tri•ous
im•age *n., v.*, im•aged, im•ag•ing
im•ag•i•nar•y
im•ag•i•na•tion
im•ag•i•na•tive
im•ag•i•na•tive•ly
im•ag•i•na•tive•ness
im•ag•ine *v.*, im•ag•ined, im•ag•in•ing

im•ag•in•er
im•be•cile
im•be•cil•ic
im•be•cil•i•ty
im•i•ta•ble
im•i•tate *v.*, im•i•tat•ed, im•i•tat•ing
im•i•ta•tion
im•i•ta•tive
im•i•ta•tive•ly
im•i•ta•tive•ness
im•i•ta•tor
im•ma•nent (inherent: cf. EMANANT; EMINENT; IMMINENT)
im•ma•te•ri•al
immaterial breach
immaterial var•i•ance
im•ma•te•ri•al•i•ty *n., pl.* im•ma•te•ri•al•i•ties
im•ma•te•ri•al•ly
im•meas•ur•a•bil•i•ty
im•meas•ur•a•ble
im•meas•ur•a•ble•ness
im•meas•ur•a•bly
im•me•di•a•cy *n., pl.* im•me•di•a•cies
im•me•di•ate
im•me•di•ate an•nu•i•ty
immediate cause
immediate pre•cur•sor
im•me•di•ate•ly
im•me•di•ate•ness
im•me•mo•ri•al
Immigr. (Immigration)
im•mi•grant (person from another country: cf. EMIGRANT)
im•mi•grate *v.*, im•mi•grat•ed, im•mi•grat•ing (to come

into a new country: cf. EMIGRATE)
im•mi•gra•tion (*citation form:* Immigr.)
im•mi•gra•tion•al
im•mi•gra•tor
im•mi•gra•to•ry
im•mi•nence
im•mi•nen•cy
im•mi•nent (impending: cf. EMANANT; EMINENT; IMMANENT)
imminent dan•ger
imminent per•il
im•mi•nent•ly
im•mi•nent•ness
im•mo•bile
im•mo•bil•i•ty
im•mo•bi•li•za•tion
im•mo•bi•lize *v.*, im•mo•bi•lized, im•mo•bi•liz•ing
im•mo•bi•liz•er
im•mor•al (violating moral standards: cf. AMORAL)
immoral con•sid•er•a•tion
immoral con•tract
im•mo•ral•i•ty *n., pl.* im•mo•ral•i•ties
im•mor•al•ly
im•mov•a•bil•i•ty
im•mov•a•ble
im•mov•a•ble•ness
im•mov•a•bles *n.pl.*
im•mov•a•bly
im•mune
im•mu•ni•ty *n., pl.* im•mu•ni•ties
immunity bath
im•mu•ni•za•tion
im•mu•nize *v.*, im•mu•nized, im•mu•niz•ing
im•mu•niz•er

im•mu•no•as•say
im•pact
im•pair
im•pair•a•ble
im•paired
impaired judg•ment
impaired oc•cu•pa•tion•al func•tion•ing
impaired so•cial func•tioning
im•pair•er
im•pair•ment
impairment of cap•i•tal
im•pale v., im•paled, im•pal•ing
im•pale•ment
im•pal•er
im•pan•el v., im•pan•eled, im•pan•el•ing
im•pan•el•ment
im•parl
im•par•lance
im•par•tial
im•par•ti•al•i•ty
im•par•tial•ly
im•passe
im•peach
im•peach•a•bil•i•ty
im•peach•able
im•peach•er
im•peach•ment
im•pe•cu•ni•ous
im•pe•cu•ni•ous•ly
im•pe•cu•ni•ous•ness
im•pede v., im•ped•ed, im•ped•ing
im•ped•er
im•ped•i•bil•i•ty
im•ped•i•ble
im•ped•i•ment
im•ped•i•men•ta n.pl.

im•ped•i•men•tal
im•ped•i•men•ta•ry
im•ped•ing•ly
im•per•a•tive
im•per•a•tive•ly
im•per•a•tive•ness
im•per•fect
imperfect trust
imperfect war
im•per•fec•tion
im•per•fect•ly
im•per•fect•ness
im•pe•ri•al
imperial pres•i•den•cy
im•pe•ri•al•ism
im•pe•ri•al•ist
im•pe•ri•al•is•tic
im•pe•ri•al•is•ti•cal•ly
im•pe•ri•al•ly
im•pe•ri•al•ness
im•per•il v., im•per•iled, im•per•il•ing
im•per•il•ment
im•pe•ri•um n., pl. im•pe•ri•a
im•per•son•ate v., im•per•so•nat•ed, im•per•so•nat•ing
im•per•son•a•tion
im•per•son•a•tor
im•per•ti•nence
im•per•ti•nen•cy n., pl. im•per•ti•nen•cies
im•per•ti•nent
im•per•ti•nent•ly
im•per•ti•nent•ness
im•per•turb•a•bil•i•ty
im•per•turb•a•ble
im•per•turb•a•ble•ness
im•per•turb•a•bly
im•per•vi•ous

im•per•vi•ous•ly
im•per•vi•ous•ness
im•pet•u•ous
im•pet•u•ous•ly
im•pet•u•ous•ness
im•pinge v., im•pinged, im•ping•ing
im•pinge•ment
im•ping•er
im•plac•a•bil•i•ty
im•plac•a•ble
im•plac•a•ble•ness
im•plac•a•bly
im•plant
im•plan•ta•tion
im•plau•si•bil•i•ty
im•plau•si•ble
im•plau•si•bly
im•plead v., im•plead•ed, im•plead•ing
im•plead•a•ble
im•plead•er
im•ple•ment
im•ple•ment•a•ble
im•ple•men•ta•tion
im•ple•ment•er
im•pli•cate v., im•pli•cat•ed, im•pli•cat•ing
im•pli•ca•tion
im•pli•ca•tive
im•pli•ca•tive•ly
im•plic•it
implicit cost
im•plic•it•ness
im•plied
implied con•di•tion
implied con•sent
implied con•tract
implied in fact
implied in law
implied pow•er
implied re•peal
implied trust

implied waiv○er

implied war○ran○ty

im•pli○ed○ly

im•plore *v.*, im•plored, im•plor•ing

im•plor•ing○ly

im○ply *v.*, im•plied, im•ply•ing (to indicate or suggest: cf. INFER)

im•pol○i•tic

im•pol○i•tic○ly

im•pol○i•tic•ness

im•pon•der•a○bil○i•ty

im•pon•der•a○ble

im•pon•der•a○ble•ness

im•pon•der•a○bly

im•port

import quo○ta

im•port•a○bil○i•ty

im•port•a○ble

im•por•tance

im•por•tant

im•por•ta•tion

im•port○er

im•por•tu•nate

im•por•tu•nate○ly

im•por•tu•nate•ness

im•por•tune *v.*, im•por•tuned, im•por•tun•ing

im•por•tun○er

im•por•tu•ni•ty *n.*, *pl.* im•por•tu•ni•ties

im•pos•a○ble

im•pose *v.*, im•posed, im•pos•ing

im•pos○er

im•po•si•tion

im•pos•si•bil○i•ty *n.*, *pl.* im•pos•si•bil○i•ties

im•pos•si•ble

im•pos•si•bly

im•post

im•post○er (customs official who classifies dutiable goods: cf. IMPOSTOR)

im•pos•tor (person posing as another: cf. IMPOSTER)

im•po•tence

im•po•ten○cy

im•po•tent

im•po•tent○ly

im•pound

im•pound•a○ble

im•pound○er

im•pound•ment

im•pov•er•ish

im•pov•er•ished

im•pov•er•ish•ment

im•prac•ti•ca○bil○i•ty

im•prac•ti•ca•ble

im•prac•ti•ca•bly

im•pre•cate *v.*, im•pre•cat○ed, im•pre•cat•ing

im•pre•ca•tion

im•pre•ca•tor

im•pre•ca•to○ry

im•pre•cise

im•pre•cise○ly

im•pre•cise•ness

im•pre•ci•sion

im•pre•scrip•ti•bil○i•ty

im•pre•scrip•ti•ble

im•pre•scrip•ti•bly

im•press *v.*, im•pressed, im•press•ing (to make an impression; to impose; to force into service; a mark: cf. EMPRESS; IMPREST)

im•press○er

im•pres•sion

im•pres•sion•a•bil○i•ty

im•pres•sion•a○ble

im•pres•sion•a○ble•ness

im•pres•sion•a○bly

im•pres•sive

im•pres•sive○ly

im•pres•sive•ness

im•press•ment

im•prest (an advance of money: cf. IMPRESS)

imprest ac•count

imprest fund

im•pri•ma•tur

im•pris○on

im•pris•on•a○ble

im•pris•on○er

im•pris•on•ment

im•prob•a○bil○i•ty *n.*, *pl.* im•prob•a○bil○i•ties

im•prob•a○ble

im•prob•a○ble•ness

im•prob•a○bly

im•prop○er

im•prop•er○ly

im•pro•pri•e○ty *n.*, *pl.* im•pro•pri•e○ties

im•prov•a○bil○i•ty

im•prov•a○ble

im•prove *v.*, im•proved, im•prov•ing

im•prove•ment

improvement claim

im•prov○er

im•prov○i•dence

im•prov○i•dent

improvident exercise of discretion

im•prov○i•dent○ly

im•pru•dence

im•pru•dent

im•pru•dent○ly

im•pu•dence
im•pu•dent
im•pu•dent•ly
im•pu•dent•ness
im•pugn
im•pugn•a•bil•i•ty
im•pugn•a•ble
im•pugn•er
im•pugn•ment
im•pulse
impulse con•trol
impulse-control dis•or•der
im•pul•sive
im•pul•sive•ly
im•pul•sive•ness
im•pul•siv•i•ty
im•put•a•ble
im•pu•ta•tion
im•pute *v.*, im•put•ed, im•put•ing
im•put•ed
imputed in•come
imputed in•ter•est
imputed knowl•edge
imputed neg•li•gence
im•put•ed•ly
im•put•er
in ab•sen•tia *Latin.*
in ab•strac•to *Latin.*
in ac•tion
in ad•ver•sum *Latin.*
in au•tre droit *Law French.*
in bank or in banc See EN BANC.
in bar
in be•ing
in blank
in bond
in ca•hoots
in cam•er•a *Latin.*
in ca•pi•te *Latin.*
in cham•bers
in chan•cer•y

in chief
in com•mon
in con•cert
in con•sid•er•a•tion of
in con•si•mi•li ca•su *Latin.*
in con•tem•pla•tion of death
in cus•to•di•a le•gis *Latin.*
in de•lic•to *Latin.*
in due course
in du•pli•cate
in ef•fect
in es•crow
in es•se *Latin.*
in ev•i•dence
in ex•ten•so *Latin.*
in ex•tre•mis *Latin.*
in fact
in fee
in fine[1] *English.* (in short; in conclusion)
in fi•ne[2] *Latin.* (at the end)
in fla•gran•te de•lic•to *Latin.*
in force
in for•ma pau•pe•ris *Latin.*
in full
in fu•tu•ro *Latin.*
in ge•ne•re *Latin.*
in good faith
in good stand•ing
in gross
in haec ver•ba *Latin.*
in-house
in in•vi•tum *Latin.*
in-kind *adv.*
in-kind *adj.*
in-kind div•i•dend
in law (constructive; as a matter of law: cf. IN-LAW; INLAW)

in-law (relative by marriage: cf. IN LAW; IN LAW)
in lieu of
in li•mi•ne *Latin.*
in lo•co pa•ren•tis *Latin.*
in me•di•as res *Latin.*
in mi•se•ri•cor•di•a *Latin.*
in pais *Law French.*
in pa•ri de•lic•to *Latin.*
in pari ma•te•ri•a *Latin.*
in per•pe•tu•i•ty
in per•pe•tu•um *Latin.*
in per•so•nam *Latin.*
in personam ac•tion
in personam judg•ment
in personam ju•ris•dic•tion
in play
in point
in pos•se *Latin.*
in pos•ses•sion
in prae•sen•ti *Latin.*
in pro•pri•a per•so•na *Latin.*
in re *Latin.*
in rem *Latin.*
in rem ac•tion
in rem judg•ment
in rem ju•ris•dic•tion
in rem mort•gage
in-serv•ice
in ses•sion
in sev•er•al•ty
in si•tu *Latin.*
in so•li•dum or in so•li•do *Latin.*
in spe•cie (specifically; in kind; in coin: cf. SPECIES)

in sta•tu quo *Latin.*

in statu quo an•te *Latin.*

in ter•ro•rem *Latin.*

in terrorem clause

in the course of

in the mat•ter of

in the or•di•nar•y course of busi•ness

in to•to *Latin.*

in tran•sit

in tran•si•tu *Latin.*

in trust

in u•te•ro *Latin.*

in va•cu•o *Latin.*

in vi•tro *Latin.*

in vitro fer•ti•li•za•tion (IVF)

in vi•vo *Latin.*

in with•er•nam

in•ac•cu•ra•cy *n., pl.* in•ac•cu•ra•cies

in•ac•cu•rate

in•ac•cu•rate•ly

in•ac•cu•rate•ness

in•ac•tion

in•ac•tive

inactive stock

in•ac•tive•ly

in•ac•tive•ness

in•ac•tiv•i•ty

in•ad•e•qua•cy *n., pl.* in•ad•e•qua•cies

in•ad•e•quate

inadequate con•sid•er•a•tion

inadequate rem•e•dy at law

in•ad•e•quate•ness

in•ad•mis•si•bil•i•ty

in•ad•mis•si•ble

in•ad•mis•si•bly

in•ad•vert•ence

in•ad•vert•en•cy *n., pl.* in•ad•vert•en•cies

in•ad•vert•ent

in•ad•vert•ent•ly

in•ad•vis•a•bil•i•ty

in•ad•vis•a•ble

in•ad•vis•a•bly

in•al•ien•a•bil•i•ty

in•al•ien•a•ble

in•al•ien•a•bly

in•ane

in•ane•ly

in•an•i•ty

in•ap•pli•ca•bil•i•ty

in•ap•pli•ca•ble

in•ap•po•site

in•ap•po•site•ly

in•ap•po•site•ness

in•ap•pro•pri•ate

in•ap•pro•pri•ate•ly

in•ap•pro•pri•ate•ness

in•ar•tic•u•late

in•ar•tic•u•late•ly

in•ar•tic•u•late•ness

in•as•much as

in•at•ten•tive

in•at•ten•tive•ly

in•at•ten•tive•ness

in•au•gu•ral

in•au•gu•rate *v.,* in•au•gu•rat•ed, in•au•gu•rat•ing

in•au•gu•ra•tion

in•au•gu•ra•tor

in•aus•pi•cious

in•aus•pi•cious•ly

in•aus•pi•cious•ness

in•au•then•tic

in•au•then•ti•cal•ly

in•au•then•tic•i•ty

in•born

Inc. (Incorporated)

in•ca•pa•bil•i•ty

in•ca•pa•ble

in•ca•pa•ble•ness

in•ca•pa•bly

in•ca•pac•i•tate *v.,* in•ca•pac•i•tat•ed, in•ca•pac•i•tat•ing

in•ca•pac•i•tat•ed

in•ca•pac•i•ta•tion

in•ca•pac•i•ty

in•car•cer•ate *v.,* in•car•cer•at•ed, in•car•cer•at•ing

in•car•cer•a•tion

in•car•cer•a•tive

in•car•cer•a•tor

in•cau•tion

in•cau•tious

in•cau•tious•ly

in•cau•tious•ness

in•cen•di•ar•y *adj., n., pl.* in•cen•di•ar•ies

in•cen•tive

incentive com•pen•sa•tion

incentive con•tract

incentive pay

incentive wage

in•cen•ti•vize *v.,* in•cen•ti•vized, in•cen•ti•viz•ing

in•cep•tion

in•cep•tive

in•cep•tive•ly

in•ces•san•cy

in•ces•sant

in•ces•sant•ly

in•ces•sant•ness

in•cest

in•ces•tu•ous

in•ces•tu•ous•ly

in•ces•tu•ous•ness

Inch•ma•ree clause

in•cho•ate

inchoate dow•er

inchoate in•ter•est

inchoate lien

inchoate of•fense

inchoate right

in•cho•ate•ly
in•cho•ate•ness
in•ci•dence
in•ci•dent
incident of own•er•
ship
incident to ar•rest
in•ci•den•tal
incidental ben•e•fi•
ci•ar•y
incidental dam•ag•es
incidental pow•er
incidental use
in•ci•den•tal•ly
in•ci•den•tal•ness
in•ci•den•tals *n.pl.*
in•cip•i•ence
in•cip•i•en•cy
in•cip•i•ent
in•cip•i•ent•ly
in•ci•sive
in•ci•sive•ly
in•ci•sive•ness
in•cite *v.,* in•cit•ed,
in•cit•ing (to stir up:
cf. INSIGHT)
in•cite•ment
in•cit•ing
in•cit•ing•ly
in•ci•vil•i•ty *n., pl.*
in•ci•vil•i•ties
in•cli•na•tion
in•cline *v.,* in•clined,
in•clin•ing
in•clined
in•clud•a•ble
in•clude *v.,* in•
clud•ed, in•clud•ing
included of•fense
in•clu•sion
in•clu•sion•ar•y
inclusionary zon•ing
in•clu•sive
in•clu•sive•ly
in•clu•sive•ness
in•cog•ni•to *to adj.,*

adv., n., pl. in•cog•
ni•tos
in•co•her•ence
in•co•her•en•cy *n.,*
pl. in•co•her•en•
cies
in•co•her•ent
in•co•her•ent•ly
in•come
income ac•count
income av•er•ag•ing
income bond
income from con•
tin•u•ing op•er•a•
tions
income from dis•con•
tin•ued operations
income fund
income in re•spect of
a de•ce•dent
income main•te•
nance
income-seek•ing ex•
pense
income shift•ing
income split•ting
income state•ment
income sum•ma•ry
income tax
income-tax ex•pense
in•com•men•su•rate
in•com•men•su•
rate•ly
in•com•men•su•
rate•ness
in•com•mu•ni•ca•do
in•com•pa•ra•
bil•i•ty
in•com•pa•ra•ble
in•com•pa•ra•ble•
ness
in•com•pa•ra•bly
in•com•pat•
i•bil•i•ty
in•com•pat•i•ble
in•com•pat•i•bly

in•com•pe•tence
in•com•pe•ten•cy
in•com•pe•tent
in•com•pe•tent•ly
in•com•plete
in•com•plete•ly
in•com•plete•ness
in•com•pre•hen•si•
bil•i•ty
in•com•pre•hen•si•
ble
in•com•pre•hen•si•
ble•ness
in•com•pre•hen•si•
bly
in•con•ceiv•
a•bil•i•ty
in•con•ceiv•a•ble
in•con•ceiv•a•ble•
ness
in•con•ceiv•a•bly
in•con•clu•sive
in•con•clu•sive•ly
in•con•clu•sive•ness
in•con•gru•i•ty *n.,*
pl. in•con•gru•i•ties
in•con•gru•ous
in•con•gru•ous•ly
in•con•gru•ous•ness
in•con•se•quen•tial
in•con•se•quen•ti•
al•i•ty
in•con•se•quen•
tial•ly
in•con•sid•er•a•ble
in•con•sid•er•ate
in•con•sid•er•ate•ly
in•con•sid•er•ate•
ness
in•con•sis•ten•cy *n.,*
pl. in•con•sist•en•
cies
in•con•sis•tent
inconsistent judg•
ments

inconsistent state•
  ment
inconsistent ver•dict
in•con•spic•u•ous
in•con•spic•u•ous•ly
in•con•spic•u•ous•
  ness
in•con•test•
  a•bil•i•ty
incontestability clause
in•con•test•a•ble
in•con•test•a•bly
in•con•tro•vert•
  i•bil•i•ty
in•con•tro•vert•i•ble
in•con•tro•vert•
  i•ble•ness
in•con•tro•vert•i•bly
in•con•ven•ience n.,
  v., in•con•ven•
  ienced, in•con•ven•
  ienc•ing
inconvenient fo•rum
in•con•ven•ient•ly
in•con•vert•
  i•bil•i•ty
in•con•vert•i•ble
in•con•vert•i•bly
in•cor•po•ra•ble
in•cor•po•rate v., in•
  cor•po•rat•ed, in•
  cor•po•rat•ing
incorporate by ref•
  er•ence
in•cor•po•rat•ed
  (Inc.)
incorporated bar
in•cor•po•rat•ed•
  ness
in•cor•po•ra•tion
incorporation by ref•
  er•ence
incorporation doc•
  trine
in•cor•po•ra•tive

in•cor•po•ra•tor
in•cor•po•re•al
incorporeal her•e•
  dit•a•ment
incorporeal prop•
  er•ty
in•cor•po•re•al•i•ty
in•cor•po•re•al•ly
in•cor•po•re•i•ty
in•cor•rect
in•cor•rect•ly
in•cor•rect•ness
in•cor•ri•gi•bil•i•ty
in•cor•ri•gi•ble
in•cor•ri•gi•ble•ness
in•cor•ri•gi•bly
in•cor•rupt•i•
  bil•i•ty
in•cor•rupt•i•ble
in•cor•rupt•i•ble•
  ness
in•cor•rupt•i•bly
in•creas•a•ble
in•crease v., in•
  creased, in•creas•
  ing, n.
in•creas•ing•ly
in•cred•i•bil•i•ty
in•cred•i•ble (unbe-
  lievable: cf. INCREDU-
  LOUS)
in•cred•i•ble•ness
in•cred•i•bly
in•cre•du•li•ty
in•cred•u•lous (unbe-
  lieving: cf. INCREDIBLE)
in•cred•u•lous•ly
in•cred•u•lous•ness
in•cre•ment
in•cre•men•tal
incremental cost
incremental rev•e•
  nue
in•cre•men•tal•ism
in•cre•men•tal•ist
in•cre•men•tal•ly

in•crim•i•nate v., in•
  crim•i•nat•ed, in•
  crim•i•nat•ing
incriminating state•
  ment
in•crim•i•na•tion
in•crim•i•na•tor
in•crim•i•na•to•ry
in•cul•pa•ble (blame-
  less: cf. CULPABLE; IN-
  CULPATORY)
in•cul•pate v., in•
  cul•pat•ed, in•cul•
  pat•ing
in•cul•pa•tion
in•cul•pa•to•ry (in-
  criminating: cf. INCULP-
  PABLE)
in•cum•ben•cy n., pl.
  in•cum•ben•cies
in•cum•bent
in•cur v., in•curred,
  in•cur•ring
in•cur•a•bil•i•ty
in•cur•a•ble (not cur-
  able: cf. INCURRABLE)
in•cur•a•ble•ness
in•cur•a•bly
in•cur•ra•ble (subject
  to being incurred: cf.
  INCURABLE)
in•de•bi•ta•tus as•
  sump•sit Latin.
in•debt•ed
in•debt•ed•ness
in•de•cen•cy n., pl.
  in•de•cen•cies
in•de•cent
indecent as•sault
indecent ex•po•sure
indecent lib•er•ties
indecent speech
in•de•cent•ly
in•de•ci•sive
in•de•ci•sive•ly
in•de•ci•sive•ness

in•de•fea•si•bil•i•ty
in•de•fea•si•ble
in•de•fea•si•bly
in•de•fen•si•bil•i•ty
in•de•fen•si•ble
in•de•fen•si•ble•
 ness
in•de•fen•si•bly
in•def•i•nite
indefinite de•liv•er•y
 con•tract
indefinite fail•ure of
 is•sue
indefinite sen•tence
in•def•i•nite•ly
in•def•i•nite•ness
in•del•i•bil•i•ty
in•del•i•ble
indelible nav•i•ga•
 bil•i•ty doc•trine
in•del•i•ble•ness
in•del•i•bly
Indem. (Indemnity)
in•dem•ni•fi•ca•tion
in•dem•ni•fi•ca•
 to•ry
in•dem•ni•fi•er
in•dem•ni•fy v., in•
 dem•ni•fied, in•
 dem•ni•fy•ing
in•dem•ni•tee
in•dem•ni•tor
in•dem•ni•ty n., pl.
 in•dem•ni•ties (cita-
 tion form: Indem.)
indemnity in•sur•
 ance
in•dent
in•den•ture n., v., in•
 den•tured, in•den•
 tur•ing
indentured serv•ant
in•den•ture•ship
Indep. (Independent)
in•de•pend•ence
in•de•pend•en•cy n.,

pl. in•de•pend•en•
 cies
in•de•pend•ent (cita-
 tion form: Indep.)
independent ac•
 count•ant
independent au•dit
independent au•di•
 tor
independent con•
 trac•tor
independent coun•sel
independent in•ter•
 ven•ing cause
independent pros•e•
 cu•tor
independent source
 rule
independent state
 grounds
independent un•ion
in•de•pend•ent•ly
in•de•scrib•
 a•bil•i•ty
in•de•scrib•a•ble
in•de•scrib•a•ble•
 ness
in•de•scrib•a•bly
in•de•struct•
 i•bil•i•ty
in•de•struct•i•ble
indestructible trust
in•de•struct•i•ble•
 ness
in•de•struct•i•bly
in•de•ter•mi•nate
indeterminate sen•
 tence
in•de•ter•mi•nate•ly
in•de•ter•mi•nate•
 ness
in•de•ter•mi•na•
 tion
in•dex n., pl. in•
 dex•es or (esp. in sci-
 entific contexts) in•
 di•ces, v.

index ar•bi•trage
index crime
index fund
in•dex•a•ble
in•dex•a•tion
in•dexed mort•gage
in•dex•ing
In•di•an
Indian coun•try
Indian res•er•va•tion
in•di•cat•a•ble
in•di•cate v., in•di•
 cat•ed, in•di•cat•
 ing
in•di•ca•tion
in•di•ca•tive
in•di•ca•tive•ly
in•di•ca•tor
in•dic•a•to•ry
in•di•ci•um n., pl. in•
 di•ci•a
in•dict (to charge with
 wrongdoing: cf. INDITE)
in•dict•a•bil•i•ty
in•dict•a•ble
indictable of•fense
in•dict•a•bly
in•dict•ee
in•dict•er or in•
 dict•or (an accuser:
 cf. INDITER)
in•dict•ment (an accu-
 sation: cf. INDITEMENT)
in•di•gence
in•dig•e•nous
indigenous peo•ples
in•dig•e•nous•ly
in•dig•e•nous•ness
in•di•gent
in•di•gent•ly
in•dig•nant
in•dig•nant•ly
in•dig•na•tion
in•dig•ni•ty n., pl.
 in•dig•ni•ties
in•di•rect

indirect cost
indirect e•lec•tion
indirect ev•i•dence
indirect in•i•ti•a•tive
indirect la•bor
indirect pri•ma•ry
indirect proof
indirect tax
in•di•rec•tion
in•di•rect•ly
in•di•rect•ness
in•dis•creet
in•dis•creet•ly
in•dis•creet•ness
in•dis•cre•tion
in•dis•crim•i•nate
in•dis•crim•i•nate•ly
in•dis•crim•i•nate•
  ness
in•dis•pen•sa•
  bil•i•ty
in•dis•pen•sa•ble
indispensable par•ty
in•dis•pen•sa•ble•
  ness
in•dis•pen•sa•bly
in•dis•put•a•ble
in•dis•put•a•ble•
  ness
in•dis•put•a•bly
in•dis•sol•u•bil•i•ty
in•dis•sol•u•ble
in•dis•sol•u•ble•
  ness
in•dis•sol•u•bly
in•dite v., in•dit•ed,
  in•dit•ing (to com-
  pose or write: cf. IN-
  DICT)
in•dite•ment (the ac-
  tion of composing a
  written work: cf. IN-
  DICTMENT)
in•dit•er (a writer: cf.
  INDICTER)
in•di•vid•u•al

individual ac•count
individual in•sur•
  ance
individual lib•er•ty
individual re•tire•
  ment ac•count (IRA)
individual retirement
  ar•range•ment (IRA)
individual re•turn
in•di•vid•u•al•ism
in•di•vid•u•al•ist
in•di•vid•u•al•is•tic
in•di•vid•u•al•is•ti•
  cal•ly
in•di•vid•u•al•i•ty
  n., pl. indi•vid•u•
  al•i•ties
in•di•vid•u•al•ly
in•di•vis•i•bil•i•ty
in•di•vis•i•ble
in•di•vis•i•ble•ness
in•di•vis•i•bly
in•dom•i•ta•bil•i•ty
in•dom•i•ta•ble
in•dom•i•ta•ble•
  ness
in•dom•i•ta•bly
in•dorse or en•dorse
  v., in•dorsed or en•
  dorsed, in•dors•ing
  or en•dors•ing (to
  sign the back of a ne-
  gotiable instrument: cf.
  ENDORSE¹)
in•dor•see or en•
  dor•see
in•dorse•ment or en•
  dorse•ment
in•dors•er or en•
  dors•er
in•duce v., in•duced,
  in•duc•ing
in•duce•ment
in•duc•er
in•duc•i•ble
in•duct

in•duc•tee
in•duc•tion
in•duc•tive
in•duc•tive•ly
in•duc•tive•ness
Indus. (Industry; Indus-
  tries; Industrial)
in•dus•tri•al (citation
  form: Indus.)
industrial de•vel•op•
  ment bond (IDB)
industrial es•pi•o•
  nage
industrial life in•sur•
  ance
industrial per•for•
  mance zon•ing
industrial psy•
  chol•o•gy
industrial re•la•tions
industrial rev•e•nue
  bond (IRB)
industrial spy
industrial un•ion
in•dus•tri•al•ly
in•dus•try n., pl. in•
  dus•tries (citation
  form for sing. and pl.:
  Indus.)
in•dus•try•wide
in•e•bri•ate v., in•e•
  bri•at•ed, in•e•bri•
  at•ing, n.
in•e•bri•a•tion
in•ef•fec•tive
ineffective as•sis•
  tance of coun•sel
in•ef•fec•tive•ly
in•ef•fec•tive•ness
in•ef•fec•tu•al
in•ef•fec•tu•al•i•ty
in•ef•fec•tu•al•ly
in•ef•fec•tu•al•ness
in•ef•fi•ca•cious
in•ef•fi•ca•cious•ly

in•ef•fi•ca•cious•
ness
in•ef•fi•cac•i•ty
in•ef•fi•ca•cy
in•ef•fi•cien•cy n.,
pl. in•ef•fi•cien•cies
in•ef•fi•cient
in•ef•fi•cient•ly
in•e•gal•i•tar•i•an
in•e•las•tic
inelastic de•mand
inelastic sup•ply
in•e•las•tic•i•ty
in•el•oi•gi•bil•i•ty
in•el•oi•gi•ble
in•el•oi•gi•bly
in•e•luc•ta•bil•i•ty
in•e•luc•ta•ble
in•e•luc•ta•bly
in•ept
in•ep•ti•tude
in•ept•ly
in•ept•ness
in•e•qual•i•ty n.,
pl. in•e•qual•i•ties
in•eq•ui•ta•ble
in•eq•ui•ta•ble•ness
in•eq•ui•ta•bly
in•eq•ui•ty n., pl. in•
eq•ui•ties (unfair-
ness: cf. INIQUITY)
in•es•ti•ma•ble
in•es•ti•ma•bly
in•evoi•ta•bil•i•ty
in•evoi•ta•ble
inevitable ac•ci•dent
inevitable dis•cov•
er•y ex•cep•tion
inevitable loss
in•evoi•ta•bly
in•ex•cus•a•bil•i•ty
in•ex•cus•a•ble
in•ex•cus•a•ble•ness
in•ex•cus•a•bly
in•ex•o•ra•bil•i•ty
in•ex•o•ra•ble

in•ex•o•ra•ble•ness
in•ex•o•ra•bly
in•ex•pe•di•ent
in•ex•pe•ri•enced
in•ex•pli•ca•bil•i•ty
in•ex•pli•ca•ble
in•ex•pli•ca•ble•
ness
in•ex•pli•ca•bly
in•ex•pres•si•ble
in•ex•pres•si•bly
in•ex•tri•ca•bil•i•ty
in•ex•tri•ca•ble
in•ex•tri•ca•ble•ness
in•ex•tri•ca•bly
in•fa•mous
infamous crime
infamous pun•ish•
ment
in•fa•mous•ly
in•fa•mous•ness
in•fa•my n., pl. in•
fa•mies
in•fan•cy n., pl. in•
fan•cies
in•fant
in•fan•ti•cid•al
in•fan•ti•cide
in•fan•tile
in•fan•ti•lism
in•fan•til•i•ty
in•fan•til•i•za•tion
in•fan•til•ize v., in•
fan•til•ized, in•fan•
til•iz•ing
in•fect
in•fect•ant
in•fect•ed•ness
in•fec•tion
in•fec•tious
infectious dis•ease
in•fec•tious•ly
in•fec•tious•ness
in•fe•lic•i•tous
in•fe•lic•i•tous•ly

in•fe•lic•i•ty n., pl.
in•fe•lic•i•ties
in•fer v., in•ferred,
in•fer•ring (to rea-
son; to draw a conclu-
sion: cf. IMPLY)
in•fer•a•ble
in•fer•a•bly
in•fer•ence
in•fer•en•tial
in•fer•en•tial•ly
in•fe•ri•or
inferior court
in•fe•ri•or•i•ty
in•fer•rer
in•feu•da•tion
in•fi•del•i•ty n., pl.
in•fi•del•i•ties
in•fill
in•firm
in•firm•a•tive
infirmative ev•i•
dence
infirmative hy•
poth•e•sis
in•fir•mi•ty n., pl.
in•fir•mi•ties
in•flame v., in•
flamed, in•flam•ing
in•flamed
in•flam•er
in•flam•ing•ly
in•flam•ma•bil•i•ty
in•flam•ma•ble
in•flam•ma•bly
in•flate v., in•flat•ed,
in•flat•ing
in•fla•tion
in•fla•tion•ar•y
inflationary spi•ral
in•flex•i•bil•i•ty
in•flex•i•ble
in•flex•i•bly
in•flict
in•flict•a•ble

in•flict•or or in•flic•tor
in•flic•tion
infliction of men•tal dis•tress
in•flic•tive
in•flu•ence *n., v.,* in•flu•enced, in•flu•enc•ing
influence ped•dler
influence ped•dling
in•flu•ence•a•ble
in•flu•enc•er
in•flu•en•tial
in•flu•en•tial•ly
Info. (Information)
in•fo•mer•cial or in•for•mer•cial
in•form
in•for•mal
in•for•mal•i•ty *n., pl.* in•for•mal•i•ties
in•for•mal•ly
in•form•ant
in•for•ma•tion (*citation form:* **Info.**)
information and be•lief
information tech•nol∘o∘gy (IT)
in•for•ma•tion∘al
informational pick•et•ing
in•formed con•sent
in•form•er
informer's priv•i•lege
in∘fra *Latin.*
infra le∘gem *Latin.*
in•fract
in•frac•tion
in•frac•tor
in•fra-struc•tural
in•fra-struc•ture
in•fringe *v.,* in•fringed, in•fring•ing
in•fringe•ment

in•fring•er
in•fu•ri•ate *v.,* in•fu•ri•at∘ed, in•fu•ri•at•ing
in•fu•ri•at∘ed
in•fu•ri•at•ing
in•fu•ri•at•ing•ly
in•gen•ious (clever: cf. INGENUOUS)
in•gen•ious•ly
in•gen•ious•ness
in•ge•nu•i∘ty *n., pl.* in•ge•nu•i•ties
in•gen•u•ous (naive: cf. INGENIOUS)
in•gen•u•ous•ly
in•gen•u•ous•ness
in•gra•ti•ate *v.,* in•gra•ti•at∘ed, in•gra•ti•at•ing
in•gra•ti•at•ing
in•gra•ti•a•tion
in•grat∘i•tude
in•gress
in•hab∘it
in•hab∘i•ta•bil∘i•ty
in•hab∘i•ta•ble
in•hab∘i•tant
in•hal•ant
inhalant a∘buse
inhalant de•pend•ence
inhalant-in•duced dis•or•der
inhalant in•tox∘i•ca•tion
in•here *v.,* in•hered, in•her•ing
in•her•ence
in•her•en∘cy *n., pl.* in•her•en•cies
inherency doc•trine
in•her•ent
inherent de•fect
inherent pow∘er
inherent right

inherent vice
in•her•ent•ly
in•her∘it
in•her∘i•ta•bil∘i•ty
in•her∘i•ta•ble
in•her∘i•ta•bly
in•her∘i•tance
inheritance tax
in•hib∘it
in•hi•bi•tion
in•hib∘i•tor
in•hib∘i•to∘ry
in•hu•man *adj.*
in•hu•mane
in•hu•man∘i∘ty *n., pl.* in•hu•man∘i•ties.
in•hu•man•ly
in•hu•man•ness
in•iq•ui•tous
in•iq•ui•tous•ly
in•iq•ui•tous•ness
in•iq•ui•ty *n., pl.* in•iq•ui•ties (evildoing: cf. INEQUITY)
in∘i•tial
initial de•ter•mi•na•tion
initial pub•lic of•fer•ing (IPO)
in∘i•tial•er
in∘i•tial•ly
in∘i•ti•ate *v.,* in∘i•ti•at∘ed, in∘i•ti•at•ing, *adj., n.*
in∘i•ti•a•tion
in∘i•ti•a•tive
in∘i•ti•a•tor
Inj. (Injury)
in•ject
in•ject•a∘ble
in•jec•tion
in•ju•di•cious
in•ju•di•cious•ly
in•ju•di•cious•ness
in•junc•tion

in•junc•tive
injunctive relief
in•junc•tive•ly
in•jur•a•ble
in•jure v., in•jured, in•jur•ing
in•jured
in•jur•er
in•ju•ri•a n., pl. in•ju•ri•ae Latin.
in•ju•ri•ous
injurious false•hood
in•ju•ri•ous•ly
in•ju•ri•ous•ness
in•ju•ry n., pl. in•ju•ries (citation form: Inj.)
in•jus•tice
in•land
inland bill of ex•change
inland ma•rine in•sur•ance
in•law (a person with full legal rights; to restore an outlaw's legal rights: cf. IN LAW; IN-LAW)
in•law•ry
in•mate
inn
in•nate
in•nate•ly
in•nate•ness
in•ner bar
inner bar•ris•ter
Inner Tem•ple
inn•keep•er
in•no•cence
in•no•cent
innocent pas•sage
in•no•cent•ly
in•noc•u•ous
in•noc•u•ous•ly
in•noc•u•ous•ness
in•no•va•tion

in•no•va•tive
in•no•va•tive•ly
in•no•va•tive•ness
Inns of Chan•cer•y
Inns of Court
in•nu•en•do n., pl. in•nu•en•dos or in•nu•en•does
in•nu•mer•a•ble (too many to count: cf. ENUMERABLE)
in•of•fi•ci•os•i•ty
in•of•fi•cious
inofficious tes•ta•ment
inofficious will
in•of•fi•cious•ness
in•op•er•a•bil•i•ty
in•op•er•a•ble
in•op•er•a•tive
in•op•er•a•tive•ness
in•op•por•tune
in•or•di•nate
in•or•di•nate•ly
in•or•di•nate•ness
in•pa•tient
in•quest
in•quir•a•ble
in•quire or (esp. Brit.) en•quire v., in•quired or en•quired, in•quir•ing or en•quir•ing
in•quir•er or (esp. Brit.) en•quir•er
in•quir•ing•ly or (esp. Brit.) en•quir•ing•ly
in•quir•y or (esp. Brit.) en•quir•y n., pl. in•quir•ies or en•quir•ies
inquiry no•tice
in•qui•si•tion

in•qui•si•tion•al
in•quis•i•tive
in•quis•i•tive•ly
in•quis•i•tive•ness
in•quis•i•tor
in•quis•i•to•ri•al
inquisitorial sys•tem
in•quis•i•to•ri•al•ly
in•quis•i•to•ri•al•ness
Ins. (Insurance)
in•sane
in•sane•ly
in•sane•ness
in•san•i•ty n., pl. in•san•i•ties
insanity de•fense
in•scru•ta•bil•i•ty
in•scru•ta•ble
inscrutable fault
in•scru•ta•ble•ness
in•scru•ta•bly
in•se•cure
in•se•cure•ly
in•se•cure•ness
in•se•cu•ri•ty n., pl. in•se•cu•ri•ties
in•sep•a•ra•bil•i•ty
in•sep•a•ra•ble
in•sep•a•ra•ble•ness
in•sep•a•ra•bly
in•side
inside job
in•sid•er
insider trad•er or in•side trad•er
insider trad•ing
in•sid•i•ous
in•sight (understanding: cf. INCITE)
in•sight•ful
in•sight•ful•ly
in•sight•ful•ness
in•sig•nif•i•cance
in•sig•nif•i•cant

in•sig•nif•i•cant•ly
in•sin•cere
in•sin•cere•ly
in•sin•cer•i•ty *n., pl.*
  in•sin•cer•i•ties
in•sin•u•ate *v.*, in•
  sin•u•at•ed, in•
  sin•u•at•ing
in•sin•u•at•ing•ly
in•sin•u•a•tion
in•sist
in•sist•ence
in•sist•ent
in•so•far as
in•sol•ven•cy *n., pl.*
  in•sol•ven•cies
in•sol•vent
in•spect
in•spect•a•bil•i•ty
in•spect•a•ble
in•spec•tion
inspection of doc•u•
  ments
in•spec•tion•al
in•spec•tor
Inst. (Institute; Institu
  tion
in•sta•bil•i•ty
in•stall
in•stal•la•tion
in•stall•er
in•stall•ment or in•
  stal•ment
installment note
installment plan
installment sale
in•stance
in•stant
instant un•sea•wor•
  thi•ness
in•stan•ta•ne•ous
in•stan•ta•ne•ous•ly
in•stan•ta•ne•ous•
  ness
in•stan•ter *Latin.*
in•stead

in•sti•gate *v.*, in•sti•
  gat•ed, in•sti•gat•
  ing
in•sti•ga•tion
in•sti•ga•tive
in•sti•ga•tor
in•sti•tute[1] *n.* (*citation*
  form: Inst.)
institute[2] *v.*, in•sti•
  tut•ed, in•sti•tut•
  ing
In•sti•tutes of Jus•
  tin•i•an
in•sti•tu•tion (*citation*
  form: Inst.)
in•sti•tu•tion•al
institutional in•ves•
  tor
in•sti•tu•tion•al•i•
  za•tion
in•sti•tu•tion•al•ize
  v., in•sti•tu•tion•
  al•ized, in•sti•tu•
  tion•al•iz•ing
in•sti•tu•tion•al•ly
in•sti•tu•tor or in•
  sti•tut•er
in•struct
in•struc•tion
in•struc•tion•al
in•struc•tions *n.pl.*
in•struc•tive
in•struc•tor
in•stru•ment
in•stru•men•tal
instrumental trust
in•stru•men•tal•i•ty
  n., pl. in•stru•men•
  tal•i•ties
in•stru•men•tal•ly
in•su•bor•di•nate
in•su•bor•di•nate•ly
in•su•bor•di•na•tion
in•suf•fi•cien•cy *n.,*
  pl. in•suf•fi•cien•
  cies

insufficiency of marks
in•suf•fi•cient
insufficient cause
insufficient ev•i•
  dence
insufficient funds
in•suf•fi•cient•ly
in•su•late *v.*, in•su•
  lat•ed, in•su•lat•
  ing
in•su•la•tion
in•su•la•tive
in•su•la•tor
in•sult
in•sult•ing
in•sult•ing•ly
in•sur•a•bil•i•ty
in•sur•a•ble
insurable in•ter•est
insurable risk
insurable ti•tle
in•sur•ance (*citation*
  form: Ins.)
insurance a•gent
insurance brok•er
insurance pol•i•cy
insurance trust
in•sure *v.*, in•sured,
  in•sur•ing (to protect
  against loss: cf. EN-
  SURE)
in•sured *n., pl.* in•
  sured or in•sureds
in•sur•er
in•sur•gence
in•sur•gen•cy *n., pl.*
  in•sur•gen•cies
in•sur•gent
in•sur•ing clause
in•sur•rec•tion
in•sur•rec•tion•al
in•sur•rec•tion•ism
in•sur•rec•tion•ist
in•tan•gi•bil•i•ty
in•tan•gi•ble
intangible as•set

intangible prop•er•ty
in•tan•gi•ble•ness
in•tan•gi•bly
in•te•grate v., in•te•grat•ed, in•te•grat•ing
integrated bar
integrated con•tract
integrated writ•ing
in•te•gra•tion
integration clause
in•te•gra•tion•ist
in•te•gra•tive
in•te•gra•tor
in•teg•ri•ty
Intell. (Intellectual)
in•tel•lect
in•tel•lec•tu•al (citation form: Intell.)
intellectual func•tion•ing
in•tellec•tual prop•er•ty
in•tel•lec•tu•al•i•ty
in•tel•lec•tu•al•i•za•tion
in•tel•lec•tu•al•ize
in•tel•lec•tu•al•ly
in•tel•li•gence
intelligence a•gen•cy
intelligence of•fice
intelligence quo•tient (IQ)
intelligence test
in•tel•li•genc•er
in•tel•li•gent
in•tel•li•gent•ly
in•tel•li•gi•bil•i•ty
in•tel•li•gi•ble
in•tel•li•gi•bly
in•tem•per•ance
in•tem•per•ate
in•tem•per•ate•ly
in•tem•per•ate•ness
in•tend
in•tend•ment

in•tent
in•ten•tion
in•ten•tion•al
intentional in•flic•tion of men•tal dis•tress
intentional tort
intentional wrong
in•ten•tion•al•ism
in•ten•tion•al•i•ty
in•ten•tion•al•ly
in•ten•tioned
in•ter a•li•a Latin.
inter pa•res Latin. (between or among equals: cf. INTER PAR•TES)
inter par•tes Latin. (between or among the parties: cf. INTER PARES)
inter se or inter se•se Latin.
inter vi•vos Latin.
inter vivos gift
inter vivos trust
in•ter•ac•tion
in•ter•ac•tive
in•ter•ac•tive•ly
in•ter•ac•tiv•i•ty
in•ter•a•gen•cy
in•ter•brand com•pe•ti•tion
in•ter•cede v., in•ter•ced•ed, in•ter•ced•ing
in•ter•ced•er
in•ter•cept
in•ter•cep•tion
in•ter•cep•tor or in•ter•cept•er
in•ter•change v., in•ter•changed, in•ter•chang•ing, n.
in•ter•change•a•bil•i•ty

in•ter•change•a•ble
in•ter•change•a•bly
in•ter•com•mon
in•ter•com•mon•age
in•ter•com•mon•er
in•ter•com•pa•ny
intercompany dis•tri•bu•tion
intercompany trans•ac•tion
in•ter•con•nect
in•ter•con•nect•ed•ness
in•ter•con•nec•tion
in•ter•course
in•ter•de•part•men•tal
in•ter•de•part•men•tal•ly
in•ter•de•pend•ence
in•ter•de•pend•en•cy
in•ter•de•pend•ent
in•ter•de•pend•ent•ly
in•ter•dict
in•ter•dic•tion
in•ter•dic•tor
in•ter•dic•to•ry
Interdisc. (Interdisciplinary)
in•ter•dis•ci•pli•nar•y (citation form: Interdisc.)
in•ter•es•se Latin.
interesse ter•mi•ni Latin.
in•ter•est
interest-bear•ing
interest-free loan
interest group
interest on law•yers' trust ac•counts (IOLTA)
in•ter•est•ed
interested par•ty

interested per•son
interested wit•ness
in•ter•est•ed•ly
in•ter•est•ed•ness
in•ter•est•ing
in•ter•est•ing•ly
in•ter•ex•change
con•nec•tion
in•ter•face
in•ter•fere v., in•ter•
fered, in•ter•fer•ing
in•ter•fer•ence
interference pro•
ceed•ing
in•ter•fer•er
interfering pat•ent
in•ter•gov•ern•
men•tal
in•ter•im
in•te•ri•or
in•ter•in•sur•ance
in•te•ri•or
in•ter•lin•e•ate v.,
in•ter•lin•e•at•ed,
in•ter•lin•e•at•ing
in•ter•lin•e•a•tion
in•ter•lock
in•ter•lock•ing di•
rec•to•rate
interlocking loans
in•ter•loc•u•to•ry
interlocutory ap•peal
interlocutory de•cree
interlocutory in•junc•
tion
interlocutory or•der
in•ter•lope v.,
in•ter•loped,
in•ter•lop•ing
in•ter•lop•er
in•ter•mar•riage
in•ter•mar•ry v.,
in•ter•mar•ried,
in•ter•mar•ry•ing
in•ter•med•dle v.,
in•ter•med•dled,
in•ter•med•dling

in•ter•med•dler
in•ter•med•dling
in•ter•me•di•ar•y n,
pl. in•ter•me•di•ar•
ies, adj.
in•ter•me•di•ate
intermediate ap•pel•
late court
intermediate scru•
ti•ny
in•ter•me•di•a•tion
in•ter•mer•chant
in•ter•min•gle v.,
in•ter•min•gled,
in•ter•min•gling
in•ter•min•gle•ment
in•ter•mit•tent
intermittent ex•plo•
sive dis•or•der
intermittent sen•
tence
in•ter•mit•tent•ly
in•ter•mod•al
intermodal trans•port
in•ter•mod•al•ism
in•tern n, v., in•
terned, in•tern•ing
in•ter•nal
internal ac•count•ing
internal au•dit
internal au•di•tor
internal re•port•ing
internal rev•e•nue
Internal Rev•e•nue
Code (citation form: I.
R.C.)
in•ter•nal•ly
in•ter•na•tion•al (ci-
tation form: Int'l)
international boy•cott
International Court of
Jus•tice (citation
form: I.C.J.)
international law
international re•la•
tions

international trade
in•ter•na•tion•al•ly
in•ter•ne•cine
in•tern•ee
In•ter•net
Internet serv•ice pro•
vid•er (ISP)
Internet te•
leph•o•ony
in•tern•ment
internment camp
in•tern•ship
in•ter•of•fice
in•ter•plead v.,
in•ter•plead•ed,
in•ter•plead•ing
in•ter•plead•er
in•ter•pos•a•ble
in•ter•pos•al
in•ter•pose v.,
in•ter•posed,
in•ter•pos•ing
in•ter•pos•er
in•ter•pos•ing•ly
in•ter•po•si•tion
in•ter•pret
in•ter•pret•
a•bil•i•ty
in•ter•pret•a•ble
in•ter•pret•a•bly
in•ter•pre•ta•tion
in•ter•pre•ta•tive
in•ter•pre•ta•tive•ly
in•ter•pret•er
in•ter•pre•tive
interpretive rule
in•ter•pre•tive•ly
Interrog. (Interroga-
tory)
in•ter•ro•ga•ble
in•ter•ro•gate v., in•
ter•ro•gat•ed, in•
ter•ro•gat•ing
in•ter•ro•gat•ing•ly
in•ter•ro•ga•tion
in•ter•ro•ga•tion•al

in•ter•ro•ga•tor
in•ter•rog•a•to•ri•ly
in•ter•rog•a•to•ry
n., pl. in•ter•rog•a•
to•ries (citation form:
Interrog.)
in•ter•ro•gee
in•ter•spous•al
interspousal im•mu•
ni•ty
interspousal trans•
ac•tion
in•ter•spous•al•ly
in•ter•state
interstate com•merce
interstate com•pact
in•ter•vene v.,
in•ter•vened,
in•ter•ven•ing
in•ter•ven•er or or
in•ter•ve•nor
in•ter•ven•ing cause
in•ter•ven•tion
in•ter•ven•tion•ism
in•ter•ven•tion•ist
in•ter•view
in•ter•view•ee
in•ter•view•er
in•tes•ta•ble
in•tes•ta•cy
in•tes•tate
intestate suc•ces•sion
in•ti•ma•cy n., pl. in•
ti•ma•cies
in•ti•mate v., in•ti•
mat•ed, in•ti•mat•
ing, adj., n.
in•ti•mate•ly
in•ti•mat•er
in•ti•ma•tion
in•tim•i•date v., in•
tim•i•dat•ed, in•
tim•i•dat•ing
in•tim•i•da•tion
in•tim•i•da•tor
Int'l (International)

in•tol•er•a•bil•i•ty
in•tol•er•a•ble
in•tol•er•a•ble•ness
in•tol•er•a•bly
in•tol•er•ance
intolerant
in•tol•er•ant•ly
in•tox•i•cant
in•tox•i•cate v., in•
tox•i•cat•ed, in•
tox•i•cat•ing
in•tox•i•cat•ed•ly
in•tox•i•cat•ing
in•tox•i•ca•tion
in tra vi•res Latin.
in•tra•brand com•
pe•ti•tion
in•trac•ta•bil•i•ty
in•trac•ta•ble
in•trac•ta•ble•ness
in•trac•ta•bly
in•tra•group stock
in•tra•net
in•tran•si•gence
in•tran•si•gen•cy
in•tran•si•gent
in•tran•si•gent•ly
in•tra•pre•neur (em-
ployee given latitude
for creativity): cf. EN
TREPRENEUR
in•tra•pre•neur•ship
in•tra•state
intrastate com•merce
in•tra•ve•nous
intravenous drug
intravenous in•jec•
tion
in•tra•ve•nous•ly
in•trigue n., v., in•
trigued, in•tri•guing
in•tri•guer
in•tri•guing•ly
in•trin•sic
intrinsic fraud
in•trin•si•cal•ly

in•tro•duce v.,
in•tro•duced,
in•tro•duc•ing
in•tro•duc•er
in•tro•duc•i•ble
in•tro•duc•tion
in•tro•duc•to•ri•ly
in•tro•duc•to•ri•
ness
in•tro•duc•to•ry
in•trude v., in•
trud•ed, in•trud•ing
in•trud•er
in•trud•ing•ly
in•tru•sion
in•tru•sive
in•tru•sive•ly
in•tru•sive•ness
in•ure or en•ure v.,
in•ured or en•ured,
in•ur•ing or en•ur•
ing
in•ured or en•ured
in•ure•ment or en•
ure•ment
Inv. (Investor; Inves
tors; Investment; In-
vestments)
in•vad•a•ble
in•vade v., in•vade,
in•vad•ing
in•vad•er
in•val•id[1] (not valid)
in•va•lid[2] (sick person)
in•val•i•date v., in•
val•i•dat•ed, in•
val•i•dat•ing
in•val•i•da•tion
in•val•i•da•tor
in•va•lid•i•ty
in•va•lid•ly
in•va•sion
invasion of pri•va•cy
in•va•sive
in•veigh
in•veigh•er

in•vei•gle v., in•vei•gled, in•vei•gling
in•vei•gle•ment
in•vei•gler
in•vent
in•vent•a•ble
in•ven•tion
in•ven•tive
in•ven•tive•ly
in•ven•tive•ness
in•ven•tor
in•ven•to•ri•a•ble
in•ven•tor•ship
inventorship en•ti•ty
in•ven•to•ry n., pl. in•ven•to•ries, v., in•ven•to•ried, in•ven•to•ry•ing
in•verse n., v., in•verse, in•vers•ing
inverse con•dem•na•tion
inverse or•der of al•ien•a•tion
in•verse•ly
in•vest
in•vest•a•ble
in•ves•ti•ga•ble
in•ves•ti•gate v., in•ves•ti•ga•ed, in•ves•ti•gat•ing
in•ves•ti•ga•tion
in•ves•ti•ga•tion•al
in•ves•ti•ga•tive
investigative priv•i•lege
in•ves•ti•ga•tor
in•ves•ti•ga•to•ry
in•ves•ti•tive
in•ves•ti•ture
in•vest•ment (citation form for sing. and pl.: Inv.)
investment ad•vis•er
investment bank
investment bank•er

investment bank•ing
investment com•pany
investment fund
investment in•come
investment tax cred•it (ITC)
investment trust
in•ves•tor (citation form for sing. and pl Inv.)
in•vid•i•ous
invidious dis•crim•i•na•tion
in•vid•i•ous•ly
in•vid•i•ous•ness
in•vi•o•la•bil•i•ty
in•vi•o•la•ble
in•vi•o•la•bly
in•vi•o•la•cy
in•vi•o•late
in•vi•o•late•ly
in•vi•o•late•ness
in•vi•ta•tion
invitation for bids (IFB)
in•vi•ta•tion•al
in•vite v., in•vit•ed, in•vit•ing
in•vi•tee
in•vit•er
in•vo•ca•ble
in•vo•ca•tion
in•voice n., v., in•voiced, in•voic•ing
in•voke v., in•voked, in•vok•ing
in•vok•er
in•vol•un•tar•i•ly
in•vol•un•tar•i•ness
in•vol•un•tar•y
involuntary bank•rupt•cy
involuntary con•fes•sion
involuntary con•vey•ance

involuntary dis•con•tin•u•ance
involuntary dis•mis•sal
involuntary man•slaugh•ter
involuntary non•suit
involuntary pub•lic fig•ure
involuntary sale
involuntary smok•ing
involuntary trans•fer
involuntary trust
IOLTA (interest on lawyers' trust accounts)
IPO (initial public offering)
ip•se dix•it Latin.
ip•so fac•to Latin.
ipso ju•re Latin.
IQ (intelligence quotient)
IRA (individual retirement account; individual retirement arrangement)
IRB (industrial revenue bond)
I.R.C. (Internal Revenue Code)
i•ron•ic
i•ron•i•cal
i•ron•i•cal•ly
i•ro•ny n., pl. i•ro•nies
ir•ra•tion•al
ir•ra•tion•al•i•ty n., pl. ir•ra•tion•al•i•ties
ir•ra•tion•al•ly
ir•re•but•ta•ble
irrebuttable pre•sump•tion
ir•rec•on•cil•a•bil•i•ty
ir•rec•on•cil•a•ble

ir•rec•on•cil•a•ble dif•fer•enc•es
ir•rec•on•cil•a•ble•ness
ir•rec•on•cil•o•a•bly
ir•re•deem•a•ble
ir•re•deem•a•bly
ir•re•duc•i•ble
ir•re•duc•i•bly
ir•re•form•a•ble
ir•ref•u•ta•bil•i•ty
ir•ref•u•ta•ble
ir•ref•u•ta•bly
ir•reg•u•lar
ir•reg•u•lar•i•ty n., pl. ir•reg•u•lar•i•ties
ir•reg•u•lar•ly
ir•rel•e•vance
ir•rel•e•van•cy n., pl. ir•rel•e•van•cies
ir•rel•e•vant
ir•rel•e•vant•ly
ir•re•me•di•a•ble•ness
ir•re•me•di•a•bly
ir•rep•a•ra•bil•i•ty
ir•rep•a•ra•ble
irreparable in•ju•ry
ir•rep•a•ra•ble•ness
ir•rep•a•ra•bly
ir•re•plev•i•a•ble

ir•re•plev•i•sa•ble
ir•re•press•i•bil•i•ty
ir•re•press•i•ble
ir•re•press•i•bly
ir•re•sist•i•bil•i•ty
ir•re•sist•i•ble
irresistible im•pulse test
ir•re•sist•i•ble•ness
ir•re•sist•i•bly
ir•re•spon•si•bil•i•ty
ir•re•spon•si•ble
ir•re•spon•si•bly
ir•re•triev•a•bil•i•ty
ir•re•triev•a•ble
irretrievable break•down of mar•riage
ir•re•triev•a•bly
ir•re•vers•i•bil•i•ty
ir•re•vers•i•ble
ir•re•vers•i•bly
ir•rev•o•ca•bil•i•ty
ir•rev•o•ca•ble
irrevocable bid
irrevocable let•ter of cred•it
irrevocable of•fer
irrevocable trust
ir•rev•o•ca•ble•ness
ir•rev•o•ca•bly
Is•lam•ic law
i•so•bu•tyl ni•trite

i•so•late v., i•so•lat•ed, i•so•lat•ing, n.
i•so•la•tion
i•so•mer
i•so•meth•a•done Controlled Subst.
i•so•tope
ISP (Internet service provider)
is•su•a•ble
is•su•ance
is•sue n., v., is•sued, is•su•ing
issue of fact
issue of law
issue pre•clu•sion
is•su•er
IT (information technology)
ITC (investment tax credit)
i•tem
i•tem•i•za•tion
i•tem•ize v., i•tem•ized, i•tem•iz•ing
itemized de•duc•tion
i•tem•iz•er
i•tin•er•an•cy
i•tin•er•ant
i•tin•er•ant•ly
IVF (in vitro fertilization)
i•vo•ry tow•er

J

J.¹ (Journal)
J.² pl. JJ (Judge; Justice)
J. Res. (Joint Resolution)
J.A. (Joint Appendix)
jac•ti•ta•tion
jactitation of mar•riage
JAG Corps (Judge Advocate General's Corps)
jail
jail de•liv•er•y
jail•a•ble
jail•bait
jail•bird
jail•break
jail•er or jail•or
jail•house
jailhouse law•yer
Jan. (January)
Jane Doe
Jan•u•ar•y (citation form: **Jan.**)
jar•gon
jar•gon•y

Ja•son clause
jay•walk
jay•walk•er
jay•walk•ing
J.D. (Juris Doctor)
jeal•ous
jealous de•lu•sion
jeal•ous•ly
jeal•ous•ness
jeal•ous•y *n., pl* jeal•
ous•ies
jeer
jeer•er
jeer•ing•ly
jell (to become definite;
to congeal: cf. GEL)
jeo•fail *Law French.*
jeop•ard•ize *v.,* jeop•
ard•ized, jeop•ard•
iz•ing
jeop•ard•ous
jeop•ard•y
jer•ry-build *v.,* jer•ry-
built, jer•ry-build•
ing (to build cheaply
and flimsily: cf. JURY-
RIG)
jerry-build•er
jerry-built
jet•sam (goods thrown
overboard: cf. JETTISON)
jet•ti•son (to discard
or throw overboard;
the act of throwing
overboard: cf. JETSAM)
jet•ti•son•a•ble
Jew•ish law
jibe *v.,* jibed, jib•ing
(to fit; to be in har-
mony or accord: vs.
jive; cf. GIBE)
ji•had
jilt
jilt•er
Jim Crow
Jim Crow law

JINS (juvenile in need
of supervision)
JJ. (Judges; Justices)
j.n.o.v. (judgment not-
withstanding the ver-
dict) See also N.O.V.
job *n., v.,* jobbed,
job•bing, *adj.*
job ac•tion
job clas•si•fi•ca•tion
job de•scrip•tion
job e•val•u•a•tion
job-hunt *v.*
job-hunt•er
job-hunt•ing
job lot
job mar•ket
job se•cur•i•ty
job spec•i•fi•ca•tion
job•ber
job•ber•y
job•less
job•less•ness
John Doe
join
join is•sue
join•a•ble
join•der (a joining: cf.
JOINER; JOINTER)
joinder of is•sue
join•er (one who joins:
cf. JOINDER; JOINTER)
joint
joint ac•count
joint ad•ven•ture
joint and last sur•vi•
vor an•nu•i•ty
joint and sev•er•al
joint and several li•
a•bil•i•ty
joint and several ob•
li•ga•tion
joint and sur•vi•vor
an•nu•i•ty
joint ap•pen•dix (*cita
tion form:* **J.A.**)

joint com•mit•tee
joint con•tract
joint cus•to•dy
joint de•fense
joint defense a•gree•
ment
joint defense priv•i•
lege
joint en•ter•prise
joint es•tate
joint li•a•bil•i•ty
joint life an•nu•i•ty
joint life in•sur•ance
joint lives
joint ob•li•ga•tion
joint own•er
joint res•o•lu•tion
(*citation form:* **J. Res.**)
joint re•turn
joint ses•sion
joint stock
joint-stock as•so•ci•
a•tion
joint-stock com•
pa•ny
joint ten•an•cy
joint ten•ant
joint tort•fea•sor
joint ven•ture
joint ven•tur•er
joint will
joint•er (a joint owner:
cf. JOINDER; JOINER)
joint•ly
jointly and sev•er•
al•ly
joint•ress
join•ture
join•tured
join•ture•less
jok•er
jos•tle *v.,* jos•tled,
jos•tling
jos•tler
jos•tling

jour•nal (*citation form:* J.)

jour•nal•ism

jour•nal•ist

jour•nal•is•tic

jour•nal•is•ti•cal•ly

jour•nal•ists' priv•i•lege

journalists' shield law

jour•ney•man *n., pl.* jour•ney•men

jour•ney•work

joy•ride *n., v.,* joy•rode, joy•rid•den, joy•rid•ing

joy•rid•er

joy•rid•ing

J.P. (Justice of the Peace)

J.P. Ct. (Justice of the Peace's Court)

J.P.M.L. (Judicial Panel on Multidistrict Litigation)

J.S.D. (Doctor of the Science of Law: from Latin *Juris Scientiae Doctor*)

Jud. (Judicial)

ju•dex *n., pl.* ju•di•ces *Latin.*

judge[1] *n. (abbr.:* J., *pl.* JJ.)

judge[2] *v.,* judged, judg•ing

judge ad•vo•cate *n., pl.* judge ad•vo•cates

judge advocate gen•er•al *n., pl.* judge advocates gen•er•al or judge advocate gen•er•als

Judge Advocate General's Corps (JAG Corps)

Judge Lynch

judge-made law

judge trial

judge•a•ble

judge•like

judge•ment (a spelling often used in British nonlegal writing: cf. JUDGMENT)

judg•er

judge•ship

judg•ing•ly

judg•ment (preferred spelling in America and in British legal writing: cf. JUDGEMENT)

judgment by de•fault

judgment cred•i•tor

judgment debt

judgment debt•or

judgment in per•so•nam

judgment in rem

judgment lien

judgment note

judgment not•with•stand•ing the ver•dict (j.n.o.v.)

judgment n.o.v. judgment notwithstanding the verdict) See also N.O.V.

judgment on the plead•ings

judgment on the ver•dict

judgment proof

judgment roll

judg•men•tal

ju•di•ca•ble

ju•di•care

ju•di•ca•tive

ju•di•ca•tor

ju•di•ca•to•ri•al

ju•di•ca•to•ry

ju•di•ca•ture

ju•di•ci•a•ble

ju•di•cial (*citation form:* Jud.)

judicial ac•tiv•ism

judicial ac•tiv•ist

judicial ad•mis•sion

judicial com•pe•tence

judicial con•serv•a•tive

judicial dis•cre•tion

judicial dis•trict

judicial e•con•o•my

judicial gloss

judicial im•mu•ni•ty

judicial leg•is•la•tion

judicial no•tice

Judicial Pan•el on Mul•ti•dis•trict Lit•i•ga•tion (*citation form:* J.P.M.L.)

judicial proc•ess

judicial re•straint

judicial re•view

judicial sale

judicial sep•a•ra•tion

judicial writ

ju•di•cial•ly

ju•di•ci•ar•i•ly

ju•di•ci•ar•y *n., pl.* ju•di•ci•ar•ies, *adj.*

ju•di•cious

ju•di•cious•ly

ju•di•cious•ness

ju•di•ci•um *n., pl.* ju•di•ci•a *Latin.*

Ju•ly (*citation form:* July)

jump

jump bail

jump•er

June (*citation form:* June)

jun•ior

junior coun•sel

junior cred•i•tor

junior in•ter•est

junior lien

junior mort•gage

junior mort•ga•gee

junior part•ner

junior se•cur•i•ty

junk bond

junk fax

junk food

junk mail

junk mail•er

junk sci•ence

junk tel•e•phone call

jun•ket

jun•ke•teer

jun•ket•er

junk•ie n., pl. junk•ies (a drug addict)

junk•y adj., junk•i•er, junk•i•est (of low quality)

jun•ta n., pl. jun•tas (a ruling group: cf. JUNTO)

jun•to n., pl. jun•tos (a cabal or clique: cf. JUNTA)

ju•ra See JUS.

ju•ral

ju•ral•ly

ju•rat

ju•ra•tion

ju•re ux•o•ris Latin.

Jurid. (Juridical)

ju•rid•i•cal (citation form: Jurid.)

juridical day

juridical per•son

ju•rid•i•cal•ly

Juris. (Jurisprudence)

Ju•ris Doc•tor (J.D.) Latin.

juris u•trum Latin.

ju•ris•con•sult

ju•ris•dic•tion

jurisdiction in per•so•nam

jurisdiction in rem

jurisdiction of (or o•ver) the case

jurisdiction of (or over) the per•son

jurisdiction qua•si in rem

jur•is•dic•tion•al

jurisdictional a•mount

jurisdictional fact

jurisdictional state•ment

jurisdictional strike

ju•ris•dic•tion•al•ly

ju•ris•pru•dence (citation form: Juris.)

jurisprudence con•stante French.

ju•ris•pru•dent

ju•ris•pru•den•tial

ju•ris•pru•den•tial•ly

ju•rist

ju•ris•tic

juristic act

juristic per•son

ju•ris•ti•cal

ju•ris•ti•cal•ly

ju•ror

ju•ry n., pl. ju•ries

jury ar•ray

jury box

jury du•ty

jury in•struc•tions

jury nul•li•fi•ca•tion

jury-pack•ing

jury pan•el

jury poll

jury-rig n., v., jury-rigged, jury-rig•ging (a makeshift arrangement; to assemble from materials at hand: cf. JERRY-BUILD)

jury room

jury sen•tenc•ing

jury tam•per•ing

jury tri•al

jury wheel

ju•ry•man n., pl. ju•ry•men

ju•ry•wom•an n., pl. ju•ry•wom•en

jus n., pl. ju•ra Latin.

jus ac•cre•scen•di Latin.

jus bel•li Latin.

jus ca•no•ni•cum Latin.

jus ci•vi•le Latin.

jus co•gens Latin.

jus com•mu•ne Latin.

jus gen•ti•um Latin.

jus ges•ti•o•nis Latin.

jus im•pe•ri•i Latin.

jus in per•so•nam Latin.

jus in rem Latin.

jus na•tu•rae Latin.

jus na•tu•ra•le Latin.

jus non scrip•tum Latin.

jus post•li•mi•ni•i Latin.

jus ra•ti•o•na•le Latin.

jus san•gui•nis Latin.

jus scrip•tum Latin.

jus so•li Latin.

jus stan•di Latin.

jus ter•ti•i Latin.

just

Just. (Justice)

just and rea•son•a•ble rates

just cause

just com•pen•sa•tion

just debts

just de•serts

just in time adv.

just-in-time adj.

jus•tice¹ (the concept

or system of law; *citation form:* **Just.**)

justice[2] (a judge; *abbr.:* **J.,** *pl.* **JJ.**)

justice in eyre

justice of the peace (*citation form:* **J.P.**)

Jus·tice of the Peace's Court (*citation form:* **J.P. Ct.**)

jus·tic·er

jus·tice's court

jus·tice·ship

jus·ti·ci·a·bil·i·ty

jus·ti·ci·a·ble

jus·ti·ci·ar

jus·ti·ci·ar·ship

jus·ti·ci·ar·y *adj., n., pl.* **jus·ti·ci·ar·ies**

jus·ti·ci·o·es *Latin.*

jus·ti·fi·a·bil·i·ty

jus·ti·fi·a·ble

justifiable hom·i·cide

jus·ti·fi·a·bly

jus·ti·fi·ca·tion

jus·ti·fi·ca·tive

jus·tif·i·ca·to·ry

jus·ti·fi·er

jus·ti·fy *v.,* **jus·ti·fied, jus·ti·fy·ing**

jus·ti·fy·ing·ly

just·ly

just·ness

Juv. (Juvenile)

Juv. Ct. (Juvenile Court)

ju·ve·nile (*citation form:* **Juv.**)

Ju·ve·nile Court (*citation form:* **Juv. Ct.**)

juvenile de·lin·quen·cy

juvenile de·lin·quent

juvenile fa·cil·i·ty

juvenile in need of su·per·vi·sion (JINS)

juvenile of·fend·er

jux·ta·pose *v.,* **jux·ta·posed, jux·ta·pos·ing**

jux·ta·po·si·tion

jux·ta·po·si·tion·al

K

Kaf·ka·esque

kan·ga·roo court

ka·put

kar·y·o·type

kar·y·o·typ·ing

K.B. (King's Bench)

K.C. (King's Counsel)

keel·age

keel·haul

keep *v.,* **kept, keep·ing,** *n.*

keep·a·bil·i·ty

keep·a·ble

keep·er

keep·sake

ken *n., v.,* **kenned, ken·ning**

Ke·ogh plan

ke·taz·o·lam *Controlled Subst.*

ke·to·bem·i·done *Controlled Subst.*

key-ex·ec·u·tive in·sur·ance

key-man insurance

key mon·ey

Keynes·i·an ec·o·nom·ics

ki·bosh

kick·back

kick·er

kid·nap *v.,* **kid·napped** or **kid·naped** or **kid·nap·ping** or **kid·nap·ing**

kid·nap·pee or **kid·nap·ee**

kid·nap·per or **kid·nap·er**

kid·nap·ping or **kid·nap·ing**

kill

kill·a·ble

kill·er

kill·ing

kin

kind

kind·heart·ed

kind·heart·ed·ly

kind·heart·ed·ness

kind·ly *adj.,* **kind·li·er, kind·li·est**

kind·ness

kin·dred

king

king·dom

king·li·ness

king·ly *adj.,* **king·li·er, king·li·est**

king·mak·er

king·mak·ing

King's Bench (*citation form:* **K.B.**)

King's Coun·sel (K.C.)

king·ship

kin·ship

kins·man *n., pl.* **kins·men**

kins·wom·an *n., pl.* **kins·wom·en**

kitch·en cab·i·net

kite *n., v.,* kit∘ed, kit•
ing
kit∘er
kith
kith and kin
Klans•man *n., pl.*
Klans•men
Klax∘on doc•trine
klep•to•ma•ni∘a
klep•to•ma•ni∘ac
knack
knave
knav•er∘y *n., pl.*
knav•er•ies
knav•ish
knav•ish∘ly
knav•ish•ness
knee-jerk *adj.*
knell
knife *n., pl.* knives, *v.,*
knifed, knif•ing
knight
knight-er•rant

knight•hood
knight•li•ness
knight∘ly
knight's serv•ice
knock
knock and an•nounce
rule
knock down *v.* (cf.
KNOCKDOWN)
knock off *v.* (cf. KNOCK-
OFF)
knock•a∘bout
knock•down *n.* (cf.
KNOCK DOWN)
knockdown price
knock•off *n.* (cf. KNOCK
OFF)
know *v.,* knew,
known, know•ing,
n.
know all men by
these pres•ents
know-how
know-it-all

know-noth•ing
know-noth•ing•ism
know•a∘bil∘i∘ty
know•a∘ble
know•a∘ble•ness
know∘er
know∘ing
know•ing∘ly
know•ing•ness
knowl•edge
knowl•edge•
a∘bil∘i∘ty
knowl•edge•a∘ble
knowl•edge•a∘ble•
ness
knowl•edge•a∘bly
known
Ko∘ran or Qur∘'an
Ko•ran∘ic
ko∘sher
kow•tow
ku∘dos *n.sing.*
kye

L

L. (Law)
l. *pl.* ll (line)
L. Rev. (Law Review)
LAAM *Controlled Subst.*
(levo-
alphacetylmethadol)
Lab.¹ (Labor; Labour)
Lab.² *pl.* **Lab.** or **Labs**
(Laboratory)
la∘bel *n., v.,* la•beled,
la•bel•ing
la•bel∘er
la•bel•ing
la∘bor (*citation form:*
Lab.)
labor camp
labor con•tract
labor dis•pute
labor force

labor-hour con•tract
labor-in•ten•sive
labor law
labor mar•ket
labor move•ment
labor or•gan∘i•za∘
tion
labor prac•tice
labor re•la∘tions
labor spy
labor stand•ards
labor un∘ion
labor un∘ion•ist
la∘bo∘ra•to•ri∘al
la∘bo∘ra•to•ri•al∘ly
la∘bo∘ra•to•ri∘an
la∘bo∘ra•to∘ry *n., pl.*
la∘bo∘ra•to•ries,
adj. (*citation form:*

Lab., *pl.* Lab. or
Labs.)
la∘bored
la∘bored∘ly
la∘bored•ness
la∘bor∘er
la∘bor•ing∘ly
la∘bo•ri∘ous
la∘bo•ri•ous∘ly
la∘bo•ri•ous•ness
la∘bor•less
la∘bor-sav•ing
la∘bour (British spell-
ing for LABOR; *citation
form:* **Lab.**)
lab∘y•rinth
lab∘y•rin•thine
lac•er•ate *v.,* lac•er•
at∘ed, lac•er•at•ing

lac•er•at•ed
lac•er•at•ing
lac•er•a•tion
lac•er•a•tive
lach•es *n.sing. Law French.*
lach•ry•mose
lach•ry•mose•ly
lach•ry•mos•i•ty
lack
lack•a•dai•si•cal
lack•a•dai•si•cal•ly
lack•a•dai•si•cal•ness
lack•ey
lack•ing
lack•lus•ter
la•con•ic
la•con•i•cal•ly
la•cu•na *n., pl.* la•cu•nae or la•cu•nas
lade *v.,* lade, lad•en, lad•ing
lad•en
laden in bulk
lad•er
lad•ing
la•dy *n., pl.* la•dies
lag *v.,* lagged, lag•ging, *n.*
lag•an
lag•gard
lag•gard•ly
lag•gard•ness
lag•ging
lais•sez faire or lais•ser-faire *n.*
laissez-faire *adj.*
laissez-faire•ism
lais•sez-pas•ser *n., pl.* lais•sez-pas•ser *French.*
lam•baste *v.,* lam•bast•ed, lam•bast•ing
lame duck *n.*

lame-duck *adj.*
lame-duck ses•sion
la•ment
la•ment•a•ble
la•ment•a•ble•ness
la•ment•a•bly
lam•en•ta•tion
la•ment•ed
la•ment•er
la•ment•er•ing•ly
lam•poon
lam•poon•er
lam•poon•er•y
lam•poon•ist
land
land a•gent
land bank
land bank•ing
land con•tract
land freeze
land-grab•ber
land grant
land mine
land of•fice
land-office busi•ness
land pat•ent
land-poor
land re•form
land trust
land use
land use plan•ning
land use reg•u•la•tion
land•ed
land•fill
land•hold•er
land•hold•ing
land•ing card
land•la•dy *n., pl.* land•la•dies
land•less
land•less•ness
land•lord
land•lord•ism
land•lord•ly

land•lord•ry
landlord's lien
land•lord•ship
land•man *n., pl.* land•men
land•mark
landmark case
landmark de•ci•sion
landmark des•ig•na•tion
landmark pre•ser•va•tion
land•own•er
land•own•er•ship
land•own•ing
land•slide
lands•man *n., pl.* lands•men
lands•men
lan•guage
lan•guish
lan•guish•ing
lan•guish•ing•ly
lao•gai *Chinese.*
lap•page
lap•ping
laps•a•ble or laps•i•ble
lapse *n., v.,* lapsed, laps•ing
lapsed
lapsed de•vise
lapsed leg•a•cy
lapsed pol•i•cy
lar•ce•ner
lar•ce•nist
lar•ce•nous
lar•ce•nous•ly
lar•ce•ny
larceny by trick
large *adj.,* larg•er, larg•est, *n.*
large-cap
large•ly
lar•gess or lar•gesse
las•civ•i•ous

las•civ•i•ous•ly
las•civ•i•ous•ness
lash
lash•er
lash•ing•ly
last an•te•ced•ent rule
last clear chance
last in, first out (LIFO)
last-in-time rule
last re•sort
last will
last will and tes•ta•ment
late charge
la•tent
latent am•bi•gu•i•ty
latent de•fect
la•tent•ly
lat•er•al
lateral sup•port
lat•er•al•ly
Lat•in side
la•ti•tat *Latin.*
lat•i•tude
laud
laud•a•bil•i•ty
laud•a•ble
laud•a•ble•ness
laud•a•bly
lau•da•num *Controlled Subst.* (tincture of opium)
laud•a•to•ri•ly
laud•a•to•ry
laud•er
laugh
laugh test
laugh•a•ble
laugh•a•ble•ness
laugh•a•bly
laugh•ing gas nitrous oxide
laugh•ing•ly
laugh•ter

laun•der
laun•der•a•bil•i•ty
laun•der•a•ble
laun•der•er
laun•der•ing
lau•re•ate
lav•ish
lav•ish•er
lav•ish•ly
lav•ish•ness
law (*citation form:* L.
   Law. (Lawyer; Lawyers; Lawyer's; Lawyers')
law-a•bid•ing
law-a•bid•ing•ness
law and or•der
law clerk
Law Court (*citation form:* Law Ct.)
Law Ct. (Law Court)
law day
Law Div. (Law Division)
Law Di•vi•sion (*citation form:* Law Div.)
law ec•cle•si•as•tic
law en•force•ment
law enforcement a•gen•cy
law enforcement of•fic•er
law French or Law French.
law-hand
law jour•nal (*citation form:* L.J.)
law Lat•in or Law Lat•in.
law lord
law mer•chant
law of finds
Law of Mo•ses
law of na•tions
law of na•ture
law of the case
law of the flag

law of the jun•gle
law of the land
law of the sea
law of war
law re•ports
law review (*citation form:* L. Rev.)
law school
Law School Ad•mis•sion Test (LSAT)
Law School Da•ta As•sem•bly Serv•ice (LSDAS)
law side
law•book
law•break•er
law•break•ing
law•ful
lawful age
lawful ar•rest
lawful heir
lawful in•ter•est
lawful is•sue
lawful mon•ey
lawful pur•pose
law•ful•ly
law•ful•ness
law•giv•er
law•giv•ing
law•less
law•less•ly
law•less•ness
law•like
law•mak•er
law•mak•ing
law•man *n., pl.* law•men
Laws of O•le•ron
law•suit
law•yer (*citation form for sing. and pl.:* Law.)
law•yer•ing
law•yer•like
law•yer•ly
lay *v.,* laid, lay•ing,

n., adj. (to put or place: cf. LIE[1])
lay day
lay fee
lay judge
lay lord
lay of the land
lay off *v.* (cf. LAYOFF)
lay on the ta•ble
lay time
lay•a•way
layaway plan
lay•man *n., pl.* lay•men
lay•off *n.* (cf. LAY OFF)
lay•per•son *n., pl.* lay•peo•ple or lay peo•ple
lay•wom•an *n., pl* lay•wom•en
la•zy *adj.*, la•zi•er, la•zi•est
LBO (leveraged buyout)
lead *v.*, led, lead•ing, *n., adj.*
lead coun•sel
lead poi•son•ing
lead•er
lead•er•less
lead•er•ship
lead•ing
leading case
leading marks
leading ques•tion
league
League of Na•tions
leak
leak•age
leak•er
learn *v.*, learned, learn•ing
learn•a•ble
learn•ed *adj*
learn•ed pro•fes•sion
learn•ed•ly

learn•ed•ness
learn•ing
learning dis•a•bil•i•ty
learning-dis•a•bled
learning dis•or•der
leas•a•ble
lease *n., v.*, leased, leas•ing
lease-pur•chase
lease•back
leased ac•cess chan•nel
lease•hold
leasehold es•tate
leasehold im•prove•ment
leasehold in•ter•est
lease•hold•er
lease•less
leash law
least re•stric•tive means
leave *v.*, left, leav•ing, *n.*
leave of court
leav•er
ledg•er
leet
leg•a•cy *n., pl.* leg•a•cies
le•gal
legal ac•tion
legal ad•ver•tis•ing
legal age
legal aid
legal aid as•so•ci•a•tion
legal aid so•ci•e•ty
legal as•set
legal as•sis•tant
legal ca•pac•i•ty
legal cap•i•tal
legal cause
legal con•clu•sion
legal cus•to•dy

legal dis•a•bil•i•ty
legal du•ty
legal es•tate
legal eth•ics
legal ex•pense
legal fic•tion
legal heir
legal hol•i•day
legal im•pos•si•bil•i•ty
legal in•ca•pac•i•ty
legal in•ter•est
legal is•sue
legal list
legal mal•prac•tice
legal mem•o•ry
legal mon•ey
legal o•pin•ion
legal own•er
legal per•son•al•i•ty
legal pre•sump•tion
legal re•al•ism
legal re•serve
legal res•i•dence
legal right
legal sec•re•tar•y
legal sep•a•ra•tion
legal ten•der
legal ti•tle
le•gal•ese
le•gal•ism
le•gal•ist
le•gal•is•tic
le•gal•is•ti•cal•ly
le•gal•i•ty *n., pl.* le•gal•i•ties
le•gal•i•za•tion
le•gal•ize *v.*, le•gal•ized, le•gal•iz•ing
le•gal•ly
leg•a•tee
le•ga•tion
le•ga•tor
leg•i•ble

leg•i•bly

Legis. Legislation; Legislative

leg•is•late *v.*, leg•is•lat•ed, leg•is•lat•ing

leg•is•la•tion (*citation form*; **Legis.**

leg•is•la•tive (*citation form*: **Legis.**

legislative con•trol

legislative coun•cil

legislative court

legislative dis•trict

legislative fact

legislative his•to•ry

legislative im•mu•ni•ty

legislative in•tent

legislative in•ves•ti•ga•tion

legislative pur•pose

legislative ve•to

leg•is•la•tive•ly

leg•is•la•tor

leg•is•la•to•ri•al

leg•is•la•tor•ship

leg•is•la•ture

le•gist

le•git•i•ma•cy

le•git•i•mate *adj., v.*, le•git•i•mat•ed, le•git•i•mat•ing, *n.*

le•git•i•mate•ly

le•git•i•mate•ness

le•git•i•ma•tion

le•git•i•ma•tize *v.* le•git•i•ma•tized, le•git•i•ma•tiz•ing

leg•i•time

le•git•i•mism

le•git•i•mist

le•git•i•mis•tic

le•git•i•mi•za•tion

le•git•i•mize *v.* le•

git•i•mized, le•git•i•miz•ing

lei•sure

lei•sure•li•ness

lei•sure•ly

lem◦on

lemon law

lend *v.*, lent, lend•ing

lend•a•ble

lend◦er

le•ni•ence

le•ni•en◦cy *n., pl.* le•ni•en•cies

le•ni•ent

le•ni•ent◦ly

len◦i◦ty *n., pl.* len◦i•ties

les•bi◦an

les•bi•an•ism

lèse-ma•jes•té *French.*

lese maj•es◦ty

le•sion

les•see

less◦en

less◦er smaller; inferior: cf. LESSOR

lesser in•clud◦ed of•fense

les•sor (grantor of a lease: cf. LESSER

lest

let *v.*, let, let•ting, *n.*

let down *v.* (cf. LET-DOWN

let or hin•drance

let•down *n.* cf. LET DOWN

le•thal

lethal weap◦on

le•thal◦i◦ty

le•thal◦ly

le•thar•gic

le•thar•gi•cal◦ly

leth•ar◦gy

let•ter

letter bomb

letter con•tract

letter of ad•vice

letter of at•torn•ment

letter of com•fort

letter of com•pli•ance

letter of cre•dence

letter of cred◦it

letter of in•tent

letter of the law

letter rul•ing

letter stock

let•tered

let•ters *n.pl.*

letters close

letters cre•den•tial

letters of ad•min•oi•stra•tion

letters of administra-tion c.t.a. (cum testamento annexo

letters of administra-tion d.b.n. de bonis non

letters of cre•dence

letters of marque and coun•ter•marque

letters of marque and re•pris◦al

letters pa•tent

letters ro•ga•to◦ry

letters tes•ta•men•ta◦ry

let•tre de ca•chet *n. pl.* let•tres de ca•chet *French.*

lettre de change *n. pl.* lettres de change *French.*

lettre de cré•ance *n. pl.* lettres de cré•ance *French.*

le•va◦ri fa•ci◦as *Latin.*

lev◦ee *n. v.* lev•eed,

lev•ee•ing a dike: a recep•tion: to build a dike: cf. LEVY

le•vée en masse *French.*

lev•el play•ing field

lev•el•head•ed

lev•el•head•ed•ly

lev•el•head•ed•ness

lev•er•age *n., v.* **lev•er•aged, lev•er•ag•ing**

lev•er•aged buy•out (LBO)

lev•er•ag•ing

lev•oi•a•ble

Le•vit•i•cal law

Le•vit•i•cus

lev•oi•ty *n., pl.* **lev•oi•ties**

le•vo-al•pha-ce•tyl-meth&spn b;a•dol (LAAM) *Controlled Subst.*

le•vo•me•thor•phan *Controlled Subst.*

le•vo•mor•a•mide *Controlled Subst.*

le•vo•phe•na•cyl•mor•phan *Controlled Subst.*

le•vor•phan•ol *Controlled Subst.*

lev•y *n. pl.* **lev•ies,** *v.* **lev•ied, lev•y•ing** a tax; conscrip•tion; to tax or con•script: cf. LEVEE

lewd

lewd•ly

lewd•ness

lex *n. pl.* **le•ges** *Latin*

lex con•trac•tus *Latin.*

lex do•mi•cil•oi•oi *Latin.*

lex fo•ori *Latin.*

lex lo•oci *Latin.*

lex loci ac•tus *Latin.*

lex loci con•trac•tus *Latin.*

lex loci de•lic•oti *Latin.*

lex mer•ca•to•ri•a *Latin.*

lex non scrip•ta *Latin.*

lex scrip•ta *Latin.*

lex ta•li•o•nis *Latin.*

lex va•li•di•ta•tis *Latin.*

Lex•is *Trademark.*

Liab. Liabi̇́lity

li•a•bil•oi•ty *n. pl.* **li•a•bil•oi•ties** *citation form:* **Liab.**

liability in•sur•ance

liability lim•oit

liability with•out fault

li•a•ble

li•ai•son

li•oar

li•obel *n., v.,* **li•beled, li•bel•ing**

libel per quod

libel per se

libel-proof

li•bel•ant

li•bel•ee

li•bel•or

li•bel•ous

libelous per quod

libelous per se

li•bel•ous•ly

lib•er•al

liberal con•struc•tion

lib•er•al•ism

lib•er•al•oi•za•tion

lib•er•al•ize *v.,* **lib•er•al•ized, lib•er•al•iz•ing**

lib•er•al•oly

lib•er•al•ness

lib•er•ate *v.* **lib•er•at•oed, lib•er•at•ing**

lib•er•oa•tion

lib•er•oa•tion•ist

lib•er•oa•tor

li•ber•oté, é•ga•li•oté, fra•ter•ni•oté *French.*

lib•er•tine

lib•er•tin•ism

lib•er•oty *n. pl.* **lib•er•ties**

li•be•rum ve•oto

Libr. Library; Libraries; Librarian; Librarians

li•brar•oi•an *citation form for sing. and pl.:* **Libr.**

li•brar•oi•an•ship

li•brar•oy *n. pl.* **li•brar•ies** *citation form for sing. and pl.:* **Libr.**

Lib•ri•o•um *Trademark.*

li•cens•a•ble

li•cense *n. v.,* **li•censed, li•cens•ing**

li•cen•see

li•cens•oer (official who gives out permits: cf. LICENSOR

li•cen•sor private grantor of a license: cf. LICENSER

li•cen•sure

li•cen•ti•ate

li•cen•ti•ate•ship

li•cen•tious

li•cen•tious•oly

li•cen•tious•ness

li•c|et *Latin.*

lic•oit

lic•oit•oly

lie[1] *v.,* lay, lain, ly•oing, *n.* to recline: to be situated: cf. LAY; LIE

lie[2] *v.,* lied, ly•oing, *n.*

to speak falsely. cf. LIE

lie de•tec•tor

liege

liege•man *n., pl* liege•men

lien

lien cred◦i•tor

lien strip•ping

lien•a◦ble

lien◦ee

lien•hold◦er

lien◦or

li◦er

lieu

lieu•ten•ant gov•er•nor (Lt. Gov.)

life *n., pl.* lives

life and death *n.*

life-and-death *adj*

life an•nu◦i◦ty

life care *n.*

life-care *adj.*

life care con•tract

life es•tate

life ex•pec•tan◦cy

life-giv◦ing

life in be◦ing *n., pl* lives in be◦ing

life in•sur•ance

life in•sur•ance trust

life in•ter•est

life or death *n.*

life-or-death *adj.*

life part•ner

life sal•vage

life sen•tence

life sup•port *n.*

life-support *adj.*

life ten•an◦cy

life ten•ant

life-threat•en•ing

life•less

life•less◦ly

life•less•ness

life•like

life•long

lif◦er

life•style

life•time

lifetime trans•fer

LIFO last in, first out

li◦gan an obsolete spelling for LAGAN

li•geance

light•er◦age

light•heart◦ed

light•heart•ed◦ly

light•heart•ed•ness

lik•a◦ble

like-kind ex•change

like-kind prop•er◦ty

like•a◦ble•ness

like•li•hood

likelihood of con•fu•sion

like◦ly *adj.*, like•li◦er, like•li•est

li◦mes *n., pl.* lim◦i•tes

li•mi◦ne *Latin.*

lim◦it

li•it or◦der

lim•it•a◦ble

lim•it•a◦ble•ness

lim◦i•ta•tion

lim◦i•ta•tion o◦ver

limitation pe•ri◦od

limitation pro•ceed•ing

limitation pro•ceed•ings

lim◦i•ta•tions pe•ri◦od

lim•it◦ed (Ltd.)

limited ad•mis•si•bil◦i◦ty

limited ap•pear•ance

limited com•pa◦ny

limited di•vorce

limited ju•ris•dic•tion

li•ited li•a•bil◦i◦ty

limited liability com•pa◦ny

limited liability part•ner•ship (L.L.P.)

limited mon•arch

limited mon•ar◦chy

limited part•ner

limited part•ne•ship (L.P.)

limited-pay•ment life in•sur•ance

limited pol◦i◦cy

limited pub•lic fo◦rum

limited-pur•pose pub-lic fig•ure

limited war

limited war•ran◦ty

lim•it•ed◦ly

lim•it•ed•ness

lim•it•less

lim•it•less◦ly

lim•it•less•ness

linch•pin

Lin•coln's Inn

line[1] *n. citation form:* l., *pl.* ll.

line[2] *v.*, lined, lin•ing

line i◦tem *n.*

line-item *ad .*

line-item ve◦to

line of bus•iness

line of com•merce

line of cred◦it

line up *v.* cf. LINEUP

lin◦e•age

lin◦e◦al

lineal de•scend•ant

lineal heir

lin◦e◦al◦ly

lin◦er bill

line◦up *n.* cf. LINE UP

lin◦go *n., pl.* lin•goes

lin•guist

lin•guis•tic

lin•guis•ti•cal•ly
lin•guis•tics *n.sing.*
link
link•age
lip serv•ice
liq•uid
liquid as•set
liq•ui•date *v.*, liq•ui•dat•ed, liq•ui•dat•ing
liq•ui•dat•ed
liquidated a•mount
liquidated claim
liquidated dam•ag•es
liquidated debt
liq•ui•dat•ing dis•tri•bu•tion
liquidating sale
liquidating trust
liq•ui•da•tion
liquidation val•ue
liq•ui•da•tor
li•quid•i•ty
liquidity ra•tio
liq•uor
lis *n.*, *pl.* li•tes *Latin.*
lis pen•dens *Latin.*
list
list•ed
listed chem•i•cal
listed se•cu•ri•ty
listed stock
list•ee
lis•ten
lis•ten•er
lis•ten•ing post
list•er
list•ing
listing a•gree•ment
lit•a•ny *n.*, *pl.* lit•a•nies
lit•er•a•cy
literacy test
lit•er•al (exact; strict: cf. LITTORAL)

literal-mind•ed
lit•er•al•ly (actually; in the strict sense of the words: cf. FIGURA-TIVELY)
lit•er•a•ry
lit•er•a•ry ex•ec•u•tor
literary prop•er•ty
literary work
lit•er•ate
lit•er•ate•ly
lit•e•ra•tim
Litig. (Litigation)
lit•i•ga•ble
lit•i•gant
lit•i•gate *v.*, lit•i•gat•ed, lit•i•gat•ing
lit•i•ga•tion (*citation form:* Litig.)
lit•i•ga•tive
lit•i•ga•tor
li•ti•gious
li•ti•gious•ly
li•ti•gious•ness
lit•ter
lit•ter•bug
lit•ter•er
lit•ter•ing
lit•to•ral (of a shore: cf. LITERAL)
Lit•vi•nov assign•ment
liv•a•ble
live *v.*, lived, liv•ing, *adj.*
live-in
live•li•hood
live•li•ly
live•li•ness
live•ly *adj.*, live•li•er, live•li•est, *adv.*
liv•en
live•ness

liv•er•y *n.*, *pl.* liv•er•ies
livery of sei•sin
live•stock *n. sing. or pl.*
liv•id
liv•id•ly
liv•id•ness
liv•ing ex•pens•es
living stand•ard
living trust
living trusts fraud
living will
L.J. (Law Journal; Lord Justice)
ll. (lines)
LL.B. (Bachelor of Laws: from Latin *Legum Bac-calaureus*)
LL.D. (Doctor of Laws: from Latin *Legum Doc-tor*)
LL.M. (Master of Laws: from Latin *Legum Magister*)
L.L.P. (Limited Liability Partnership)
load
load fund
load line
load-line mark
loan
loan com•mit•ment
loan for con•sump•tion
loan for use
loan guar•an•tee
loan o•rig•i•na•tion
loan par•tic•i•pa•tion
loan shark
loan val•ue
loan•er (an item on loan: cf. LONER)
loan•shark•ing
loath *adj.*

loathe v., loathed,
loath•ing
loath•ing
loath•ing•ly
loath•some
loathsome dis•ease
loath•some•ly
loath•some•ness
lob•by n., pl. lob•
bies, v., lob•bied,
lob•by•ing
lob•by•ing
lob•by•ist
Loc. (Local)
loc. cit. (loco citato)
lo•cal (citation form:
Loc.)
local ac•tion
local a•gent
local as•sess•ment
local con•tent
local coun•sel
local gov•ern•ment
local im•prove•ment
local improvement
as•sess•ment
local law
local op•tion
local rules
local un•ion
lo•cal•i•ty n., pl. lo•
cal•i•ties
locality test
lo•cal•iz•a•ble
lo•cal•i•za•tion
lo•cal•ize v., lo•cal•
ized, lo•cal•iz•ing
lo•cal•ized am•ne•
sia
lo•cal•ly
lo•cal•ness
lo•cat•a•ble
lo•cate v., lo•cat•ed,
lo•cat•ing
lo•ca•tion
lo•ca•tion•al

lo•ca•tion•al•ly
lo•ca•tor
lock-in
lock out v. (cf. LOCK-
OUT)
lock up (cf. LOCKUP)
lock•down
locked in
lock•out n. (cf. LOCK
OUT)
lock•step
lock•up n. (cf. LOCK UP)
lo•co ci•ta•to (loc.
cit.) Latin.
loco pa•ren•tis Latin
lo•cus n., pl. lo•ci
locus con•trac•tus
Latin.
locus cri•mi•nis Latin.
locus de•lic•ti Latin.
locus re•i si•tae Latin.
locus si•gil•li (L.S.)
Latin.
locus stan•di Latin.
lode•star
lodestar rate
lodge v., lodged,
lodg•ing
lodg•er
lodg•ing
lodg•ment
log•ger•head
log•ic
log•i•cal
log•i•cal•ly
lo•gis•tic
lo•gis•ti•cal
lo•gis•ti•cal•ly
lo•gis•tics n.sing.
log•jam
lo•go n., pl. lo•gos
lo•go•type
log•roll
log•roll•er
log•roll•ing
loi•ter

loi•ter•er
loi•ter•ing
loi•ter•ing•ly
lon•er (person acting
alone: cf. LOANER)
long ac•count
long-arm ju•ris•dic•
tion
long-arm stat•ute
long-last•ing
long-lived
long-range
long suit
long-term adj.
long-term as•set
long-term cap•i•tal
gain
long-term care
long-term con•tract
long-term debt
long-term li•a•
bil•i•ty
long-term mem•o•ry
long•shore
longshore and har•
bor work•ers
long•shore•man n.,
pl. long•shore•men
long•shore•work•er
look back v.
look-back adj.
look-back pe•ri•od
look out v. (cf. LOOK-
OUT)
look•out n. (cf. LOOK
OUT)
loop•hole
loose adj., loos•er,
loos•est, adv., v.,
loosed, loos•ing
loose•leaf
looseleaf serv•ice
loot
loot•er
loot•ing
Lo•phoph•o•ra wil•

liam•si•i Le•maire Controlled Subst. (peyote)

lo•pra•zo•o•lam Controlled Subst.

lo•qua•cious

lo•qua•cious•ly

lo•qua•cious•ness

lo•quac•i•ty

lo•raz•o•e•opam Controlled Subst.

lord

Lord Chan•cel•lor or Lord High Chan•cel•lor n., pl. Lord Chan•cel•lors or Lord High Chan•cel•lors

Lord Jus•tice (L.J.) n., pl. Lords Jus•tic•es

Lord Spir•it•u•al n., pl. Lords Spir•it•u•al

Lord Tem•po•ral n., pl. Lords Tem•po•ral

lord•ship

lor•me•taz•e•opam Controlled Subst.

lose v., lost, los•ing

los•er

loss

loss cau•sa•tion

loss lead•er

loss-lead•ing

loss of con•sor•tium

loss of earn•ing ca•pac•i•ty

loss of fu•ture earn•ing ca•pac•i•ty

loss of life's en•joy•ments

loss of so•ci•e•ty and con•sor•ti•um

loss of wag•es

loss ra•tio

loss-spread•ing

lost

lost cause

lost pol•i•cy

lost will

lot•ter•y n., pl. lot•ter•ies

lov•a•bil•i•ty

lov•a•ble

lov•a•ble•ness

lov•a•bly

love v., loved, lov•ing

lov•ing

lov•ing•ly

low den•si•ty zon•ing

low-in•come hous•ing

low-lev•el

low pressure n.

low-pres•sure adj.

low•down

low•er

low•er cham•ber

lower court

lower house

lower of cost or mar•ket

low•est re•spon•si•ble bid•der

low•life

low•li•ness

low•ly adj., low•li•er, low•li•est

loy•al

loy•al•ist

loy•al•ly

loy•al•ty n., pl. loy•al•ties

loyalty oath

L.P. (Limited Partnership)

L.S. (locus sigilli)

LSAT Trademark. (Law School Admission Test)

LSD Controlled Subst. (lysergic acid diethyla-mide: abbr. from German lysergsäure-diäthylamid)

LSDAS (Law School Data Assembly Service)

Lt. Gov. (Lieutenant Governor)

Ltd. (Limited)

lu•bri•cious

lu•bri•cious•ly

lu•bric•i•ty

lu•cid

lucid in•ter•val

lu•cid•i•ty

lu•cid•ly

lu•cid•ness

lu•cra•tive

lucrative bail•ment

lu•cra•tive•ly

lu•cra•tive•ness

lu•cre

lu•gu•bri•ous

lu•gu•bri•ous•ly

lu•gu•bri•ous•ness

luke•warm

luke•warm•ly

luke•warm•ness

lu•mi•nar•y n., pl. lu•mi•nar•ies

lump sum n.

lump-sum adj.

lump-sum dis•tri•bu•tion

lump-sum pay•ment

lump-sum set•tle•ment

lum•pen

lum•pen•pro•le•tar•i•at

lu•na•cy n., pl. lu•na•cies

lu•na•tic

lure n., v., lured, lur•ing

lur•ing•ly

lust
lust•ful
lust•ful•ly
lust•ful•ness
lux•u•ri•ate v.,
  lux•u•ri•at•ed,
  lux•u•ri•at•ing
lux•u•ri•ous
lux•u•ri•ous•ly

lux•u•ri•ous•ness
lux•u•o•ry n., pl.
  lux•u•ries
luxury tax
ly•ing by
lying in wait
lynch
lynch law
lynch•er

lynch•ing
ly•ser•gic ac•id Con-
  trolled Subst.
lysergic acid am•ide
  Controlled Subst.
lysergic acid di•
  eth•yl•am•ide (LSD)
  Controlled Subst.

M

m. (noon: from Latin
  meridies)
M&A (mergers and ac-
  quisitions)
M.A. (Master of Arts:
  from Latin Magister
  Artium)
MAAP (multiple arbi-
  trary amplicon profil-
  ing)
ma•ca•bre
mace n. (medieval
  weapon; ceremonial
  staff)
Mace n. Trademark.
  (incapacitating spray)
Mace or mace v.,
  Maced or maced,
  Mac•ing or mac•ing
  (to attack with Mace)
mace•bear•er
mac•er
Mach. (Machine; Ma-
  chinery)
Mach•i•a•vel•li•an
Mach•i•a•vel•li•an•
  ism
Mach•i•a•vel•li•
  an•ly
Mach•i•a•vel•lism
mach•i•nate v.,
  mach•i•nat•ed,
  mach•i•nat•ing
mach•i•na•tion

mach•i•na•tor
ma•chine[1] n. (citation
  form: Mach.)
machine[2] v., ma•
  chined, ma•chin•ing
ma•chin•er•y (citation
  form: Mach.)
ma•chis•mo
ma•cho n., pl. ma•
  chos
mac•ro•ec•o•nom•ic
mac•ro•ec•o•nom•
  ics
mac•ro•e•con•o•
  mist
mac•ro•so•ci•
  ol•o•gy
MACRS (modified accel-
  erated cost recovery
  system)
mad adj., mad•der,
  mad•dest
mad•am[1] n., pl. mes•
  dames (polite term of
  address for women)
madam[2] n., pl. mad•
  ams (brothel manager)
ma•dame n., pl. mes•
  dames French. (title of
  respect for married or
  older women; English
  abbr.: Mme.; French
  abbr.: Mme)
mad•den

mad•den•ing (exas-
  perating: cf. MADDING)
mad•den•ing•ly
mad•ding (frenzied: cf.
  MADDENING)
mad•ly
mad•man n., pl. mad•
  men
MADSP (modified ag-
  gregate deemed sales
  price)
mad•wom•an n., pl.
  mad•wom•en
Ma•fi•a
ma•fi•o•so n., pl.
  ma•fi•o•si or ma•
  fi•o•sos
Mag. (Magistrate; Mag-
  azine)
mag•a•zine (citation
  form: Mag.)
mag•i•cal think•ing
Magis. Ct. (Magistrate's
  Court)
mag•is•te•ri•al
mag•is•te•ri•al•ly
mag•is•tra•cy n., pl.
  mag•is•tra•cies
mag•is•trate (Mag.)
Mag•is•trate's Court
  (citation form: Magis.
  Ct.)
mag•is•trate•ship

mag•na as•si•sa *Latin.*

Magna Car•ta or Magna Char•ta *Latin.*

magna cum lau•de *Latin.*

mag•na•nim•i•ty *n., pl.* mag•na•nim•i•ties

mag•nan•i•mous

mag•nan•i•mous•ly

mag•nan•i•mous•ness

mag•nate (successful person: cf. MAGNET)

mag•net (something that attracts: cf. MAGNATE)

magnet school

mag•nil•o•quence

mag•nil•o•quent

mag•nil•o•quent•ly

mag•ni•tude

mag•num

mail fraud

mail or•der *n.*

mail-order *adj., v.*

mail-order di•vorce

mail•a•bil•i•ty

mail•a•ble

mailable mat•ter

mail•box rule

mailed fist

mail•er

maim

maim•er

main brief

main pur•pose doc•trine

main•line *v.,* main•lined, main•lin•ing, *adj.*

main•our *Law French.*

main•per•na•ble

main•per•nor

main•prise or main•prize *n., v.,* main•prised or main•prized, main•pris•ing or main•priz•ing

main•stream

main•stream•ing

main•tain

main•tain•a•bil•i•ty

main•tain•a•ble

main•tain•er (a person or thing that maintains generally: cf. MAINTAINOR)

main•tain•or (an outsider who helps maintain a lawsuit: cf. MAINTAINER)

main•te•nance

maintenance and cure

maintenance of mem•ber•ship

maintenance treat•ment

maj•es•ty *n., pl.* maj•es•ties

ma•jor

major life ac•tiv•i•ty

major med•i•cal in•sur•ance

major/mi•nor fault rule or major-mi•nor fault rule

ma•jor•i•tar•i•an

ma•jor•i•tar•i•an•ism

ma•jor•i•ty *n., pl.* ma•jor•i•ties

majority-mi•nor•i•ty dis•trict

majority o•pin•ion

make *v.,* made, mak•ing, *n.*

make a rec•ord

make bail

make law

make whole

mak•er

Ma•kis a•gree•ment

ma•la fi•de *adv. Latin.* (in bad faith: cf. MALA FIDES)

mala fi•des *n.sing. Latin.* (bad faith: cf. MALA FIDE)

mal•ad•ap•ta•tion

mal•a•dapt•ed

mal•a•dap•tive

mal•ad•just•ed

mal•ad•min•is•ter

mal•ad•min•is•tra•tion

mal•ad•min•is•tra•tor

mal•a•droit

mal•a•droit•ly

mal•a•droit•ness

mal•ap•por•tioned

mal•ap•por•tion•ment

mal•a•prop•ism

ma•lar•key

mal•con•tent

M.A.L.D. (Master of Arts in Law and Diplomacy)

mal•dis•trib•ut•ed

mal•dis•tri•bu•tion

male chau•vin•ism

male chau•vin•ist

mal•e•dic•tion

mal•e•dic•tive

mal•e•dic•to•ry

mal•e•fac•tion

mal•e•fac•tor

mal•e•fac•tress

ma•lef•ic

ma•lef•i•cence

ma•lef•i•cent

ma•lev•o•lence

ma•lev•o•lent

mal•fea•sance

mal•fea•sant

mal•ice

malice a•fore•thought

malice in fact

malice in law

ma•li•cious

malicious in•ju•ry

malicious mis•chief

malicious pros•e•cu•tion

ma•li•cious•ly

ma•li•cious•ness

ma•lign

ma•lig•nan•cy n., pl. ma•lig•nan•cies

ma•lig•nant

ma•lig•nant•ly

ma•lign•er

ma•lig•ni•ty

ma•lign•ly

Mal•o•ki

ma•lin•ger

ma•lin•ger•er

ma•lin•ger•ing

mall (shopping complex; public green: cf. MAUL)

mal•le•a•bil•i•ty

mal•le•a•ble

mal•le•a•ble•ness

mal•le•a•bly

Mal•linc•krodt trust

mal•nour•ished

mal•nu•tri•tion

ma•lo a•ni•mo Latin.

mal•prac•tice

malpractice in•sur•ance

mal•prac•ti•tion•er

mal•treat

mal•treat•er

mal•treat•ment

ma•lum n., pl. ma•la Latin.

malum in se n., pl. mala in se Latin.

malum pro•hi•bi•tum n., pl. mala pro•hi•bi•ta Latin.

mal•ver•sa•tion

man n., pl. men

man•a•cle n., v., man•a•cled, man•a•cling

man•age v., man•aged, man•ag•ing

man•age•a•bil•i•ty

man•age•a•ble

man•age•a•ble•ness

man•age•a•bly

man•aged care

managed cur•ren•cy

man•age•ment (citation form: Mgmt.)

management ac•count•ing

management au•dit

management con•sult•ant

management con•sult•ing

management fee

management in•for•ma•tion sys•tem (MIS)

management re•port•ing

man•ag•er

man•a•ge•ri•al

managing a•gent

man•bote

man•da•mus n., pl. man•da•mus•es, v., man•da•mused, man•da•mus•ing

man•dant

man•da•tar•y n., pl. man•da•tar•ies (recipient of a mandate: cf. MANDATORY)

man•date v., man•dat•ed, man•dat•ing

man•da•tor

man•da•to•ri•ly

man•da•to•ry adj. (compulsory: cf. MANDATARY)

mandatory in•junc•tion

mandatory in•struc•tion

mandatory pre•sump•tion

mandatory sen•tenc•ing

mandatory sub•ject of ne•go•ti•a•tion

man•da•tum n., pl. man•da•ta Latin.

ma•neu•ver

ma•neu•ver•a•bil•i•ty

ma•neu•ver•a•ble

ma•neu•ver•er

man•han•dle v., man•han•dled, man•han•dling

ma•ni•a

ma•ni•ac

ma•ni•a•cal

man•ic

manic-de•pres•sion

manic-de•pres•sive

manic-depressive ill•ness

manic dis•or•der

manic ep•i•sode

man•i•fest

man•i•fest•a•ble

man•i•fes•ta•tion

man•i•fest•er

man•i•fest•ly

man•i•fest•ness

man•i•fes•to n., pl. man•i•fes•toes

man•i•fold adj. (of many kinds or parts: cf. MANYFOLD)

ma•nip•u•la•bil•i•ty

ma•nip•u•la•ble

ma•nip•u•lat•a•ble

ma•nip•u•late v.,
  ma•nip•u•lat•ed,
  ma•nip•u•lat•ing

ma•nip•u•la•tion

ma•nip•u•la•tive

ma•nip•u•la•tive•ly

ma•nip•u•la•tor

ma•nip•u•la•to•ry

man•kind

man•ner (method; custom: cf. MANOR)

man•nered

man•ner•ism

man•ner•ly

ma•no a ma•no Spanish.

man•or (estate: cf. MANNER)

ma•no•ri•al•ism

man•pow•er

man•slaugh•ter

man•slay•er

man•steal•ing

man•sue•tude

man•u•al

ma•nu•cap•ti•o Latin.

ma•nu•cap•tion

ma•nu•cap•tor

man•u•fac•ture v.,
  man•u•fac•tured,
  man•u•fac•tur•ing,
  n.

man•u•fac•tur•er (citation form: Mfr.)

man•u•fac•tur•er's a•gent

manufacturer's brand

manufacturer's li•a•bil•i•ty

man•u•fac•tur•ing (citation form: Mfg.)

manufacturing cost

manufacturing o•ve•rhead

man•u•mis•sion

man•u•mit v.,
  man•u•mit•ted,
  man•u•mit•ting

man•u•mit•ter

ma•nus n., pl.
  ma•nus Latin.

man•u•script (citation form: ms., pl. mss.)

man•y•fold adv. (by many times: cf. MANIFOLD)

mar v., marred, mar•ring

Mar. (March; Maritime)

ma•raud

ma•raud•er

ma•raud•ing

March (citation form: Mar.)

ma•re clau•sum Latin.

ma•re li•be•rum Latin.

mar•gin

margin ac•count

margin call

margin of safe•ty

margin rate

margin trans•ac•tion

mar•gin•al

marginal cost

marginal cost•ing

marginal rev•e•nue

mar•gin•al•i•ty

mar•gin•al•ly

ma•ri•hua•na Controlled Subst. (spelling in federal drug laws)

ma•ri•jua•na Controlled Subst. (usual spelling)

ma•rine

marine belt

marine in•sur•ance

marine pol•lu•tion

marine risks pol•i•cy

marine sal•vage

marine serv•ice con•tract

mar•i•ner

Mar•i•nol Trademark.

mar•i•tal

marital com•mu•ni•ca•tions priv•i•lege

marital de•duc•tion

marital prop•er•ty

marital rape

marital sta•tus

marital ther•a•py

mar•i•time (citation form: Mar.)

maritime ar•rest

maritime at•tach•ment

maritime belt

maritime but lo•cal

maritime com•mon law

maritime con•tract

maritime gar•nish•ment

maritime ju•ris•dic•tion

maritime law

maritime lien

maritime tort

mark (a visible feature; to make a mark: cf. MARQUE)

mark down v. (cf. MARKDOWN)

mark up v. (cf. MARKUP)

mark•down n. (cf. MARK DOWN)

marked

marked im•prove•ments

mark•ed•ly

mark•ed•ness

mark•er

marker gene
mar•ket (*citation form:* Mkt.)
market al•lo•ca•tion
market cap•i•tal•i•za•tion
market di•vi•sion
market e•con•o•my
market ex•ten•sion merg•er
market fol•low•ing
market ma•nip•u•la•tion
market or•der
market pow•er
market price
market re•search
market share
market shar•ing
market tim•ing
market val•ue
mar•ket•a•bil•i•ty
mar•ket•a•ble
marketable se•cur•i•ty
marketable ti•tle
mar•ket•a•bly
mar•ket•eer
mar•ket•er
mar•ket•ing (*citation form:* Mktg.)
marketing risk
mar•ket•place
marketplace of i•deas
mark•ing
marks•man *n., pl.* marks•men
marks•wom•an *n., pl.* marks•wom•en
mark•up *n.* (cf. MARK UP)
Mar•kush claim
marque (retaliatory seizure: cf. MARK)
marque and re•pris•al

mar•riage
marriage li•cense
marriage of con•ven•ience
marriage po•rtion
marriage set•tle•ment
mar•riage•a•bil•i•ty
mar•riage•a•ble
mar•riage•a•ble•ness
mar•ry *v.,* mar•ried, mar•ry•ing
mar•shal *n., v.,* mar•shaled, mar•shal•ing (an officer; to assemble: vs. *Marshall;* cf. MARTIAL)
mar•shal•cy
mar•shal•er
mar•shal•ing
marshaling as•sets
marshaling liens
mar•shal•ship
mar•tial (military: cf. MARSHAL)
martial law
Mar•tin•dale-Hub•bell *Trademark.*
mar•tyr
mar•tyr•dom
mar•tyr•i•za•tion
mar•tyr•ize *v.,* mar•tyr•ized, mar•tyr•iz•ing
Mary Car•ter a•gree•ment
mask work
mas•och•ism
mas•och•ist
mas•och•is•tic
mas•och•is•ti•cal•ly
mas•quer•ade *v.,* mas•quer•ad•ed, mas•quer•ad•ing
mas•quer•ad•er

mass lay•off
mass ma•rket
mass me•di•a
mass move•ment
mass-pro•duce *v.,* mass-pro•duced, mass-pro•duc•ing.
mass-pro•duc•er
mass-pro•duc•i•ble
mass pro•duc•tion
mass psy•chol•o•gy
mass tran•sit
Mas•sa•chu•setts busi•ness trust
Massachusetts trust
mas•sa•cre *n., v.,* mas•sa•cred, mas•sa•cring
mas•sa•crer
mas•sage *v.,* mas•saged, mas•sag•ing, *n.*
massage par•lor
mas•seur
mas•seuse
mas•ter
master a•gree•ment
master and serv•ant
master lim•it•ed part•ner•ship
Mas•ter of Arts (M.A. or A.M.)
Master of Arts in Law and Di•plo•ma•cy (M.A.L.D.)
Master of Busi•ness Ad•min•i•stra•tion (M.B.A.)
Master of Laws (LL.M.)
Master of Sci•ence (M.S.)
Master of the Rolls (M.R.)
master plan
mas•ter•ful

mas•ter•ful•ly
mas•ter•ful•ness
mas•ter•li•ness
mas•ter•ly
mas•ter•mind
mas•ter•piece
mas•ter's de•gree
mas•ter•ship
mas•ter•y
mas•tur•bate v.,
  mas•tur•bat•ed,
  mas•tur•bat•ing
mas•tur•ba•tion
mas•tur•ba•to•ry
matched or•der
match•mak•er
ma•te•ri•al (sub-
  stance; pertinent: cf.
  MATÉRIEL)
material al•le•ga•
  tion
material al•ter•a•
  tion
material breach
material fact
material is•sue
material mis•rep•re•
  sen•ta•tion
material rep•re•sen•
  ta•tion
material var•i•ance
material wit•ness
ma•te•ri•al•ism
ma•te•ri•al•ist
ma•te•ri•al•i•ty
ma•te•ri•al•i•za•
  tion
ma•te•ri•al•ize v.,
  ma•te•ri•al•ized,
  ma•te•ri•al•iz•ing
ma•te•ri•al•ly
ma•te•ri•al•man n.,
  pl. ma•te•ri•al•men
ma•te•ri•al•man's
  lien
ma•té•ri•el or ma•

te•ri•el (equipment:
  cf. MATERIAL)
ma•ter•nal
maternal line
ma•ter•nal•ism
ma•ter•nal•is•tic
ma•ter•nal•ly
ma•ter•ni•ty
maternity leave
mat•ri•cid•al
mat•ri•cide
Matrim. (Matrimonial)
mat•ri•mo•ni•al (ci-
  tation form: Matrim.)
matrimonial ac•tion
matrimonial dom•i•
  cile
mat•ri•mo•ny
ma•tron
mat•ter
matter in deed
matter of course n.
matter-of-course adj.
matter of fact n.
matter-of-fact adj.
matter-of-fact•ly
matter-of-fact•ness
matter of law
matter of rec•ord
mat•u•ra•tion
ma•ture adj., ma•
  tur•er, ma•tur•est,
  v., ma•tured, ma•
  tur•ing
mature mi•nor
ma•ture•ly
ma•tu•ri•ty
maturity date
maud•lin
maud•lin•ly
maud•lin•ness
maul (to injure; a ham-
  mer: cf. MALL)
mau•so•le•um n., pl.
  mau•so•le•ums or
  mau•so•le•a

mav•er•ick
mawk•ish
mawk•ish•ly
mawk•ish•ness
max•im
max•i•mal
max•i•mi•za•tion
max•i•mize v.,
  max•i•mized,
  max•i•miz•ing
max•i•mum n., pl.
  max•i•mums or (esp.
  in scientific contexts)
  max•i•ma
maximum se•cu•ri•ty
  n.
maximum-security adj.
May (citation form:
  May)
may•hem
may•or
may•or•al
may•or•al•ty
May•or's Court
maz•in•dol Controlled
  Subst.
M.B.A. (Master of Busi-
  ness Administration)
MBE (Multistate Bar Ex-
  amination)
Mc•Car•thy•ism
M.D.[1] (Middle District)
M.D.[2] (Doctor of Medi-
  cine: from Latin Medi-
  cinae Doctor)
MDA Controlled Subst.
  (methylenedioxyam-
  phetamine)
MDMA Controlled
  Subst. (methylenediox-
  ymethamphetamine)
me•a cul•pa Latin.
mean v., meant,
  mean•ing, adj.,
  mean•er, mean•est,
  n. (to signify; cruel or

base; the average: cf.
MESNE; MIEN)
mean•spir•it•ed
mean•ing
mean•ing•ful
mean•ing•ful re•la•
tion•ship
mean•ing•ful•ly
mean•ing•ful•ness
mean•ing•less
mean•ing•less•ly
mean•ing•less•ness
mean•ly
mean•ness
means
means test
means test•ing
mean•while
meas•ure n., v.,
meas•ured, meas•
ur•ing
measure of dam•
ag•es
meas•ured
meas•ured•ly
meas•ured•ness
meas•ure•ment
meas•ur•ing life
me•bu•ta•mate Con-
trolled Subst.
me•chan•ic
me•chan•i•cal
mechanical e•quiv•a•
lent
mechanical pat•ent
me•chan•i•cal•ly
me•chan•ic's lien
mech•an•ism
mech•a•nis•tic
mech•a•nis•ti•cal•ly
mech•a•ni•za•tion
mech•a•nize v.,
mech•a•nized,
mech•a•niz•ing
mec•lo•qua•lone
Controlled Subst.

Med. (Mediator; Medi-
cine; Medical)
me•daz•e•pam Con-
trolled Subst.
med•dle v., med•
dled, med•dling (to
interfere: vs. (medal)
med•dler
med•dle•some (intru-
sive: cf. METTLESOME)
med•dle•some•ly
med•dle•some•ness
med•dling•ly
Me•dellín car•tel
me•di•a See MEDIUM.
me•di•a•cy
me•di•al
me•di•al•ly
me•di•an
me•di•ate v., me•di•
at•ed, me•di•at•
ing, adj.
me•di•ate•ly
me•di•ate•ness
me•di•a•tion
me•di•a•tive
me•di•a•ti•za•tion
me•di•a•tize v., me•
di•a•tized, me•di•
a•tiz•ing
me•di•a•tor (Med.)
me•di•a•to•ri•al
me•di•a•tor•ship
me•di•a•to•ry
med•i•ca•ble
Med•i•caid
med•i•cal (citation
form: Med.)
medical de•vice
medical ex•am•in•er
medical ex•pense
medical ju•ris•pru•
dence
medical mal•prac•tice
medical sav•ings ac•
count (MSA)

med•i•cal•i•za•tion
med•i•cal•ize v.,
med•i•cal•ized,
med•i•cal•iz•ing
med•i•cal•ly
med•i•ca•ment
Med•i•care
med•i•cate v.,
med•i•cat•ed,
med•i•cat•ing
med•i•ca•tion
med•i•ca•tive
me•dic•i•nal
me•dic•i•nal•ly
med•i•cine (citation
form: Med.)
med•i•co•le•gal
med•i•gap in•sur•
ance
me•di•o•cre
me•di•oc•ri•ty n., pl.
me•di•oc•ri•ties
med•i•tate v.,
med•i•tat•ed,
med•i•tat•ing
med•i•tat•ing•ly
med•i•ta•tion
med•i•ta•tive
med•i•ta•tive•ly
med•i•ta•tive•ness
med•i•ta•tor
me•di•um n., pl.
me•di•a or me•di•
ums, adj.
medium of ex•change
meek adj., meek•er,
meek•est
meek•ly
meek•ness
meet v., met, meet•
ing, n., adj. (to come
together; a contest; fit-
ting: cf. METE)
meet•ing
meeting com•pe•ti•
tion

meeting of cred•i•
tors

meeting of the minds

meet•ly

me•fen•o•rex *Con-
trolled Subst.*

meg•a•lo•ma•ni•a

meg•a•lo•ma•ni•ac

meg•a•lo•ma•ni•a•
cal

meg•a•lo•ma•ni•a•
cal•ly

Meg•an's law

Meg•an's Law

mei•o•sis *n., pl.* mei•
o•ses

mel•an•cho•li•a

me•lan•chol•ic

mel•an•chol•i•cal•ly

mel•an•chol•y

me•lee

mel•io•ra•ble

mel•io•rate *v.,* mel•
io•rat•ed, mel•io•
rat•ing

mel•io•ra•tion

mel•io•ra•tive

mel•io•ra•tor

mel•o•dra•ma

mel•o•dra•mat•ic

mel•o•dra•mat•i•
cal•ly

mel•o•dra•mat•ics *n.
sing.*

melt•down

Mem. See memoran-
dum.

mem. See memoran-
dum.

mem•ber

member state

membership cor•po•
ra•tion

me•men•to *n., pl.*
me•men•tos or me•
men•toes

memento mo•ri *Latin.*

Mem'l (Memorial)

mem•o *n., pl.*
mem•os

mem•oir

mem•o•ra•bil•i•a
n.pl.

mem•o•ra•bil•i•ty

mem•o•ra•ble

mem•o•ra•ble•ness

mem•o•ra•bly

mem•o•ran•da See
MEMORANDUM.

mem•o•ran•dum *n.,
pl.* mem•o•ran•da
(*citation forms:* **Mem.**
for a litigant's brief;
mem. for a short judicial decision)

memorandum clause

memorandum de•ci•
sion

memorandum of law

memorandum of
points and au•
thor•i•ties

memorandum of
un•der•stand•ing

memorandum o•pin•
ion

memorandum or•der

me•mo•ri•al (*citation
form:* **Mem'l**)

me•mo•ri•al•i•za•
tion

me•mo•ri•al•ize *v.,*
me•mo•ri•al•ized,
me•mo•ri•al•iz•ing

mem•o•riz•a•ble

mem•o•ri•za•tion

mem•o•rize *v.,*
mem•o•rized,
mem•o•riz•ing

mem•o•riz•er

mem•o•ry *n., pl.*
mem•o•ries

memory im•pair•
ment

men•ace *n., v.,* men•
aced, men•ac•ing

men•ac•er

men•ac•ing

men•ac•ing•ly

men•da•cious

men•da•cious•ly

men•da•cious•ness

men•dac•i•ty *n., pl.*
men•dac•i•ties

men•di•can•cy

men•di•cant

me•ni•al

me•ni•al•ly

mens *n., pl.* men•tes
Latin.

mens re•a *Latin.*

men•sa et tho•ro
Latin.

men•stru•al ex•trac•
tion

men•sur•a•bil•i•ty

men•sur•a•ble

men•su•ra•tion

men•su•ra•tive

men•tal

mental age

mental an•guish

mental ca•pac•i•ty

mental con•di•tion

mental cru•el•ty

mental de•fect

mental dis•a•bil•i•ty

mental dis•ease

mental dis•or•der

mental health

mental health in•sur•
ance

mental ill•ness

mental im•pair•ment

mental res•er•va•
tion

mental re•tar•da•
tion

mental state
men•tal•ly
men•tee
men•tion
men•tion•a•ble
men•tion•er
men•tor
men•tor•ing
men•tor•ship
me•per•i•dine *Controlled Subst.*
meph•o•bar•bi•tal *Controlled Subst.*
me•pro•ba•mate *Controlled Subst.*
mer•can•tile
mer•can•til•ism
mer•can•til•ist
mer•can•til•is•tic
mer•ce•nar•i•ly
mer•ce•nar•i•ness
mer•ce•nar•y *adj., n.*
mer•ce•nar•ies
mer•chan•dis•a•ble
mer•chan•dise *n. v.,* mer•chan•dised, mer•chan•dis•ing
mer•chan•dis•er
mer•chan•dis•ing
merchandising group
mer•chant
merchant ma•rine
merchant whole•sal•er
mer•chant•a•bil•i•ty
mer•chant•a•ble
merchantable qual•i•ty
merchantable ti•tle
mer•ci•ful
mer•ci•ful•ly
mer•ci•ful•ness
mer•ci•less
mer•ci•less•ly
mer•ci•less•ness

mer•cy *n., pl.* mer•cies
mercy kill•ing
mere *adj.,* mer•est
mere•ly
mer•e•tri•cious (illicit; vulgar; specious: cf. MERITORIOUS)
meretricious re•la•tion•ship
mer•e•tri•cious•ly
mer•e•tri•cious•ness
merge *v.,* merged, merg•ing
merg•er
merger clause
merger of law and eq•ui•ty
merg•ers and ac•qui•si•tions (M&A)
mer•it
merit in•crease
merit pay
merit rat•ing
merit sys•tem
mer•it•ed•ly
mer•it•less
mer•i•toc•ra•cy *n., pl.* mer•i•toc•ra•cies
mer•i•to•ri•ous (praiseworthy: cf. MERETRICIOUS
meritorious de•fense
mer•i•to•ri•ous•ly
mer•i•to•ri•ous•ness
mer•its *n.pl.*
mes•cal
mescal but•ton
mes•ca•line *Controlled Subst.*
mes•mer•i•za•tion
mes•mer•ize *v.,* mes•mer•ized, mes•mer•iz•ing
mes•mer•iz•er

mesn•al•ty
mesne *Law French.* (intermediate: cf. MEAN; MIEN)
mesne lord
mesne proc•ess
mesne prof•its
mes•sage (communication: cf. MASSAGE)
mes•sen•ger
messenger RNA
mes•suage
mes•ter•o•o•lone *Controlled Subst.*
me•tab•o•lism
me•tab•o•lite
met•a•eth•i•cal
met•a•eth•ics
met•a•phor
met•a•phor•ic
met•a•phor•i•cal
met•a•phor•i•cal•ly
met•a•phor•i•cal•ness
me•taz•o•o•cine *Controlled Subst.*
mete *v.,* met•ed, met•ing, *n.* (to allot; a boundary: cf. MEET)
me•ter maid
metes and bounds
meth•a•done *Controlled Subst.*
methadone main•te•nance
meth•am•phet•a•mine *Controlled Subst.*
meth•an•di•e•none *Controlled Subst.*
meth•an•dra•none *Controlled Subst.*
meth•an•dri•ol *Controlled Subst.*
meth•an•dro•sten•o•lone *Controlled Subst.*

meth•aq•ua•lone *Controlled Subst.*

meth•cath•oi•none *Controlled Subst.*

Meth•oe•drine *Trademark.*

me•the•no•lone *Controlled Subst.*

meth•od

me•thod•oi•cal

me•thod•oi•cal•ly

me•thod•oi•cal•ness

meth•od•less

meth•od•oo•log•oi•cal

meth•od•oo•log•oi•cal•ly

meth•od•ol•oo•gist

meth•od•ol•oo•gy *n., pl.* meth•od•ol•oo•gies

meth•oo•hex•oi•tal *Controlled Subst.*

meth•oo•trex•ate

meth•yl•de•sor•phine *Controlled Subst.*

meth•yl•ene•di•ox•oy•am•phet•a•mine (MDA) *Controlled Subst.*

meth•yl•ene•di•ox•oy•meth&sp brk;am•phet•oa•mine (MDMA) *Controlled Subst.*

meth•yl•hy•dro•mor•phine *Controlled Subst.*

meth•yl•phen•oi•date *Controlled Subst.*

meth•yl•phe•no•bar•bi•tal *Controlled Subst.*

meth•yl•tes•tos•ter•one *Controlled Subst.*

meth•o•y•pry•lon *Controlled Subst.*

me•tic•ou•los•oi•ty

me•tic•ou•lous

me•tic•ou•lous•ly

me•tic•ou•lous•ness

mé•tier

met•oo•pon *Controlled Subst.*

Metro. (Metropolitan)

me•trop•oo•lis *n., pl.* me•trop•oo•lís•es

met•ro•pol•oi•tan (*citation form:* Metro.)

met•tle (courage; temperament: vs. *metal*)

met•tle•some (spirited: cf. MEDDLESOME)

Mfg. (Manufacturing)

Mfr. (Manufacturer)

Mgmt. (Management)

mi•bo•le•rone *Controlled Subst.*

mi○cro•cosm

mic○ro•cos•mic

mi○cro•ec○o•nom○ic

mi○cro•ec○o•nom○ics

mi○cro•e•con○o•mist

mi○cro•en•vi•ron•ment

mi○cro•en•vi•ron•men•tal

mi○cro•man•age *v.,* mi○cro•man•aged, mi○cro•man•ag•ing

mi○cro•man•age•ment

mi○cro•or•gan•ism

mi○cro•so•ci•ol○o○gy

mi•daz○o•lam *Controlled Subst.*

mid-cap

mid•dle class *n.*

Mid•dle Dis•trict (*citation form:* M.D.)

middle-in•come hous•ing

middle man•age•ment

Middle Tem•ple

middle-class *adj.*

mid•dle•man *n., pl.* mid•dle•men

mid-lev○el

mid•night

mid•night dead•line

midrash *n., pl.* mid•ra•shim or mid•ra•shoth Hebrew.

Mid•rash Ag•ga•dah

Midrash Ha•la•khah

mid-term cap•oi•tal gain

mid•wife *n., pl.* mid•wives, *v.,* mid•wifed or mid•wived, mid•wif•ing or mid•wiv•ing

mid•wife○ry

mien (demeanor: cf. MEAN, MESNE)

mif○e○pris•tone

might

might and main

might○i○ly

might○i•ness

might○y *adj.,* might○i•er, might○i•est

mi•gra•to○ry

migratory di•vorce

migratory spe•cies

mile•age (rate per mile; number of miles: cf. MILLAGE)

mil○i•tan○cy

mil○i•tant

mil○i•tant•ly

mil○i•tant•ness

mil○i•taro•i○ly

mil○i•taro•i•ness

mil○i•ta•rism

mil○i•ta•rist

mil•i•ta•ri•za•tion
mil•i•ta•rize v.,
mil•i•ta•rized,
mil•i•ta•riz•ing
mil•i•tar•y adj., n., pl
mil•i•tar•ies
mil•i•tar•y court
military gov•ern•
ment
military gov•er•nor
military-in•dus•tri•al
com•plex
military ju•ris•dic•
tion
military law
military of•fense
military tri•bu•nal
mil•i•tate v., mil•i•
tat•ed, mil•i•tat•
ing
mi•li•tia
mill
mill rate
mill•age (tax rate in
mills per dollar: cf.
MILEAGE)
Mill•er trust
Mil•town Trademark.
mi•me•sis
mi•met•ic
mimetic drug
mi•met•i•cal•ly
Min. (Mineral)
min•a•ble
mind
mind-bog•gling
mind-bog•gling•ly
mind•ful
mind•ful•ly
mind•ful•ness
mind•less
mind•less•ly
mind•less•ness
mine n., v., mined,
min•ing, pron.
mine•field

min•er (one who en-
gages in mining: cf.
MINOR)
min•er•al (citation
form: Min.)
mineral deed
mineral lease
mineral rights
mine•work•er
min•i•mal
min•i•mal•ly
min•i•mi•za•tion
min•i•mize v., min•i•
mized, min•i•miz•
ing
min•i•miz•er
min•i•mum n., pl.
min•i•mums or (esp.
in scientific contexts)
min•i•ma
minimum con•tacts
minimum lend•ing
rate
minimum month•ly
main•te•nance
needs al•low•ance
(MMMNA)
minimum se•cu•ri•ty
n.
minimum-security adj.
minimum sen•tence
minimum tax
minimum wage n.
minimum-wage adj.
min•ing
mining claim
mining lease
min•ion
minion of the law
min•is•ter
minister plen•i•po•
ten•ti•ar•y
minister res•i•dent
n., pl. ministers
res•i•dent

minister with•out
port•fo•li•o
min•is•te•ri•al
ministerial act
ministerial func•tion
ministerial trust
min•is•te•ri•al•ly
min•is•try n., pl.
min•is•tries
min•i•tri•al
Min•ne•so•ta
Mul•ti•pha•sic Per•
son•al•i•ty In•ven•
to•ry (MMPI)
mi•nor (a young per-
son; not serious: cf.
MINER)
minor in need of
su•per•vi•sion
(MINS)
minor of•fense
mi•nor•i•ty n., pl.
mi•nor•i•ties, adj.
minority group
minority in•ter•est
minority o•pin•ion
minority rep•re•sen•
ta•tion
minority set-a•side
minority stock•hold•
ers
MINS (minor in need of
supervision)
mi•nus•cule
min•ute¹ n., v., min•
ut•ed, min•ut•ing
(a span of time or a
note; to note down)
mi•nute² adj., mi•
nut•er, mi•nut•est
(tiny)
mi•nute•ly
mi•nute•ness
min•utes n.pl.
mi•nu•ti•a n., pl. mi•
nu•ti•ae
mi•nu•ti•al

Mi•ran○da rule
Miranda warn•ing
Mi•ran•dize *v.*, Mi•ran•dized, Mi•ran•diz•ing
mire *v.*, mired, mir•ing
mir•ror sub•sid○i•ar○y
MIS (management information system)
mis•ad•ven•ture
mis•al•le•ga•tion
mis•al•lege *v.*, mis•al•leged, mis•al•leg•ing
mis•an•drist
mis•an•dry
mis•an•thrope
mis•an•throp○ic
mis•an•throp○i•cal○ly
mis•an•thro•pist
mis•an•thro○py
mis•ap•pli•ca•tion
mis•ap•ply *v.*, mis•ap•plied, mis•ap•ply•ing
mis•ap•pre•hend
mis•ap•pre•hen•sion
mis•ap•pro•pri•ate *v.*, mis•ap•pro•pri•at○ed, mis•ap•pro•pri•at•ing
mis•ap•pro•pri•a•tion
mis•be•got•ten
mis•be•have *v.*, mis•be•haved, mis•be•hav•ing
mis•be•hav○er
mis•be•hav•ior
mis•brand
mis•brand○ed
mis•brand•ing
mis•cal•cu•late *v.*,

mis•cal•cu•lat○ed,
mis•cal•cu•lat•ing
mis•cal•cu•la•tion
mis•car•riage
miscarriage of jus•tice
mis•car○ry *v.*, mis•car•ried, mis•car•ry•ing
mis•ceg○e○na•tion
mis•cel•la•ne•ous
mis•cel•la•ne•ous○ly
mis•cel•la•ne•ous•ness
mis•cel•la○ny *n.*, *pl.* mis•cel•la•nies
mis•chance
mis•charge *v.*, mis•charged, mis•charg•ing, *n.*
mis•chief
mis•chief-mak○er
mis•chief-mak•ing
mis•chie•vous
mis•chie•vous○ly
mis•chie•vous•ness
mis•com•mu•ni•cate *v.*, mis•com•mu•ni•cat○ed, mis•com•mu•ni•cat•ing
mis•com•mu•ni•ca•tion
mis•con•ceive *v.*, mis•con•ceived, mis•con•ceiv•ing
mis•con•cep•tion
mis•con•duct
mis•con•struc•tion
mis•con•strue *v.*, mis•con•strued, mis•con•stru•ing
mis•cop○y *v.*, mis•cop•ied, mis•cop○y•ing, *n.*, *pl.* mis•cop•ies
mis•cre•an○cy
mis•cre•ant

mis•date *v.*, mis•dat○ed, mis•dat•ing
mis•deed
mis•de•liv•er
mis•de•liv•er○y
mis•de•mean•ant
mis•de•mean○or
mis•de•scribe *v.*, mis•de•scribed, mis•de•scrib•ing
mis•de•scrip•tion
mis•de•scrip•tive
mis•di•ag•nose *v.*, mis•di•ag•nosed, mis•di•ag•nos•ing
mis•di•ag•no•sis *n.*, *pl.* mis•di•ag•no•ses
mis•di•rect
mis•di•rec•tion
mise *Law French.*
mis•er•a○ble
mis•er•a○bly
mi•se•ri•cor•di○a *Latin.*
mis•er○y *n.*, *pl.* mis•er•ies
mis•fea•sance
mis•fea•sor
mis•fit
mis•giv•ing
mis•guid○ed
mis•guid•ed○ly
mis•guid•ed•ness
mis•han•dle *v.*, mis•han•dled, mis•han•dling
mis•hap
mis•hear *v.*, mis•heard, mis•hear•ing
Mish•nah
mis•i○den•ti•fi•ca•tion
mis•i○den•ti•fy *v.*, mis•i○den•ti•fied, mis•i○den•ti•fy•ing

mis•im•pres•sion
mis•in•form
mis•in•for•ma•tion
mis•in•ter•pret
mis•in•ter•pret•a•ble
mis•in•ter•pre•ta•tion
mis•in•ter•pret•er
mis•join•der
mis•judge *v.*, mis•judged, mis•judg•ing
mis•judg•ment
mis•la•bel *v.*, mis•la•beled, mis•la•bel•ing
mis•lay *v.*, mis•laid, mis•lay•ing
mis•lead *v.*, mis•led, mis•lead•ing
mis•lead•ing
mis•lead•ing•ly
mis•lead•ing•ness
mis•man•age *v.*, mis•man•aged, mis•man•ag•ing
mis•man•age•ment
mis•man•ag•er
mis•no•mer
mi•sog•y•nist
mi•sog•y•nis•tic
mi•sog•y•nous
mi•sog•y•ny
mi•so•pros•tol
mis•plead *v.*, mis•plead•ed, mis•plead•ing
mis•plead•ing
mis•pri•sion
misprision of fel•on•y
misprision of trea•son
mis•quo•ta•tion
mis•quote *v.*, mis•quot•ed, mis•quot•ing, *n.*
mis•read *v.*, mis•read, mis•read•ing
mis•re•port
mis•rep•re•sent
mis•rep•re•sen•ta•tion
mis•rule *v.*, mis•ruled, mis•rul•ing
mis•sing
mis•sion
mis•sive
mis•speak *v.*, mis•spoke, mis•spok•en, mis•speak•ing
mis•spend *v.*, mis•spent, mis•spend•ing
mis•state•ment
mis•step
mis•tak•a•ble
mis•take *n., v.*, mis•took, mis•tak•en, mis•tak•ing
mistake of fact
mistake of law
mis•tak•en
mis•tak•en•ly
mis•tak•en•ness
mis•trans•late *v.*, mis•trans•lat•ed, mis•trans•lat•ing
mis•trans•la•tion
mis•treat
mis•treat•ment
mis•tress
mis•tri•al
mis•trust
mis•trust•ful
mis•trust•ful•ly
mis•trust•ful•ness
mis•un•der•stand *v.*, mis•un•der•stood, mis•un•der•stand•ing

mis•un•der•stand•ing
mis•use *n., v.*, mis•used, mis•us•ing
mis•us•er
mit•i•ga•ble
mit•i•gate *v.*, mit•i•gat•ed, mit•i•gat•ing
mit•i•gat•ing cir•cum•stance
mitigating fac•tor
mitigating meas•ure
mit•i•ga•tion
mitigation of dam•ag•es
mi•to•chon•dri•a See MITOCHONDRION.
mi•to•chon•dri•al DNA
mitochondrial DNA test•ing
mi•to•chon•dri•on *n., pl.* mi•to•chon•dri•a
mi•to•sis *n., pl* mi•to•ses
mi•tot•ic
mit•ti•mus *n , pl.* mit•ti•mus•es
mixed
mixed ac•tion
mixed cost
mixed e•con•o•my
mixed nui•sance
mixed question of law and fact
mix•ed•ness
Mkt. (Market)
Mktg. (Marketing)
MMMNA (minimum monthly maintenance needs allowance)
MMPI (Minnesota Multiphasic Personality Inventory)

M'Nagh•ten rule
M'Naghten test
M.O. (modus operandi)
mob *n., v.,* mobbed,
  mob•bing
mob rule
mo•bi•liz•a•ble
mo•bi•li•za•tion
mo•bi•lize *v.,* mo•bi•
  lized, mo•bi•liz•ing
mo•bi•liz•er
mock•up
Mod. (Modern)
mod•al *adj.* (of a
  mode: cf. MODEL)
mo•dal•i•ty *n., pl.*
  mo•dal•i•ties
mode
mod•el *n , adj., v.,*
  mod•eled, mod•el•
  ing (example; exem-
  plary; to serve as an
  example: cf. MODAL)
model law
Model Pe•nal Code
Model Rules of Pro•
  fes•sion•al Con•
  duct
model stat•ute
mod•er•ate *n., adj.,*
  v., mod•er•at•ed,
  mod•er•at•ing
mod•er•a•tor
mod•ern (*citation
  form:* **Mod.**)
mod•est
mod•est•ly
mod•es•ty
mod•i•fi•a•bil•i•ty
mod•i•fi•a•ble
mod•i•fi•a•ble•ness
mod•i•fi•ca•tion
mod•i•fi•ca•to•ry
mod•i•fied ac•cel•
  er•at•ed cost re•

cov•er•y sys•tem
  (MACRS)
modified ag•gre•gate
  deemed sales price
  (MADSP)
modified life in•sur•
  ance
mod•i•fi•er
mod•i•fy *v.,* mod•i•
  fied, mod•i•fy•ing
mod•u•late *v.,*
  mod•u•lat•ed,
  mod•u•lat•ing
mod•u•la•tion
mod•u•la•tor
mo•dus *n., pl* mo•di
  Latin
modus o•pe•ran•di
  (M.O.) *n., pl.* modi
  o•pe•ran•di *Latin.*
modus vi•ven•di
  Latin.
moi•e•ty *n., pl.* moi•
  e•ties
mole
mo•lec•u•lar
mol•e•cule
mo•lest
mo•les•ta•tion
mo•lest•er
mo•lest•ful
mol•li•fi•a•ble
mol•li•fi•ca•tion
mol•li•fi•er
mol•li•fy *v.,* mol•li•
  fied, mol•li•fy•ing
mol•li•fy•ing•ly
mo•men•tous
mo•men•tous•ly
mo•men•tous•ness
mo•men•tum *n., pl.*
  mo•men•ta or mo•
  men•tums
mom•my track
mon•arch
mo•nar•chal

mo•nar•chi•cal
mon•ar•chism
mon•ar•chy *n., pl.*
  mon•ar•chies
mon•e•tar•i•ly
mon•e•ta•rism
mon•e•ta•rist
mon•e•tar•y
mon•e•ti•za•tion
mon•e•tize *v.,*
  mon•e•tized,
  mon•e•tiz•ing
mon•ey
money chang•ing
money counts
money dam•ag•es
money fund
money had and re•
  ceived
money judg•ment
money laun•der•ing
money mar•ket
money market ac•
  count
money mar•ket cer•
  tif•i•cate
money market fund
money of ac•count
money or•der
money-pur•chase
  plan
money sup•ply
mon•ey•chang•er
mon•ey•lend•er
mon•ism
mon•ist
mo•ni•tion
monition pe•ri•od
mon•i•tor
mon•o•clo•nal
  an•ti•bod•y
mo•nog•a•mous
mo•nog•a•mous•ly
mo•nog•a•mous•
  ness
mo•nog•a•my

mon○o•ma•ni•a
mon○o•ma•ni•ac
mon○o•ma•ni•a•cal
mon○o•ma•ni•a•cal○ly
mo•nop○o•lism
mo•nop○o•list
mo•nop○o•lis•tic
mo•nop○o•lis•ti•cal○ly
mo•nop○o•li•za•tion
mo•nop○o•lize v.,
    mo•nop○o•lized,
    mo•nop○o•liz•ing
mo•nop○o•ly n., pl.
    mo•nop○o•lies
monopoly pow○er
mo•nop•so•nist
mo•nop•so•nis•tic
mo•nop•so○ny n., pl.
    mo•nop•so•nies
monopsony pow○er
mon•strous
mon•strous○ly
mon•strous•ness
month-to-month ten•
    an○cy
mon○u•ment
mon○u•men•tal
mon○u•men•tal•ism
mon○u•men•tal○i○ty
mon○u•men•tal○ly
mood-al○ter•ing sub•
    stance
mood dis•or•der
mood ep○i•sode
moon•light
moon•shine
moon•shin○er
moon•shin•ing
moot (debatable; purely
    hypothetical; to de-
    bate; to render aca-
    demic: cf. MUTE)
moot court
moot○er

moot•ness
mor○al (ethical; a les-
    son: cf. MORALE)
moral cer•tain○ty
moral con•sid•er○a•
    tion
moral haz•ard
moral ob•li•ga•tion
moral rights
moral tur•pi•tude
mo•rale (emotional
    state: cf. MORAL)
mor•al•ist
mor•al•is•tic
mor•al•is•ti•cal○ly
mo•ral○i○ty
mor•al•i•za•tion
mor•al•ize v., mor•
    al•ized, mor•al•iz•
    ing
mor•al○ly
mor•als n.pl.
mo•rass
mor○a•tor○i○um n.,
    pl. mor○a•tor○i○a or
    mor○a•tor○i○ums
mo•rbid
mor•bid○i○ty
mor•dant
more def○i•nite
    state•ment
mor•ga•nat○ic mar•
    riage
morgue
mor○i•bund
mor○i•bun•di○ty
mor○i•bund○ly
morning-af○ter pill
morn•ing loan
mor•pher○i•dine Con-
    trolled Subst.
mo•rphine Controlled
    Subst.
morphine meth○yl•
    bro•mide Controlled
    Subst.

morphine meth○yl•
    sul•fo•nate Con
    trolled Subst.
morphine-N-ox○ide
    Controlled Subst.
mort d'an•ces•tor
    Law French.
mor•tal
mor•tal○i○ty n., pl.
    mor•tal○i•ties
mortality ta•ble
mor•tal○ly
mort•gage n., v.,
    mort•gaged, mort•
    gag•ing
mortgage bank•ing
mortgage bond
mortgage com•pa○ny
mortgage cred○i•tor
mortgage debt○or
mortgage fore•clo•
    sure
mortgage in•sur•ance
mortgage loan
mortgage loan com•
    mit•ment
mortgage note
mortgage real es•tate
    in•vest•ment trust
mortgage serv•ic•ing
mortgage ware•
    hous○ing
mort•gage•a○ble
mort•ga•gee
mortgagee clause
mortgagee in pos•
    ses•sion
mort•ga•gor
mor•tis cau○sa Latin.
mort•main Law
    French.
mortmain stat•ute
Mo•sa○ic law
most-fa•vored na•
    tion n.

most-favored-nation *adj.*

most-favored-nation clause

moth○er

Moth○er Hub○bard clause

mother-in-law *n., pl.* mothers-in-law

moth•er•hood

moth•er•ing

moth•er•less

moth•er○ly

mo•tion

motion in li•mi○ne

motion pa•pers

mo•ti•vate *v.,* mo•ti• vat○ed, mo•ti•vat• ing

mo•ti•va•tion

mo•ti•va•tor

mo•tive

mo○tor

motor ve•hi•cle

motor vehicle theft

motor vot○er law

mourn

mourn○er

mourn•ful

mourn•ful○ly

mourn•ful•ness

mourn•ing

mouth•piece

mov•a○bil•i○ty

mov•a○ble

mov•a○bles

mov•a○bly

mov•ant (person mak- ing a motion in court: cf. MOVER)

move *v.,* moved, mov•ing, *n.*

move•ment

mov○er (one who moves generally: cf. MOVANT)

moving-av•er•age meth○od

mov•ing ex•pense

moving vi○o•la•tion

MPT (Multistate Perfor- mance Test)

M.R. (Master of the Rolls)

M.S. (Master of Sci ence)

ms. *pl.* **mss** (manu script)

MSA (medical savings account)

muck•rake *v.,* muck• raked, muck•rak•ing

muck•rak○er

mud•dle *v.,* mud• dled, mud•dling, *n.*

mud•sling○er

mud•sling•ing

muf○ti *n., pl.* muf•tis

mug *v.,* mugged, mug•ging, *n.*

mug•shot

muj○ta•hid

mulct

mu•li○er

mulier puis○ne *Law French.*

mu•li•er○ty

mul○lah

mul○ti•cul•tur○al

mul○ti•cul•tur•al• ism

mul○ti•dis•trict lit○i• ga•tion

mul○ti•em•ploy○er bar•gain•ing

multiemployer pen• sion plan

mul○ti•fac•to•ri○al

mul○ti•fac•to•ri• al○ly

mul○ti•fam○i•ly

mul○ti•far○i○ous

mul○ti•far○i•ous• ness

mul○ti•lat•er○al

multilateral a○gree• ment

multilateral trea○ty

mul○ti•lat•er•al•ism

mul○ti•lat•er•al○ly

mul○ti•lev○el

mul○ti•lin•gual

mul○ti•lin•gual•ism

mul○ti•lin•gual○ly

mul○ti•me•di○a

multimedia mar•ket

mul○ti•mod○al

multimodal car•riage of goods

mul○ti•mod•al•ism

mul○ti•na•tion○al

mul○ti•par○ty

mul•ti•ple

multiple ar•bi•trar○y am•pli•con pro•fil• ing (MAAP)

multiple dam•ag○es

multiple hear•say

multiple list•ing

multiple per•son• al○i○ty

multiple personality dis•or•der

multiple sen•tence

mul•ti•pli•a○ble

mul•ti•pli•ca•tion

mul•ti•pli•ca•tive

mul•ti•plic○i○ty *n., pl.* mul•ti•plic○i•ties

mul•ti•pli○er

multiplier ef•fect

mul•ti•ply *v.,* mul•ti• plied, mul•ti•ply• ing, *adv.*

mul○ti•pronged

mul○ti•pur•pose

mul○ti•ra•cial

mul○ti•state
Multistate Bar Ex•
am•in○a•tion (MBE)
Multistate Per•for•
mance Test (MPT)
mul○ti•tude
mul○ti•tu•di•nous
mul○ti•tu•di•nous○ly
mul○ti•tu•di•nous•
ness
mul○ti•use
mul○ti•us○er
mum○bo jum○bo
Mun. (Municipal)
Mun. Ct. (Municipal
Court)
Mun•chau•sen (or
Munch•hau•sen or
Munch•hau•sen's)
syn•drome
Munchausen (or
Munchhausen or
Munchhausen's) syn-
drome by prox○y
mun•dane
mun•dane•ness
mu•nic○i•pal (citation
form: **Mun.**)
municipal bond
municipal bond fund
municipal char•ter
municipal cor•po•ra•
tion
Mu•nic○i•pal Court
(citation form: **Mun.
Ct.**)
municipal law
municipal or•di•
nance
municipal se•cur○i•ty
mu•nic○i•pal•ism
mu•nic○i•pal○i○ty n.,

pl. mu•nic○i•pal○i•
ties
mu•nic○i•pal○ly
mu•ni•ment
mu•ni•ments of
ti○tle
mu•ni•tion
munitions n.pl.
mu•ni•tions list
mu•rage
mur•der
mur•der○er
mur•der•ess
mur•der•ous
mur•der•ous○ly
mur•der•ous•ness
mur•drum
mus•cle re•lax•ant
mu•si○cal work
must-car○ry pro•vi•
sion
mus•ter
Mut. (Mutual)
mu•ta•bil○i○ty
mu•ta•ble
mu•ta•ble•ness
mu•ta•bly
mu•ta•gen○e•sis
mu•ta•tion
mu•ta•tis mu•tan•
dis Latin.
mute adj., n., v.,
mut○ed, mut•ing (si-
lent; one who remains
silent; to muffle: cf.
MOOT)
mute○ly
mute•ness
mu•ti•late v., mu•ti•
lat○ed, mu•ti•lat•
ing
mu•ti•la•tion

mu•ti•la•tive
mu•ti•la•tor
mu•ti•neer
mu•ti•nous
mu•ti•nous○ly
mu•ti•nous•ness
mu•ti○ny n., pl. mu•
ti•nies, v., mu•ti•
nied, mu•ti•ny•ing
mu•tu○al (citation
form: **Mut.**)
mutual fund
mutual in•sur•ance
mutual insurance
com•pa•ny
mutual mis•take
mutual re•leas○es
mutual sav•ings bank
mu•tu•al○i○ty
mu•tu•al○i○za•tion
mu•tu•al•ize v., mu•
tu•al•ized, mu•tu•
al•iz•ing
mu•tu•al○ly
my•ro•phine Con-
trolled Subst.
mys•te•ri•ous
mys•te•ri•ous○ly
mys•te•ri•ous•ness
mys•ter○y n., pl.
mys•ter•ies
mys•ti•fi•ca•tion
mys•ti•fied○ly
mys•ti•fi○er
mys•ti○fy v., mys•ti•
fied, mys•ti•fy•ing
mys•ti•fy•ing○ly
myth
myth○i•cal
myth○i•cal○ly

N

N. (North; Northern)

n. *pl.* nn (note; footnote; endnote)

N.A. (National Association)

nab•i•lone *Controlled Subst.*

na•bob

NAFTA (North American Free Trade Agreement)

na•ïf *n.* (cf. NAIVE)

nail and mail

na•ive *adj.* (cf. NAÏF)

na•ive•ly

na•ive•té

na•ked

naked trust

na•ked•ly

na•ked•ness

nal•or•phine *Controlled Subst.*

name *n., v.,* named, nam•ing, *adj.*

name brand

name-drop•per

name-drop•ping

name•a•ble or nam•a•ble

named in•sured

name•less

name•less•ly

name•less•ness

name•ly

nam•er

nan•dro•lone *Controlled Subst.*

nan•ny tax

Na•po•le•on•ic Code

narc or nark

nar•cis•sism

nar•cis•sist

nar•cis•sis•tic

narcissistic per•son•al•i•ty dis•or•der

nar•co•a•nal•y•sis

nar•co•lep•sy

nar•co•lep•tic

nar•co•sis

nar•cot•ic

narcotic drug

nar•cot•i•cal•ly

nark See NARC.

nar•rate *v.,* nar•rat•ed, nar•rat•ing

nar•ra•tion

nar•ra•tive

narrative ev•i•dence

nar•ra•tive•ly

nar•ra•tor

nar•row

nar•row con•struc•tion

narrow im•prove•ment

narrow in•ter•pre•ta•tion

narrow-mind•ed

narrow-mind•ed•ly

narrow-mind•ed•ness

nar•row•ly

nar•row•ness

nas•cence

nas•cen•cy

nas•cent

NASDAQ (National Association of Securities Dealers Automated Quotations)

nas•ti•ly

nas•ti•ness

nas•ty *adj.,* nas•ti•er, nas•ti•est

Nat. (Natural)

na•tion

nation-state

na•tion•al (*citation form:* Nat'l)

National As•so•ci•a•tion of Se•cu•ri•ties Deal•ers Au•to•mat•ed Quo•ta•tions (NASDAQ)

national bank

national brand

national cem•e•ter•y

national e•mer•gen•cy

national for•est

national mon•u•ment

national park

national rec•re•a•tion ar•e•a

national sea•shore

national se•cu•ri•ty

na•tion•al•ism

na•tion•al•ist

na•tion•al•is•tic

na•tion•al•is•ti•cal•ly

na•tion•al•i•ty *n.,* na•tion•al•i•ties

na•tion•al•i•za•tion

na•tion•al•ize *v.,* na•tion•al•ized, na•tion•al•iz•ing

na•tion•al•ly

na•tion•hood

na•tion•wide

na•tive

na•tive•ly

na•tive•ness

na•tiv•i•ty *n.,* na•tiv•i•ties

Nat'l (National)

nat•u•ral (*citation form:* Nat.)

natural af•fec•tion

natural-born

natural-born cit•i•zen

natural caus•es

natural child

natural con•se•quence

natural death

natural dis•as•ter

natural guard•i•an

natural heir

natural jus•tice

natural law

natural lib•er•ty

natural mo•nop•o•o•ly

natural ob•ject of boun•ty

natural par•ent

natural per•son

natural re•source

natural right

nat•u•ral•i•za•tion

naturalization pro•ceed•ing

nat•u•ral•ize v., nat•u•ral•ized, nat•u•ral•iz•ing

naturalized cit•i•zen

nat•u•ral•ly

nat•u•ral•ness

na•ture

naught or nought (nothing) See also NOUGHT.

nav•i•ga•bil•i•ty

nav•i•ga•ble

navigable wa•ters

nav•i•ga•tion

nav•i•ga•tion•al

nav•i•ga•tor

nay

nay•say•er

N.B. (nota bene)

N.D. (Northern District)

n.d. (no date)

N.E. (North Eastern Reporter)

ne ex•e•at *Latin.*

ne in•jus•te vex•es *Latin.*

neb•u•lous

neb•u•lous•ly

neb•u•lous•ness

nec•es•sar•ies *n.pl.*

nec•es•sar•y

necessary par•ty

nec•es•si•tous

necessitous cir•cum•stances

nec•es•si•tous•ly

nec•es•si•tous•ness

nec•es•si•ty *n., pl.* nec•es•si•ties

nec•ro•phil•i•a

née or nee

need•ful (necessary; needed: cf. NEEDY)

need•ful•ly

need•ful•ness

need•i•ly

need•i•ness

nee•dle *n., v.,* nee•dled, nee•dling

needle ex•change pro•gram

need•less

need•less•ly

need•less•ness

need•y *adj.,* need•i•er, need•i•est (poor; in need: cf. NEEDFUL)

ne'er-do-well

ne•far•i•ous

ne•far•i•ous•ly

ne•far•i•ous•ness

ne•gate *v.,* ne•gat•ed, ne•gat•ing

ne•ga•tion

neg•a•tive *adj., n., adv., v.,* neg•a•tived, neg•a•tiv•ing, *interj.*

negative act

negative am•or•ti•za•tion

negative as•sur•ance

negative a•ver•ment

negative clear•ance

negative con•di•tion

negative con•fir•ma•tion

negative cov•e•nant

negative du•ty

negative ease•ment

negative float

negative in•come

negative income tax

negative op•tion

negative plea

negative pledge

negative preg•nant

negative rules of in•ven•tlon

neg•a•tive•ly

neg•a•tive•ness

neg•a•tiv•ism

neg•a•tiv•ist

neg•a•tiv•is•tic

neg•a•tiv•i•ty

neg•a•tor

Negl. (Negligence)

ne•glect

neglect of du•ty

ne•glect•ed

neglected child

ne•glect•ed•ness

ne•glect•er

ne•glect•ful

ne•glect•ful•ly

ne•glect•ful•ness

neg•li•gence (*citation form:* Negl.)

negligence in law

negligence per se

neg•li•gent

negligent hom•i•cide

negligent in•flic•tion of e•mo•tion•al dis•tress

negligent man•
  slaugh•ter
neg•li•gent•ly
neg•li•gi•bil•i•ty
neg•li•gi•ble
neg•li•gi•ble•ness
neg•li•gi•bly
ne•go•ti•a•bil•i•ty
ne•go•ti•a•ble
negotiable docu•
  ment of ti•tle
negotiable in•stru•
  ment
negotiable pa•per
ne•go•ti•ate v., ne•
  go•ti•at•ed, ne•
  go•ti•at•ing
ne•go•ti•at•ed plea
negotiated rule•mak•
  ing
ne•go•ti•a•tion
ne•go•ti•a•tor
neif Law French.
neif•ty
neigh•bor
neigh•bor•hood
neigh•bor•ing
neighboring rights
neigh•bor•li•ness
neigh•bor•ly
nem. con. (nemine con-
  tradicente)
Nem•bu•tal Trade-
  mark.
nem•e•sis n., pl.
  nem•e•ses
ne•mi•ne con•tra•
  di•cen•te (nem.
  con.) Latin.
nemine dis•sen•ti•
  en•te Latin.
ne•mo n.sing. Latin.
ne•o•na•tal
ne•o•nate
ne•o•na•ti•cide
ne•o•na•tol•o•gy

ne•o•phyte
neph•ew
nep•o•tism
nep•o•tist
nep•o•tis•tic
nerve gas
nerve-rack•ing
nerv•ous
nerv•ous•ly
nerv•ous•ness
net adj., n., v., net•
  ted, net•ting
net as•set val•ue
net as•sets
net cap•i•tal gains
net change
net con•tract
net cur•rent as•sets
net es•tate
net in•come
net lease
net list•ing
net na•tion•al prod•
  uct (NNP)
net op•er•at•ing in•
  come
net operating loss
net po•si•tion
net pres•ent val•ue
net prof•it
net re•a•liz•a•ble
  val•ue
net sales
net weight
net worth
net•ta•ble
net•ting proc•ess
net•work
net•work•ing
neu•ro•cog•ni•tive
  func•tion•ing
neu•ro•log•i•cal
neurological def•i•cit
neu•ro•log•i•cal•ly
neu•rol•o•gy

neu•ro•psy•chi•at•
  ric
neu•ro•psy•chi•a•
  try
neu•ro•psy•cho•
  log•i•cal
neu•ro•psy•
  chol•o•gy
neu•ro•sis n., pl.
  neu•ro•ses
neu•rot•ic
neu•rot•i•cal•ly
neu•tral
neu•tral•ism
neu•tral•ist
neu•tral•i•ty
neu•tral•ize v., neu•
  tral•ized, neu•tral•
  iz•ing
neu•tral•iz•er
neu•tral•ly
nev•er•the•less
new
new mat•ter
new prom•ise
new se•ries (citation
  form: n.s.)
new tri•al
new•ly
newly dis•cov•ered
  ev•i•dence
news n.sing.
news re•lease
Newsl. (Newsletter)
news•let•ter (citation
  form: Newsl.)
new•speak
news•wor•thi•ness
news•wor•thy
Nex•is Trademark. (a
  computerized research
  service: cf. NEXUS)
next friend
next of kin
nex•us n., pl. nex•

us•es (a connection: cf. NEXIS)

NGO (nongovernmental organization)

ni•ce•ty n., pl. ni•ce•ties

niche

nick•el-and-dime adj., v., nick•el-and-dimed or nick•eled-and-dimed, nick•el-and-dim•ing or nick•el•ing-and-dim•ing

nic•o•co•deine Controlled Subst.

nic•o•mor•phine Controlled Subst.

nic•o•tine

nicotine de•pend•ence

nicotine with•draw•al

nic•o•tin•ism

nic•o•tin•ize v., nic•o•tin•ized, nic•o•tin•iz•ing

niece

nig•gard•li•ness

nig•gard•ly

nig•gle v., nig•gled, nig•gling

nig•gler

nig•gling

nig•gling•ly

night court

night watch•man

night•time

ni•hil Latin.

nihil de•bet Latin.

ni•hil•ism

ni•hil•ist

ni•hil•is•tic

nil

nim•ble div•i•dend

NIMBY or Nimby (not in my backyard)

Nim•by•ism

ni•me•taz•e•pam Controlled Subst.

ni•si Latin.

nisi pri•us Latin.

nit•pick

nit•pick•er

nit•pick•ing

ni•traz•e•pam Controlled Subst.

nn. (notes; footnotes; endnotes)

NNP (net national product)

no adv., adj., n., pl. noes, interj.

No. (Number)

no-ac•tion let•ter

no bill

no con•test

no date (citation form: n.d.)

no-fault

no-fault di•vorce

no-fault in•sur•ance

no-knock

no-load fund

no-non•sense

no-par

no-par stock

no place (citation form: n.p.)

no-re•turn

no-smok•ing

no-strike

no-strike clause

no•bil•i•ty n., pl. no•bil•i•ties

no•ble adj., no•bler, no•blest, n.

no•ble•ness

Noerr-Pen•ning•ton doc•trine

nol. pros. (nolle prose-qui)

nol-pros v., nol-prossed, nol-pros•sing

no•lens vo•lens Latin.

nol•le pro•se•qui (nol. pros.) Latin.

no•lo con•ten•de•re Latin.

no•men n., pl. no•mi•na Latin.

nomen ju•ris Latin.

no•men•cla•tive

no•men•cla•tur•al

no•men•cla•ture

nom•i•nal

nominal cap•i•tal

nominal con•sid•er•a•tion

nominal dam•ag•es

nominal de•fend•ant

nominal part•ner

nominal plain•tiff

nominal trust

nominal val•ue

nominal wag•es

nom•i•nal•ly

nom•i•nate v., nom•i•nat•ed, nom•i•nat•ing

nom•i•na•tion

nom•i•na•tive

nom•i•na•tor

nom•i•nee

nominee trust

no•mog•ra•pher

no•mog•ra•phy

nom•o•thet•ic

nom•o•thet•i•cal

non Latin.

non as•sump•sit Latin.

non com•pos Latin.

non compos men•tis Latin.

non est *Latin.*

non est fac•tum *Latin.*

non est in•ven•tus *Latin.*

non li•cet *Latin.*

non li•quet *Latin.*

non ob•stan•te (non obst.) *Latin.*

non obstante ve•re• dic•to (n.o.v.) *Latin.*

non pros. (non prose- quitur)

non-pros v., non- prossed, non-pros• sing

non pro•se•qui•tur (non pros.) *Latin.*

non seq. (non sequitur)

non se•qui•tur (non seq.) *Latin.*

non su•i ju•ris *Latin.*

non vult *Latin.*

non vult con•ten• de•re *Latin.*

non•a•bat•a•ble

non•a•bu•sive

non•a•bu•sive•ly

non•ac•cel•er•a•tion

non•ac•cept•ance

non•ac•cess

non•ac•ci•den•tal

non•ac•com•mo•da• tion

non•ac•count• a•bil•i•ty

non•ac•cred•it•ed

nonacq. (nonacquies- cence)

non•ac•qui•es•cence (*citation form:* non- acq.)

non•ac•tion•a•ble

non•ac•tion•a•bly

non•ad•dict•ing

non•ad•dict•ive

non•ad•ja•cent

non•ad•just•a•ble

non•age[1] or non-age (state of being under legal age: cf. NONAGE[2])

no•nage[2] (a one-ninth portion of a decedent's movable property, for- merly paid to the clergy: cf. NONAGE[1])

non•ag•gres•sion

non•a•ligned

non•a•lign•ment

non•a•nal•o•gous

nonanalogous art

non•ap•par•ent

non•ap•peal• a•bil•i•ty

non•ap•peal•a•ble

non•ap•pear•ance

non•ap•pli•ca• bil•i•ty

non•ap•point•ive

non•ar•bi•tra•ble

non•as•sess•a• bil•i•ty

non•as•sess•a•ble

nonassessable stock

non•as•sign• a•bil•i•ty

non•as•sign•a•ble

non•as•sign•a•bly

non•at•tend•ance

non•bail•a•ble

non•bank

non•bel•lig•er•en•cy

non•bel•lig•er•ent

non•bill•a•ble

non•bind•ing

nonbinding res•o•lu• tion

non•bind•ing•ly

non•bind•ing•ness

non•call•a•ble

non•can•cel•a•ble

noncancelable pol•i•cy

non•can•di•date

non•cap•i•tal

non•ca•pri•cious

non•ca•pri•cious•ly

non•ca•pri•cious• ness

non•cash

non•cha•lance

non•cha•lant

non•cha•lant•ly

non•char•i•ta•ble

non•cit•a•ble

non•cit•i•zen

non•com•bat•ant

non•com•mer•cial

non•com•mis•sioned of•fi•cer

non•com•mit•tal

non•com•pet•ing

non•com•pe•ti•tion a•gree•ment

non•com•pet•i•tive

non•com•pet•i• tive•ly

non•com•pet•i•tive• ness

non•com•pli•ance

non•com•pli•ant

non•com•pul•so• ri•ly

non•com•pul•so•ri• ness

non•com•pul•so•ry

non•con•flict•ing

non•con•form•ance

non•con•form•ing

nonconforming goods

nonconforming use

non•con•form•ist

non•con•form•i•ty

non•con•fron•ta• tion

non•con•fron•ta• tion•al

non•con•sent

non•con•sent•ing

non•con•test•a•bil•i•ty
noncontestability clause
non•con•tes•ta•tion
non•con•trac•tu•al
non•con•tra•dic•to•ry *adj., n., pl.*
non•con•tra•dic•to•ries
non•con•trib•u•ting
non•con•trib•u•to•ry
noncontributory pen•sion plan
non•con•tro•ver•sial
non•con•vert•i•bil•i•ty
non•con•vert•i•ble
non•co•op•er•a•tion
non•cred•i•ble
non•crim•i•nal
non•cum•u•la•tive
noncumulative pre•ferred stock
non•cur•rent as•set
noncurrent li•a•bil•i•ty
non•cus•to•di•al
noncustodial par•ent
non•dead•ly
non•de•bat•a•ble
non•de•ferred in•ter•com•pa•ny trans•ac•tion
non•del•e•ga•ble
nondelegable duty
non•de•mise
non•de•pre•ci•a•ble
non•der•o•ga•ble
non•de•script
non•det•ri•men•tal
non•det•ri•men•tal•ly
non•dis•clo•sure

nondisclosure of ma•te•ri•al facts
non•dis•cov•er•a•ble
non•dis•cre•tion•a•ry
nondiscretionary trust
non•dis•crim•i•na•tion
non•dis•crim•i•na•to•ry
non•doc•tri•naire
non•dog•mat•ic
non•dom•i•nant
non•dra•mat•ic work
non•drink•er
non•du•ra•ble
non•ec•o•nom•ic loss
non•en•ti•ty *n., pl.* non•en•ti•ties
non•es•sen•tial
none•the•less
non•ex•clu•sive
nonexclusive li•cense
nonexclusive list•ing
non•ex•clu•siv•i•ty
non•ex•ist•ence
non•ex•ist•ent
non•ex•ploi•tive
non•ex•tra•dit•a•ble
non•fea•sance
non•for•feit•a•bil•i•ty
non•for•fei•ture ben•e•fit
nonforfeiture val•ue
non•for•tu•i•tous
non•for•tu•i•tous•ly
non•for•tu•i•tous•ness
non•fraud•u•lent
non•fraud•u•lent•ly
non•free•hold
nonfreehold es•tate
non•ful•fill•ment

non•func•tion•al
non•ger•mane
nongermane a•mend•ment
non•gov•ern•men•tal or•gan•i•za•tion (NGO)
non•hab•it•a•bil•i•ty
non•hab•it•a•ble
non•haz•ard•ous
non•he•red•i•tar•y
non•her•it•a•bil•i•ty
non•her•it•a•ble
non-hor•i•zon•tal mer•ger
non•im•pair•ment
non•in•clu•sive
non•in•clu•sive•ly
non•in•clu•sive•ness
non•in•fring•ing use
non•in•ju•ri•ous
non•in•ju•ri•ous•ly
non•in•ju•ri•ous•ness
non•in•ter•course
non•in•ter•est•ed
non•in•ter•fer•ence
non•in•ter•ven•tion
non•is•sue
non•i•tem•ized
nonitemized de•duc•tion
non•join•der
non•judg•men•tal
non•judg•men•tal•ly
non•ju•di•cial
non•ju•di•cial•ly
non•ju•ror
non•ju•ry tri•al
non•jus•ti•ci•a•bil•i•ty
non•jus•ti•ci•a•ble
non•law•yer
non•le•gal

non•le•thal
non•lev•i•a•ble
non•li•a•ble
non•li•bel•ous
non•lit•er•al
non•li•ti•gious
non•mail•a•bil•i•ty
non•mail•a•ble
nonmailable mat•ter
non•ma•jor•i•ty *adj.,
n., pl.* non•ma•
jor•i•ties
non•ma•li•cious
non•ma•li•cious•ly
non•ma•li•cious•
ness
non•mar•i•tal
non•mar•ket•
a•bil•i•ty
non•mar•ket•a•ble
non•mar•riage•
a•bil•i•ty
non•mar•riage•a•ble
non•match•ing
non•mem•ber
non•min•is•te•ri•al
non•min•is•te•ri•
al•ly
non•mi•nor•i•ty *adj.,
n., pl.* non•mi•
nor•i•ties
non•nar•cot•ic
non•nav•i•ga•
bil•i•ty
non•nav•i•ga•ble
nonnavigable wa•ters
non•ne•go•ti•
a•bil•i•ty
non•ne•go•ti•a•ble
nonnegotiable
doc•u•ment of
ti•tle
nonnegotiable in•
stru•ment
non•no•ti•fi•ca•tion
plan

non•nu•cle•ar
non•ob•vi•ous
non•ob•vi•ous•ness
non•oc•cur•rence
non•of•fend•er
non•op•er•at•ing
ex•pen•ses
nonoperating in•ter•
est
nonoperating
rev•e•nues
non•o•pi•ate
non•or•gan•ic
nonorganic men•tal
dis•or•der
non•par stock
non•par•tic•i•pant
non•par•tic•i•pat•
ing
non•par•tic•i•pa•
tion
non•par•ti•san
non•pat•ent•
a•bil•i•ty
non•pat•ent•a•ble
non•path•o•log•i•
cal
non•pay•ing
non•pay•ment
non•pend•ing
non•per•form•ance
non•per•form•ing
non•per•son
non•plus *v.,* non•
plussed *or* non•
plused, non•plus•
sing *or* non•plus•
ing, *n.*
non-point-source pol•
lu•tion
non•prac•tic•ing
non•pre•scrip•tion
non–pro ra•ta
non–pro rata dis•tri•
bu•tion
non•prob•lem•at•ic

non•pro•duc•tive
non•pro•duc•tive•ly
non•pro•duc•tive•
ness
non•pro•duc•tiv•i•ty
non•pro•fes•sion•al
non•pro•fes•sion•
al•ism
non•prof•it
nonprofit cor•po•ra•
tion
nonprofit or•gan•i•
za•tion
non•pro•lif•er•a•
tion
non•pub•lic fo•rum
non•qual•i•fied
nonqualified pen•sion
plan
nonqualified stock
op•tion
non•rec•og•ni•tion
non•re•course
nonrecourse debt
non•re•course loan
non•re•cur•ring
nonrecurring charge
non•res•i•dence
non•res•i•den•cy
non•res•i•dent
nonresident al•ien
nonresident mo•tor•
ist stat•ute
non•res•i•den•tial
non•re•sis•tance
non•re•spon•sive
non•re•strict•ed
non•re•tro•ac•
tiv•i•ty
non•re•us•a•ble
non•sal•a•ried
non•sched•uled
non•sec•tar•i•an
non-self-ex•e•cut•ing
non-self-executing
trea•ty

non-self-gov•ern•ing
non•sense
non•sen•si•cal
non•sen•si•cal•ly
non•sen•si•cal•ness
non•sig•na•to•ry
adj., n., pl. non•sig•na•to•ries
non•slan•der•ous
non•smok∘er
non•smok•ing
non•stan•dard
non•start∘er
non•stat∘u•to∘ry
non•stock cor•po•ra•tion
non•stop
non•strike•a∘ble or non•strik•a∘ble
non•suit
non•sup•port
non•sus•tain•a∘ble
non•tar•get
non•tar•iff bar•ri∘er
non•tax ac•count•ing
non•tax•a∘bil∘i∘ty
non•tax•a∘ble
nontaxable ex•change
non•tax•a∘bly
non•tech•ni•cal
non•ten•ured
non•trans•fer•a∘bil∘i∘ty
non•trans•fer•a∘ble
nontransferable li•cense
non•triv•i∘al
non•un•ion
nonunion shop
non•us∘er
non•vi•a•bil∘i∘ty
non•vi•a•ble
non•vi•o•lence
non•vi•o•lent

non•vi•tal
non•void•a∘ble
non•vot∘er
non•war•rant∘ed
non•work•ing
noose
nor•a∘cy•meth∘a•dol *Controlled Subst.*
nor•di•az∘e∘pam *Controlled Subst.*
nor•eth•an•dro•lone *Controlled Subst.*
nor•lev•or•pha•nol *Controlled Subst.*
norm
nor•mal
nor•mal∘i∘ty
nor•mal•i•za•tion
nor•mal•ize *v.,* nor•mal•ized, nor•mal•iz•ing
nor•mal∘ly
nor•mal•ness
nor•ma•tive
nor•ma•tive∘ly
nor•ma•tiv∘i∘ty
nor•meth∘a•done *Controlled Subst.*
norm•less
nor•mor•phine *Controlled Subst.*
nor•pi•pa•none *Controlled Subst.*
north (N.)
North A∘mer∘i•can Free Trade A∘gree•ment (NAFTA)
North East•ern Re•port∘er *citation form:* N.E.)
North West•ern Re-porter *(citation form:* N.W.)
north•ern (N.)
Northern Dis•trict *(citation form:* N.D.)

nos•ci•tur a so•ci∘is *Latin*
nos•trum *n. pl.* nos•trums
not-for-prof∘it cor•po•ra•tion
not found
not guilt∘y
not guilty by rea•son of in•san∘i∘ty
not in my back•yard (NIMBY or Nimby)
not prov∘en
not suf•fi•cient funds (NSF)
no∘ta be∘ne (N.B.) *Latin*
no•ta•ble
no•ta•ble•ness
no•ta•bly
no•tar•i∘al
notarial act
no•tar•i•al∘ly
no•tar•i•za•tion
no•ta•rize *v.* no•ta•rized, no•ta•riz•ing
no•ta∘ry *n., pl.* no•ta•ries
notary pub•lic *n., pl* notaries pub•lic
no•ta•ry•ship
note¹ *(citation forms·* n., *pl.* nn. in citations to footnotes or end-notes in another work, note, *pl.* notes, in cross-references to footnotes or endnotes within one s own work, and in citations to all other kinds of notes)
note² *v.,* not∘ed, not•ing
note bro•ker
note pay•a∘ble *n. pl.* notes pay•a∘ble

note re•ceiv•a•ble *n.,*
pl. notes re•ceiv•
a•ble

note ver•bale *n., pl.*
notes ver•bales
French.

note•hold•er

not∘er

note•wor•thi•ness

note•wor•thy

no•tice *n., v.,* no•
ticed, no•tic•ing

notice by pub•li•ca•
tion

notice of ap•pear•
ance

notice of dep∘o•si•
tion

notice of dis•hon•or

notice of mo•tion

notice of pro•test

notice of suit

notice of tri•al

notice plead•ing

notice to cred∘i•tors

notice to pro•duce

notice to quit

no•tice•a•bil∘i•ty

no•tice•a•ble

no•tice•a•bly

no•ti•fi•a•ble

no•ti•fi•ca•tion

notification plan

no•ti•fi•er

no•ti•fy *v.,* no•ti•
fied, no•ti•fy•ing

no•to•ri•e•ty

no•to•ri•ous

notorious pos•ses•
sion

no•to•ri•ous•ly

no•to•ri•ous•ness

not•with•stand•ing

nought or naught (the
numeral zero; a ci-

pher) See also entry
for NAUGHT.

nou•veau pau•vre *n.,*
pl. nou•veaux pau•
vres *French.*

nouveau riche *n., pl.*
nou•veaux riches
French.

Nov. (November)

n.o.v. (notwithstanding
the verdict: from Latin
non obstante veredicto)

no•va•tion

nov∘el

novel dis•sei•sin

nov•el∘ty

No•vem•ber (*citation
form:* Nov.)

nox•ious

nox•ious∘ly

nox•ious•ness

no∘yade *n., v.* no•
yad∘ed, no∘yad•ing

n.p. (no place)

n.s. (new series)

NSF (not sufficient
funds)

NSF check

nu•ance

nu•anced

nu•cle∘ar

nuclear DNA

nuclear en•er∘gy

nuclear non•pro•lif•
er∘a•tion

nuclear pro•lif•er∘a•
tion

nuclear waste

nu•cle∘ic ac∘id

nu•cle•o•tide

nu•cle∘us *n., pl* nu•
cle∘i

nude *adj.,* nud∘er,
nud∘est, *n.*

nude con•tract

nu•di∘ty

nu∘dum pac•tum
Latin.

nu•ga•to∘ry

nui•sance

nuisance per se

nuisance tax

nul dis•sei•sin *Law
French.*

nul tiel *Law French.*

nul tiel rec∘ord

nul tort *Law French.*

null

null and void

nul∘la bo∘na *Latin.*

nul•li•fi•ca•tion

nul•li•fi∘er

nul•li•fy *v.,* nul•li•
fied, nul•li•fy•ing

nul•li∘ty *n., pl.* nul•
li•ties

nul•li∘us fi•li∘us
Latin.

nullius ju∘ris *Latin.*

num•ber (*citation
form:* No.)

num•bered ac•count

num•bers game

numbers rack•et

numbers run•ning

nu•mer•ous

nu•mer•ous∘ly

nu•mer•ous•ness

nunc pro tunc *Latin.*

nun•ci∘o *n., pl.* nun•
ci∘os

nun•cu•pate *v.,* nun•
cu•pat∘ed, nun•cu•
pat•ing

nun•cu•pa•tive

nuncupative will

nu∘per o∘bi∘it *Latin.*

nup•tial

nup•tial∘ly

nup•tials *n., pl.*

Nu•rem•berg tri∘al

Nuremberg Tri•bu•
nal

nurs•ing home

nursing home fraud

nur•tur•ance

nur•tur•ant

nur•ture v., nur•
tured, nur•tur•ing

nur•tur•er

N.W. (North Western
Reporter)

nym•pho•ma•ni•a

O

OASDI (Old-Age, Survi-
vors, and Disability In-
surance)

oath n., pl. oaths

oath-help•er

oath of of•fice

oath or af•fir•ma•
tion

ob•du•ra•cy

ob•du•rate

ob•du•rate•ly

o•be•di•ence

o•be•di•ent

o•be•di•ent•ly

o•bei•sance

o•bei•sant

o•bei•sant•ly

o•bey

o•bey•a•ble

o•bey•er

ob•fus•cate v., ob•
fus•cat•ed, ob•fus•
cat•ing

ob•fus•ca•tion

ob•fus•ca•to•ry

ob•i•ter Latin.

obiter dic•tum n., pl.
obiter dic•ta Latin.

ob•ject

ob•jec•tion

ob•jec•tion•
a•bil•i•ty

ob•jec•tion•a•ble

ob•jec•tion•a•ble•
ness

ob•jec•tion•a•bly

ob•jec•tive

objective test

ob•jec•tive•ly

ob•jec•tiv•ism

ob•jec•tiv•ist

ob•jec•ti•vis•tic

ob•jec•tiv•i•ty

ob•jec•tor

ob•li•ga•ble

ob•li•gate v., ob•li•
gat•ed, ob•li•gat•
ing

obligate gene

ob•li•ga•ti•o n., pl.
ob•li•ga•ti•o•nes
Latin.

ob•li•ga•tion

ob•li•ga•tion•al

obligational au•
thor•i•ty

ob•li•ga•tive

ob•li•ga•tor

ob•li•ga•to•ri•ly

ob•li•ga•to•ri•ness

o•blig•a•to•ry

o•blige v., o•bliged,
o•blig•ing

o•bliged

o•blig•ed•ly

o•blig•ed•ness

o•li•gee

o•blig•ing

o•blig•ing•ly

o•blig•ing•ness

ob•li•gor

o•blique

o•blique•ly

o•blique•ness

ob•lit•er•ate v., ob•

lit•er•at•ed, ob•lit•
er•at•ing

ob•lit•er•a•tion

ob•lit•er•a•tive

ob•lit•er•a•tor

ob•liv•i•on

ob•liv•i•ous

ob•liv•i•ous•ly

ob•liv•i•ous•ness

ob•lo•quy n., pl. ob•
lo•quies

ob•nox•ious

ob•nox•ious•ly

ob•nox•ious•ness

ob•rep•tion

ob•rep•ti•tious

ob•rep•ti•tious•ly

ob•ro•ga•tion

ob•scene

ob•scene•ly

ob•scen•i•ty n., pl.
ob•scen•i•ties

ob•scure adj., v., ob•
scured, ob•scur•ing

ob•scure•ly

ob•scu•ri•ty n., pl.
ob•scu•ri•ties

ob•se•qui•ous

ob•se•qui•ous•ly

ob•se•qui•ous•ness

ob•serv•a•bil•i•ty

ob•serv•a•ble

ob•serv•a•bly

ob•serv•ance

ob•serv•ant

ob•serv•ant•ly

ob•ser•va•tion

ob•ser•va•tion•al

ob•ser•va•tion•al•ly
ob•serve *v.*, ob•
  served, ob•serv•ing
ob•serv∘er
ob•sess
ob•sessed
ob•sess•ing•ly
ob•ses•sion
ob•ses•sion∘al
ob•ses•sive
obsessive-com•pul•
  sive
obsessive-compulsive
  dis•or•der
obsessive-compulsive
  per•son•al∘i∘ty dis-
  order
ob•ses•sor
ob•so•les•cence
ob•so•les•cent
ob•so•les•cent•ly
ob•so•lete *adj., v.*,
  ob•so•let∘ed, ob•
  so•let•ing
ob•sta•cle
ob•sti•na•cy *n., pl*
  ob•sti•na•cies
ob•sti•nate
ob•sti•nate•ly
ob•sti•nate•ness
ob•strep•er•ous
ob•strep•er•ous•ly
ob•strep•er•ous•
  ness
ob•struct
ob•struc•tion
obstruction of jus•
  tice
ob•struc•tion•ism
ob•struc•tion•ist
ob•struc•tion•is•tic
ob•struc•tive
ob•struc•tive•ly
ob•struc•tive•ness
ob•struc•tor
ob•tain

ob•tain•a•bil•i•ty
ob•tain•a•ble
ob•tain•ment
ob•tru•sive
ob•tru•sive•ly
ob•tru•sive•ness
ob•tuse
ob•tuse•ly
ob•tuse•ness
ob•vi•a•ble
ob•vi•ate *v.*, ob•vi•
  at∘ed, ob•vi•at•ing
ob•vi•a•tion
ob•vi•ous
ob•vi•ous•ly
ob•vi•ous•ness
oc•ca•sion
oc•ca•sion∘al
oc•ca•sion•al•ly
oc•cu•pan•cy *n., pl*
  oc•cu•pan•cies
oc•cu•pant
oc•cu•pa•tion
oc•cu•pa•tion∘al
occupational dis•ease
occupational haz•ard
occupational in•ju•ry
occupational safe∘ty
  and health
oc•cu•pa•tion•al•ly
oc•cu•pi•a•ble
oc•cu•pied
oc•cu•pi∘er
oc•cu•py *v.*, oc•cu•
  pied, oc•cu•py•ing
occupy the field
oc•cu•py•ing claim•
  ant
oc∘cur *v.*, oc•curred,
  oc•cur•ring
oc•cur•rence
o∘cean bill of lad•ing
ocean dump•ing
och•loc•ra∘cy
och•lo•crat∘ic
Oct. (October)

Oc•to•ber (*citation
  form:* Oct.)
OD *n., pl.* **OD's**, *v.*,
  OD'd, **OD'ing** (over
  dose)
odd lot *n*
odd-lot *adj.*
odd-lot•ter
o∘di•ous
o∘di•ous•ly
o∘di•ous•ness
o∘di∘um
of age
of coun•sel
of course
of grace
of rec∘ord
of right
of the es•sence
Off. (Office)
off-board
off-bud•get
off-hire clause
off-the-board
off-the-books
off the rec∘ord *adv.*
off-the-record *adj.*
of•fend
of•fend∘er
of•fense
of•fen•sive
offensive speech
of•fen•sive•ly
of•fen•sive•ness
of∘fer
offer of com•pro•
  mise
offer of proof
of•fer•a∘ble
of•fer∘ee
of•fer•ing
offering cir•cu•lar
offering price
of•fer∘or

of•fice (*citation form:* Off.)
of•fice•hold•er
of•fi•cer
officer hours
officer of the court
of•fi•cial (authorita tive: cf. OFFICIOUS)
official im•mu•ni•ty
of•fi•cial•ly
of•fi•ci•ate *v.*, of•fi• ci•at•ed, of•fi•ci• at•ing
of•fi•ci•a•tor
of•fi•cious (meddle- some: cf. OFFICIAL)
officious in•ter•med• dler
officious will
of•fi•cious•ly
of•fi•cious•ness
off•set *n., adj., v.,* off•set, off•set•ting
off•shore
offshore oil and gas drill•ing
offshore struc•tures
offshore work•ers
of•ten
OGI (ordinary gross in- come)
OID (original issue dis- count)
oil and gas lease
Old-Age, Sur•vi•vors, and Dis•a•bil•i•ty In•sur•ance (OASDI)
Old Bai•ley
old-boy net•work
old-girl network
O•le•ron Laws (or Rules) of
ol•i•garch
ol•i•gar•chic
ol•i•gar•chi•cal
ol•i•gar•chi•cal•ly

ol•i•gar•chy *n., pl.* ol•i•gar•chies
ol•i•gop•oo•lis•tic
ol•i•gop•oo•ly
ol•i•gop•so•nis•tic
ol•i•gop•so•ny
om•buds•man *n., pl.* om•buds•men
om•buds•per•son *n., pl.* om•buds•per• sons
om•buds•wom•an *n, pl.* om•buds• wom•en
om•i•nous
om•i•nous•ly
om•i•nous•ness
o•mis•si•ble
o•mis•sion
o•mis•sive
o•mis•sive•ly
o•mit *v.,* o•mit•ted, o•mit•ting
o•mit•ter
om•ni•bus
omnibus bill
omnibus clause
om•ni•mark
on ac•count
on all fours
on ap•prov•al
on bail
on be•half of (*citation form:* ex rel.)
on board bill of lad• ing
on com•mis•sion
on con•sent
on con•sign•ment
on cred•it
on de•mand
on in•for•ma•tion and be•lief
on its face
on-line or on•line
on-line bank•ing

on mar•gin
on no•tice
on or a•bout
on or be•fore
on pa•pers
on point
on sight
on the brief
on the job *adv.*
on-the-job *adj.*
on-the-job train•ing
on the mer•its
on the plead•ings
on the rec•ord *adv.*
on-the-record *adj.*
on the re•la•tion of (*citation form:* ex rel.)
on•com•ing
one per•son, one vote
one-sid•ed
one-sid•ed•ly
one-sid•ed•ness
on•er•ous
on•er•ous•ly
on•er•ous•ness
on•go•ing
on•line See ON-LINE.
on•o•mas•tic
on•set
on•slaught
on•to•log•oi•cal
on•to•log•oi•cal•ly
on•tol•oo•gist
on•tol•oo•gy
o•nus[1] *n., pl.* o•nus•es *English.*
o•nus[2] *n., pl.* o•ne•ra *Latin.*
o•nus pro•ban•di *Latin.*
Op. (Opinion; Opinions)
o•pac•i•ty *n., pl.* o•pac•i•ties
o•paque
o•paque•ly

o•paque•ness
o•pen
open ac•count
open and no•to•ri•ous
open and notorious pos•ses•sion
open-and-shut
open-book cred•it
open cit•y
open cor•po•ra•tion
open court
open door n.
open-door adj.
open-end
open-end cred•it
open-end in•vest•ment com•pa•ny
open-end mort•gage bond
open-end•ed
open-ended del•e•ga•tion
open-end•ed•ness
open fields doc•trine
open hous•ing n.
open-housing adj.
open list•ing
open mar•ket n.
open-market adj.
open meet•ing
open-mind•ed
open-mind•ed•ly
open-mind•ed•ness
open mort•gage pol•i•cy
open or•der
open pol•i•cy
open price term
open reg•is•try
open sea•son
open shop
open the door
o•pen•ing
opening state•ment
o•pen•ly

o•pen•ness
op•er•a•bil•i•ty
op•er•a•ble
op•er•a•bly
op•er•ate v., op•er•ated, op•er•at•ing
op•er•at•ing
operating budg•et
operating ex•pense
operating in•come
operating in•ter•est
operating lease
op•er•a•tion
operation of law
op•er•a•tion•al
operations in•come
op•er•a•tive
operative part
operative words
op•er•a•tive•ly
op•er•a•tive•ness
op•er•a•tor
o•pi•ate n., adj., v., o•pi•at•ed, o•pi•at•ing
o•pi•at•ic
o•pin•ion (citation form for sing. and pl.: Op.)
opinion ev•i•dence
o•pin•ion•at•ed
o•pi•oid
opioid a•buse
opioid an•tag•o•nist
opioid de•pend•ence
opioid-in•duced dis•or•der
opioid in•tox•i•ca•tion
opioid with•draw•al
o•pi•um Controlled Subst.
opium de•riv•a•tive
opium pop•py Controlled Subst. (Papaver somniferum L.)

op•po•nent
op•por•tune
op•por•tune•ly
op•por•tune•ness
op•por•tun•ism
op•por•tun•ist
op•por•tu•ni•ty n., pl op•por•tu•ni•ties
opportunity cost
opportunity fund
opportunity to be heard
op•pos•a•ble
op•pose v., op•posed, op•pos•ing
op•pos•er
op•pos•ing
op•pos•ing•ly
op•po•site (contrary: cf. APPOSITE)
op•po•si•tion
op•po•si•tion•al
oppositional de•fi•ant dis•or•der
op•press
op•press•i•ble
op•pres•sion
op•pres•sive
op•pres•sive•ly
op•pres•sive•ness
op•pres•sor
op•pro•bri•ous
op•pro•bri•ous•ly
op•pro•bri•ous•ness
op•pro•bri•um
opt
opt out
op•ti•mism
op•ti•mist
op•ti•mis•tic
op•ti•mis•ti•cal•ly
op•ti•mi•za•tion
op•ti•mize v., op•ti•mized, op•ti•miz•ing

op•ti•mum *n.*, *pl* op•tio•ma or op•ti•mums, *adj.*

op•tion

option con•tract

op•tion•a•ble

op•tion○al

optional writ

op•tion•al○ly

op•tion○ee

OR (own recognizance)

o○ral (by mouth; spoken: cf. AURAL; VERBAL)

oral ar•gu•ment

oral con•tract

oral trust

oral will

o○ral○ly

or○a•tor

or○a•tor○i•cal

or○a•tor○i•cal○ly

or○a•to○ry

or•dain

or•deal

or○der

order bill of lad•ing

order in•stru•ment

order ni○si

order nunc pro tunc

order of busi•ness

Order of the Coif

order of the day[1] (custom; common occurrence)

order of the day[2] or or•ders of the day (agenda)

order pa○per

order to show cause

or•der•a•ble

or•dered

ordered lib•er○ty

or•der○er

or•der•li•ness

or•der○ly *adj., adv., n., pl.* or•der•lies

orderly mar•ket•ing a○gree•ment

or•di•nance (a local law: cf. ORDNANCE)

or•di•nar○i•ly

or•di•nar○i•ness

or•di•nar○y *adj., n., pl.* or•di•nar•ies

ordinary and nec•es•sar○y

ordinary care

ordinary course of busi•ness

ordinary gross in•come (OGI)

ordinary in•come

ordinary life in•sur•ance

ordinary neg•li•gence

ordinary pru•dence

ordinary re•pairs

ordinary risks of em•ploy•ment

ordinary sea•man

ordinary skill

ordinary wear and tear

ord•nance (military weaponry: cf. ORDINANCE)

Org. (Organization; Organizing)

or•gan○ic

organic law

organic men•tal dis•or•der

organic stat•ute

or•gan•i•cal○ly

or•ga•nic○i•ty

or•gan•i•sa•tion (a British spelling for ORGANIZATION)

or•gan•ism

or•gan•iz•a•bil○i•ty

or•gan•iz•a•ble

or•gan•i•za•tion (*citation form:* **Org.**)

or•gan•i•za•tion•al

organizational pick•et•ing

or•gan•i•za•tion•al○ly

or•gan•ize *v.*, or•gan•ized, or•gan•iz•ing

or•gan○i•zed

organized crime

organized la•bor

or•gan•iz○er

or•gan•iz•ing (*citation form:* **Org.**)

or○i•gin

o○rig○i•nal

original en○try

original in•tent

original is○sue

original issue dis•count (OID)

original ju•ris•dic•tion

original pack•age doc•trine

original writ

o○rig○i•nal•ism

o○rig○i•nal○i•ty

o○rig○i•nal○ly

o○rig○i•nate *v.*, o○rig○i•nat•ed, o○rig○i•nat•ing

o○rig○i•na•tion

origination fee

o○rig○i•na•tor

or•na•men•tal

or•na•men•tal○i•ty

or•na•men•tal○ly

or•na•men•ta•tion

or•ner•i•ness

or•ner○y *adj.*, or•ner○i•er, or•ner○i•est

o○ro•tund

o‧ro‧tun‧di‧ty
or‧phan
or‧phan‧age
or‧phan‧hood
Orphans' Court (*citation form:* **Orphans' Ct.**)
Orphans' Ct. (Orphans' Court)
or‧tho‧dox
or‧tho‧dox‧y *n., pl.* or‧tho‧dox‧ies
Or‧well‧i‧an
os‧ten‧si‧ble
ostensible au‧thor‧i‧ty
ostensible own‧er‧ship
ostensible part‧ner
os‧ten‧si‧bly
OTC (over-the-counter)
oth‧er‧wise
ought
oust
oust‧er
out
out-and-out
out of court
out-of-court
out-of-court set‧tle‧ment
out of or‧der
out-of-pock‧et ex‧pense
out on bail
out‧build‧ing
out‧cast (a rejected person; cf. OUTCASTE)
out‧caste (one put out of his or her caste or having no caste; cf. OUTCAST)
out‧come
out‧cry *n., pl.* out‧cries
outer bar

outer bar‧ris‧ter
outer space
out‧go‧ing
out‧growth
out‧land‧ish
out‧land‧ish‧ly
out‧land‧ish‧ness
out‧law
outlaw strike
out‧law‧ry *n., pl.* out‧law‧ries
out‧pa‧tient
out‧per‧form
out‧place *v.,* out‧placed, out‧plac‧ing
out‧place‧ment
out‧put *n., adj., v.,* out‧put‧ted or out‧put, out‧put‧ting
output con‧tract
out‧rage *n., v.,* out‧raged, out‧rag‧ing
out‧ra‧geous
out‧ra‧geous‧ly
out‧ra‧geous‧ness
out‧rank
out‧right
out‧side
outside coun‧sel
outside di‧rec‧tor
out‧source *v.,* out‧sourced, out‧sourc‧ing
out‧sourc‧ing
out‧stand‧ing
outstanding check
outstanding shares
out‧stand‧ing‧ly
out‧stand‧ing‧ness
out‧vote *v.,* out‧vot‧ed, out‧vot‧ing
out‧ward
out‧ward‧ly
o‧ver
over the count‧er *adv.*

over-the-counter (OTC) *adj.*
over-the-counter drug
over-the-counter mar‧ket
over-the-counter stock
o‧ver‧age
o‧ver‧breadth
o‧ver‧broad
o‧ver‧build *v.,* o‧ver‧built, o‧ver‧build‧ing
o‧ver‧cer‧ti‧fi‧ca‧tion
o‧ver‧cer‧ti‧fy *v.,* o‧ver‧cer‧ti‧fied, o‧ver‧cer‧ti‧fy‧ing
o‧ver‧charge *v.,* o‧ver‧charged, o‧ver‧charg‧ing
o‧ver‧charg‧er
o‧ver‧claim
o‧ver‧claim‧ing
o‧ver‧come *v.,* o‧ver‧came, o‧ver‧com‧ing
o‧ver‧dos‧age
o‧ver‧dose (OD) *n., v.,* o‧ver‧dosed, o‧ver‧dos‧ing
o‧ver‧draft
overdraft check‧ing ac‧count
o‧ver‧draw *v.,* o‧ver‧drew, o‧ver‧drawn, o‧ver‧draw‧ing
o‧ver‧drawn
over‧due
o‧ver‧ex‧tend
o‧ver‧ex‧tend‧ed
o‧ver‧ex‧ten‧sion
o‧ver‧haul
o‧ver‧head
o‧ver‧hear *v.,* o‧ver‧

heard, o∘ver•hear•ing
o∘ver•hear∘er
o∘ver•in•sur•ance
o∘ver•in•sure *v.*, o∘ver•in•sured, o∘ver•in•sur•ing
o∘ver•in•sured
o∘ver•is•sue *n.*, *v.*, o∘ver•is•sued, o∘ver•is•su•ing
o∘ver•lap *v.*, o∘ver•lapped, o∘ver•lap•ping, *n.*
o∘ver•lay *v.*, o∘ver•laid, o∘ver•lay•ing, *n.* (to place over; something placed over: cf. OVERLIE)
o∘ver•lie *v.*, o∘ver•lay, o∘ver•lain, o∘ver•ly•ing (to lie over: cf. OVERLAY)
o∘ver•lord
o∘ver•night
o∘ver•pay *v.*, o∘ver•paid, o∘ver•pay•ing
o∘ver•pay•ment
o∘ver•qual∘i•fied
o∘ver•reach
o∘ver•reach∘er
o∘ver•reach•ing
o∘ver•re•act
o∘ver•re•ac•tion
o∘ver•ride *v.*, o∘ver•rode, o∘ver•rid•den, o∘ver•rid•ing, *n.*
o∘ver•rid•ing
overriding roy∘al∘ty

o∘ver•rule *v.*, o∘ver•ruled, o∘ver•rul•ing
o∘ver•rul∘er
o∘ver•run *v.*, o∘ver•ran, o∘ver•run, o∘ver•run•ning, *n.*
o∘ver•see *v.*, o∘ver•saw, o∘ver•seen, o∘ver•see•ing
o∘ver•se∘er
o∘ver•sight
o∘ver•sim•pli•fi•ca•tion
o∘ver•sim•pli∘fy *v.*, o∘ver•sim•pli•fied, o∘ver•sim•pli•fy•ing
o∘ver•sub•scribe *v.*, o∘ver•sub•scribed, o∘ver•sub•scrib•ing
o∘ver•sub•scrip•tion
o∘vert
overt act
o∘ver•time
o∘ver•val∘u•a•tion
o∘ver•val∘ue *v.*, o∘ver•val∘ued, o∘ver•val•u•ing
o∘ver•view
o∘ver•whelm
o∘ver•whelm•ing
o∘ver•whelm•ing∘ly
o∘ver•whelm•ing•ness
o∘ver•with•hold *v.*, o∘ver•with•held, o∘ver•with•hold•ing
o∘ver•work
o∘ver•wrought

o∘ver•zeal•ous
o∘ver•zeal•ous∘ly
o∘ver•zeal•ous•ness
owe *v.*, owed, ow∘ing
ow∘ing
own re•cog•ni•zance (OR)
own∘er
owner-oc•cu•pied
owner-oc•cu•pi∘er
owner of rec•ord
owner-op•er∘a•tor
owner pro hac vi∘ce
own•ers' eq∘ui∘ty
own•er•ship
ox•an•dro•lone *Controlled Subst.*
ox•az∘e∘pam *Controlled Subst.*
ox•az∘o•lam *Controlled Subst.*
ox∘y•co•done *Controlled Subst.*
ox∘y•mes•te•rone *Controlled Subst.*
ox∘y•meth∘o•lone *Controlled Subst.*
ox∘y•mo•ron *n.*, *pl.* ox∘y•mo∘ra
ox∘y•mo•ron∘ic
ox∘y•mor•phone *Controlled Subst.*
o∘yer *Law French.*
oyer and ter•mi•ner
oyer et terminer *Law French.*
o∘yez or o∘yes *Law French.*

P

P. (Pacific Reporter; Procedure)

p. *pl.* **pp.** (page)

P&L (profit and loss; profit and loss statement)

P.A. (Professional Association)

PAC *n., pl.* **PAC's** or **PACs** (political action committee)

Pac. (Pacific)

Pac-Man de•fense

pac•i•fi•a•ble

Pa•cif•ic (*citation form:* **Pac.**)

Pacific Re•port•er (*citation form:* **P.**)

pac•i•fi•ca•tion

pac•i•fism

pac•i•fist

pac•i•fis•tic

pac•i•fis•ti•cal•ly

pac•i•fy *v.,* **pac•i•fied, pac•i•fy•ing**

pack date

pack•age

package deal

package li•cense

package store

pack•ag•er

pact

pac•tum *n., pl.* **pac•ta** *Latin.*

pad•dy wag•on

pae•an (expression of praise: cf. PEON)

page¹ (a leaf of printed matter; *citation form for internal cross-references:* **p.,** *pl.* **pp.** Pages in outside sources are cited by

number alone, without the word *page* or any abbreviation.)

page² *n., v.,* **paged, pag•ing** (an attendant; to summon)

paid-in cap•i•tal

paid-in sur•plus

paid-up pol•i•cy

paid-up stock

pain

pain and suf•fer•ing

pain dis•or•der

pain•ful

pain•ful•ly

pain•ful•ness

pain•less

pain•less•ly

pain•less•ness

pains•tak•ing

pains•tak•ing•ly

pains•tak•ing•ness

pair

paired vote

pais *Law French.*

pal•a•din

pa•lav•er

pa•lav•er•er

pal•i•mo•ny

pal•li•ate *v.,* **pal•li•at•ed, pal•li•at•ing**

pal•li•a•tion

pal•li•a•tive

palliative care

pal•li•a•tive•ly

pal•li•a•tor

palm

palm off

palm•er

palm•ing off

pal•pa•bil•i•ty

pal•pa•ble

palpable il•le•gal•i•ty

pal•pa•ble•ness

pal•pa•bly

pal•tri•ly

pal•tri•ness

pal•try *adj.,* **pal•tri•er, pal•tri•est**

pam•phlet

pam•phlet•eer

pan•a•ce•a

pan•a•ce•an

pan•dect (a comprehensive compilation or digest)

Pan•dects (the digest of Roman law under Justinian)

pan•der

pan•der•er

pan•der•ing

Pan•do•ra's box

pan•el *n., v.,* **pan•eled, pan•el•ing.**

pan•han•dle *v.,* **pan•han•dled, pan•han•dling**

pan•han•dler

pan•han•dling

pan•ic *n., adj., v.,* **pan•icked, pan•ick•ing**

panic at•tack

panic dis•or•der

panic re•ac•tion

panic-strick•en

pan•ick•y

pan•o•ply *n., pl.* **pan•o•plies,** *v.,* **pan•o•plied, pan•o•ply•ing**

pa•pa•raz◦zo *n., pl.*
  pa•pa•raz◦zi
Pa•pa•ver som•ni•
  fe•rum L. *Controlled
  Subst.* (opium poppy)
pa◦per
paper chase
paper pat•ent
paper prof•it
pa•pers *n., pl.*
par
par ex•cel•lence
  French.
par val◦ue
par value stock
para. (paragraph)
par◦a•chute *n., v.,*
  par◦a•chut◦ed,
  par◦a•chut•ing
par◦a•digm
par◦a•dig•mat◦ic
par◦a•dig•mat◦i•
  cal◦ly
par◦a•dox
par◦a•dox◦i•cal
par◦a•dox◦i•cal◦i•ty
par◦a•dox◦i•cal◦ly
par◦a•dox◦i•cal•ness
par◦a•gon
par◦a•graph (*citation
  form:* ¶ *or* **para.,** *pl.*
  ¶¶ *or* **paras.**)
par◦a•hex◦yl *Con-
  trolled Subst.*
par◦a•judge
par•al•de•hyde *Con-
  trolled Subst.*
par◦a•le•gal
par◦a•lip•sis *n., pl.*
  par◦a•lip•ses
par•al•lel *adj., n., v.,*
  par•al•leled, par•
  al•lel•ing
parallel ci•ta•tion
par•al•lel•a◦ble
par•al•lel•ism

par•al•lel•less
par•al•lel◦ly
pa•ral◦y•sis *n., pl.*
  pa•ral◦y•ses
par◦a•lyt◦ic
par◦a•lyt◦i•cal◦ly
par◦a•lyze *v.,* par◦a•
  lyzed, par◦a•lyz•ing
par◦a•lyz◦er
par◦a•lyz•ing
par◦a•lyz•ing◦ly
par◦a•med◦ic
par◦a•med◦i•cal
par◦a•me•thox•y•
  am•phet◦a•mine
  (PMA) *Controlled
  Subst.*
par◦a•mil◦i•ta•rist
par◦a•mil◦i•tar◦y
  adj., n., pl. par◦a•
  mil◦i•tar•ies
par◦a•mount
paramount title
par◦a•mount◦cy
par◦a•mount◦ly
par◦a•mour
par◦a•noi◦a
par◦a•noi◦ac
par◦a•noid
paranoid i◦de•a•tion
paranoid per•son•
  al◦i•ty dis•or•der
paranoid schizo◦o•
  phre•ni◦a
paranoid schizo◦o•
  phren◦ic
par◦a•pher•na•lia *n,
  sing. or pl.*
par◦a•phil◦i◦a
par◦a•phil◦i◦ac
par◦a•phras•a◦ble
par◦a•phrase *n., v.,*
  par◦a•phrased,
  par◦a•phras•ing
par◦a•phras◦er

pa•raph•ra•sis *n., pl.*
  pa•raph•ra•ses
par◦a•phras•tic
par◦a•phras•ti•cal◦ly
par◦a•prax◦is *n., pl.*
  par◦a•prax◦es
par◦a•pro•fes•
  sion◦al
par◦a•site
par◦a•sit◦ic
par◦a•sit◦i•cal
par◦a•sit◦i•cal◦ly
par◦a•sit◦i•cal•ness
par◦a•sit•ism
par◦a•si•tize *v.,*
  par◦a•si•tized,
  par◦a•si•tiz•ing
par◦a•stat◦al
par◦a•tax◦ic
parataxic dis•tor•tion
par◦a•vail
par•cel
par•ce•nar◦y
par•ce•ner
par•don
par•don•a◦ble
par•don•a◦ble•ness
par•don•a◦bly
par•don◦er
pa•rens pa•tri◦ae
  Latin.
par•ent
parent com•pa◦ny
parent cor•po•ra•
  tion
parent-in-law *n., pl.*
  parents-in-law
par•ent•age
pa•ren•tal (of a par-
  ent: cf. PARENTERAL)
parental con•sent
parental consent re•
  quire•ment
parental kid•nap•
  ping
parental leave

parental li•a•bil•i•ty
parental ne•glect
parental no•ti•fi•ca•tion
parental re•spon•si•bil•i•ty law
parental right
pa•ren•tal•ly
par•en•ter•al (taken into the body other than through the digestive tract: cf. PARENTAL)
par•en•ter•al•ly
pa•ren•the•sis *n., pl.* pa•ren•the•ses
pa•ren•the•size *v.,* pa•ren•the•sized, pa•ren•the•siz•ing
pa•ren•thet•ic
pa•ren•thet•i•cal
pa•ren•thet•i•cal•ly
parent•ing
pa•ri cau•sa *Latin.*
pari de•lic•to *Latin.*
pari ma•te•ri•a *Latin.*
pari pas•su *Latin.*
pari ra•ti•o•ne *Latin.*
pa•ri•ah
pa•ri•ah•dom
pa•ri•e•tal
parietal rules
parietals *n.pl.*
par•ish
Parish Court (*citation form:* Parish Ct.)
Parish Ct. (Parish Court)
par•i•ty
park
park•ing
Parl. (Parliament; Parliamentary)
par•lance
par•lay
par•ley *n., pl.* par•

leys, *v.,* par•leyed, par•ley•ing
par•lia•ment (*citation form:* Parl.)
par•lia•men•tar•i•an
par•lia•men•tar•i•an•ism
par•lia•men•tar•i•ly
par•lia•men•ta•ry (*citation form:* Parl.)
parliamentary gov•ern•ment
parliamentary law
parliamentary prac•tice
parliamentary pro•ce•dure
parliamentary sys•tem
parliamentary writ
par•lous
pa•ro•chi•al
parochial school
pa•ro•chi•al•ism
pa•ro•chi•al•ist
pa•ro•chi•al•ly
pa•ro•chi•al•ness
par•o•di•a•ble
par•o•dist
par•o•dis•tic
par•o•dis•ti•cal•ly
par•o•dy *n., pl.* par•o•dies, *v.,* par•o•died, par•o•dy•ing
pa•rol (oral; extrinsic; an oral statement: cf. PAROLE)
parol ar•rest
parol ev•i•dence
parol evidence rule
parol trust
pa•rol•a•ble
pa•role *n., v.,* pa•roled, pa•rol•ing (conditional release

from prison; to release conditionally: cf. PA•ROL)
parole of•fi•cer
parole rev•o•ca•tion
parole vi•o•la•tion
pa•rol•ee
par•ox•ysm
par•ox•ys•mal
par•ox•ys•mal•ly
par•ri•a•ble
par•ri•cid•al
par•ri•cide
par•ri•cer
par•ry *v.,* par•ried, par•ry•ing
pars *n., pl.* par•tes *Latin.*
par•si•mo•ni•ous
par•si•mo•ni•ous•ly
par•si•mo•ni•ous•ness
par•si•mo•ny
par•son's writ of right
part (*citation form:* pt.)
part per•for•mance
part time *n.*
part-time *adj., adv.*
part-tim•er
par•take *v.,* par•took, par•tak•en, par•tak•ing
par•tak•er
par•tial
partial breach
partial dis•a•bil•i•ty
partial dis•clo•sure
partial e•vic•tion
partial in•tes•ta•cy
partial liq•ui•da•tion
partial lock•out
partial ver•dict
par•ti•al•i•ty *n., pl.* par•ti•al•i•ties

(bias; fondness: cf.
PARTIALNESS)
par•tial•ly
par•tial•ness (incom-
pleteness: cf. PARTIAL-
ITY)
par•ti•ceps *adj., n., pl.*
par•ti•ci•pes *Latin.*
particeps cri•mi•nis
Latin.
par•tic•i•pant
par•tic•i•pate *v.,*
par•tic•i•pat•ed,
par•tic•i•pat•ing
participating in•sur•
ance
participating pre•
ferred stock
par•tic•i•pat•ing•ly
par•tic•i•pa•tion
par•tic•i•pa•tive
par•tic•i•pa•tive•ly
par•tic•i•pa•tor
par•tic•i•pa•to•ry
participatory de•
moc•ra•cy
par•tic•u•lar
particular av•er•age
particular es•tate
particular lien
particular ten•ant
par•tic•u•lar•ism
par•tic•u•lar•ist
par•tic•u•lar•is•tic
par•tic•u•lar•is•ti•
cal•ly
par•tic•u•lar•i•ty
par•tic•u•lar•i•za•
tion
par•tic•u•lar•ize *v.,*
par•tic•u•lar•ized,
par•tic•u•lar•iz•ing
par•tic•u•lar•ly
par•tic•u•lars *n.pl.*
par•ti•san

par•ti•san•ism
par•ti•san•ry
par•ti•san•ship
par•ti•tion
par•ti•tion•a•ble
par•ti•tion•ar•y
par•ti•tion•er (one
who partitions real
property: cf. PARTITION-
IST)
par•ti•tion•ist (advo-
cate of partitioning a
region into two na-
tions: cf. PARTITIONER)
part•ner
part•ner•less
part•ner•ship
partnership a•gree•
ment
par•ty *n., pl.* par•ties
party ag•grieved
party de•fend•ant
party in in•ter•est
party join•der
party line
party lin•er
party of the first part
party plain•tiff
party pol•itics
party wall
par•ty•ism
par•ty•less
pass
pass a•long *v.* (cf.
PASSALONG)
pass mus•ter
pass off
pass o•ver
pass through *v.*
pass-through *n., adj.*
pass up
pass•a•ble (accepta-
ble; able to pass or be
passed: vs. *passible*)
pass•a•bly
pas•sage

pass•a•long *n., adj.*
(cf. PASS ALONG)
pass•book
passbook sav•ings
ac•count
passed div•i•dend
pas•sen•ger
pas•sim *Latin.*
pass•ing off
pas•sion
pas•sion•ate
pas•sion•ate•ly
pas•sion•ate•ness
pas•sive
passive ac•tiv•i•ty
loss lim•i•ta•tions
passive ag•gres•sion
passive-ag•gres•sive
passive-aggressive
per•son•al•i•ty
passive for•eign in•
vest•ment com•
pa•ny
passive in•come
passive loss
passive re•sist•ance
passive smok•ing
passive trust
pas•sive•ly
pas•sive•ness
pas•siv•i•ty
pass•port
pass•port•less
pass•word
past con•sid•er•a•
tion
past due
past re•col•lec•tion
re•cord•ed
pat. (patent)
pat. pend. (patent
pending)
pa•ten•cy
pat•ent[1] *n., v., adj.*
(exclusive right to an
invention; to grant or

receive a patent; protected by a patent; *citation form:* **Pat.**)
pa•tent² *adj.* (open to view; obvious)
pa•tent am•bi•gu•i•ty
pa•tent de•fect
pat•ent in•fringe•ment
pat•ent in•ter•fer•ence
pat•ent med•i•cine
pat•ent of•fice
pat•ent pend•ing (pat. pend.)
pat•ent right
pat•ent•a•bil•i•ty
pat•ent•a•ble
patentable sub•ject mat•ter
pat•ent•a•bly
pat•ent•ee
pat•ent•or (one who obtains a patent: cf. PATENTOR)
pa•tent•ly
patently of•fen•sive
pat•en•tor (grantor of a patent: cf. PATENTER)
pa•ter•fa•mil•i•as *n., pl.* pa•tres•fa•mil•i•as or pa•ter•fa•mil•i•as•es
pa•ter•nal
paternal line
pa•ter•nal•ism
pa•ter•nal•ist
pa•ter•nal•is•tic
pa•ter•nal•is•ti•cal•ly
pa•ter•nal•ly
pa•ter•ni•ty
paternity ac•tion
paternity in•dex (PI)

paternity pro•ceed•ing
paternity suit
paternity test
pa•thet•ic (evoking pity or contempt: cf. BATHETIC)
pa•thet•i•cal•ly
path•o•gen
path•o•gen•e•sis
path•o•gen•ic
path•o•ge•nic•i•ty
path•o•log•i•cal
pathological gam•bling
pathological li•ar
path•o•log•i•cal•ly
pa•thol•o•gist
pa•thol•o•gy *n., pl.* pa•thol•o•gies
path•o•phys•i•o•log•i•cal
path•o•phys•i•ol•o•gy
pa•thos (tender or sad quality: cf. BATHOS)
pa•tient
pa•tres•fa•mil•i•as *See* PATERFAMILIAS.
pa•tri•a po•tes•tas *Latin.*
pa•tri•ar•chal
pa•tri•ar•chal•ism
pa•tri•ar•chal•ly
pa•tri•ar•chic
pa•tri•ar•chi•cal
pa•tri•ar•chi•cal•ly
pa•tri•arch•y *n., pl.* pa•tri•arch•ies
pa•tri•ate *v.,* pa•tri•at•ed, pa•tri•at•ing
pa•tri•a•tion
pa•tri•cian
pat•ri•cid•al
pat•ri•cide
pat•ri•mo•ni•al

pat•ri•mo•ni•al•ly
pat•ri•mo•ny *n., pl.* pat•ri•mo•nies
pa•tri•ot
pa•tri•ot•ic
pa•tri•ot•i•cal•ly
pa•tri•ot•ism
pa•trol *v.,* pa•trolled, pa•troll•ing
patrol car
pa•trol•ler
pa•trol•man *n., pl.* pa•trol•men
pa•trol•wom•an *n., pl.* pa•trol•wom•en
pa•tron
pa•tron•age
pa•tron•al
pa•tron•ess
pa•tron•i•za•tion
pa•tron•ize *v.,* pa•tron•ized, pa•tron•iz•ing
pa•tron•iz•er
pa•tron•iz•ing
pa•tron•iz•ing•ly
pat•sy *n., pl.* pat•sies
pat•tern
pattern bar•gain•ing
pattern of rack•et•eer•ing ac•tiv•i•ty
pau•ci•ty
pau•per
pau•per•age
pau•per•dom
pau•per•ism
pau•per•i•za•tion
pau•per•ize *v.* pau•per•ized, pau•per•iz•ing
pawn
pawn tick•et
pawn•a•ble
pawn•age
pawn•bro•ker
pawn•bro•king

pawn•ee

pawn•or usual spelling: cf. PAWNOR)

paw•nor spelling used in legal contexts as correlative for PAWNEE: cf. PAWNER)

pawn•shop

pay *v.*, paid, pay•ing, *n.*

pay back *v.* (cf. PAY-BACK)

pay en•vel•ope

pay in *v.*

pay-in *n.*

pay off *v.* (cf. PAYOFF)

pay on death (POD)

pay out *v.* (cf. PAYOUT)

pay o•ver

pay-per-view

pay tel•e•vi•sion

pay•a•bil•i•ty

pay•a•ble

payable after sight

payable on de•mand

payable to bear•er

payable to or•der

pay•a•bly

pay•back *n.* (cf. PAY-BACK)

pay•ee

pay•er (spelling used in nonlegal contexts: cf. PAYOR)

pay•load

pay•ment

payment bond

pay•off *n., adj.* (cf. PAY-OFF)

pay•o•o•la

pay•or (spelling used in legal contexts, esp. as correlative for PAYEE: cf. PAYER)

payor bank

pay•out *n.* (cf. PAY-OUT)

payout ra•tio

pay•roll

payroll costs

payroll tax

P.C. (Professional Corporation; Privy Council)

PCP *Controlled Subst.* _ phencyclidine)

PCR (polymerase chain reaction)

p/e (price-earnings ratio)

peace

peace of•fi•cer

peace•a•ble

peaceable as•sem•bly

peaceable pos•ses•sion

peace•a•ble•ness

peace•a•bly

peace•ful

peaceful as•sem•bly

peaceful en•joy•ment

peaceful pos•ses•sion

peace•ful•ly

peace•ful•ness

peace•keep•er

peace•keep•ing

peacekeeping mis•sion

peace•mak•er

peace•mak•ing

peace•time

peas•ant

peas•ant•like

peas•ant•ry

pec•ca•bil•i•ty

pec•ca•ble

pec•ca•dil•lo *n., pl.* pec•ca•dil•loes or pec•ca•dil•los

pec•can•cy

pec•cant

pec•cant•ly

pec•cu•late *v.* pec•cu•lat•ed, pec•cu•lat•ing

pec•cu•la•tion

pec•cu•la•tor

pe•cu•liar

peculiar in•sti•tu•tion

pe•cu•li•ar•i•ty *n., pl.* pe•cu•li•ar•i•ties

pe•cu•li•ar•ly

pe•cu•ni•ar•i•ly

pe•cu•ni•ar•y

pecuniary dam•ag•es

pecuniary in•ju•ry

pecuniary in•ter•est

ped•ant

pe•dan•tic

pe•dan•ti•cal•ly

ped•ant•ry *n., pl.* ped•ant•ries

ped•dle *v.*, ped•dled, ped•dling

ped•dler

ped•dling

ped•er•ast

ped•er•as•ty

ped•es•tal•ism

pe•des•tri•an

pe•des•tri•an•ism

pe•di•at•ric

pe•di•at•rics *n.sing.*

pe•do•phile

pe•do•phil•i•a

pe•do•phil•ic

peep

peep show

peep•er

Peep•ing Tom

peer (one of equal rank; member of nobility: cf. PIER)

peer of the realm

peer pres•sure

peer re•view
peer review or•
  gan•i•za•tion (PRO)
peer•age
peer•less
peer•less•ly
peer•less•ness
peg n., v., pegged,
  peg•ging
peine forte et dure
  Law French.
pej•o•ra•tion
pe•jo•ra•tive
pe•jo•ra•tive•ly
pell-mell
pem•o•line Controlled
  Subst.
pe•nal
penal code
penal in•sti•tu•tion
penal law
penal ser•vi•tude
penal stat•ute
pe•nal•i•ty
pe•nal•iz•a•ble
pe•nal•i•za•tion
pe•nal•ize v., pe•
  nal•ized, pe•nal•iz•
  ing
pe•nal•ly
pen•al•ty n., pl. pen•
  al•ties
penalty clause
penalty phase
pen•ance
pend
pend•ant n. (cf. PEND-
  ENT)
pen•den•cy n., pl.
  pen•den•cies
pend•ent adj. (cf.
  PENDANT)
pendent ju•ris•dic•
  tion
pen•den•ote li•te
  Latin.

pen•dent•ly
pend•ing
pen•e•tra•bil•i•ty
pen•e•tra•ble
pen•e•tra•bly
pen•e•trate v.,
  pen•e•trat•ed,
  pen•e•trat•ing
pen•e•trat•ing
pen•e•trat•ing•ly
pen•e•trat•ing•ness
pen•e•tra•tion
pen•e•tra•tive
pen•e•tra•tor
pe•nile
pe•nis n., pl. pe•
  nis•es or
  (esp. in scientific contexts) pe•nes
pen•i•tence
pen•i•tent
pen•i•ten•tial
pen•i•ten•tial•ly
pen•i•ten•tia•ry n.,
  pl. pen•i•ten•tia•
  ries, adj.
pen•i•tent•ly
pen•ni•less
pen•ni•less•ly
pen•ni•less•ness
penny stock
pe•no•log•i•cal
pe•nol•o•gist
pe•nol•o•gy
pen•sion
pension fund
pension plan
pen•sion•a•ble
pen•sion•a•bly
pen•sion•er
pen•sion•less
pen•ta•zo•cine Con-
  trolled Subst.
pen•to•bar•bi•tal
  Controlled Subst.

Pen•to•thal Trade-
  mark.
pe•num•bra n., pl.
  pe•num•bras or
  esp. in scientific con-
  texts pe•num•brae
pe•num•bral
penumbral right
pen•u•ry
pe•on (landless la-
  borer; one forced to
  work off a debt: cf.
  PAEAN
pe•on•age
peo•ple n., v., peo•
  pled, peo•pling
pep•per•corn
per English and Latin.
per an•num Latin.
  (annual; annually: cf.
  PER ANUM)
per a•num Latin.
  anal; anally: cf. PER
  ANNUM
per cap•i•ta Latin.
per con•tra Latin.
per cu•ri•am Latin.
per curiam o•pin•ion
per di•em Latin.
per os Latin.
per pro. (per procura-
  tionem or per procura-
  tion)
per proc. (per procura-
  tionem or per procura-
  tion)
per pro•cu•ra•tion
  (per proc. or per pro.
  or p.p.)
per pro•cu•ra•ti•o•
  nem (per proc. or
  per pro. or p.p.)
  Latin.
per quae ser•vi•ti•a
  Latin.
per quod Latin.
per se Latin.

per se rule
per stir•pes *Latin.*
per•ceiv•a•bil•i•ty
per•ceiv•a•ble
per•ceiv•a•bly
per•ceive *v.,* per•ceived, per•ceiv•ing
per•ceiv•er
per•cent
per•cent•age
percentage de•ple•tion
percentage lease
percentage of com•ple•tion–cap•i•tal•ized cost meth•od of ac•count•ing
percentage of com•ple•tion meth•od of ac•count•ing
per•cen•tile
per•cept (a mental impression; a thing perceived: cf. PRECEPT)
per•cep•ti•bil•i•ty
per•cep•ti•ble
per•cep•ti•bly
per•cep•tion
per•cep•tion•al
per•cep•tive
per•cep•tive•ly
per•cep•tive•ness
per•cep•tu•al
perceptual dis•tor•tion
perceptual dis•turb•ance
per•cep•tu•al•ly
per•cip•i•ence
per•cip•i•en•cy
per•cip•i•ent
percipient wit•ness
Per•co•dan *Trademark.*
per•emp•to•ri•ly

per•emp•to•ri•ness
per•emp•to•ry
peremptory chal•lenge
peremptory ex•cep•tion
peremptory in•struc•tion
peremptory plea
peremptory writ
per•fect
perfect com•pe•ti•tion
perfect war
per•fect•ed
perfected se•cu•ri•ty in•ter•est
per•fect•er
per•fect•i•bil•i•ty
per•fect•i•ble
per•fec•tion
per•fec•tive
per•fid•i•ous
per•fid•i•ous•ly
per•fid•i•ous•ness
per•fi•dy *n., pl.* per•fi•dies
per•force
per•form
per•form•a•ble
per•for•mance
performance bond
performance com•pen•sa•tion plan
performance e•val•u•a•tion
performance rat•ing
performance shares
per•form•er
performing rights so•ci•e•ty
per•func•to•ri•ly
per•func•to•ri•ness
per•func•to•ry
per•oil *n., v.,* per•iled, per•il•ing

per•il•ous
per•il•ous•ly
per•il•ous•ness
per•ils of the sea
pe•ri•od
pe•ri•od•ic
periodic es•tate
periodic ex•pense
periodic rate
periodic ten•an•cy
pe•ri•od•i•cal
pe•ri•od•i•cal•ly
pe•riph•er•al
pe•riph•er•al•ly
pe•riph•er•y *n., pl.* pe•riph•er•ies
pe•riph•ra•sis *n., pl.* pe•riph•ra•ses
pe•riph•ras•tic
pe•ri•phras•ti•cal•ly
per•jure *v.,* per•jured, per•jur•ing
per•jured
per•jur•er
per•ju•ri•ous
per•ju•ri•ous•ly
per•ju•ri•ous•ness
per•ju•ry *n., pl.* per•ju•ries
perk
perm. (permanent)
per•ma•nence
per•ma•nen•cy
per•ma•nent (*citation forms:* **Perm.** in a name; **perm.** in descriptive material)
permanent a•bode
permanent dis•a•bil•i•ty
permanent in•junc•tion
permanent in•ju•ry
permanent nui•sance
permanent res•i•dence

per•ma•nent•ly
per•me•ate v., per•
  me•at•ed, per•me•
  at•ing
per•mis•si•bil•i•ty
per•mis•si•ble
per•mis•si•ble•ness
per•mis•si•bly
per•mis•sion
per•mis•sive
permissive coun•ter•
  claim
permissive join•der
permissive pre•sump•
  tion
permissive sub•ject of
  ne•go•ti•a•tion
permissive use
permissive waste
per•mis•sive•ly
per•mis•sive•ness
per•mit v., per•mit•
  ted, per•mit•ting, n.
per•mit•ted
per•mit•ted•ly
per•mit•tee
per•nan•cy
per•ni•cious
per•ni•cious•ly
per•ni•cious•ness
per•nor
per•o•rate v., per•o•
  rat•ed, per•o•rat•
  ing
per•o•ra•tion
per•o•ra•tion•al
perp
per•pe•tra•ble
per•pe•trate v., per•
  pe•trat•ed, per•pe•
  trat•ing
per•pe•tra•tion
per•pe•tra•tor
per•pet•u•al
perpetual lease

perpetual suc•ces•
  sion
perpetual trust
per•pet•u•al•i•ty
per•pet•u•al•ly
per•pet•u•al•ness
per•pet•u•ate v.,
  per•pet•u•at•ed,
  per•pet•u•at•ing
per•pet•u•a•tion
per•pet•u•a•tor
per•pe•tu•i•ty n., pl
  per•pe•tu•i•ties
per•plex
per•plexed
per•plex•ed•ly
per•plex•ed•ness
per•plex•ing
per•plex•ing•ly
per•plex•i•ty n., pl.
  per•plex•i•ties
per•qui•site (benefit:
  cf. PREREQUISITE)
Pers. (Personal)
per•se•cute v., per•
  se•cut•ed, per•se•
  cut•ing
per•se•cut•ing•ly
per•se•cu•tion
per•se•cu•tion•al
per•se•cu•tive
per•se•cu•tive•ness
per•se•cu•tor
per•se•cu•to•ry
persecutory de•lu•
  sion
per•se•ver•ance
per•sev•er•ate v.,
  per•sev•er•at•ed,
  per•sev•er•at•ing
per•sev•er•a•tion
per•sev•er•a•tive
per•sist
per•sist•ence
per•sist•en•cy
per•sist•ent

persistent de•lu•
  sion•al dis•or•der
persistent veg•e•ta•
  tive state
per•sist•ent•ly
per•sist•er
per•sis•tive
per•sis•tive•ly
per•sis•tive•ness
per•son
person ag•grieved
person in need of
  su•per•vi•sion
  (PINS)
per•so•na¹ n., pl.
  per•so•nas or (esp.
  in technical contexts)
  per•so•nae
per•so•na² n., pl.
  per•so•nae Latin.
persona gra•ta n., pl.
  per•so•nae gra•tae
  Latin.
persona non gra•ta
  n., pl. per•so•nae
  non gra•tae Latin.
per•son•a•ble
per•son•a•ble•ness
per•son•a•bly
per•son•age
per•son•al (citation
  form:
  Pers.)
personal ac•tion
personal de•fense
personal ef•fects
personal ex•emp•
  tion
personal hold•ing
  com•pa•ny
personal holding com-
  pany tax
personal in•come tax
personal in•ju•ry (PI)
personal judg•ment

personal ju•ris•dic•tion
personal know•ledge
personal lib•er•ty
personal loan
personal prop•er•ty
personal rep•re•sent•a•tive
personal serv•ice
personal service cor•po•ra•tion
personal serv•i•ces (or service) con•tract
personal trust
per•son•al•i•ty n., pl. per•son•al•i•ties (character; temperament: cf. PERSONALTY)
personality change
personality dis•or•der
personality in•ven•to•ry
personality test•ing
per•son•al•ly
per•son•al•ty (personal property: cf. PERSONALITY)
per•so•nam Latin.
per•son•hood
per•son•nel
personnel a•gen•cy
Persp. (Perspective; Perspectives)
per•spec•tive (citation form for sing. and pl.: Persp.)
per•spi•ca•cious (keenly observant: cf. PERSPICUOUS)
per•spi•ca•cious•ly
per•spi•cac•i•ty
per•spi•cu•ous (clearly presented: cf. PERSPICACIOUS)
per•spi•cu•ous•ly

per•spi•cu•ous•ness
per•suad•a•bil•i•ty
per•suad•a•ble
per•suade v., per•suad•ed, per•suad•ing
per•suad•er
per•sua•si•ble
per•sua•sion
per•sua•sive
persuasive au•thor•i•ty
per•sua•sive•ly
per•sua•sive•ness
per•tain
per•ti•na•cious
per•ti•na•cious•ly
per•ti•na•cious•ness
per•ti•nac•i•ty
per•ti•nence
per•ti•nen•cy
per•ti•nent
pertinent art
per•ti•nent•ly
per•turb
per•turb•a•bil•i•ty
per•turb•a•ble
per•tur•ba•tion
per•vade v., per•vad•ed, per•vad•ing
per•vad•er
per•vad•ing•ly
per•va•sive
pervasive pub•lic fig•ure
per•va•sive•ly
per•va•sive•ness
per•verse
per•verse•ly
per•verse•ness
per•ver•sion
per•ver•si•ty
per•vert
per•vert•ed
pes•ti•cid•al

pes•ti•cide
pes•ti•fer•ous
pes•ti•lence
pes•ti•lent
pes•ti•len•tial
Pet. (Petition; Petitioner)
pe•tard
peth•i•dine Controlled Subst.
pet•it Law French.
petit (or pet•ty) ju•ror
petit (or petty) ju•ry
petit (or petty) lar•ce•ny
petit (or petty) ser•jeant•y
petit (or petty) trea•son
pe•ti•ti•o prin•ci•pi•i Latin.
pe•ti•tion (citation form: Pet.)
pe•ti•tion•a•ble
pe•ti•tion•ar•y
pe•ti•tion•er (citation form: Pet'r or Pet.)
pet•i•to•ry
petitory ac•tion
Pet'r (Petitioner)
pet•ori•chlor•al Controlled Subst.
pet•o•ro•dol•lar
pet•ti•fog v., pet•ti•fogged, pet•ti•fog•ging
pet•ti•fog•ger
pet•ti•fog•ger•y
pet•ti•fog•ging
pet•ti•ly
pet•ti•ness
pet•ty adj., pet•ti•er, pet•ti•est
petty as•size
petty av•er•age

petty cash

petty ju•ror See PETIT JUROR.

petty ju•ry See PETIT JURY.

petty lar•ce•ny See PETIT LARCENY.

petty of•fense

petty pat•ent

petty ser•jeant•y See PETIT SERJEANTY.

petty ses•sions

petty trea•son See PETIT TREASON.

pet•u•lance

pet•u•lant

pet•u•lant•ly

pe•yo•te *Controlled Subst.* (Lophophora williamsii Lemaire)

phan•tom

phantom count

phantom stock

Pharm. (Pharmaceutics; Pharmaceutical)

phar•ma•ceu•ti•cal (*citation form:* **Pharm.**)

phar•ma•ceu•tics *n. sing.* (*citation form:* **Pharm.**)

phar•ma•cist

phar•ma•co•log•ic

phar•ma•co•log•i•cal

pharmacological ef•fect

phar•ma•co•log•i•cal•ly

phar•ma•col•o•gist

phar•ma•col•o•gy

phar•ma•co•poe•ia or phar•ma•co•pe•ia

phar•ma•cy *n., pl.* phar•ma•cies

phase *n., v.,* phased, phas•ing (an aspect or stage; to change gradually: cf. FAZE)

phase out *v.* (cf. PHASE OUT)

phase•out *n.* (cf. PHASE OUT)

Ph.D. (Doctor of Philosophy: from Latin *Philosophiae Doctor*)

phe•na•dox•one *Controlled Subst.*

phe•nam•pro•mide *Controlled Subst.*

phe•naz•o•cine *Controlled Subst.*

phen•cy•cli•dine (PCP) *Controlled Subst.*

phencyclidine a•buse

phencyclidine de•pend•ence

phencyclidine-induced dis•or•der

phencyclidine in•tox•i•ca•tion

phen•di•met•ra•zine *Controlled Subst.*

phen-fen See FEN-PHEN.

phen•met•ra•zine *Controlled Subst.*

phe•no•bar•bi•tal *Controlled Subst.*

phe•nom•e•na See PHENOMENON.

phe•nom•e•nal

phe•nom•e•nal•ly

phe•nom•e•no•log•i•cal

phe•nom•e•no•log•i•cal•ly

phe•nom•e•nol•o•gist

phe•nom•e•nol•o•gy

phe•nom•e•non *n., pl.* phe•nom•e•na

or (in sense of a remarkable person)

phe•nom•e•nons

phe•no•mor•phan *Controlled Subst.*

phe•no•per•o•i•dine *Controlled Subst.*

phe•no•type

phe•no•typ•ic

phe•no•typ•i•cal

phe•no•typ•i•cal•ly

phen•ter•mine *Controlled Subst.* See also FENFLURAMINE-PHENTERMINE.

phen•yl•ac•e•tone (P2P) *Controlled Subst.*

phen•yl•al•kyl•a•mine

Phil. (Philosophical; Philosophy)

Phil•a•del•phi•a law•yer

phil•an•throp•ic

phil•an•throp•i•cal

phil•an•throp•i•cal•ly

phi•lan•thro•py

phi•los•o•pher

phil•o•soph•i•cal (*citation form:* **Phil.**)

phil•o•soph•i•cal•ly

phil•o•soph•i•cal•ness

phi•los•o•phy *n., pl.* phi•los•o•phies (*citation form:* **Phil.**)

pho•bi•a

pho•bic

pho•bi•cal•ly

phol•co•dine *Controlled Subst.*

pho•ni•ness

pho•no•gram

pho•no•re•cord

pho•ny *adj.,* pho•

ni•er, pho•ni•est,
n., pl. pho•nies, v.,
pho•nied, pho•ny•
ing
pho•to•graph
pho•tog•ra•pher
pho•to•graph•ic
pho•tog•ra•phy
phys•i•cal (of the
body: cf. FISCAL)
physical dis•
a•bil•i•ty
physical im•pair•
ment
physical in•ca•
pac•i•ty
phys•i•cal•ly
phy•si•cian
physician-as•sist•ed
su•i•cide
physician-pa•tient
priv•i•lege
physician's as•sis•
tant
phys•i•o•log•i•cal
physiological de•
pend•ence
phys•i•o•log•i•
cal•ly
phys•i•ol•o•gist
phys•i•ol•o•gy
PI (paternity index; per-
sonal injury; private
investigator)
pic•a•yune
pick•et
pick•et•er
pick•et•ing
pick•pock•et
pic•tur•a•ble
pic•ture n., v., pic•
tured, pic•tur•ing
pid•dling
piece n., v., pieced,
piec•ing
piece rate

piece•meal
piece•work
piece•work•er
pier (a dock: cf. PEER)
pier to pier
pierce v., pierced,
pierc•ing
pierce the cor•po•
rate veil
pi•geon
pigeon drop
pig•nus n., pl. pig•
no•ra Latin.
pil•fer
pil•fer•age
pil•fer•er
pil•lage v., pil•laged,
pil•lag•ing, n.
pil•lag•er
pil•lo•ry n., pl. pil•
lo•ries, v., pil•lo•
ried, pil•lo•ry•ing
pi•lot
pilot wa•ters
pi•lot•age
pi•min•o•o•dine Con-
trolled Subst.
pimp
pi•naz•e•pam Con-
trolled Subst.
pink-col•lar
pink slip
PINS (person in need of
supervision)
pin•striped
pi•o•neer
pioneer pat•ent
pipe bomb
pipe•line n., v., pipe•
lined, pipe•lin•ing
pi•pra•drol Controlled
Subst.
pi•ra•cy n., pl. pi•ra•
cies
pi•rate n., v., pi•
rat•ed, pi•rat•ing

pi•rat•ic
pi•rat•i•cal
pi•rat•i•cal•ly
pi•ri•tra•mide Con-
trolled Subst.
pis•ca•ory n., pl. pis•
ca•ries
pis•tol
pit•e•ous
pit•e•ous•ly
pit•e•ous•ness
pit•fall
pit•i•a•ble
pit•i•a•ble•ness
pit•i•a•bly
pit•i•er
pit•i•ful
pit•i•ful•ly
pit•i•ful•ness
pit•tance
pit•y n., pl. pit•ies, v.,
pit•ied, pit•y•ing
pit•y•ing•ly
P/L (profit and loss)
Pl. (Plaintiff)
place
place of a•bode
place of busi•ness
place of de•liv•er•y
place of em•ploy•
ment
pla•ce•bo n., pl. pla•
ce•bos or pla•ce•
boes
placebo ef•fect
place•hold•er
place•ment
plac•i•to•ry
pla•ci•tum n., pl. pla•
ci•ta Latin.
placitum co•ro•nae
n., pl. placita co•ro•
nae Latin.
pla•gia•rism
pla•gia•rist
pla•gia•rize v., pla•

gia•rized, pla•gia•
riz•ing

pla•gia•riz•er

plague n., v., plagued,
pla•guing

plain clothes n.pl. (cf.
PLAINCLOTHES)

plain Eng•lish

plain er•ror

plain lan•guage

plain mean•ing

plain-spo•ken

plain view doc•trine

plain-clothes adj. (cf.
PLAIN CLOTHES)

plainclothes of•fi•cer

plain•clothes•man n.,
pl. plain•clothes•
men

plaint

plain•tiff (citation
form: Pl.)

plaintiff in er•ror

plan n., v., planned,
plan•ning

Plan. (Planning)

plan of li•qui•da•
tion

plan of re•or•gan•i•
za•tion

planned u•nit de•
vel•op•ment

plan•ning (citation
form: Plan.)

plant

plant pat•ent

plat n., v., plat•ted,
plat•ting

plat•form

plat•i•tude

plat•i•tu•di•nous

plau•si•bil•i•ty

plau•si•ble

plausible de•ni•
a•bil•i•ty

plau•si•ble•ness

plau•si•bly

p.l.c. (public limited
company)

plea

plea bar•gain n.

plea-bargain v.,
plea-bar•gained,
plea-bar•gain•ing

plea bar•gain•er

plea bar•gain•ing

plea in a•bate•ment

plea in bar

plead v., plead•ed or
pled, plead•ing

plead•a•ble

plead•er

plead•ing

plead•ing•ly

pleas of the crown (or
Crown)

pleb•i•scite

pledge n., v., pledged,
pledg•ing

pledge•a•ble

pledg•ee

pledg•er (one who
makes a pledge or
promise of any kind:
cf. PLEDGOR)

pledg•or (one who
pledges property as se-
curity: cf. PLEDGER)

ple•na•ri•ly

ple•na•ry or
plen•a•ry adj., n., pl.
ple•na•ries or
plen•a•ries

plenary ac•tion

plenary ju•ris•dic•
tion

plenary pow•er

plenary pro•ceed•ing

plenary ses•sion

plen•i•po•ten•ti•
ar•y n., pl. plen•i•

po•ten•ti•ar•ies,
adj.

ple•no ju•re Latin.

ple•num n., pl. ple•
nums or ple•na

ple•o•nasm

ple•o•nas•tic

ple•o•nas•ti•cal•ly

pleth•o•o•ra

ple•thor•ic

plight

plight•er

Plim•soll line

Plimsoll mark

plot n., v., plot•ted,
plot•ting

plot•tage

plot•ter

plow

plow•back n.

ploy

plun•der

plun•der•a•ble

plun•der•age

plu•ral

plural mar•riage

plu•ral•ism

plu•ral•ist

plu•ral•is•tic

plu•ral•is•ti•cal•ly

plu•ral•i•ty n., pl.
plu•ral•i•ties

plurality o•pin•ion

plu•ri•es writ

plu•ri•lat•er•al

plurilateral trade
a•gree•ment

plu•toc•ra•cy n., pl.
plu•toc•ra•cies

plu•to•crat

plu•to•crat•ic

plu•to•crat•i•cal•ly

p.m. (after noon: from
Latin post meridiem)

PMA Controlled Subst.

(paramethoxyamphet-amine)

pmbl. (preamble)

PMS (premenstrual syn-drome)

pneu∘mo∘co∘ni∘o∘sis

poach

poachºer

poach•ing

pockºet

pocket part

pocket veºto n.

pocket-veºto v., pocket-ve•toed, pocket-ve•to•ing

POD (pay on death)

point

point and bend rule

point of in•for•ma•tion

point of law

point of orºder

point of pur•chase n.

point-of-purchase adj.

point-of-purchase ad•ver•tis•ing

point of sale n.

point-of-sale adj.

point-of-sale ter•mi•nal

point of serv•ice n.

point-of-service adj.

point of view

point re•served

point-source pol•lu•tion

point sys•tem

point•less

point•less∘ly

point•less•ness

poi•son

poison-pen adj.

poison pill

poi•son∘er

poi•son∘ous

poisonous tree

poi•son•ousl∘y

poi•son•ous•ness

Pol. (Political; Politics)

po•lar∘i∘za∘tion

po•lar•ize v., po•lar•ized, po•lar•iz•ing

po•lar•ized

po•lice n., v., po•liced, po•lic•ing

police ac•tion

police chase

police court

police of•fi•cer

police powºer

police state

po•lice•man n., pl. po•lice•men

po•lice•wom∘an n., pl. po•lice•wom∘en

pol∘i∘cy n., pl. pol∘i∘cies (citation form: Pol'y)

policy game

policy loan

pol∘i∘cy•hold∘er

pol∘i∘tic

po•lit∘i∘cal (citation form: **Pol.**)

political ac•tion com•mit•tee (PAC)

political a∘sy•lum

political con•tri•bu•tion

political crime

political e∘con∘o∘mist

political e∘con∘o∘my

political lib•er∘ty

political of•fice

political pa•tron•age

political pris•on∘er

political ques•tion

political ref∘u•gee

political right

political rights a∘nal∘y•sis

political sci•ence

political sci•en•tist

po•lit∘i∘cal∘ly (in a way that involves poli-tics: cf. POLITICLY)

pol∘i•ti•cian

po•lit∘i∘ci∘za∘tion

po•lit∘i∘cize v., po•lit∘i∘cized, po•lit∘i∘ciz•ing

pol∘i•tick

pol∘i•tick•ing

pol∘i∘tic∘ly (tactfully; diplomatically: cf. PO-LITICALLY)

po•lit∘i∘co n., pl. po•lit∘i∘cos

pol∘i•tics n.sing. or pl.

pol∘i∘ty n., pl. pol∘i•ties

poll

poll tax

poll the ju∘ry

poll watch∘er

poll•book

pol•lic∘i•ta•tion

poll•ing booth

polling place

polls n.pl.

pol•lute v., pol•lut∘ed, pol•lut•ing

pol•lut∘ed

pol•lut∘er

pol•lu•tion

pollution-con•trol bond

pollution cred∘it

pol•troon

Pol'y (Policy)

pol∘y•an•drist (a woman with more than one husband: cf. POLYGAMIST; POLYGYNIST)

pol∘y•an•drous

pol○y•an•dry
pol○y•drug use
po•lyg○a•mist (a per-
son with more than
one spouse: cf. POLYAN-
DRIST; POLYGYNIST)
po•lyg○a•mous
po•lyg○a•mous•ly
po•lyg○a•my
pol○y•graph
po•lyg•raph○er
pol○y•graph○ic
po•lyg•ra•phist
po•lyg○y•nist (a man
with more than one
wife: cf. POLYANDRIST;
POLYGYNIST)
po•lyg○y•nous
po•lyg○y○ny
pol○y•mer○ase chain
re•ac•tion (PCR)
po○ly•mor•phism
po○ly•sub•stance
de•pend•ence
pom•pos○i○ty n., pl.
pom•pos○i•ties
pom•pous
pom•pous○ly
pom•pous•ness
pon•der
pon•der•a○ble
pon•der○er
Pon○zi scheme
pool
pooled trust
pool○er
pool•ing
pooling a○gree•ment
pooling ar•range•
ment
pooling of in○ter•ests
poor
pop○u•lar
popular sov•er•
eign○ty
popular vote

pop○u•lar○i○ty
pop○u•lar○ly
pop○u•la•tion
pop○u•lism
pop○u•list
pork
pork bar•rel n.
pork-barrel adj.
pork-barrel leg•is•la•
tion
pork○chop•per
por•nog•ra•pher
por•no•graph○ic
por•no•graph○i•
cal○ly
por•nog•ra•phy
port
port au•thor○i○ty
port bill of lad•ing
port cus•toms reg○u•
la•tions
port of call
port of en○try
port•a○bil○i○ty
por•tal-to-por•tal pay
port•fo•li○o n., pl.
port•fo•li○os
por•tion
por•tion•a○ble
po•si•tion
po•si•tion•al
po•si•tion○er
pos○i•tive
positive con•fir•ma•
tion
positive law
pos○i•tive○ly
pos○i•tiv○ism
pos○i•tiv•ist
pos○i•tiv•is•tic
pos○i•tiv•is•ti•cal○ly
pos•se English and
Latin.
posse co○mi•ta•tus
Latin.
pos•sess

pos•ses•sion
possession is nine
points of the law
possession is nine-
tenths of the law
pos•ses•sor
pos•ses•so•ri•ness
pos•ses•so○ry
possessory action
possessory as•size
possessory es•tate
possessory in○ter•est
possessory lien
pos•si•bil○i○ty
possibility of re•
vert○er
pos•si•ble
pos•si•bly
post English and Latin.
post bail
post dis•sei•sin
post fac•tum Latin.
post hoc Latin.
post hoc er○go prop•
ter hoc Latin.
post li○tem mo○tam
Latin.
post-o○bit
post-obit bond
post o○bi•tum Latin.
post•ac•qui•si•tion
part year
post•au•dit
post•con•vic•tion
postconviction
rem•e○dy
post•date v., post•
dat○ed, post•dat•
ing
post○ed land
pos•ter○i○ty
post-ex•pi•ra•tion
post•hu•mous
post•hu•mous○ly
post•hu•mous•ness
post•hyp•not○ic

post•hyp•not•ic sug•ges•tion
post•hyp•not•i•cal•ly
post•ing
post•li•mi•ni•um *Latin.*
post•lim•i•o•ny
post•man
post•mor•tem
post•na•tus *n., pl.* post•na•ti *Latin.*
post•nup•tial
post•par•tum
post•pon•a•ble
post•pone *v.,* post•poned, post•pon•ing
post•pone•ment
post•pon•er
pos•tre•mo•gen•i•ture
post•struc•tur•al•ism
post•struc•tur•al•ist
post•trau•mat•ic stress dis•or•der (PTSD)
post•tri•al
posttrial mo•tion
posttrial rem•e•dy
pos•tu•late *n., v.,* pos•tu•lat•ed, pos•tu•lat•ing
pos•tu•la•tion
pos•tu•la•tion•al
po•ten•cy
po•tent
po•ten•tial
po•ten•ti•al•i•ty *n., pl.* po•ten•ti•al•i•ties
po•ten•tial•ly
po•ten•ti•ate *v.,* po•ten•ti•at•ed, po•ten•ti•at•ing
po•ten•ti•a•tion

po•ten•ti•a•tor
po•tent•ly
po•tes•tas *n., pl.* po•tes•ta•tes *Latin.*
pound
pound•age
pour o•ver *v.*
pour-o•ver *or* pour•o•ver *adj.*
pour-over (or pourover) trust
pov•er•ty
poverty-strick•en
powder burn
powder keg
pow•er
power coup•led with an in•ter•est
power of ac•cept•ance
power of al•ien•a•tion
power of ap•point•ment
power of at•tor•ney
power of sale
power of ter•mi•na•tion
pow•er•ful
pow•er•ful•ly
pow•er•ful•ness
pow•er•less
pow•er•less•ly
pow•er•less•ness
p.p. (per procurationem or per procuration)
pp. (pages)
Prac. (Practical; Practice; Practitioner; Practitioners)
prac•ti•ca•bil•i•ty
prac•ti•ca•ble
prac•ti•ca•bly
prac•ti•cal (*citation form:* **Prac.**)

prac•ti•cal•i•ty *n., pl.* prac•ti•cal•i•ties
prac•ti•cal•ly
prac•ti•cal•ness
prac•tice (*citation form:* **Prac.**)
prac•tic•er
prac•ti•cum *n., pl.* prac•ti•cums
prac•tise *v.,* prac•tised, prac•tis•ing (British spelling for PRACTICE as a verb)
prac•tis•er (British spelling for PRACTICER)
prac•ti•tion•er (*citation form for sing. and pl.:* **Prac.**)
prae•ci•pe *Latin.*
praecipe in ca•pi•te *Latin.*
praecipe quod red•dat *Latin.*
prae•di•al
prae•di•al•i•ty
prae•mu•ni•re *Latin.*
prae•sen•ti *Latin.*
prae•tor
prae•to•ri•al
prae•to•ri•an
prag•mat•ic
prag•mat•i•cal•ly
prag•ma•tism
prag•ma•tist
praise *v.,* praised, prais•ing
praise•wor•thi•ly
praise•wor•thi•ness
praise•wor•thy
pray (to petition: cf. PREY)
prayer[1] (a humble request)
pray•er[2] (one who prays)
prayer for re•lief

pra•ze•pam *Controlled Subst.*
pre•ac•qui•si•tion part year
pre•am•ble (*citation form:* pmbl.)
pre•au•dit
pre•car•i•ous
pre•car•i•ous•ly
pre•car•i•ous•ness
prec○a○tive
prec○a○to○ry
precatory lan•guage
precatory trust
precatory words
pre•cau•tion
pre•cau•tion•ar•y
pre•ced•a○ble
pre•cede *v.,* pre•ced○ed, pre•ced•ing
pre•ce•dence *or* prec○e○dence
pre•ce•den○cy *or* prec○e○den○cy
prec○e○dent[1] *n.*
pre•ce•dent[2] *adj.*
prec○e○dent○ed
prec○e○den•tial
pre•cept (a writ, warrant, order, or rule: cf. PERCEPT)
pre•cep•tive
pre•cep•tive○ly
pre•cinct
pre•cip○i•tant
pre•cip○i•tate *v.,* pre•cip○i•tat○ed, pre•cip○i•tat•ing, *adj., n.*
pre•cip○i•tate○ly
pre•cip○i•tate•ness
pre•cip○i•tat•ing
pre•cip○i•ta•tion
pre•cip○i•ta•tive
pre•cip○i•ta•tor
pre•cip○i•tous

pre•cip○i•tous•ly
pre•cip○i•tous•ness
pre•cise
pre•cise○ly
pre•cise•ness
pre•ci•sion
pre•clud•a○ble
pre•clude *v.,* pre•clud○ed, pre•clud•ing
pre•clu•sion
pre•clu•sive
pre•clu•sive○ly
pre•cog•ni•tion
pre•con•di•tion
pre•con•scious
pre•con•scious○ly
pre•con•tract
pre•cur•sive
pre•cur•sor
pre•cur•so○ry
pre•date *v.,* pre•dat○ed, pre•dat•ing
pre•da•tion
pred○a•tor
pred○a•to•ri○ly
pred○a•to•ri•ness
pred○a•to○ry
predatory pric•ing
pre•de•cease *v.,* pre•de•ceased, pre•de•ceas•ing
pred○e○ces•sor
pre•de•ter•mi•na•tion
pre•de•ter•mi•na•tive
pre•de•ter•mine *v.,* pre•de•ter•mined, pre•de•ter•min•ing
pre•de•ter•mined
pred○i•ca•bil○i○ty
pred○i•ca•ble
pred○i•ca•bly
pre•dic○a•ment
pred○i•cate *v.,*

pred○i•cat○ed, pred○i•cat•ing, *adj., n.*
predicate crime
predicate of•fense
pred○i•ca•tion
pred○i•ca•tion○al
pred○i•ca•tive
pred○i•ca•tive○ly
pre•dict
pre•dict•a○bil○i○ty
pre•dict•a○ble
pre•dict•a○bly
pre•dic•tion
pre•dic•tive
pre•dic•tive○ly
pre•dic•tive•ness
pre•dic•tor
pre•di•lec•tion
pre•dis•pose *v.,* pre•dis•posed, pre•dis•pos•ing
pre•dis•posed
pre•dis•pos•ed○ly
pre•dis•pos•ed•ness
pre•dis•pos•ing
predisposing fac•tor
pre•dis•po•si•tion
pre•dis•po•si•tion○al
pre•dom○i•nance
pre•dom○i•nant
predominant con•tacts a○nal○y•sis
pre•dom○i•nate *v.,* pre•dom○i•nat○ed, pre•dom○i•nat•ing
pre•e○lec•tion
pre•em○i•nence
pre•em○i•nent
pre•em○i•nent○ly
pre•empt
pre•emp•tion
pre•emp•tive
preemptive pric•ing
preemptive right
pre•emp•tive○ly

pre•en•force•ment
pre•ex•ist
pre•ex•ist•ence
pre•ex•ist•ing
preexisting con•di•tion
preexisting du•ty
pref○a•to•ri•ly
pref○a•to○ry
pre•fect
pre•fec•tur○al
pre•fec•ture
pre•fer *v.*, pre•ferred, pre•fer•ring
pref•er•a○bil○i•ty
pref•er•a○ble
pref•er•a○bly
pref•er•ence
preference share
pref•er•en•tial
preferential shop
preferential tar•iff
preferential vot•ing
pref•er•en•tial•ism
pref•er•en•tial•ist
pref•er•en•tial•ly
pre•ferred
preferred cred○i•tor
preferred stock
pre•fer•red○ly
pre•fer•red•ness
pre•fer•rer
preg•nan○cy *n., pl.* preg•nan•cies
pregnancy dis•crim○i•na•tion
preg•nant
pre•hear•ing
prehearing con•fer•ence
pre•judge *v.*, pre•judged, pre•judg•ing
pre•judg○er
pre•judg•ment

prejudgment in○ter•est
prejudgment rem○e○dy
prej○u•dice *n., v.*, prej○u•diced, prej○u•dic○ing
prej○u•diced
prej○u•diced•ly
prej○u•di○cial
prejudicial ef•fect
prejudicial er○ror
prejudicial pub•lic○i○ty
prej○u•di•cial○ly
prej○u•di•cial•ness
pre•lim○i•nar○i○ly
pre•lim○i•nar○y
preliminary hear•ing
preliminary in•junc•tion
preliminary state•ment
pre•lit○i•ga•tion
Pre•lu•din *Trademark.*
pre•mar○i•tal a○gree•ment
pre•mature
pre•mature○ly
pre•ma•tu•ri○ty
pre•med○i•tate *v.*, pre•med○i•tat○ed, pre•med○i•tat○ing
pre•med○i•tat○ed
pre•med○i•tat○ed○ly
pre•med○i•ta•tion
pre•men•stru○al syn•drome (PMS)
pre•merg○er no•ti•fi•ca•tion
pre•mier (leading; prime minister: cf. PRE-MIERE)
pre•miere *n. v.*, pre•miered, pre•mier•ing, *adj.* (first perfor-

mance; to give the first performance; ini-tial or principal: cf. PREMIER)
pre•mier•ship
prem•ise
prem○i•ses *n.pl.*
pre•mi○um
premium loan
pre•mo•ni•tion
pre•mon○i•to○ry
pre•na•tal
prenatal tort
pre•na•tal○ly
pre•no•tice
pre•no•ti•fi•ca•tion
pre•nup•tial
prenuptial a○gree•ment
pre•paid
prepaid ex•pense
prepaid in•sur•ance
prepaid in○ter•est
prepaid le○gal serv•ic○es
prepaid rent
prep○a•ra•tion
pre•par○a•tive
pre•par○a•tive○ly
pre•par○a•to○ry
pre•pare *v.*, pre•pared, pre•par•ing
pre•par○ed•ness
pre•par○er
pre•pay *v.*, pre•paid, pre•pay•ing
pre•pay•a○ble
pre•pay•ment
prepayment pen•al○ty
pre•pon•der•ance
preponderance of the ev○i•dence
pre•pon•der•ant
pre•pon•der•ate *v.*,

pre•pon•der•at∘ed,
pre•pon•der•at∘ing
pre•pos•ter•ous
pre•pos•ter•ous•ly
pre•pos•ter•ous•
ness
pre•req•ui•site (pre-
condition: cf. PERQUI-
SITE)
Prerog. (Prerogative)
Prerog. Ct. (Prerogative
Court
pre•rog∘a•tive (*cita-
tion form:* **Prerog.**)
Pre•rog∘a•tive Court
(*citation form:* **Prerog.
Ct.**)
prerogative writ
pre•screen
pre•screen•ing
pre•scrib•a∘ble
pre•scribe v. pre•
scribed, pre•scrib•
ing (to dictate; to
claim a property right
by virtue of prior use:
cf. PROSCRIBE)
pre•scrib∘er
pre•scrip•ti•ble
pre•scrip•tion
pre•scrip•tive
prescriptive ease•
ment
pre•scrip•tive•ly
pre•scrip•tive•ness
pre•sei•zure
preseizure ju•di•cial
re•view
pre•sence
pres•ent¹ *adj., n.*
pre•sent² *v.*
present dan•ger
pres•ent es•tate
pres•ent in∘ter•est
pres•ent pos•ses•
so∘ry es•tate

pres•ent rec•ol•lec•
tion re•freshed
pres•ent sense im•
pres•sion
pres•ent val∘ue
pres•en•ta•tion
pre•sen•tence in•
ves•ti•ga•tion
pre•sen•tence re•
port
pre•sen•tial sea
pre•sent•ment
pres•ents *n.pl.*
pre•side v., pre•
sid∘ed, pre•sid•ing
pres∘i•den∘cy n., pl.
pres∘i•den•cies
pres∘i•dent
president-e∘lect
president pro tem•
po∘re (or pro tem)
pres∘i•den•tial
presidential gov•ern•
ment
presidential pri•
ma∘ry
pres∘i•den•tial∘ly
pre•sid∘er
pre•sid•ing judge
presiding of•fi•cer
press
press re•lease
pres•sure n., v., pres•
sured, pres•sur•ing
pressure group
pre•sub•scrip•tion
pre•sum•a∘ble
pre•sum•a∘bly
pre•sume v., pre•
sumed, pre•sum•ing
pre•sumed
presumed intent
pre•sum∘er
pre•sump•tion
presumption of fact

presumption of in•
no•cence
presumption of law
presumption of le•
git∘i•ma∘cy
presumption of sur•
vi•vor•ship
pre•sump•tive
presumptive heir
presumptive trust
pre•sump•tive•ly
pre•sump•tu•ous
pre•sump•tu•ous•ly
pre•sump•tu•ous•
ness
pre•sup•pose v., pre•
sup•posed, pre•
sup•pos•ing
pre•sup•po•si•tion
pre•tend
pre•tend∘ed
pre•tend∘er
pre•tense
pre•ten•sion
pre•ten•tious
pre•ten•tious•ly
pre•ten•tious•ness
pret•er•oi•tion
pre•ter•le•gal
pret•er•mis•sion
pret•er•mit v., pret•
er•mit•ted, pret•er•
mit•ting
pretermitted heir
pret•er•mit•ter
pre•text
pre•tex•tu•al
pre•tri∘al
pretrial con•fer•ence
pretrial de•ten•tion
pretrial dis•cov•er∘y
pretrial mo•tion
pretrial or∘der
pre•vail
pre•vail∘er
pre•vail•ing

prevailing par•ty
prevailing wage
prevailing wage laws
prev•a•lence
prev•a•lent
prev•a•lent•ly
pre•var•i•cate v.,
  pre•var•i•cat•ed,
  pre•var•i•cat•ing
pre•var•i•ca•tion
pre•var•i•ca•tor
pre•vent
pre•vent•a•bil•i•ty
pre•vent•a•ble
pre•vent•a•tive
pre•vent•a•tive•ly
pre•vent•er
pre•ven•tion
pre•ven•tive
preventive de•ten•
  tion
pre•ven•tive•ly
pre•vi•ous
previous ques•tion
pre•vi•ous•ly
prey (a victim; to vic
  timize: f. PRAY)
prey•er
price n., v., priced,
  pric•ing
price-cap reg•u•la•
  tion
price con•trol
price-cut•ter
price cut•ting
price dis•crim•i•na•
  tion
price-earn•ings ra•tio
  (p/e)
price fix•ing
price guar•an•tee
price in•dex
price lead•er
price pro•tec•tion
price reg•u•la•tion
price sup•port

price u•ni•form•i•ty
price war
pri•ma fac•i•e Latin.
prima facie case
prima facie ev•i•
  dence
prima facie proof
pri•ma•cy
pri•mae im•pres•si•
  o•nis Latin.
pri•ma•ri•ly
pri•ma•ri•ness
pri•ma•ry adj., n., pl.
  pri•ma•ries
primary au•thor•i•ty
primary boy•cott
primary care
primary-care phy•si•
  cian
primary du•ty doc•
  trine
primary e•lec•tion
primary ju•ris•dic•
  tion
primary li•a•bil•i•ty
primary mar•ket
primary men•tal dis•
  or•der
primary pick•et•ing
primary pur•pose
primary-si•tus pick•
  et•ing
primary source
prime adj., n., v.,
  primed, prim•ing
prime con•trac•tor
prime in•ter•est rate
prime min•is•ter
prime rate
prim•er
pri•mo•gen•i•tar•y
pri•mo•gen•i•ture
pri•mus in•ter pa•res
  Latin.
princ. (principle)
prin•ci•pal (foremost;

a person directly re-
sponsible; a capital
sum: cf. PRINCIPLE)
principal cred•i•tor
principal debt•or
principal ob•li•gee
principal ob•li•gor
principal reg•is•ter
principal sum
prin•ci•pal•i•ty n., pl
  prin•ci•pal•i•ties
prin•ci•ple (citation
  form: princ.; a rule or
  guideline: cf. PRINCIPAL)
print•ed mat•ter
print•ing (citation
  form: prtg.)
pri•on
pri•or
prior ad•ju•di•ca•
  tion
prior art
prior bad act
prior con•vic•tion
prior in•con•sis•tent
  state•ment
prior lien
prior re•straint
pri•or•i•ty n., pl. pri•
  or•i•ties
pri•sage
pris•on
prison camp
prison psy•cho•sis
pris•on•er
prisoner of con•
  science
prisoner of war
pri•va•cy
pri•vate
private at•tor•ney
  gen•er•al
private bill
private car•riage
private car•ri•er
private com•pan•y

private cor•po•ra•
tion
private de•tec•tive
private en•ter•prise
private foun•da•tion
private in•ter•na•
tion•al law
private in•ves•ti•ga•
tor (PI)
private la•bel
private law
private let•ter rul•ing
private nui•sance
private place•ment
private prop•er•ty
private pros•e•cu•tor
private right of ac•
tion
private sec•tor
private trust
private wrong
pri•va•teer
pri•vate•ly
privately held cor•
po•ra•tion
pri•va•ti•za•tion
pri•va•tize v., pri•
va•tized, pri•va•
tiz•ing
priv•i•lege n., v.,
priv•i•leged, priv•i•
leg•ing
privilege a•gainst
self-in•crim•i•na•
tion
priv•i•leged
privileged com•mu•
ni•ca•tion
privileged mo•tion
privileged ves•sel
priv•i•le•ges and
im•mu•ni•ties
priv•i•ty
privity of con•tract
privity of es•tate
priv•y adj., priv•i•er,

priv•i•est, n., pl.
priv•ies
Priv•y Coun•cil (cita-
tion form: **P.C.**)
prize n., v., prized,
priz•ing
prize case
prize court
prize pro•ceed•ings
pro English and Latin.
PRO (peer review or-
ganization)
pro bo•no Latin.
pro bono pu•bli•co
Latin.
pro con•fes•so Latin.
pro fi•ne Latin.
pro for•ma Latin.
pro forma fi•nan•cial
state•ment
pro forma in•voice
pro hac vi•ce Latin.
pro in•ter•es•se
su•o Latin.
pro ra•ta Latin.
pro rata dis•tri•bu•
tion
pro se Latin.
pro tan•to Latin.
pro tem
pro tem•po•re Latin.
Prob. (Probate)
Prob. Ct. (Probate
Court)
prob•a•bi•lism
prob•a•bi•lis•tic
prob•a•bil•i•ty n., pl.
prob•a•bil•i•ties
probability of pa•ter•
ni•ty
prob•a•ble
probable cause
probable cause hear•
ing
prob•a•bly

pro•bate[1] n., adj. (citation form: **Prob.**)
probate[2] v., pro•
bat•ed, pro•bat•ing
Probate Court (citation
form: **Prob. Ct.**)
pro•ba•tion
probation of•fi•cer
probation rev•o•ca•
tion
probation vi•o•la•
tion
pro•ba•tion•al
pro•ba•tion•ar•y
pro•ba•tion•er
prob•a•tive
probative val•ue
prob•a•tive•ly
pro•bi•ty
prob•lem
prob•lem•at•ic
prob•lem•at•i•cal
prob•lem•at•i•cal•ly
Prob•lems (citation
form:
Probs.)
Probs. (Problems)
Proc. (Proceedings; Procedure)
pro•ce•den•do Latin.
procedendo ad ju•di•
ci•um Latin.
pro•ce•dur•al
procedural due proc•
ess
procedural law
procedural rule
procedural un•con•
scion•a•bil•i•ty
pro•ce•dur•al•ism
pro•ce•dur•al•ly
pro•ce•dure
pro•ceed
pro•ceed•er
pro•ceed•ing

pro•ceed•ings *n. pl.*
(citation form: **Proc.**)

pro•ceeds *n. pl.*

pro•cès-ver•bal *n*, *pl*
pro•cès-ver•baux
French.

proc•ess

process pat•ent

process serv•er

pro•ces•su•al

pro•chein a•mi *Law
French.*

pro•claim

pro•claim•er

proc•la•ma•tion

pro•cliv•i•ty *n., pl*
pro•cliv•i•ties

pro•com•pet•i•tive

pro•cras•ti•nate *v.*,
pro•cras•ti•nat•ed,
pro•cras•ti•nat•ing

pro•cras•ti•nat•
ing•ly

pro•cras•ti•na•tion

pro•cras•ti•na•tive

pro•cras•ti•na•
tive•ly

pro•cras•ti•na•tive•
ness

pro•cras•ti•na•tor

pro•cras•ti•na•to•ry

proc•tor

proctor in ad•mi•
ral•ty

proc•to•ri•al

proc•to•ri•al•ly

proc•tor•ship

pro•cur•a•ble

pro•cur•ance

proc•u•ra•tion

proc•u•ra•tor

proc•u•ra•to•ri•al

proc•u•ra•to•ry

pro•cure *v.*, pro•
cured, pro•cur•ing

pro•cure•ment

procurement con•
tract

pro•cur•er

pro•cur•ess

pro•cur•ing cause

Prod. (Product; Produc
tion)

pro•di•tion

prod•ro•mal

pro•drome

pro•duce[1] *v.*, pro•
duced, pro•duc•ing

prod•uce[2] or pro•
duce *n*

pro•duc•er

pro•duc•i•bil•i•ty

pro•duc•i•ble

pro•duc•ing cause

prod•uct (citation
form: **Prod.**)

product claim

product ex•ten•sion
merg•er

product li•a•bil•i•ty
See PRODUCTS LIABILITY.

product mark

product of na•ture

product safe•ty

pro•duc•tion (citation
form: **Prod.**)

production of doc•u•
ments

production pay•ment

pro•duc•tive

pro•duc•tive•ly

pro•duc•tive•ness

pro•duc•tiv•i•ty

products (or product)
li•a•bil•i•ty

Prof. (Profession·ı Professional; Professor)

pro•fane *adj., v.*, pro•
faned, pro•fan•ing

pro•fan•i•ty

pro•fert

pro•fes•si•o ju•ris
Latin.

pro•fes•sion (citation
form: **Prof.**)

pro•fes•sion•al (cita
tion forms: **Prof.** in
periodical names;
Prof'l in case names)

professional as•so•
ci•a•tion (P.A.)

professional cor•po•
ra•tion (P.C.)

professional crim•i•
nal

professional eth•ics

professional mal•
prac•tice

professional re•spon•
si•bil•i•ty

professional serv•ice
cor•po•ra•tion

pro•fes•sion•al•ly

pro•fes•sor (Prof.)

pro•fes•so•ri•al

pro•fes•so•ri•al•ly

prof•fer

prof•fer•er

pro•fi•cien•cy

proficiency test

pro•fi•cient

pro•fi•cient•ly

pro•file *n., v.*, pro•
filed, pro•fil•ing

prof•it

pro•fit à pren•dre
Law French.

pro•fit à ren•dre *Law
French.*

profit and loss (P&L or
P/L)

profit and loss ac•
count

profit and loss state•
ment (P&L)

profit mar•gin

profit mo•tive

profit shar•ing n.
profit-sharing adj.
profit-sharing plan
profit tak•ing
prof•it•a•bil•i•ty
prof•it•a•ble
prof•it•a•bly
prof•it•eer
prof•it•er
Prof'l (Professional)
prof•li•ga•cy
prof•li•gate
prof•li•gate•ly
pro•found men•tal
re•tar•da•tion
prog•e•ny
pro•ges•tin
prog•no•sis n., pl
prog•no•ses
pro•gram n., v., pro•
grammed or pro•
gramed, pro•gram•
ming or pro•gram•
ing
program trad•ing
pro•gramme (British
spelling for PROGRAM
except in sense of a
computer program or
to program a com-
puter)
pro•gram•mer
pro•gram•ming
prog•ress¹ n.
pro•gress² v.
prog•ress pay•ment
pro•gres•sion
pro•gres•sive
progressive tax
pro•gres•sive•ly
pro•gres•sive•ness
pro•gres•siv•ism
pro•gres•siv•i•ty
pro•hep•ta•zine Con-
trolled Subst.
pro•hib•it

pro•hib•it•ed
prohibited de•grees
of con•san•
guin•i•ty
pro•hi•bi•tion
pro•hi•bi•tion•ar•y
pro•hi•bi•tion•ist
pro•hib•i•tive
pro•hib•i•tive•ness
pro•hib•i•tor or pro•
hib•it•er
pro•hib•i•tor•i•ly
pro•hib•i•to•ry
prohibitory in•junc•
tion
proj•ect¹ n.
pro•ject² v.
pro•jec•tion
pro•jet French
pro•lep•sis n., pl.
pro•lep•ses
pro•le•tar•i•an
pro•le•tar•i•at
pro•lif•er•ate v.,
pro•lif•er•at•ed,
pro•lif•er•at•ing
pro•lif•er•a•tion
pro•lif•er•a•tive
pro•lif•ic
pro•lif•i•ca•cy
pro•lif•i•cal•ly
pro•li•fic•i•ty
pro•lif•ic•ness
pro•lix
pro•lix•i•ty
pro•lix•ly
pro•long
pro•lon•ga•tion
prom•is•cu•i•ty
pro•mis•cu•ous
pro•mis•cu•ous•ly
pro•mis•cu•ous•ness
prom•ise n., v.,
prom•ised, prom•
is•ing
prom•is•ee

prom•is•er (usual
spelling in nonlegal
contexts: cf. PROMISOR;
PROMISSOR)
prom•is•ing
prom•is•ing•ly
prom•i•sor (usual
spelling in legal con-
texts: cf. PROMISER;
PROMISSOR)
pro•mis•sor Latin. (a
term used in Roman
and civil law contexts:
cf. PROMISER; PROMISOR)
prom•is•so•ri•ly
prom•is•so•ry
promissory es•top•
pel
promissory note
promissory war•
ran•ty
pro•mot•a•bil•i•ty
pro•mot•a•ble
pro•mote v., pro•
mot•ed, pro•mot•
ing
pro•mot•er
promoting pros•ti•
tu•tion
pro•mo•tion
pro•mo•tion•al
prompt
prompt•ly
prompt•ness
prom•ul•gate v.,
prom•ul•gat•ed,
prom•ul•gat•ing
prom•ul•ga•tion
prom•ul•ga•tor
prong
pro•nounce v., pro•
nounced, pro•
nounc•ing
pronounce sen•tence
pro•nounce•a•ble
pro•nounce•ment

pro•nounc∘er
proof
proof of claim
proof of loss
proof of serv•ice
Prop. (Property)
prop∘a•gan∘da
pro•pen•si∘ty n., pl.
  pro•pen•si•ties
prop∘er
proper par∘ty
proper vice
pro•per∘dine Con-
  trolled Subst.
prop•er∘ly
prop•er•ty n., pl.
  prop•er•ties (citation
  form: **Prop.**)
property in•sur•ance
property right
property set•tle•
  ment
property tax
pro•phy•lac•tic
pro•phy•lac•ti•cal∘ly
pro•phy•lax∘is
pro•pi•ram Controlled
  Subst.
pro•po•nent
pro•por•tion
pro•por•tion∘al
proportional rep•re•
  sen•ta•tion
pro•por•tion•al∘i∘ty
pro•por•tion•al∘ly
proportionally e∘qual
pro•por•tion•ate
pro•por•tion•ate•
  ness
pro•pos•a∘ble
pro•pos∘al
pro•pose v., pro•
  posed, pro•pos•ing
pro•posed
proposed rule
pro•pos∘er

prop∘o•si•tion
prop∘o•si•tion∘al
pro•pos∘i•tus n., pl.
  pro•pos∘i∘ti
pro•pound
pro•pound∘er
pro•pri∘a per•so∘na
  Latin.
pro•pri•e•tar∘i∘ly
pro•pri•e•tar∘y adj.,
  n., pl. pro•pri•e•
  tar•ies See also Pty.
proprietary drug
proprietary in•for•
  ma•tion
proprietary lease
pro•pri•e•tor
pro•pri•e•to•ri∘al
pro•pri•e•to•ri∘al∘ly
pro•pri•e•tor•ship
pro•pri•e∘ty n., pl
  pro•pri•e•ties
pro•pri∘o ju∘re Latin.
proprio mo∘tu Latin.
proprio no•mi∘ne
  Latin.
pro•rat•a∘ble
pro•rate v., pro•
  rat∘ed, pro•rat•ing
pro•ra•tion
pro•ro•ga•tion
pro•rogue v., pro•
  rogued, pro•ro•
  guing
pro•scrib•a∘ble
pro•scribe v., pro•
  scribed, pro•scrib•
  ing (to condemn or
  prohibit; cf. prescribe)
pro•scrib∘er
pro•scrip•tion
pro•scrip•tive
pro•script•ive∘ly
pros∘e∘cut•
  a∘bil∘i∘ty
pros∘e∘cut•a∘ble

pros∘e∘cute v.,
  pros∘e∘cut∘ed,
  pros∘e∘cut•ing
pros∘e∘cut•ing at•
  tor•ney
prosecuting wit•ness
pros∘e∘cu•tion
pros∘e∘cu•tor
pros∘e∘cu•to•ri∘al
prosecutorial dis•cre•
  tion
prosecutorial mis•
  con•duct
pros∘e∘cu•to∘ry
pros∘e•cu•trix n., pl
  pros∘e•cu•tri•ces
pros•pect
pros•pect•ing
pro•spec•tive
prospective dam•
  ag∘es
pro•spec•tive∘ly
pro•spec•tive•ness
pros•pec•tor
pro•spec•tus n., pl.
  pro•spec•tus∘es
pros•per
pros•per∘i∘ty
pros•per•ous
pros•per•ous∘ly
pros•per•ous•ness
pros•ta•glan•din
pros•ti•tute n., v.,
  pros•ti•tut∘ed,
  pros•ti•tut•ing
pros•ti•tu•tion
pros•ti•tu•tor
pro•te•ase in•hib∘i•
  tor
pro•tect
pro•tect∘ed per•son
protected speech
pro•tect∘ee
pro•tect∘i•bil∘i∘ty
pro•tect∘i•ble
protectible work

pro•tec•tion
protection mon•ey
protection order
protection rack•et
pro•tec•tion•al
pro•tec•tion•ism
pro•tec•tion•ist
pro•tec•tion•is•tic
pro•tec•tive
protective cus•to•dy
protective or•der
protective tar•iff
protective trust
pro•tec•tive•ly
pro•tec•tive•ness
pro•tec•tor
pro•tec•tor•ate
pro•tein
pro•test
protest vote
pro•test•a•ble
prot•es•ta•tion
pro•test•er or pro•
  tes•tor
pro•test•ing•ly
pro•test•ive
pro•thon•o•tar•i•al
pro•thon•o•tar•y n.,
  pl. pro•thon•o•tar•
  ies
pro•to•col
pro•to•typ•al
pro•to•type
pro•to•typ•ic
pro•to•typ•i•cal
pro•to•typ•i•cal•ly
pro•tract
pro•tract•ed
pro•tract•ed•ly
pro•tract•ed•ness
pro•tract•i•ble
pro•trac•tive
prov. (provisional)
prov•a•bil•i•ty
prov•a•ble

prov•a•ble•ness
prov•a•bly
prove v., proved or
  prov•en, prov•ing
prov•er
pro•vid•a•ble
pro•vide v., pro•
  vid•ed, pro•vid•ing
pro•vid•ed
prov•i•dence
prov•i•den•cy
providency in•quir•y
prov•i•dent
prov•i•dent•ly
prov•i•dent•ness
prov•ince
pro•vi•sion
pro•vi•sion•al (cita-
  tion form: **prov.**)
provisional gov•ern•
  ment
provisional or•der
provisional re•lief
provisional rem•e•dy
pro•vi•sion•al•i•ty
pro•vi•sion•al•ly
pro•vi•sion•al•ness
pro•vi•so n., pl. pro•
  vi•sos
pro•vo•ca•teur
prov•o•ca•tion
prov•o•ca•tion•al
pro•voc•a•tive
pro•voc•a•tive•ly
pro•voc•a•tive•ness
pro•voke v., pro•
  voked, pro•vok•ing
pro•vok•er
pro•vost
provost court
pro•vost•ship
prox•i•mate
proximate cause
proximate dam•ag•es
prox•i•mate•ly
prox•i•mate•ness

prox•im•i•ty
prox•y n., pl. prox•ies
proxy do•nor
proxy fight
proxy state•ment
Pro•zac Trademark.
prtg. (printing)
pru•dence
pru•dent
prudent per•son rule
pru•den•tial
pru•den•ti•al•i•ty
pru•den•tial•ly
pru•den•tial•ness
pru•dent•ly
pru•ri•ence
pru•ri•en•cy
pru•ri•ent
prurient in•ter•est
pru•ri•ent•ly
P.S.C. (Public Service
  Commission)
pseu•do•nym
pseu•don•y•mous
pseu•don•y•mous•ly
pseu•don•y•mous•
  ness
pseu•do•science
pseu•do•sci•en•tif•ic
pseu•do•sci•en•
  tif•i•cal•ly
pseu•do•sci•en•tist
psil•o•cin (a hallucino-
  gen) See also PSILOCYN.
psil•o•cy•bin Con-
  trolled Subst.
psil•o•cyn Controlled
  Subst. (spelling in federal drug laws, pre-
  sumably for PSILOCIN)
psy•che
psy•che•del•ic
psychedelic drug
psychedelic ex•pe•ri•
  ence
psy•che•del•i•cal•ly

psy•chi•at•ric
psy•chi•at•ri•cal•ly
psy•chi•a•trist
psy•chi•a•try
psy•chic
psy•chi•cal•ly
psy•cho•ac•tive
psychoactive sub•stance
psy•cho•a•nal•y•sis
psy•cho•an•a•lyt•ic
psy•cho•an•a•lyt•i•cal
psy•cho•an•a•lyt•i•cal•ly
psy•cho•an•a•lyze v., psy•cho•an•a•lyzed, psy•cho•an•a•lyz•ing
psy•cho•bab•ble
psy•cho•dy•nam•ic
psy•cho•dy•nam•i•cal•ly
psy•cho•dy•nam•ics n., sing.
psy•cho•gen•ic (of mental origin: cf. PSY-CHOTOGENIC)
psychogenic am•ne•sia
psychogenic fugue
Psychol. (Psychological; Psychology)
psy•cho•log•i•cal (citation form: Psychol.)
psychological de•pend•ence
psychological test•ing
psychological war•fare
psy•chol•o•gist
psy•chol•o•gy n., pl. psy•chol•o•gies (citation form: Psychol.)
psy•cho•mo•tor

psychomotor ag•i•ta•tion
psy•cho•neu•ro•sis n., pl. psy•cho•neu•ro•ses
psy•cho•path
psy•cho•path•ic
psychopathic per•son•al•i•ty
psy•cho•path•o•log•ic
psy•cho•path•o•log•i•cal
psy•cho•path•o•log•i•cal•ly
psy•cho•pa•thol•o•gist
psy•cho•pa•thol•o•gy
psy•chop•a•thy n., pl. psy•chop•a•thies
psy•cho•phar•ma•co•log•ic
psy•cho•phar•ma•co•log•i•cal
psy•cho•phar•ma•co•log•i•cal•ly
psy•cho•phar•ma•col•o•gist
psy•cho•phar•ma•col•o•gy
psy•cho•phys•i•o•log•ic
psy•cho•phys•i•o•log•i•cal
psy•cho•phys•i•o•log•i•cal•ly
psy•cho•phys•i•ol•o•gist
psy•cho•phys•i•ol•o•gy
psy•cho•sis n., pl. psy•cho•ses
psy•cho•so•cial
psychosocial stres•sor
psy•cho•so•cial•ly
psy•cho•so•mat•ic

psy•cho•so•mat•i•cal•ly
psy•cho•sur•ger•y
psy•cho•ther•a•peu•tic
psy•cho•ther•a•peu•ti•cal•ly
psy•cho•ther•a•peu•tics n., sing.
psy•cho•ther•a•pist
psychotherapist-pa•tient priv•i•lege
psy•cho•ther•a•py n., pl. psy•cho•ther•a•pies
psy•chot•ic
psychotic de•ni•al
psychotic dis•or•der
psy•chot•i•cal•ly
psy•chot•o•gen
psy•chot•o•gen•ic (causing psychosis: cf. PSYCHOGENIC)
psy•chot•o•mi•met•ic
psy•cho•tro•pic
psychotropic drug
pt. (part)
PTP (publicly traded partnership)
PTSD (posttraumatic stress disorder)
Pty. (abbr. for Proprietary used in Australian company names)
Pub. (Public; Publishing)
pub•lic (citation form: Pub.)
public-ac•cess chan•nel
public-access tel•e•vi•sion
public ac•com•mo•da•tion
public ac•count•ant
public ac•count•ing

public act

public ad•min•is•tra•tion

public ad•min•is•tra•tor

public af•fairs

public as•sis•tance

public bill

public charge

public com•pa•ny

public con•tract

public con•ven•ience and ne•ces•si•ty

public cor•po•ra•tion

public debt

public de•fend•er

public do•main

public ease•ment

public en•e•my

public fig•ure

public fo•rum

public funds

public good

public health

public hear•ing

public hous•ing

public im•prove•ment

public in•de•cen•cy

public in•ter•est

public interest, con•ven•ience, and ne•ces•si•ty

public interest law

public in•ter•na•tion•al law

public in•tox•i•ca•tion

public lands

public law

public-li•a•bil•i•ty in•sur•ance

public life

public lim•it•ed com•pa•ny (p.l.c.)

public meet•ing

public ne•ces•si•ty

public no•tice

public notice ad•ver•tis•ing

public nui•sance

public of•fer•ing

public of•fice

public of•fic•er

public per•son•al•i•ty

public pol•i•cy

public prop•er•ty

public pros•e•cu•tor

public pur•pose

public rec•ord

public re•la•tions

public safe•ty

public sale

public sec•tor

public serv•ant

public serv•ice

Public Service Com•mis•sion (*citation forms:* **P.S.C.** as a judicial body; **Pub. Serv. Comm'n** as a party)

public-service cor•po•ra•tion

public stat•ute

public tri•al

public trust

public use

Public U•til•i•ties Com•mis•sion (*citation forms:* **P.U.C.** as a judicial body; **Pub. Util. Comm'n** as a party)

public u•til•i•ty

public ware•house

public wel•fare

public works

public wrong

pub•li•ca•tion

pub•li•cist

pub•lic•i•ty

publicity pic•ket•ing

pub•lic•ly

publicly held cor•po•ra•tion

publicly trad•ed part•ner•ship (PTP)

publicly traded stock

pub•lish

pub•lish•a•ble

pub•lish•er

pub•lish•ing (*citation form:* **Pub.** in periodical names; **Publ'g** in case names)

P.U.C. (Public Utilities Commission)

puff

puff•er

puff•ing

puff•ing•ly

pug•na•cious

pug•na•cious•ly

pug•na•cious•ness

pug•nac•i•ty

puis•ne *Law French.*

Pull•man ab•sten•tion

pul•mo•nar•y dis•ease

punc•ta•tim *Latin.*

punc•til•i•o *n., pl.* punc•til•i•os

punc•til•i•ous

punc•til•i•ous•ly

punc•til•i•ous•ness

punc•tu•al

punc•tu•al•i•ty

punc•tu•al•ly

pun•dit

pun•di•to•ry

pun•ish

pun•ish•a•bil•i•ty

pun•ish•a•ble

pun•ish•er

pun•ish•ment

pu•ni•tive

punitive dam•a•ges
pu•ni•tive•ly
pu•ni•tive•ness
pu•pil
pu•pil•lar•i•ty or
  pu•pi•lar•i•ty
pur au•tre vie *Law
  French.*
pur•chas•a•bil•i•ty
pur•chase *v.*, pur•
  chased, pur•chas•
  ing, *n.*
purchase mon•ey
  mort•gage
purchase money re•
  sult•ing trust
purchase or•der
pur•chas•er
purchaser for val•ue
pur•chas•ing pow•er
pure *adj.*, pur•er,
  pur•est
pure de•moc•ra•cy
pur•ga•tion
purge *v.*, purged,
  pur•ging, *n.*
purge•a•ble
purg•er
purg•ing
pu•ri•fi•ca•tion
pu•ri•fi•ca•to•ry
pu•ri•fied
pu•ri•fi•er
pu•ri•fy *v.*, pu•ri•
  fied, pu•ri•fy•ing

pu•rine
pu•ri•tan•oi•cal
pu•ri•tan•oi•cal•ly
pu•ri•tan•ism
pu•ri•ty
pur•loin
pur•loin•er
pur•port
pur•port•ed
pur•port•ed•ly
pur•pose *n.*, *v.*, pur•
  posed, pur•pos•ing
pur•pose•ful
pur•pose•ful•ly
pur•pose•ful•ness
pur•pose•ly
pur•pos•ive
pur•pos•ive•ly
pur•pos•ive•ness
pur•pres•ture
purse snatch•er
purse snatch•ing
pur•su•a•ble
pur•su•ance
pur•su•ant
pur•sue *v.*, pur•sued,
  pur•su•ing
pur•su•er
pur•suit
pursuit of hap•pi•
  ness
pur•vey
pur•vey•ance
pur•vey•or

pur•view
push
push•er
push•o•ver
push•y *adj.*,
  push•i•er, push•i•
  est
pu•sil•la•nim•i•ty
pu•sil•lan•i•mous
pu•sil•lan•i•mous•ly
put *v.*, put, put•ting,
  n.
put down *v.* (cf. PUT-
  DOWN)
put in is•sue
put op•tion
pu•ta•tive
putative fa•ther
putative mar•riage
putative spouse
pu•ta•tive•ly
put•down *n.* (cf. PUT
  DOWN)
pyr•a•mid
pyramid scheme
pyramid sell•ing
pyr•a•mid•ing
py•rim•i•dine
py•ro•ma•ni•a
py•ro•ma•ni•ac
py•ro•ma•ni•a•cal
pyr•o•val•er•one
  Controlled Subst.
Pyr•rhic vic•to•ry

Q

Q. (Quarterly)
Q clear•ance
Q-ra•tio
qa•di *n.*, pl. qa•dis
Q.B. (Queen's Bench)
Q.C. (Queen's Counsel)

Q.E.D. (quod erat de•
  monstrandum)
qq.v. See Q.V.
Q-TIP trust (qualified
  terminable interest
  property trust)
qua *English and Latin.*

Quaa•lude *Trademark.*
quack
quack•er•y *n.*, *pl.*
  quack•er•ies
quad•ren•ni•al
quad•ren•ni•al•ly
quad•ren•ni•um *n.*,

pl. quad•ren•ni•a, quad•ren•ni•ums

quae vi○de (qq.v.) *Latin.* See Q.V.

quae○re *Latin.*

quag•mire

qual○i•fi•a•ble

qual○i•fi•ca•tion

qual○i•fi•ca•to•ry

qual○i•fied

qualified de•ferred com•pen•sa•tion plan

qualified dis•claim•er

qualified es•tate

qualified fee

qualified in•come trust

qualified in•dorse•ment

qualified o•pin•ion

qualified pen•sion plan

qualified pre•re•tire•ment sur•vi•vor an•nu•i○ty

qualified priv○i•lege

qualified prop•er•ty

qualified pros•pect

qualified re•port

qualified small busi•ness

qualified stock op•tion

qualified ter•mi•na•ble in•ter•est prop•er○ty (Q-TIP) trust

qualified vot○er

qual○i•fied○ly

qual○i•fied•ness

qual○i•fy *v.,* qual○i•fied, qual○i•fy○ing

qualify as an ex•ec○u•tor

qualify as an ex•pert

qualify for tax-ex•empt sta○tus

qualify to do busi•ness

qual○i•ta•tive

qual○i•ta•tive•ly

qual○i•ty *n., pl.* qual○i•ties, *adj.*

quality as•sur•ance

quality au○dit

quality con•trol

quality of life *n.*

quality-of-life *adj.*

qualm

quan•da○ry *n., pl.* quan•da•ries

quan○do *Latin.*

quan○go *n., pl.* quan•gos

quan•ti•fi•a•ble

quan•ti•fi•a•bly

quan•ti•fi•ca•tion

quan•ti○fy *v.,* quan•ti•fied, quan•ti•fy•ing

quan•ti•ta•tive

quan•ti•ta•tive•ly

quan•ti•ta•tive•ness

quan•ti○ty *n., pl.* quan•ti•ties

quan•tum *n., pl.* quan○ta, *adj. English and Latin.*

quantum me•ru○it *Latin.*

quantum va•le•bant *Latin.*

quantum va•le•bat *Latin.*

quar•an•ti○a•ble

quar•an•tine *n., v.,* quar•an•tined, quar•an•tin•ing

quar•an•tin○er

qua○re *Latin.*

quare clau•sum fre•git *Latin.*

quare e○je•cit *Latin.*

quare im•pe•dit *Latin.*

quar•rel *n., v.,* quar•reled, quar•el•ing.

quar•rel○er

quar•rel•ing○ly

quar•rel•some

quar•rel•some○ly

quar•rel•some•ness

quar•ter

quarter ses•sions

quar•ter•age

quar•ter•ing of troops

quar•ter○ly *(citation form:* Q.*)*

quar•tile

quash

qua○si *English and Latin.*

quasi-au•ton○o•mous

quasi-com•mu•ni○ty prop•er○ty

quasi con•tract

quasi-contract *or* quasi-con•trac•tu○al sal•vage

quasi-con•trac•tu○al

quasi cor•po•ra•tion

quasi de•lict

quasi de•re•lict *n.*

quasi-derelict *adj.*

quasi ex con•trac•tu *Latin.*

quasi in rem *Latin.*

quasi in rem ac•tion

quasi in rem ju•ris•dic•tion

quasi-ju•di•cial

quasi-of•fi•cial

quasi-pub•lic cor•po•ra•tion

quasi-sus•pect clas•
si•fi•ca•tion
quasi-leg•is•la•tive
quay
quay•age
qua•ze•pam *Con-
trolled Subst.*
queen
Queen's Bench (*cita-
tion form:* Q.B.)
Queen's Coun•sel
(Q.C.)
quell
quell•a◦ble
quell◦er
quer◦u•lous
quer◦u•lous◦ly
quer◦u•lous◦ness
que◦ory *n., pl.* que•
ries, *v.,* que•ried,
que•ry•ing
que•ry•ing◦ly
quest
quest◦er
ques•tion
question of fact
question of law
ques•tion◦a•bil◦i◦ty
ques•tion•a◦ble
ques•tion•a◦ble•ness
ques•tion◦a•bly
ques•tion◦er
ques•tion•ing
ques•tion•ing◦ly
ques•tion•naire
questions pres•
ent◦ed
qui *Latin.*
qui tam *Latin.*
qui◦a *Latin.*

quia do•mi•nus re•
mi•sit cu•ri•am
Latin.
quia emp•to•res
Latin.
quia ti◦met *Latin.*
quib•ble *n., v.,* quib•
bled, quib•bling
quib•bler
quib•bling
quib•bling◦ly
quick
quick as•sets
quick ra◦tio
quick◦en
quick•en•ing
quick◦ie strike
quid *Latin.*
quid pro quo *n., pl*
quid pro quos
quid pro quo ha•
rass•ment
qui◦et
quiet en•joy•ment
quiet ti◦tle
qui•et•ing title
qui•e•tus *n., pl.* qui•
e•tus◦es
quin•tes•sence
quin•tes•sen•tial
quin•tes•sen•tial◦ly
quit *v.,* quit or (esp. in
sense of surrendering
premises) quit•ted,
quit•ting, *adj.*
quit•claim
quitclaim deed
quit•ta•ble
quit•tance
quit•ter

quix◦o•tic
quix◦o•ti•cal◦ly
quiz *v.,* quizzed, quiz•
zing, *n., pl.* quiz•zes
quo *Latin.*
quo a◦ni◦mo *Latin.*
quo ju◦re *Latin.*
quo mi◦nus *Latin.*
quo war•ran◦to *Latin.*
quod *Latin.*
quod e◦i de•for•
ce◦at *Latin.*
quod e◦rat de•mon•
stran•dum (Q.E.D.)
Latin.
quod per•mit•tat
Latin.
quod vi◦de (q.v.) *pl.*
quae vi◦de (qq.v.)
Latin
quo•rum *n., pl.* quo•
rums
quo◦ta
quota sys•tem
quot◦a•bil◦i◦ty
quot◦a•ble
quot◦a•bly
quo•ta•tion
quote *v.,* quot•ed,
quot•ing, *n.*
quot◦ed bid
quot◦er
quo•tient
quotient ver•dict
Qur◦'an *Arabic.* See
KORAN.
q.v. *pl.* **qq.v.** (which
see: from Latin *quod
vide, pl. quae vide*)

R

R. (Rule; Rules; Rex, Regina)

R&D (research and development)

R-rat•ed

ra•bo•bi *n.*, *pl.* rab•bis

rab•ble-rous•er

rab•ble-rous•ing

rab•oid

rab•id•o•i•ty

rab•id•o•ly

rab•id•ness

race

race cod•ing

race norm•ing

rac•o•e•meth•or•phan *Controlled Subst.*

rac•o•e•mor•a•mide *Controlled Subst.*

rac•o•e•mor•phan *Controlled Subst.*

ra•cial

racial dis•crim•i•na•tion

ra•cial•ly re•stric•tive cov•e•nant

rac•ism

rac•ist

rack

rack-rent[1] **or** rack rent *n.*

rack-rent[2] *v.*

rack-rent•er

rack•et

rack•et•eer

Racketeer In•flu•enced and Cor•rupt Or•gan•i•za•tions Act (RICO)

rack•e•teer•ing

ra•di•a•tion

rad•i•cal

rad•i•cal•ism

rad•i•cal•i•za•tion

rad•i•cal•ize *v.*, rad•i•cal•ized, rad•i•cal•iz•ing

rad•i•cal•ly

rad•i•cal•ness

ra•di•o•ac•tive

radioactive waste

ra•di•o•ac•tive•ly

ra•di•o•ac•tiv•i•ty

ra•di•o•im•mu•no•as•say (RIA)

raf•fle *n.*, *v.*, raf•fled, raf•fling

rage *n.*, *v.*, raged, rag•ing

rag•ing•ly

raid

raid•er

raid•ing

rail•age

rail•road[1] *n.* (*citation form:* **R.R.**)

railroad[2] *v.*, rail•road•ed, rail•road•ing

rail•way (*citation form:* **Ry.**)

rain•mak•er

rain•mak•ing

rais•a•ble

raise *v.*, raised, rais•ing, *n.* (to elevate: *cf.* RAZE)

raised check

rais•er

rais•ing por•tions

rai•son d'é•tat *n.*, *pl.* rai•sons d'é•tat *French.*

rai•son d'ê•tre *n.*, *pl.* rai•sons d'ê•tre *French.*

rake *v.*, raked, rak•ing

rake off *v.*

rake-off *n.*

rak•ish

rak•ish•ly

rak•ish•ness

ral•li•er

ral•ly *v.*, ral•lied, ral•ly•ing, *n.*, *pl.* ral•lies

ram•i•fi•ca•tion

ram•i•fy *v.*, ram•i•fied, ram•i•fy•ing

ram•page *n.*, *v.*, ram•paged, ram•pag•ing

ram•pag•er

ram•pan•cy

ramp•ant

ramp•ant•ly

ran•cor

ran•cored

ran•cor•ous

ran•cor•ous•ly

ran•cor•ous•ness

ran•dom

random am•pli•fied po•ly•mor•phic DNA (RAPD)

random match

random-match prob•a•bil•i•ty

ran•dom•ly

ran•dom•ness

range•land

rang•er

rank

rank and file *n.*

rank-and-file *adj.*

rank•ing

ran•kle *v.*, ran•kled, ran•kling

ran•sack

ran•sack•er

ran•som

ran•som•er
rap sheet
ra•pa•cious
ra•pa•cious•ly
ra•pa•cious•ness
ra•pac•i•ty
rape n., v., raped,
 rap•ing
rape shield law
rap•ine
rap•ist
rap•por•teur French.
rap•proche•ment
ras•cal
ras•cal•i•ty n., pl.
 ras•cal•i•ties
ras•cal•ly
rash
rash•ly
rash•ness
ra•sure
rat•a•bil•i•ty
rat•a•ble
ratable prop•er•ty
rat•a•ble•ness
rat•a•bly
rate n., v., rat•ed,
 rat•ing
rate base
rate of ex•change
rate of in•ter•est
rate of re•turn
rate-of-re•turn price
 reg•u•la•tion
rate reg•u•la•tion
rate•mak•ing
rate•pay•er
rate•pay•ing
rat•er
rath•er
rat•i•fi•ca•tion
rat•i•fi•er
rat•i•fy v., rat•i•fied,
 rat•i•fy•ing
rat•ing

ra•tio¹ n., pl. ra•tios
 English. (quotient of
 two numbers)
ra•ti•o² n., pl. ra•ti•
 o•nes *Latin.* (reason;
 rationale)
ra•ti•o de•ci•den•di
 Latin.
ra•ti•o le•gis *Latin.*
ra•tion
ra•tion•al
rational ba•sis test
ra•tion•ale
ra•tion•al•ism
ra•tion•al•ist
ra•tion•al•i•ty
ra•tion•al•i•za•tion
ra•tion•al•ize v., ra•
 tion•al•ized, ra•
 tion•al•iz•ing
ra•tion•al•iz•er
ra•tion•al•ly
rat•tle v., rat•tled,
 rat•tling, n.
rat•trap
rau•cous
rau•cous•ly
rau•cous•ness
rav•age v., rav•aged,
 rav•ag•ing, n.
rave v., raved, rav•
 ing, n., adj.
rav•ing
rav•ing•ly
rav•ish
rav•ish•er
rav•ish•ment
ravishment de gard
ravishment of ward
raze v., razed, raz•ing
 (to tear down: cf.
 RAISE)
raz•er
Rd. (Road)
re *Latin.*

re•a n., pl. re•ae
 Latin.
re•ac•quire v., re•ac•
 quired, re•ac•quir•
 ing
re•ac•quired stock
re•ac•qui•si•tion
re•act
re•ac•tion
reaction for•ma•tion
re•ac•tion•al
re•ac•tion•al•ly
re•ac•tion•ar•y adj.,
 n., pl. re•ac•tion•
 ar•ies
re•ac•ti•vate
re•ac•ti•va•tion
re•ac•tive
re•ac•tive•ly
re•ac•tive•ness
re•ac•tor
read v., read, read•
 ing, n.
read•a•bil•i•ty
read•a•ble
read•er
read•i•ly
read•i•ness
read•ing
reading dis•or•der
re•ad•ju•di•cate v.,
 re•ad•ju•di•cat•ed,
 re•ad•ju•di•cat•ing
re•ad•ju•di•ca•tion
re•ad•just
re•ad•just•a•ble
re•ad•just•er
re•ad•just•ment
re•ad•mit v., re•ad•
 mit•ted, re•ad•mit•
 ting
re•ad•mit•tance
read•y adj.,
 read•i•er, read•i•
 est, v., read•ied,
 read•y•ing, n., interj.

ready, wil·ling, and
a·ble
re·af·firm
re·af·fir·ma·tion
reaffirmation a·gree·
ment
re·al
real ac·tion
real as·set
real cov·e·nant
real de·fense
real ear·nings
real es·tate
real estate a·gent
real estate brok·er
real estate in·vest·
ment trust (REIT)
real estate mort·gage
in·vest·ment con·
duit (REMIC)
real estate tax
real ev·i·dence
real in·come
real par·ty in in·ter·
est
real prop·er·ty
real wa·ges
re·al·ien·ate v., re·
al·ien·at·ed, re·al·
ien·at·ing
re·al·ien·a·tion
re·a·lign
re·a·lign·ment
re·al·ism
re·al·ist
re·al·ist·ic
re·al·ist·i·cal·ly
re·al·i·ty n., pl. re·
al·i·ties the state of
being real; a real
thing: cf. REALTY)
re·al·iz·a·bil·i·ty
re·al·iz·a·ble
realizable val·ue
re·al·iz·a·bly
re·al·i·za·tion

re·al·ize v., re·al·
ized, re·al·iz·ing
re·al·le·ga·tion
re·al·lege v., re·al·
leged, re·al·leg·ing
re·al·lot·ment
re·al·ly
realm
re·al·po·li·tik German.
re·al·po·li·tik·er
Re·al·tor Service
Mark.
re·al·ty (land and
things attached to it:
cf. REALITY)
re·an·a·lyze v., re·
an·a·lyzed, re·
an·a·lyz·ing
re·ap·point
re·ap·point·ment
re·ap·por·tion
re·ap·por·tion·ment
re·ap·prais·al
re·ap·praise v., re·
ap·praised, re·ap·
prais·ing
re·ap·pro·pri·ate v.,
re·ap·pro·pri·
at·ed, re·ap·pro·
pri·at·ing
re·ap·pro·pri·a·tion
rear-end v.
re·ar·gue v., re·ar·
gued, re·ar·gu·ing
re·ar·gu·ment
re·arm
rea·son
reason of state
rea·son·a·ble
reasonable be·lief
reasonable care
reasonable com·pen·
sa·tion
reasonable doubt
reasonable force

reasonable man
reasonable man
stand·ard
reasonable mar·i·ner
reasonable no·tice
reasonable per·son
reasonable person
stand·ard
reasonable re·li·ance
reasonable val·ue
reasonable vic·tim
stand·ard
reasonable wom·an
stand·ard
rea·son·a·ble·ness
rea·son·a·bly
reasonably fore·see·
a·ble
reasonably pru·dent
mar·i·ner
reasonably pru·dent
per·son
rea·soned
reasoned de·ci·
sion-mak·ing
rea·son·ing
re·as·sert
re·as·ser·tion
re·as·sess
re·as·sess·ment
re·as·sur·ance
re·as·sure v., re·as·
sured, re·as·sur·ing
re·as·sur·er
re·as·sur·ing·ly
re·at·tach·ment
re·at·trib·ute v., re·
at·trib·ut·ed, re·
at·trib·ut·ing
re·at·tri·bu·tion
re·au·dit
re·au·thor·i·za·tion
re·au·thor·ize v., re·
au·thor·ized, re·
au·thor·iz·ing
re·bat·a·ble

re•bate n., v., re•
bat∘ed, re•bat•ing
re•bat∘er
re∘bel[1] v., re•belled,
re•bel•ling
reb∘el[2] n., adj.
re•bel•lion
re•bel•lious
re•bel•lious∘ly
re•bel•lious•ness
re∘bid v., re∘bid, re•
bid•ding, n.
re•birth
re•born
re•buff
re•build v., re•built,
re•build•ing
re•buk∘a•ble
re•buke v., re•buked,
re•buk•ing, n.
re•buk∘er
re•buk•ing∘ly
re∘bus sic stan•ti•bus
Latin.
re∘but v., re•but•ted,
re•but•ting
re•but∘ta•ble
rebuttable pre•sump•
tion
re•but∘tal
rebuttal ev∘i•dence
re•but•ter
Rec. (Record
re•cal•ci•trance
re•cal•ci•tran∘cy
re•cal•ci•trant
re•call
re•call∘a•ble
re•cant
re•can•ta•tion
re•cant∘er
re•cap∘i•tal∘i•za•
tion
re•cap∘i•tal•ize v.,
re•cap∘i•tal•ized,
re•cap∘i•tal•iz•ing

re•ca•pit∘u•late v.,
re•ca•pit∘u•lat∘ed,
re•ca•pit∘u•lat•ing
re•ca•pit∘u•la•tive
re•ca•pit∘u•la•to∘ry
re•cap•tion
re•cap•tur∘a•ble
re•cap•ture v., re•
cap•tured, re•cap•
tur•ing, n.
re•cede v. re•ced∘ed,
re•ced•ing
re•ceipt
re•ceipt∘or
re•ceiv∘a•ble
re•ceive v., re•ceived,
re•ceiv•ing
re•ceived-for-ship•
ment bill of lad•ing
re•ceiv∘er
receiver gen∘er∘al n.,
pl. re•ceiv•ers gen•
eral
receiver pen•den∘te
li∘te
re•ceiv•er•ship
re•ceiv•ing sto•len
prop•er∘ty
re•cen∘cy
re•cent
re•cent∘ly
re•cent•ness
re•cep•tion
re•cep•tive
re•cep•tive∘ly
re•cep•tive•ness
re•cep•tiv∘i∘ty
re•cer•ti•fi•ca•tion
re•cer•ti•fy v., re•
cer•ti•fied, re•cer•
ti•fy•ing
re•cess
re•ces•sion
re•ces•sion∘al (per-
taining to a recess: cf.
RECESSIONARY

re•ces•sion•ar∘y
(pertaining to an eco-
nomic recession: cf.
RECESSIONAL
re•ces•sive trait
re•cid∘i•vate v., re•
cid∘i•vat∘ed, re•
cid∘i•vat•ing
re•cid∘i•vism
re•cid∘i•vist
re•cid∘i•vis•tic
re•cip∘i•ent
re•cip•ro•cal
reciprocal ben∘e•fi•
ci∘ar•ies
reciprocal deal•ing
reciprocal in•sur•ance
reciprocal neg∘a•tive
ease•ment
reciprocal trusts
reciprocal wills
re•cip•ro•cal∘ly
re•cip•ro•cate v., re•
cip•ro•cat∘ed, re•
cip•ro•cat•ing
re•cip•ro•ca•tion
re•cip•ro•ca•tor
re•cip•roc∘i∘ty
reciprocity a∘gree•
ment
re•cit∘a•ble
re•cit∘al
rec∘i•ta•tion
re•cite v., re•cit∘ed,
re•cit•ing
re•cit∘er
reck•less
reckless dis•re•gard
reckless driv•ing
reckless en•dan•ger•
ment
reckless hom∘i•cide
reck•less∘ly
reck•less•ness
reck∘on
reck•on•ing

re-claim (to seek to recover possession of)

re•claim (to make usable or profitable)

re•claim•a•ble

re•claim•er

re•cla•ma•tion

re•clas•si•fi•ca•tion

re•clas•si•fy v., re•clas•si•fied, re•clas•si•fy•ing

rec•luse

re•cod•i•fi•ca•tion

re•cod•i•fy v., re•cod•i•fied, re•cod•i•fy•ing

rec•og•ni•tion

recognition of judg•ments

recognition pick•et•ing

rec•og•ni•tion•al

re•cog•ni•tor

re•cog•niz•a•bil•i•ty

re•cog•niz•a•ble

re•cog•niz•a•bly

re•cog•ni•zance

rec•og•nize v., rec•og•nized, rec•og•niz•ing

recognized mar•ket

re•cog•ni•zee

rec•og•niz•er (one who recognizes: cf. RE-COGNIZOR)

re•cog•ni•zor (one who enters into a recognizance: cf. RECOGNIZER)

re-col•lect (to gather up again

rec•ol•lect (to call to mind

rec•ol•lec•tion

re•com•bi•nant DNA

re•com•bi•na•tion

rec•om•mend

rec•om•men•da•tion

rec•om•mend•a•to•ry

re•com•mit v., re•com•mit•ted, re•com•mit•ting

re•com•mit•ment

re•com•mit•tal

rec•om•pen•sa•ble

rec•om•pense v., rec•om•pensed, rec•om•pens•ing, n.

rec•om•pens•er

re•com•pu•ta•tion

re•com•pute v., re•com•put•ed, re•com•put•ing

rec•on•cil•a•bil•i•ty

rec•on•cil•a•ble

rec•on•cil•a•bly

rec•on•cile v., rec•on•ciled, rec•on•cil•ing

rec•on•cil•er

rec•on•cil•i•a•tion

rec•on•cil•i•a•to•ry

rec•on•cil•ing

rec•on•cil•ing•ly

rec•on•dite

rec•on•dite•ly

rec•on•dite•ness

re•con•duct

re•con•duc•tion

re•con•firm

re•con•fir•ma•tion

re•con•nais•sance

re•con•noi•ter

re•con•sid•er

re•con•sid•er•a•tion

reconsideration en banc

re•con•sign

re•con•sign•ment

re•con•sti•tute v.,

re•con•sti•tut•ed, re•con•sti•tut•ing

re•con•struct

re•con•struct•i•ble

re•con•struc•tion (the act of reconstructing)

Re•con•struc•tion (post–Civil War period)

re•con•struc•tive

re•con•vene v., re•con•vened, re•con•ven•ing

re•con•ven•tion

re•con•ver•sion

re•con•vert

re•con•vert•er

re•con•vey

re•con•vey•ance

rec•ord[1] n., adj. (citation form: Rec.)

re•cord[2] v.

rec•ord date

rec•ord no•tice

rec•ord own•er

rec•ord pi•ra•cy

rec•ord ti•tle

re•cord•a•ble

re•cor•da•tion

re•cord•ed rec•ol•lec•tion

re•cord•er

recorder of deeds

re•cord•ing

recording sec•re•tar•y

recording stat•ute

rec•ord•keep•ing

re-count (to count again)

re•count (to narrate)

re•coup

re•coup•a•ble

re•coup•ment

re•course

re•cov•er (to cover
again)
re•cov•er (to obtain
judicially; to get back)
re•cov•er•a•bil•i•ty
re•cov•er•a•ble
re•cov•ered
mem•o•ry
re•cov•er•or
re•cov•er•y n., pl.
re•cov•er•ies
rec•re•ance
rec•re•an•cy
rec•re•ant
rec•re•ant•ly
rec•re•a•tion
rec•re•a•tion•al
recreational drug
recreational drug use
recreational use
re•crim•i•nal•i•za•
tion
re•crim•i•nal•ize v., re•
crim•i•nal•ized,
re•crim•i•nal•iz•ing
re•crim•i•nate v., re•
crim•i•nat•ed, re•
crim•i•nat•ing
re•crim•i•na•tion
re•crim•i•na•tive
re•crim•i•na•tor
re•crim•i•na•to•ry
re•cross
re•cross-ex•am•i•
na•tion or recross
ex•am•i•na•tion
re•cruit
re•cruit•a•ble
re•cruit•er
re•cruit•ment
rec•ti•fi•a•ble
rec•ti•fi•ca•tion
rec•ti•fi•er
rec•ti•fy v., rec•ti•
fied, rec•ti•fy•ing
rec•ti•tude

rec•ti•tu•di•nous
rec•ti•tu•din•ous•ly
rec•to Latin.
rec•tum n., pl. rec•ta
Latin.
re•cu•per•ate v., re•
cu•per•at•ed, re•
cu•per•at•ing
re•cu•per•a•tion
re•cu•per•a•tive
re•cur v., re•curred,
re•cur•ring
re•cur•rence
re•cur•rent
re•cur•rent•ly
re•cur•ring
re•cur•ring•ly
re•cus•al
re•cuse v., re•cused,
re•cus•ing
re•cy•cla•bil•i•ty
re•cy•cla•ble
re•cy•cle v., re•cy•
cled, re•cy•cling
re•cy•cler
red-hand•ed
red-hand•ed•ly
red-hand•ed•ness
red her•ring
red-her•ring pro•
spec•tus
red-light dis•trict
red tape
re•dact
re•dac•tion
re•dac•tion•al
re•dac•tor
red•dend•um Latin.
re•deem
re•deem•a•bil•i•ty
re•deem•a•ble
redeemable bond
redeemable se•cu•
ri•ty
re•deem•a•bly
re•deem•er

re•deem•ing
re•def•i•ni•tion
re•de•liv•er
re•de•liv•er•y n., pl.
re•de•liv•er•ies
redelivery bond
re•de•mise n., v. re•
de•mised, re•de•
mis•ing
re•demp•tion
redemption pe•ri•od
redemption price
re•demp•tive
re•demp•tive•ly
re•demp•to•ry
re•de•ploy
re•de•ploy•ment
re•de•pos•it
re•de•ter•mi•na•
tion
re•de•ter•mine v.,
re•de•ter•mined,
re•de•ter•min•ing
re•de•vel•op
re•de•vel•op•er
re•de•vel•op•ment
red•hi•bi•tion
red•hib•i•to•ry
re•di•rect
redirect ex•am•i•na•
tion
re•di•rec•tion
re•dis•count
rediscount rate
re•dis•seise v., re•
dis•seised, re•dis•
seis•ing
re•dis•sei•sin
re•dis•sei•sor
re•dis•trib•ute v., re•
dis•trib•ut•ed, re•
dis•trib•ut•ing
re•dis•tri•bu•tion
re•dis•tri•bu•tion•al
re•dis•trib•u•tive
re•dis•trict

red•line v., red•lined, red•lin•ing
red•lin•er
red•lin•ing
re•dou•ble v., re•dou•bled, re•dou•bling
re•doubt•a•ble
re•doubt•a•ble•ness
re•doubt•a•bly
re•doubt•ed
re•dound
re•draft
re•dress
re•dress•a•ble
re•dress•er
re•duce v., re•duced, re•duc•ing
reduced paid-up in•sur•ance
re•duc•i•bil•i•ty
re•duc•i•ble
re•duc•i•bly
re•duc•ti•o ad ab•sur•dum Latin.
re•duc•tion
reduction in force
reduction in•to pos•ses•sion
reduction to prac•tice
re•duc•tion•ism
re•duc•tion•ist
re•duc•tion•is•tic
re•duc•tive
re•duc•tive•ly
re•duc•tive•ness
re•duc•tiv•ism
re•duc•tiv•ist
re•dun•dan•cy n., pl. re•dun•dan•cies
re•dun•dant
re•dun•dant•ly
re•dux
Re•dux Trademark.
re•ed•u•cate v., re•

ed•u•cat•ed, re•ed•u•cat•ing
re•ed•u•ca•tion
re•ed•u•ca•tive
re•em•pha•size v., re•em•pha•sized, re•em•pha•siz•ing
re•en•act
re•en•act•ment
reenactment rule
re•en•gin•eer
re•en•gin•eer•ing
re•en•list
re•en•list•ment
re•en•ter
re•en•trant
re•en•try n, pl re•en•tries
re•es•tab•lish
re•es•tab•lish•ment
reeve
re•ex•am•in•a•ble
re•ex•am•i•na•tion
re•ex•am•ine v., re•ex•am•ined, re•ex•am•in•ing
re•ex•am•in•er
re•ex•change n., v. re•ex•changed, re•ex•chang•ing
Ref. (Referee; Refining)
re•feoff•ment
re•ofer v., re•ferred, re•fer•ring
ref•er•a•ble
ref•er•ee (Ref.)
ref•er•ence
ref•er•en•dum¹ n., pl. ref•er•en•dums (a vote on a measure submitted to the peo•ple)
referendum² n., pl. ref•er•en•da (a measure submitted to the people for a vote)

re•fer•ral
re•fer•rer
re•fin•a•ble
re•fi•nance v., re•fi•nanced, re•fi•nanc•ing
re•fi•nanc•ing
re•fine v., re•fined, re•fin•ing
re•fine•ment
re•fin•er
re•fin•ing (citation form: **Ref.**)
re•flect
re•flec•tion
re•flec•tive
re•flex
re•flex•ive
re•fo•cus v., re•fo•cused, re•fo•cus•ing
re•form
re•form•a•bil•i•ty
re•form•a•ble
ref•or•ma•tion
re•form•a•to•ry n., pl. re•form•a•to•ries
re•form•er
re•frain
re•fresh
re•fresh•er
re•fresh•er course
ref•uge
ref•u•gee
re•fund
refund an•nu•i•ty
re•fund•a•bil•i•ty
re•fund•a•ble
re•fund•er
re•fund•ment
re•fus•a•ble
re•fus•al
refusal to deal
re•fuse¹ v., re•fused, re•fus•ing

ref•use² *n.*

re•fus•er

re•fut•a•bil•i•ty

re•fut•a•ble

re•fut•a•bly

ref•u•ta•tion

re•fute *v.*, re•fut•ed, re•fut•ing

re•fut•er

Reg. (Register; Registered; Regulation; Regulatory)

Reg. U.S. Pat. & Tm. Off. (Registered U.S. Patent and Trademark Office)

re•gain

re•gain•a•ble

re•gal

re•gal•i•ty *n.*, re•gal•i•ties

re•gal•ly

re•gal•ness

re•gard

re•gard•ing

re•gard•less

re•gen•cy *n., pl.* re•gen•cies, *adj.*

re•gent

reg•i•cid•al

reg•i•cide

re•gime

reg•i•men

reg•i•ment

reg•i•men•ta•tion

re•gi•na (R.) *n., pl.* re•gi•nae *Latin.*

re•gi•nal

re•gion

re•gion•al (*citation form:* **Reg'l**)

re•gion•al•ism

re•gion•al•ist

re•gion•al•is•tic

reg•is•ter (*citation form:* **Reg.**)

register of deeds

register of ships

register of wills

register of writs

reg•is•tered (reg.)

registered bond

registered check

registered let•ter

registered mail

registered rep•re•sent•a•tive

registered se•cu•ri•ty

registered trade•mark

Registered U.S. Pat•ent and Trade•mark Of•fice (Reg. U.S. Pat. & Tm. Off.)

registered vot•er

reg•is•tra•bil•i•ty

reg•is•tra•ble

reg•is•trant

reg•is•trar

registrar of deeds

reg•is•tra•tion

registration state•ment

reg•is•try *n., pl.* reg•is•tries

registry of deeds

Reg'l (Regional)

reg•nal

re•grate *v.*, re•grat•ed, re•grat•ing

re•grat•er

re•grat•ing

re•gress

re•gres•sion

re•gres•sive

regressive tax

re•gres•sive•ly

re•gres•sive•ness

re•gres•sor

re•gret *v.*, re•gret•ted, re•gret•ting

re•gret•ful

re•gret•ful•ly

re•gret•ful•ness

re•gret•ta•ble

re•gret•ta•ble•ness

re•gret•ta•bly

re•group

reg•u•la•ble

reg•u•lar

regular check•ing ac•count

regular course of busi•ness

regular meet•ing

regular on its face

regular ses•sion

reg•u•lar•i•ty

reg•u•lar•ize *v.*, reg•u•lar•ized, reg•u•lar•iz•ing

reg•u•lar•ly

reg•u•late *v.*, reg•u•lat•ed, reg•u•lat•ing

reg•u•lat•ed in•dus•try

regulated in•vest•ment com•pa•ny

reg•u•la•tion (*citation form:* **Reg.**)

reg•u•la•tor

reg•u•la•to•ry (*citation form:* **Reg.**)

regulatory a•gen•cy

regulatory crime

regulatory of•fense

regulatory tak•ing

re•ha•bil•i•tate *v.*, re•ha•bil•i•tat•ed, re•ha•bil•i•tat•ing

re•ha•bil•i•ta•tion

re•ha•bil•i•ta•tive

re•ha•bil•i•ta•tor

re•hear *v.*, re•heard, re•hear•ing

re•hear•ing (*citation form:* **reh'g**)

rehearing en banc

reh'g (rehearing)
re•hire v., re•hired,
 re•hir•ing, n.
re•hos•pi•tal•i•za•
 tion
re•hos•pi•tal•ize v.,
 re•hos•pi•tal•ized,
 re•hos•pi•tal•iz•
 ing
re•house v., re•
 housed, re•hous•ing
reign
re•ig•nite v., re•ig•
 nit•ed, re•ig•nit•
 ing
re•ig•ni•tion
re•im•burs○a•ble
re•im•burse v., re•
 im•bursed, re•im•
 burs•ing
re•im•burse•ment
re•im•burs○er
re•im•pose v., re•im•
 posed, re•im•pos•
 ing
re•im•po•si•tion
re•im•pris○on
re•im•pris•on•ment
re•in•cor•po•rate v.,
 re•in•cor•po•
 rat○ed, re•in•cor•
 po•rat•ing
re•in•cor•po•ra•tion
re•in•cur v., re•in•
 curred, re•in•cur•
 ring
re•in•dict
re•in•dict•ment
re•in•dorse v., re•in•
 dorsed, re•in•dors•
 ing
re•in•dorse•ment
re•in•force v., re•in•
 forced, re•in•forc•
 ing
re•in•force•ment
re•in•forc○er

re•in•state v., re•in•
 stat○ed, re•in•stat•
 ing
re•in•state•ment
reinstatement pick•
 et•ing
re•in•sti•tute v., re•
 in•sti•tut○ed, re•
 in•sti•tut•ing
re•in•sti•tu•tion
re•in•sur•ance
re•in•sure v., re•in•
 sured, re•in•sur•ing
re•in•sur○er
re•in•ter•pret
re•in•ter•pre•ta•tion
re•in•ter•view
re•in•tro•duce v., re•
 in•tro•duced, re•in•
 tro•duc•ing
re•in•tro•duc•tion
re•in•vent
re•in•ven•tion
re•in•vest
re•in•ves•ti•gate v.,
 re•in•ves•ti•
 gat○ed, re•in•ves•
 ti•gat•ing
re•in•ves•ti•ga•tion
re•in•vest•ment
re•is•su○a•ble
re•is•sue n., v., re•is•
 sued, re•is•su•ing
REIT (real estate invest-
 ment trust)
re•it•er•a○ble
re•it•er•ate v., re•it•
 er•at○ed, re•it•er•
 at•ing
re•it•er○a•tion
re•it•er○a•tive
re•ject
re•ject•a○ble
re•ject○ee
re•ject○er
re•jec•tion

re•jec•tive
re•join
re•join•der
Rel. (Relations) See also
 EX REL.
re•lapse v., re•lapsed,
 re•laps•ing
re•laps○er
re•late v., re•lat○ed,
 re•lat•ing
re•lat○ed
related com•pa○ny
related par○ty
related party trans•
 ac•tion
related per•son
re•lat•ed•ness
re•lat○er (a narrator:
 cf. RELATOR)
re•la•tion
relation back
re•la•tions (citation
 form: Rel.)
re•la•tion•ship
rel○a•tive
rel○a•tive•ly
rel○a•tive•ness
rel○a•tiv•ism
rel○a•tiv○i•ty
re•la•tor (an inform-
 ant at whose instance
 an action is com-
 menced: cf. RELATER)
re•la•trix n., pl. re•
 la•tri•ces
re•lax•ant
re•lax○a•ti○o n., pl.
 re•lax○a•ti•o•nes
 Latin.
re•leas•a○bil○i•ty
re•leas•a○ble
re-lease v., re-leased,
 re-leas•ing, n. (to
 lease anew; a new
 lease)
re•lease v., re•leased,

re•leas•ing, *n.* (to let
go; a letting go)
release on own re•
cog•ni•zance (ROR)
re•leas•ee
re•leas•er (one who
lets go of anything: cf.
RELEASER)
re•lea•sor (one who
gives up a right or
claim against another:
cf. RELEASER)
rel•o•e•ga•ble
rel•o•e•gate *v.*,
rel•o•e•gat•ed,
rel•o•e•gat•ing
rel•o•e•ga•tion
re•lent
re•lent•less
re•lent•less•ly
re•lent•less•ness
rel•o•e•vance
rel•o•e•van•cy
rel•o•e•vant
relevant mar•ket
rel•o•e•vant•ly
re•li•a•bil•i•ty
re•li•a•ble
re•li•a•bly
re•li•ance
re•li•ant
re•li•ant•ly
re•li•cense *v.*, re•li•
censed, re•li•cens•
ing
rel•ict
re•lic•tion
re•lief
re•lieve *v.*, re•lieved,
re•liev•ing
re•li•gion
re•li•gi•os•i•ty
re•li•gious
religious law
religious test
re•li•gious•ly

re•li•gious•ness
re•lin•quish
re•lin•quish•er
re•lin•quish•ment
re•lit•i•gate *v.*, re•
lit•i•gat•ed, re•
lit•i•gat•ing
re•lit•i•ga•tion
re•live *v.*, re•lived,
re•liv•ing
re•lo•cate *v.*, re•lo•
cat•ed, re•lo•cat•
ing
re•lo•ca•tion
re•luc•tance
re•luc•tant (unwilling;
disinclined: cf. RETI•
CENT)
re•luc•tant•ly
re•ly *v.*, re•lied, re•
ly•ing
rem *Latin.*
re•main
re•main•der
re•main•der•man *n.*,
pl. re•main•der•
men
re•mains *n.pl.*
re•mand
re•mar•gin
re•mark
re•mark•a•ble
re•mark•a•ble•ness
re•mark•a•bly
re•mar•riage
re•mar•ry *v.*, re•
mar•ried, re•mar•
ry•ing
re•me•di•a•ble
re•me•di•a•ble•ness
re•me•di•a•bly
re•me•di•al
remedial leg•is•la•
tion
remedial stat•ute
re•me•di•al•ly

re•me•di•a•tion
re•me•di•less
rem•e•dy *n.*, *pl.*
rem•e•dies, *v.*,
rem•e•died,
rem•e•dy•ing
re•mem•ber
re•mem•ber•er
re•mem•brance
re•mem•branc•er
REMIC (real estate
mortgage investment
conduit)
rem•i•fen•ta•nil *Con-
trolled Subst.*
re•mind
re•mind•er
rem•i•nis•cent
rem•i•nis•cent•ly
re•mise *v.*, re•mised,
re•mis•ing
remise, re•lease, and
quit•claim
re•miss
re•mis•sion
re•miss•ly
re•miss•ness
re•mit *v.*, re•mit•ted,
re•mit•ting, *n.*
re•mit•ta•ble
re•mit•tance
re•mit•tee
re•mit•ter
re•mit•ti•tur *Latin.*
re•mon•strance
re•mon•strant
re•mon•strate *v.*, re•
mon•strat•ed, re•
mon•strat•ing
re•mon•strat•ing•ly
re•mon•stra•tion
re•mon•stra•tive
re•mon•stra•tive•ly
re•mon•stra•tor
re•morse
re•morse•ful

re•morse•ful•ly
re•morse•ful•ness
re•morse•less
re•morse•less•ly
re•morse•less•ness
re•mote *adj.*, re•
mot•er, re•mot•est,
n.
remote cause
remote dam•ag•es
re•mote•ly
re•mote•ness
re•mov•a•bil•i•ty
re•mov•a•ble
re•mov•al
removal case
re•move *v.*, re•
moved, re•mov•ing,
n.
re•mov•er
re•mu•ner•a•bil•i•ty
re•mu•ner•a•ble
re•mu•ner•a•bly
re•mu•ner•ate *v.*, re•
mu•ner•at•ed, re•
mu•ner•at•ing
re•mu•ner•a•tion
re•mu•ner•a•tive
re•mu•ner•a•tive•
ness
re•mu•ner•a•tor
rend *v.*, rent, rend•
ing
ren•der
ren•der•a•ble
ren•der•er
ren•dez•vous *n.*, *pl.*
ren•dez•vous, *v.*,
ren•dez•voused,
ren•dez•vous•ing
rend•i•ble
ren•di•tion
ren•e•gade
re•nege *v.*, re•neged,
re•neg•ing
re•neg•er

re•ne•go•ti•a•ble
renegotiable-rate
mort•gage
re•ne•go•ti•ate *v.*,
re•ne•go•ti•at•ed,
re•ne•go•ti•at•ing
re•ne•go•ti•a•tion
re•new
re•new•a•bil•i•ty
re•new•a•ble
renewable en•er•gy
renewable re•source
re•new•a•bly
re•new•al
renewal lease
re•new•er
re•no•ti•fi•ca•tion
re•no•ti•fy *v.*, re•
no•ti•fied, re•no•
ti•fy•ing
re•nounce *v.*, re•
nounced, re•nounc•
ing
re•nounce•a•ble
re•nounce•ment
re•nounc•er
re•nown
re•nowned
rent
rent-a-judge
rent charge *n.*, *pl.*
rents charge or rent
charg•es
rent con•trol
rent-free
rent seck *n.*, *pl.* rents
seck
rent serv•ice *n.*, *pl.*
rents serv•ice or
rent serv•ic•es
rent sta•bi•li•za•tion
rent strike
rent•a•bil•i•ty
rent•a•ble
rent•al
rent•er

re•nun•ci•a•ble
re•nun•ci•a•tion
re•nun•ci•a•tive
re•nun•ci•a•to•ry
ren•voi *French.*
re•o ab•sen•te *Latin.*
re•oc•cu•pa•tion
re•oc•cu•py *v.*, re•
oc•cu•pied, re•oc•
cu•py•ing
re•oc•cur *v.*, re•oc•
curred, re•oc•cur•
ring
re•oc•cur•rence
re•of•fend
re•of•fer
re•o•pen
re•o•pen•er clause
Reorg. (Reorganization)
re•or•gan•i•za•tion
(*citation form:* Reorg.)
reorganization plan
re•or•gan•ize *v.*, re•
or•gan•ized, re•or•
gan•iz•ing
re•or•ganiz•er
Rep. (Report; Reports;
Reporter; Representa-
tive)
re•pair
re•pair•a•bil•i•ty
re•pair•a•ble (fixable,
esp. by mechanical
means: cf. REPARABLE)
re•pair•er
rep•a•ra•ble (remedi-
able or compensable,
esp. through an action
at law: cf. REPAIRABLE)
rep•a•ra•tion
rep•a•ra•tions *n.pl.*
re•par•ti•tion
re•pa•tri•a•ble
re•pa•tri•ate *v.*, re•
pa•tri•at•ed, re•
pa•tri•at•ing, *n.*

re•pa•tri•a•tion
re•pay v., re•paid,
 re•pay•ing
re•pay•a•bil•i•ty
re•pay•a•ble
re•pay•ment
re•peal
re•peal•a•bil•i•ty
re•peal•a•ble
re•peal•er
re•peat
repeat of•fend•er
re•peat•a•bil•i•ty
re•peat•a•ble
re•peat•er
re•pel v., re•pelled,
 re•pel•ling
re•pel•lant n. (cf. RE-
 PELLENT)
re•pel•lent adj. (cf. RE-
 PELLANT)
re•pel•lent•ly
re•pent
re•pent•ance
re•pent•ant
re•pent•ant•ly
re•pent•er
re•per•cus•sion
re•per•cus•sive
re•pe•ti•tion (to peti-
 tion anew)
rep•e•ti•tion (the act
 of repeating; a civil
 law action for return
 of something given by
 mistake)
rep•e•ti•tious
rep•e•ti•tious•ly
rep•e•ti•tious•ness
re•pet•i•tive
re•pet•i•tive•ly
re•pet•i•tive•ness
re•phrase v., re•
 phrased, re•phras•
 ing
repl. (replacement)

re•place
re•place•a•bil•i•ty
re•place•a•ble
re•place•ment (cita-
 tion form: repl.)
replacement cost
replacement in•sur•
 ance
replacement val•ue
re•plac•er
re•plead v., re•
 plead•ed, re•plead•
 ing
re•plead•er
re•pledge v., re•
 pledged, re•pledg•
 ing, n.
re•plen•ish
re•plen•ish•er
re•plen•ish•ment
re•plete
re•plev•i•a•ble
re•plev•in
replevin bond
re•plev•i•sa•ble
re•plev•y v., re•plev•
 ied, re•plev•y•ing,
 n., pl. re•plev•ies
rep•li•ca•ble
rep•li•cate v., rep•li•
 cat•ed, rep•li•cat•
 ing
rep•li•ca•tion
rep•li•ca•tive
re•pli•er
re•ply v., re•plied,
 re•ply•ing, n., pl.
 re•plies
reply brief
re•po n., pl. re•pos
re•port (citation form
 for sing. and pl.: Rep.)
re•port•a•ble
re•port•age
re•port•ed
re•port•ed•ly

re•port•er (citation
 form: Rep. or Rptr.)
rep•or•to•ri•al
rep•or•to•ri•al•ly
re-pose v., re-posed,
 re-pos•ing (to pose
 again)
re•pose n., v., re•
 posed, re•pos•ing
 (to lie or rest; to
 place)
re•po•si•tion
re•pos•i•to•ry n., pl.
 re•pos•i•tor•ies
re•pos•sess
re•pos•sess•a•ble
re•pos•sess•a•bly
re•pos•ses•sion
re•pos•ses•sor
rep•re•hen•si•ble
rep•re•hen•si•ble•
 ness
rep•re•hen•si•bly
re-pre•sent (to present
 anew)
rep•re•sent (to stand
 in for; to state)
rep•re•sent•
 a•bil•i•ty
rep•re•sent•a•ble
rep•re•sen•ta•tion
representation e•lec•
 tion
rep•re•sen•ta•
 tion•al
rep•re•sent•a•tive
representative ac•tion
representative ca•
 pac•i•ty
representative de•
 moc•ra•cy
rep•re•sent•a•
 tive•ly
rep•re•sent•a•tive•
 ness

re•press (to press anew)

re•press (to keep down)

re•pressed

repressed mem•o•ry

re•press•i•ble

re•pres•sion

re•pres•sive

re•pres•sive•ly

re•pres•sive•ness

re•prieve v., re•prieved, re•priev•ing, n.

re•priev•er

rep•ri•mand

rep•ri•mand•er

re•pris•al

re•pris•es n.pl.

re•pri•va•tize v., re•pri•va•tized, re•pri•va•tiz•ing

re•proach

re•proach•a•ble

re•proach•a•ble•ness

re•proach•a•bly

re•proach•er

re•proach•ful

re•proach•ful•ly

re•proach•ful•ness

rep•ro•ba•cy

rep•ro•bate n., adj., v., rep•ro•bat•ed, rep•ro•bat•ing

rep•ro•ba•tion

rep•ro•ba•tive

Reprod. (Reproduction; Reproductive)

re•pro•duce v., re•pro•duced, re•pro•duc•ing

re•pro•duc•er

re•pro•duc•i•bil•i•ty

re•pro•duc•i•ble

re•pro•duc•tion (citation form: **Reprod.**)

re•pro•duc•tive (citation form: **Reprod.**)

re-proof v. (to proofread again)

re•proof n. (a rebuke; the act of rebuking)

re•pro•pose v., re•pro•posed, re•pro•pos•ing

re•pros•e•cute v., re•pros•e•cut•ed, re•pros•e•cut•ing

re•prov•a•ble

re•prov•a•ble•ness

re-prove v., re-proved, re-proved or re-prov•en, re-prov•ing (to prove again)

re•prove v., re•proved, re•prov•ing (to criticize)

re•prov•er

re•prov•ing•ly

re•pub•lic

re•pub•li•can

republican form of gov•ern•ment

Republican par•ty

re•pub•li•can•ism

re•pub•li•ca•tion

re•pub•lish

re•pub•lish•a•ble

re•pub•lish•er

re•pu•di•ate v., re•pu•di•at•ed, re•pu•di•at•ing

re•pu•di•a•tion

re•pu•di•a•to•ry

re•pug•nance

re•pug•nan•cy n., pl. re•pug•nan•cies

re•pug•nant

re•pug•nant•ly

re•pulse v., re•pulsed, re•puls•ing

re•pul•sion

re•pul•sive

re•pul•sive•ly

re•pul•sive•ness

re•pur•chase v., re•pur•chased, re•pur•chas•ing, n., adj.

repurchase a•gree•ment

re•pur•chas•er

rep•u•ta•bil•i•ty

rep•u•ta•ble

rep•u•ta•ble•ness

rep•u•ta•bly

rep•u•ta•tion

rep•u•ta•tion•al

re•pute n., v., re•put•ed, re•put•ing

re•put•ed

re•put•ed•ly

re•qual•i•fi•ca•tion

re•qual•i•fy v., re•qual•i•fied, re•qual•i•fy•ing

re•quest

request for ad•mis•sions

request for pro•duc•tion of doc•u•ments

request for pro•pos•als (RFP)

request for quo•ta•tions (RFQ)

re•quest•er

re•ques•tion

requests for in•struc•tions

requests to charge

re•quir•a•ble

re•quire v., re•quired, re•quir•ing

re•quire•ment

requirements con•tract

re•quir•er
req•ui•site
req•ui•site•ly
req•ui•site•ness
req•ui•si•tion
re•qui•si•tion•er
re•quit•al
re•quite v., re•quit•ed, re•quit•ing
re•reg•is•ter
re•reg•is•tra•tion
re•reg•ou•late v., re•reg•ou•lat•ed, re•reg•ou•lat•ing
re•reg•ou•la•tion
re•rent
re•rent•al
res n., pl. res Latin.
Res. (Research; Resolution)
res ad•ju•di•ca•ta Latin.
res a•li•e•na Latin.
res com•mu•nes n.pl. Latin.
res co•ro•nae Latin.
res ges•tae n.pl. Latin.
res in•te•gra Latin.
res ip•sa lo•qui•tur Latin.
res ju•di•ca•ta Latin.
res no•va Latin.
res nul•li•us Latin.
res pu•bli•ca Latin.
res pu•bli•cae n.pl. Latin.
re•sal•a•ble Latin.
re•sale
resale price main•ten•ance
re•sched•ule v., re•sched•uled, re•sched•ul•ing
re•scind
re•scind•a•ble
re•scis•si•ble

re•scis•sion
re•scis•so•ry
re•script
res•cu•a•ble
res•cue v., res•cued, res•cu•ing
res•cu•er
re-search v. (to search again: cf. RESEARCH²)
re•search¹ n. (citation form: **Res.**)
research² v. (to investi•gate: cf. RE-SEARCH)
research and de•vel•op•ment (R&D)
re•seg•re•gate v., re•seg•re•gat•ed, re•seg•re•gat•ing
re•seg•re•ga•tion
re•sell v., re•sold, re•sell•ing
re•sell•er
re•sem•blance
re•sem•ble v., re•sem•bled, re•sem•bling
re•sent
re•sen•tence v., re•sen•tenced, re•sen•tenc•ing
re•sent•ful
re•sent•ful•ly
re•sent•ful•ness
re•sent•ment
re•serv•a•ble
re•ser•va•tion
re-serve v., re-served, re-serv•ing (to serve again)
re•serve v., re•served, re•serv•ing, n., adj. (to hold back; something held back)
reserve bank
reserve clause
reserve cur•ren•cy

reserve for bad debts
reserve fund
reserve re•quire•ment
re•served
reserved gate
reserved point
reserved pow•er
reserved ques•tion
re•serv•ist
re•set•tle v., re•set•tled, re•set•tling
re•set•tle•ment
re•side v., re•sid•ed, re•sid•ing
res•i•dence
res•i•den•cy n., pl. res•i•den•cies
residency re•quire•ment
res•i•dent
resident a•gent
resident al•ien
resident com•mis•sion•er
res•i•den•tial
residential fa•cil•i•ty
residential treat•ment
re•sid•u•al
residual pow•er
residual val•ue
re•sid•u•al•ly
re•sid•u•als n.pl.
re•sid•u•ar•y
residuary be•quest
residuary clause
residuary de•vise
residuary de•visee
residuary es•tate
residuary law
residuary leg•a•cy
residuary leg•a•tee
res•i•due
re•sid•u•um n., pl. re•sid•u•a
re-sign (to sign again)

re•sign (to give up a position)
res•ig•na•tion
re•signed
re•sign•ed•ly
re•sign•ed•ness
re•sil•ience
re•sil•ien•cy
re•sist
re•sist•ance
re•sist•ant
re•sist•er
re•sist•i•bil•i•ty
re•sist•i•ble
re•sist•i•bly
re•sist•ing an of•fi•cer
resisting ar•rest
re•sist•ing•ly
re•sis•tive
re•sis•tive•ly
re•sis•tive•ness
re•so•cial•i•za•tion
Resol. (Resolution)
res•o•lute
res•o•lu•tion (citation form: Res. or Resol.)
re•sol•u•tive
resolutive con•di•tion
re•sol•u•to•ry
resolutory con•di•tion
re•solv•a•bil•i•ty
re•solv•a•ble
re•solve v., re•solved, re•solv•ing, n.
re•solved
re•solv•er
res•o•nance
res•o•nant
res•o•nant•ly
res•o•nate v., res•o•nat•ed, res•o•nat•ing
re•sort

re-sound (to sound again)
re•sound (to reverberate)
re•sound•ing
re•sound•ing•ly
re•source
re•source•ful
re•source•ful•ly
re•source•ful•ness
re•source•less
Resp. (Response; Responsibility; Respondent)
re•spect
re•spect•a•bil•i•ty
re•spect•a•ble
re•spect•a•bly
re•spect•er
re•spect•ful
re•spect•ful•ly
re•spect•ful•ness
re•spec•tive
re•spec•tive•ly
res•pi•ra•tor
re•spite n., v., re•spit•ed, re•spit•ing
respite ser•vi•ces
re•spond
re•spon•de•at su•pe•ri•or Latin.
re•spond•ent (citation form: Resp't or Resp.)
re•spon•den•ti•a Latin.
respondentia bond
respondentia lien
re•spond•er
re•sponse (citation form: Resp.)
re•spon•si•bil•i•ty n., pl. re•spon•si•bil•i•ties (citation form: Resp.)
responsibility-for-con•vey•ance clause

re•spon•si•ble
responsible bid•der
re•spon•si•ble•ness
re•spon•si•bly
re•spon•sive
responsive plead•ing
re•spon•sive•ness
Resp't (Respondent)
rest (to cease introducing evidence: cf. WREST)
rest, res•i•due, and re•main•der
re•state v., re•stat•ed, re•stat•ing
re•state•ment
Restatement of the Law
res•ti•tu•tion
res•ti•tu•tion•ar•y (pertaining to or derived from the law of restitution: cf. RESTITUTIVE; RESTITUTORY)
res•ti•tu•tive (tending to restore: cf. RESTITUTIONARY)
res•ti•tu•to•ry (pertaining to the general concept of restitution: cf. RESTITUTIONARY)
re•stor•a•ble
res•to•ra•tion
re•stor•a•tive
re•store v., re•stored, re•stor•ing
re•stor•er
re-strain (to strain again)
re•strain (to stay or hold back)
re•strain•a•bil•i•ty
re•strain•a•ble
re•strained
re•strain•ing or•der
re•straint

restraint of mar•riage
restraint of princ•es
restraint of trade
restraint on al•ien•a•tion
re•strict
re•strict∘ed
restricted for•eign cur•ren∘cy
restricted stock
re•strict∘ed∘ly
re•strict•ed•ness
re•stric•tion
restriction en∘do∘nu•cle∘ase
restriction en•zyme
restriction frag•ment length pol∘y•morph•ism (RFLP)
re•stric•tive
restrictive cov∘e∘nant
restrictive in•dorse•ment
re•stric•tive∘ly
re•stric•tive•ness
re•struc•ture v., re•struc•tured, re•struc•tur∘ing
re•struc•tur•ing
re•sub•mis•sion
re•sub•mit v., re•sub•mit•ted, re•sub•mit•ting
re•sult
re•sult•ant
re•sult•ing
resulting trust
resulting use
re•sum∘a•ble
re•sume v., re•sumed, re•sum•ing
ré•su∘mé or re•su∘mé or re•su∘me n.
re•sum•mons v., re•

sum•monsed, re•sum•mons•ing
re•sump•tion
re•sur•face v., re•sur•faced, re•sur•fac∘ing
re•surge v., re•serged, re•serg•ing
re•sur•gence
re•sur•gent
res∘ur•rect
res∘ur•rec•tion
re•sus•ci•tate v., re•sus•ci•tat∘ed, re•sus•ci•tat•ing
re•sus•ci•ta•tion
re•sus•ci•ta•tive
re•sus•ci•ta•tor
re•swear v., re•swore, re•sworn, re•swear•ing
re•tail
retail in•stall•ment con•tract
retail installment sale
retail sale
re•tail∘er
re•tail•ing
re•tain
re•tain•a∘bil∘i∘ty
re•tain•a∘ble
re•tain•age
re•tained
retained ear•nings
retained o∘ver•rid∘ing roy•al∘ty
re•tain∘er
re•tain∘ing lien
re•tal∘i∘ate v., re•tal∘i∘at∘ed, re•tal∘i∘at•ing
re•tal∘i∘a•tion
re•tal∘i∘a•to∘ry
retaliatory dis•charge
retaliatory e∘vic•tion
re•tard

re•tard•ant
re•tard∘a•tion
re•tard∘ed
re•tard∘er
re•tar•get
re•ten•tion
re•ten•tive
re•ten•tive∘ly
re•ten•tive•ness
re•think v., re•thought, re•think•ing
ret∘i•cence
ret∘i•cent (reserved; inclined not to speak: cf. RELUCTANT)
ret∘i•cent∘ly
ret∘i•nue
re•tire v., re•tired, re•tir•ing
re•tired
re•tir∘ee
re•tire•ment
retirement an•nu•i∘ty
retirement ben∘e∘fits
retirement plan
re•ti•tle v., re•ti•tled, re•ti•tling
re•tool
re•tool•a∘ble
re•tor•sion
re•tort
re•tract
re•tract•a∘bil∘i∘ty
re•tract•a∘ble
re•trac•tion
re•trac•tor
re•train
re•train∘ee
re•trans•mis•sion
re•trans•mit v. re•trans•mit•ted, re•trans•mit•ting
re•tra•xit Latin.
re-treat (to treat again)

re•treat (to withdraw)
retreat to the wall
re•treat•er
re•trench
re•trench•er
re•trench•ment
re•tri•al
ret•ri•bu•tion
ret•rib•u•tive
ret•rib•u•tive•ly
re•trib•u•tiv•ism
re•trib•u•tiv•ist
re•triev•a•bil•i•ty
re•triev•a•ble
re•triev•al
re•trieve v., re•
    trieved, re•triev•ing
ret•ro•ac•tive
retroactive ef•fect
retroactive law
ret•ro•ac•tive•ly
ret•ro•ac•tiv•i•ty
ret•ro•cede v.,
    ret•ro•ced•ed,
    ret•ro•ced•ing
ret•ro•ces•sion
ret•ro•ces•sion•aire
ret•ro•grade
retrograde am•ne•sia
ret•ro•gress
ret•ro•gres•sion
ret•ro•gres•sive
ret•ro•gres•sive•ly
ret•ro•spect
ret•ro•spec•tion
ret•ro•spec•tive
ret•ro•spec•tive•ly
ret•ro•spec•tive•
    ness
ret•ro•vi•rus n., pl.
    ret•ro•vi•rus•es
re•turn
return date
return day
return of serv•ice

return of writs
return on as•sets
return on eq•ui•ty
return on in•vest•
    ment
return on in•vest•
    ments
return on net as•sets
return re•ceipt
re•turn•a•bil•i•ty
re•turn•a•ble
re•turn•ee
re•type v., re•typed,
    re•typ•ing
re•u•ni•fi•ca•tion
re•u•ni•fy v., re•
    u•ni•fied, re•u•ni•
    fy•ing
re•un•ion
re•u•nit•a•ble
re•u•nite v., re•
    u•nit•ed, re•u•nit•
    ing
re•us n., pl. re•i Latin.
re•us•a•bil•i•ty
re•us•a•ble
re•use v., re•used,
    re•us•ing
re•u•ti•li•za•tion
re•u•ti•lize v., re•
    u•ti•lized, re•u•ti•
    liz•ing
Rev. (Review; Revised;
    Revision; Revenue
rev. (revised; revision)
Rev. Proc. (Revenue
    Procedure)
Rev. Rul. (Revenue Rul•
    ing
re•val•i•date v., re•
    val•i•dat•ed, re•
    val•i•dat•ing
re•val•i•da•tion
re•val•u•ate v., re•
    val•u•at•ed, re•
    val•u•at•ing

re•val•u•a•tion
re•val•ue v., re•val•
    ued, re•val•u•ing
re•vanche French.
re•vanch•ism
re•vanch•ist
rev'd (reversed)
re•veal
re•veal•a•ble
re•veal•er
re•veal•ing
re•veal•ing•ly
rev•e•la•tion
re•vel•o•a•tive
re•vel•o•a•to•ry
re•ven•di•cate v., re•
    ven•di•cat•ed, re•
    ven•di•cat•ing (to
    reclaim: cf. REVINDI-
    CATE)
re•ven•di•ca•tion
re•venge n., v., re•
    venged, re•veng•
    ing
re•venge•ful
re•venge•ful•ly
re•venge•ful•ness
re•veng•er
rev•e•nue (citation
    form: Rev.)
revenue bill
revenue bond
revenue en•hance•
    ment
revenue law
revenue meas•ure
revenue neu•tral
revenue of•fi•cer
Revenue Pro•ce•dure
    (citation form: Rev.
    Proc.)
Revenue Rul•ing (cita-
    tion form: Rev. Rul.)
revenue shar•ing n.
revenue-sharing adj.
revenue stamp

revenue tar•iff

rev•e•nu•er

rev•e•nues

re•ver•ber•ant

re•ver•ber•ant•ly

re•ver•ber•ate *v.*, re•ver•ber•at•ed, re•ver•ber•at•ing

re•ver•ber•a•tion

re•ver•ber•a•tive

re•ver•i•fi•ca•tion

re•ver•i•fy *v.*, re•ver•i•fied, re•ver•i•fy•ing

re•ver•sal

re•verse *adj., n., v.,* re•versed, re•vers•ing

reverse ac•qui•si•tion

reverse an•nu•i•ty mort•gage

reverse dis•crim•i•na•tion

reverse-en•gi•neer

reverse en•gi•neer•ing

reverse FOIA suit

reverse mort•gage

reverse pas•sing off

reverse stock split

reverse tran•scrip•tase

reverse tri•an•gu•lar merg•er

re•versed (*citation form:* rev'd)

reversed and re•mand•ed

re•vers•i•bil•i•ty

re•vers•i•ble

reversible er•ror

re•vers•i•bly

re•vers•ing (*citation form:* rev'g

re•ver•sion

re•ver•sion•ar•y

reversionary an•nu•i•ty

reversionary in•ter•est

re•ver•sion•er

re•vert

re•vert•er

re•vert•i•bil•i•ty

re•vert•i•ble

re•vest

rev'g (reversing)

re•view (*citation form:* Rev.)

re•view•a•bil•i•ty

re•view•a•ble

re•vile *v.*, re•viled, re•vil•ing

re•vile•ment

re•vil•er

re•vil•ing•ly

re•vin•di•cate *v.*, re•vin•di•cat•ed, re•vin•di•cat•ing (to vindicate anew: cf. RE-VENDICATE

re•vin•di•ca•tion

re•vis•a•ble

re•vise *v.*, re•vised, re•vis•ing

re•vised (*citation forms:* Rev. in title of a work; rev. in descriptive material)

re•vis•er or re•vi•sor

re•vi•sion (*citation forms:* Rev. in title of a work; rev. in descriptive material

re•vi•sion•ar•y

re•vi•sion•ism

re•vi•sion•ist

re•vis•it

re•vi•so•ry

re•vi•tal•i•za•tion

re•vi•tal•ize *v.*, re•vi•tal•ized, re•vi•tal•iz•ing

re•viv•al

re•vive *v.*, re•vived, re•viv•ing

re•viv•er (one who revives something: cf. REVIVOR

re•vi•vor (the reviving of a proceeding that has abated: cf. REVIVER

rev•o•ca•bil•i•ty

rev•o•ca•ble

revocable trust

rev•o•ca•bly

rev•o•ca•tion

rev•o•ca•to•ry

re•voke *v.*, re•voked, re•vok•ing

re•vok•er

re•volt

re•volt•er

re•volt•ing

re•volt•ing•ly

rev•o•lu•tion

rev•o•lu•tion•ar•i•ly

rev•o•lu•tion•ar•i•ness

rev•o•lu•tion•ar•y *adj., n.,* rev•o•lu•tion•ar•ies

rev•o•lu•tion•ist

rev•o•lu•tion•ize *v.*, rev•o•lu•tion•ized, rev•o•lu•tion•iz•ing

re•volv•a•ble

re•volve *v.*, re•volved, re•volv•ing

re•volv•er

re•volv•ing

revolving charge ac•count

revolving cred•it

revolving door

revolving fund

revolving loan
re•volv•ing•ly
re•vote *v.*, re•vot○ed,
 re•vot•ing, *n.*
re•vulsed
re•vul•sion
re•vul•sive
re•ward
re•ward•a○ble
re•ward•a○ble•ness
re•ward○a•bly
re•ward○er
re•ward•ing
re•word
re•work
re•write *v.*, re•wrote,
 re•writ•ten, re•
 writ•ing, *n.*
rex (R.) *n.*, *pl.* re○ges
 Latin.
re•zone *v.*, re•zoned,
 re•zon•ing
re•zon•ing
RFLP (restriction frag-
 ment length polymor-
 phism)
RFP (request for propos-
 als)
RFQ (request for quota-
 tions)
rhet○o•ric
rhe•tor○i•cal
rhetorical de•vice
rhetorical ques•tion
rhe•tor○i•cal○ly
rhe•tor○i•cal•ness
rhet○o•ri•cian
Rho•di○an law
RIA (radioimmunoas-
 say)
ri•bo•nu•cle○ic ac○id
 (RNA)
Rich•ard Roe
RICO (Racketeer Influ-
 enced and Corrupt Or-
 ganizations Act)

rid *v.*, rid or rid•ded,
 rid•ding
rid•dance
ride *v.*, rode, rid•den,
 rid•ing, *n.*
rid○er
rid•er•less
rid•er•ship
ride•shar•ing
rid○i•cule *n.*, *v.*,
 rid○i•culed, rid○i•
 cul•ing
ri•dic○u•lous
ri•dic○u•lous○ly
ri•dic○u•lous•ness
rife
rife•ness
ri○fle *n.*, *v.*, ri•fled,
 ri•fling
ri•fler
rift
rig *v.*, rigged, rig•
 ging, *n.*
rigged bid•ding
right
right in per•so•nam
right in rem
right of ac•tion
right of an•ga○ry
right of a○sy•lum
right of e○lec•tion
right of en○try
right of first re•
 fus○al
right of pri•va○cy
right of re•demp•
 tion
right of re•en•try
right of re○ply
right of search
right of sur•viv•or•
 ship
right of way
right, ti○tle, and in•
 ter•est
right to bear arms

right to com•ment
right to coun•sel
right to die
right to ef•fec○tive
 as•sis•tance of
 coun•sel
right to know
right to pri•va○cy
right to re•main si•
 lent
right to trav○el
right-to-work law
right•a○ble
right○er
right•ful
rightful heir
right•ful○ly
right•ful•ness
right○ly
right•ness
rights (*citation form·*
 Rts.)
rights is○sue
rights of•fer•ing
rights on
rig○id
ri•gid○i•ty
rig•id○ly
rig•id•ness
rig○or
rigor mor•tis *Latin*
rig•or•ous
rig•or•ous○ly
rig•or•ous•ness
rile *v.*, riled, ril•ing
ri○ot
Riot Act
ri•ot○er
ri•ot•ous
ri•ot•ous○ly
ri•ot•ous•ness
rip *v.*, ripped, rip•
 ping, *n.*
rip off *v.* (cf. RIPOFF)
ri•par○i•an

riparian land

riparian own∘er

riparian right

ripe *adj* , rip∘er, rip∘est

ripe for re∙view

ripe∙ness

ripeness doc∙trine

rip∙off *n.* (cf. RIP OFF)

ri∙poste *n* , *v.*, ri∙post∘ed, ri∙post∙ing

rise *v.*, rose, ris∘en, ris∙ing, *n.*

ris∙i∘ble

ris∙ing of the court

risk

risk ar∙bi∙trage

risk-ben∘e∙fit a∘nal∘y∙sis

risk cap∘i∙tal

risk man∙age∙ment

risk man∙ag∘er

risk of loss

risk of non∙per∙sua∙sion

risk spread∙ing *n*

risk-spreading *adj.*

risk trans∙fer∙ence

risk∘er

risk∘i∘ly

risk∘i∙ness

risk∙less

risk∙tak∘er

risk∘y *adj.*, risk∘i∘er, risk∘i∙est

ris∙qué

Rit∘a∙lin *Trademark.*

ri∘val *n* , *adj.*, *v.*, ri∙valed, ri∙val∙ing

ri∘val∘ry *n.*, *pl.* ri∙val∙ries

rive *v.*, rived, rived or riv∘en, riv∙ing

riv∘en

riv∘et

RNA (ribonucleic acid)

RNA fin∙ger∙print∙ing

RNA pol∘y∙mer∙ase

road (Rd.)

road rage

road test *n*

road-test *v.*

road∙block

rob *v.*, robbed, rob∙bing

rob∙ber

rob∙ber∘y *n* , *pl* rob∙ber∙ies

robe *n.*, *v* , robed, rob∙ing

Rob∙ert's Rules of Or∘der

rob∙ing room

ro∙ga∙tion

rog∘a∙to∘ry

rogue *n.*, *v* , rogued, ro∙guing, *adj.*

rogues' gal∙ler∘y

ro∙guish

ro∙guish∙ly

ro∙guish∙ness

Ro∙hyp∘nol *Trademark.*

roist∘er

roist∙er∘er

roist∙er∙ous

roist∙er∙ous∘ly

role (one's function or part: cf. ROLL)

role-play

role-play∙ing

roll (a list or record: f. ROLE)

roll call

roll o∘ver *v.* (cf. ROLL∘OVER)

roll∙back

roll∙o∘ver *n.*, *adj.* cf. ROLL OVER)

rollover mort∙gage

Ro∘man law

ro∙mance *n* *v.*, ro∙manced, ro∙manc∙ing

ro∙man∙tic

ro∙man∙ti∙ci∙za∙tion

ro∙man∙ti∙cize *v.* ro∙man∙ti∙cized, ro∙man∙ti∙ciz∙ing

room∘er

room∙ing house

roor∙back

root of ti∘tle

ROR (release on own recognizance)

ros∙ter

ros∙trum *n* , *pl* ros∙trums or ros∙tra

Roth IRA

rou∙é

rough∙neck

round lot

roust∙a∘bout

rout (an unlawful assembly verging on riot: cf. ROUTE)

route *n.*, *v* , rout∘ed, rout∙ing (a path or method: f. ROUT)

route of ad∙min∙is∙tra∙tion

rou∙tine

rou∙tine∘ly

rou∙tine∙ness

rou∙tin∘i∙za∙tion

rou∙tin∙ize *v.* rou∙tin∙ized, rou∙tin∙iz∙ing

rov∙ing wire∙tap

row∙di∘ly

row∙di∙ness

row∘dy *n* , *pl.* row∙dies, *adj.*, row∙di∘er, row∙di∙est

row∙dy∙ism

roy∘al

roy∙al∘ly

roy•al•ty n., pl. roy•al•ties

roy•al•ty-free li•cense

Rptr. (Reporter)

R.R. (Railroad)

Rts. (Rights)

RU 486

rub•bish

ru•bric

ruck•ous n., pl. ruck•us•es

rude adj., rud•er, rud•est

rude•ly

rude•ness

rud•i•ment

rud•i•men•ta•ry

rue•ful

rue•ful•ly

rue•ful•ness

ru•in

ru•in•a•tion

ru•in•er

ru•in•ous

ru•in•ous•ly

ru•in•ous•ness

Rul. (Ruling)

rule[1] n. (citation form for sing. and pl.: **R.**)

rule[2] v., ruled, rul•ing

rule ab•so•lute n., pl. rules ab•so•lute

rule a•gainst ac•cu•mu•la•tions

rule against per•pe•tu•i•ties

rule in Shel•ley's Case

rule in Wild's Case

rule ni•si n., pl. rules ni•si

rule of four

rule of law

rule of len•i•ty

rule of rea•son

rule to show cause

rule•mak•ing

rulemaking au•thor•i•ty

rul•er

rules com•mit•tee

rules of court

rules of ev•i•dence

rules of nav•i•ga•tion

Rules of O•le•ron

rules of or•der

rules of prac•tice

rules of pro•ce•dure

rules of pro•fes•sion•al con•duct

rules of the road

rul•ing (citation form: **Rul.**)

ru•mi•nate v., ru•mi•nat•ed, ru•mi•nat•ing

ru•mi•na•tion

ru•mi•na•tive

ru•mi•na•tive•ly

ru•mor

ru•mor•mon•ger

rump

rump ses•sion

run v., ran, run, run•ning, n.

run a•way v. (cf. RUNAWAY)

run with the land

run•a•way n., adj. (cf. RUN AWAY)

runaway grand ju•ry

runaway jury

runaway shop

run•ner

run•ner-up

run•ning ac•count

running cov•e•nant

running days

running of the stat•ute of lim•i•ta•tions

run•off

runoff e•lec•tion

ru•ral

ru•ral•ly

ruse

rus•tle v., rus•tled, rus•tling, n.

rus•tler

rus•tling

ruth

ruth•ful

ruth•ful•ly

ruth•ful•ness

ruth•less

ruth•less•ly

ruth•less•ness

Ry. (Railway)

S

S. (Senate; Senate Bill; South; Southern; Southern Reporter; Surrogate)

S&L (savings and loan association)

S cor•po•ra•tion

Sab•bath

sab•o•tage n., v., sab•o•tag•ed, sab•o•tag•ing

sab•o•teur

sa•cred

sa•cred•ly

sa•cred•ness

sac•ri•fice n., v., sac•ri•ficed, sac•ri•fic•ing

sac•ri•fice•a•ble
sac•ri•fic•er
sac•ri•fi•cial
sac•ri•lege
sac•ri•le•gious
sac•ri•le•gious•ly
sac•ri•le•gious•ness
sac•ro•sanct
sac•ro•sanc•ti•ty
sac•ro•sanct•ness
sa•dism
sa•dist
sa•dis•tic
sa•dis•ti•cal•ly
sa•do•mas•o•chism
sa•do•mas•o•chist
sa•do•mas•o•chis•tic
safe n., adj., saf•er, saf•est
safe berth
safe-con•duct
safe-de•pos•it box
safe har•bor
safe house
safe port
safe•crack•er
safe•crack•ing
safe•guard
safe•keep•ing
safe•ly
safe•ness
safe•ty n., pl. safe•ties
safety-de•pos•it box
safety en•gi•neer•ing
safety net
safety valve
sa•ga•cious
sa•ga•cious•ly
sa•ga•cious•ness
sa•gac•i•ty
said
sail•or's will

sal•a•bil•i•ty
sal•a•ble
sal•a•bly
sa•la•cious
sa•la•cious•ly
sa•la•cious•ness
sa•lac•i•ty
sal•a•ried
sal•a•ry n , pl sal•a•ries
sale
sale and lease•back
sale by sam•ple
sale in gross
sale on ap•prov•al
sale or re•turn
sales n pl.
sales con•tract
sales fi•nance com•pa•ny
sales rep•re•sent•a•tive
sales tax
sales•per•son n , pl sales•peo•ple
Sal•ic law
sa•li•ence
sa•li•ent
sa•li•ent•ly
sa•loon
SALT (Strategic Arms Limitation Talks)
sal•u•tar•i•ly
sal•u•tar•i•ness
sal•u•tar•y
salv•a•ble
sal•vage
salvage a•ward
salvage loss
salvage val•ue
sal•vage•a•bil•i•ty
sal•vage•a•ble
sal•vag•er
salve v., salved, salv•ing
salved prop•er•ty

sal•vo¹ Latin
sal•vo² n , pl sal•vos English
sal•vor
same
sam•ple n., adj., v., sam•pled, sam•pling
sa•nae men•tis Latin.
sanc•ti•mo•ni•ous
sanc•ti•mo•ni•ous•ly
sanc•ti•mo•ni•ous•ness
sanc•tion
sanc•tion•a•ble
sanc•tion•er
sanc•tions
sanc•tu•ar•y n , pl sanc•tu•ar•ies
sane adj., san•er, san•est
sane•ly
sane•ness
san•i•tar•y
sanitary code
san•i•ta•tion
san•i•ty
sanity hear•ing
sa•pi•ence
sa•pi•ent
sa•pi•ent•ly
sar•casm
sar•cas•tic
sar•cas•ti•cal•ly
sat•el•lite
sat•ire
sa•tir•i•cal
sa•tir•i•cal•ly
sa•tir•i•cal•ness
sat•o•rist
sat•o•riz•a•ble
sat•o•rize v., sat•o•rized, sat•o•riz•ing
sat•is•fac•tion
satisfaction piece
sat•is•fac•to•ri•ly

sat•is•fac•to•ri•ness
sat•is•fac•to•ry
satisfactory ev•i•
dence
satisfactory ti•tle
sat•is•fi•a•ble
sat•is•fi•er
sat•is•fy v., sat•is•
fied, sat•is•fy•ing
sat•u•rate v., sat•u•
rat•ed, sat•u•rat•
ing
Sat•ur•day-night
spe•cial
Sat•ya•gra•ha San•
skrit.
sa•ty•ri•a•sis
sauf-con•duit n. pl
sauf-con•duits Law
French and French
Sav. (Savings)
sav•a•ble
sav•age adj , n., v.,
sav•aged, sav•
ag•ing
sav•age•ly
sav•age•ness
sav•age•ry n., pl.
sav•age•ries
save n., v., saved,
sav•ing
save harm•less
save harmless
a•gree•ment
save harmless clause
sav•er
sav•ing
saving clause
saving to suit•ors
clause
sav•ings (citation form:
Sav.)
savings ac•count
savings and loan as•
so•ci•a•tion (S&L)
savings bank

savings bond
savings clause
Savings In•cen•tive
Match Plan for Em•
ploy•ees
(SIMPLE)
sav•ior
say-so n , pl. say-sos
scab n., v., scabbed,
scab•bing
scab•rous
scaf•fold
scale n., v., scaled,
scal•ing
scalp
scalp•er
scalp•ing
scan•dal
scan•dal•i•za•tion
scan•dal•ize v., scan•
dal•ized, scan•dal•
iz•ing
scan•dal•iz•er
scan•dal•mon•ger
scan•dal•ous
scandalous mat•ter
scan•dal•ous•ly
scan•dal•ous•ness
scath•ing
scath•ing•ly
scat•o•log•i•cal
sca•tol•o•gy
Sc.D. (Doctor of Sci
ence: from Latin Scien
tiae Doctor)
sce•nar•i•o n., pl.
sce•nar•i•os
scène à faire French.
Sch. (School; Schools)
sched. (schedule)
sched•ule[1] n. (citation
form: sched.
schedule[2] v., sched•
uled, sched•ul•ing
schedule (or Schedule)

I con•trolled sub•
stance
schedule (or Schedule)
II con•trolled sub•
stance
schedule (or Schedule
III con•trolled sub•
stance
schedule (or Schedule)
IV con•trolled sub•
stance
schedule (or Schedule)
V con•trolled sub•
stance
sched•uled debt
scheduled drug
scheduled prop•er•ty
sched•ul•er
sched•ul•ing
scheme
scheme or ar•ti•fice
to de•fraud
scheme to de•fraud
schism
schis•mat•ic
schiz•o•af•fec•tive
dis•or•der
schiz•oid
schizoid per•son•
al•i•ty disorder
schiz•o•phre•ni•a
schiz•o•phre•ni•
form disorder
schiz•o•typ•al
schizotypal dis•or•
der
schizotypal per•son•
al•i•ty dis•or•der
schol•ar
schol•ar•ly
schol•ar•ship
scho•las•tic
scho•las•ti•cal•ly
school (citation form
for sing and pl : Sch.)
school tax

school•ing
Sci. (Science; Sciences; Scientific)
sci. fa. (scire facias)
sci•ence (*citation form for sing. and pl :* **Sci.**)
sci•en•ter *Latin*
sci•en•tif•ic (*citation form:* **Sci.**)
scientific meth•od
sci•en•tif•i•cal•ly
sci•en•tist
scil•i•cet *Latin*
scin•til•la
scin•til•late *v.,* scin•til•lat•ed, scin•til•lat•ing
scin•til•lat•ing
scin•til•lat•ing•ly
scin•til•la•tion
sci•on
sci•re fa•ci•as (**sci. fa.**) *Latin*
scis•sion
scoff•law
scold
scold•a•ble
scold•er
scold•ing
scold•ing•ly
scope
scope of a•gen•cy
scope of au•thor•i•ty
scope of em•ploy•ment
scope of ex•am•i•na•tion
scope of ex•per•tise
scope of re•view
scorched earth
scored test
scorn
scorn•er
scorn•ful
scorn•ful•ly
scorn•ful•ness

Scot. (Scotland; Scottish)
scot-free
Scotch ver•dict
Scot•land (**Scot.**)
Scotland Yard
Scots law
Scot•tish (**Scot.**)
scoun•drel
scoun•drel•ly
scourge *n* , *v.,* scourged, scourg•ing
scrap val•ue
scream
screed
screen
screen•a•ble
screen•er
scrip (a certificate. cf. SCRIPT)
scrip div•i•dend
script (handwriting; text to be read: cf. SCRIP)
scriv•en
scriv•en•er
scriv•en•er's er•ror
scriv•en•ing
scru•ple *n., v.,* scru•pled, scru•pling
scru•pu•los•i•ty
scru•pu•lous
scru•pu•lous•ly
scru•pu•lous•ness
scru•ta•bil•i•ty
scru•ta•ble
scru•ti•nize *v.,* scru•ti•nized, scru•ti•niz•ing
scru•ti•niz•er
scru•ti•ny *n., pl.* scru•ti•nies
scur•ril•oi•ty *n., pl* scur•ril•oi•ties
scur•ril•ous
scur•ril•ous•ly

scur•ril•ous•ness
scu•tage
scut•tle *v.,* scut•tled, scut•tling
scut•tle•butt
S.D. (Southern District)
S.E. (South Eastern Reporter)
se de•fen•den•do *Latin.*
sea
sea•bed
seabed min•ing
sea•far•ing na•tion
sea•go•ing ves•sel
seal
seal•a•ble
sealed
sealed and de•liv•ered
sealed bid
sealed bid•ding
sealed de•po•o•si•tion
sealed ev•o•i•dence
sealed in•dict•ment
sealed in•stru•ment
sealed ob•li•ga•tion
sealed rec•ord
sealed ver•dict
sea•man *n* , *pl.* sea•men
sea•man's will
sea•man•ship
search
search and sei•zure
search war•rant
search•a•ble
search•a•ble•ness
search•er
search•ing
search•ing•ly
search•ing•ness
sea•shore
sea•son
sea•son•a•ble
   (timely: cf. SEASONAL)

sea•son•a•ble•ness
sea•son•a•bly
sea•son•al (relating to the time of year: cf. SEASONABLE)
seasonal em•ploy•ment
seasonal un•em•ploy•ment
sea•son•al•ly
sea•son•al•ness
sea•son•ing
seat
seat∘ed land
sea•wor•thi•ness
sea•wor•thy *adj.*, sea•wor•thi∘er, sea•wor•thi∘est
Sec. (Section [of an organization]; Security; Securities)
sec. (section [of a statute])
sec. leg. (secundum legem)
se•cede *v.*, se•ced∘ed, se•ced•ing
se•ced∘er
se•ces•sion
se•ces•sion∘al
se•ces•sion•ist
se•clud∘ed
se•clud•ed∘ly
se•clud•ed•ness
se•clu•sion
sec∘o∘bar•bi•tal *Controlled Subst.*
sec•ond
second-class cit∘i•zen
second de•gree
second-degree crime
second-degree mur•der
second de•liv•er•ance
second lien

second-look doc•trine
second mort•gage
second-rate
second read•ing
second sur•charge
sec•ond•ar∘i•ly
secondarily li•a•ble
sec•ond•ar∘i•ness
sec•ond•ar∘y *n., pl.* sec•ond•ar•ies
secondary au•thor∘i•ty
secondary boy•cott
secondary care
secondary dis•tri•bu•tion
secondary ease•ment
secondary fi•nanc•ing
secondary li•a•bil∘i•ty
secondary mar•ket
secondary mean•ing
secondary mort•gage mar•ket
secondary of•fer•ing
secondary pick•et•ing
secondary-si•tus pick•et•ing
secondary source
sec•ond∘er
sec•ond•hand
secondhand goods
secondhand smoke
se•cre∘cy
se•cret
secret a∘gent
secret bal•lot
secret coun•sel
secret part•ner
secret po•lice
secret serv•ice
secret trust
sec•re•tar•i∘al
sec•re•tar•i∘at

sec•re•tar∘y *n., pl.* sec•re•tar•ies
secretary-gen•er∘al *n., pl.* secretaries-general
sec•re•tar•y•ship
se•crete *v.*, se•cret∘ed, se•cret•ing
se•cret∘ly
sect
sec∘ta *n., pl.* sec•tae *Latin.*
sec•tar•i∘an
sec•tar•i•an•ism
sec•tion[1] (*citation form:* + or sec.; *pl.* ++ or secs.) (part of a statute: cf. SECTION[2])
section[2] (*citation form:* Sec.) (part of an organization: cf. SEC•TION[1])
sec•tor
sec•tor∘al
sec∘u•lar
secular busi•ness
sec∘u•lar•ism
sec∘u•lar•ist
sec∘u•lar∘i•za•tion
sec∘u•lar•ize *v.*, sec∘u•lar•ized, sec∘u•lar•iz•ing
sec∘u•lar∘ly
se•cun•dum *Latin.*
secundum ae•quum et bo∘num *Latin.*
secundum al•le•ga∘ta et pro•ba∘ta *Latin.*
secundum le∘gem (sec. leg.) *Latin.*
se•cur•a∘ble
se•cure *adj.*, se•cur∘er, se•cur•est, *v.*, se•cured, se•cur•ing
se•cured

secured cred○i•tor
secured debt
secured loan
secured par•ty
secured trans•ac•tion
se•cure○ly
se•cure•ness
se•cur○er
se•cu•ri•ties acts
securities bro•ker
securities ex•change
securities fraud
securities of•fer•ing
se•cu•ri•ti•za•tion
se•cu•ri•tize *v.*, se•cu•ri•tized, se•cu•ri•tiz•ing
se•cu•ri○ty *n.*, *pl.* se•cu•ri•ties (*citation form for sing. and pl : Sec.*)
security a○gree•ment
security de•pos○it
security for costs
security in•ter•est
security risk
sed *Latin.*
sed quae○re *Latin.*
sed vi○de *Latin.*
se•da•tion
sed○a•tive
sedative a○buse
sedative de•pend•ence
sedative-in•duced dis•or•der
sedative in•tox○i•ca•tion
sedative with•draw○al
se•di•tion
se•di•tious
seditious li○bel
se•di•tious○ly
se•di•tious•ness

se•duce *v.*, se•duced, se•duc○ing
se&duc○er
se•duc○i○ble or se•duce•a○ble
se•duc•tion
se•duc•tive
se•duc•tive○ly
se•duc•tive•ness
se•duc•tress
se•du•li○ty
sed○u•lous
sed○u•lous○ly
sed○u•lous•ness
see *v.*, saw, see•ing
See•ing Eye *Trademark*
Seeing Eye dog
seek *v.*, sought, seek•ing
seek○er
seem
seem•ing
seem•ing○ly
seem•ing•ness
seem•li•ness
seem○ly *adj.*, seem•li○er, seem•li•est
seg•ment
seg•re•ga•ble
seg•re•gate *v.*, seg•re•gat○ed, seg•re•gat•ing
seg•re•gat○ed
seg•re•gat•ed○ly
seg•re•gat•ed•ness
seg•re•ga•tion
seg•re•ga•tion○al
seg•re•ga•tive
sei•gneur *French.*
sei•gneu•ri•age *French.*
sei•gneu•ri○al *French*
sei•gneu•rie *French.*
sei•gneur○y *n*, *pl*
sei•gneur•ies

seign•ior
seign•ior•age
seign•ior○y *n.*, *pl*
seign•ior•ies
sei•gno•ri•al
seise *v.*, seised, seis•ing (to vest with a freehold estate: f. SEIZE)
seised
sei•sin
seiz•a○ble
seize *v.*, seized, seiz•ing (to take possession of: cf. SEISE)
seiz•er or sei•zor
sei•zure
se•lect
select com•mit•tee
se•lec•ta•bil○i•ty
se•lec•ta•ble
se•lect•ee
se•lec•tion
se•lec•tive am•ne•sia
selective con•sci•en•tious ob•jec•tor
selective en•force•ment
selective in•cor•po•ra•tion
selective pros○e•cu•tion
selective serv•ice
se•lec•tiv○i•ty
se•lect○ly
se•lect•man *n*, *pl* se•lect•men
se•lect•ness
se•lec•tor
self *n.*, *pl* selves, *adj. pron*
self-a○base•ment
self-ab•ne•ga•tion
self-ab•sorbed
self-ab•sorp•tion

self-ac•tu•al•i•za•
tion
self-ad•min•is•ter∘ed
self-ad•min•is•ter•
ing
self-ad•min•is•tra•
tion
self-ag•gran•dize•
ment
self-ag•gran•diz•ing
self-ag•gran•diz•
ing∘ly
self-ap•point∘ed
self-ap•point•ment
self-as•sert•ing∘ly
self-as•ser•tion
self-as•ser•tive
self-as•ser•tive∘ly
self-as•ser•tive•ness
self-as•sess•ment
self-as•sur•ance
self-as•sured
self-as•sur•ed•ness
self-au•then•ti•cat•
ing
self-au•thor•ized
self-au•thor•iz•ing
self-a∘vowed
self-cen•sor•ship
self-cen•tered
self-cen•tered∘ly
self-cen•tered•ness
self-char•ac•ter∘i•
za•tion
self-com•mit•ment
self-con•dem•na•tion
self-con•dem•na•
to∘ry
self-con•fessed
self-con•fi•dence
self-con•fi•dent
self-con•fi•dent•ly
self-con•fine•ment
self-con•flict
self-con•grat∘u•la•
to∘ry

self-con•scious
self-con•scious∘ly
self-con•scious•ness
self-con•tained
self-con•tam∘i•na•
ting
self-con•tam∘i•na•
tion
self-con•tra•dict•ing
self-con•tra•dic•tion
self-con•tra•dic•
to∘ry
self-con•trol
self-con•vict∘ed
self-cor•rect•ing
self-deal•ing
self-de•ceiv•ing
self-de•cep•tion
self-de•feat•ing
self-de•fense
self-de•fen•sive
self-de•fin•ing
self-def∘i•ni•tion
self-dep•re•cat•ing
self-dep•re•cat•
ing∘ly
self-dep•re•ca•tion
self-dep•re•ca•to∘ry
self-dep•ri•va•tion
self-de•scribed
self-de•scrip•tion
self-de•struc•tion
self-de•struc•tive
self-de•ter•mi•na•
tion
self-de•ter•mined
self-de•ter•min•ing
self-di•ag•no•sis
self-di•rect∘ed
self-di•rect•ing
self-di•rec•tion
self-dis•ci•pline
self-dis•ci•plined
self-doubt
self-doubt•ing

self-dram∘a•ti•za•
tion
self-dram∘a•tiz•ing
self-ed∘u•cat∘ed
self-ed∘u•ca•tion
self-ef•face•ment
self-ef•fac•ing
self-em•ployed
self-em•ploy•ment
self-employment in•
come
self-employment tax
self-en•forc•ing
self-es•teem
self-ev∘i•dent
self-ev∘i•dent∘ly
self-ex•am∘i•na•tion
self-ex∘e•cut•ing
self-executing trea∘ty
self-ex•plan∘a•to∘ry
self-ful•fill•ing
self-fulfilling proph•
e∘cy
self-ful•fill•ment
self-gov•erned
self-gov•ern•ing
self-gov•ern•ment
self-help
self-help∘er
self-in•crim∘i•nat•
ing
self-in•crim∘i•na•
tion
self-in•crim∘i•na•
to∘ry
self-in•dul•gence
self-in•dul•gent
self-in•dul•gent∘ly
self-in•flict∘ed
self-in•flic•tion
self-in•sur•ance
self-in•sure *v.*,
self-in•sured,
self-in•sur•ing
self-in•sured
self-in•sur∘er

self•in•ter•est
self•in•ter•est•ed
self•in•ter•est•ed•
 ness
self•jus•ti•fi•ca•tion
self•jus•ti•fy•ing
self-knowl•edge
self-less
self-less•ly
self-less•ness
self-lim•it•ing
self-liq•ui•dat•ing
self-med•i•ca•tion
self-mo•ti•vat•ed
self-mo•ti•va•tion
self-or•dain•ed
self-own•er•ship
self-per•cep•tion
self-per•pet•u•at•ing
self-pit•y
self-pit•y•ing
self-pit•y•ing•ly
self-pos•sessed
self-pos•ses•sion
self-pres•er•va•tion
self-pro•claim•ed
self-pro•fessed
self-pro•mot•er
self-pro•mot•ing
self-pro•mo•tion
self-prov•ing
self-ques•tion•ing
self-reg•u•lat•ed
self-reg•u•lat•ing
self-reg•u•la•tion
self-reg•u•la•tive
self-reg•u•la•to•ry
self-re•li•ance
self-re•li•ant
self-rep•li•cat•ing
self-rep•li•ca•tion
self-rep•re•sen•ta•
 tion
self-re•proach
self-re•proach•ing

self-re•spect
self-re•spect•ing
self-re•strained
self-re•straint
self-re•veal•ing
self-rev•e•la•tion
self-re•vel•a•to•ry
self-right•eous
self-right•eous•ly
self-right•eous•ness
self-sac•ri•fice
self-sac•ri•fi•cial
self-sac•ri•fic•ing
self-sat•is•fac•tion
self-sat•is•fied
self-sat•is•fy•ing
self-se•lect•ed
self-se•lec•tion
self-serv•ing
self-set•tled trust
self-styled
self-suf•fi•cien•cy
self-suf•fi•cient
self-sup•port•ed
self-sup•port•ing
self-sus•tain•ing
self-taught
self-trained
self-val•i•dat•ing
self-worth
self•ish
self•ish•ly
self•ish•ness
self•same
sell v., sold, sell•ing
 (to offer for money; cf.
 CELL)
sell-back n.
sell off v.
sell-off n.
sell out v. cf SELLOUT
sell short
sell•a•ble
sell•er

sell•er's (or sell•ers')
 mar•ket
seller's op•tion
sell•out n. (cf. SELL
 OUT)
se•man•tic
se•man•ti•cal•ly
se•man•tics n.sing.
sem•ble Law French.
se•men
sem•i•an•nu•al
sem•i•an•nu•al•ly
sem•i•au•ton•o•
 mous
sem•i•au•ton•o•o•my
sem•i•con•duc•tor
semiconductor chip
sem•i•lit•er•a•cy
sem•i•lit•er•ate
sem•i•nal
sem•i•nal•i•ty
sem•i•nal•ly
sem•i•nude
sem•i•nu•di•ty
sem•i•per•ma•nent
sem•i•po•lit•i•cal
sem•i•pri•vate
sem•i•pro•fes•sion•
 al
sem•i•pub•lic
sem•i•se•ri•ous
sem•i•syn•thet•ic
semisynthetic drug
Sem•tex
Sen. (Senator)
Sen•ate (citation form.
 S.)
Sen•ate Bill (citation
 form: S.)
sen•a•tor (Sen.)
sen•a•to•ri•al
senatorial cour•te•sy
senatorial dis•trict
sen•a•to•ri•al•ly
send v. sent, send•
 ing

send-up or send•up *n.*
send•er
se•nes•cence
se•nes•cent
se•nile
senile de•men•tia
se•nil•i•ty
sen•ior
senior cit•i•zen
senior cred•i•tor
senior in•ter•est
senior lien
senior mon•ey
senior mort•gage
senior mort•ga•gee
senior part•ner
senior se•cu•ri•ty
sen•ior•i•ty
seniority rule
seniority sys•tem
sen•sa•tion
sen•sa•tion•al
sen•sa•tion•al•ism
sen•sa•tion•al•ist
sen•sa•tion•al•is•tic
sen•sa•tion•al•ize *v.*,
   sen•sa•tion•al•ized,
   sen•sa•tion•al•iz•
   ing
sen•sa•tion•al•ly
sense *n., v.,* sensed,
   sens•ing
sense•less
sense•less•ly
sense•less•ness
sen•si•bil•i•ty *n., pl.*
   sen•si•bil•i•ties
sen•si•ble
sen•si•ble•ness
sen•si•bly
sen•si•tive
sen•si•tive•ly
sen•si•tiv•i•ty *n., pl.*
   sen•si•tiv•i•ties
sensitivity train•ing
sen•si•ti•za•tion

sen•si•tize *v.*, sen•si•
   tized, sen•si•tiz•ing
sen•su•al (pertaining
   to the senses: cf. CEN-
   SUAL)
sen•tence *n., v.,* sen•
   tenced, sen•
   tenc•ing
sen•tenc•er
sen•tenc•ing
sentencing guide•
   lines
sentencing hear•ing
SEP (simplified em-
   ployee pension)
sep•a•ra•bil•i•ty
separability clause
sep•a•ra•ble
separable con•tro•
   ver•sy
sep•a•ra•bly
sep•a•rate *v.*, sep•a•
   rat•ed, sep•a•rat•
   ing, *adj., n*
separate ac•tion
separate but e•qual
separate main•te•
   nance
separate o•pin•ion
separate prop•er•ty
separate re•turn
separate tri•al
sep•a•rate•ly
sep•a•rate•ness
sep•a•ra•tion
separation a•gree•
   ment
separation anx•i•
   e•ty
separation anxiety
   dis•or•der
separation of church
   and state
separation of pow•
   ers
sep•a•ra•tism

sep•a•ra•tist
Sept. (September)
Sep•tem•ber (*citation
   form:* **Sept.**)
se•quence *n., v.,* se•
   quenced, se•quenc•
   ing
se•quen•tial
se•quen•tial•ly
se•ques•ter
se•ques•tra•ble
se•ques•trate *v.*, se•
   ques•trat•ed, se•
   ques•trat•ing
se•ques•tra•tion
se•ques•tra•tor
ser. (series; serial; seri-
   als)
serf
serf•dom
ser•gean•cy (the posi-
   tion of sergeant: cf.
   SERJEANTY)
ser•geant (a military
   or quasi-military officer: cf. SERJEANT AT
   LAW)
sergeant at arms *n.,
   pl.* ser•geants at
   arms
ser•geant•ship
se•ri•al (*citation form
   for sing. and pl.:* **ser.**)
serial bond
serial note
se•ri•a•tim
se•ries *n.pl.* (*citation
   form for sing. and pl.:*
   ser.)
series bonds
se•ri•ous
se•ri•ous•ly
se•ri•ous•ness
ser•jeant at law (a
   former rank of barris-
   ters: cf. SERGEANT)

ser•jeant•y a land tenure with obligation to render services to the king: cf. SER-GEANCY

se•ro•log•ic

se•ro•log•i•cal

se•ro•log•i•cal•ly

se•rol•o•gist

se•rol•o•gy

Serv. Service

serv•a•ble

serv•ant

serve v., served, serv•ing

serv•ice¹ n. adj. (cita-tion form: **Serv.**

service² v. serv•iced, serv•ic•ing

service by mail

service by pub•li•ca•tion

service charge

service con•tract

service mark (SM)

service of proc•ess

serv•ice•a•bil•i•ty

serv•ice•a•ble

serv•ice•a•bly

serv•ic•es n pl.

ser•vi•ent

servient es•tate

servient ten•ement

ser•vi•tude

Sess. Session; Sessions

ses•sion citation form for sing. and pl.: **Sess.**)(a sitting or term of a court or legisla-ture: cf. CESSION)

session laws

ses•sion•al

set . set, set•ting, n. adj.

set a•side .

set-aside n.

set back v. (cf. SETBACK)

set down

set down for tri•al

set forth

set free

set off v. cf. SETOFF

set out

set up v. cf. SETUP

set•back n. cf. SET BACK

set•ting

set•tle v. set•tled, set•tling

set•tle•a•bil•i•ty

set•tle•a•ble

set•tled•ness

set•tle•ment

set•tle•ment op•tion

set•tler one who oc-cupies land or resolves a matter: cf. SETTLOR

set•tlor (one who grants property or cre-ates a trust: cf. SET-TLER

set•up n. cf. SET UP

sev•en years' ab•sence

sev•er

sev•er•a•bil•i•ty

severability clause

sev•er•a•ble

severable con•tract

severable stat•ute

sev•er•al

several li•a•bil•i•ty

sev•er•al•ly

severally li•a•ble

sev•er•al•ty n. pl. sev•er•al•ties

sev•er•ance

severance pay

severance tax

se•vere adj., se•ver•er, se•ver•est

se•vere•ly

se•ver•i•ty

sew•er serv•ice

sex

sex a•buse

sex-based dis•crim•i•na•tion

sex discrimination

sex-linked char•ac•ter•is•tic

sex ob•ject

sex-plus dis•crim•i•na•tion

sex•ism

sex•ist

sex•u•al

sexual a•buse

sexual as•sault

sexual de•vi•a•tion

sexual ha•rass•ment

sexual o•ri•en•ta•tion

sexual pred•a•tor

sexual pref•er•ence

sex•u•al•i•ty

sex•u•al•ly

sexually trans•mit•ted dis•ease (STD)

shack•le n. v. shack•led, shack•ling

shad•ow

shadow coun•sel

shadow mon•ey

shad•ow•er

Shaf•i•'i

shake v. shook, shak•en, shak•ing, n.

shake down v. cf. SHAKEDOWN

shake•down n. cf. SHAKE DOWN

shak•en ba•by syn•drome

shake•out *n.*

shall

sham *n. adj.*
shammed, sham•
ming

sham plead•ing

sham trans•ac•tion

shame *n.* . shamed,
sham•ing

shame•ful

shame•ful•ly

shame•ful•ness

shame•less

shame•less•ly

shame•less•ness

shang•hai *v.* shang•
haied, shang•hai•
ing

share *n., v.,* shared,
shar•ing

share ac•count

share and share
a•like

share cer•tif•i•cate

share draft

share•a•ble or shar•
a•ble

share•crop *v.* share•
cropped, share•
crop•ping

share•crop•per

shared-ap•pre•ci•a•
tion mort•gage

shared-eq•ui•ty
mort•gage

shared psy•chot•ic
dis•or•der

share•hold•er

shareholder de•
riv•a•tive ac•tion

share•hold•ers' eq•
ui•ty

share•hold•ing

shar•er

sha•ri•a'ah or sha•
ri•a

shark re•pel•lent

sharp

sharp prac•tice

sharp•shoot•er

sharp•shoot•ing

shav•a•ble

shave . shaved,
shav•ing

shelf reg•is•tra•tion

shell

shell com•pa•ny

shell cor•po•ra•tion

Shel•ley's Case, rule
in

shel•ter

shel•tered

shel•ter•er

shel•ter•ing trust

shel•ter•ing•ly

Shep•ard•ize *v.,*
Shep•ard•ized,
Shep•ard•iz•ing
Trademark.

Shep•ard's *Trademark.*

sher•iff

sher•iff•al•ty *n. pl.*
sher•iff•al•ties

sher•iff•dom

sher•iff's sale

sher•iff•wick

shield law

shift

shift dif•fer•en•tial

shift the bur•den of
proof

shift•ing ex•ec•u•
to•ry in•ter•est

shifting use

shift•less

shift•less•ly

shift•less•ness

shill

shin•gle

ship *n. v.* shipped,
ship•ping

ship mort•gage

ship re•pair•er

ship•build•er

ship•build•ing

ship•ment

ship•per

ship•ping

shipping or•der

ship's hus•band

ship's pa•pers

ship•wreck

shirk

shirk•er

shiv

shock

shock•a•bil•i•ty

shock•a•ble

shock•er

shock•ing

shoot . shot, shoot•
ing, *n.*

shoot•er

shoot•ing gal•ler•y

shoot•out

shop *n. v.* shopped,
shop•ping

shop book

shop-book ex•cep•
tion to the hear•say
rule

shop-book rule

shop com•mit•tee

shop right

shop right rule

shop stew•ard

shop•lift

shop•lift•er

shop•lift•ing

shore *n.* . shored,
shor•ing

short

short cov•er•ing

short-lived

short-pe•ri•od re•
turn

short po•si•tion

short rate

short sale
short sell•er
short sell•ing
short shrift
short sum•mons
short-swing prof•its
short tan•dem re•peat (STR)
short-tem•pered
short-term *adj.*
short-term cap•i•tal gain
short-term debt
short-term fi•nanc•ing
short-term loan
short-term mem•o•o•ry
short•age
short•change *v.* short•changed, short•chang∘ing
short•chang∘er
short•com•ing
short•fall
short•ness
short•sight∘ed
short•sight•ed∘ly
short•sight•ed•ness
shot•gun *n. adj., v.* shot•gunned, shot•gun•ning
should
shoul•der hol•ster
show *v.,* showed, shown or showed, show∘ing
show cause
show off *v.*
show-off *n.*
show tri∘al
show up *v.*
show•a∘ble
show•ing
show∘up *n.*
shriev∘al
shriev•al∘ty

shrink *v.,* shrank, shrunk, shrink•ing, *n.*
shrink-wrap
shrink•a∘ble
shrink•age
shut-in rent∘al
shut-in roy•al∘ty
shy•ster
shy•ster•ism
sib•ling ri•val∘ry dis•or•der
sic *Latin.*
sick day
sick leave
sick pay
side
side arm *n.*
side ef•fect
side•bar
side•line *n., v.* side•lined, side•lin•ing
side•swipe *v.* side•swiped, side•swip•ing, *n.*
side•swip∘er
side•track
side•ways at•tri•bu•tion of stock own•er•ship
sideways merg∘er
SIDS sudden infant death syndrome
siege
siege men•tal∘i•ty
sight vision: cf. CITE, SITE
sight draft
sign
sign•age
sig•nal *n. adj. v,* sig•naled, sig•nal•ing
sig•nal∘er
sig•na•to∘ry *n. pl.* sig•na•to•ries, *adj*

sig•na•ture
signature card
signed, sealed, and de•liv•ered
sign∘er
sig•nif∘i•cance
sig•nif∘i•cant
significant oth∘er
sig•ni•fi•ca•tion
sig•nif∘i•ca•tive
sig•nif∘i•ca•tive∘ly
sig•nif∘i•ca•tive•ness
sig•ni•fier
sig•ni•fy *v.* sig•ni•fied, sig•ni•fy•ing
si•lence *n., v.* si•lenced, si•lenc∘ing
si•lenc∘er
si•lent
silent a∘larm
silent part•ner
si•lent∘ly
sil∘i•cone
sil∘i•co•sis
sil∘i•cot∘ic
sil•li∘ly
sil•li•ness
sil∘ly *ad.* sil•li∘er sil•li•est
sim∘i•lar
sim∘i•lar∘i∘ty *n. pl* sim∘i•lar∘i∘ties
sim∘i•lar∘ly
sim∘i•le
si•mil∘i•tude
sim•ple *adj.* sim•pler sim•plest
SIMPLE Savings Incentive Match Plan for Employees
simple as•sault
simple bat•ter∘y
simple con•tract
simple debt
simple in•ter•est

simple lar•ce○ny
simple ma•jor•i○ty
simple neg•li•gence
simple ob•li•ga•tion
simple trust
sim•ple-mind•ed
sim•ple-mind•ed○ly
sim•ple-mind•ed• •
ness
sim•ple•ness
sim•plic•i•ter *Latin.*
sim•plic○i•ty
sim•pli•fi•ca•tion
sim•pli•fied em•
ploy○ee pen•sion
(SEP)
sim•pli•fy *v.,* sim•
pli•fied, sim•pli•fy•
ing
sim•plis•tic
sim•plis•ti•cal○ly
sim•ply
sim○u•la•crum *n., pl.*
sim○u•la•cra
sim○u•late *v.,* sim○u•
lat○ed, sim○u•lat•
ing
simulated sale
sim○u•la•tion
sim○u•la•tive
sim○u•la•tor
si•mul•ta•ne•i○ty
si•mul•ta•ne•ous
simultaneous death
simultaneous pub•li•
ca•tion
si•mul•ta•ne•ous○ly
si•mul•ta•ne•ous•
ness
sin *n., v.,* sinned, sin•
ning
sin tax
sin•cere *adj.,* sin•
cer○er, sin•cer•est
sin•cere○ly
sin•cer○i○ty

si○ne *Latin.*
sine di○e *Latin.*
sine pro○le *Latin.*
sine qua non *Latin.*
si•ne•cure
sin•ful
sin•ful○ly
sin•ful•ness
sin•gle *adj., v.,* sin•
gled, sin•gling, *n.*
single em•ploy○er
plan
single-hand○ed
single-hand•ed○ly
single-hand•ed•ness
single-mind○ed
single-mind•ed○ly
single-mind•ed•ness
single-name pa○per
single-pre•mi○um life
in•sur•ance
single pub•li•ca•tion
rule
single-sex *adj.*
single tax *n.*
single-tax *adj.*
sin•gly
sin•is•ter
sin•is•ter○ly
sin•is•ter•ness
sink *v.,* sank, sunk,
sink•ing *n.*
sink•ing fund
sire *n., v.,* sired, sir•
ing
sis•ter
sister cor•po•ra•tion
sister-in-law *n., pl.*
sis•ters-in-law
sister state
sis•ter•hood
sis•ter○ly
sit *v.,* sat, sit•ting
sit-down strike
sit-in *n.*
site *n., v.,* sit○ed, sit•

ing (location: cf. CITE;
SIGHT)
sit•ting
sitting en banc
sitting in bank
sitting in cam•er○a
sit○u•ate *v.,* sit○u•
at○ed, sit○u•at•ing,
adj.
sit○u•at○ed
sit○u•a•tion
sit○u•a•tion•al
situational drug use
sit•u•a•tion•al○ly
si○tus[1] *n., pl.* si•
tus○es *English.*
si○tus[2] *n., pl.* si○tus
Latin.
situs pick•et•ing
S.J.D. (Doctor of Juridical Science: from Latin
*Scientiae Juridicae Doc-
tor*)
skep•tic
skep•ti•cal
skep•ti•cal○ly
skep•ti•cism
skill
skill-less
skill-less•ness
skilled
skilled la○bor
skilled nurs•ing fa•
cil○i○ty
skill•ful
skill•ful○ly
skill•ful•ness
skim *v.,* skimmed,
skim•ming
skim•mer
skip *v.,* skipped, skip•
ping, *n.*
skip per•son
skip trace
skip trac○er
skip trac•ing

skul•dug•ger•y *n.*

sky mar•shal

sky•jack

sky•jack•er

sky•jack•ing

slack•er

slam *v.*, slammed, slam•ming

slam•ming

slan•der

slander of ti•tle

slander per quod

slander per se

slan•der•er

slan•der•ous

slanderous per quod

slanderous per se

slan•der•ous•ly

slan•der•ous•ness

slap *n.*, *v.*, slapped, slap•ping

slap•dash

slap•hap•py *adj.*, slap•hap•pi•er, slap•hap•pi•est

SLAPP *n.*, SLAPPed, SLAPP•ing (Strategic Lawsuit Against Public Participation)

SLAPP suit

slash

slash•er

slate *n.*, *v.*, slat•ed, slat•ing

slat•tern

slat•tern•li•ness

slat•tern•ly

slaugh•ter

slaugh•ter•er

slave *n.*, *v.*, slaved, slav•ing

slave driv•er

slave la•bor

slave labor camp

slave ship

slave trade

slave-trad•ing

slave•hold•er

slave•hold•ing

slave•like

slav•er

slav•er•y

slav•ish

slav•ish•ly

slav•ish•ness

slay *v.*, slew, slain, slay•ing

slay•er

sleaze

slea•zi•ly

slea•zi•ness

slea•zy *adj.*, slea•zi•er, slea•zi•est

sleuth

sleuth•like

slick

slick•ly

slick•ness

slid•ing scale

slight

slip *v.*, slipped, slip•ping, *n.*

slip and fall *v.*

slip-and-fall *adj.*, *n.*

slip law

slip o•pin•ion

slow code

slow vi•rus

slow•down *n.*

slump

slur *n.*, *v.*, slurred, slur•ring

slush fund

SM (service mark)

small busi•ness

small business cor•po•ra•tion

small-cap

small claims court

small-sav•er cer•tif•i•cate

smart mon•ey

smear

smear cam•paign

smear•er

smoke *n.*, *v.*, smoked, smok•ing

smok•er

smok•ing

smoking gun

smoth•er

smug•gle *n.* *v.*, smug•gled, smug•gling

smug•gler

smug•gling

smut

smut•ty *adj.*, smut•ti•er, smut•ti•est

sna•fu

sneak *v.*, sneaked, sneak•ing, *n.*

sneak thief

sneer

sneer•er

sneer•ing•ly

snide *adj.*, snid•er, snid•est

snide•ly

snide•ness

sniff

snif•fing

snob

snob•ber•y *n.*, *pl.* snob•ber•ies

snob•bish

snob•bish•ly

snob•bish•ness

snoop

snoop•er

snort

snort•er

snort•ing

snuff

so or•dered

so•ber *adj.*, so•ber•er, so•ber•est

so•ber•ly

so•bri•e◦ty
sobriety check•point
sobriety test
Soc. (Social; Sociologi-
cal; Sociology)
soc•age
soc•ag◦er
so•cia•bil◦i◦ty
so•cia•ble
so•cia•bly
so•cial (*citation form:*
Soc.)
social con•tract
social con•trol
social cost
social Dar•win•ism
social Dar•win•ist
social drink•ing
social guest
social in•sur•ance
social in•ter•ac•tion
social jus•tice
social psy•chol◦o◦gy
social se•cu•ri◦ty
social security dis•
a◦bil◦i◦ty
social se•cu•ri•ty tax
social wel•fare
so•cial•ism
so•cial•ist
so•cial•is•tic
so•cial•is•ti•cal◦ly
so•cial•iz•a◦ble
so•cial◦i•za•tion
so•cial•ize *v.*, so•
cial•ized, so•cial•iz•
ing
so•cial•iz◦er
so•cial◦ly
so•cial•ness
so•ci•e•tal
societal norms
so•ci•e•tal◦ly
so•ci•e◦ty (*citation
form:* Soc'y)
so◦ci◦o◦cul◦tur◦al

so◦ci◦o◦ec◦o◦nom◦ic
so◦ci◦o◦ec◦o◦
nom◦i◦cal◦ly
so◦ci◦o◦ec◦o◦nom•
ics *n.sing.*
so◦ci◦o◦e•con◦o•
mist
so◦ci◦o◦log◦i◦cal (*ci
tation form:* Soc.)
so◦ci◦o◦log◦i◦cal◦ly
so•ci•ol◦o◦gist
so•ci•ol◦o◦gy (*cita
tion form:* Soc.)
so◦ci◦o◦path
so◦ci◦o◦path◦ic
sociopathic per•son•
al◦i◦ty
so•ci•op◦a•thy
so◦ci◦o◦po•lit◦i•cal
so◦ci◦o◦psy•cho•
log◦i◦cal
So•crat◦ic meth•od
Soc'y (Society)
so•di◦um am◦y•tal
sodium pen•to•thal
sod◦om•ize *v.*,
sod◦om•ized,
sod◦om•iz◦ing
sod•om◦y
soft
soft-core
soft-core por•nog•
ra•phy
soft drug
soft land•ing
soft law
soft line *n.*
soft-line *adj.*
soft-lin◦er
soft mon◦ey
soft-ped◦al *v.*,
soft-ped•aled,
soft-ped•al•ing
soft sell *n.*
soft-sell *adj.*
soft◦ly

soft•ness
soft•ware
software li•cense
software pi•ra•cy
soke
sol•ace *n., v.*, sol•
aced, sol•ac•ing
so•la•ti◦um *n., pl.*
so•la•ti◦a
sol•dier's will
sole
sole ac◦tor doc•trine
sole cus•to◦dy
sole dis•cre•tion
sole pro•pri•e•tor•
ship
sole-source
sole◦ly
sol•emn
so•lem•ni◦fy *v.*, so•
lem•ni•fied, so•
lem•ni•fy◦ing
so•lem•ni◦ty *n., pl.*
so•lem•ni•ties
sol•em•ni•za•tion
sol•em•nize *v.*, sol•
em•nized, sol•em•
niz◦ing
sol•em•niz◦er
sol•emn◦ly
sole•ness
Solic. (Solicitor; Solicitors; Solicitors'; Solicitor's)
so•lic◦it
so•lic◦i•ta•tion
so•lic◦i•tor (*citation
form for sing. and pl.:*
Solic.)
solicitor gen•er◦al *n.,
pl.* so•lic◦i•tors gen•
eral
so•lic◦i•tor•ship
so•lic◦i•tous
so•lic◦i•tous◦ly
so•lic◦i•tous•ness

so•lic•i•tude
sol•i•dar•i•ty
sol•ip•sism
sol•ip•sist
sol•ip•sis•tic
sol•i•tar•y
solitary con•fine•
    ment
so•lon
so•lu•tion
solve v., solved, solv•
    ing
sol•ven•cy
sol•vent
sol•vent•ly
so•mat•ic
somatic hal•lu•ci•na•
    tion
so•mat•i•cal•ly
so•mat•i•cize v., so•
    mat•i•cized, so•
    mat•i•ciz•ing
so•mat•i•za•tion
somatization dis•or•
    der
so•mat•o•form
somatoform dis•or•
    der
son
son-in-law n., pl. sons-
    in-law
Son of Sam law
soph•ism
soph•ist
so•phis•tic
so•phis•ti•cal
so•phis•ti•cal•ly
so•phis•ti•cat•ed
sophisticated in•ves•
    tor
so•phis•ti•ca•tion
soph•ist•ry n., pl.
    soph•ist•ries
sor•did
sor•did•ly
sor•did•ness

sor•ri•ly
sor•ri•ness
sor•row
sor•row•ful
sor•row•ful•ly
sor•ry adj., sor•ri•er,
    sor•ri•est
sound
sound and dis•pos•
    ing mind and
    mem•o•ry
sound bite
sound in con•tract
sound in tort
sound mind
sound ti•tle
sound•ly
sound•ness
source n., v., sourced,
    sourc•ing
source code
source code es•crow
source of in•come
sourc•es of the law
sourc•ing
south (S.)
South East•ern Re•
    port•er (citation form:
    S.E.)
South West•ern Re•
    port•er (citation form:
    S.W.)
south•ern (S.)
South•ern blot
Southern blot•ting
Southern Dis•trict (ci-
    tation form: S.D.)
Southern Re•port•er
    (citation form: S.)
sov•er•eign
sovereign im•mu•
    ni•ty
sov•er•eign•ly
sov•er•eign•ty n., pl.
    sov•er•eign•ties
space chart•er

space law
spam n., v., spammed,
    spam•ming
spar v., sparred, spar•
    ring
spas•mod•ic
speak v., spoke,
    spok•en, speak•ing
speak•er
speak•er•ship
speak•ing de•mur•
    rer
speaking mo•tion
speak•ing ob•jec•
    tion
spec. (special)
spe•cial (citation
    forms: **Spec.** in a
    name; **spec.** in de-
    scriptive material)
special act
special a•gent
special ap•pear•ance
special as•sess•ment
special as•sump•sit
special check•ing ac•
    count
special cir•cum•
    stances
special com•mit•tee
special con•tract
special coun•sel
special court-mar•tial
special dam•ag•es
special de•mur•rer
special div•i•dend
special ed•u•ca•tion
special e•lec•tion
special ex•cep•tion
special grand ju•ry
special guard•i•an
special in•dorse•ment
special in•ter•est n.
special-interest adj.
special in•ter•rog•a•
    to•ries

special ju•ris•dic•tion
special ju∘ry
special law
special leg•is•la•tion
special lim∘i•ta•tion
special mas•ter
special meet•ing
special needs trust
special plea
special plead•ing
special pow∘er of
  ap•point•ment
special power of at•
  tor•ney
special pro•ceed•ing
special pros∘e•cu•tor
special ques•tions
special-rev∘e•nue
  debt
special rule
special ses•sion
special term
special trust
special use
special use per•mit
special use val•u•a•
  tion
special ver•dict
special war•ran∘ty
special warranty deed
Special Weap•ons
  and Tac•tics (SWAT)
spe•cial•ist
spe•cial∘i•za•tion
spe•cial•ize v., spe•
  cial•ized, spe•cial•
  iz•ing
spe•cial•ly
spe•cial∘ty n., pl.
  spe•cial•ties
specialty debt
spe•cie n.sing. (coined
  money: cf. SPECIES; IN
  SPECIE)
spe•cies n., pl. spe•
  cies (a type of plant or

animal: cf. SPECIE; IN
  SPECIE)
spe•cif•ic
specific be•quest
specific claim
specific de•ni∘al
specific de•vise
specific in•tent
specific leg∘a∘cy
specific lien
specific per•for•
  mance
specific re•lief
specific res•ti•tu•tion
spe•cif∘i•cal∘ly
spec∘i•fi•ca•tion
spec∘i•fic∘i•ty
spec∘i•fied-risk
  pol∘i∘cy
spec∘i•fi∘er
spec∘i•fy v., spec∘i•
  fied, spec∘i•fy•ing
spec∘i•men
spe•cious
spe•cious∘ly
spe•cious•ness
spec•trum n., pl.
  spec•tra or spec•
  trums
spectrum al•lo•ca•
  tion
spec∘u•late v.,
  spec∘u•late
spec∘u•la•tion
spec∘u•la•tive
speculative dam•
  ag∘es
speculative risk
spec∘u•la•tive∘ly
spec∘u•la•tive•ness
spec∘u•la•tor
speech
speech plus
speech•less
speech•less∘ly
speech•less•ness

speed n., v., sped or
  (in sense of exceeding
  the speed limit or
  speeding up)
  speed∘ed, speed•ing
speed lim∘it
speed-up or speed•
  up n
speed∘er
speed∘i∘ly
speed∘i•ness
speed•ing
speed∘y adj., speed•
  i∘er, speed•i•est
speedy tri∘al
spell
spell•bind∘er
spell•bind•ing
spell•bound
spend v., spent,
  spend•ing
spend•a∘ble
spend∘er
spend•thrift
spendthrift trust
spes suc•ces•si∘o•nis
  Latin.
sphere of in•flu•ence
spill
spill•age
spin v., spun, spin•
  ning, n.
spin con•trol
spin doc•tor
spin off v.
spin-off or spin•off n.
spin•ster
spin•ster•hood
spir∘it of the law
spir•it∘ed
spir•it•ed∘ly
spir•it•ed•ness
spir•it•less
spir•it•less∘ly
spir•it•less•ness
spir•its n.pl.

spir•it•u•al

spir•it•u•al•i•ty

spir•it•u•al•ly

spir•it•u•al•ness

spite *n.*, *v.*, spit•ed, spit•ing

spite fence

spite•ful

spite•ful•ly

spite•ful•ness

spleen

spleen•ful

spleen•ful•ly

split *v.*, split, split•ting

split-dol•lar in•sur•ance

split off *v.*

split-off *n.*

split roll

split-roll tax

split sen•tence

split up *v.*

split-up *n.*

split•ta•ble

spoil *v.*, spoiled, spoil•ing

spoil•a•ble

spoil•age

spoil•er

spoils *n.pl.*

spoils sys•tem

spokes•man *n.*, *pl.* spokes•men

spokes•per•son *n.*, *pl.* spokes•peo•ple

spokes•wom•an *n.*, *pl.* spokes•wom•en

spo•li•ate *v.*, spo•li•at•ed, spo•li•at•ing

spo•li•a•tion

spo•li•a•tor

spon•sion

spon•sor

spon•so•ri•al

spon•sor•ship

spon•ta•ne•ous

spontaneous a•bor•tion

spontaneous com•bus•tion

spontaneous dec•la•ra•tion

spontaneous ex•cla•ma•tion

spontaneous state•ment

spon•ta•ne•ous•ly

spon•ta•ne•ous•ness

spo•rad•ic

spo•rad•i•cal•ly

spo•rad•i•cal•ness

spot *n.*, *v.*, spot•ted, spot•ting, *adj.*

spot check *n.*

spot-check *v.*

spot mar•ket

spot price

spot trad•ing

spot zon•ing

spous•al

spous•al a•buse

spousal priv•i•lege

spousal rape

spousal sup•port

spous•al•ly

spouse

spouse•hood

spouse•less

spous•e's e•lec•tion

spouse's e•lec•tive share

spouse's stat•u•to•ry share

spread *v.*, spread, spread•ing, *n.*

spread op•tion

spread up•on the rec•ord

spread•sheet

spring *v.*, sprang, sprung, spring•ing, *n.*, *adj.*

spring•ing

springing ex•ec•u•to•ry in•ter•est

springing pow•er of at•tor•ney

springing trust

springing use

spring•ing•ly

sprink•ling trust

spu•ri•ous

spu•ri•ous•ly

spu•ri•ous•ness

spurn

spy *n.*, *v.* spied, spy•ing

spy•ing

squab•ble *v.*, squab•bled, squab•bling, *n.*

squad

squad car

squan•der

squan•der•er

square *n.*, *v.*, squared, squar•ing, *adj.*, squar•er, squar•est

square•ly

squat *v.* squat•ted, squat•ting

squat•ter

squat•ter•dom

squeeze *v.*, squeezed, squeez•ing, *n.*

squeeze out *v.*

squeeze-out *n.*, *adj.*

squeez•er

squire *n.*, *v.* squired, squir•ing

S.S. (Steamship; Steamships)

SSI (Supplemental Security Income)

St. (State; Street)

sta•bil•i•ty

sta•bi•li•za•tion

sta•bi•lize v., sta•bi•lized, sta•bi•liz•ing
sta•bi•liz•er
sta•ble adj., sta•bler, sta•blest
sta•bly
staff n., pl. staffs or (in sense of a rod or pole) staves, adj., v.
staff•er
stag•fla•tion
stag•nate v., stag•nat•ed, stag•nat•ing
stag•na•tion
stake
stake•hold•er
stale adj., stal•er, stal•est
stale check
stale claim
stale•ly
stale•ness
stalk
stalk•er
stalk•ing
stalk•ing-horse
stalk•ing•ly
stall
stall•age
stal•wart
stal•wart•ly
stal•wart•ness
stamp
stamp tax
stanch (to stop a flow: cf. STAUNCH)
stand v., stood, stand•ing, n.
stand bail
stand by v. (cf. STANDBY)
stand down v.
stand-down n.
stand mute

stand•ard
standard cost
standard de•duc•tion
standard of care
standard of liv•ing
standard of proof
standard of re•view
stand•ard•iz•a•ble
stand•ard•i•za•tion
stand•ard•ize v., stand•ard•ized, stand•ard•iz•ing
stand•ard•iz•er
stand•ards n.pl.
standards pick•et•ing
standby n., pl. stand•bys, adj. (cf. STAND BY)
standby coun•sel
standby let•ter of cred•it
standby loan com•mit•ment
stand•ing
standing com•mit•tee
standing or•der
stand•off n.
stand•out n.
Stan•ford-Bi•net test
stan•o•o•lone Controlled Subst.
stan•o•o•zo•lol Controlled Subst.
sta•ple
Star Cham•ber
star cham•ber pro•ceed•ing
sta•re de•ci•sis Latin.
start
START (Strategic Arms Reduction Treaty)
start up v.
start-up n., adj.
star•va•tion wag•es
stash
Stat. (Statistical; Statistics; Statute; Statutes;

United States Statutes at Large)
state¹ n., adj. (citation form: St.)
state² v., stat•ed, stat•ing
state ac•tion
state aid
state bank
state of mind
state of the art n.
state-of-the-art v.
state of war
state po•lice
state re•li•gion
state se•cret
state vis•it
state•craft
stat•ed
stated cap•i•tal
stated meet•ing
stated term
stated val•ue
state•hood
state•hood•er
state•house
state•less
stateless per•son
stateless ves•sel
state•less•ness
state•ment
statement of changes in fi•nan•cial po•si•tion
statement of changes in own•ers' eq•ui•ty
statement of claim
statement of fi•nan•cial po•si•tion
statement of op•er•a•tions
statement of re•tained earn•ings
statement of the case

statement sav•ings
  ac•count
state's at•tor•ney
state's ev∘i∘dence
states' right∘er
states' rights
states•man *n., pl.*
  states•men
states•man•like
states•man∘ly
states•man•ship
stat∘ic
stat∘i∘cal∘ly
sta•tim *Latin.*
stat•ism
stat•ist
sta•tis•tic
sta•tis•ti•cal *(citation
  form:* **Stat.**)
sta•tis•ti•cal∘ly
statistically sig•nif∘i•
  cant
sta•tis•tics *n.sing. or
  pl. (citation form:*
  Stat.)
sta•tus[1] *n., pl.* sta•
  tus∘es *English.*
sta•tus[2] *n., pl.* sta•tus
  Latin.
status crime
status of•fend∘er
status of•fense
status quo *Latin.*
status quo an∘te
  Latin.
stat∘u•ta•ble
stat•ute *(citation form
  for sing. and pl.:*
  Stat.)
statute of frauds
statute of lim∘i•ta•
  tions
Statute of Qui∘a
  Emp•to∘res
statute of re•pose
Statute of Us∘es

Statute of Wills
Stat•utes at Large *(ci-
  tation form:* **Stat.**)
statutes of de•scent
  and dis•tri•bu•tion
Statutes of Mort•
  main
Statutes of Prae•mu•
  ni∘re
stat∘ut•ist
stat∘u•to•ri∘ly
stat∘u•to∘ry
statutory ab•sten•
  tion
statutory con•struc•
  tion
statutory crime
statutory du∘ty
statutory em•ploy∘er
statutory ex•cep•tion
statutory law
statutory lien
statutory list
statutory ob•li•ga•
  tion
statutory of•fense
statutory rape
statutory re•demp•
  tion
statutory right
statutory share
staunch *(steadfast: cf.*
  STANCH)
stay
stay of ex∘e•cu•tion
stay of pro•ceed•ings
stay on ap•peal
STD *(sexually transmit-
  ted disease)*
stead•fast
stead•fast∘ly
stead•fast•ness
steal *v.,* stole, sto•len,
  steal•ing, *n.*
steal•a∘ble
steal∘er

stealth
stealth∘i∘ly
stealth∘y
steam•ship *(citation
  form for sing. and pl.:*
  S.S.)
steer•ing com•mit•
  tee
stel•lion•ate
ste•nog•ra•pher
sten∘o∘graph∘ic
ste•nog•ra•phy
step *n., v.* stepped,
  step•ping
step trans•ac•tion
step up *v.*
step-up *adj., n.*
step•broth∘er
step•child *n., pl.*
  step•chil•dren
step•daugh•ter
step•fa•ther
step•moth∘er
step•par•ent
stepped-down ba∘sis
stepped-up basis
step•sib•ling
step•sis•ter
step•son
ster∘e∘o∘type *n., v.,*
  ster∘e∘o∘typed,
  ster∘e∘o∘typ•ing
ster∘e∘o∘typed
stereotyped be•hav•
  ior
ster∘e∘o∘typ∘er
ster∘e∘o∘typ∘ic
ster∘e∘o∘typ∘i•cal
ster∘e∘o∘typ∘i•cal∘ly
ster•ile
ste•ril∘i∘ty
ster∘i•li•za•tion
ster∘i•lize *v.,* ster∘i•
  lized, ster∘i•liz•ing
ster•oid
ste•roi•dal

stet[1] *Latin.*

stet[2] *v.,* stet•ted,
stet•ting

ste•ve•dore *n., v.,*
ste•ve•dored, ste•
ve•dor•ing

stew•ard

stew•ard•ship

sti•fle *v.,* sti•fled, sti•
fling

sti•fling

sti•fling•ly

stig•o•ma *n., pl.* stig•
ma•ta *or* stig•mas

stig•ma•ti•za•tion

stig•ma•tize *v.,* stig•
ma•tized, stig•ma•
tiz•ing

stig•ma•tiz•er

still•birth

still•born

stim•u•lant

sti•pend

stip•u•la•ble

stip•u•late *v.,* stip•u•
lat•ed, stip•u•lat•
ing

stipulated dam•ag•es

stipulated fact

stip•u•la•tion

stip•u•la•tor

stip•u•la•to•ry

stirps *n., pl.* stir•pes

stock

stock ap•pre•ci•a•
tion right

stock as•soc•i•a•tion

stock bo•nus plan

stock book

stock brok•er•age

stock buy•back

stock cer•tif•i•cate

stock com•pa•ny

stock cor•po•ra•tion

stock div•i•dend

stock ex•change

stock in trade *or*
stock-in-trade

stock in•sur•ance
com•pa•ny

stock is•sue

stock ledg•er

stock ma•nip•u•la•
tion

stock mar•ket

stock op•tion

stock pow•er

stock re•demp•tion

stock re•pur•chase

stock rights

stock split

stock sub•scrip•tion

stock trans•fer

stock transfer a•gent

stock transfer tax

stock war•rant

stock with par val•ue

stock with•out par
value

stock•brok•er

stock•brok•er•age

stock•brok•ing

stock•hold•er

stockholder de•riv•a•
tive ac•tion

stockholder of rec•
ord

stock•hold•ers' eq•
ui•ty

stock•job•ber

stock•job•ber•y

stock•job•bing

stolen prop•er•ty

stone•wall

stone•wall•er

stone•wall•ing

stool pi•geon

stool•ie

stop *v.,* stopped,
stop•ping, *n.*

stop and frisk

stop clause

stop-lim•it or•der

stop-loss

stop-loss clause

stop-loss or•der

stop no•tice

stop or•der

stop pay•ment order

stop price

stop•page

stoppage in tran•sit

store *n., v.,* stored,
stor•ing, *adj.*

stor•er

stow•age

stow•a•way

STR (short tandem re-
peat)

strad•dle *n., v.,* strad•
dled, strad•dling

straight (unswerving;
unmodified; honest: cf.
STRAIT)

straight bank•rupt•cy

straight bill of lad•
ing

straight face

straight-face test

straight-faced

straight-fac•ed•ly

straight life in•sur•
ance

straight-line de•pre•
ci•a•tion

straight•en (to make
or become straight: cf.
STRAITEN)

straight•ly

straight•ness

strait (a narrows; a dif-
ficult or dire situation:
cf. STRAIGHT)

strait-laced

strait-lac•ed•ly

strait-lac•ed•ness

strait•en (to put into

difficulty; to restrict:
cf. STRAIGHTEN)
strait•jack•et
stran•ger
stran•gle v., stran•
gled, stran•gling
stran•gle•hold
stran•gu•late v.,
stran•gu•lat•ed,
stran•gu•lat•ing
stran•gu•la•tion
stran•gu•la•tive
stran•gu•la•to•ry
strat∘a•gem
stra•te•gic
Strategic Arms Lim∘i•
ta•tion Talks (SALT)
Strategic Arms Re•
duc∘tion Trea∘ty
(START)
Strategic Law•suit
A∘gainst Pub•lic
Par•tic∘i•pa•tion
See SLAPP.
stra•te•gi•cal∘ly
strat∘e∘gy n., pl.
strat∘e∘gies
stra•toc•ra∘cy n., pl.
stra•toc•ra•cies
strat∘o•crat
strat∘o•crat∘ic
straw man
straw pur•chase
straw pur•chas∘er
straw vote
stream of com•merce
street (St.)
street cer•tif∘i•cate
street crime
street drug
street name
street-smart
street smarts
street-wise or street•
wise
street•walk∘er

street•walk•ing
strength
strength∘en
strength•en∘er
stress
stress re•ac•tion
stres•sor
stretch out v.
stretch-out or stretch•
out n.
strict
strict con•struc•tion
strict fore•clo•sure
strict li•a•bil∘i•ty
strict scru•ti∘ny
strict∘ly
strict•ness
stri•den•cy
stri•dent
stri•dent∘ly
strife
strike v., struck, struck
or (esp. in sense of af-
flicting) strick∘en,
strik•ing, n.
strike ben∘e•fit
strike fund
strike price
strike suit
strike•a∘ble or strik•
a∘ble
strike•break∘er
strike•break•ing
strike•less
strik∘er
strik•ing price
string ci•ta•tion
string cite
strin•gent
strin•gent∘ly
strip v., stripped,
strip•ping, n.
strip search
strong
strong-arm
strong-arm rob•ber∘y

strong hand
strong∘ly
strong•man n., pl.
strong•men
struck ju∘ry
struc•tur∘al
struc•tur•al•ism
struc•tur•al•ist
struc•tur•al∘ly
strych∘nine
stub•born
stub•born∘ly
stub•born•ness
Stud. (Studies)
stu•dent
stud•ies (citation form:
Stud.)
stud∘y n., pl. stud•
ies, v., stud∘ied,
stud•y•ing
stul•ti•fi•ca•tion
stul•ti•fi∘er
stul•ti∘fy v., stul•ti•
fied, stul•ti•fy•ing
stul•ti•fy•ing∘ly
stun v., stunned,
stun•ning
stun gun
stu•pe•fac•tion
stu•pe•fac•tive
stu•pe•fi∘er
stu•pe∘fy v., stu•
pe∘fied, stu•pe•fy•
ing
stu•pe•fy•ing∘ly
stu•pid
stu•pid∘i•ty
stu•pid∘ly
stu•por
stu•por•ous
Sturm und Drang Ger-
man.
style n., v., styled,
styl•ing
su∘a spon∘te Latin.
su•a•bil∘i•ty

su•a•ble
su•a•bly
sua•sion
sua•sive
sua•sive•ly
sua•sive•ness
sub *Latin.*
sub ju•di•ce *Latin.*
sub mo•do *Latin.*
sub nom. (sub nomine)
sub no•mi•ne *Latin*
(*citation form:* sub
nom.)
sub ro•sa *Latin.*
sub si•gil•lo *Latin.*
sub si•len•ti•o *Latin.*
sub•a•gen•cy *n., pl.*
sub•a•gen•cies
sub•a•gent
sub•av•er•age
sub•cat•e•go•ry *n.,*
pl. sub•cat•e•go•
ries
sub•chap•ter
Subchapter C cor•po•
ra•tion
sub•char•ter
sub•class
sub•com•bi•na•tion
Sub•comm. (Subcom-
mittee
sub•com•mit•tee (*ci-*
tation form: Sub-
comm.
sub•con•scious
sub•con•scious•ly
sub•con•tract
sub•con•trac•tor
sub•cul•ture
sub•del•e•ga•tion
sub•de•mise *n., v.*
sub•de•mised, sub•
de•mis•ing
sub•dis•trib•u•tor
sub•dis•trict
sub•di•vid•a•ble

sub•di•vide *v.,* sub•
di•vid•ed, sub•di•
vid•ing
sub•di•vid•er
sub•di•vi•sion
sub•du•a•ble
sub•due *v.,* sub•
dued, sub•du•ing
sub•dued
sub•freight
sub•ge•ner•ic
sub•ge•nus *n., pl.*
sub•gen•e•ra
sub•group
sub•in•feu•da•tion
sub•ja•cen•cy
sub•ja•cent
subjacent sup•port
sub•ja•cent•ly
sub•ject
subject mat•ter ju•
ris•dic•tion
subject to
subject to o•pen
sub•ject•a•bil•i•ty
sub•ject•a•ble
sub•ject•ed•ly
sub•ject•ed•ness
sub•jec•tive
subjective test
sub•jec•tive•ly
sub•jec•tive•ness
sub•jec•tiv•ism
sub•jec•tiv•ist
sub•jec•ti•vis•tic
sub•jec•ti•vis•ti•
cal•ly
sub•jec•tiv•i•ty
sub•ju•ga•ble
sub•ju•gate *v.,* sub•
ju•gat•ed, sub•ju•
gat•ing
sub•ju•ga•tion
sub•ju•ga•tor
sub•lease *n., v.,* sub•
leased, sub•leas•ing

sub•les•see
sub•les•sor
sub•let *v.,* sub•let,
sub•let•ting, *n.*
sub•li•cense *n., v.,*
sub•li•censed, sub•
li•cens•ing
sub•li•cen•see
sub•li•ma•tion
sub•lim•i•nal
sub•lim•i•nal•ly
sub•lit•to•ral
sub•ma•chine gun
sub•mar•ket
sub•mis•si•ble
sub•mis•sion
sub•mis•sive
sub•mis•sive•ly
sub•mis•sive•ness
sub•mit *v.* sub•mit•
ted, sub•mit•ting
sub•mit•ta•ble
sub•mit•ter
sub•nor•mal
sub•op•ti•mal
sub•or•di•nate *adj.,*
n., v., sub•or•di•
nat•ed, sub•or•di•
nat•ing
subordinate lien
subordinate se•cu•
ri•ty
sub•or•di•nat•ed
subordinated de•
ben•ture
sub•or•di•nate•ly
sub•or•di•nate•ness
sub•or•di•na•tion
(making secondary or
subservient: cf. SUBOR-
NATION)
subordination
a•gree•ment
subordination clause
sub•or•di•na•tive
sub•orn

sub•or•na•tion (urg-
ing a person commit a
wrong, esp. perjury:
cf. SUBORDINATION

subornation of per•
jury

sub•or•na•tive

sub•or•nee

sub•orn•er

sub•poe•na *n., pl.*
sub•poe•nas, *v.,*
sub•poe•naed, sub•
poe•na•ing

subpoena ad tes•ti•
fi•can•dum

subpoena du•ces
te•cum

sub•rep•tion

sub•rep•ti•tious

sub•rep•ti•tious•ly

sub•ro•gate *v.,* sub•
ro•gat•ed, sub•ro•
gat•ing

sub•ro•ga•tion

sub•ro•gee

sub•ro•gor

sub•sam•ple

sub•scrib•a•ble

sub•scribe *v.,* sub•
scribed, sub•scrib•
ing

sub•scribed and
sworn to

subscribed stock

sub•scrib•er

sub•scrib•er•ship

sub•scrip•tion

sub•scrip•tive

sub•scrip•tive•ly

sub•sec•re•tar•i•at

sub•sec•tion

sub•se•quent

sub•se•quent•ly

sub•serve *v.,* sub•
served, sub•serv•ing

sub•ser•vi•ence

sub•ser•vi•en•cy

sub•ser•vi•ent

sub•ser•vi•ent•ly

sub•side *v.,* sub•
sid•ed, sub•sid•ing

sub•sid•ence

sub•sid•er

sub•sid•i•ar•i•ly

sub•sid•i•ar•i•ness

sub•sid•i•ar•y *adj.,
n., pl.* sub•sid•i•ar•
ies

subsidiary cor•por•a•
tion

subsidiary ledg•er

subsidiary rights

sub•si•diz•a•ble

sub•si•di•za•tion

sub•si•dize *v.,* sub•
si•dized, sub•si•
diz•ing

sub•si•diz•er

sub•si•dy *n., pl.* sub•
si•dies

sub•sist

sub•sist•ence

subsistence al•low•
ance

subsistence farm•ing

sub•spe•cial•ty

sub•spe•cies *n., pl.*
sub•spe•cies

sub•stance

substance a•buse

substance de•pend•
ence

substance-in•duced
anx•i•e•ty dis•or•
der

substance-induced
de•lir•i•um

substance-induced
disorder

substance-induced
mood disorder

substance-induced

per•sist•ing am•
nes•tic disorder

substance-induced
persisting de•men•
tia

substance-induced
psy•chot•ic dis•or•
der

substance-induced
sex•u•al dys•func•
tion

substance-induced
sleep dis•or•der

substance in•tox•i•
ca•tion

substance-re•lat•ed
dis•or•der

substance use disor-
der

substance with•
draw•al

sub•stance•less

sub•stand•ard

sub•stan•tial

substantial ca•
pac•i•ty test

substantial com•pli•
ance

substantial ev•i•
dence

substantial im•pact
test

substantial jus•tice

substantial per•for•
mance

substantial sim•i•
lar•i•ty

sub•stan•tial•i•ty

sub•stan•tial•ly

sub•stan•tial•ness

sub•stan•ti•a•ta•ble

sub•stan•ti•ate *v.,*
sub•stan•ti•at•ed,
sub•stan•ti•at•ing

sub•stan•ti•a•tion

sub•stan•ti•a•tive

sub•stan•ti•a•tor

sub•stan•tive

substantive due proc•ess

substantive ev•i•dence

substantive law

substantive right

substantive rule

substantive un•con•scion•a•bil•i•ty

sub•stan•tive•ly

sub•stan•tive•ness

sub•sti•tut•a•bil•i•ty

sub•sti•tut•a•ble

sub•sti•tute n., v., sub•sti•tut•ed, sub•sti•tut•ing, adj.

sub•sti•tut•ed

substituted ba•sis

substituted serv•ice

sub•sti•tut•er

sub•sti•tu•tion

sub•sti•tu•tion•al

sub•sti•tu•tion•al•ly

sub•sti•tu•tion•ar•y

sub•sti•tu•tive

sub•sti•tu•tive•ly

sub•ten•an•cy

sub•ten•ant

sub•ten•ure

sub•ter•fuge

sub•ti•tle n., v., sub•ti•tled, sub•ti•tling

sub•tle adj., sub•tler, sub•tlest

sub•tle•ty n., pl. sub•tle•ties

sub•to•tal n., v., sub•to•taled, sub•to•tal•ing

sub•tract

sub•trac•tion

sub•trac•tive

sub•type

sub•ur•ban

sub•ur•ban•ite

sub•ur•ban•oi•za•tion

sub•ur•ban•ize v., sub•ur•ban•ized, sub•ur•ban•iz•ing

sub•ur•bi•a

sub•ven•tion

sub•ven•tion•ar•y

sub•ver•sion

sub•ver•sive

subversive ac•tiv•i•ty

sub•ver•sive•ly

sub•ver•sive•ness

sub•vert

sub•vert•er

suc•ceed

suc•ceed•a•ble

suc•ceed•er

suc•ceed•ing

suc•cess

suc•cess•ful

suc•cess•ful•ly

suc•cess•ful•ness

suc•ces•sion

succession tax

suc•ces•sive

suc•ces•sive•ly

suc•ces•sive•ness

suc•ces•sor

successor in in•ter•est

suc•ces•sors and as•signs

suc•cinct

suc•cinct•ly

suc•cinct•ness

suc•cor

suc•cor•a•ble

suc•cor•er

Suchapter S cor•po•ra•tion

suck•er

sud•den

sudden e•mer•gen•cy doc•trine

sudden in•fant death syn•drome (SIDS)

sud•den•ly

sud•den•ness

sue v., sued, su•ing

sue out

su•er

su•fen•ta•nil Controlled Subst.

suf•fer

suf•fer•a•ble

suf•fer•a•ble•ness

suf•fer•a•bly

suf•fer•ance

suf•fer•er

suf•fer•ing

suf•fice v., suf•ficed, suf•fic•ing

suf•fi•cien•cy

suf•fi•cient

sufficient cause

sufficient ev•i•dence

suf•fi•cient•ly

suf•fo•cate v., suf•fo•cat•ed, suf•fo•cat•ing

suf•fo•cat•ing•ly

suf•fo•ca•tion

suf•fo•ca•tive

suf•frage

suf•fra•gist

sug•gest

sug•gest•er

sug•gest•i•bil•i•ty

sug•gest•i•ble

sug•gest•i•bly

sug•ges•tion

suggestion of in•ter•est

sug•ges•tive

sug•ges•tive•ly

sug•ges•tive•ness

su•i ge•ne•ris Latin.

sui ju•ris Latin.

su•i•ci•dal

suicidal i•de•a•tion

su•i•ci•dal•ly

su•i•cide

suicide clause

suicide pact

suit

suit•a•bil•i•ty

suit•a•ble

suit•or

sul•fon•di•eth•yl• meth•ane *Controlled Subst.*

sul•fon•eth•yl• meth•ane *Controlled Subst.*

sul•fon•meth•ane *Controlled Subst.*

sum *n.*, *v.*, **summed, sum•ming**

sum cer•tain

sum-of-the-years'-dig• its meth•od of de• pre•ci•a•tion

sum up

sum∘ma cum lau∘de *Latin.*

sum•mar∘i•ly

sum•mar∘i•ness

sum•ma•riz•a•ble

sum•ma•ri•za•tion

sum•ma•rize *v.*, **sum• ma•rized, sum•ma• riz•ing**

sum•ma•riz∘er

sum•ma∘ry *n.*, *pl.* **sum•ma∘ries,** *adj.*

summary ac•tion

summary con•vic• tion

summary court-mar• tial

summary judg•ment

summary ju•ris•dic• tion

summary pro•ceed• ing

summary proc•ess

summary tri∘al

sum•ma•tion

sum•mit

summit meet•ing

sum•mit•eer

sum•mit∘ry

sum•mon *v.*, **sum• moned, sum•mon• ing** (to call: cf. SUM-MONS)

sum•mon•a•ble

sum•mon•er

sum•mons *n.*, *pl.* **sum•mons∘es,** *v.*, **sum•monsed, sum• mons•ing** (enforcea-ble demand to appear; to serve such a de-mand: cf. SUMMON)

sum•mons∘a•ble

sum•mum bo∘num *Latin.*

sump•tu•ar∘y

sumptuary law

Sun•day clos•ing law

sunk∘en

sun•set

sunset clause

sunset law

sun•shine law

su∘o ju∘re *Latin.*

suo nom∘i∘ne *Latin.*

Sup. (Supreme)

Sup. Ct. (Supreme Court)

Sup. Ct. Err. (Supreme Court of Errors)

Sup. Jud. Ct. (Supreme Judicial Court)

Super. (Superior)

Super. Ct. (Superior Court)

su∘per due proc∘ess

su∘per•a∘bil∘i•ty

su∘per•a∘ble

su∘per∘a•bun•dance

su∘per∘a•bun•dant

su∘per∘a•bun• dant∘ly

su∘per•er∘o∘gate *v.*, su∘per•er∘o∘ gat∘ed, su∘per• er∘o∘gat•ing

su∘per•er∘o∘ga•tion

su∘per•er∘o∘ga•tor

su•per•fi∘cial

su•per•fi∘ci•al∘i∘ty

su•per•fi∘cial∘ly

su•per•flu•i∘ty *n.*, *pl* su•per•flu∘i•ties

su•per•flu•ous

su•per•flu•ous∘ly

su∘per•fund

su∘per•hu∘man

su∘per•in•tend

su∘per•in•tend• en∘cy

su∘per•in•tend•ent

su•pe•ri∘or (*citation form:* Super.)

Superior Court (*cita-tion form:* Super. Ct.)

superior lien

su•pe•ri•or∘i∘ty

su•pe•ri•or∘ly

su∘per•ja•cent

superjacent wa•ters

su∘per•ma•jor∘i∘ty *n.*, *pl.* su∘per•ma• jor∘i•ties

su∘per•pa•tri∘ot

su∘per•pa•tri•ot∘ic

su∘per•pa•tri•ot∘i• cal∘ly

su∘per•pa•tri•ot•ism

su∘per•sed•a∘ble

su∘per•sede *v.*, su∘per•sed∘ed, su∘per•sed•ing

su∘per•se•de∘as *Latin.*

supersedeas bond

su•per•sed•er
su•pe•rsed•ing cause
su•per•sen•ior•i•ty
su•per•ses•sion
su•per•sti•tion
su•per•sti•tious
superstitious trust
superstitious use
su•per•sti•tious•ly
su•per•sti•tious•ness
su•per•vene v.,
su•per•vened,
su•per•ven•ing
su•per•ven•ience
su•per•ven•ien•er
su•per•ven•ient
su•per•ven•ing
supervening cause
supervening neg•li•
gence
su•per•ven•tion
su•per•vise v.,
su•per•vised,
su•per•vis•ing
supervised vis•it•a•
tion
su•per•vi•sion
su•per•vi•sor
su•per•vi•sor•ship
su•per•vi•so•ry
sup•ple•ment
sup•ple•men•tal
supplemental af•fi•
da•vit
supplemental an•
swer
supplemental com•
plaint
supplemental ju•ris•
dic•tion
supplemental plead•
ing
supplemental reg•is•
ter
Supplemental Se•cu•
ri•ty In•come (SSI)

sup•ple•men•tal•ly
sup•ple•men•ta•ry
supplementary pro•
ceed•ing
sup•ple•men•ta•tion
sup•pli•ant
sup•pli•ant•ly
sup•pli•cant
sup•pli•cate v., sup•
pli•cat•ed, sup•pli•
cat•ing
sup•pli•cat•ing•ly
sup•pli•er
sup•ply v., sup•plied,
sup•ply•ing, n.
sup•port
support lev•el
support mort•gage
support trust
sup•port•a•bil•i•ty
sup•port•a•ble
sup•port•er
sup•port•ive
sup•pos•a•ble
sup•pose
sup•posed
sup•pos•ed•ly
sup•pos•er
sup•pos•ing
sup•po•si•tion
sup•po•si•tion•al
sup•po•si•tion•al•ly
sup•po•si•tious
sup•pos•i•ti•tious
sup•pos•i•ti•tious•ly
sup•pos•i•ti•tious•
ness
sup•pos•i•tive
sup•press
sup•pres•sant
sup•press•i•ble
sup•pres•sion
suppression hear•ing
suppression of ev•i•
dence
sup•pres•sive

sup•pres•sive•ly
sup•pres•sor
su•pra Latin
su•pra•lit•to•ral
su•pra•na•tion•al
su•pra•pro•test
su•prem•o•a•cy
Supremacy Clause
su•preme (citation
form: Sup.)
Supreme Court (cita
tion form: Sup. Ct.)
Supreme Court of Er•
rors (citation form:
Sup. Ct. Err.)
Supreme Court of Ju•
di•ca•ture
Supreme Court of the
U•nit•ed States
Supreme Ju•di•cial
Court (citation form:
Sup. Jud. Ct.)
sur Law French.
Sur. (Surety)
sur•cease v., sur•
ceased, sur•ceas•
ing, n.
sur•charge n., v., sur•
charged, sur•
charg•ing
sur•charg•er
sur•e•ty n., pl. sur•e•
ties (citation form:
Sur.)
surety bond
sur•e•ty•ship
suretyship bond
surf (to skim or search
haphazardly: cf. SERF)
sur•feit
sur•geon
sur•ger•y n., pl. sur•
ger•ies
sur•gi•cal
sur•gi•cal•ly
sur•li•ness

sur•ly *adj.*, sur•li•er, sur•li•est
sur•mis•a•ble
sur•mise *v.*, sur•mised, sur•mis•ing
sur•mis•er
sur•mount
sur•mount•a•ble
sur•mount•er
sur•name
sur•pass
sur•pass•a•ble
sur•pass•er
sur•pass•ing
sur•pass•ing•ly
sur•plus
sur•plus•age
sur•prise *n.*, *v.*, sur•prised, sur•pris•ing
sur•pris•ing
sur•pris•ing•ly
Surr. Ct. (Surrogate's Court)
sur•real
sur•re•al•is•tic
sur•re•al•is•ti•cal•ly
sur•re•but•tal
sur•re•but•ter
sur•re•join•der
sur•ren•der
surrender val•ue
sur•ren•der•er
sur•re•ply
surreply brief
sur•rep•ti•tious
sur•rep•ti•tious•ly
sur•rep•ti•tious•ness
sur•ro•ga•cy
sur•ro•gate (S.)
surrogate moth•er
surrogate moth•er•hood
Sur•ro•gate's Court (*citation form:* **Surr. Ct.**)
sur•ro•gate•ship

sur•round
sur•round•ing
sur•round•ings *n pl*
sur•tax
Surv. (Survey)
sur•veil *v.*, sur•veilled, sur•veil•ling
sur•veil•lance
sur•vey (*citation form:* **Surv.**)
sur•vey•a•ble
sur•vey•or
sur•viv•a•bil•i•ty
sur•viv•a•ble
sur•viv•al
survival stat•ute
sur•vive *v.*, sur•vived, sur•viv•ing
sur•viv•ing spouse
sur•vi•vor
sur•vi•vor•ship
survivorship an•nu•i•ty
sus•cep•ti•bil•i•ty
sus•cep•ti•ble
sus•cep•ti•bly
sus•pect
suspect clas•si•fi•ca•tion
sus•pect•i•ble
sus•pend
sus•pend•ed sen•tence
sus•pend•i•bil•i•ty
sus•pend•i•ble
sus•pense
sus•pense•ful
sus•pen•sion
suspension of the pow•er of al•ien•a•tion
sus•pen•sive
suspensive con•di•tion
sus•pen•sive•ly
sus•pi•cion

sus•pi•cious
sus•tain
sus•tain•a•bil•i•ty
sus•tain•a•ble
sus•tained re•mis•sion
sus•tain•ed•ly
sus•tain•er
sus•tain•ing•ly
sus•te•nance
su•ze•rain
su•ze•rain•ty *n.*, *pl.* su•ze•rain•ties
S.W. (South Western Reporter)
SWAT (Special Weapons and Tactics)
SWAT team
sway
sway•a•ble
sway•er
swear *v.*, swore, sworn, swear•ing
swear or af•firm
swear•er
swear•ing con•test
sweat eq•ui•ty
sweat•ing sys•tem
sweat•shop
sweep ac•count
sweep•stakes
sweet•heart
sweetheart con•tract
sweetheart deal
swin•dle *v.*, swin•dled, swin•dling
swin•dle•a•ble
swin•dler
swing *v.*, swung, swing•ing, *n.*, *adj.*
swing vote
sworn
sworn state•ment
sworn to
syc•o•phant
syc•o•phan•tic

syc○o•phan•ti•cal○ly

syc○o•phant•ism

syl•la•bus *n., pl.* syl•
la•bus○es or syl•
la○bi

syl•lo•gism

syl•lo•gis•tic

syl•lo•gis•ti•cal○ly

sym•bi•o•sis *n., pl.*
sym•bi•o•ses

sym•bi•ot•ic

sym•bi•ot•i•cal○ly

sym•bol

sym•bol○ic

symbolic de•liv•er○y

symbolic speech

sym•bol○i•cal○ly

sym•bol•ism

sym•bol○i•za•tion

sym•bol•ize *v.,* sym•
bol•ized, sym•bol•
iz○ing

Symp. (Symposium)

sym•pa•thet○ic

sym•pa•thet○i•cal○ly

sym•pa•thize *v.,*
sym•pa•thized,
sym•pa•thiz○ing

sym•pa•thiz○er

sym•pa•thiz○ing○ly

sym•pa•tho•mi•
met○ic

sym•pa•thy

sympathy strike

sym•po•si○um *n., pl.*
sym•po•si○a or
sym•po•si○ums (*ci-
tation form:* **Symp.**)

symp•tom

symp•to•mat○ic

symp•to•mat○i•
cal○ly

symp•tom○a•
tol○o○gy

syn•al•lag•mat○ic

syn•chro•ni•za•tion

syn•chro•nize *v.,*
syn•chro•nized,
syn•chro•niz○ing

syn•dic

syn•dic○al

syn•di•cal•ism

syn•di•cal•ist

syn•di•cal•is•tic

syn•di•cat•a•ble

syn•di•cate *n., v.,*
syn•di•cat○ed, syn•
di•cat○ing

syn•di•ca○tion

syn•di•ca•tor

syn•drome

syn•er•gism

syn•er•gist

syn•er•gis•tic

syn•er•gis•ti•cal○ly

syn•er○gy *n., pl.* syn•
er•gies

syn○o•nym

syn•on○y•mous

syn•on○y•mous○ly

syn•on○y•mous•ness

syn•op•sis *n., pl.*
syn•op•ses

syn•op•tic

syn•op•ti•cal○ly

syn•the•sis *n., pl.*
syn•the•ses

syn•the•sist

syn•the•size *v.,* syn•
the•sized, syn•the•
siz○ing

syn•the•siz○er

syn•thet○ic

synthetic fuel

syn•thet○i•cal○ly

sy•ringe

Sys. (System; Systems)

sys•tem (*citation form
for sing. and pl.:* **Sys.**)

sys•tem•at○ic (using a
system: cf. SYSTEMIC)

sys•tem•at○i•cal○ly

sys•tem○ic (pervading
or pertaining to a sys-
tem: cf. SYSTEMATIC)

sys•tem○i•cal○ly

T

T (thymine)

ta•ble¹ (*citation form:*
tbl.)

table² *v.,* ta•bled, ta•
bling

table of au•thor○i•
ties

tab•loid

ta○boo *adj., n., pl.* ta•

boos, *v.,* ta•booed,
ta•boo○ing

ta•bu○la ra○sa *n., pl.*
ta•bu○lae ra○sae
Latin.

tab○u•la•ble

tab○u•lar

tab○u•lar○ly

tab○u•late *v.,* tab○u•

lat○ed, tab○u•lat•
ing

tab○u•la•tion

tab○u•la•tor

tac○it

tacit ad•mis•sion

tac•it○ly

tac•it•ness

tac○i•tur•ni○ty

tack (a direction or

course of action; to
add on: cf. TACT)

tack•ing

tact (diplomatic sensi
bility: cf. TACK)

tact•ful

tact•ful•ly

tact•ful•ness

tac•tic

tac•ti•cal

tac•ti•cal•ly

tac•ti•cian

tac•tics n.sing. or pl.

tac•tile hal•lu•ci•na•
tion

tact•less

tact•less•ly

tact•less•ness

tag n., v., tagged,
tag•ging

tag•gant

tail (limitation of an estate: cf. TALE)

tail spe•cial

taint

taint•ed

taint•less

taint•less•ly

taint•less•ness

tak•a•ble

take v., took, tak•en,
tak•ing

take by em•i•nent
do•main

take down v. (cf. TAKE-
DOWN)

take for pub•lic use

take-home pay

take on sub•mis•sion

take out v. (cf. TAKE
OUT)

take o•ver v. (cf. TAKE-
OVER)

take the Fifth
A•mend•ment

take the stand

take•down n., adj. (·f.
TAKE DOWN)

take•out n., adj. (cf.
TAKE OUT)

take•o•ver n., adj. (cf.
TAKE OVER)

tak•er

tak•ing

tale n., pl. tales (a
story: cf. TAIL; TALES)

tal•ent

tal•ent•ed

ta•les n.sing. or pl. (an
order summoning ad
ditional jurors; such
jurors: cf. TALE)

ta•les•man n., pl. ta•
les•men (supplemen-
tal juror: cf. TALISMAN)

tal•i•oon

tal•is•man n., pl. tal•
is•mans (powerful or
influential object or
concept: cf. TALESMAN)

tal•is•man•ic

tal•is•man•i•cal•ly

talk

talk•er

tal•ly n., pl. tal•lies,
v., tal•lied, tal•ly•
ing

Tal•mud

Tal•mud•ic

tam•per

tam•per•er

tan•gent

tan•gen•tial

tan•gen•ti•al•i•ty

tan•gen•tial•ly

tan•gi•bil•i•ty

tan•gi•ble

tangible as•set

tangible form

tangible prop•er•ty

tan•gi•ble•ness

tan•gi•bly

tan•gle v., tan•gled,
tan•gling, n.

tan•gled

tan•gle•ment

tan•ta•mount

tap v., tapped, tap•
ping, n.

tar•di•o

tar•di•ness

tar•dy adj., tar•di•er,
tar•di•est

tare (allowance for
weight of packaging:
cf. TEAR[1])

tare weight

tar•get

target-be•ne•fit plan

target com•pa•ny

tar•get•able

tar•iff

tar•nish

tar•nish•er

tar•nish•ment

Ta•ser Trademark.

task

task force

taste v., tast•ed, tast•
ing, n.

taste•ful

taste•ful•ly

taste•ful•ness

taste•less

taste•less•ly

taste•less•ness

tat•tle v., tat•tled,
tat•tling, n.

tat•tler

taunt

taunt•er

taunt•ing•ly

tau•to•log•i•cal

tau•to•log•i•cal•ly

tau•tol•o•gy n., pl.
tau•tol•o•gies

tax

tax ac•count•ing

tax an•tic•i•pa•tion note

tax at•tri•bute

tax a•void•ance

tax base

tax be•ne•fit rule

tax brack•et

tax cer•tif•i•cate

Tax Court (*citation forms*: **T.C.**, for United States Tax Court; **T.C.** or **Tax. Ct.**, for various state courts)

tax cred•it

Tax Ct. Tax Court)

tax-de•duct•i•ble

tax de•duc•tion

tax deed

tax de•fer•ral

tax-de•ferred

tax-deferred an•nu•i•ty

tax dis•trict

tax e•va•sion

tax-ex•empt

tax-exempt in•come

tax-exempt or•gan•i•za•tion

tax ex•emp•tion

tax ex•pend•i•ture

tax fraud

tax-free

tax-free bond

tax-free liq•ui•da•tion

tax-free roll•o•ver

tax ha•ven

tax home

tax in•cen•tive

tax lien

tax prac•ti•tion•er

tax pref•er•ence i•tem

tax rate

tax re•fund

tax re•turn

tax sale

tax shel•ter

tax-shel•tered

tax stamp

tax ti•tle

tax year

tax•a•bil•i•ty

tax•a•ble

taxable costs

taxable dis•tri•bu•tion

taxable es•tate

taxable gift

taxable in•come

taxable ter•mi•na•tion

taxable year

tax•a•bly

tax•a•tion (*citation form*: **Tax'n**)

taxation of costs

tax•a•tion with•out rep•re•sen•ta•tion

tax•er

tax•ing

tax•ing•ly

Tax'n (Taxation)

tax•pay•er

taxpayer suit

tax•pay•ing

tbl. (table)

T.C. (Tax Court; United States Tax Court)

Tchr. (Teacher; Teachers)

teach *v.*, taught, teach•ing

teach•a•bil•i•ty

teach•a•ble

teach•a•ble•ness

teach•er (*citation form*: **Tchr.**)

team (to join in a cooperative effort: cf. TEEM)

team•ing

teaming a•gree•ment

tear[1] *v.*, tore, torn, tear•ing, *n.* (to rip; a rip: cf. TARE)

tear[2] (a drop from the eye: cf. TIER[1])

tear gas *n.*

tear-gas *v.*, tear-gassed, tear-gas•sing

tear•a•ble

tear•ful

tear•ful•ly

tear•ful•ness

tease *v.*, teased, teas•ing, *n.*

teas•ing•ly

Tech. (Technology; Technical; Technique)

tech•ni•cal (*citation form*: **Tech.**)

tech•ni•cal•i•ty *n.*, *pl.* tech•ni•cal•i•ties

tech•ni•cal•ly

tech•ni•cal•ness

tech•ni•cian

tech•nique (*citation form*: **Tech.**)

tech•no•ban•dit

tech•no•crat

tech•no•log•i•cal

tech•no•log•i•cal•ly

tech•nol•o•gy *n.*, *pl.* tech•nol•o•gies (*citation form*: **Tech.**)

te•di•ous

te•di•ous•ly

te•di•ous•ness

te•di•um

teem (to abound or swarm: cf. TEAM)

teem•ing

Tel. (Telephone; Telegraph)

tel•e•cast *v.*, tel•e•cast•ed, tel•e•cast•ing, *n.*

tel•e•cast•er
Telecomm.
  (Telecommunication;
  Telecommunications)

tel•e•com•mu•ni•
  ca°tion (*citation form:*
  Telecomm.)

tel°e•com•mu•ni•
  ca°tions *n.sing.* (*citation form:* **Telecomm.**)

tel°e•com•mute *v.*,
  tel°e•com•mut°ed,
  tel°e•com•mut°ing

tel°e•com•mut°er

tel°e•com•mut•ing

tel°e•con•fer•ence
  n., *v.*, tel°e•con•
  fer•enced, tel°e•
  con•fer•enc°ing

tel°e•con•fer•enc•
  ing

tel°e•gen°ic

tel°e•gen°i•cal•ly

tel°e•graph (*citation
  form:* **Tel.**)

tel°e•mar•ket•er

tel°e•mar•ket•ing

tel•e•o•log°i•cal

tel•e•o•log°i•cal•ly

tel•e•ol•o°gy

tel°e•phone (*citation
  form:* **Tel.**)

tel°e•phone ex•
  change

telephone ha•rass•
  ment

telephone so•lic•i•
  ta°tion

tel°e•phon°er

tel°e•phon°ic

tel°e•phon°i•cal•ly

tel°e•phon°y

tel°e•vi•sion

tell *v.*, told, tell•ing

tell•a°ble

tell°er

tell•ing

tell•ing°ly

tell•tale

te•maz°e•pam *Con-
  trolled Subst.*

tem•er•ar•i•ous
  (reckless; rash: cf. TIM-
  OROUS)

tem•er•ar•i•ous•ly

tem•er•ar•i•ous•
  ness

tem•er•i°ty

temp. (temporary)

tem•per

tem•per•a•ment

tem•per•a•men•tal

tem•per•a•men•
  tal°ly

tem•per•ance

tem•per•ate

tem•per•ate°ly

tem•per•ate•ness

tem•pered

tem•pest

tem•pes•tu•ous

tem•pes•tu•ous°ly

tem•pes•tu•ous•ness

tem•po•ral

tem•po•ral°ly

tem•po•ral•ness

tem•po•rar•i°ly

tem•po•rar•i•ness

tem•po•rar•y (*citation
  forms:* **Temp.** in a
  name; **temp.** in de
  scriptive material,*

temporary al•i•
  mo°ny

temporary dis•
  a•bil•i•ty

temporary in•junc•
  tion

temporary in•
  san°i•ty

temporary re•lief

temporary rem•e•dy

temporary re•strain•
  ing or•der (TRO)

tem•po•ri•za°tion

tem•po•rize *v.*, tem•
  po•rized, tem•po•
  riz•ing

tem•po•riz°er

tem•po•riz•ing°ly

tempt

tempt•a°ble

temp•ta°tion

temp°ter

tempt•ing

tempt•ing°ly

tempt•ress

ten•a•bil•i°ty

ten•a°ble

ten•a•ble•ness

ten•a°bly

te•na•cious

te•na•cious°ly

te•na•cious•ness

te•nac°i•ty

ten•an°cy *n.*, *pl.* ten•
  an•cies

tenancy at suf•fer•
  ance

tenancy at will

tenancy by the en•
  tire°ty

tenancy for life

tenancy for years

tenancy from year to
  year

tenancy in com•mon

tenancy in fee

tenancy in part•ner•
  ship

tenancy in tail

ten•ant (person in pos-
  session of land: cf.
  TENET)

tenant at suf•fer•
  ance

tenant at will

tenant by the en•tire•ty
tenant farm•er
tenant for life
tenant for years
tenant from year to year
tenant in ca•pi•te
tenant in com•mon
tenant in fee
tenant in tail
tenant par•a•vail
ten•ant•a•ble
tenantable re•pair
ten•ant•less
ten•ant•ry
ten•den•cy n., pl. ten•den•cies
ten•den•tious
ten•den•tious•ly
ten•den•tious•ness
ten•der
tender-heart•ed
tender of•fer
tender years
ten•der•a•bil•i•ty
ten•der•a•ble
ten•der•er
ten•e•ment
tenement house
ten•e•men•tal
ten•e•men•ta•ry
ten•e•ment•ed
te•nen•dum *Latin.*
ten•et (a belief or pri - ciple: cf. TENANT)
ten•or
tense
tense•ly
tense•ness
ten•sion
ten•ta•tive
tentative trust
ten•ta•tive•ly
ten•ta•tive•ness

ten•ter•hooks *n.pl.*
ten•u•ous
ten•u•ous•ly
ten•u•ous•ness
ten•ure
ten•ured
ten•u•ri•al
ten•u•ri•al•ly
te•rat•o••gen
te•rat•o••gen•e•sis
te•rat•o••gen•ic
term
term bond
term in•sur•ance
term life in•sur•ance
term lim•its
term of art
term of of•fice
term of years
term pol•i•cy
term•er (one serving a specified term in office or prison: cf. TERMOR)
ter•mi•na•bil•i•ty
ter•mi•na•ble
terminable in•ter•est
terminable prop•er•ty
ter•mi•na•ble•ness
ter•mi•na•bly
ter•mi•nal
terminal dis•claim•er
ter•mi•nal•ly
ter•mi•nate *v.,* ter•mi•nat•ed, ter•mi•nat•ing
ter•mi•na•tion
ter•mi•na•tive
ter•mi•na•tive•ly
ter•mi•na•tor
ter•mi•ner *Law French.*
ter•mi•no•log•i•cal
ter•mi•no•log•i•cal•ly
ter•mi•nol•o•gy *n.*

pl. ter•mi•nol•o•gies
ter•mi•nus *n., pl.* ter•mi•ni
terminus a quem *Latin.*
terminus a quo *Latin.*
terminus ad quem *Latin.*
ter•mor (holder of an estate for a term of years: cf. TERMER)
terms and con•di•tions
Terr. (Territory; Territorial)
ter•ra nul•li•us *Latin.*
ter•rae et te•ne•men•ta *Latin.*
ter•ri•ble
ter•ri•ble•ness
ter•ri•bly
ter•ri•er
ter•ri•fi•er
ter•ri•fy *v.,* ter•ri•fied, ter•ri•fy•ing
ter•ri•fy•ing•ly
ter•ri•to•ri•al *(citation form:* **Terr.**)
territorial court
territorial ju•ris•dic•tion
territorial sov•er•eign•ty
territorial wa•ters
ter•ri•to•ri•al•ism
ter•ri•to•ri•al•ist
ter•ri•to•ri•al•i•ty
ter•ri•to•ri•al•i•za•tion
ter•ri•to•ry *n., pl.* ter•ri•to•ries *(citation form:* **Terr.**)
ter•ror
ter•ro•rem *Latin.*
ter•ror•ism

ter•ror•ist

ter•ror•is•tic

ter•ror•i•za•tion

ter•ror•ize *v.*, ter•
ror•ized, ter•ror•iz•
ing

ter•ror•iz•er

terse *adj.*, ters•er,
ters•est

terse•ly

terse•ness

ter•ti•ar•y

tertiary care

test

test case

test•a•bil•i•ty

test•a•ble

tes•ta•cy

tes•ta•ment

tes•ta•men•ta•ry

testamentary ca•
pac•i•ty

testamentary gift

testamentary guard•
i•an

testamentary in•tent

testamentary pow•er
of ap•point•ment

testamentary trust

tes•ta•men•tum *n* ,
pl. tes•ta•men•ta
Latin.

tes•tate

tes•ta•tor

tes•ta•trix *n.*, *pl.* tes•
ta•tri•ces

tes•te *Latin and Eng-
lish.*

test•er

tes•ti•fi•er

tes•ti•fy *v*, tes•ti•
fied, tes•ti•fy•ing

tes•ti•ly

tes•ti•mo•ni•al

testimonial priv•i•
lege

tes•ti•mo•ni•um
clause

tes•ti•mo•ny *n.*, *pl.*
tes•ti•mo•nies

tes•ti•ness

test•ing

tes•to•lac•tone *Con-
trolled Subst.*

tes•tos•ter•one *Con-
trolled Subst.*

tes•ty *adj.*, tes•ti•er,
tes•ti•est

tête-à-tête *n.*, *pl.* tête-
à-tête or (*English*)
tête-à-têtes, *adj.*,
adv. French.

tet•ra•hy•dro•can•
nab•i•nol (THC) *Con-
trolled Subst.*

tet•raz•e•pam *Con-
trolled Subst.*

text

text•book

tex•tu•al

tex•tu•al•ly

tha•lid•o•mide

thal•weg or tal•weg
German.

thalweg (or talweg)
doc•trine

than•a•to•log•i•cal

than•a•tol•o•gist

than•a•tol•o•gy

than•a•tos

than•a•tot•ic

thank

thank•ful

thank•less

THC *Controlled Subst.*
(tetrahydrocannabinol)

the•a•ter or the•a•
tre

the•at•ri•cal

the•at•ri•cal•ism

the•at•ri•cal•i•ty

the•at•ri•cal•ly

the•at•rics *n.sing. or
pl.*

the•ba•con *Controlled
Subst.*

the•ba•ine *Controlled
Subst.*

theft

thence

thence•forth

thence•for•ward

then•yl•fen•ta•nyl
Controlled Subst.

the•oc•ra•cy *n.*, *pl.*
the•oc•ra•cies

the•o•crat•ic

the•o•crat•i•cal•ly

the•o•ret•i•cal

the•o•ret•i•cal•ly

the•o•rize *v.*, the•o•
rized, the•o•riz•ing

the•o•ry *n.*, *pl.* the•
o•ries

ther•a•peu•tic

ther•a•peu•ti•cal•ly

ther•a•pist

ther•a•py *n.*, *pl.*
ther•a•pies

there•a•bout

there•af•ter

there•at

there•by

there•for (for that; on
that account: cf. THERE-
FORE)

there•fore (conse-
quently: cf. THEREFOR)

there•from

there•in

there•in•af•ter

there•in•be•fore

there•in•to

there•of

there•on

there•to

there•to•fore

there•un•der

there•un•to
there•up∘on
there•with
these pres•ents
the•sis *n., pl.* the•ses
Thib∘o∘daux ab•sten•tion
thick-skinned
thief *n., pl.* thieves
thieve *v.* thieved, thiev•ing
thiev•er∘y *n., pl.* thiev•er•ies
thiev•ing
thiev•ing∘ly
thiev•ish
thiev•ish∘ly
thiev•ish∘ness
thin *adj.,* thin•ner, thin•nest
thin cor•po∘ra•tion
thin in•cor•po∘ra•tion
thin-skinned
thing
thing in ac•tion
thing of val∘ue
things per•son∘al
things re∘al
think *v.,* thought, think•ing
think tank
think•a∘ble
think•a∘ble•ness
think•a∘bly
think∘er
thin∘ly
thin•ness
thi•o•fen•ta•nyl *Controlled Subst.*
thi•o•pen∘tal so•di∘um
third
third de•gree *n.*
third-degree *adj.*
third par∘ty *n.*

third-party *adj.*
third-party ac•tion
third-party ben•e∘fi•ci•ar∘y
third-party beneficiary con•tract
third-party check
third-party claim
third-party com•plaint
third-party de•fend•ant
third-party in•sur•ance
third-party plain•tiff
third-party prac•tice
third read•ing
third∘ly
Tho∘ra•zine *Trademark.*
thor∘ough
thor∘ough•fare
thor∘ough•go∘ing
thor∘ough∘ly
thor∘ough•ness
though
thought
thought broad•cast•ing de∘lu•sion
thought dis•or∘der
thought in•ser•tion delusion
thought•ful
thought•ful∘ly
thought•ful•ness
thought•less
thought•less∘ly
thought•less•ness
thrall
thrall•dom
threat
threat∘en
threat•en∘er
threat•en•ing
threat•en•ing∘ly
three-card mon∘te

three-judge court
three-mile lim∘it
three-strikes law
thresh•old
threshold is∘sue
threshold ques•tion
threshold show•ing
thrift
thrift in•sti•tu•tion
thrift∘i∘ly
thrift∘i•ness
thrift∘y *adj.,* thrift•i∘er, thrift•i•est
throe *n., pl.* throes (spasm; agony; anguished struggle: cf. THROW)
throne
through
through bill of lad•ing
through trans•port
through•out
throw *v.,* threw, thrown, throw•ing, *n.* (to hurl; a hurling: cf. THROE)
throw•back rule
thug
thug•ger∘y
thug•gish
thumb•screw
thus
thwart
thwart∘er
thy•mine (T)
tick∘et
ticket scalp∘er
ticket scalp•ing
tick•et•less
tick•ler
tie *v.,* tied, ty∘ing
tie in *v.*
tie-in *adj., n.*
tie-in a∘gree•ment
tie-in ar•range•ment

tied prod•uct

tier¹ (a layer or level: cf. TEAR²)

ti∘er² (one who en-gages in tying: cf. TIRE)

tight-fist∘ed

ti•le•tam•ine-zo∘laz∘e∘pam *Controlled Subst.*

ti•li•dine *Controlled Subst.*

tim•ber rights

time *n., adj., v.,* timed, tim•ing

time-and-ma•te•ri•als con•tract

time-barred

time bill

time chart∘er

time de•pos∘it

time dis•count

time draft

time-hon•ored

time im•me•mo•ri∘al

time of the es•sence

time of war

time out of mind

time, place, and man•ner

time price

time-price doc•trine

time served

time-share *v.,* time-shared, time-shar•ing, *n.*

time-shar∘er

time-shar•ing

time-test∘ed

time•less

time•li•ness

time•ly *adj.,* time•li∘er, time•li•est

tim∘id

ti•mid∘i•ty

tim•id∘ly

tim•ing

tim•or•ous (fearful: cf. TEMERARIOUS)

tim•or•ous∘ly

tim•or•ous•ness

tin par•a•chute

tinc•ture of o∘pi∘um *Controlled Subst.*

tip *n., v.,* tipped, tip•ping

tip off *v.*

tip-off *n.*

tip•pee

tip•per

tip•staff *n., pl.* tip•staffs or tip•staves

tire *v.,* tired, tir•ing, *n.* (to exhaust or be-come exhausted; a wheel: cf. TIER²)

tit. (title)

tithe *n., v.,* tithed, tith•ing

tith•ing

tit•il•late *v.,* tit•il•lat∘ed, tit•il•lat•ing

tit•il•lat•ing∘ly

tit•il•la•tion

tit•il•la•tive

ti∘tle *n., adj. (citation form:* tit.)

title *v.,* ti•tled, ti•tling

title com•pa∘ny

title in•sur•ance

title re•cord•ing sys•tem

title reg•is•tra•tion system

title search

tit∘u•lar

TM (trademark)

TMA *Controlled Subst.* (trimethoxyamphet-amine)

to-do *n., pl.* to-dos

to wit

to•bac•co *n., pl.* to•bac•cos

to•bac•co•less

toc•sin (an alarm bell: cf. TOXIN)

TOD (transfer on death)

toe•hold

to•geth∘er

to∘ken

token pay•ment

to•ken•ism

tol•er•a∘bil∘i•ty

tol•er•a∘ble

tol•er•a∘ble•ness

tol•er•a∘bly

tol•er•ance

tol•er•ant

tol•er•ate *v.,* tol•er•at∘ed, tol•er•at•ing

tol•er•a•tion

tol•er•a•tive

tol•er•a•tor

toll

tol∘u•ene

tomb•stone ad

ton•nage

ton•tine

top-heav∘y plan

top∘ic

top∘i•cal

top∘i•cal∘i•ty *n., pl.* top∘i•cal•i•ties

top•less

top•less•ness

To∘rah

tor•ment

tor•ment•ed∘ly

tor•ment•ing∘ly

tor•men•tor or tor•ment∘er

Tor•rens ti∘tle sys•tem

tor•rent

tor•ren•tial

tort

tort•fea•sor

tor•tious (constituting a tort: cf. TORTIOUS; TORTUROUS)

tortious in•ter•fer•ence with con•tract

tor•tious◦ly

tor•tu•ous (twisting; circuitous; devious: cf. TORTIOUS; TORTUROUS)

tor•tu•ous◦ly

tor•tu•ous•ness

tor•tur•a◦ble

tor•ture

tor•tured

tor•tur◦er

tor•tur•ous (painful: f. TORTIOUS; TORTUOUS)

tor•tur•ous◦ly

to◦tal adj., n. v., to•taled, to•tal•ing

total breach

total dis•a◦bil◦i◦ty

total loss

total re•turn

to•tal◦i•tar•i◦an

to•tal◦i•tar•i•an•ism

to•tal◦i◦ty n., pl. to•tal◦i•ties

to•tal◦ly

to◦to Latin.

Tot•ten trust

touch and con•cern

touch-and-go adj.

touch and stay

tough

tough-mind•ed

tough-mind•ed◦ly

tough-mind•ed•ness

tour de force n., pl. tours de force French.

tour of du◦ty

Tou•rette's dis•or•der

tout

tow•age

---

town

town man•ag◦er

town meet•ing

town•ship

tox◦ic

toxic e◦mis•sion

toxic emission cred◦it

toxic psy•cho•sis

toxic waste

tox◦i•cal◦ly

tox◦i•cant

tox•ic◦i•ty n., pl. tox◦i•ties

tox◦i•co•log◦ic

tox◦i•co•log◦i•cal

tox◦i•co•log◦i•cal◦ly

tox◦i•col◦o◦gist

tox◦i•col◦o◦gy

tox◦in (a poison: cf. TOCSIN

tox•oid

Tr. (Trust; Trusts; Transcript)

trace n., v., traced, trac◦ing

trace ev◦i•dence

trace•a•bil◦i◦ty

trace•a◦ble

trace•a◦bly

trac◦er

track (a trail; to trail: cf. TRACT)

track marks

track•a◦bil◦i◦ty

track•a◦ble

track◦er

tract (a plot of land; an organ system; a writ-ing: cf. TRACK

trac•ta•bil◦i◦ty

trac•ta•ble

trac•ta•ble•ness

trac•ta•bly

trade n., v., trad◦ed, trad•ing, adj.

trade ac•cept•ance

---

trade as•so•ci•a•tion

trade bal•ance

trade bar•ri•er

trade coun•cil or trades coun•cil

trade cred◦it

trade def◦i•cit

trade dis•count

trade draft

trade dress

trade in v.

trade-in n., adj.

trade li◦bel

trade name

trade off v.

trade-off n.

trade or busi•ness

trade reg◦u•la•tion

trade se•cret

trade sur•plus

trade un◦ion

trade un•ion•ism

trade un•ion•ist

trade us◦age

trade•mark

trad◦er

trad•ing with the en•emy

tra•di•tion

tra•di•tion◦al

traditional law

traditional pub•lic fo◦rum

tra•di•tion•al•ism

tra•di•tion•al•ist

tra•di•tion•al◦ly

tra•di•tion•ar◦y ev◦i•dence

tra•duce v., tra•duced, tra•duc◦ing

tra•duce•ment

tra•duc◦er

tra•duc◦ing◦ly

traf•fic n., v., traf•ficked, traf•fick•ing

traffic court
traffic of•fense
traffic reg∘u•la•tion
traf•fick∘er
traf•fick•ing
trag∘e∘dy n., pl.
  trag∘e•dies
trag∘ic
trag∘i•cal∘ly
trag∘i•cal•ness
trail
trail•a∘ble
trail∘er
train
train•a∘bil∘i∘ty
train•a∘ble
train∘ee
train∘ee•ship
train∘er
train•ing
training school
trait
trai•tor
trai•tor•ous
trai•tor•ous∘ly
trai•tor•ous•ness
trai•tor•ship
tramp
tramp ship•ping
tramp steam∘er
tramp∘er
tran•quil
tran•quil∘i•za•tion
tran•quil•ize v., tran•
  quil•ized, tran•quil•
  iz•ing
tran•quil•iz∘er
tran•quil•li∘ty or
  tran•quil∘i∘ty See
  also DOMESTIC TRANQUIL-
  ITY.
tran•quil∘ly
trans. (translation;
  translator)
trans•act
trans•ac•tion

transaction of busi•
  ness
trans•ac•tion∘al
transactional im•mu•
  ni∘ty
trans•ac•tion•al∘ly
trans•ac•tor
trans•bound∘a∘ry
transboundary air
  pol•lu•tion
tran•scend
tran•scend•ence
tran•scend•ent
tran•scend•ent∘ly
tran•scend•ent•ness
tran•scend•ing∘ly
Transcon. (Transconti-
  nental)
trans•con•ti•nen•tal
  citation form: Trans-
  con.)
tran•scribe v. tran•
  scribed, trans•scrib•
  ing
tran•scrib∘er
tran•script *citation
  form:* Tr)
transcript of rec∘ord
tran•scrip•tase
tran•scrip•tion
trans•fer v., trans•
  ferred, trans•fer•
  ring, n., adj.
transfer a∘gent
transfer in con•tem•
  pla•tion of death
transfer on death
  (TOD)
transfer pay•ment
transfer tax
trans•fer•a∘bil∘i∘ty
trans•fer•a∘ble
trans•fer∘ee
trans•fer•ence
trans•fer∘or (one who
  conveys an interest in

  property: cf. TRANSFER-
  RER)
trans•ferred ba∘sis
transferred in•tent
trans•fer•rer (a person
  or thing that
  transfers generally: cf.
  TRANSFEROR)
trans•fix
trans•form
trans•form•a∘ble
trans•for•ma•tion
trans•for•ma•tion∘al
trans•for•ma•tive
trans•form•ing
trans•gen∘ic
trans•gress
trans•gres•sion
trans•gres•sive
transgressive trust
trans•gres•sive∘ly
trans•gres•sor
tran•sience
tran•sient
transient ju•ris•dic•
  tion
tran•sient∘ly
tran•sient•ness
tran•sit n., v., tran•
  sit∘ed, tran•sit•ing
tran•si•tion
tran•si•tion∘al
tran•si•tion•al∘ly
tran•si•to•ri∘ly
tran•si•to•ri•ness
tran•si•to∘ry
transitory ac•tion
transitory un•sea•
  wor•thi•ness
trans•lat•a∘bil∘i∘ty
trans•lat•a∘ble
trans•late v., trans•
  lat∘ed, trans•lat•ing
trans•la•tion (citation
  form: trans.)
trans•la•tion∘al

trans•la•tion•al•ly
trans•la•tor (*citation form:* **trans.**)
trans•mis•si•bil•i•ty
trans•mis•si•ble
trans•mis•sion
trans•mis•sive
trans•mit *v.*, trans•mit•ted, trans•mit•ting
trans•mit•ta•ble
trans•mit•tal
trans•mit•ter
trans•na•tion•al (*citation form:* **Transnat'l**)
transnational cor•po•ra•tion
trans•na•tion•al•ism
trans•na•tion•al•ly
Transnat'l (Transnational)
Transp. (Transport; Transportation)
trans•par•en•cy *n.*, *pl.* trans•par•en•cies
trans•par•ent
trans•par•ent•ly
trans•par•ent•ness
trans•port (*citation form:* **Transp.**)
trans•port•a•ble
trans•port•a•bly
trans•por•ta•tion (*citation form:* **Transp.**)
trans•por•tive
trans•sex•u•al
trans•sex•u•al•ism
trans•sex•u•al•i•ty
trans•ship *v.*, trans•shipped, trans•ship•ping
trans•ship•ment
trans•ship•ping
trau•ma *n.*, *pl.* trau•mas or trau•ma•ta

trau•mat•ic
trau•mat•i•cal•ly
trau•ma•tism
trau•ma•ti•za•tion
trau•ma•tize *v.*, trau•ma•tized, trau•ma•tiz•ing
tra•vail
tra•vaux pré•pa•ra•toires *n.pl. French.*
trav•el *v.*, trav•eled, trav•el•ing
trav•el ex•pense
trav•el•a•ble
trav•el•er
trav•el•er's check
tra•vers•a•ble
trav•erse *v.*, trav•ersed, trav•ers•ing, *n.*
trav•erse ju•ry
tra•vers•er
trav•es•ty *n.*, *pl.* trav•es•ties, *v.*, trav•es•tied, trav•es•ty•ing
treach•er•ous
treach•er•ous•ly
treach•er•ous•ness
treach•er•y *n.*, *pl.* treach•er•ies
Treas. (Treasury
trea•son
trea•son•a•ble
trea•son•a•bly
trea•son•ous
trea•son•ous•ly
treas•ure *n.*, *v.*, treas•ured, treas•ur•ing
treasure sal•vage
treasure-trove
treas•ur•er
treas•ur•er•ship
treas•ur•y *n.*, *pl.* treas•ur•ies (*citation form:* **Treas.**)

Treas•ur•y bill
Treasury bond
Treasury cer•tif•i•cate
Treasury note
treasury stock
trea•tise
treat•ment
treatment mo•dal•i•ty
treatment pro•gram
trea•ty *n.*, *pl.* trea•ties
tre•ble *adj.*, *v.*, tre•bled, tre•bling
treble dam•age suit (or **action**)
treble dam•ag•es
tre•bly
tre•buck•et
tren•bo•lone *Controlled Subst.*
trench•an•cy
trench•ant
trench•ant•ly
trep•i•da•tion
tres•ai•el *Law French*.
tres•pass
trespass de bo•nis as•por•ta•tis
trespass de e•jec•ti•o•ne fir•mae
trespass for mesne prof•its
trespass in e•ject•ment
trespass on the case
trespass on the spe•cial case
trespass qua•re clau•sum fre•git
trespass to chat•tels
trespass to try ti•tle
trespass vi et ar•mis
tres•pass•er
tri•a•ble

Tri•ads
tri•al
trial bal•ance
trial brief
trial by am•bush
trial by bat•tle
trial by ju•ry
trial by or•deal
trial by sur•prise
trial by wag•er of bat•tle
trial by wager of law
trial cal•en•dar
trial court
trial de no•vo
trial dock•et
trial ex•am•in•er
trial law•yer
tri•an•gu•lar re•or•gan•i•za•tion
tri•az•o•lam *Controlled Subst.*
Trib. (Tribune; Tribunal)
trib•al
tribal coun•cil
Tribal Court (*citation form:* Tribal Ct.)
Tribal Ct. (Tribal Court)
tribal lands
tribal sov•er•eign•ty
trib•al•ly
tribe
trib•ou•la•tion
tri•bu•nal (*citation form:* Trib.)
trib•une (*citation form:* Trib.)
trib•ute
tri•chot•o•mous
tri•chot•o•mous•ly
tri•chot•o•my *n., pl.* tri•chot•o•mies
trick
trick•er

trick•er•oy *n., pl.* trick•er•ies
trick•le-down
trick•le-down the•o•ry
tri•er of fact
tri•fle *n., v.,* tri•fled, tri•fling
tri•fler
tri•fling
tri•fling•ly
tri•fling•ness
trigamist
trig•a•mous
trig•a•my
trig•ger
trig•ger-hap•py
trig•ger•ing
trig•ger•man *n., pl.* trig•ger•men
tril•o•gy *n., pl.* tril•o•gies
tri•me•per•oi•dine *Controlled Subst.*
tri•mes•ter
tri•me•thox•y•am•phet•o•a•mine (TMA) *Controlled Subst.*
trip in•sur•ance
tri•par•tite
tri•ple *adj., n., v.,* tri•pled, tri•pling
trip•li•cate *n., v.,* trip•li•cat•ed, trip•li•cat•ing, *adj.*
trip•wire
trite *adj.,* trit•er, trit•est
trite•ly
trite•ness
tri•umph
tri•um•phal
tri•um•phant
tri•umph•er
triv•i•oa *n.pl.*
triv•i•al

triv•i•al•oi•ty *n., pl.* triv•i•al•oi•ties
triv•i•al•oi•za•tion
triv•i•al•ize *v.,* triv•i•al•ized, triv•i•al•iz•ing
triv•i•al•ly
TRO (temporary restraining order)
trou•ble *n., v.,* trou•bled, trou•bling
trou•bled
trou•bled•ly
trou•bled•ness
trou•ble•shoot *v.,* trou•ble•shoot•ed or trou•ble•shot, trou•ble•shoot•ing
trou•ble•shoot•er
trou•ble•shoot•ing
trou•ble•some
trou•ble•some•ly
trou•ble•some•ness
trou•bling
trou•bling•ly
tro•ver
trover and con•ver•sion
tru•an•cy
tru•ant
truant of•fic•er
truce
true *adj.,* tru•er, tru•est
true bill
true cop•y
tru•ism
tru•ly
trun•cate *v.,* trun•cat•ed, trun•cat•ing
trun•ca•tion
trun•cheon
trust (*citation form for sing. and pl.:* Tr.)
trust ac•count
trust com•pa•ny

trust cor•pus
trust deed
trust es•tate
trust ex de•lic•to
trust ex ma•le•fi•
  ci•o
trust fund
trust in•den•ture
trust in•stru•ment
trust in•ter vi•vos
trust of•fi•cer
trust prop•er•ty
trust re•ceipt
trust res
trust state
trust ter•ri•to•ry
trust the•o•ry ju•ris•
  dic•tion
trust wid•ow
trust wid•ow•er
trust•a•bil•i•ty
trust•a•ble
trust•ee
trustee ad li•tem
trustee de son tort
trustee ex ma•le•fi•
  ci•o
trustee in bank•
  rupt•cy
trustee proc•ess
trust•ee•ship
trust•er (one who
  trusts: cf. TRUSTOR)
trust•ful
trust•ful•ly
trust•ful•ness
trust•i•ly
trust•i•ness
trust•ing
trust•ing•ly
trust•ing•ness
trus•tor (one who cre-
  ates a trust: cf.
  TRUSTER)
trusts and es•tates
trust•wor•thi•ly

trust•wor•thi•ness
trust•wor•thy
trust•y adj., trust•
  i•er, trust•i•est, n,
  pl. trust•ies
truth n., pl truths
truth•ful
truth•ful•ly
truth•ful•ness
try v., tried, try•ing,
  n., pl. tries
try ti•tle
tryst
tu quo•que Latin.
tub•man
tu•mult
tu•mul•tu•ar•y
tu•mul•tu•ous
tu•mul•tu•ous•ly
tu•mul•tu•ous•ness
tur•ba•ry n., pl. tur•
  ba•ries
tur•bu•lence
tur•bu•lent
tur•bu•lent•ly
turf
turf war
tur•moil
turn
turn a•round v. (cf.
  TURNAROUND)
turn o•ver v. (cf. TURN-
  OVER)
turn state's ev•i•
  dence
turn•a•ble
turn•a•round n. (cf.
  TURN AROUND)
turn•coat
turn•key n.
turnkey con•tract
turnkey op•er•a•tion
turn•o•ver n. (cf. TURN
  OVER)
turnover du•ty of
  safe con•di•tion

turnover du•ty to
  warn
turnover or•der
turnover pro•ceed•
  ing
tur•pi•tude
tus•sle v., tus•sled,
  tus•sling, n.
tu•tor
tu•to•ri•al
tu•tor•ship
twad•dle n., v.,
  twad•dled, twad•
  dling
twelve-mile lim•it
Twin•kie de•fense
twist
twist•ed
twist•ed•ly
twist•ing
twist•ing•ly
two-faced
two-fac•ed•ly
two-fac•ed•ness
two-name pa•per
two-par•ty sys•tem
two-step sealed bid•
  ding
two-tier wage plan
ty•coon
ty•ing
tying a•gree•ment
tying ar•range•ment
tying pro•duct
typ•al
type n., v., typed,
  typ•ing
typ•i•cal
typ•i•cal•i•ty
typ•i•cal•ly
typ•i•cal•ness
typ•i•fi•ca•tion
typ•i•fi•er
typ•i•fy v., typ•i•
  fied, typ•i•fy•ing
typ•ist

ty•po n., pl. ty•pos
ty•po•graph•i•cal
   er•ror
ty•ran•ni•cal
ty•ran•ni•cal•ly

ty•ran•ni•cal•ness
ty•ran•ni•cid•al
ty•ran•ni•cide
tyr•an•nous
tyr•an•nous•ly

tyr•an•ny n., pl. tyr•
   an•nies
tyranny of the ma•
   jor•i•ty
ty•rant
ty•ro n., pl. ty•ros

U

U. (University, Universi-
   ties)
u•ber•ri•ma fi•des
   Latin.
u•bi Latin.
u•biq•ui•tous
u•biq•ui•tous•ly
u•biq•ui•ty
UCR (Uniform Crime
   Report)
u•kase
'u•la•ma or u•le•ma
   n.pl.
ul•lage
ullage-to-ullage rule
ul•te•ri•or
ulterior mo•tive
ul•te•ri•or•ly
ul•ti•mate
ultimate con•sum•er
ultimate fact
ultimate is•sue
ultimate pur•chas•er
ultimate us•er
ul•ti•mate•ly
ul•ti•mate•ness
ul•ti•ma•tum n., pl
   ul•ti•ma•tums or
   ul•ti•ma•ta
ul•ti•mo•gen•i•
   tar•y
ul•ti•mo•gen•i•ture
ul•tra Latin.
ultra vi•res Latin.
ul•tra•haz•ard•ous
ultrahazardous ac•
   tiv•i•ty

ul•tra•na•tion•al•
   ism
ul•tra•na•tion•al•ist
um•brage
um•brel•la
um•brel•la pol•i•cy
um•pir•age
um•pire n., v., um•
   pired, um•pir•ing
U.N. (United Nations)
u•na vo•ce Latin.
un•a•bashed
un•a•bash•ed•ly
un•a•bat•ed
un•a•bat•ed•ly
un•a•bet•ted
un•a•ble
un•ac•com•mo•
   dat•ed
un•ac•com•pa•nied
unaccompanied
   mi•nor
un•ac•count•a•ble
un•ac•count•a•bly
un•ac•count•ed-for
un•ac•crued
un•ac•knowl•edged
un•ad•ju•di•cat•ed
unadjudicated claim
un•ad•just•ed
un•a•dul•ter•at•ed
un•a•dul•ter•at•
   ed•ly
un•ad•vised
un•ad•vis•ed•ly
un•ad•vis•ed•ness
un•af•fect•ed

un•af•fect•ed•ly
un•af•fect•ed•ness
un•af•fil•i•at•ed
un•af•ford•
   a•bil•i•ty
un•af•ford•a•ble
un•a•fraid
un•al•ien•a•ble
un•al•ter•a•ble
un•al•ter•a•bly
un•am•big•u•ous
un•am•big•u•ous•ly
un•am•big•u•ous•
   ness
un•a•mend•a•ble
un•a•mend•ed
un•a•merce•a•ble
un•a•merced
un-A•mer•i•can
u•na•nim•i•ty
u•nan•i•mous
unanimous de•ci•sion
unanimous o•pin•ion
unanimous ver•dict
u•nan•i•mous•ly
un•an•swer•a•ble
un•an•swer•a•ble•
   ness
un•an•swer•a•bly
un•an•swered
un•a•pol•o•get•ic
un•a•pol•o•get•i•
   cal•ly
un•ap•par•ent
un•ap•peal•a•ble
un•ap•pealed
un•ap•point•a•ble

un•ap•point•ed
un•ap•por•tioned
un•ap•praised
un•ap•pre•ci•at•ed
un•ap•pro•pri•at•ed
un•ap•proved
un•ap•prov•ing
un•ap•prov•ing•ly
un•ar•gu•a•ble
un•ar•gu•a•bly
un•ar•gued
un•armed
unarmed rob•ber•y
un•as•cer•tain•a•ble
un•as•cer•tain•a•bly
un•as•cer•tained
un•a•shamed
un•a•sham•ed•ly
un•as•sail•a•bil•i•ty
un•as•sail•a•ble
un•as•sail•a•ble•
   ness
un•as•sail•a•bly
un•as•sailed
un•as•sim•i•lat•ed
un•at•tend•ed
un•at•test•ed
un•au•dit•ed
un•au•then•ti•
   cat•ed
un•au•thor•ized
unauthorized prac•
   tice
un•a•vail•a•bil•i•ty
un•a•vail•a•ble
unavailable wit•ness
un•a•vail•ing
un•a•vail•ing•ly
un•a•void•a•bil•i•ty
un•a•void•a•ble
unavoidable ac•ci•
   dent
unavoidable de•te•
   ri•o•ra•tion
un•a•void•a•bly

un•a•vowed
un•a•ware
un•a•ware•ly
un•a•ware•ness
un•a•wares
un•bal•anced
un•bear•a•ble
un•bear•a•ble•ness
un•bear•a•bly
un•be•known
un•be•knownst
un•be•liev•a•ble
un•be•liev•a•bly
un•bi•ased
un•bid•den
un•born
un•brand•ed
un•brib•a•ble
un•bridge•a•ble
un•bridged
un•bri•dled
un•bun•dle *v.*, un•
   bun•dled, un•bun•
   dling
un•bun•dling
un•cen•sor•a•ble
un•cen•sored
un•cer•tain
un•cer•tain•ly
un•cer•tain•ty *n.*, *pl.*
   un•cer•tain•ties
un•cer•tif•i•cat•ed
uncertificated se•cu•
   ri•ty
uncertificated share
un•char•ac•ter•is•tic
un•char•ac•ter•is•ti•
   cal•ly
un•charged
un•char•tered
un•chaste
un•chaste•ly
un•chas•tened
un•chaste•ness
un•chas•ti•ty

un•checked
un•clean hands
unclean hands de•
   fense
unclean hands doc•
   trine
un•co•erced
un•col•lat•er•al•ized
un•col•lect•ed
uncollected funds
un•com•mer•cial
un•com•mit•ted
un•com•mon
un•com•mon•ly
un•com•pel•la•ble
un•com•pelled
un•com•pro•mis•ing
un•com•pro•mis•
   ing•ly
un•com•pro•mis•
   ing•ness
un•con•di•tion•al
unconditional dis•
   charge
unconditional re•
   lease
un•con•di•tion•
   al•i•ty
un•con•di•tion•al•ly
un•con•di•tion•al•
   ness
un•con•firmed
un•con•scion•
   a•bil•i•ty
un•con•scion•a•ble
unconscionable
   a•gree•ment
un•con•scion•a•bly
un•con•scious
un•con•scious•ly
un•con•scious•ness
un•con•sent•ed
unconsented use
un•con•sent•ing
Unconsol. (Unconsoli-
   dated)

un•con•sol•o•i•dat•ed
(*citation form:* Uncon-
sol.)
un•con•sti•tu•
tion•al
un•con•sti•tu•tion•
al•i•o•ty
un•con•sti•tu•tion•
al•ly
un•con•sum•mat•ed
un•con•test•ed
uncontested di•vorce
un•con•tra•dict•ed
un•con•trol•la•ble
uncontrollable im•
pulse test
un•con•trol•la•bly
un•con•tro•vert•ed
un•con•vinced
un•con•vin•ci•ble
un•con•vinc•ing
un•co•op•er•o•a•tive
un•co•op•er•o•a•
tive•ly
un•co•op•er•o•a•tive•
ness
un•cop•y•right•
a•ble
un•cop•y•right•ed
un•cor•rect•a•ble
un•cor•rect•ed
un•cor•rob•o•o•rat•ed
un•cov•ered
un•dan•ger•ous
un•daunt•ed
un•daunt•ed•ly
un•daunt•ed•ness
un•de ni•hil ha•bet
Latin.
un•de•ceit•ful
un•de•cep•tive
un•de•cep•tive•ly
un•de•cep•tive•ness
un•de•cid•ed
un•de•clared
undeclared war

un•de•fend•a•ble
un•de•fend•ed
un•de•fined
un•dem•o•o•crat•ic
un•dem•o•o•crat•i•
cal•ly
un•de•ni•a•ble
un•de•ni•a•bly
un•de•pend•a•ble
un•de•pend•a•ble•
ness
un•de•pend•a•bly
un•de•pre•ci•at•ed
un•der
under col•or of law
under cov•er *adv.* (cf.
UNDERCOVER)
under oath
under pro•test
under seal
under sec•re•tar•y
n., pl. under sec•re•
tar•ies
under-sec•re•tar•y•
ship
under the count•er
adv.
under-the-counter *adj.*
under the in•flu•ence
under way
un•der•age
un•der•bid *v.*,
un•der•bid,
un•der•bid•ding
un•der•bid•der
un•der•boss
un•der•cap•o•i•tal•i•
za•tion
un•der•cap•o•i•tal•ize
v., un•der•cap•o•i•
tal•ized, un•der•
cap•o•i•tal•iz•ing
un•der•charge *v.,*
un•der•charged,
un•der•charg•ing
un•der•com•pen•

sate *v.,* un•der•
com•pen•sat•ed,
un•der•com•pen•
sat•ing
un•der•com•pen•sa•
tion
un•der•count
un•der•cov•er *adj.*
(cf. UNDER COVER)
un•der•cut *v.,*
un•der•cut,
un•der•cut•ting
un•der•de•vel•oped
un•der•dog
un•der•em•ployed
un•der•em•ploy•
ment
un•der•fund
un•der•fund•ed
un•der•go *v.,*
un•der•went,
un•der•gone,
un•der•go•ing
un•der•ground
un•der•hand•ed
un•der•hand•ed•ly
un•der•hand•ed•
ness
un•der•in•sur•ance
un•der•in•sure *v.,*
un•der•in•sured,
un•der•in•sur•ing
un•der•in•sured
un•der•lease *n., v.,*
un•der•leased,
un•der•leas•ing
un•der•les•see
un•der•let *v.,*
un•der•let, un•der•
let•ting
un•der•lie *v.,*
un•der•lay, un•der•
lain, un•der•ly•ing
un•der•ly•ing
un•der•mine *v.,*
un•der•mined,
un•der•min•ing

un○der•pay *v.*,
un○der•paid,
un○der•pay•ing
un○der•pay•ment
underpayment pen•
al○ty
un○der•pin *v.*,
un○der•pinned,
un○der•pin•ning
un○der•pin•ning
un○der•price *v.*,
un○der•priced,
un○der•pric•ing
un○der•priv•i•leged
un○der•pro•duc•tive
un○der•pro•duc•
tiv○i○ty
un○der•re•port
un○der•sec•re•tar•
i○at
un○der•sell
un○der•sell○er
un○der•sign
un○de•rsigned
un○der•stand *v.*,
un○der•stood,
un○der•stand•ing
un○der•stand•
a○bil○i○ty
un○der•stand•a○ble
un○der•stand•a○bly
un○der•stand•ing
un○der•stand•ing○ly
un○der•state *v.*,
un○der•stat○ed,
un○der•stat•ing
un○der•stat•ed•ness
un○der•state•ment
un○der•take *v.*,
un○der•took,
un○der•ta•ken,
un○der•tak•ing
un○der•tak○er
un○der•tak•ing
un○der•ten•an○cy
un○der•ten•ant

un○der•u•ti•li•za•
tion
un○der•u•ti•lize *v.*,
un○der○u•ti•lized,
un○der○u•ti•liz•ing
un○der•val•u•a•tion
un○der•val○ue *v.*,
un○der•val○ued,
un○der•val○u•ing
un○der•with•hold *v.*,
un○der•with•held,
un○der•with•hold•
ing
un○der•with•hold•
ing
un○der•write *v.*,
un○der•wrote,
un○der•writ•ten,
un○der•writ•ing
un○der•writ○er
un○der•writ•ing
underwriting syn•di•
cate
un•de•sir•a•bil○i○ty
un•de•sir•a○ble
undesirable dis•
charge
un•de•sir•a○bly
un•de•vel○oped
un•dis•closed
undisclosed prin•ci•
pal
un•dis•put○ed
un•dis•put•ed○ly
un•dis•trib•ut○ed
prof•its
un•di•vid○ed
undivided frac•
tion○al in•ter•est
undivided interest
undivided prof•its
undivided profits tax
un•doc•u•ment○ed
undocumented al○ien
un•do•ing
un•doubt○ed

un•doubt•ed○ly
un○due
undue in•flu•ence
un•du○ly
un•earned
unearned in•come
unearned in•cre•
ment
unearned in•ter•est
unearned sur•plus
un•em•ploy•
a○bil○i○ty
un•em•ploy•a○ble
un•em•ployed
un•em•ploy•ment
unemployment
ben○e•fit
unemployment com•
pen•sa•tion
unemployment in•
sur○ance
un•en•force•
a○bil○i○ty
un•en•force•a○ble
un•en•forced
un•en•forc•ed○ly
un•e○qual
un•e○qualled
un•e○qual○ly
un•e•quiv○o•cal
un•e•quiv○o•cal○ly
un•e•quiv○o•cal•
ness
un•es•cheat•a○ble
un•es•cheat○ed
un•eth○i•cal
un•eth○i•cal○ly
un•ex•cep•tion•
a○ble
un•ex•cep•tion•
a○ble•ness
un•ex•cep•tion•
a○bly
un•ex•cep•tion•al
un•ex•cep•tion•al○ly
un•ex○e•cut○ed trust

un•ex•er•cised
un•ex•pect•ed
un•ex•pect•ed•ly
un•ex•pect•ed•ness
un•fair
unfair com•pe•ti•tion
unfair la•bor prac•tice
unfair meth•ods of com•pe•ti•tion
unfair trade practice
un•fair•ly
un•fair•ness
un•faith•ful
un•faith•ful•ly
un•faith•ful•ness
un•fa•vor•a•ble
un•fa•vor•a•ble•ness
un•fa•vor•a•bly
un•fea•si•bil•i•ty
un•fea•si•ble
un•fea•si•ble•ness
un•fea•si•bly
un•feigned
un•fit
unfit par•ent
un•fit•ness
un•for•giv•ing
un•for•giv•ing•ness
un•for•tu•nate
un•for•tu•nate•ly
un•for•tu•nate•ness
un•found•ed
un•found•ed•ly
un•found•ed•ness
un•fraud•u•lent
un•fraud•u•lent•ly
un•ful•filled threat
un•fund•ed
unfunded man•date
un•grate•ful
un•grate•ful•ly
un•grate•ful•ness

un•guard•ed
un•guard•ed•ly
un•guard•ed•ness
un•hab•it•a•ble
un•hab•it•a•ble•ness
un•hab•it•a•bly
un•harmed
un•hinged
u•ni•cam•er•al
u•ni•cam•er•al•ism
u•ni•cam•er•al•ly
Unif. (Uniform)
u•ni•fied
unified bar
unified es•tate and gift tax
u•ni•form (*citation form:* Unif.)
Uniform Acts
Uniform Crime Re•port (UCR)
Uniform Laws
Uniform Of•fense Clas•si•fi•ca•tion (UOC)
Uniform Sys•tem of Ci•ta•tion See BLUE-BOOK.
u•ni•form•i•ty *n., pl.* u•ni•form•i•ties
u•ni•fy *v.,* u•ni•fied, u•ni•fy•ing.
u•ni•lat•er•al
unilateral con•tract
unilateral mis•take
u•ni•lat•er•al•ism
u•ni•lat•er•al•ist
u•ni•lat•er•al•i•ty
u•ni•lat•er•al•ly
un•im•ag•o•i•na•ble
un•im•ag•o•i•na•ble•ness
un•im•ag•o•i•na•bly
un•im•ag•ined

un•im•peach•a•bil•i•ty
un•im•peach•a•ble
un•im•peach•a•ble•ness
un•im•peach•a•bly
un•im•por•tant
un•im•proved
unimproved land
un•in•cor•po•rat•ed
unincorporated as•so•ci•a•tion
un•in•dict•a•ble
un•in•dict•ed
unindicted co-con•spir•a•tor
un•in•sur•a•ble
uninsurable risk
un•in•sured
uninsured mo•tor•ist
uninsured motorist in•sur•ance
un•in•tel•li•gent
un•in•tel•li•gent•ly
un•in•tel•li•gi•bil•i•ty
un•in•tel•li•gi•ble
un•in•tel•li•gi•bly
un•in•tend•ed
un•in•ten•tion•al
un•in•ten•tion•al•ly
un•in•ter•est•ed (bored: cf. DISINTER-ESTED)
un•in•ter•est•ed•ly
un•in•ter•est•ed•ness
un•ion
union bust•er
union-bust•ing
union cer•ti•fi•ca•tion
union la•bel
union-made
union rec•og•ni•tion
union scale

union shop
un•ion•ism
un•ion•ist
un•ion•is•tic
un•ion•i•za•tion
un•ion•ize *v.,* un•
ion•ized, un•ion•iz•
ing
un•ion•ized
un•ion•iz∘er
u∘nique
u∘nique∘ly
u∘nique•ness
un•is•sued stock
u∘nit
unit cost
unit in•vest•ment
trust
unit of pro•duc•tion
unit own•er•ship
unit price
unit pric•ing
unit trust
u∘ni•tar∘i•ness
u∘ni•tar∘y
u∘nit∘ed
united front
United Na•tions
(U.N.)
United States (U.S.)
United States At•tor•
ney
United States Code
(*citation form:* U.S.C.)
United States Court
of Ap•peals
United States Court
of Appeals for the
Armed Forc∘es (*cita-
tion form:* C.A.A.F.)
United States Court
of Appeals for the
Fed•er∘al Cir•cuit
(*citation form:* Fed.
Cir.)
United States Court

of Fed•er∘al Claims
(*citation form:* Fed.
Cl.)
United States Court
of In•ter•na•tion∘al
Trade (*citation form:*
Ct. Int'l Trade)
United States Court
of Vet•er•ans Ap•
peals (*citation form:*
Vet. App.)
United States Dis•
trict Court
United States Phar•
ma•co•pe∘ia (USP)
United States Re•
ports (*citation form:*
U.S.)
United States Stat•
utes at Large (*cita-
tion form:* Stat.)
United States Su•
preme Court (infor-
mal name for the Su-
PREME COURT OF THE
UNITED STATES)
United States Tax
Court (*citation form:*
T.C.)
u∘nit•ed∘ly
u∘nit•ed•ness
u∘ni•trust
u∘ni∘ty *n., pl.* u∘ni•
ties
unity of in•ter•est
unity of pos•ses•sion
unity of time
unity of ti∘tle
Univ. (University)
u∘ni•ver•sal
universal ju•ris•dic•
tion
universal life in•sur•
ance
universal mit•i•ga•
tion
universal suf•frage

u∘ni•ver•sal∘i∘ty *n.,
pl.* u∘ni•ver•sal∘i•
ties
u∘ni•verse
u∘ni•ver•si∘ty *n., pl.*
u∘ni•ver•si•ties (*ci-
tation forms:* U., *pl.* U.
, in periodical
names; Univ., *pl.* Un-
ivs., in case names)
un•just
unjust en•rich•ment
un•just∘ly
un•just•ness
un•know•a∘ble
un•know•ing
un•know•ing∘ly
un•knowl•edge•a•
ble
un•known
un•lade *v.,* un•
lad∘ed, un•lad•ing
un•law•ful
unlawful ar•rest
unlawful as•sem•bly
unlawful de•tain∘er
unlawful dis•tress
unlawful en∘try
unlawful pick•et•ing
unlawful re•straint
unlawful search
un•law•ful∘ly
un•law•ful•ness
un•law•yer•like
un•law•yer∘ly
un•li•censed
un•lim•it∘ed
unlimited li•a•
bil∘i∘ty
un•lim•it•ed∘ly
un•liq•ui•dat∘ed
unliquidated claim
unliquidated dam•
ag∘es
unliquidated debt
un•list∘ed

unlisted se•cu•ri•ty
un•load
un•load•er
un•loan•a•ble
un•mail•a•ble
unmailable mat•ter
un•man•age•a•
  bil•i•ty
un•man•age•a•ble
un•man•age•a•bly
un•mar•ket•a•ble
unmarketable ti•tle
un•mar•ried
un•mer•i•to•ri•ous
un•mit•i•gat•ed
un•mit•i•gat•ed•ly
un•mo•ti•vat•ed
un•nat•u•ral
unnatural act
un•nat•u•ral•ly
un•nat•u•ral•ness
un•nec•es•sar•y
unnecessary hard•
  ship
un•ob•vi•ous
un•ob•vi•ous•ly
un•ob•vious•ness
un•oc•cu•pied
un•op•pos•a•ble
un•op•posed
un•par•lia•men•
  ta•ry
un•pa•rol•a•ble
un•pat•ent•
  a•bil•i•ty
un•pat•ent•a•ble
un•pat•ent•ed
un•per•son
un•per•suad•a•ble
un•per•suad•a•bly
un•per•suad•ed
un•per•sua•sive
un•per•sua•sive•ly
un•per•sua•sive•
  ness

un•pop•u•lar
un•pop•u•lar•i•ty
un•pop•u•lar•ly
un•prec•e•dent•ed
un•prec•e•den•tial
un•pre•dict•
  a•bil•i•ty
un•pre•dict•a•ble
un•pre•dict•a•bly
un•prej•u•diced
un•pre•vent•a•ble
un•prin•ci•pled
un•prin•ci•pled•ness
un•priv•i•leged
unprivileged com•
  mu•ni•ca•tion
un•pro•fes•sion•al
unprofessional con•
  duct
un•pro•fes•sion•
  al•ly
un•prof•it•a•bil•i•ty
un•prof•it•a•ble
un•prof•it•a•bly
un•pro•tect•ed
unprotected speech
un•pro•tect•i•ble
un•pub•lished
unpublished work
un•qual•i•fied
un•qual•i•fied•ly
un•qual•i•fied•ness
un•re•al•ized
unrealized ap•pre•ci•
  a•tion
unrealized gain
unrealized loss
un•rea•son•a•ble
unreasonable re•
  straint of trade
unreasonable search
unreasonable search
  and sei•zure
un•rea•son•a•ble•
  ness
un•rea•son•a•bly

un•rec•og•nized
un•re•deem•a•ble
un•re•deem•a•bly
un•re•deemed
un•re•lat•ed
unrelated busi•ness
  in•come
un•re•spon•sive
un•re•spon•sive•ly
un•re•spon•sive•
  ness
un•re•strict•ed
unrestricted stock
un•re•strict•ed•ly
un•re•view•
  a•bil•i•ty
un•re•view•a•ble
un•sat•is•fi•a•ble
un•sat•is•fied
un•scru•pu•lous
un•scru•pu•lous•ly
un•scru•pu•lous•
  ness
un•seal
un•seal•a•ble
un•sealed
un•seat
un•sea•wor•thi•ness
un•sea•wor•thy
unseaworthy ves•sel
un•se•cured
unsecured cred•i•tor
unsecured loan
un•set•tled
un•set•tled•ness
un•sev•er•a•ble
un•sev•ered
un•skilled
unskilled la•bor
un•slan•der•ous
un•so•lic•it•ed
un•sound
unsound mind
un•sound•ly
un•sound•ness

un•speak•a◦ble
un•speak•a◦ble•ness
un•speak•a◦bly
un•suc•cess•ful◦ly
un•su•per•vised
un•sus•tain•a◦ble
un•sus•tain•a◦bly
un•sworn
unsworn state◦ment
un•ten•a•bil◦i◦ty
un•ten•a◦ble
un•ten•a◦ble•ness
un•ten•a◦bly
un•ten•ant•a◦ble
un•test◦ed
un•think•a◦ble
un•think•a◦bly
un•think◦ing
un•time•li◦ness
un•time◦ly
un•trace•a◦ble
un•tried
un•true
un•truth
un•truth•ful
un•truth•ful◦ly
un•truth•ful•ness
un•u◦su◦al
un•u◦su•al◦ly
un•u◦su•al•ness
un•ut•ter•a◦ble
un•ut•ter•a◦bly
un•val•ued
un•var•nished
un•want◦ed (not de-
   sired: cf. UNWONTED)
un•want◦ed•ness
un•wel•come
un•wel•comed
un•wel•come•ness
un•wel•com◦ing
un•wit•nessed
un•wit•ting
un•wit•ting◦ly
un•wit•ting•ness

un•wont◦ed (unusual:
   cf. UNWANTED)
un•wont◦ed◦ly
un•wont◦ed•ness
un•wor•thi◦ly
un•wor•thi•ness
un•wor•thy *adj.*, un•
   wor•thi◦er, un•
   wor•thi◦est
un•writ•ten
unwritten con•sti•
   tu•tion
unwritten law
UOC (Uniform Offense
   Classification)
up-or-out *adj.*
up•braid (to censure:
   cf. ABRADE)
up•braid◦er
up•bring•ing
up•date *v.*, up•
   dat◦ed, up•dat•ing
up•heav◦al
up•hold *v.*, up•held,
   up•hold•ing
up•hold◦er
up•keep
up◦per cham•ber
upper house
upper man•age•ment
up◦set price
up◦side
up•stream
upstream merg◦er
up•turn
u◦ra-cil
Urb. (Urban)
ur◦ban (*citation form:*
   Urb.)
urban home•stead◦er
urban home•stead•
   ing
urban re•new◦al
ur•gen◦cy *n.*, *pl.* ur•
   gen•cies

u◦ri•nal•y•sis *n.*, *pl.*
   u◦ri•nal•y•ses
u◦rine test◦ing
U◦ru•guay Round
U.S. (United States;
   United States Reports)
us•a◦bil◦i◦ty
us•a◦ble
us•a◦bly
us◦age
usage of trade
us•ance
U.S.C. (United States
   Code)
use *v.*, used,
   us◦ing, *n.*
use and ben◦e•fit
use im•mu•ni◦ty
use tax
used goods
us◦ee
use•ful
useful arts
useful life
use•ful◦ly
use•ful•ness
use•less
use•less◦ly
use•less•ness
us◦er
user fee
us◦er's fee
USP (United States
   Pharmacopeia)
u◦su◦al
usual cov◦e•nants
usual place of a◦bode
usual place of busi•
   ness
u◦su•al◦ly
u◦su•al•ness
u◦su•ca•pi◦on or
   u◦su•cap•tion
u◦su•fruct
u◦su•fruc•tu•ar◦y

|

adj., n., pl. **u•su•**
fruc•tu•ar•ies
u•su•o•ra *n., pl.* **u•su•**
rae *Latin.*
u•su•rer
u•su•ri•ous
u•su•ri•ous•ly
u•su•ri•ous•ness
u•surp
u•sur•pa•tion
u•sur•pa•tive
u•surp•er
u•su•o•ry *n., pl.* **u•su•**
ries
u•sus *n., pl.* **u•si**
Latin.
u•ti pos•si•de•tis
Latin.

Util. *pl.* **Util.** or **Utils.**
(Utility)
u•til•oi•tar•i•an
u•til•oi•tar•i•an•ism
u•til•oi•ty *n., pl.*
u•til•oi•ties, *adj. (citation form:* **Util.,** *pl.*
Util. or **Utils.**)
utility mod•el
utility pat•ent
u•til•iz•a•ble
u•til•i•za•tion
u•til•ize *v.,* **u•ti•**
lized, u•til•iz•ing
u•til•iz•er
ut•most
utmost care
utmost re•sist•ance

u•to•pi•a
u•to•pi•an
u•trum *Latin.*
ut•ter
utter bar
utter bar•ris•ter
ut•ter•a•ble
ut•ter•ance
ut•ter•er
ut•ter•ing
uttering a forged in•
stru•ment
ut•ter•ly
ux. (uxor)
ux•or (ux.) *n., pl.*
ux•o•res *Latin.*

V

v.[1] (abbr. for VERSUS
used in case names:
cf. vs.)
v.[2] (vide)
V chip
va•can•cy *n., pl.* **va•**
can•cies
va•cant
va•cat•a•ble
va•cate *v.,* **va•cat•ed,**
va•cat•ing
va•ca•tion
va•ca•tur *Latin.*
vac•il•late *v.,* **vac•il•**
lat•ed, vac•il•lat•
ing
vac•il•lat•ing•ly
vac•il•la•tion
vac•il•la•to•ry
va•cu•i•ty
vac•u•ous
va•di•um *n., pl.*
va•di•a *Latin.*
va•gi•na *n., pl.* **va•**
gi•nas or (esp. in sci-

entific contexts) **va•**
gi•nae
vag•i•nal
va•gran•cy
va•grant
vague *adj.,* **va•guer,**
va•guest
vague•ly
vague•ness
vain
val•id
val•i•date *v.,* **val•i•**
dat•ed, val•i•dat•
ing
val•i•da•tion
val•i•da•tor
va•lid•i•ty
val•id•ly
Val•i•um *Trademark.*
val•u•a•ble
valuable con•sid•
er•a•tion
val•u•a•ble•ness
val•u•a•bly

val•u•ate *v.,* **val•u•**
at•ed, val•u•at•ing
val•u•a•tion
val•ue *n., v.,* **val•ued,**
val•u•ing
value-add•ed tax
(VAT)
value date
value fund
val•ued pol•i•cy
van•dal
van•dal•ism
van•dal•ize *v.,* **van•**
dal•ized, van•dal•
iz•ing
van•guard
van•ish
van•ish•ing•ly
van•quish
van•quish•a•ble
van•quish•er
van•quish•ment
van•tage
vantage point
var•i•a•bil•i•ty

var•i•a•ble
variable an•nu•i•ty
variable cost
variable life in•sur•ance
variable-rate mort•gage (VRM)
var•i•a•bly
var•i•ance
var•i•ant
var•i•a•tion
var•i•ous
var•i•ous•ly
var•i•ous•ness
var•y v., var•ied, var•y•ing
vas•sal
vas•sal•age
VAT (value-added tax)
vault
V.C. (Vice Chancellor)
veg•e•ta•tive state
ve•he•mence
ve•he•ment
ve•he•ment•ly
ve•hi•cle
ve•hic•u•lar
vehicular hom•i•cide
vehicular man•slaugh•ter
veil
veiled
vel non *Latin*.
ve•loc•i•ty n., pl. ve•loc•i•ties
ve•nal (bribable; corrupt: cf. VENIAL)
ve•nal•i•ty
ve•nal•ly
vend
vend•ee
vend•i•bil•i•ty
vend•i•ble
ven•dor
ven•dor's lien
ven•due

ven•er•a•tion (revering: cf. FENERATION)
venge•ance
venge•ful
venge•ful•ly
venge•ful•ness
ve•ni•al (excusable; not seriously wrong: cf. VENAL)
ve•ni•re *Latin and English*.
venire de no•vo *Latin*.
venire fa•ci•as *Latin*.
venire facias de no•vo *Latin*.
venire facias tot ma•tro•nas *Latin*.
ve•ni•re•man n., pl. ve•ni•re•men
ve•ni•re•mem•ber
ven•ter[1] n., pl. ven•ters *English*.
ven•ter[2] n., pl. ven•tres *Latin*.
ven•tre n., pl. ven•tres *Law French*.
ven•ture
venture cap•i•tal
venture cap•i•tal•ism
venture cap•i•tal•ist
ven•tur•er
ven•ue
ve•rac•i•ty n., pl. ve•rac•i•ties
ver•bal (in words; spoken or written: cf. ORAL)
verbal act
ver•bal•i•za•tion
ver•bal•ize v., ver•bal•ized, ver•bal•iz•ing
ver•bal•iz•er
ver•bal•ly
ver•ba•tim

verbatim et li•te•ra•tim *Latin*.
ver•bi•age
ver•bose
ver•bose•ly
ver•bose•ness
ver•bos•i•ty
ver•bo•ten *German*.
ver•bum n., pl. ver•ba *Latin*.
ver•dict
ver•i•fi•a•bil•i•ty
ver•i•fi•a•ble
ver•i•fi•ca•tion
ver•i•fied
verified com•plaint
verified cop•y
ver•i•fi•er
ver•i•fy v., ver•i•fied, ver•i•fy•ing
ver•i•ta•ble
ver•i•ta•ble•ness
ver•i•ta•bly
ve•ri•tas *Latin*.
ver•i•ty n., pl. ver•i•ties
ver•sus (abbreviated as v. in case names; as vs. in other contexts)
ver•ti•cal
vertical com•bi•na•tion
vertical di•vest•oi•ture
vertical in•te•gra•tion
vertical mar•ket al•lo•ca•tion
vertical market di•vi•sion
vertical mer•ger
vertical price fix•ing
vertical priv•i•ty
vertical re•straint
vertical un•ion
ver•ti•cal•ly

ves•sel
vest
vest○ed
vested es•tate
vested in in•ter•est
vested in pos•ses•sion
vested in•ter•est
vested pen•sion
vested re•main•der
vested right
vested rights the•o○ry
vest•ing
vesting or○der
ves•tur○al
ves•ture
vet v., vet•ted, vet•ting
Vet. App. (United States Court of Veterans Appeals)
vet•er○an
vet•er•ans' in•sur•ance
veterans' pref•er•ence
ve○to n. pl. ve○tos, v. ve•toed, ve•to•ing
veto pow○er
ve•to○er
vex
vex○a•tious
vexatious lit○i•ga•tion
vex○a•tious○ly
vex○a•tious•ness
vi et ar○mis Latin.
vi○a me○di○a Latin.
vi•a•bil○i○ty
vi•a•ble
vi•a•bly
vi•car○i•ous
vicarious li•a•bil○i○ty
vi•car○i•ous○ly

vi•car○i•ous•ness
vice
vice-chair
vice chair•man or vice-chair•man n., pl. vice chair•men or vice-chair•men
vice-chair•man•ship
vice chan•cel•lor or vice-chan•cel•lor (V.C.)
vice-chan•cel•lor•ship
vice con•sul or vice-con•sul
vice-con•su•lar
vice-con•su•late
vice-con•sul•ship
vice-pres○i•den○cy n., pl. vice-pres○i•den•cies
vice pres○i•dent or vice-pres○i•dent (V.P.)
vice-pres○i•den•tial
vice-re•gen○cy n., pl. vice-re•gen•cies
vice re•gent or vice-re•gent
vice squad
vice ver○sa
vice•ge•ral
vice•ge•ren○cy n., pl. vice•ge•ren•cies
vice•ge•rent
vice•re•gal
vice•re•gal○ly
vice•reine
vice•roy
vice•roy•al○ty n., pl. vice•roy•al•ties
vice•roy•ship
vic○i•nage
vic○i•nal
vi•cin○i○ty n., pl. vi•cin○i•ties

vi•cious
vi•cious○ly
vi•cious•ness
vi•cis•si•tude
vi•cis•si•tu•di•nous
vic•tim
victim im•pact state•ment
vic•tim•hood
vic•tim○i•za•tion
vic•tim•ize v., vic•tim•ized, vic•tim•iz•ing
vic•tim•iz○er
vic•tim•less
victimless crime
vic•tims' rights
vic•to•ri•ous
vic•to•ri•ous○ly
vic•to•ri•ous•ness
vic•to○ry
vi○de (v.) Latin
vide an○te Latin.
vide in○fra Latin.
vide post Latin.
vide su○pra Latin.
vi○de•li•cet (viz.) Latin.
vid•e○o pi○ra•cy
video will
vid•e•o•con•fer•ence
vid•e•o•con•fer•enc•ing
vie v., vied, vy○ing
vi○er
view
view•a•ble
view○er
view•point
vig○i•lance
vigilance com•mit•tee
vig○i•lant
vig○i•lan•te
vig○i•lan•te•ism

vig•oi•lan•tism
vig•oi•lant•ly
vig•or
vig•or•ish
vig•or•ous
vig•or•ous•ly
vig•or•ous•ness
vile *adj.*, vil•er, vil•est
vil•oi•fi•ca•tion
vil•oi•fi•er
vil•oi•fy *v.*, vil•oi•fied, vil•oi•fy•ing
vill
vil•lage
vil•lag•er
vil•lain (a criminal or scoundrel: cf. VILLEIN)
vil•lain•ous
vil•lain•ous•ly
vil•lain•ous•ness
vil•lain•y *n.*, *pl.* vil•lain•ies
vil•lein (a member of a certain feudal class: cf. VILLAIN)
villein serv•ice
villein soc•age
vil•lein•age
vin•cu•lo ma•tri•mo•ni•i *Latin.*
vin•cu•lum matri•monii *Latin.*
vin•di•ca•bil•oi•ty
vin•di•ca•ble
vin•di•cate *v.* vin•di•cat•ed, vin•di•cat•ing
vin•di•ca•tion
vin•di•ca•tive tending to clear or justify: cf. VINDICTIVE)
vin•di•ca•tor
vin•di•ca•to•ry
vin•dic•tive (vengeful. cf. VINDICATIVE)
vindictive dam•ag•es

vin•dic•tive•ly
vin•dic•tive•ness
vi•o•la•bil•oi•ty
vi•o•la•ble
vi•o•la•bly
vi•o•late *v.*, vi•o•lat•ed, vi•o•lat•ing
vi•o•la•tion
vi•o•la•tive
vi•o•la•tor
vi•o•lence
vi•o•lent
violent crime
violent pre•sump•tion
vi•o•lent•ly
vir *n.*, *pl.* vi•ori *Latin.*
vi•oral
vir•tu•al
vir•tu•al•oi•ty
vir•tu•al•ly
vir•tue
vir•tu•ous
vir•tu•ous•ly
vir•tu•ous•ness
vir•u•lence
vir•u•len•cy
vir•u•lent
vi•orus *n.*, *pl.* vi•rus•es
vis *n.*, *pl.* vi•ores
vis-à-vis *French.*
vis ma•jor *Latin.*
vi•osa *n.*, *v.*, vi•saed, vi•sa•ing
Vis•by rules
vis•cer•al
vis•cer•al•ly
vis•oi•bil•oi•ty
vis•oi•ble
vis•oi•bly
vi•sion
vi•sion•ar•oi•ness
vi•sion•ar•oy *adj., n.*, *pl.* vi•sion•ar•ies
vis•it

vis•it•a•ble
vis•it•a•tion
visitation rights
vis•it•a•tion•al
vis•oi•tor
vis•u•al
visual hal•lu•ci•na•tion
vis•u•al•iz•a•ble
vis•u•al•oi•za•tion
vis•u•al•ize *v.*, vis•u•al•ized, vis•u•al•iz•ing
vis•u•al•ly
vi•ota[1] *n.*, *pl.* vi•otas *English.*
vi•ota[2] *n.*, *pl.* vi•otae *Latin.*
vi•otal
vital sta•tis•tics
vi•tal•oi•ty
vi•tal•oi•za•tion
vi•tal•ize *v.*, vi•tal•ized, vi•tal•iz•ing
vi•tal•iz•er
vi•tal•ly
vi•tal•ness
vi•ti•ate *v.*, vi•ti•at•ed, vi•ti•at•ing
vi•ti•a•tion
vi•ti•a•tor
vi•tu•per•ate *v.*, vi•tu•per•at•ed, vi•tu•per•at•ing
vi•tu•per•a•tion
vi•tu•per•a•tive
vi•tu•per•a•tive•ly
vi•tu•per•a•tor
vi•va vo•ce *Latin.*
viv•id
viv•id•ly
viv•id•ness
viv•oi•fy *v.*, viv•oi•fied, viv•oi•fy•ing
viz. (videlicet)
vo•ca•tion

vo•ca•tion∘al

vocational ed∘u•ca•tion

vo•ca•tion•al∘ly

vo•cif•er•ous

vo•cif•er•ous∘ly

vo•cif•er•ous•ness

voice *n., v.,* voiced, voic•ing

voice mail

voice-stress an∘a•lyz∘er

voice vote

voice•less

voice•less∘ly

voice•less•ness

voice•print

voice•print•ing

void

void ab i∘ni•ti∘o

void for vague•ness

void mar•riage

void•a∘ble

voidable mar•riage

voidable pre•fer•ence

void•a∘ble•ness

void•ance

void∘ed

void∘er

void•ness

voir dire *Law French.*

vol. (volume)

vol∘a•tile

volatile chem∘i•cal

volatile in•hal•ant

volatile sol•vent

volatile stock

volatile sub•stance

volatility

vol∘a•til∘i•ty in∘dex

vo•li•tion

vo•li•tion∘al

vo•li•tion•al∘ly

vol∘ou•bil∘i∘ty

vol∘ou•ble

vol∘ou•bly

vol•ume (*citation form:* vol.)

vo•lu•mi•nous

vo•lu•mi•nous∘ly

vo•lu•mi•nous•ness

vol•un•tar∘i∘ly

vol•un•tar∘i•ness

vol•un•ta•rism

vol•un•ta•rist

vol•un•ta•ris•tic

vol•un•tar∘y

voluntary ap•pear•ance

voluntary ar•bi•tra•tion

voluntary as•so•ci•a•tion

voluntary bank•rupt∘cy

voluntary com•mit•ment

voluntary con•fes•sion

voluntary con•vey•ance

voluntary debt

voluntary de•fer•ral plan

voluntary dis•con•tin•u•ance

voluntary dis•mis•sal

voluntary man•slaugh•ter

voluntary non•suit

voluntary pi∘lot

voluntary trans•fer

voluntary trust

voluntary waste

vol•un•teer

vol•un•teer•ism

vot•a∘ble

vote *n., v.,* vot∘ed, vot•ing

vot∘er

voter qual∘i•fi•ca•tion

vot•ing rights

voting se•cu•ri∘ty

voting stock

voting trust

vouch

vouch∘ee

vouch∘er

vouch•er•a∘ble

vouch•ing in

vouch•safe *v.,* vouch•safed, vouch•saf•ing

vow

voy•age *n., v.,* voy•aged, voy•ag•ing

voyage char•ter

voyage clause

voy•ag∘er

vo•yeur

vo•yeur•ism

vo•yeur•is•tic

vo•yeur•is•ti•cal∘ly

V.P. (Vice President)

VRM (variable-rate mortgage)

vs. (abbr. for VERSUS used in general contexts, but not usually in case names: cf. v.)

vul•gar

vul•gar∘i∘ty

vul•gar∘ly

vul•ner•a∘bil∘i∘ty

vul•ner•a∘ble

vul•ner∘a•bly

W

W. (West; Western)
wage *n., v.*, waged, wag•ing
wage and price con•trol
wage con•tin•u•a•tion plan
wage earn∘er
wage earn•er's plan
wage scale
wa∘ger
wager of bat•tle
wager of law
wa•ger∘er
wa•ger•ing con•tract
wait
wait and see doc•trine
wait and see zon•ing
wait•ing pe•ri∘od
waive *v.*, waived, waiv•ing
waiv∘er (relinquishment: cf. WAVER)
waiver by e∘lec•tion
waiver of pre•mi∘um
waiver of tort
walk•out *n.*
Wall Street
Wall Street law firm
wan•gle *v.*, wan•gled, wan•gling, *n.* (to contrive: cf. WRAN-GLE)
wan•gler
want (a lack; a need; a desire: cf. WONT)
want of con•sid•er∘a•tion
want of ju•ris•dic•tion
want of pros∘e∘cu•tion

want∘ed
wanted per•son
wan•ton
wan•ton∘ly
wan•ton•ness
war
war crime
war crimes tri•bu•nal
war pow∘er
war risk in•sur•ance
ward
ward of the court
war•den
war•den•ship
ward∘er
ward•ship
ware•house *n., v.*
    ware•housed, ware•hous•ing
warehouse re•ceipt
ware•house•man *n.*, *pl.* ware•house•men
ware•house•man's lien
ware•hous∘er
ware•hous•er's lien
war•fare
war∘i∘ly
war∘i•ness
war•lord
warn
warn∘er
warn•ing
war•rant
warrant of ar•rest
warrant of e∘vic•tion
war•rant•a∘ble
war•rant∘ed
war•ran•tee
war•ran•ti∘a char•tae *Latin.*
war•ran•ties of ti∘tle

war•rant•less
warrantless ar•rest
warrantless search
war•ran•tor
war•ran∘ty *n., pl.* war•ran•ties
warranty deed
warranty of fit•ness for a par•tic•u•lar pur•pose
warranty of hab•it•a∘bil∘i•ty
warranty of mer•chant•a∘bil∘i•ty
warranty of qui∘et en•joy•ment
warranty of ti∘tle
warranty of work•man•like per•for•mance
war•time
war∘y *adj.*, war•i∘er, war•i•est
wash
wash out *v.* (cf. WASH-OUT)
wash sale
washed up
wash•out *n.* (cf. WASH OUT)
waste *n., v.*, wast∘ed, wast•ing
waste•ful
waste•ful∘ly
waste•ful•ness
wast•ing as∘set
wasting prop•er∘ty
wasting trust
watch•dog
watch•ful
watch•ful∘ly
watch•ful•ness
wa∘ter

water rights
wa•tered stock
wa•ter•er
wa•ter•front
wa•ters *n.pl.*
wa•ter•shed
wa•ter•way
wa•ver (to vacillate: cf. WAIVER)
wa•ver•er
way
way•bill
way•go•ing crop
way•lay *v.*, way•laid, way•lay•ing
way•lay•er
way•leave
ways and means
way•ward
way•ward•ly
way•ward•ness
W.D. (Western District)
weak
weak•en
weak•ly
weak•ness
weal
wealth
wealth tax
wealth•y *adj.*, wealth•i•er, wealth•i•est
weap•on
weap•oned
weap•on•less
weap•ons of•fense
wear and tear
Web See WORLD WIDE WEB.
Web site
Wechs•ler In•tel•li•gence Scales
wed *v.*, wed•ded, wed•ded or wed, wed•ding
wed•lock

week (*citation form:* Wk.)
week•end sen•tence
week•ly (*citation form:* Wkly.)
weigh
weigh•er
weight of the ev•i•dence
weight•i•ly
weight•i•ness
weight•y *adj.* weight•i•er, weight•i•est
wel•come *adj.*, *v.*, wel•comed, wel•com•ing, *n.*, *interj.*
wel•fare
welfare ec•o•nom•ics
welfare fund
welfare ho•tel
welfare state
well-ad•vised
well-be•ing
well-con•ceived
well-con•sid•ered
well-de•fined
well-dis•posed
well-doc•u•ment•ed
well-e•quipped
well-es•tab•lished
well-found•ed
well-ground•ed
well-in•formed
well-in•ten•tioned
well-known
well-mean•ing
well-nigh
well-plead•ed
well-pleaded com•plaint rule
well-pre•pared
well-rea•soned
well-suit•ed
well•ness

welsh
welsh•er
west (W.)
west•ern (W.)
West•ern Dis•trict (*citation form:* W.D.)
West•law *Trademark.*
wharf *n.*, *pl.* wharves or wharfs
wharf•age
Whar•ton rule
what•ev•er
what•so•ev•er
when is•sued
where
where•a•bouts *n.pl.*
where•as
where•by
where•fore
where•from
where•in
where•in•to
where•of
where•on
where•so•ev•er
where•to
where•un•to
where•up•on
wher•ev•er
where•with
where•with•al
whip *v.*, whipped, whip•ping, *n.*
whip•lash
whip•ping post
whip•saw
whipsaw strike
whis•tle•blow•er
whistleblower law
white-col•lar
white-collar crime
white-collar work•er
white knight
white lie
white mar•ket

white pa∘per
white-shoe law firm
White•a•cre
whole
whole law
whole life in•sur•ance
whole•sale n., adj., adv., v., whole•saled, whole•sal•ing
wholesale price in∘dex
whole•sal∘er
whol∘ly
wholly owned sub•sid•i•ar∘y
whore
WIC pro•grams (Women, Infants, and Children programs)
wick∘ed
wick•ed•ly
wick•ed•ness
wid∘ow
wid•ow∘er
wid•ow∘er's al•low•ance
widower's e∘lec•tion
widower's e∘lec•tive (or stat∘u•to∘ry) share
wid∘ow's al•low•ance
widow's e∘lec•tion
widow's e∘lec•tive (or stat∘u•to∘ry) share
wife n., pl. wives
wife a∘buse
wife∘ly
wild•cat strike
wild•cat•ter
wil•der•ness
wilderness ar∘e∘a
wild•ing
wild•life

Wild's Case, rule in
will
will con•test
will∘er
will•ful
willful and ma•li•cious
willful and wan•ton
willful ne•glect
will•ful∘ly
will•ful•ness
will∘ing buy∘er–will∘ing sell∘er rule
wind up v., wound up, wind•ing up
wind•fall
windfall prof∘it
windfall prof•its tax
win•dow of op•por•tu•ni∘ty
wine
wire n., adj., v., wired, wir•ing
wire fraud
wire trans•fer
wire•tap n., v., wire•tapped, wire•tap•ping
wire•tap•per
with all faults
with prej•u•dice
with re•course
with strong hand
with•draw v., with•drew, with•drawn, with•draw•ing
with•draw•a∘ble
with•draw∘al
withdrawal syn•drome
with•draw∘er
with•er•nam
with•hold v., with•held, with•hold•ing
with•hold∘er

with•hold•ing ev∘i•dence
withholding tax
with∘in
with•out
without day
without prej∘u•dice
without re•course
with•stand v., with•stood, with•stand•ing
wit•ness
witness list
witness my hand and seal
witness stand
witness tam•per•ing
wit•ness•ing part
wit•ting
wit•ting∘ly
Wk. (Week)
Wkly. (Weekly)
woe•ful
woe•ful∘ly
woe•ful•ness
wom∘an n., pl. wom∘en
woman suf•frage
Women, In•fants, and Chil•dren pro•grams (WIC programs)
wont (customary practice; accustomed: cf. WANT)
wont∘ed
wont•ed∘ly
wont•ed•ness
word∘i∘ly
word∘i•ness
word•ing
words ac•tion•a∘ble in them•selves
words of art
words of lim∘i•ta•tion

words of ne•go•ti•a•bil•i•ty

words of pro•cre•a•tion

words of pur•chase

word•y *adj.*, word•i•er, word•i•est

work

work made for hire

work of au•thor•ship

work out *v.* (cf. WORK-OUT)

work pro•duct

work product doc•trine

work re•lease *n.*

work-release *adj.*

work rules

work stop•page

work•a•bil•i•ty

work•a•ble

work•er

worker buy•out

work•ers' com•pen•sa•tion

workers' compensation act

workers' compensation in•sur•ance

work•fare

work•house

work•ing

working as•set

working cap•i•tal

working hy•poth•e•sis

working pa•pers

work•man•like

work•out *n.* (cf. WORK-OUT)

work•place

works *n.pl.*

work•week

World Court

world mark

World Wide Web (the Web)

world•ly

worldly pos•ses•sions

wor•ried

wor•ri•er

wor•ri•some

wor•ry *v.*, wor•ried, wor•ry•ing, *n.*, *pl.* wor•ries

worse

wors•en

wor•ship

wor•ship•er

wor•ship•ful

worst

worst-case sce•nar•i•o

worth

wor•thi•er ti•tle

wor•thi•ly

wor•thi•ness

worth•less

worth•less•ly

worth•less•ness

worth•while

wor•thy *adj.*, wor•thi•er, wor•thi•est, *n.*, *pl.* wor•thies

would-be

wound

wran•gle *n.*, *v.*, wran•gled, wran•gling (to argue or dispute: cf. WANGLE)

wran•gler

wrap•a•round *adj.*,

wraparound mort•gage

wrath

wrath•ful

wrath•ful•ly

wrath•ful•ness

wreak

wreak•er

wreck

wreck•age

wreck•er

wrest (to tear away: cf. REST)

wrest•er

writ

writ de con•su•e•tu•di•ni•bus et ser•vi•ti•is

writ de e•jec•ti•o•ne fir•mae

writ de ho•mi•ne re•ple•gi•an•do

writ de o•di•o et a•ti•a

writ de ra•ti•o•na•bi•li par•te

writ de ra•ti•o•na•bi•li•bus di•vi•sis

writ de ven•tre in•spi•ci•en•do

writ of ad quod dam•num

writ of ad•meas•ure•ment

writ of ai•el

writ of ar•rest

writ of as•sis•tance

writ of as•size

writ of as•soil•er

writ of at•tach•ment

writ of at•taint

writ of au•di•ta que•re•la

writ of bes•ai•el

writ of ca•pi•as

writ of cer•ti•o•ra•ri

writ of ces•sa•vit

writ of co•ram no•bis

writ of coram vo•bis

writ of cos•in•age

writ of course

writ of cov•e•nant

writ of debt

writ of de•ceit

writ of de•liv•er•y

writ of det•oi•nue

writ of di•em clau•sit ex•tre•mum

writ of dis•trin•gas

writ of dow•er

writ of dower un•de ni•hil ha•bet

writ of ease

writ of e•ject•ment

writ of e•lec•tion

writ of e•le•git

writ of en•try

writ of entry qua•re e•je•cit

writ of entry sur a•bate•ment

writ of entry sur al•ien•a•tion

writ of entry sur dis•sei•sin

writ of entry sur in•tru•sion

writ of er•ror

writ of error co•ram no•bis

writ of error coram vo•bis

writ of es•cheat

writ of e•strepe•ment

writ of ex•e•cu•tion

writ of ex•emp•tion

writ of ex•i•gent

writ of ex•i•gi fa•ci•as

writ of ex•tent

writ of fi•e•ri fa•ci•as

writ of for•me•don

writ of ha•be•as cor•pus

writ of in•quir•y

writ of ju•ris u•trum

writ of jus•ti•ci•es

writ of la•ti•tat

writ of le•va•ri fa•ci•as

writ of main•prise

writ of man•da•mus

writ of man•u•cap•tion

writ of man•u•mis•sion

writ of mesne

writ of ne ex•e•at

writ of ne in•jus•te vex•es

writ of neif•ty

writ of nu•per ob•i•it

writ of par•lia•ment

writ of par•ti•tion

writ of pos•ses•sion

writ of post dis•sei•sin

writ of prae•ci•pe

writ of praecipe quod red•dat

writ of prae•mu•ni•re

writ of priv•i•lege

writ of pro•ce•den•do

writ of procedendo ad ju•di•ci•um

writ of pro•hi•bi•tion

writ of pro•tec•tion

writ of qua•re im•pe•dit

writ of quo ju•re

writ of quo war•ran•to

writ of quod e•i de•for•ce•at

writ of quod per•mit•tat

writ of rav•ish•ment de gard

writ of ravishment of ward

writ of re•at•tach•ment

writ of re•cap•tion

writ of re•dis•sei•sin

writ of re•plev•in

writ of res•ti•tu•tion

writ of re•sum•mons

writ of re•view

writ of right

writ of right close

writ of right de ra•ti•o•na•bi•li par•te

writ of right in ca•pi•te

writ of right of ad•vow•son

writ of right of dow•er

writ of right of ward

writ of right pa•tent

writ of right qui•a do•mi•nus re•mi•sit cu•ri•am

writ of right up•on dis•claim•er

writ of sci•re fa•ci•as

writ of sec•ond de•liv•er•ance

writ of second sur•charge

writ of sei•sin

writ of se•ques•tra•tion

writ of sub•poe•na

writ of sum•mons

writ of su•per•se•de•as

writ of tres•ai•el

writ of tres•pass

writ of tri•al

writ of ve•ni•re fa•ci•as

writ of war•ran•ti•a char•tae

writ of waste

writ per quae ser•vi•
ti•a
writ up•on the case
write v., wrote, writ•
ten, writ•ing
write down v.
write-down n.
write in v.
write-in n., adj.
write off v.
write-off n.
write up v.
write-up n.

writ•er
writ•ing o•blig•a•
to•ry
writ•ten con•sti•tu•
tion
written con•tract
written-down val•ue
written law
wrong
wrong•do•er
wrong•do•ing
wrong•ful
wrongful birth

wrongful con•cep•
tion
wrongful death
wrongful dis•charge
wrongful dis•hon•or
wrongful life
wrongful ter•mi•na•
tion
wrong•ful•ly
wrong•ful•ness
wrong•ly
wrong•ness

XYZ

X-rat•ed
Xan•ax *Trademark.*
xe•no•cur•ren•cy
xe•no•graft
xe•no•graft•ing
xe•no•phobe
xe•no•pho•bi•a
xe•no•pho•bic
xe•no•trans•plant
xe•no•trans•plan•
ta•tion
xe•ro•graph•ic
xe•rog•ra•phy
XYY male
ya•hoo•ism
yard•bird
yard•stick
Y.B. (Yearbook; Year
Book)
yea
year
year-and-a-day rule
Year Book (*citation
form:* Y.B.)
year-end
year-round
year to date (YTD)
year•book (*citation
form:* Y.B.)

year•long
year•ly
yeas and nays
yea•say•er
yel•low-dog con•
tract
yeo•man n., pl. yeo•
men
yeo•man•ly
yeo•man•ry
yes adv., adj., n., pl.
yes•es, interj.
yes-man n., pl. yes-
men
yes-no ques•tion
yes-or-no question
yield
yield to ma•tu•ri•ty
(YTM)
yield•er
York-Ant•werp rules
Young•er ab•sten•
tion
Your Hon•or
Youth Court (*citation
form:* Youth Ct.)
Youth Ct. (Youth
Court)
youth•ful of•fend•er

youth•ful•ness
YTD (year to date)
YTM (yield to maturity)
zeal
zeal•less
zeal•ot
zeal•ot•ry
zeal•ous
ze•ro n., pl. ze•ros,
v., ze•roed, ze•ro•
ing, adj.
ze•ro-bal•ance ac•
count
ze•ro-cou•pon bond
ze•ro-sum adj.
ze•ro-tol•er•ance adj.
zo•laz•e•pam See TI-
LETAMINE-ZOLAZEPAM.
zol•pi•dem Controlled
Subst.
zon•al
zone n., v. zoned,
zon•ing
zone of em•ploy•
ment
zone of rule•mak•ing
zon•ing
zy•gos•i•ty
zy•gote

OUTLINE OF UNITED STATES GOVERNMENT AGENCIES AND OTHER GOVERNMENTAL BODIES

This list shows the principal organizational units and selected subunits of the United States government, arranged hierarchically. Conventional abbreviations, informal names, and other information are given in parentheses following the organization names.

In cases where the officer heading a government body has a title of particular note, that title is given in italics and parentheses under the name of the body, unless it is obvious from the name of the organizational unit itself (as in, for example, the Office of the United States Trade Representative). In most other cases, the heads of government bodies are referred to simply as the Chairman, Director, Commissioner, or Administrator of the unit in question, except that high-level subdivisions of executive departments are usually headed by an Under Secretary or Assistant Secretary of the department.

Certain courts established by Congress under Article I of the Constitution are treated here as part of the judicial branch of government because they carry out an essentially judicial function, even though they technically do not exercise what the Constitution calls "the judicial Power of the United States" as do the courts established under Article III.

LEGISLATIVE BRANCH

The Congress of the United States

The Senate

(Head: Majority Leader. Presiding Officer: President of the Senate, who is the Vice President of the United States)

Committee on Agriculture, Nutrition, and Forestry
Committee on Appropriations
Committee on Armed Services
Committee on Banking, Housing, and Urban Affairs
Committee on the Budget
Committee on Commerce, Science, and Transportation
Committee on Energy and Natural Resources
Committee on Environment and Public Works
Committee on Finance
Committee on Foreign Relations
Committee on Governmental Affairs
Committee on Indian Affairs
Committee on the Judiciary
Committee on Labor and Human Resources
Committee on Rules and Administration
Committee on Small Business
Committee on Veterans' Affairs
Select Committee on Ethics
Select Committee on Intelligence
Special Committee on Aging

The House of Representatives
(Speaker)

- Committee on Agriculture
- Committee on Appropriations
- Committee on Banking and Financial Services
- Committee on the Budget
- Committee on Commerce
- Committee on Education and the Workforce
- Committee on Government Reform and Oversight
- Committee on House Oversight
- Committee on International Relations
- Committee on the Judiciary
- Committee on National Security
- Committee on Resources
- Committee on Rules
- Committee on Science
- Committee on Small Business
- Committee on Standards of Official Conduct
- Committee on Transportation and Infrastructure
- Committee on Veterans' Affairs
- Committee on Ways and Means
- Permanent Select Committee on Intelligence

Joint Committees

- Joint Committee on the Library
- Joint Committee on Printing
- Joint Committee on Taxation
- Joint Economic Committee (JEC)

Legislative Branch Agencies

Architect of the Capitol

Congressional Budget Office (CBO)

General Accounting Office (GAO)
(Comptroller General of the United States)

Government Printing Office (GPO)
(Public Printer)
    Government Printing Office Style Board
    Superintendent of Documents
        Documents Sales Service
        Office of Electronic Information
           Dissemination

Library of Congress (LC)
(Librarian of Congress)
    Congressional Research Service (CRS)
    United States Copyright Office
    Law Library
    Library Services

United States Botanic Garden

JUDICIAL BRANCH

Courts

The Supreme Court of the United States
(Chief Justice of the United States)

United States Courts of Appeals
    (One for each of twelve geographic regions: the
    First Circuit through the Eleventh Circuit plus
    the District of Columbia Circuit)

United States Court of Appeals for the Federal
    Circuit

United States District Courts
    (One for each of 91 geographic districts: from
    one to four in each state, plus one for the
    District of Columbia and one for Puerto Rico.
    Each such court includes a unit called the
    Bankruptcy Court for that district.)

Judicial Panel on Multidistrict Litigation

Territorial Courts
(One District Court each for Guam, the Virgin Islands, and the Northern Mariana Islands)

United States Court of Federal Claims (Fed. Cl.)

United States Court of International Trade (Ct. Int'l Trade)

United States Tax Court (T.C.)

United States Court of Appeals for the Armed Forces (C.A.A.F.)

United States Court of Veterans Appeals (Vet. App.)

District of Columbia Court of Appeals

Superior Court of the District of Columbia

Judicial Branch Agencies

Administrative Office of the United States Courts

Federal Judicial Center (FJC)

United States Sentencing Commission (USSC)

EXECUTIVE BRANCH

The President of the United States

The Cabinet

The Vice President of the United States

Executive Office of the President

The White House Office

Office of the Vice President of the United States

Council of Economic Advisers (CEA)

Council on Environmental Quality (CEQ)

National Security Council (NSC)
(The President of the United States)

Office of Administration

Office of Management and Budget (OMB)

Office of National Drug Control Policy (ONDCP)

Office of Policy Development
Domestic Policy Council
National Economic Council

Office of Science and Technology Policy (OSTP)

Office of the United States Trade Representative
(USTR)

Executive Departments

Department of Agriculture (USDA)
(Secretary of Agriculture)
Farm and Foreign Agricultural Services mission
Commodity Credit Corporation (CCC)
Farm Service Agency (FSA)
Foreign Agricultural Service (FAS)
Risk Management Agency
Food, Nutrition, and Consumer Services
(FNCS) mission
Center for Nutrition Policy and Promotion
(CNPP)
Food and Nutrition Service (FNS)
Food Safety mission
Food Safety and Inspection Service (FSIS)
Marketing and Regulatory Programs mission
Agricultural Marketing Service (AMS)
Animal and Plant Health Inspection Service
(APHIS)
Grain Inspection, Packers, and Stockyards
Administration (GIPSA)

Natural Resources and Environment mission
  Forest Service
  Natural Resources Conservation Service
    (NRCS)
Research, Education, and Economics mission
  Agricultural Research Service (ARS)
  Cooperative State Research, Education, and
    Extension Service (CSREES)
  Economic Research Service (ERS)
  National Agricultural Statistics Service
    (NASS)
Rural Development mission
  Rural Business-Cooperative Service (RBS)
  Rural Housing Service (RHS)
  Rural Utilities Service (RUS)
Alternative Agricultural Research and
    Commercialization (AARC) Corporation

Department of Commerce (DOC)
(Secretary of Commerce)
  Bureau of Export Administration (BXA)
  Economic Development Administration (EDA)
  Economics and Statistics Administration (ESA)
  Bureau of the Census
  Bureau of Economic Analysis (BEA)
  International Trade Administration (ITA)
  Minority Business Development Agency
    (MBDA)
  National Oceanic and Atmospheric
    Administration (NOAA)
    National Marine Fisheries Service (NMFS)
    National Weather Service (NWS)
  National Telecommunications and Information
    Administration (NTIA)

Patent and Trademark Office (PTO)
(Commissioner of Patents and Trademarks)
Technology Administration
Office of Technology Policy (OTP)
National Institute of Standards and
Technology (NIST)
National Technical Information Service (NTIS)
Department of Defense (DOD)
(Secretary of Defense)
Joint Chiefs of Staff (JCS)
(Chairman of the Joint Chiefs of Staff)
Department of the Air Force
(Secretary of the Air Force)
United States Air Force (USAF)
(Chief of Staff of the Air Force)
Department of the Army
(Secretary of the Army)
United States Army (USA)
(Chief of Staff of the Army)
Department of the Navy
(Secretary of the Navy)
United States Marine Corps (USMC)
(Commandant of the Marine Corps)
United States Navy (USN)
(Chief of Naval Operations)
United States Coast Guard (USCG)
(Normally a unit of the Department of
Transportation; operates as a service
in the Navy in time of war or at the
President's direction.)
(Commandant)
Other Defense Agencies, Offices, and Activities
Ballistic Missile Defense Organization (BMDO)

Department of Defense Education Activity (DODEA)

Defense Advanced Research Projects Agency (DARPA)

Defense Intelligence Agency (DIA)

Defense Prisoner of War/Missing Personnel Office (DPMO)

Defense Security Assistance Agency

Defense Special Weapons Agency (DSWA)

Defense Technology Security Administration (DTSA)

National Imagery and Mapping Agency (NIMA)

National Security Agency/Central Security Service (NSA/CSS)

Nuclear and Chemical and Biological (NCB) Defense Programs

Office of Civilian Health and Medical Program of the Uniformed Services (OCHAMPUS)

Department of Education (ED)
(Secretary of Education)

Office for Civil Rights (OCR)

Office of Bilingual Education and Minority Languages Services (OBEMLA)

Office of Educational Research and Improvement (OERI)

Office of Elementary and Secondary Education (OESE)

Office of Postsecondary Education (OPE)

Office of Special Education and Rehabilitative Services (OSERS)

Office of Vocational and Adult Education (OVAE)

Department of Energy (DOE)
(Secretary of Energy)
    Energy Programs
        Energy Information Administration
        Office of Energy Efficiency and Renewable
            Energy
        Office of Fossil Energy
    Environmental Management Programs
        Office of Civilian Radioactive Waste
            Management
        Office of Environmental Management
        Office of Fissile Materials Disposition
    National Security Programs
        Office of Defense Programs
        Office of Nonproliferation and National
            Security
    Science and Technology Programs
        Office of Energy Research
        Office of Nuclear Energy,Science, and
            Technology
    Federal Energy Regulatory Commission (FERC)
Department of Health and Human Services (HHS)
(Secretary of Health and Human Services)
    Administration for Children and Families (ACF)
        Administration for Native Americans (ANA)
        Administration on Children, Youth, and
            Families (ACYF)
        Administration on Developmental
            Disabilities (ADD)
        Office of Child Support Enforcement (CSE)
        Office of Community Services
        Office of Family Assistance (OFA)
        Office of Refugee Resettlement (ORR)

Administration on Aging (AOA)
Agency for Health Care Policy and Research
    (AHCPR)
Agency for Toxic Substances and Disease
    Registry (ATSDR)
Centers for Disease Control and Prevention (CDC)
    National Center for Chronic Disease
        Prevention and Health Promotion
        (NCCDPHP)
    National Center for Environmental Health
        (NCEH)
    National Center for Health Statistics (NCHS)
    National Center for HIV, STD, and TB
        Prevention (NCHSTP)
    National Center for Infectious Diseases (NCID)
    National Center for Injury Prevention and
        Control (NCIPC)
    National Institute for Occupational Safety
        and Health (NIOSH)
Food and Drug Administration (FDA)
Health Care Financing Administration (HCFA)
Health Resources and Services Administration
    (HRSA)
    Bureau of Health Professions (BHPr)
    Bureau of Health Resources Development
    Bureau of Primary Health Care (BPHC)
    HIV/AIDS Bureau (HAB)
    Maternal and Child Health Bureau (MCHB)
Indian Health Service (IHS)
Public Health Service (PHS)
    Office of the Surgeon General
    Agency for Health Care Policy and Research
        (AHCPR)

Bureau of Medical Services
Bureau of State Services
National Institutes of Health (NIH)
    National Cancer Institute (NCI)
    National Eye Institute (NEI)
    National Heart, Lung, and Blood Institute (NHLBI)
    National Human Genome Research Institute (NHGRI)
    National Institute of Allergy and Infectious Diseases (NIAID)
    National Institute of Arthritis and Musculoskeletal and Skin Diseases (NIAMS)
    National Institute of Child Health and Human Development (NICHD)
    National Institute of Dental Research (NIDR)
    National Institute of Diabetes and Digestive and Kidney Diseases (NIDDK)
    National Institute of Environmental Health Sciences (NIEHS)
    National Institute of General Medical Sciences (NIGMS)
    National Institute of Mental Health (NIMH)
    National Institute of Neurological Disorders and Stroke (NINDS)
    National Institute of Nursing Research
    National Institute on Aging (NIA)
    National Institute on Alcohol Abuse and Alcoholism (NIAAA)

National Institute on Deafness and Other
    Communication Disorders (NIDCD)
National Institute on Drug Abuse (NIDA)
Office of AIDS Research
Substance Abuse and Mental Health Services
    Administration (SAMHSA)
    Center for Mental Health Services (CMHS)
    Center for Substance Abuse Prevention
        (CSAP)
    Center for Substance Abuse Treatment
        (CSAT)

Department of Housing and Urban Development (HUD)
(Secretary of Housing and Urban Development)
Office of Community Planning and
    Development
Office of Fair Housing and Equal Opportunity
Office of Federal Housing Enterprise Oversight
Office of Housing and Federal Housing
    Administration (FHA)
    (Federal Housing Commissioner)
Office of Lead Hazard Control
office of Policy Development and Research
Office of Public and Indian Housing
Government National Mortgage Association
    (GNMA or Ginnie Mae)

Department of the Interior (DOI)
(Secretary of the Interior)
Bureau of Indian Affairs (BIA)
Bureau of Land Management (BLM)
Bureau of Reclamation
Minerals Management Service (MMS)
National Park Service

Office of Insular Affairs
Office of Surface Mining Reclamation and
      Enforcement (OSM)
United States Fish and Wildlife Service
United States Geological Survey (USGS)

Department of Justice (DOJ)
(Attorney General of the United States)
Offices
    Asset Forfeiture Management Staff (AFMS)
    Community Relations Service
    Executive Office for United States Trustees
    Executive Office for United States Attorneys
        (EOUSA)
    Office of Information and Privacy
    Office of Intelligence Policy and Review
    Office of Legal Counsel
    Office of Professional Responsibility
    Office of the Pardon Attorney
    Office of the Solicitor General
    Office of Tribal Justice (OTJ)
Divisions
    Antitrust Division
    Civil Division
        Appellate Staff
        Commercial Litigation Branch
        Federal Programs Branch
        Office of Consumer Litigation
        Office of Immigration Litigation
        Torts Branch
    Civil Rights Division
        Appellate Section
        Coordination and Review Section
        Criminal Section

Disability Rights Section
Educational Opportunities Section
Employment Litigation Section
Housing and Civil Enforcement Section
Office of Special Counsel for Immigration
Related Unfair Employment Practices
Special Litigation Section
Voting Section
Criminal Division
Appellate Section
Asset Forfeiture/Money Laundering
Section
Child Exploitation and Obscenity Section
(CEOS)
Computer Crime and Intellectual Property
Section (CCIPS)
Executive Office for the Organized Crime
Drug Enforcement Task Force
(Executive Office for OCDETF)
Fraud Section
Internal Security Section
International Criminal Investigative
Training Assistance Program
Narcotic and Dangerous Drug Section
(NDDS)
Office of Enforcement Operations
Office of International Affairs
Office of Policy and Legislation (OPL)
Office of Professional Development and
Training
Office of Special Investigations
Organized Crime and Racketeering
Section

Public Integrity Section
Terrorism and Violent Crime Section
Environment and Natural Resources
Division
Appellate Section
Environmental Crimes Section
Environmental Defense Section
Environmental Enforcement Section
General Litigation Section
Indian Resources Section
Land Acquisition Section
Policy, Legislation, and Special Litigation
Section
Wildlife and Marine Resources Section
Tax Division
Bureaus
Bureau of Prisons
Drug Enforcement Administration (DEA)
Federal Bureau of Investigation (FBI)
Immigration and Naturalization Service
(INS)
Office of Justice Programs (OJP)
Bureau of Justice Assistance (BJA)
Bureau of Justice Statistics (BJS)
Corrections Program Office (CPO)
Drug Court Program Office (DCPO)
National Institute of Justice (NIJ)
Office for Victims of Crime (OVC)
Office of Juvenile Justice and
Delinquency Prevention (OJJDP)
Missing Children's Program
Violence Against Women Office (VAWO)
United States Marshals Service

United States National Central
Bureau—International Criminal
Police Organization (USNCB or
Interpol—Washington)
Boards
Executive Office for Immigration Review
Board of Immigration Appeals
Foreign Claims Settlement Commission of
the United States
Office of Community Oriented Policing
Services (COPS)
United States Parole Commission

Department of Labor (DOL)
(Secretary of Labor)
Office of the Deputy Secretary of Labor
Administrative Review Board
Benefits Review Board (BRB)
Board of Service Contract Appeals
Bureau of International Labor Affairs (ILAB)
Employees' Compensation Appeals Board
(ECAB)
Wage Appeals Board
Women's Bureau (WB)
Bureau of Labor Statistics (BLS)
Employment and Training Administration (ETA)
Bureau of Apprenticeship and Training
Federal Unemployment Insurance Service
Office of Job Corps Programs
Office of Job Training Programs
Office of Regional Management
Office of Trade Adjustment Assistance
Office of Work-Based Learning

Office of Worker Retraining and Adjustment
Programs
Senior Community Service Employment
Program (SCSEP)
United States Employment Service (USES)
Employment Standards Administration (ESA)
Office of Federal Contract Compliance
Programs (OFCCP)
Office of Labor-Management Standards
(OLMS)
Office of Workers' Compensation Programs
(OWCP)
Wage and Hour Division (WHD)
Mine Safety and Health Administration
(MSHA)
Occupational Safety and Health Administration
(OSHA)
Pension and Welfare Benefits Administration
(PWBA)
Veterans' Employment and Training Service
(VETS)

Department of State (State)
(Secretary of State)

Bureau of Consular Affairs
Bureau of Democracy, Human Rights, and
Labor
Bureau of Economic and Business Affairs
Bureau of Intelligence and Research
Bureau of International Communications and
Information Policy
Bureau of International Narcotics and Law
Enforcement Affairs

Bureau of International Organization Affairs
Bureau of Oceans and International
    Environmental and Scientific Affairs
Bureau of Political-Military Affairs
Bureau of Population, Refugees, and Migration
Foreign Service Institute
United States Mission to the United Nations
    *(United States Representative to the United
    Nations)*

Department of Transportation (DOT)
(Secretary of Transportation)

Bureau of Transportation Statistics (BTS)
Federal Aviation Administration (FAA)
Federal Highway Administration (FHWA)
Federal Railroad Administration (FRA)
Federal Transit Administration (FTA)
Maritime Administration (MARAD)
National Highway Traffic Safety Administration
    (NHTSA)
Research and Special Programs Administration
    (RSPA)
    Office of Emergency Transportation
    Office of Hazardous Materials Safety
    Office of Pipeline Safety
    Transportation Safety Institute
Saint Lawrence Seaway Development
    Corporation (SLSDC)
Surface Transportation Board (STB)
United States Coast Guard (USCG) (Operates as
    a service of the Navy in time of war or at
    the President's direction.)
    (Commandant)

Department of the Treasury (Treasury)
(Secretary of the Treasury)
- Bureau of Alcohol, Tobacco, and Firearms (ATF)
- Bureau of Engraving and Printing (BEP)
- Bureau of the Public Debt (BPD)
- Federal Law Enforcement Training Center (FLETC)
- Financial Crimes Enforcement Network (FinCEN)
- Financial Management Service (FMS)
- Internal Revenue Service (IRS)
- Office of the Comptroller of the Currency (OCC)
- Office of the Treasurer of the United States
- Office of Thrift Supervision (OTS)
- United States Customs Service (USCS)
- United States Mint (USM)
- United States Secret Service (USSS)

Department of Veterans Affairs (VA)
(Secretary of Veterans Affairs)
- Board of Veterans' Appeals (BVA)
- National Cemetery System (NCS)
- Veterans Benefits Administration (VBA)
- Veterans Health Administration

Selected Independent Establishments, Government Corporations, and Interagency Programs
- African Development Foundation
- Central Intelligence Agency (CIA)
(Director of Central Intelligence)
- Commodity Futures Trading Commission (CFTC)
- Consumer Product Safety Commission (CPSC)

Corporation for National and Community Service
    AmeriCorps
        AmeriCorps*National Civilian Community
            Corps (AmeriCorps*NCCC)
        AmeriCorps*State and National
        AmeriCorps*VISTA (Volunteers in Service to
            America)
    Learn and Serve America
    National Senior Service Corps (Senior Corps)

Defense Nuclear Facilities Safety Board (DNFSB)

Environmental Protection Agency (EPA)
    Air and Radiation
    Enforcement and Compliance Assurance
    International Activities
    Policy, Planning, and Evaluation
    Prevention, Pesticides, and Toxic Substances
    Research and Development
    Solid Waste and Emergency Response
    Water

Equal Employment Opportunity Commission
    (EEOC

Export-Import Bank of the United States (Ex-Im
    Bank)

Farm Credit Administration (FCA)

Federal Communications Commission (FCC)
    Cable Services Bureau
    Common Carrier Bureau
    Compliance and Information Bureau
    International Bureau
    Mass Media Bureau
    Office of Engineering and Technology
    Wireless Telecommunications Bureau

Federal Deposit Insurance Corporation (FDIC)
Federal Election Commission (FEC)
Federal Emergency Management Agency (FEMA)
Federal Housing Finance Board
Federal Labor Relations Authority (FLRA)
Federal Maritime Commission (FMC)
Federal Mediation and Conciliation Service (FMCS)
Federal Mine Safety and Health Review
    Commission
Federal Prison Industries (UNICOR)
Federal Reserve System (the Fed)
    Board of Governors of the Federal Reserve
        System (the Fed)
    Federal Reserve Banks
        (one in each of twelve geographic regions,
        with branch banks in 25 additional cities)
    Consumer Advisory Council
    Federal Advisory Council
    Federal Open Market Committee
    Thrift Institutions Advisory Council
Federal Retirement Thrift Investment Board
Federal Trade Commission (FTC)
    Bureau of Competition
    Bureau of Consumer Protection
    Bureau of Economics
General Services Administration (GSA)
Inter-American Foundation
Merit Systems Protection Board (MSPB)
National Aeronautics and Space Administration
    (NASA)

National Archives and Records Administration
    (NARA)
National Capital Planning Commission (NCPC)
National Credit Union Administration (NCUA)
National Foundation on the Arts and the
    Humanities
  Institute of Museum and Library Services
    (IMLS)
  National Endowment for the Arts (NEA)
  National Endowment for the Humanities (NEH)
National Institute for Literacy
National Labor Relations Board (NLRB)
National Mediation Board (NMB)
National Railroad Passenger Corporation (Amtrak)
National Science Foundation (NSF)
National Transportation Safety Board (NTSB)
Nuclear Regulatory Commission (NRC)
Occupational Safety and Health Review
    Commission (OSHRC)
Office of Government Ethics (OGE)
Office of Personnel Management (OPM)
Office of Special Counsel (OSC)
Organized Crime Drug Enforcement Task Force
    (OCDETF)
Peace Corps
Pension Benefit Guaranty Corporation (PBGC)
Postal Rate Commission (PRC)
Railroad Retirement Board (RRB)
Securities and Exchange Commission (SEC)

Division of Corporation Finance
Division of Enforcement
Division of Investment Management
Division of Market Regulation
Office of Compliance Inspections and
    Examinations
Office of Municipal Securities
Office of Investor Education and Assistance

Selective Service System (SSS)

Small Business Administration (SBA)
Office of Advocacy
Office of Business Initiatives
Office of Financial Assistance
Office of Government Contracting
Office of International Trade
Office of Minority Enterprise Development
Office of Native American Affairs
Office of Small Business Development Centers
Office of Surety Guarantees
Office of Technology
Office of Veterans' Affairs (OVA)
Office of Women's Business Ownership
    (OWBO)

Social Security Administration (SSA)

Tennessee Valley Authority (TVA)

Trade and Development Agency (TDA)

United States Arms Control and Disarmament
    Agency (ACDA)

United States Commission on Civil Rights
    (USCCR)

United States Information Agency (USIA)

Bureau of Educational and Cultural Affairs

Bureau of Information

International Broadcasting Bureau

United States International Development
Cooperation Agency (IDCA)

Agency for International Development (USAID
or AID)

Overseas Private Investment Corporation
(OPIC)

United States International Trade Commission
(USITC)

United States Postal Service (USPS)

Selected Quasi-Official and Private Agencies (established by Congress to fulfill a public purpose, but not officially part of the government)

Fannie Mae (the name under which the Federal
National Mortgage Association does business)

Freddie Mac (the name under which the Federal
Home Loan Mortgage Corporation does
business)

Legal Services Corporation (LSC)

Sallie Mae (the name under which the Student
Loan Marketing Association and affiliated
companies do business)

Securities Investor Protection Corporation (SIPC)

Smithsonian Institution

State Justice Institute

United States Institute for Peace

INTERNATIONAL ORGANIZATIONS

This is a selected list of the principal multinational bodies through which governments and businesses of the world seek to cooperate on matters of international concern. First is the United Nations with its six principal organs and selected subsidiary bodies, its specialized agencies, and a selection of related organizations. Second is a listing of the principal organizational components of the European Union, and selected other consultative and specialized EU agencies. Third is a selection of other major international organizations, with emphasis on organizations in which the United States participates.

Many international bodies have official names in more than one language; the English forms are given here. Conventional abbreviations, short forms of names, and other information are given in parentheses following the organization names. Abbreviations that do not seem a good match for the names are usually derived from an earlier name for the organization or a non-English form of the name.

UNITED NATIONS (U.N.)

General Assembly

Main Committees

Disarmament and International Security
Committee (First Committee)

Economic and Financial Committee (Second
Committee)

Social, Humanitarian and Cultural Committee
(Third Committee)

Special Political and Decolonization Committee
(Fourth Committee)

Administrative and Budgetary Committee (Fifth
Committee)

Legal Committee (Sixth Committee)

Other bodies

Advisory Board on Disarmament Matters

Advisory Committee of the United Nations
Programme of Assistance in the
Teaching, Study, Dissemination and
Wider Appreciation of International Law

Committee on Contributions

Committee on Relations with the Host Country

Committee on the Peaceful Uses of Outer Space
(COPUOS)

Conference on Disarmament (CD)

High-Level Open-Ended Working Group on the
Financial Situation of the United Nations

Informal Open-Ended Working Group on an
Agenda for Peace

International Civil Service Commission (ICSC)

International Criminal Court Preparatory
Committee

International Law Commission (ILC)

Special Committee on Peace-keeping Operations

United Nations Commission on International
Trade Law (UNCITRAL)

United Nations Disarmament Commission
(UNDC)

United Nations Scientific Committee on the
Effects of Atomic Radiation (UNSCEAR)

Security Council

Committee on Admission of New Members

Military Staff Committee

Peacekeeping and Related Operations

Military Armistice Commission in Korea

Neutral Nations Supervisory Commission in
Korea (NNSC)

United Nations Civilian Police Mission in Haiti
(MIPONUH)

United Nations Command in Korea

United Nations Iraq-Kuwait Observation
Mission (UNIKOM)

United Nations Military Observer Group in
India and Pakistan (UNMOGIP)

United Nations Mission in Bosnia and
Herzegovina (UNMIBH)

United Nations Special Commission (UNSCOM)

*Special Tribunals for the Prosecution of Persons
Responsible for Genocide and Other Serious
Violations of International Humanitarian Law*

International Criminal Tribunal for Rwanda

International Criminal Tribunal for the Former
Yugoslavia

Economic and Social Council (ECOSOC)

Commission for Social Development (CSD)

Commission on Crime Prevention and Criminal
Justice

Commission on Human Rights (CHR)

Commission on Human Settlements (Habitat)

Commission on Narcotic Drugs (CND)

Commission on Population and Development

Commission on Science and Technology for Development

Commission on Sustainable Development (CSD)

Commission on the Status of Women (CSW)

Committee on Economic, Social and Cultural Rights

Committee on Non-Governmental Organizations

Inter-Agency Committee on Women

Statistical Commission

Trusteeship Council (Inactive—no territories left under United Nations trusteeship)

International Court of Justice (I.C.J.)

Secretariat

Executive Office of the Secretary-General

Administrative Committee on Coordination (ACC)

Department for Development Support and Management Services

Department for Economic and Social Information and Policy Analysis

Department for Policy Coordination and Sustainable Development

Department of Humanitarian Affairs

Department of Peace-keeping Operations

Department of Political Affairs

Office of Legal Affairs

Specialized Agencies (United States a member of each except for the two noted)

Food and Agriculture Organization (FAO)

International Civil Aviation Organization (ICAO)

International Fund for Agricultural Development (IFAD)

International Labour Organization (ILO)

International Maritime Organization (IMO)

International Monetary Fund (IMF)

International Telecommunication Union (ITU)

United Nations Educational, Scientific and Cultural Organization (UNESCO) (United States not a member)

United Nations Industrial Development Organization (UNIDO) (United States no longer a member)

Universal Postal Union (UPU)

World Bank Group
    International Bank for Reconstruction and Development (IBRD or World Bank)
    International Centre for Settlement of Investment Disputes (ICSID)
    International Development Association (IDA)
    International Finance Corporation (IFC)
    Multilateral Investment Guarantee Agency (MIGA)

World Health Organization (WHO)

World Intellectual Property Organization (WIPO)

World Meteorological Organization (WMO)

Other United Nations–Related Organizations
(United States a member or participant
in almost all)

Commission on the Limits of the Continental Shelf

Committee Against Torture (CAT)

Committee on the Elimination of Discrimination Against Women (CEDAW)

Committee on the Elimination of Racial Discrimination (CERD)

Committee on the Rights of the Child

Convention on Biological Diversity (CBD)

Convention on International Trade in Endangered Species of Wild Fauna and Flora (CITES)

Convention on the Conservation of Migratory Species of Wild Animals (CMS or Bonn Convention)

Global Environment Facility (GEF)

Human Rights Committee

Intergovernmental Panel on Climate Change (IPCC)

International Atomic Energy Agency (IAEA)

International Consultative Group on Food Irradiation (ICGFI)

International Narcotics Control Board (INCB)

International Research and Training Institute for the Advancement of Women (ISTRAW)

International Seabed Authority

International Trade Centre UNCTAD/WTO (ITC)

International Tribunal on the Law of the Sea

International Union for the Protection of New Varieties of Plants (UPOV)

Office of the United Nations High Commissioner for Human Rights

Office of the United Nations High Commissioner for Refugees (UNHCR)

Ozone Secretariat

United Nations Capital Development Fund (UNCDF)

United Nations Children's Fund (UNICEF)

United Nations Conference on Trade and Development (UNCTAD)

United Nations Development Fund for Women (UNIFEM)

United Nations Development Programme (UNDP)

United Nations Environment Programme (UNEP)

United Nations Framework Convention on Climate Change (UNFCCC)

United Nations Institute for Disarmament Research (UNIDIR)

United Nations Institute for Training and Research (UNITAR)

United Nations International Drug Control Programme (UNDCP)

United Nations Interregional Crime and Justice Research Institute (UNICRI)

United Nations Population Fund (UNFPA)

United Nations Research Institute for Social Development (UNRISD)

United Nations Volunteers (UNV)

World Food Programme (WFP)

World Tourism Organization (WTO)

World Trade Organization (WTO); successor to the General Agreement on Tariffs and Trade (GATT)

THE EUROPEAN UNION (EU)

Original Organizations (traditionally referred to collectively as the European Community or the European Communities (EC))

> European Coal and Steel Community (ECSC)
>
> European Economic Community (EEC or Common Market), now officially named the European Community (EC)
>
> European Economic Energy Community (Euratom)

Principal Legislative, Judicial, Policy Making, and Financial Bodies

> Council of the European Union
>
> Court of Justice
>
> European Commission
>
> European Council
>
> European Court of Auditors
>
> European Investment Bank (EIB)
>
> European Parliament

Other Consultative and Functional Bodies

> Committee of the Regions
>
> Economic and Social Committee
>
> European Agency for Safety and Health at Work
>
> European Agency for the Evaluation of Medicinal Products (EMEA)
>
> European Environment Agency (EEA)
>
> European Foundation for the Improvement of Living and Working Conditions
>
> European Monetary Institute (EMI)

European Monitoring Centre for Drugs and Drug Addiction

Office for Harmonization in the Internal Market (Trade Marks and Designs) (OHIM)

OTHER INTERNATIONAL ORGANIZATIONS
(* means United States is a member or participant.)

*African Development Bank Group

*Arctic Council

*Asian Development Bank (ADB)

*Asia-Pacific Economic Cooperation (APEC)

Association of Caribbean States (ACS)

Association of South East Asian Nations (ASEAN)

Benelux Economic Union

Black Sea Economic Cooperation (BSEC)

Caribbean Community and Common Market (CARICOM)

Central African Customs and Economic Union (UDEAC)

Central American Common Market (CACM)

Central European Initiative (CEI)

*Colombo Plan for Cooperative Economic and Social Development in Asia and the Pacific

The Commonwealth (formerly the British Commonwealth)

Commonwealth of Independent States (CIS)

Council of Europe

*Customs Co-operation Council (CCC); official name of the World Customs Organization (WCO)

*European Bank for Reconstruction and
  Development (EBRD)

European Economic Area (EEA)

European Free Trade Association (EFTA)

European Organization for Nuclear Research (CERN)

European Space Agency (ESA)

*Fund for the Protection of the World Cultural and
  Natural Heritage

*Group of Seven (G-7)

*Group of Eight (G-8)

*Group of Ten (G-10)

*Hague Conference on Private International Law

*Inter-American Defense Board

*Inter-American Development Bank (IDB)

*International Bureau of Weights and Measures

*International Chamber of Commerce (ICC)

*International Council for the Exploration of the
  Seas (ICES)

*International Criminal Police Organization (ICPO
  or Interpol)

*International Energy Agency (IEA)

*International Institute for the Unification of
  Private Law

*International Mobile Satellite Organization
  (Inmarsat)

*International Organization for Legal Metrology

*International Organization for Migration

*International Telecommunications Satellite
  Organization (Intelsat)

*International Union for Conservation of Nature and Natural Resources (IUCN or World Conservation Union)

*International Whaling Commission

*Interparliamentary Union

Latin American Economic System (LAES)

Latin American Integration Association (LAIA)

League of Arab States (Arab League)

Nonaligned Movement (NAM)

Nordic Council

*North American Free Trade Agreement (NAFTA)

*North Atlantic Cooperation Council

*North Atlantic Treaty Organization (NATO)

*Organization for Economic Cooperation and Development (OECD)

*Organization for Security and Cooperation in Europe (OSCE)

*Organization for the Prevention of Chemical Weapons

Organization of African Unity (OAU)

*Organization of American States (OAS)

Organization of Arab Petroleum Exporting Countries (OAPEC)

Organization of the Islamic Conference (OIC)

Organization of the Petroleum Exporting Countries (OPEC)

*Pan American Health organization (PAHO)

*Partnership for Peace

*Permanent Court of Arbitration

South Asian Association for Regional Cooperation
    (SAARC)

*South Pacific Commission (SPC)

Southern African Development Community
    (SADC)

Western European Union (WEU)

*World Customs Organization (WCO) (working
    name of the Customs Co-operation Council
    (CCC))

GEOGRAPHIC ABBREVIATIONS FOR THE UNITED STATES AND CANADA: CITATION FORMS AND POSTAL DESIGNATIONS

United States

Jurisdiction	Legal Citation Form	Official Postal Abbreviation
United States	U.S.	
Alabama	Ala.	AL
Alaska	Alaska	AK
American Samoa	Am. Sam.	AS
Arizona	Ariz.	AZ
Arkansas	Ark.	AR
Armed Forces the Americas		AA
Armed Forces Europe		AE
Armed Forces Pacific		AP
California	Cal.	CA
Colorado	Colo.	CO
Connecticut	Conn.	CT
Delaware	Del.	DE
District of Columbia	D.C.	DC
Florida	Fla.	FL
Georgia	Ga.	GA
Guam	Guam	GU
Hawaii	Haw.	HI

Jurisdiction	Legal Citation Form	Official Postal Abbreviation
Idaho	Idaho	ID
Illinois	Ill.	IL
Indiana	Ind.	IN
Iowa	Iowa	IA
Kansas	Kan.	KS
Kentucky	Ky.	KY
Louisiana	La.	LA
Maine	Me.	ME
Maryland	Md.	MD
Massachusetts	Mass.	MA
Michigan	Mich.	MI
Minnesota	Minn.	MN
Mississippi	Miss.	MS
Missouri	Mo.	MO
Montana	Mont.	MT
Nebraska	Neb.	NE
Nevada	Nev.	NV
New Hampshire	N.H.	NH
New Jersey	N.J.	NJ
New Mexico	N.M.	NM
New York	N.Y.	NY
North Carolina	N.C.	NC
North Dakota	N.D.	ND
Northern Mariana Islands	N. Mar. I.	MP
Ohio	Ohio	OH
Oklahoma	Okla.	OK
Oregon	Or.	OR
Pennsylvania	Pa.	PA
Puerto Rico	P.R.	PR
Rhode Island	R.I.	RI

Jurisdiction	Legal Citation Form	Official Postal Abbreviation
South Carolina	S.C.	SC
South Dakota	S.D.	SD
Tennessee	Tenn.	TN
Texas	Tex.	TX
Utah	Utah	UT
Vermont	Vt.	VT
Virginia	Va.	VA
Virgin Islands [of the United States]	V.I.	VI
Washington [state]	Wash.	WA
West Virginia	W. Va.	WV
Wisconsin	Wis.	WI
Wyoming	Wyo.	WY

Areas Formerly Administered by the United States

Jurisdiction	Legal Citation Form	Official Postal Abbreviation
Canal Zone[1]	C.Z.	
Federated States of Micronesia[2]		FM
Republic of the Marshall Islands[2]		MH
Republic of Palau[2]		PW

---

[1] Returned to Panama on April 1, 1982; citation form used primarily in connection with matters that arose before that date.

[2] Now a sovereign nation; but by agreement with the United States, for the first several years of independence its international mail is handled by the United States Postal Service, and mail from the U.S. to the new nation is treated as if it were still U.S. domestic mail.

Canada

Jurisdiction	Legal Citation Form	Official Postal Abbreviation
Canada	Can.	
Alberta	Alta.	AB
British Columbia	B.C.	BC
Manitoba	Man.	MB
New Brunswick	N.B.	NB
Newfoundland	Nfld.	NF
Northwest Territories	N.W.T.	NT
Nova Scotia	N.S.	NS
Ontario	Ont.	ON
Prince Edward Island	P.E.I.	PE
Québec	Que.	QC
Saskatchewan	Sask.	SK
Yukon	Yukon	YT